CW00686719

INTRODUCTION

Many Christians today are passing out copies of the New Testament (which often include the Psalms and Proverbs from the Old Testament) in their effort to share God's Word with others. Of course, that is a wonderful idea, but I suggest there is now an increasing problem with this approach. You see, most people who receive these New Testaments have been trained by the secular world, which comes through the influence of the news media, movies, internet, public schools, and even many Christian schools/colleges, to believe in evolution and millions of years. They have been taught a set of foundational beliefs that cause them to doubt or even totally disbelieve the truth of God's Word in Genesis. Ultimately, this creates doubt and disbelief in regard to the whole of the Bible, including the gospel message of the New Testament.

When only the New Testament portion of the Bible is given to "evolutionized" people, they do not receive the book of Genesis, which gives them the true account of origins. Genesis is foundational to an understanding of the gospel and all Christian doctrine, including the biggest social and ethical issues of our day. In this increasingly secularized culture, people no longer fully understand the gospel message and the origin of sin and death as found in Genesis — and thus our need of a Savior. Not only that, but because of what people have been taught in regard to origins and social issues, such as sexuality, identity, abortion, racism, and more, many have great doubts (or full-blown unbelief) that God's Word can be totally trusted.

When Christians pass out New Testaments and tell people they need to start with the book of John to understand the gospel, something key is being missed. As people learn of the good news of the gospel, they also need to have an understanding of the bad news in Genesis: our sin in Adam and that we are alienated from our Creator and are in need of a Savior. In today's world, people who read the New Testament only, by and large, rarely understand the gospel and the full meaning of the Christian faith because they have little understanding of the foundations of the gospel and how all Christian doctrine connects.

In addition, because of what people have been taught in our culture, as mentioned above, people are already skeptical about trusting the Bible they have been handed. In a culture that has little or no understanding of the Bible, Christians can be more effective when they start to share their faith at the beginning — in Genesis — so unbelievers will understand the Bible's full message of repentance and need for a Savior.

With this special edition of the Legacy Standard Bible, we have sought to give readers an overview of the Christian faith and the message of the gospel in the following manner: by presenting it the way God does in His Word, and that's by starting at the Bible's beginning. In today's world, we need to communicate a message of the true God — our Creator God. Christians need to give the account of the true history of the world concerning creation, the first man and woman, the fall of man, the entrance of sin and death, and the promise of the Savior fulfilled in the person of Jesus Christ. It is an essential approach to take into a world that knows little, for example, of the meaning and origin of sin or why Christ, the Creator, stepped into history to be our Savior.

This special edition of the LSB contains the entire book of Genesis to communicate a timeline of history from the beginning of time to Christ and then to the new heavens and new earth to come. The Bible's message starting with Genesis is all about what God has done for the salvation of humankind. By including Genesis with the entire New Testament + Psalms & Proverbs, this edition seeks to give individuals a "big picture" understanding of the gospel so that they might receive Christ into their life as Lord and Savior.

I believe this will be blessed by God to become a powerful evangelistic resource to reach a skeptical culture with the precious gospel message.

— Ken Ham

**LEGACY
STANDARD
BIBLE**

GENESIS
NEW TESTAMENT
PSALMS AND PROVERBS

Published by
STEADFAST BIBLES
a division of
Three Sixteen Publishing

Southern California

ISBN: 978-1-63664-048-8
SKU: SBLS0295

ISBN: 978-1-63664-047-1
SKU: SBLS0296

ISBN: 978-1-63664-400-4
SKU: SBLS0312

ISBN: 978-1-63664-401-1
SKU: SBLS0313

CONTENTS

Genesis

The New Testament

Psalms and Proverbs

CONTENTS

FOREWORD

Scriptural Promise

*"The grass withers, the flower fades,
But the word of our God stands forever."*

Isaiah 40:8

The Legacy Standard Bible has been produced with the conviction that the words of Scripture as originally penned in Hebrew, Aramaic, and Greek are the eternal Word of God. The Holy Scriptures speak with authority to each generation, giving wisdom that leads to salvation, that people may serve Christ to the glory of God. Because it is God-breathed (2 Tim 3:16), every word of it is inspired, every word is true, and every word must be conveyed to every nation, tribe, people, and tongue (Rev 7:9), so that every word can be taught and obeyed (Josh 23:14; Matt 28:20; John 17:17).

The Fourfold Aim of The Lockman Foundation

1. These publications shall be true to the original Hebrew, Aramaic, and Greek.
2. They shall be grammatically correct.
3. They shall be understandable.
4. They shall give the Lord Jesus Christ His proper place, the place which the Word gives Him; therefore, no work will ever be personalized.

PREFACE TO THE
LEGACY STANDARD BIBLE

In the history of English Bible translations, the King James Version is the most well known. This time-honored version of 1611, itself a revision of the Bishops' Bible of 1568, became the basis for the English Revised Version, which appeared in 1881 (New Testament) and 1885 (Old Testament). Its American counterpart, a product of both British and American scholarship, was published in 1901. Recognizing the values of the American Standard Version, The Lockman Foundation felt an urgency to preserve the ASV while incorporating recent discoveries of Hebrew and Greek textual sources and rendering it into more current English. This resulted in the New American Standard Bible, a translation based upon the time-honored principles of translation of the ASV and KJV, along with other linguistic tools and biblical scholarship.

The Legacy Standard Bible reflects another iteration of such preservation and refinement. Worked on by a core translation team in conjunction with pastors and educators from different countries, it is designed to honor, maintain, and advance the tradition represented by the NASB.

Principles of Translation

Key Principles: The Legacy Standard Bible has worked to uphold the style and translational choices of the NASB as much as possible. Even more, it has endeavored to follow through on the NASB's stated intent to be true to the original Hebrew, Aramaic, and Greek. While the interpreter, teacher, and pastor have the goal of understanding what the text means, the translator is to provide them with what the text says. Consistently, the goal of this translation is to be a window into the original text. Within that goal, this revision has focused upon accuracy and consistency. It has checked that words and grammar have been carried over properly. It also established rules for the consistent translation of terms within their various nuances. This allows the reader to more easily reconstruct what the original texts said. It also helps the reader more easily trace the flow of argument within a text, identify when the same word is used in another passage, and make connections between texts.

There are limits to the application of this philosophy. In this edition, a word might not be translated consistently in order to maintain a highly familiar rendering of a text or to preserve a wordplay in the text that advances the inspired author's message. Moreover, because Scripture is a literary masterpiece, some linguistic features could not be transferred to this translation, not even by a note. Nevertheless, ensuring that the original languages are precisely rendered paves the way for careful readers to discover these insights for themselves.

In this way, the LSB upholds the philosophy that a translation does not replace pastors or teachers but rather depends upon faithful believers and the church to study and live out what has been written (Acts 8:30–31). Translation is a tool for the church and must be done in that context so that each word of Scripture may be taught and lived.

Modern English Usage: The attempt has been made to render the grammar and terminology in contemporary English. When word-for-word literalness was determined unacceptable to the modern reader, a change was made in the direction of a more current English idiom. In the instances where this has been done, the more literal rendering has been indicated in the notes. There are a few exceptions to this procedure. Of note, while an effort has been made to incorporate conjunctions as much as possible, the conjunction "and" is occasionally not translated at the beginning of sentences because of differences in style between ancient and modern writing. Punctuation is a relatively modern invention, and ancient writers often linked most of their sentences with "and" or other connectives.

Alternative Readings: In addition to the more literal renderings, notations have been made to include readings of variant manuscripts, explanatory equivalents of the text, and alternate translations that may bring out a play on words difficult to maintain in the text. These notations have been used specifically to assist the reader in comprehending the terms used by the original author.

Names of God: In the Scriptures, the name of God is significant and understandably so. Traditionally, the translation "God" renders the Hebrew word *Elohim*. Likewise, the word "Lord" is a translation of *Adonai*. In the LSB, God's covenant name is rendered as Yahweh. The meaning and implication of this name is God's self-deriving, ongoing, and never-ending existence. Exodus 3:14–15 shows that God Himself considered it important for His people to know His name. The effect of revealing God's name is His distinction from other gods and His expression of intimacy with the nation of Israel. Such a dynamic is a prevalent characteristic of the Scriptures as Yahweh appears in the OT over 6,800 times.

In addition to Yahweh, the full name of God, the OT also includes references to God by a shorter version of His name, Yah. By itself, God's name "Yah" may not be as familiar, but the appearance of it is recognizable in Hebrew names and words (e.g. Zechar-*iah*, meaning Yah remembers, and Hallelu-*jah*, meaning praise Yah!). God's shortened name "Yah" is predominantly found in poetry and praise.

The translation "Yahweh" is substantiated by scholarly reconstruction as well as by historical discussions in Theodoret, Epiphanius, Clement of Alexandria, Origen, and Aquila. Consequently, those latter individuals affirm the usage of God's covenant name in the period of the early church. Preserving this in translation foundationally records what is present in the OT text. It also allows proper distinction between God's personal name and the title "Lord" (*Adonai*), which emphasizes God's authority. Even more, it helps the reader to engage God with the name which He gifted to His people. Thus, the reintroduction of God's personal name into the translation of the OT is a feature that enhances the precision, intensity, and clarity of the biblical text in English.

The NT uses the term "Lord" (*Kurios*) to translate Yahweh. The LSB maintains the translation "Lord" and does not change those instances to Yahweh. In cases when "Lord" explicitly translates Yahweh in a quotation of the OT, a footnote is provided stating such in certain editions. Nevertheless, the LSB maintains the translation of "Lord" in the NT for the same reason it upholds Yahweh in the OT: because that is what is written in the original text. Just as translations preserve the distinct wording between an OT passage and its quotation in the NT, so this distinction is preserved.

While there may be several factors behind this shift from Yahweh to Lord, for the apostles, one purpose centers on the declaration that Jesus Christ is Lord. Because the NT writers rendered Yahweh as Lord, they showed that Jesus is both Lord over all (even over Caesar, Acts 25:26) and none other than Yahweh Himself (Acts 2:25, 34, 36). Hence, the term "Lord" is a profound title showing Christ's supremacy in heaven and earth. That being said, the significance of this title presumes that one understands the movement from Yahweh to Lord. By rendering what is written in both the OT and NT, one can observe this shift and the fullness of its theological import.

The Terminology of Slave: The NASB has already translated the Greek term *doulos* frequently as "slave" in the NT. The LSB made this consistent across the NT. This upholds the lexical definition of the term, its consistent translation, and its distinction from other terms that do denote a "servant." Such consistency also highlights a biblical theological reality that Christians were slaves of sin but now are slaves of Christ (Rom 6:16–22). Biblical writers did not shy from this term because it condemned a wicked form of slavery (i.e., to sin, Satan, and death), highlighted the power of redemption, and affirmed one's total submission to the lordship of Christ.

In the OT, the Hebrew term *ebed* has more flexibility than *doulos* in the NT. For the word *ebed*, the notion of servant and slave can be present in describing one's relationship with God and man. The Messiah is the suffering Servant (Isa 52:13; cf. Acts 3:26) even as Israel was a slave of Egypt (Deut 5:15) but now a slave of God (Lev 25:55). Likewise, Joseph's brothers call themselves Joseph's servants (Gen 44:9; *ebed*) but later in the same verse they say they are willing to become Joseph's slaves (Gen 44:9; again *ebed*). All of this demonstrates that *ebed* can have both the notion of servant and slave. For this reason, the NT translates *ebed* not merely with *doulos* but other words (e.g., *pais*). The apostles recognized that *ebed* can have different nuances that go beyond "slave." Accordingly, in human relationships, the term "servant" is used for *ebed* when talking about one's general submission to another as opposed to economic ownership (slave). In relationships between man and God, slave is used unless *ebed* occurs with a personal name (e.g., My servant David). This formulation conforms to the nuances of the word and also connects well with NT usage of slave. This translation principle also often brings out that God's people emphasize their total subjection to their loving God (by calling themselves His slaves) even as He uses them uniquely as His servants in His plan.

Units of Measurement and Currency: Because this translation is designed to bring the reader to what was originally written, the LSB maintains the unit of measurement and currency used in the original writing. For clarity, conversions into both American and metric units are provided in the notes for measurements. This allows for the LSB to serve the entire English-speaking world by not choosing one country's unit of measurement or currency over another.

Hebrew Text: The Legacy Standard Bible utilizes the latest edition of Rudolf Kittel's *Biblia Hebraica* together with the most recent light from lexicography, cognate languages, and the Dead Sea Scrolls.

Hebrew Tenses, Aspect, and Stem: While recognizing the challenges of the Hebrew verbal system, the approach of the LSB has been guided by the Hebrew verb's form in light of its immediate and broad contexts. Thus, fundamentally, the LSB works to express distinctively the various verb forms. When appropriate, the translators have brought out various emphases of the verbal stem such as simple active, simple middle-passive, factitive, causative, and iterative. The translation has also attempted to capture the complete, ongoing, habitual, inceptive, and resultative aspect of the verb. Finally, the translators took into account temporal adverbials and the syntactic constructions surrounding the verb to identify its tense.

Greek Text: The Legacy Standard Bible has the benefit of a number of critical Greek texts in determining the best variant reading to translate. The 27th edition of Eberhard Nestle's *Novum Testamentum Graece*, supplemented by the 28th edition in the General Epistles, serves as the base text. On every variant reading the *Society of Biblical Literature GNT* as well as the *Tyndale House GNT* were also consulted. In the end, each decision was based upon the current available manuscript evidence.

Greek Tenses, Moods, and Syntax: A distinction was observed in the treatment of the Greek aorist tense and the Greek imperfect tense. Aorists are usually simple past tense in the indicative (e.g., "He did."). Imperfects are usually rendered as English past progressive (e.g., "He was doing") or inceptive (e.g., "He began to do"). "Began" is italicized if it renders an imperfect tense, in order to distinguish it from the Greek verb for "begin." In some contexts the Greek imperfect is conveyed better as a simple past tense (e.g., "had an illness for many years" would be preferable to "was having an illness for many years" and would be understood in the same way).

On the other hand, not all aorists have been rendered as English pasts ("He did"). Judging from the context in which they occur, some needed to be rendered as English perfects ("He has done"), or even as past perfects ("He had done") to make proper sense.

In addition to aorists and imperfects, the translators have been sensitive to bring out in English the perfect tense indicative and participle as conveying a current state initiated in the past ("one who has been born of God," cf. 1 John 5:1).

Imperatives: As for the distinction between aorist and present imperatives, the translators have usually rendered these imperatives as simple commands, rather than attempting a fine distinction as "Begin to do!" (for the aorist imperative), or, "Continually do!" (for the present imperative).

Participles: The LSB has also tried to convey the presence and function of each Greek participle. They often are translated temporally ("After Jesus entered Capernaum, he entered the synagogue"). This limits a translation reflecting what grammarians call the "attendant circumstance" function of the participle. While the translators do not question that function, the desire is to show the reader when there is a dependent participle which usually leads to a temporal or causal idea as conveyed in context.

Questions: In the rendering of negative questions introduced by the particle *me-* (which always expects the answer "No"), the LSB maintains the wording of the Greek text as opposed to adding a phrase at the end of the question (e.g., "He will not do this, will he?"). This allows for questions that truly have such phrasing to stand out (John 18:25). Readers are trusted to determine, given the context and the wording of the question, that a negative response is intended.

The Commitments of the Legacy Standard Bible

The Legacy Standard Bible aspires to be a legacy preserved—to uphold the work and tradition that is found in translations from the KJV, ASV, to NASB.

The Legacy Standard Bible aspires to be a legacy performed—to advance the commitments of past translations by bringing forth features of the original text relative to accuracy and consistency.

The Legacy Standard Bible aspires to be a legacy passed on—to equip generations to study Scripture and continue the philosophy of being a window into the original text for the glory of God.

The Lockman Foundation

EXPLANATION OF
GENERAL FORMAT

Paragraphs are designated by bold face verse numbers or letters.

Quotation Marks are used in the text in accordance with modern English usage.

Personal Pronouns are capitalized when pertaining to Deity. While descriptions about God are not capitalized, those which are used indisputably as direct titles for God are.

Italics are used in the text to indicate words which are not found in the original Hebrew, Aramaic, or Greek but implied by it. Italics are used in the footnotes to signify alternate readings for the text. Roman text in the footnote alternate readings is the same as italics in the Bible text.

Small Caps in the NT are used in the text to indicate OT quotations or obvious references to OT texts. Variations of OT wording are found in NT citations depending on whether the NT writer translated from a Hebrew text, used existing Greek or Aramaic translations, or paraphrased the material. It should be noted that modern rules for the indication of direct quotation were not used in biblical times; thus, the ancient writer would use exact quotations or references to quotation without specific indication of such.

Asterisks are used to mark present tense verbs in Greek which have been translated with an English past tense in order to conform to modern usage (i.e., historical presents). The translators recognized that in some contexts the present tense seems more unexpected and unjustified to the English reader than a past tense would have been. But Greek authors frequently used the present tense for the sake of heightened vividness, thereby transporting their readers in imagination to the actual scene at the time of occurrence. However, the translators felt that it would be wise to change these historical presents to English past tenses.

ABBREVIATIONS AND
SPECIAL MARKINGS

Aram	=	Aramaic
DSS	=	Dead Sea Scrolls
Gr	=	Greek translation of O.T. (Septuagint or LXX) or Greek text of N.T.
Heb	=	Hebrew text, usually Masoretic
Lat	=	Latin
M.T.	=	Masoretic text
Syr	=	Syriac
Lit	=	A literal translation
Or	=	An alternate translation justified by the Hebrew, Aramaic, or Greek
[]	=	In text, brackets indicate words probably not in the original writings
[]	=	In margin, brackets indicate references to a name, place, or thing similar to, but not identical with that in the text
Approx.	=	approximately
cf	=	compare
f, ff	=	following verse or verses
mg	=	Refers to a marginal reading on another verse
ms, mss	=	manuscript, manuscripts
v, vv	=	verse, verses

GENESIS

LEGACY STANDARD BIBLE

Creation

1 In the beginning God created the heavens and the earth. ² And the earth was formless and void, and darkness was over the surface of the deep, and the Spirit of God was hovering over the surface of the waters. ³ Then God said, "Let there be light"; and there was light. ⁴ And God saw that the light was good; and God separated the light from the darkness. ⁵ And God called the light day, and the darkness He called night. And there was evening and there was morning, one day.

6 Then God said, "Let there be an expanse in the midst of the waters, and let it separate the waters from the waters." ⁷ So God made the expanse and separated the waters which were below the expanse from the waters which were above the expanse; and it was so. ⁸ And God called the expanse heaven. And there was evening and there was morning, a second day.

9 Then God said, "Let the waters below the heavens be gathered into one place, and let the dry land appear"; and it was so. ¹⁰ And God called the dry land earth, and the gathering of the waters He called seas; and God saw that it was good. ¹¹ Then God said, "Let the earth sprout vegetation, plants yielding seed, *and* fruit trees on the earth bearing fruit after their kind with seed in them"; and it was so. ¹² And the earth brought forth vegetation, plants yielding seed after their kind, and trees bearing fruit with seed in them, after their kind; and God saw that it was good. ¹³ And there was evening and there was morning, a third day.

14 Then God said, "Let there be lights in the expanse of the heavens to separate the day from the night, and let them be for signs and for seasons and for days and years; ¹⁵ and let them be for lights in the expanse of the heavens to give light on the earth"; and it was so. ¹⁶ So God made the two great lights, the greater light to rule the day, and the lesser light to rule the night, and *also* the stars. ¹⁷ And God placed them in the expanse of the heavens to give light on the earth, ¹⁸ and to rule the day and the night, and to separate the light from the darkness; and God saw that it was good. ¹⁹ And there was evening and there was morning, a fourth day.

20 Then God said, "Let the waters swarm with swarms of living creatures, and let birds fly above the earth across the face of the expanse of the heavens." ²¹ And God created the great sea monsters and every living creature that moves, with which the waters swarmed after their kind, and every winged bird after its kind; and God saw that it was good. ²² Then God blessed them, saying, "Be fruitful and multiply, and fill the waters in the seas, and let the birds multiply on the earth." ²³ And there was evening and there was morning, a fifth day.

24 Then God said, "Let the earth bring forth living creatures after their kind: cattle and creeping things and beasts of the earth after their kind"; and it was so. ²⁵ God made the beasts of the earth after their kind, and the cattle after their kind, and every creeping thing of the ground after its kind; and God saw that it was good.

26 Then God said, "Let Us make man in Our image, according to Our likeness, so that they will have dominion over the fish of the sea and over the birds of the

sky and over the cattle and over all the earth and over every creeping thing that creeps on the earth." 27 And God created man in His own image, in the image of God He created him; male and female He created them. 28 God blessed them, and God said to them, "Be fruitful and multiply, and fill the earth, and subdue it; and have dominion over the fish of the sea and over the birds of the sky and over every living thing that creeps on the earth." 29 Then God said, "Behold, I have given to you every plant yielding seed that is on the surface of all the earth, and every tree which has *the* fruit of *the* tree yielding seed; it shall be food for you; 30 and to every beast of the earth and to every bird of the sky and to every thing that creeps on the earth which has life, *I have given* every green plant for food"; and it was so. 31 And God saw all that He had made, and behold, it was very good. And there was evening and there was morning, the sixth day.

2 Thus the heavens and the earth were completed, and all their hosts. 2 And on the seventh day God completed His work which He had done, and He rested on the seventh day from all His work which He had done. 3 Then God blessed the seventh day and sanctified it, because on it He rested from all His work which God had created in making *it*.

The Generations of the Heavens and the Earth

4 These are the generations of the heavens and the earth when they were created, in the day that Yahweh God made earth and heaven. 5 Now no shrub of the field was yet in the earth, and no plant of the field had yet grown, for Yahweh God had not caused it to rain upon the earth, and there was no man to cultivate the ground. 6 But a stream would rise from the earth and water the whole surface of the ground. 7 Then Yahweh God formed man of dust from the ground and breathed into his nostrils the breath of life; and so the man became a living being. 8 And Yahweh God planted a garden in Eden, toward the east; and there He placed the man whom He had formed. 9 And out of the ground Yahweh God caused to grow every tree that is desirable in appearance and good for food; the tree of life also in the midst of the garden, and the tree of the knowledge of good and evil.

10 Now a river went out of Eden to water the garden; and from there it divided and became four rivers. 11 The name of the first is Pishon; it is the one that went around the whole land of Havilah, where there is gold. 12 Now the gold of that land is good; the bdellium and the onyx stone are there. 13 And the name of the second river is Gihon; it is the one that went around the whole land of Cush. 14 And the name of the third river is Tigris; it is the one that went east of Asshur. And the fourth river is the Euphrates.

15 Then Yahweh God took the man and set him in the garden of Eden to cultivate it and keep it. 16 And Yahweh God commanded the man, saying, "From any tree of the garden you may surely eat; 17 but from the tree of the knowledge of good and evil, you shall not eat from it; for in the day that you eat from it you will surely die."

18 Then Yahweh God said, "It is not good for the man to be alone; I will make him a helper suitable for him." 19 And out of the ground Yahweh God had formed every beast of the field and every bird of the sky, and He brought *each* to the man to see what he would call it; and whatever the man called a living creature, that was its name. 20 And the man gave names to all the cattle and to the

birds of the sky and to every beast of the field; but for Adam there was not found a helper suitable for him. [21] So Yahweh God caused a deep sleep to fall upon the man, and he slept; then He took one of his ribs and closed up the flesh at that place. [22] And Yahweh God fashioned the rib, which He had taken from the man, into a woman, and He brought her to the man. [23] Then the man said,

"This one finally is bone
      of my bones,
   And flesh of my flesh;
   This one shall be called Woman,
   Because this one
         was taken out of Man."

[24] Therefore a man shall leave his father and his mother, and cleave to his wife; and they shall become one flesh. [25] And the man and his wife were both naked and were not ashamed.

Adam and Eve Sent Out
from the Garden

3 Now the serpent was more crafty than any beast of the field which Yahweh God had made. And he said to the woman, "Indeed, has God said, 'You shall not eat from any tree of the garden'?" [2] And the woman said to the serpent, "From the fruit of the trees of the garden we may eat; [3] but from the fruit of the tree which is in the midst of the garden, God said, 'You shall not eat from it, and you shall not touch it, lest you die.'" [4] And the serpent said to the woman, "You surely will not die! [5] For God knows that in the day you eat from it your eyes will be opened, and you will be like God, knowing good and evil." [6] Then the woman saw that the tree was good for food, and that it was a delight to the eyes, and that the tree was desirable to make *one* wise, so she took from its fruit and ate; and she gave also to her husband with her, and he ate. [7] And the

eyes of both of them were opened, and they knew that they were naked; and they sewed fig leaves together and made themselves loin coverings.

8 Then they heard the sound of Yahweh God walking in the garden in the cool of the day, and the man and his wife hid themselves from the presence of Yahweh God in the midst of the trees of the garden. [9] Yahweh God called to the man and said to him, "Where are you?" [10] And he said, "I heard the sound of You in the garden, and I was afraid because I was naked; so I hid." [11] And He said, "Who told you that you were naked? Have you eaten from the tree of which I commanded you not to eat?" [12] And the man said, "The woman whom You gave *to be* with me, she gave to me from the tree, and I ate." [13] Then Yahweh God said to the woman, "What is this you have done?" And the woman said, "The serpent deceived me, and I ate." [14] And Yahweh God said to the serpent,

"Because you have done this,
      Cursed are you more than any
            of the cattle,
      And more than every
            beast of the field;
      On your belly you will go,
      And dust you will eat
      All the days of your life;
   [15]   And I will put enmity
      Between you and the woman,
      And between your seed
            and her seed;
      He shall bruise you on the head,
      And you shall bruise him
            on the heel."

[16] To the woman He said,

"I will greatly multiply
      Your pain and conception,
      In pain you will bear children;
   Your desire will be for your husband,
   And he will rule over you."

¹⁷Then to Adam He said, "Because you have listened to the voice of your wife and have eaten from the tree about which I commanded you, saying, 'You shall not eat from it';

Cursed is the ground
   because of you;
In pain you will eat of it
All the days of your life.
¹⁸ "Both thorns and thistles
   it shall grow for you;
And you will eat
   the plants of the field;
¹⁹ By the sweat of your face
You will eat bread,
Till you return to the ground,
Because from it you were taken;
For you are dust,
And to dust you shall return."

20 Now the man called his wife's name Eve, because she was the mother of all *the* living. ²¹Then Yahweh God made garments of skin for Adam and his wife, and He clothed them.

22 Then Yahweh God said, "Behold, the man has become like one of Us to know good and evil; and now, lest he send forth his hand and take also from the tree of life and eat and live forever"— ²³therefore Yahweh God sent him out from the garden of Eden, to cultivate the ground from which he was taken. ²⁴So He drove the man out; and at the east of the garden of Eden He stationed the cherubim and the flaming sword which turned every direction to guard the way to the tree of life.

Cain and Abel

4 Now the man knew his wife Eve, and she conceived and gave birth to Cain, and she said, "I have gotten a man with *the help of* Yahweh." ² And again, she gave birth to his brother Abel. Abel was a keeper of flocks, but Cain was a cultivator of the ground. ³So it happened in the course of time that Cain brought an offering to Yahweh of the fruit of the ground. ⁴Abel, on his part, also brought of the firstborn of his flock and of their fat portions. And Yahweh had regard for Abel and for his offering; ⁵but for Cain and for his offering He had no regard. So Cain became very angry, and his countenance fell. ⁶Then Yahweh said to Cain, "Why are you angry? And why has your countenance fallen? ⁷If you do well, will not *your countenance* be lifted up? And if you do not do well, sin is lying at the door; and its desire is for you, but you must rule over it." ⁸Then Cain spoke to Abel his brother; and it happened when they were in the field, that Cain rose up against Abel his brother and killed him. **9** Then Yahweh said to Cain, "Where is Abel your brother?" And he said, "I do not know. Am I my brother's keeper?" ¹⁰And He said, "What have you done? The voice of your brother's blood is crying out to Me from the ground. ¹¹And now, cursed are you from the ground, which has opened its mouth to receive your brother's blood from your hand. ¹²When you cultivate the ground, it will no longer yield its strength to you; you will be a vagrant and a wanderer on the earth." ¹³And Cain said to Yahweh, "My punishment is too great to bear! ¹⁴Behold, You have driven me this day from the face of the ground; and from Your face I will be hidden, and I will be a vagrant and a wanderer on the earth, and it will be that whoever finds me will kill me." ¹⁵So Yahweh said to him, "Therefore whoever kills Cain, vengeance will be taken on him sevenfold." And Yahweh appointed a sign for Cain, so that no one who found him would strike him.

16 Then Cain went out from the presence of Yahweh and settled in the land of Nod, east of Eden.

17 Then Cain knew his wife, and she

conceived and gave birth to Enoch; and he built a city and called the name of the city Enoch, after the name of his son. [18] Now to Enoch was born Irad, and Irad was the father of Mehujael, and Mehujael was the father of Methushael, and Methushael was the father of Lamech. [19] And Lamech took for himself two wives: the name of the one was Adah, and the name of the other, Zillah. [20] And Adah gave birth to Jabal; he was the father of those who live in tents and have livestock. [21] And his brother's name was Jubal; he was the father of all those who play the lyre and pipe. [22] As for Zillah, she also gave birth to Tubal-cain, the forger of all implements of bronze and iron; and the sister of Tubal-cain was Naamah.

[23] And Lamech said to his wives,

"Adah and Zillah,
Hear my voice,
You wives of Lamech,
Give ear to my word,
For I have killed a man
for striking me;
And a boy for wounding me;
[24] If Cain is avenged sevenfold,
Then Lamech seventy-sevenfold."

[25] Then Adam knew his wife again; and she gave birth to a son and named him Seth, for she said, "God has set for me another seed in place of Abel, for Cain killed him." [26] And to Seth, to him also, a son was born; and he called his name Enosh. Then men began to call upon the name of Yahweh.

The Generations of Adam

5 This is the book of the generations of Adam. In the day when God created man, He made him in the likeness of God. [2] He created them male and female, and He blessed them and named them Man in the day when they were created.

3 When Adam had lived 130 years, he became the father of a son in his own likeness, according to his image, and named him Seth. [4] Then the days of Adam after he became the father of Seth were 800 years, and he became the father of other sons and daughters. [5] So all the days that Adam lived were 930 years, and he died.

6 And Seth lived 105 years and became the father of Enosh. [7] Then Seth lived 807 years after he became the father of Enosh, and he had other sons and daughters. [8] So all the days of Seth were 912 years, and he died.

9 And Enosh lived 90 years and became the father of Kenan. [10] Then Enosh lived 815 years after he became the father of Kenan, and he became the father of other sons and daughters. [11] So all the days of Enosh were 905 years, and he died.

12 And Kenan lived 70 years and became the father of Mahalalel. [13] Then Kenan lived 840 years after he became the father of Mahalalel, and he became the father of other sons and daughters. [14] So all the days of Kenan were 910 years, and he died.

15 And Mahalalel lived 65 years and became the father of Jared. [16] Then Mahalalel lived 830 years after he became the father of Jared, and he became the father of other sons and daughters. [17] So all the days of Mahalalel were 895 years, and he died.

18 And Jared lived 162 years and became the father of Enoch. [19] Then Jared lived 800 years after he became the father of Enoch, and he became the father of other sons and daughters. [20] So all the days of Jared were 962 years, and he died.

21 And Enoch lived 65 years and became the father of Methuselah. [22] Then Enoch walked with God 300 years after he became the father of Methuselah, and he became the father of *other* sons and daughters. ²³ So all the days of Enoch were 365 years. ²⁴ Enoch walked with God; and he was not, for God took him.

25 And Methuselah lived 187 years and became the father of Lamech. ²⁶ Then Methuselah lived 782 years after he became the father of Lamech, and he became the father of *other* sons and daughters. ²⁷ So all the days of Methuselah were 969 years, and he died.

28 And Lamech lived 182 years and became the father of a son. ²⁹ Now he called his name Noah, saying, "This one will give us rest from our work and from the pain of our hands *arising* from the ground which Yahweh has cursed." ³⁰ Then Lamech lived 595 years after he became the father of Noah, and he became the father of *other* sons and daughters. ³¹ So all the days of Lamech were 777 years, and he died.

32 And Noah was 500 years old, and Noah became the father of Shem, Ham, and Japheth.

The Nephilim and the Daughters of Men

6 Now it happened, when men began to multiply on the face of the land, and daughters were born to them, ² that the sons of men were good *in appearance*; and they took wives for themselves, whomever they chose. ³ Then Yahweh said, "My Spirit shall not strive with man forever because he indeed is flesh; nevertheless his days shall be 120 years." ⁴ The Nephilim were on the earth in those days, and also afterward, when the sons of God came in to the daughters of men, and they bore *children* to them. Those were the mighty men who *were* of old, men of renown.

5 Then Yahweh saw that the evil of man was great on the earth, and that every intent of the thoughts of his heart was only evil continually. ⁶ And Yahweh regretted that He had made man on the earth, and He was grieved in His heart. ⁷ And Yahweh said, "I will blot out man whom I have created from the face of the land, from man to animals to creeping things and to birds of the sky; for I regret that I have made them." ⁸ But Noah found favor in the eyes of Yahweh.

The Generations of Noah

9 These are the generations of Noah. Noah was a righteous man, blameless among *those in* his generations; Noah walked with God. ¹⁰ And Noah became the father of three sons: Shem, Ham, and Japheth.

11 Now the earth was corrupt before God, and the earth was filled with violence. ¹² And God saw the earth, and behold, it was corrupt; for all flesh had corrupted their way upon the earth.

13 Then God said to Noah, "The end of all flesh has come before Me; for the earth is filled with violence because of them; and behold, I am about to destroy them with the earth. ¹⁴ Make for yourself an ark of gopher wood; you shall make the ark with rooms, and you shall cover it inside and out with pitch. ¹⁵ Now this is how you shall make it: the length of the ark ¹300 cubits, its breadth 50 cubits, and its height 30 cubits. ¹⁶ You shall make a window for the ark, and complete it to one cubit from the top; and set the door of the ark in the side of it; you shall make it with lower, second, and third decks. ¹⁷ As for Me, behold

---

1. Approx. 450 ft. long, 75 ft. wide, and 45 ft. high or 135 m, 23 m, and 14 m

I am bringing the flood of water upon the earth, to destroy all flesh in which is the breath of life, from under heaven; everything that is on the earth shall breathe its last. ¹⁸ But I will establish My covenant with you; and you shall enter the ark—you and your sons and your wife and your sons' wives with you. ¹⁹ And of every living thing of all flesh, you shall bring two of every *kind* into the ark, to keep *them* alive with you; they shall be male and female. ²⁰ Of the birds after their kind, and of the animals after their kind, of every creeping thing of the ground after its kind, two of every *kind* will come to you to keep *them* alive. ²¹ As for you, take for yourself some of all food which is edible, and gather *it* to yourself; and it shall be for food for you and for them." ²² Thus Noah did; according to all that God had commanded him, so he did.

Noah and the Flood

7 Then Yahweh said to Noah, "Enter the ark, you and all your household, for you *alone* I have seen *to be* righteous before Me in this generation. ² You shall take with you of every clean animal by sevens, a male and his female; and of the animals that are not clean, two, a male and his female; ³ also of the birds of the sky, by sevens, male and female, to keep *their* seed alive on the face of all the earth. ⁴ For after seven more days, I will send rain on the earth forty days and forty nights; and I will blot out from the face of the land every living thing that I have made." ⁵ And Noah did according to all that Yahweh had commanded him.

6 Now Noah was six hundred years old when the flood of water came upon the earth. ⁷ Then Noah and his sons and his wife and his sons' wives with him entered the ark because of the water of the flood. ⁸ Of clean animals and animals that are not clean and birds and everything that creeps on the ground, ⁹ by twos they came to Noah into the ark, male and female, as God had commanded Noah. ¹⁰ Now it happened after the seven days, that the water of the flood came upon the earth. ¹¹ In the six hundredth year of Noah's life, in the second month, on the seventeenth day of the month, on this day all the fountains of the great deep split open, and the floodgates of the sky were opened. ¹² Then the rain came upon the earth for forty days and forty nights.

13 On this very day Noah and Shem and Ham and Japheth, the sons of Noah, and Noah's wife and the three wives of his sons with them, entered the ark, ¹⁴ they and every beast after its kind, and all the cattle after their kind, and every creeping thing that creeps on the earth after its kind, and every bird after its kind— every fowl, every winged creature. ¹⁵ So they came to Noah into the ark, by twos of all flesh in which was the breath of life. ¹⁶ And those that entered, male and female of all flesh, entered as God had commanded him; and Yahweh closed *it* behind him.

17 Then the flood came upon the earth for forty days, and the water multiplied and lifted up the ark, so that it rose above the earth. ¹⁸ And the water prevailed and multiplied greatly upon the earth, and the ark went on the surface of the water. ¹⁹ And the water prevailed more and more upon the earth, so that all the high mountains under all the heavens were covered. ²⁰ The water prevailed fifteen cubits higher, and the mountains were covered. ²¹ And all flesh that moved on the earth breathed its last, that is birds and cattle and beasts and every swarming thing that swarms upon the earth, as well as all mankind.

²² All in whose nostrils was the breath of the spirit of life—of all that was on the dry land—died. ²³ Thus He blotted out every living thing that was upon the face of the land, from man to animals to creeping things and to birds of the sky, and they were blotted out from the earth; and only Noah remained, and those that were with him in the ark. ²⁴ And the water prevailed upon the earth 150 days.

The Water Dries Up

8 Then God remembered Noah and all the beasts and all the cattle that were with him in the ark; and God caused a wind to pass over the earth, and the water subsided. ² Also the fountains of the deep and the floodgates of the sky were closed, and the rain from the sky was restrained; ³ and the water receded from the earth, going *forth* and returning, and at the end of 150 days the water decreased. ⁴ In the seventh month, on the seventeenth day of the month, the ark rested upon the mountains of Ararat. ⁵ Now the water decreased steadily until the tenth month; in the tenth *month*, on the first day of the month, the tops of the mountains appeared.

6 Then it happened at the end of forty days, that Noah opened the window of the ark which he had made; ⁷ and he sent out a raven, and it went out *flying* back and forth until the water was dried up from the earth. ⁸ Then he sent out a dove from him, to see if the water was abated from the face of the land; ⁹ but the dove found no resting place for the sole of its foot, so it returned to him into the ark, for the water was on the surface of all the earth. Then he stretched out his hand and took it and brought it into the ark to himself. ¹⁰ Then he waited yet another seven days; and again he sent out the dove from the ark. ¹¹ And the

dove came to him toward evening, and behold, in its beak was a freshly picked olive leaf. So Noah knew that the water was abated from the earth. ¹² Then he waited yet another seven days and sent out the dove; but it did not return to him again.

13 Now it happened in the six hundred and first year, in the first *month*, on the first of the month, the water was dried up from the earth. Then Noah removed the covering of the ark and looked, and behold, the surface of the ground was dried up. ¹⁴ In the second month, on the twenty-seventh day of the month, the earth was dry. ¹⁵ Then God spoke to Noah, saying, ¹⁶ "Go out of the ark, you and your wife and your sons and your sons' wives with you. ¹⁷ Bring out with you every living thing of all flesh that is with you, birds and animals and every creeping thing that creeps on the earth, that they may swarm on the earth, and that they may be fruitful and multiply on the earth." ¹⁸ So Noah went out, and his sons and his wife and his sons' wives with him. ¹⁹ Every beast, every creeping thing, and every bird, everything that moves on the earth, went out by their families from the ark.

Yahweh's Covenant with Noah

20 Then Noah built an altar to Yahweh and took of every clean animal and of every clean bird and offered burnt offerings on the altar. ²¹ And Yahweh smelled the soothing aroma; and Yahweh said to Himself, "I will never again curse the ground because of man, for the intent of man's heart is evil from his youth; and I will never again strike down every living thing as I have done.

²² "While all the days
    of the earth *remain*,
  Seedtime and harvest,
  And cold and heat,

And summer and winter,
And day and night
Shall not cease."

9 And God blessed Noah and his sons and said to them, "Be fruitful and multiply, and fill the earth. ² And the fear of you and the terror of you will be on every beast of the earth and on every bird of the sky; with everything that creeps on the ground, and all the fish of the sea, into your hand they are given. ³ Every moving thing that is alive shall be food for you; as *with* the green plant, I give all to you. ⁴ However, flesh with its life, *that is*, its blood, you shall not eat. ⁵ Surely I will require your lifeblood; from every living thing I will require it. And from *every* man, from each man's brother I will require the life of man.

⁶ "Whoever sheds man's blood,
By man his blood shall be shed,
For in the image of God
He made man.

⁷ "As for you, be fruitful and multiply;
Swarm on the earth
and multiply in it."

8 Then God spoke to Noah and to his sons with him, saying, ⁹ "As for Me, behold, I establish My covenant with you and with your seed after you; ¹⁰ and with every living creature that is with you, the birds, the cattle, and every beast of the earth with you; of all that comes out of the ark, even every beast of the earth. ¹¹ Indeed I establish My covenant with you; and all flesh shall never again be cut off by the water of the flood, and there shall never again be a flood to destroy the earth." ¹² Then God said, "This is the sign of the covenant which I am giving *to be* between Me and you and every living creature that is with you, for all successive generations; ¹³ I put My bow in the cloud, and it shall be for a sign of a covenant between Me and the earth. ¹⁴ And it will be, when I bring a cloud over the earth, that the bow will be seen in the cloud, ¹⁵ and I will remember My covenant, which is between Me and you and every living creature of all flesh; and never again shall the water become a flood to destroy all flesh. ¹⁶ So the bow shall be in the cloud, and I will look upon it, to remember the everlasting covenant between God and every living creature of all flesh that is on the earth." ¹⁷ And God said to Noah, "This is the sign of the covenant which I have established between Me and all flesh that is on the earth."

Noah's Three Sons

18 Now the sons of Noah who went out of the ark were Shem and Ham and Japheth; and Ham was the father of Canaan. ¹⁹ These three *were* the sons of Noah, and from these the whole earth was scattered abroad.

20 Then Noah began *to be* a man of the land and planted a vineyard. ²¹ And he drank of the wine and became drunk and uncovered himself inside his tent. ²² Then Ham, the father of Canaan, saw the nakedness of his father and told his two brothers outside. ²³ But Shem and Japheth took the garment and laid it upon both their shoulders and walked backward and covered the nakedness of their father; and their faces were turned backward, so that they did not see their father's nakedness. ²⁴ Then Noah awoke from his wine, and he knew what his youngest son had done to him. ²⁵ So he said,

"Cursed be Canaan;
A servant of servants
He shall be to his brothers."

²⁶ And he said,
"Blessed be Yahweh,
The God of Shem;
And let Canaan be his servant.

27 "May God enlarge Japheth,
And let him dwell in the tents
    of Shem;
And let Canaan be his servant."

28 And Noah lived 350 years after the flood. 29 So all the days of Noah were 950 years, and he died.

The Generations of Shem, Ham, and Japheth

10 Now these are the generations of Shem, Ham, and Japheth, the sons of Noah; and sons were born to them after the flood.

2 The sons of Japheth *were* Gomer and Magog and Madai and Javan and Tubal and Meshech and Tiras. 3 The sons of Gomer *were* Ashkenaz and Riphath and Togarmah. 4 The sons of Javan *were* Elishah and Tarshish, Kittim and Dodanim. 5 From these the coastlands of the nations were separated into their lands, every one according to his tongue, according to their families, into their nations.

6 The sons of Ham *were* Cush and Mizraim and Put and Canaan. 7 The sons of Cush *were* Seba and Havilah and Sabtah and Raamah and Sabteca; and the sons of Raamah *were* Sheba and Dedan. 8 Now Cush was the father of Nimrod; he began to be a mighty one on the earth. 9 He was a mighty hunter before Yahweh; therefore it is said, "Like Nimrod a mighty hunter before Yahweh." 10 The beginning of his kingdom was Babel and Erech and Accad and Calneh, in the land of Shinar. 11 From that land he went out to Assyria and built Nineveh and Rehoboth-Ir and Calah, 12 and Resen between Nineveh and Calah; that is the great city. 13 Mizraim was the father of Ludim and Anamim and Lehabim and Naphtuhim 14 and Pathrusim and Casluhim (from whom came the Philistines) and Caphtorim.

15 Canaan was the father of Sidon, his firstborn, and Heth 16 and the Jebusite and the Amorite and the Girgashite 17 and the Hivite and the Arkite and the Sinite 18 and the Arvadite and the Zemarite and the Hamathite; and afterward the families of the Canaanite were scattered. 19 The border of the Canaanite extended from Sidon as you go toward Gerar, as far as Gaza; as you go toward Sodom and Gomorrah and Admah and Zeboiim, as far as Lasha. 20 These are the sons of Ham, according to their families, according to their tongues, by their lands, by their nations.

21 Also to Shem, the father of all the children of Eber, *and* the older brother of Japheth, children were born. 22 The sons of Shem *were* Elam and Asshur and Arpachshad and Lud and Aram. 23 The sons of Aram *were* Uz and Hul and Gether and Mash. 24 Arpachshad was the father of Shelah; and Shelah was the father of Eber. 25 Now two sons were born to Eber; the name of the one *was* Peleg, for in his days the earth was divided; and his brother's name *was* Joktan. 26 And Joktan was the father of Almodad and Sheleph and Hazarmaveth and Jerah 27 and Hadoram and Uzal and Diklah 28 and Obal and Abimael and Sheba 29 and Ophir and Havilah and Jobab; all these were the sons of Joktan. 30 Now their settlement extended from Mesha as you go toward Sephar, the hill country of the east. 31 These are the sons of Shem, according to their families, according to their tongues, by their lands, according to their nations.

32 These are the families of the sons of Noah, according to their generations, by their nations; and out of these the nations were separated on the earth after the flood.

The Tower of Babel

11 Now the whole earth had the same language and the same words.

² And it happened as they journeyed east, that they found a plain in the land of Shinar and settled there. ³ Then they said to one another, "Come, let us make bricks and burn *them* thoroughly." And they had brick for stone, and they had tar for mortar. ⁴ And they said, "Come, let us build for ourselves a city, and a tower whose top *will reach* into heaven, and let us make for ourselves a name, lest we be scattered over the face of the whole earth." ⁵ Then Yahweh came down to see the city and the tower which the sons of men had built. ⁶ And Yahweh said, "Behold, they are one people, and they all have the same language. And this is what they have begun to do. So now nothing which they purpose to do will be impossible for them. ⁷ Come, let Us go down and there confuse their language, so that they will not understand one another's language." ⁸ So Yahweh scattered them from there over the face of the whole earth; and they stopped building the city. ⁹ Therefore its name was called Babel, because there Yahweh confused the language of the whole earth; and from there Yahweh scattered them over the face of the whole earth.

The Generations of Shem

10 These are the generations of Shem. Shem was 100 years old and became the father of Arpachshad two years after the flood; ¹¹ and Shem lived 500 years after he became the father of Arpachshad, and he became the father of *other* sons and daughters.

12 And Arpachshad lived 35 years and became the father of Shelah; ¹³ and Arpachshad lived 403 years after he became the father of Shelah, and he became the father of *other* sons and daughters.

14 And Shelah lived 30 years and became the father of Eber; ¹⁵ and Shelah lived 403 years after he became the father of Eber, and he became the father of *other* sons and daughters.

16 And Eber lived 34 years and became the father of Peleg; ¹⁷ and Eber lived 430 years after he became the father of Peleg, and he became the father of *other* sons and daughters.

18 And Peleg lived 30 years and became the father of Reu; ¹⁹ and Peleg lived 209 years after he became the father of Reu, and he became the father of *other* sons and daughters.

20 And Reu lived 32 years and became the father of Serug; ²¹ and Reu lived 207 years after he became the father of Serug, and he became the father of *other* sons and daughters.

22 And Serug lived 30 years and became the father of Nahor; ²³ and Serug lived 200 years after he became the father of Nahor, and he became the father of *other* sons and daughters.

24 Nahor lived 29 years and became the father of Terah; ²⁵ and Nahor lived 119 years after he became the father of Terah, and he became the father of *other* sons and daughters.

26 And Terah lived 70 years and became the father of Abram, Nahor, and Haran.

The Generations of Terah

27 Now these are the generations of Terah. Terah became the father of Abram, Nahor, and Haran; and Haran became the father of Lot. ²⁸ And Haran died in the presence of Terah his father in the land of his birth, in Ur of the Chaldeans. ²⁹ Abram and Nahor took wives for themselves. The name of Abram's wife was Sarai; and the name of Nahor's wife was Milcah, the daughter of Haran, the father of Milcah and the father of Iscah. ³⁰ And Sarai was barren; she had no child. **31** And Terah took Abram his son, and

Lot the son of Haran, his grandson, and Sarai his daughter-in-law, his son Abram's wife; and they went out together from Ur of the Chaldeans in order to go to the land of Canaan; and they came as far as Haran and settled there. ³² And the days of Terah were 205 years; and Terah died in Haran.

Yahweh Appears to Abram

12 And Yahweh said to Abram,
"Go forth from your land,
And from your kin
And from your father's house,
To the land which I will show you;
² And I will make you a great nation,
And I will bless you,
And make your name great;
And so you shall be a blessing;
³ And I will bless those who bless you,
And the one who curses you
I will curse.
And in you all the families
of the earth will be blessed."

4 So Abram went forth as Yahweh had spoken to him; and Lot went with him. Now Abram was seventy-five years old when he departed from Haran. ⁵ So Abram took Sarai his wife and Lot his brother's son, and all their possessions which they had accumulated, and the persons which they had acquired in Haran, and they departed to go forth to the land of Canaan; thus they came to the land of Canaan. ⁶ And Abram passed through the land as far as the site of Shechem, to the oak of Moreh. Now the Canaanite *was* then in the land. ⁷ Then Yahweh appeared to Abram and said, "To your seed I will give this land." So he built an altar there to Yahweh who had appeared to him. ⁸ Then he proceeded from there to the mountain on the east of Bethel, and he pitched his tent with Bethel on the west and Ai on the east; and there he built an altar to Yahweh and called upon the name of Yahweh. ⁹ And Abram journeyed on, continuing toward the Negev.

Abram and Sarai in Egypt

10 Now there was a famine in the land; so Abram went down to Egypt to sojourn there, for the famine was severe in the land. ¹¹ And it happened as he drew near to entering Egypt, that he said to Sarai his wife, "Now behold, I know that you are a woman beautiful in appearance; ¹² and it will be when the Egyptians see you, that they will say, 'This is his wife'; and they will kill me, but they will let you live. ¹³ Please say that you are my sister so that it may go well with me because of you, and that I may live on account of you." ¹⁴ Now it happened when Abram came into Egypt, that the Egyptians saw that the woman was very beautiful. ¹⁵ And Pharaoh's officials saw her and praised her to Pharaoh; and the woman was taken into Pharaoh's house. ¹⁶ Therefore he treated Abram well because of her; and sheep and oxen and donkeys and male and female servants and female donkeys and camels came into his possession.

17 But Yahweh struck Pharaoh and his house with great plagues because of Sarai, Abram's wife. ¹⁸ Then Pharaoh called Abram and said, "What is this you have done to me? Why did you not tell me that she was your wife? ¹⁹ Why did you say, 'She is my sister,' so that I took her for myself as a wife? So now, here is your wife, take her and go." ²⁰ So Pharaoh commanded *his* men concerning him; and they sent him away with his wife and all that belonged to him.

Abram and Lot Separate

13 So Abram went up from Egypt to the Negev, he and his wife and all that belonged to him, and Lot with him.

2 Now Abram was very rich in livestock, in silver and in gold. ³ And he went on his journeys from the Negev as far as Bethel, to the place where his tent had been at the beginning, between Bethel and Ai, ⁴ to the place of the altar which he had made there formerly; and there Abram called upon the name of Yahweh.

5 Now Lot, who was going with Abram, also had flocks and herds and tents. ⁶ And the land could not sustain them while living together, for their possessions were so abundant that they were not able to live together. ⁷ And there was strife between the herdsmen of Abram's livestock and the herdsmen of Lot's livestock. Now the Canaanite and the Perizzite were living then in the land.

8 So Abram said to Lot, "Please let there be no strife between you and me, nor between my herdsmen and your herdsmen, for we are brothers. ⁹ Is not the whole land before you? Please separate from me; if *to* the left, then I will go to the right; or if *to* the right, then I will go to the left." ¹⁰ Then Lot lifted up his eyes and saw all the valley of the Jordan, that it was well watered everywhere—*this was* before Yahweh destroyed Sodom and Gomorrah—like the garden of Yahweh, like the land of Egypt as you go to Zoar. ¹¹ So Lot chose for himself all the valley of the Jordan, and Lot journeyed eastward. Thus they separated from each other. ¹² Abram lived in the land of Canaan, while Lot lived in the cities of the valley and moved his tents as far as Sodom. ¹³ Now the men of Sodom were evil and sinners, exceedingly so, against Yahweh.

14 And Yahweh said to Abram, after Lot had separated from him, "Now lift up your eyes and look from the place where you are, northward and southward and eastward and westward; ¹⁵ for all the land which you see, I will give it to you and to your seed forever. ¹⁶ And I will make your seed as the dust of the earth, so that if anyone can number the dust of the earth, then your seed can also be numbered. ¹⁷ Arise, walk about the land through its length and breadth; for I will give it to you." ¹⁸ Then Abram moved his tent and came and lived by the oaks of Mamre, which are in Hebron, and there he built an altar to Yahweh.

Kings of the Valley Take Lot

14 And it happened in the days of Amraphel king of Shinar, Arioch king of Ellasar, Chedorlaomer king of Elam, and Tidal king of Goiim, ² *that* they made war with Bera king of Sodom, and with Birsha king of Gomorrah, Shinab king of Admah, and Shemeber king of Zeboiim, and the king of Bela (that is, Zoar). ³ All these came as allies to the valley of Siddim (that is, the Salt Sea). ⁴ Now for twelve years they had served Chedorlaomer, but the thirteenth year they rebelled. ⁵ So in the fourteenth year Chedorlaomer and the kings that were with him, came and struck the Rephaim in Ashteroth-karnaim and the Zuzim in Ham and the Emim in Shaveh-kiriathaim, ⁶ and the Horites in their Mount Seir, as far as El-paran, which is by the wilderness. ⁷ Then they turned back and came to En-mishpat (that is, Kadesh). And they struck all the country of the Amalekites, and also the Amorites, who were living in Hazazon-tamar. ⁸ And the king of Sodom and the king of Gomorrah and the king of Admah and the king of Zeboiim and the king of Bela (that is, Zoar) came out; and they arranged *themselves* for battle against them in the valley of Siddim, ⁹ against Chedorlaomer king of Elam and Tidal king of Goiim and Amraphel king of Shinar and Arioch king of

Ellasar, four kings against five— [10] now the valley of Siddim was full of tar pits— and the kings of Sodom and Gomorrah fled, and they fell into them; but those who remained behind fled to the hill country. [11] Then they took all the possessions of Sodom and Gomorrah and all their food supply and departed. [12] They also took Lot, Abram's nephew, and his possessions and departed; now he was living in Sodom.

[13] Then a fugitive came and told Abram the Hebrew. Now he was dwelling by the oaks of Mamre the Amorite, brother of Eshcol and brother of Aner, and these were in a covenant with Abram. [14] So Abram heard that his relative had been taken captive, and he led out his trained men, born in his house, 318 *in number*, and went in pursuit as far as Dan. [15] And he divided his *men* against them by night, he and his servants, and struck them and pursued them as far as Hobah, which is north of Damascus. [16] And he brought back all the possessions, and he also brought back his relative Lot with his possessions and also the women and the people.

Melchizedek Blesses Abram

[17] Then after he came back from striking down Chedorlaomer and the kings who were with him, the king of Sodom went out to meet him at the valley of Shaveh (that is, the King's Valley). [18] And Melchizedek king of Salem brought out bread and wine; now he was a priest of God Most High. [19] Then he blessed him and said,

"Blessed be Abram
    of God Most High,
  Possessor of heaven and earth;
[20] And blessed be God Most High,
    Who has delivered your enemies
      into your hand."

Then he gave him a tenth of all. [21] And the king of Sodom said to Abram, "Give the people to me, but take the possessions for yourself." [22] Then Abram said to the king of Sodom, "I have raised my hand to Yahweh God Most High, possessor of heaven and earth, [23] that I will not take a thread or a sandal strap or anything that is yours, so that you would not say, 'I have made Abram rich.' [24] I will take nothing except what the young men have eaten, and the share of the men who went with me, Aner, Eshcol, and Mamre; let them take their share."

Yahweh Cuts a Covenant with Abram

15 After these things the word of Yahweh came to Abram in a vision, saying,

  "Do not fear, Abram,
    I am a shield to you;
    Your reward shall be very great."

[2] And Abram said, "O Lord Yahweh, what will You give me, as I go on being childless, and the heir of my house is Eliezer of Damascus?" [3] And Abram said, "Since You have given no seed to me, behold, one born in my house is my heir." [4] Then behold, the word of Yahweh came to him, saying, "This one will not be your heir; but one who will come forth from your own body, he shall be your heir." [5] And He brought him outside and said, "Now look toward the heavens, and number the stars, if you are able to number them." And He said to him, "So shall your seed be." [6] Then he believed in Yahweh; and He counted it to him as righteousness. [7] And He said to him, "I am Yahweh who brought you out of Ur of the Chaldeans, to give you this land to possess it." [8] And he said, "O Lord Yahweh, how may I know that I will possess it?" [9] So He said to him, "Bring Me a three year old heifer, and a three year old female goat, and a three year old ram, and a turtledove, and a

young pigeon." ¹⁰ Then he brought all these to Him and split them into parts down the middle and laid each part opposite the other; but he did not split apart the birds. ¹¹ Then the birds of prey came down upon the carcasses, and Abram drove them away.

12 Now it happened that when the sun was going down, a deep sleep fell upon Abram; and behold, terror *and* great darkness fell upon him. ¹³ Then *God* said to Abram, "Know for certain that your seed will be sojourners in a land that is not theirs, and they will be enslaved and mistreated four hundred years. ¹⁴ But I will also judge the nation to whom they are enslaved, and afterward they will come out with many possessions. ¹⁵ As for you, you shall go to your fathers in peace; you will be buried at a good old age. ¹⁶ Then in the fourth generation they will return here, for the iniquity of the Amorite is not yet complete."

17 Now it happened that the sun had set, and it was very dark, and behold, *there appeared* a smoking oven and a flaming torch which passed between these pieces. ¹⁸ On that day Yahweh cut a covenant with Abram, saying,

"To your seed I have given this land,
From the river of Egypt
       as far as the great river,
       the river Euphrates:
¹⁹ the Kenite and the Kenizzite and the Kadmonite ²⁰ and the Hittite and the Perizzite and the Rephaim ²¹ and the Amorite and the Canaanite and the Girgashite and the Jebusite."

Sarai and Hagar

16 Now Sarai, Abram's wife, had borne him no *children*, and she had an Egyptian servant-woman whose name was Hagar. ² So Sarai said to Abram, "Now behold, Yahweh has shut my *womb* from bearing *children*. Please go in to my servant-woman; perhaps I will obtain children through her." And Abram listened to the voice of Sarai. ³ And after Abram had lived ten years in the land of Canaan, Abram's wife Sarai took Hagar the Egyptian, her servant-woman, and gave her to her husband Abram as his wife. ⁴ So he went in to Hagar, and she conceived. Then she saw that she had conceived, so her mistress became contemptible in her sight. ⁵ And Sarai said to Abram, "May the violence done to me be upon you. I gave my servant-woman into your embrace, but she saw that she had conceived, so I became contemptible in her sight. May Yahweh judge between you and me." ⁶ But Abram said to Sarai, "Behold, your servant-woman is in your hand; do to her what is good in your sight." So Sarai afflicted her, and she fled from her presence.

7 Now the angel of Yahweh found her by a spring of water in the wilderness, by the spring on the way to Shur. ⁸ And he said, "Hagar, Sarai's servant-woman, where have you come from and where are you going?" And she said, "I am fleeing from the presence of my mistress Sarai." ⁹ Then the angel of Yahweh said to her, "Return to your mistress and humble yourself under her hands." ¹⁰ Moreover, the angel of Yahweh said to her, "I will greatly multiply your seed so that they will be too many to be counted." ¹¹ And the angel of Yahweh said to her further,

"Behold, you are with child,
    And you will bear a son;
    And you shall call his name
        Ishmael,
    Because Yahweh has heard
        your affliction.
¹² "And he will be a wild donkey
        of a man,

His hand *will be*
    against everyone,
And everyone's hand *will be*
    against him;
And he will dwell in the face of all
    his brothers."

[13] Then she called the name of Yahweh who spoke to her, "You are a God who sees"; for she said, "Have I even remained alive here after seeing Him?" [14] Therefore the well was called Beer-lahai-roi; behold, it is between Kadesh and Bered.

[15] So Hagar bore Abram a son; and Abram called the name of his son, whom Hagar bore, Ishmael. [16] Now Abram was eighty-six years old when Hagar bore Ishmael to him.

Circumcision, the Sign of the Covenant

17 Now it happened that when Abram was ninety-nine years old, Yahweh appeared to Abram and said to him,
  "I am God Almighty;
  Walk before Me and be blameless,
[2] so that I may confirm My covenant
    between Me and you,
  And that I may multiply you
    exceedingly."

[3] Then Abram fell on his face, and God spoke with him, saying,
[4] "As for Me, behold,
  My covenant is with you,
  And you will be the father
    of a multitude of nations.
[5] "And no longer shall your name
    be called Abram,
  But your name shall be Abraham;
  For I have made you the father
    of a multitude of nations.

[6] "And I will make you exceedingly fruitful, and I will make nations of you, and kings will go forth from you. [7] And I will establish My covenant between Me and you and your seed after you throughout their generations for an everlasting covenant, to be God to you and to your seed after you. [8] And I will give to you and to your seed after you, the land of your sojournings, all the land of Canaan, for an everlasting possession; and I will be their God."

[9] God said further to Abraham, "Now as for you, you shall keep My covenant, you and your seed after you throughout their generations. [10] This is My covenant, which you shall keep, between Me and you and your seed after you: every male among you shall be circumcised. [11] And you shall be circumcised in the flesh of your foreskin, and it shall be the sign of the covenant between Me and you. [12] And every male among you who is eight days old shall be circumcised throughout your generations, one who is born in the house or one who is bought with money from any foreigner, who is not of your seed. [13] A *servant* who is born in your house or who is bought with your money shall surely be circumcised; thus shall My covenant be in your flesh for an everlasting covenant. [14] But an uncircumcised male who is not circumcised in the flesh of his foreskin, that person shall be cut off from his people; he has broken My covenant."

Sarah Will Bear Isaac

[15] Then God said to Abraham, "As for Sarai your wife, you shall not call her name Sarai, but Sarah *shall be* her name. [16] And I will bless her, and indeed I will give you a son by her. Then I will bless her, and she shall be *a mother of* nations; kings of peoples will come from her." [17] Then Abraham fell on his face and laughed and said in his heart, "Will *a son* be born to a man one hundred years old? And will Sarah, who is ninety years old, bear *a son*?" [18] And Abraham said to God, "Oh that Ishmael might live before You!" [19] But God said,

"No, but Sarah your wife will bear you a son, and you shall call his name Isaac; and I will establish My covenant with him for an everlasting covenant for his seed after him. ²⁰ As for Ishmael, I have heard you; behold, I will bless him and will make him fruitful and will multiply him exceedingly. He shall become the father of twelve princes, and I will make him a great nation. ²¹ But My covenant I will establish with Isaac, whom Sarah will bear to you at this season next year." ²² So He finished talking with him, and God went up from Abraham.

23 Then Abraham took Ishmael his son, and all who were born in his house and all who were bought with his money, every male among the men of Abraham's household, and circumcised the flesh of their foreskin in the very same day, as God had spoken with him. ²⁴ Now Abraham was ninety-nine years old when he was circumcised in the flesh of his foreskin. ²⁵ And Ishmael his son was thirteen years old when he was circumcised in the flesh of his foreskin. ²⁶ In the very same day Abraham was circumcised, and Ishmael his son. ²⁷ Now all the men of his household, who were born in the house or bought with money from a foreigner, were circumcised with him.

Yahweh Appears to Abraham

18 Then Yahweh appeared to him by the oaks of Mamre, while he was sitting at the tent door in the heat of the day. ² And he lifted up his eyes and looked, and behold, three men were standing nearby; he saw, and he ran from the tent door to meet them, and he bowed himself to the earth, ³ and he said, "My Lord, if now I have found favor in Your sight, please do not pass Your servant by. ⁴ Please let a little water

be brought and wash your feet, and rest yourselves under the tree; ⁵ and let me bring a piece of bread, that you may refresh your hearts; after that you may pass on, since in such a manner you have passed *by* your servant." And they said, "So you shall do, as you have said." ⁶ So Abraham hurried into the tent to Sarah and said, "Hurry, prepare *¹*three seahs of fine flour, knead *it*, and make bread cakes." ⁷ Abraham also ran to the herd and took a tender and choice calf and gave *it* to *his* young man, and he hurried to prepare it. ⁸ Then he took curds and milk and the calf which he had prepared, and placed *it* before them; and he was standing by them under the tree, and they ate.

9 Then they said to him, "Where is Sarah your wife?" And he said, "There, in the tent." ¹⁰ And He said, "I will surely return to you at this time next year; and behold, Sarah your wife will have a son." And Sarah was listening at the tent door which was behind him. ¹¹ Now Abraham and Sarah were old, advanced in age; Sarah was past childbearing. ¹² And Sarah laughed to herself, saying, "After I am worn out, shall I have pleasure, my lord being old also?" ¹³ And Yahweh said to Abraham, "Why did Sarah laugh, saying, 'Shall I indeed bear *a son*, when I am *so* old?' ¹⁴ Is anything too difficult for Yahweh? At the appointed time I will return to you, at this time next year, and Sarah will have a son." ¹⁵ Then Sarah denied *it* however, saying, "I did not laugh"; for she was afraid. And He said, "No, but you did laugh."

Yahweh and Abraham
Speak About Sodom

16 Then the men rose up from there and looked down toward Sodom; and

---

1. Approx. 21 qt. or 23 l, a seah was approx. 7 qt. or 7.7 l

Abraham was walking with them to send them off. ¹⁷ Now Yahweh said, "Shall I conceal from Abraham what I am about to do, ¹⁸ since Abraham will surely become a great and mighty nation, and in him all the nations of the earth will be blessed? ¹⁹ For I have known him, so that he may command his children and his household after him, that they keep the way of Yahweh to do righteousness and justice, so that Yahweh may bring upon Abraham what He has spoken about him." ²⁰ So Yahweh said, "The outcry of Sodom and Gomorrah is indeed great, and their sin is exceedingly grave. ²¹ I will go down now and see whether they have done entirely according to its outcry, which has come to Me; and if not, I will know." ²² Then the men turned away from there and went toward Sodom, while Abraham was still standing before Yahweh. ²³ Then Abraham came near and said, "Will You indeed sweep away the righteous with the wicked? ²⁴ Suppose there are fifty righteous within the city; will You indeed sweep *it* away and not spare the place for the sake of the fifty righteous who are in it? ²⁵ Far be it from You to do such a thing, to put to death the righteous with the wicked, so that the righteous and the wicked are *treated* alike. Far be it from You! Shall not the Judge of all the earth do justice?" ²⁶ So Yahweh said, "If I find in Sodom fifty righteous within the city, then I will spare the whole place on their account." ²⁷ And Abraham answered and said, "Now behold, I have ventured to speak to the Lord, although I am *but* dust and ashes. ²⁸ Suppose the fifty righteous are lacking five, will You destroy the whole city because of five?" And He said, "I will not destroy *it* if I find forty-five there." ²⁹ Then he spoke to Him yet again and said, "Suppose forty are found there?"

And He said, "I will not do *it* on account of the forty." ³⁰ Then he said, "Oh may the Lord not be angry, and I shall speak; suppose thirty are found there?" And He said, "I will not do *it* if I find thirty there." ³¹ And he said, "Now behold, I have ventured to speak to the Lord; suppose twenty are found there?" And He said, "I will not destroy *it* on account of the twenty." ³² Then he said, "Oh may the Lord not be angry, and I shall speak only this once; suppose ten are found there?" And He said, "I will not destroy *it* on account of the ten." ³³ And as soon as He had finished speaking to Abraham, Yahweh departed, and Abraham returned to his place.

Yahweh Destroys Sodom and Gomorrah

19 Then the two angels came to Sodom in the evening as Lot was sitting in the gate of Sodom. Lot saw *them* and rose to meet them and bowed down *with his* face to the ground. ² And he said, "Now behold, my lords, please turn aside into your servant's house, and spend the night, and wash your feet; then you may rise early and go on your way." They said however, "No, but we shall spend the night in the square." ³ Yet he pressed them strongly, so they turned aside to him and entered his house; and he made a feast for them and baked unleavened bread, and they ate. ⁴ Before they lay down, the men of the city, the men of Sodom, surrounded the house, from young to old, all the people from every quarter; ⁵ and they called to Lot and said to him, "Where are the men who came to you tonight? Bring them out to us that we may know them." ⁶ But Lot went out to them at the doorway and shut the door behind him, ⁷ and said, "Please, my brothers, do not act wickedly. ⁸ Now behold, I have two daughters who have not known a man;

please let me bring them out to you, and do to them what is good in your eyes; only do nothing to these men, inasmuch as they have come under the shelter of my roof." [9] But they said, "Step aside." Furthermore, they said, "This one came to sojourn, and already he is persistently acting like a judge; now we will treat you more wickedly than them." So they pressed hard against Lot and stepped up to break the door. [10] But the men reached out their hands and brought Lot into the house with them and shut the door. [11] And they struck the men who were at the doorway of the house with blindness, from small to great, so that they wearied *themselves trying* to find the doorway.

12 Then the *two* men said to Lot, "Whom else have you here? A son-in-law, and your sons, and your daughters, and everyone you have in the city, bring *them* out of the place; [13] for we are about to destroy this place because their outcry has become great before Yahweh, so Yahweh has sent us to destroy it." [14] And Lot went out and spoke to his sons-in-law, who were to marry his daughters, and said, "Get up, get out of this place, for Yahweh will destroy the city." But he appeared to his sons-in-law to be jesting.

15 Now at the breaking of dawn, the angels urged Lot, saying, "Get up, take your wife and your two daughters who are here, lest you be swept away in the punishment of the city." [16] But he hesitated. So the men seized his hand and the hand of his wife and the hands of his two daughters, for the compassion of Yahweh *was* upon him; and they brought him out and put him outside the city. [17] Now it happened, as they brought them outside, one said, "Escape for your life! Do not look behind you, and do not stay anywhere in the valley; escape to the mountains, lest you be swept away."

[18] But Lot said to them, "Oh no, my lords! [19] Now behold, your servant has found favor in your sight, and you have magnified your lovingkindness, which you have shown me by preserving my life; but I cannot escape to the mountains, lest calamity overtake me and I die; [20] now behold, this town is near *enough* to flee to, and it is small. Please, let me escape there (is it not small?) that my life may be preserved." [21] And he said to him, "Behold, I grant you this request also, that I will not overthrow the city of which you have spoken. [22] Hurry, escape there, for I cannot do anything until you arrive there." Therefore the name of the city was called Zoar.

23 The sun had risen over the earth when Lot came to Zoar. [24] And Yahweh rained on Sodom and Gomorrah brimstone and fire from Yahweh out of heaven, [25] and He overthrew those cities, and all the valley, and all the inhabitants of the cities, and what grew on the ground. [26] Then his wife, from behind him, looked *back*, and she became a pillar of salt.

27 Now Abraham arose early in the morning *and went* to the place where he had stood before Yahweh; [28] and he looked down toward Sodom and Gomorrah, and toward all the land of the valley, and he saw, and behold, the smoke of the land went up like the smoke of a furnace.

29 Thus it happened, when God destroyed the cities of the valley, that God remembered Abraham and sent Lot out of the midst of the overthrow, when He overthrew the cities in which Lot lived.

Lot and His Daughters

30 And Lot went up from Zoar and stayed in the mountains, and his two daughters with him; for he was afraid to stay in Zoar; and he stayed in a cave, he and his two daughters. [31] Then the firstborn said to the younger, "Our father is old, and there is not a man on earth to come in to us after the manner of the earth. ³²Come, let us make our father drink wine, and let us lie with him that we may preserve *our* seed through our father." ³³So they made their father drink wine that night, and the firstborn went in and lay with her father; and he did not know when she lay down or when she arose. ³⁴Now it happened on the following day, that the firstborn said to the younger, "Behold, I lay last night with my father; let us make him drink wine tonight also; and you go in and lie with him, that we may preserve *our* seed through our father." ³⁵So they made their father drink wine that night also, and the younger arose and lay with him; and he did not know when she lay down or when she arose. ³⁶Thus both the daughters of Lot conceived by their father. ³⁷And the firstborn bore a son and called his name Moab; he is the father of the Moabites to this day. ³⁸As for the younger, she also bore a son and called his name Ben-ammi; he is the father of the sons of Ammon to this day.

Abraham Lies to Abimelech

20 And Abraham journeyed from there toward the land of the Negev and settled between Kadesh and Shur; then he sojourned in Gerar. ²And Abraham said of Sarah his wife, "She is my sister." So Abimelech king of Gerar sent and took Sarah. ³But God came to Abimelech in a dream of the night and said to him, "Behold, you are a dead man because of the woman whom you have taken, for she is married." ⁴(Now Abimelech had not come near her.) Then he said, "Lord, will You kill a nation, even *though* righteous? ⁵Did he not himself say to me, 'She is my sister'? And she herself also said, 'He is my brother.' In the integrity of my heart and the innocence of my hands I have done this."

⁶Then God said to him in the dream, "Indeed, I know that in the integrity of your heart you have done this, and I also held you back from sinning against Me; therefore I did not let you touch her. ⁷So now, return the man's wife, for he is a prophet, and he will pray for you, and you will live. But if you do not return *her*, know that you shall surely die, you and all who are yours."

⁸So Abimelech arose early in the morning and called all his servants and told all these things in their hearing; and the men were greatly afraid. ⁹Then Abimelech called Abraham and said to him, "What have you done to us? And how have I sinned against you, that you have brought on me and on my kingdom a great sin? You have done to me things that ought not to be done." ¹⁰And Abimelech said to Abraham, "What have you seen, that you have done this thing?" ¹¹And Abraham said, "Because I said, surely there is no fear of God in this place, and they will kill me because of my wife. ¹²Besides, she actually is my sister, the daughter of my father, but not the daughter of my mother, and she became my wife; ¹³and it happened when God caused me to wander from my father's house, that I said to her, 'This is the lovingkindness which you will show to me: everywhere we go, say of me, "He is my brother." ' " ¹⁴Abimelech then took sheep and oxen and male and female slaves and gave them to Abraham and returned his wife Sarah to him. ¹⁵And Abimelech said, "Behold, my land is before you; settle wherever it is good in your sight." ¹⁶To Sarah he said, "Behold, I have given your brother one thousand pieces of silver; behold, it is your vindication before all who are with you, and before all you are cleared."

¹⁷ And Abraham prayed to God, and God healed Abimelech and his wife and his maidservants, so that they bore *children.* ¹⁸ For Yahweh had utterly shut all the wombs of the household of Abimelech because of Sarah, Abraham's wife.

Isaac Is Born

21 Now Yahweh visited Sarah as He had said, and Yahweh did for Sarah as He had promised. ² So Sarah conceived and bore a son to Abraham in his old age, at the appointed time of which God had spoken to him. ³ And Abraham called the name of his son who was born to him, whom Sarah bore to him, Isaac. ⁴ Then Abraham circumcised his son Isaac when he was eight days old, as God had commanded him. ⁵ Now Abraham was one hundred years old when his son Isaac was born to him. ⁶ And Sarah said, "God has made laughter for me; everyone who hears will laugh with me." ⁷ And she said, "Who would have said to Abraham that Sarah would nurse children? Yet I have borne *him* a son in his old age."

Sarah Sends Hagar Away

8 And the child grew and was weaned, and Abraham made a great feast on the day that Isaac was weaned. ⁹ And Sarah saw the son of Hagar the Egyptian, whom she had borne to Abraham, laughing *in jest.* ¹⁰ Therefore she said to Abraham, "Drive out this maidservant and her son! The son of this maidservant shall not be an heir with my son, with Isaac." ¹¹ And the matter distressed Abraham greatly because of his son. ¹² So God said to Abraham, "Do not be distressed because of the boy and your maidservant; whatever Sarah tells you, listen to her voice, for through Isaac your seed shall be named. ¹³ And of the son of the maidservant I will make a

nation also, because he is your seed." ¹⁴ So Abraham rose early in the morning and took bread and a skin of water and gave *them* to Hagar, putting *them* on her shoulder, and *gave her* the child, and sent her away. So she went and wandered about in the wilderness of Beersheba.

15 When the water in the skin was finished, she put the child under one of the bushes. ¹⁶ Then she went and sat down opposite him, about a bowshot away, for she said, "Do not let me see when the child dies." And she sat opposite him and lifted up her voice and wept. ¹⁷ Then God heard the voice of the boy crying; and the angel of God called to Hagar from heaven and said to her, "What is the matter with you, Hagar? Do not fear, for God has heard the voice of the boy where he is. ¹⁸ Arise, lift up the boy, and hold him by the hand, for I will make a great nation of him." ¹⁹ Then God opened her eyes, and she saw a well of water; and she went and filled the skin with water and gave the boy a drink.

20 And God was with the boy, and he grew; and he lived in the wilderness and was an archer. ²¹ And he lived in the wilderness of Paran, and his mother took a wife for him from the land of Egypt.

A Covenant with Abimelech

22 Now it happened at that time, that Abimelech and Phicol, the commander of his army, spoke to Abraham, saying, "God is with you in all that you do; ²³ so now, swear to me here by God that you will not deal falsely with me or with my offspring or with my posterity, but according to the lovingkindness that I have shown you, you shall show me and the land in which you have sojourned." ²⁴ And Abraham said, "I swear it." ²⁵ But Abraham reproved Abimelech about the well of water which the servants of

Abimelech had seized. ²⁶ And Abimelech said, "I do not know who has done this thing; you did not tell me, nor did I hear of it until today." ²⁷ So Abraham took sheep and oxen and gave them to Abimelech, and the two of them cut a covenant. ²⁸ Then Abraham set seven ewe lambs of the flock by themselves. ²⁹ And Abimelech said to Abraham, "What do these seven ewe lambs mean, which you have set by themselves?" ³⁰ He said, "You shall take these seven ewe lambs from my hand so that it may be a witness to me, that I dug this well." ³¹ Therefore he called that place Beersheba, because there the two of them swore *an oath.* ³² So they cut a covenant at Beersheba; and Abimelech and Phicol, the commander of his army, arose and returned to the land of the Philistines. ³³ And *Abraham* planted a tamarisk tree at Beersheba, and there he called upon the name of Yahweh, the Everlasting God. ³⁴ And Abraham sojourned in the land of the Philistines for many days.

The Offering of Isaac

22 Now it happened after these things, that God tested Abraham and said to him, "Abraham!" And he said, "Here I am." ² Then He said, "Take now your son, your only one, whom you love, Isaac, and go forth to the land of Moriah, and offer him there as a burnt offering on one of the mountains of which I will tell you." ³ So Abraham rose early in the morning and saddled his donkey and took two of his young men with him and Isaac his son; and he split wood for the burnt offering and arose and went to the place of which God had told him. ⁴ On the third day Abraham lifted up his eyes and saw the place from a distance. ⁵ And Abraham said to his young men, "Stay here with the donkey while I and the boy go over there; and we will worship, and we will return to you." ⁶ Then Abraham took the wood of the burnt offering and put it on Isaac his son, and he took in his hand the fire and the knife. So the two of them walked on together.

7 Then Isaac spoke to Abraham his father and said, "My father!" And he said, "Here I am, my son." And he said, "Behold, the fire and the wood, but where is the lamb for the burnt offering?" ⁸ And Abraham said, "God will provide for Himself the lamb for the burnt offering, my son." So the two of them walked on together.

9 Then they came to the place of which God had told him; and Abraham built the altar there and arranged the wood and bound his son Isaac and put him on the altar, on top of the wood. ¹⁰ And Abraham stretched out his hand and took the knife to slay his son. ¹¹ But the angel of Yahweh called to him from heaven and said, "Abraham, Abraham!" And he said, "Here I am." ¹² And He said, "Do not stretch out your hand against the boy, and do nothing to him; for now I know that you fear God, since you have not withheld your son, your only one, from Me." ¹³ Then Abraham lifted up his eyes and saw, and behold, *there was* a ram after *it had been* caught in the thicket by its horns; and Abraham went and took the ram and offered it up for a burnt offering in the place of his son. ¹⁴ And Abraham called the name of that place Yahweh Will Provide, as it is said this day, "In the mount of Yahweh it will be provided."

15 Then the angel of Yahweh called to Abraham a second time from heaven, ¹⁶ and said, "By Myself I have sworn, declares Yahweh, because you have done this thing and have not spared your son, your only one, ¹⁷ indeed I

will greatly bless you, and I will greatly multiply your seed as the stars of the heavens and as the sand which is on the seashore; and your seed shall possess the gate of his enemies. [18] In your seed all the nations of the earth shall be blessed, because you have listened to My voice." [19] So Abraham returned to his young men, and they arose and walked together to Beersheba; and Abraham lived at Beersheba.

[20] Now it happened after these things, that it was told to Abraham, saying, "Behold, Milcah also has borne children to your brother Nahor: [21] Uz his firstborn and Buz his brother and Kemuel the father of Aram [22] and Chesed and Hazo and Pildash and Jidlaph and Bethuel." [23] And Bethuel was the father of Rebekah. These eight Milcah bore to Nahor, Abraham's brother. [24] And his concubine, whose name was Reumah, also bore Tebah and Gaham and Tahash and Maacah.

Sarah's Death and Burial

23 And Sarah lived 127 years; *these were* the years of the life of Sarah. [2] Sarah died in Kiriath-arba (that is, Hebron) in the land of Canaan; and Abraham came to mourn for Sarah and to weep for her. [3] Then Abraham rose from before his dead and spoke to the sons of Heth, saying, [4] "I am a sojourner and a foreign resident among you; give me a possession for a burial site among you that I may bury my dead out of my sight." [5] And the sons of Heth answered Abraham, saying to him, [6] "Hear us, my lord, you are a mighty prince among us; bury your dead in the choicest of our burial sites; none of us will refuse you his burial sites for burying your dead." [7] So Abraham rose and bowed to the people of the land, the sons of Heth. [8] And he spoke with them, saying, "If it is your desire *for me* to bury my dead out of my sight, hear me, and meet with Ephron the son of Zohar for me, [9] that he may give me the cave of Machpelah which belongs to him, which is at the end of his field; for the full price let him give it to me in your presence as a possession for a burial site." [10] Now Ephron was sitting among the sons of Heth; and Ephron the Hittite answered Abraham in the hearing of the sons of Heth, *even* of all who went in at the gate of his city, saying, [11] "No, my lord, hear me; I give you the field, and I give you the cave that is in it. In the sight of the sons of my people I give it to you; bury your dead." [12] And Abraham bowed before the people of the land. [13] And he spoke to Ephron in the hearing of the people of the land, saying, "If you will only please hear me; I will give the silver for the field, accept *it* from me that I may bury my dead there." [14] Then Ephron answered Abraham, saying to him, [15] "My lord, hear me; a piece of land worth *f* four hundred shekels of silver, what is that between me and you? So bury your dead." [16] So Abraham heard Ephron; and Abraham weighed out for Ephron the silver which he had named in the hearing of the sons of Heth, four hundred shekels of silver, commercial standard.

[17] So Ephron's field, which was in Machpelah, which faced Mamre, the field and the cave which was in it, and all the trees which were in the field, that were within all the confines of its border, were deeded over [18] to Abraham as purchased in the sight of the sons of Heth, before all who came in at the gate of his city. [19] After this, Abraham buried Sarah his wife in the cave of the

---

1. Approx. 10 lb. or 4.4 kg, a shekel was approx. 0.4 oz. or 11 gm

field at Machpelah facing Mamre (that is, Hebron) in the land of Canaan. ²⁰ So the field and the cave that is in it were deeded over to Abraham for a possession for a burial site by the sons of Heth.

A Wife for Isaac

24 Now Abraham was old, advanced in age; and Yahweh had blessed Abraham in every way. ² And Abraham said to his servant, the oldest of his household, who ruled over all that he owned, "Please place your hand under my thigh, ³ and I will make you swear by Yahweh, the God of heaven and the God of earth, that you shall not take a wife for my son from the daughters of the Canaanites, among whom I live, ⁴ but you will go to my land and to my kin, and take a wife for my son Isaac." ⁵ And the servant said to him, "Suppose the woman is not willing to follow me to this land; should I indeed take your son back to the land from where you came?" ⁶ Then Abraham said to him, "Beware lest you take my son back there! ⁷ Yahweh, the God of heaven, who took me from my father's house and from the land of my kin, and who spoke to me and who swore to me, saying, 'To your seed I will give this land,' He will send His angel before you, and you will take a wife for my son from there. ⁸ But if the woman is not willing to follow you, then you will be free from this oath of mine; only do not take my son back there." ⁹ So the servant placed his hand under the thigh of Abraham his master and swore to him concerning this matter.

10 Then the servant took ten camels from the camels of his master, and he went with all kinds of good things of his master's in his hand. So he arose and went to Mesopotamia, to the city of Nahor. ¹¹ And he made the camels kneel down outside the city by the well of water at evening time, the time when the women go out to draw water. ¹² And he said, "O Yahweh, the God of my master Abraham, please cause *this* to happen before me today, and show lovingkindness to my master Abraham. ¹³ Behold, I am standing by the spring of water, and the daughters of the men of the city are coming out to draw water; ¹⁴ now may it be that the young woman to whom I say, 'Please let down your jar so that I may drink,' and she says, 'Drink, and I will give *water* to your camels to drink also'—*may* she *be the one* whom You have decided for Your servant Isaac; and by this I will know that You have shown lovingkindness to my master."

Rebekah Goes with Abraham's Servant

15 And before he had finished speaking, behold, Rebekah who was born to Bethuel the son of Milcah, the wife of Abraham's brother Nahor, was coming out with her jar on her shoulder. ¹⁶ Now the young woman was very beautiful in appearance, a virgin, and no man had known her; and she went down to the spring and filled her jar and came up. ¹⁷ Then the servant ran to meet her and said, "Please give me a little water to drink from your jar." ¹⁸ And she said, "Drink, my lord"; and she quickly lowered her jar to her hand and gave him a drink. ¹⁹ Now when she had finished giving him a drink, she said, "I will draw also for your camels until they have finished drinking." ²⁰ So she hurried and emptied her jar into the watering channel and ran again to the well to draw, and she drew for all his camels. ²¹ Meanwhile, the man was gazing at her in silence, to know whether Yahweh had made his journey successful or not. **22** Now it happened that when the camels had finished drinking, the man took a gold ring weighing a half-shekel and two bracelets for her wrists weighing ten shekels in gold, ²³ and said, "Whose daughter are you? Please tell me, is there a place for us to lodge in your father's house?" ²⁴ And she said to him, "I am the daughter of Bethuel, the son of Milcah, whom she bore to Nahor." ²⁵ And she said to him, "We have plenty of both straw and feed, and a place to lodge in." ²⁶ Then the man bowed low and worshiped Yahweh. ²⁷ And he said, "Blessed be Yahweh, the God of my master Abraham, who has not forsaken His lovingkindness and His truth toward my master; as for me, Yahweh has guided me in the way to the house of my master's brothers."

28 Then the young woman ran and told her mother's household about these things. ²⁹ Now Rebekah had a brother whose name was Laban; and Laban ran outside to the man at the spring. ³⁰ Now it happened, when he saw the ring and the bracelets on his sister's wrists, and when he heard the words of Rebekah his sister, saying, "This is what the man said to me," he came out to the man; and behold, he was standing by the camels at the spring. ³¹ And he said, "Come in, blessed of Yahweh! Why do you stand outside since I have prepared the house and a place for the camels?" ³² So the man came into the house. Then Laban unloaded the camels, and he gave straw and feed to the camels, and water to wash his feet and the feet of the men who were with him. ³³ Then *food* was set before him to eat, but he said, "I will not eat until I have spoken my words." And he said, "Speak!" ³⁴ So he said, "I am Abraham's servant. ³⁵ And Yahweh has greatly blessed my master, so he has become great; and He has given him flocks and herds, and silver and gold, and male slaves and female slaves, and camels and donkeys. ³⁶ Now Sarah my master's wife bore a son to my master in her old age, and he has given him all that he has. ³⁷ And my master made me swear, saying, 'You shall not take a wife for my son from the daughters of the Canaanites, in whose land I live; ³⁸ but you shall go to my father's house and to my family, and take a wife for my son.' ³⁹ Then I said to my master, 'Suppose the woman does not follow me.' ⁴⁰ And he said to me, 'Yahweh, before whom I have walked, will send His angel with you and will make your journey successful, and you will take a wife for my son from my family and from my father's house. ⁴¹ Then you will be free from my oath, when you come to my relatives. Now if they do not give her to you, you will be free from my oath.'

42 "So I came today to the spring and said, 'O Yahweh, the God of my master Abraham, if now You will make my journey on which I go successful; ⁴³ behold, I am standing by the spring of water, and may it be that the maiden who comes out to draw, and to whom I say, "Please let me drink a little water from your jar"; ⁴⁴ and she will say to me, "You drink, and I will draw for your camels also"; she is the woman whom Yahweh has decided upon for my master's son.'

45 "Before I had finished speaking in my heart, behold, Rebekah was coming out with her jar on her shoulder, and she went down to the spring and drew, and I said to her, 'Please give me a drink.' ⁴⁶ Then she hurried and lowered her jar from her *shoulder* and said, 'Drink, and I will also give *water* to your camels to drink'; so I drank, and she also gave *water* to the camels to drink. ⁴⁷ Then I asked her and said, 'Whose daughter are you?' And she said, 'The daughter of Bethuel, Nahor's son, whom Milcah bore to him'; and I put the ring on her nose and the bracelets on her wrists.

⁴⁸ And I bowed low and worshiped Yahweh; and I blessed Yahweh, the God of my master Abraham, who had guided me in the true way to take the daughter of my master's relative for his son. ⁴⁹ So now if you are going to show lovingkindness and truth with my master, tell me; and if not, tell me, that I may turn to the right or to the left."

50 Then Laban and Bethuel answered and said, "The matter comes from Yahweh; *so* we cannot speak to you bad or good. ⁵¹ Behold, Rebekah is before you, take *her* and go, and let her be the wife of your master's son, as Yahweh has spoken."

52 Now it happened that when Abraham's servant heard their words, he bowed himself to the ground before Yahweh. ⁵³ The servant brought out articles of silver and articles of gold, and garments, and gave them to Rebekah; he also gave precious things to her brother and to her mother. ⁵⁴ Then he and the men who were with him ate and drank and spent the night. And then they arose in the morning, and he said, "Send me away to my master." ⁵⁵ But her brother and her mother said, "Let the young woman stay with us *a few* days, or *even* ten; afterward she will go." ⁵⁶ And he said to them, "Do not delay me, since Yahweh has made my way successful. Send me away that I may go to my master." ⁵⁷ And they said, "We will call the young woman and ask about her wishes." ⁵⁸ Then they called Rebekah and said to her, "Will you go with this man?" And she said, "I will go." ⁵⁹ Thus they sent away their sister Rebekah and her nurse with Abraham's servant and his men. ⁶⁰ And they blessed Rebekah and said to her,

"May you, our sister,
    Become thousands
        of ten thousands,

And may your seed possess
    The gate of those who hate him."

⁶¹ Then Rebekah arose with her young women, and they mounted the camels and went after the man. So the servant took Rebekah and went.

Rebekah Becomes Isaac's Wife

62 Now Isaac had come from going to Beer-lahai-roi, for he was living in the land of the Negev. ⁶³ And Isaac went out to muse in the field toward evening; and he lifted up his eyes and looked, and behold, camels were coming. ⁶⁴ And Rebekah lifted up her eyes and saw Isaac and dismounted from the camel. ⁶⁵ Then she said to the servant, "Who is that man walking in the field to meet us?" And the servant said, "He is my master." Then she took her veil and covered herself. ⁶⁶ And the servant recounted to Isaac all the things that he had done. ⁶⁷ Then Isaac brought her into his mother Sarah's tent, and he took Rebekah, and she became his wife, and he loved her. Thus, Isaac was comforted after his mother's *death*.

The Death of Abraham

25 Now Abraham took another wife, whose name was Keturah. ² And she bore to him Zimran and Jokshan and Medan and Midian and Ishbak and Shuah. ³ Now Jokshan was the father of Sheba and Dedan. And the sons of Dedan were Asshurim and Letushim and Leummim. ⁴ And the sons of Midian *were* Ephah and Epher and Hanoch and Abida and Eldaah. All these *were* the sons of Keturah. ⁵ And Abraham gave all that he had to Isaac; ⁶ but to the sons of the concubines which Abraham had, Abraham gave gifts while he was still living, and he sent them away from his son Isaac eastward, to the land of the east.

7 These are the days of the years of Abraham's life that he lived, 175 years. ⁸ And Abraham breathed his last and died in a good old age, an old man and full *of days*; and he was gathered to his people. ⁹ Then his sons Isaac and Ishmael buried him in the cave of Machpelah, in the field of Ephron the son of Zohar the Hittite, facing Mamre, ¹⁰ the field which Abraham bought from the sons of Heth; there Abraham was buried with Sarah his wife. ¹¹ Now it happened after the death of Abraham, that God blessed his son Isaac; and Isaac lived by Beer-lahai-roi.

The Generations of Ishmael

12 Now these are the generations of Ishmael, Abraham's son, whom Hagar the Egyptian, Sarah's servant-woman, bore to Abraham; ¹³ and these are the names of the sons of Ishmael, by their names, in the order of their birth: Nebaioth, the firstborn of Ishmael, and Kedar and Adbeel and Mibsam ¹⁴ and Mishma and Dumah and Massa, ¹⁵ Hadad and Tema, Jetur, Naphish, and Kedemah. ¹⁶ These are the sons of Ishmael and these are their names, by their villages, and by their camps; twelve princes according to their tribes. ¹⁷ These are the years of the life of Ishmael, 137 years; and he breathed his last and died and was gathered to his people. ¹⁸ And they dwelt from Havilah to Shur which is east of Egypt as one goes toward Assyria; he settled in the face of all his brothers.

The Generations of Isaac

19 Now these are the generations of Isaac, Abraham's son: Abraham became the father of Isaac; ²⁰ and Isaac was forty years old when he took Rebekah, the daughter of Bethuel the Aramean of Paddan-aram, the sister of Laban the Aramean, to be his wife. ²¹ And Isaac entreated Yahweh on behalf of his wife because she was barren; and Yahweh was moved by his entreaty. So Rebekah his wife conceived. ²² But the children struggled together within her; and she said, "If it is so, why then am I this *way?*" So she went to inquire of Yahweh. ²³ And Yahweh said to her,

"Two nations are in your womb;
　And two peoples will be separated
　　from your body;
　And one people shall be stronger
　　than the other;
　And the older shall serve
　　the younger."

²⁴ And her days to give birth were fulfilled, and behold, there were twins in her womb. ²⁵ And the first came forth red, all over like a hairy garment; and they named him Esau. ²⁶ Afterward his brother came forth with his hand holding on to Esau's heel, so his name was called Jacob; and Isaac was sixty years old when she gave birth to them.

Esau Sells His Birthright

27 And the boys grew up; Esau became a skillful hunter, a man of the field, but Jacob was a peaceful man, living in tents. ²⁸ Isaac loved Esau because he had an appetite for *hunted* game, but Rebekah loved Jacob.

29 And Jacob had cooked stew. And Esau came in from the field, and he was famished. ³⁰ Then Esau said to Jacob, "Please give me a swallow from the red stuff—this red stuff, for I am famished." Therefore his name was called Edom. ³¹ But Jacob said, "First sell me your birthright." ³² And Esau said, "Behold, I am about to die; so of what *use* then is the birthright to me?" ³³ And Jacob said, "First swear to me"; so he swore to him and sold his birthright to Jacob. ³⁴ So Jacob gave Esau bread and lentil stew; and he ate and drank and rose and went away. Thus Esau despised his birthright.

Yahweh Establishes the Oath with Isaac

26 Now there was a famine in the land, besides the previous famine that had occurred in the days of Abraham. So Isaac went to Gerar, to Abimelech king of the Philistines. ² And Yahweh appeared to him and said, "Do not go down to Egypt; dwell in the land of which I shall tell you. ³ Sojourn in this land, and I will be with you and bless you, for to you and to your seed I will give all these lands, and I will establish the oath which I swore to your father Abraham. ⁴ And I will multiply your seed as the stars of heaven, and I will give your seed all these lands; and by your seed all the nations of the earth shall be blessed; ⁵ because Abraham listened to My voice and kept My charge, My commandments, My statutes, and My laws."

Isaac and Abimelech

6 So Isaac lived in Gerar. ⁷ Then the men of the place asked about his wife. And he said, "She is my sister," for he was afraid to say, "my wife," *thinking,* "lest the men of the place kill me on account of Rebekah, for she is beautiful in appearance." ⁸ Now it happened, when he had been there a long time, that Abimelech king of the Philistines looked out through a window and saw, and behold, Isaac was caressing his wife Rebekah. ⁹ Then Abimelech called Isaac and said, "Behold, surely she is your wife! How then did you say, 'She is my sister'?" And Isaac said to him, "Because I said, 'Lest I die on account of her.'" ¹⁰ And Abimelech said, "What is this you have done to us? One of the people might easily have lain with your wife, and you would have brought guilt upon us." ¹¹ So Abimelech commanded all the people,

saying, "He who touches this man or his wife shall surely be put to death."

12 And Isaac sowed in that land and reaped in the same year one hundredfold. And Yahweh blessed him, ¹³ and the man became great and continued to grow greater until he became very great; ¹⁴ and he had possessions of flocks and possessions of herds and many servants, so that the Philistines were jealous of him. ¹⁵ Now all the wells which his father's servants had dug in the days of Abraham his father, the Philistines stopped up by filling them with earth. ¹⁶ Then Abimelech said to Isaac, "Go away from us, for you are too mighty for us." ¹⁷ And Isaac departed from there and camped in the valley of Gerar and settled there.

The Quarrel over the Wells

18 Then Isaac dug again the wells of water which had been dug in the days of his father Abraham, but the Philistines had stopped them up after the death of Abraham; and he called them by the same names by which his father had called them. ¹⁹ Then Isaac's servants dug in the valley and found there a well of flowing water. ²⁰ And the herdsmen of Gerar contended with the herdsmen of Isaac, saying, "The water is ours!" So he named the well Esek, because they quarreled with him. ²¹ Then they dug another well, and they contended over it also, so he called it Sitnah. ²² Then he moved away from there and dug another well, and they did not contend over it; so he named it Rehoboth, and he said, "At last Yahweh has made room for us, and we will be fruitful in the land."

23 And he went up from there to Beersheba. ²⁴ And Yahweh appeared to him that night and said,

"I am the God of your father Abraham;
Do not fear, for I am with you.

I will bless you
> and multiply your seed,
For the sake of My servant
> Abraham."

²⁵ So he built an altar there and called upon the name of Yahweh and pitched his tent there; and there Isaac's servants dug out a well.

Isaac's Oath with Abimelech

26 Now Abimelech came to him from Gerar with his adviser Ahuzzath and Phicol the commander of his army. ²⁷ And Isaac said to them, "Why have you come to me, since you hate me and have sent me away from you?" ²⁸ Then they said, "We see plainly that Yahweh has been with you; so we said, 'Let there now be an oath between us—between you and us—and let us cut a covenant with you, ²⁹ that you will do us no harm, just as we have not touched you and have done to you nothing but good and have sent you away in peace. You are now the blessed of Yahweh.'" ³⁰ Then he made them a feast, and they ate and drank. ³¹ In the morning they arose early, and each swore to the other; then Isaac sent them away, and they departed from him in peace. ³² Now it happened on that day, that Isaac's servants came in and told him about the well which they had dug and said to him, "We have found water." ³³ So he called it Shibah; therefore the name of the city is Beersheba to this day.

34 And Esau was forty years old, and he took as a wife Judith the daughter of Beeri the Hittite, and *also* Basemath the daughter of Elon the Hittite; ³⁵ and they brought bitterness to Isaac and Rebekah.

Isaac Calls to Bless Esau

27 Now it happened that when Isaac was old and his eyes were too dim to see, that he called his older son Esau and said to him, "My son." And he said to him, "Here I am." ² And Isaac said, "Behold now, I am old, *and* I do not know the day of my death. ³ So now, please take up your gear, your quiver and your bow, and go out to the field and hunt game for me; ⁴ and prepare a savory dish for me such as I love, and bring it to me that I may eat, so that my soul may bless you before I die."

5 Now Rebekah was listening while Isaac was speaking to his son Esau. Then Esau went to the field to hunt for game to bring *to Isaac*. ⁶ But Rebekah spoke to her son Jacob, saying, "Behold, I heard your father speaking to your brother Esau, saying, ⁷ 'Bring me *some* game and prepare a savory dish for me, that I may eat and bless you in the presence of Yahweh before my death.' ⁸ So now, my son, listen to my voice as I command you. ⁹ Go now to the flock and get for me two choice young goats from there, that I may prepare them *as* a savory dish for your father, such as he loves. ¹⁰ Then you shall bring *it* to your father, that he may eat, so that he may bless you before his death." ¹¹ Then Jacob answered his mother Rebekah, "Behold, Esau my brother is a hairy man, and I am a smooth man. ¹² Perhaps my father will feel me, then I will be as a mocker in his sight, and I will bring upon myself a curse and not a blessing." ¹³ But his mother said to him, "Your curse be on me, my son; only listen to my voice, and go, get *them* for me." ¹⁴ So he went and got *them* and brought *them* to his mother; and his mother made a savory dish such as his father loved. ¹⁵ Then Rebekah took the best garments of Esau her elder son, which were with her in the house, and she put them on Jacob her younger son. ¹⁶ And she put the skins of the young goats on his hands and on the smooth part of his neck. [17] She also gave the savory dish and the bread, which she had prepared into the hand of her son Jacob.

Isaac Blesses Jacob and Esau

18 Then he came to his father and said, "My father." And he said, "Here I am. Who are you, my son?" [19] And Jacob said to his father, "I am Esau your firstborn; I have done as you told me. Rise up, please, sit and eat of my game, that your soul may bless me." [20] Then Isaac said to his son, "How is it that you have found it so quickly, my son?" And he said, "Because Yahweh your God caused *it* to happen to me." [21] Then Isaac said to Jacob, "Please come near, that I may feel you, my son, whether you are really my son Esau or not." [22] So Jacob came near to Isaac his father, and he felt him and said, "The voice is the voice of Jacob, but the hands are the hands of Esau." [23] And he did not recognize him because his hands were hairy like his brother Esau's hands; so he blessed him. [24] And he said, "Are you really my son Esau?" And he said, "I am." [25] So he said, "Bring *it* near to me, and I will eat of my son's game, that my soul may bless you." And he brought *it* near to him, and he ate; he also brought *it* wine, and he drank. [26] Then his father Isaac said to him, "Please come near and kiss me, my son." [27] So he came near and kissed him; and he smelled the smell of his garments, and then he blessed him and said,

"See, the smell of my son
    Is like the smell of a field
        which Yahweh has blessed;
[28] Now may God give you
        of the dew of heaven,
    And of the fatness of the earth,
    And an abundance of grain
        and new wine;

[29] May peoples serve you,
    And nations bow down to you;
    Be master of your brothers,
    And may your mother's sons
        bow down to you.
    Cursed be those who curse you,
    And blessed be those who
        bless you."

30 Now it happened that as soon as Isaac had finished blessing Jacob, and Jacob had hardly gone out from the presence of Isaac his father, that Esau his brother came in from his hunting. [31] Then he also made a savory dish and brought it to his father; and he said to his father, "Let my father arise and eat of his son's game, that your soul may bless me." [32] And Isaac his father said to him, "Who are you?" And he said, "I am your son, your firstborn, Esau." [33] Then Isaac trembled exceedingly violently and said, "Who was he then that hunted game and brought *it* to me, so that I ate of all *of it* before you came and blessed him? Indeed, he shall be blessed." [34] As Esau heard the words of his father, he cried out with an exceedingly great and bitter cry and said to his father, "Bless me, me also, O my father!" [35] And he said, "Your brother came deceitfully and has taken away your blessing." [36] Then he said, "Is he not rightly named Jacob, for he has supplanted me these two times? He took away my birthright, and behold, now he has taken away my blessing." And he said, "Have you not reserved a blessing for me?" [37] But Isaac answered and said to Esau, "Behold, I have made him your master, and all his *fellow* brothers I have given to him as servants; and with grain and new wine I have sustained him. Now as for you then, what can I do, my son?" [38] And Esau said to his father, "Do you have only one blessing, my father? Bless me, *even* me also, O my father." So Esau lifted his voice and wept.

39 Then Isaac his father answered and said to him,

"Behold, away from the fatness
of the earth shall be
your habitation,
And away from the dew of heaven
from above.
40 "By your sword you shall live,
And your brother you shall serve;
But it shall be when you
become restless,
That you will break his yoke
from your neck."

41 So Esau bore a grudge against Jacob because of the blessing with which his father had blessed him; and Esau said in his heart, "The days of mourning for my father are near; then I will kill my brother Jacob." **42** Then the words of her elder son Esau were told to Rebekah. So she sent and called her younger son Jacob and said to him, "Behold, your brother Esau is consoling himself concerning you *by planning* to kill you. **43** So now, my son, listen to my voice, and arise, flee to Haran, to my brother Laban! **44** Stay with him a few days, until your brother's wrath subsides, **45** until your brother's anger against you subsides and he forgets what you did to him. Then I will send and get you from there. Why should I be bereaved of you both in one day?"

46 Then Rebekah said to Isaac, "I am tired of living because of the daughters of Heth; if Jacob takes a wife from the daughters of Heth, like these, from the daughters of the land, what good will my life be to me?"

Jacob Is Sent to Laban

28 So Isaac called Jacob and blessed him and commanded him and said to him, "You shall not take a wife from the daughters of Canaan. **2** Arise, go to Paddan-aram, to the house of Bethuel your mother's father; and from there take to yourself a wife from the daughters of Laban your mother's brother. **3** May God Almighty bless you and make you fruitful and multiply you, that you may become an assembly of peoples. **4** May He also give you the blessing of Abraham, to you and to your seed with you, that you may possess the land of your sojournings, which God gave to Abraham." **5** Then Isaac sent Jacob away, and he went to Paddan-aram to Laban, son of Bethuel the Aramean, the brother of Rebekah, the mother of Jacob and Esau.

6 And Esau saw that Isaac had blessed Jacob and sent him away to Paddan-aram to take for himself a wife from there, *and that* when he blessed him he commanded him, saying, "You shall not take a wife from the daughters of Canaan," **7** and that Jacob had listened to his father and his mother and had gone to Paddan-aram. **8** So Esau saw that the daughters of Canaan were displeasing in the sight of his father Isaac; **9** and Esau went to Ishmael and took Mahalath, the daughter of Ishmael, Abraham's son, the sister of Nebaioth, to be his wife, besides the wives that he had.

Jacob's Dream

10 Then Jacob departed from Beer-sheba and went toward Haran. **11** And he reached a certain place and spent the night there because the sun had set; and he took one of the stones of the place and put it under his head and lay down in that place. **12** Then he had a dream, and behold, a ladder stood on the earth with its top touching heaven; and behold, the angels of God were ascending and descending on it. **13** And behold, Yahweh stood above it and said, "I am Yahweh, the God of your father Abraham and the God of Isaac; the land on which you lie, I will give it to you and to your seed. ¹⁴ And your seed will also be like the dust of the earth, and you will spread out to the west and to the east and to the north and to the south; and in you and in your seed all the families of the earth shall be blessed. ¹⁵ Behold, I am with you and will keep you wherever you go. And I will bring you back to this land; for I will not forsake you until I have done what I have promised you." ¹⁶ Then Jacob awoke from his sleep and said, "Surely Yahweh is in this place, and I did not know it." ¹⁷ And he was afraid and said, "How fearsome is this place! This is none other than the house of God, and this is the gate of heaven."

¹⁸ So Jacob rose early in the morning and took the stone that he had put under his head and set it up as a pillar and poured oil on its top. ¹⁹ And he called the name of that place Bethel; however, previously the name of the city had been Luz. ²⁰ Then Jacob made a vow, saying, "If God will be with me and will keep me on this journey on which I am going, and will give me food to eat and garments to wear, ²¹ and I return to my father's house in peace, then Yahweh will be my God. ²² Now this stone, which I have set up as a pillar, will be God's house, and of all that You give me I will surely give a tenth to You."

Jacob's Love for Rachel

29 Then Jacob took up his journey and came to the land of the sons of the east. ² And he looked, and behold, a well in the field, and behold, three flocks of sheep were lying there beside it, for from that well they gave *water* to the flocks to drink. Now the stone on the mouth of the well was large. ³ And all the flocks would be gathered there, and they would roll the stone from the mouth of the well and give *water* to the sheep to drink and return the stone back to its place on the mouth of the well.

⁴ And Jacob said to them, "My brothers, where are you from?" And they said, "We are from Haran." ⁵ Then he said to them, "Do you know Laban the son of Nahor?" And they said, "We know *him*." ⁶ And he said to them, "Is it well with him?" And they said, "It is well, and here is Rachel his daughter coming with the sheep." ⁷ And he said, "Behold, it is still high day; it is not time for the livestock to be gathered. Give *water* to the sheep to drink, and go, pasture them." ⁸ But they said, "We cannot, until all the flocks are gathered, and they roll the stone from the mouth of the well; then we give *water* to the sheep to drink."

⁹ While he was still speaking with them, Rachel came with her father's sheep, for she was a shepherdess. ¹⁰ Now it happened, when Jacob saw Rachel the daughter of Laban his mother's brother and the sheep of Laban his mother's brother, Jacob came near and rolled the stone from the mouth of the well and gave *water* to the flock of Laban his mother's brother to drink. ¹¹ Then Jacob kissed Rachel and lifted his voice and wept. ¹² And Jacob told Rachel that he was a relative of her father and that he was Rebekah's son, and she ran and told her father.

¹³ So it happened that when Laban heard the report of Jacob his sister's son, he ran to meet him, and he embraced him and kissed him and brought him to his house. Then he recounted to Laban all these things. ¹⁴ And Laban said to him, "Surely you are my bone and my flesh." And he stayed with him one month.

¹⁵ Then Laban said to Jacob, "Because you are my relative, should you therefore serve me for nothing? Tell

me, what shall your wages be?" ¹⁶ Now Laban had two daughters; the name of the older was Leah, and the name of the younger was Rachel. ¹⁷ And Leah's eyes were weak, but Rachel was beautiful in form and beautiful in appearance. ¹⁸ Now Jacob loved Rachel, so he said, "I will serve you seven years for your younger daughter Rachel." ¹⁹ And Laban said, "It is better that I give her to you than to give her to another man; stay with me." ²⁰ So Jacob served seven years for Rachel, and they were in his sight but a few days because of his love for her.

Laban Deceives Jacob

²¹ Then Jacob said to Laban, "Give *me* my wife, for my days are fulfilled, that I may go in to her." ²² And Laban gathered all the men of the place and made a feast. ²³ Now it happened in the evening that he took his daughter Leah and brought her to him; and *Jacob* went in to her. ²⁴ Laban also gave his servant-woman Zilpah to his daughter Leah as a servant-woman. ²⁵ Now it happened in the morning that, behold, it was Leah! And he said to Laban, "What is this you have done to me? Was it not for Rachel that I served with you? Why then have you deceived me?" ²⁶ But Laban said, "It is not the practice in our place to give the younger before the firstborn. ²⁷ Fulfill the week of this one, and we will give you the other also for the service which you shall serve with me for another seven years." ²⁸ And Jacob did so and fulfilled her week, and he gave him his daughter Rachel as his wife. ²⁹ Laban also gave his servant-woman Bilhah to his daughter Rachel as her servant-woman. ³⁰ So *Jacob* went in to Rachel also, and indeed he loved Rachel more than Leah, and he served with Laban for another seven years.

³¹ And Yahweh saw that Leah was unloved, and He opened her womb, but Rachel was barren. ³² So Leah conceived and bore a son and named him Reuben, for she said, "Because Yahweh has seen my affliction; surely now my husband will love me." ³³ Then she conceived again and bore a son and said, "Because Yahweh has heard that I am unloved, He has therefore given me this *son* also." So she named him Simeon. ³⁴ And she conceived again and bore a son and said, "Now this time my husband will be joined to me because I have borne him three sons." Therefore he was named Levi. ³⁵ And she conceived again and bore a son and said, "This time I will praise Yahweh." Therefore she named him Judah. Then she stopped bearing.

The Sons of Jacob

30 Then Rachel saw that she bore Jacob no children, so she became jealous of her sister; and she said to Jacob, "Give me children, or else I die." ² Then Jacob's anger burned against Rachel, and he said, "Am I in the place of God, who has withheld from you the fruit of the womb?" ³ And she said, "Here is my maidservant Bilhah, go in to her that she may bear on my knees, that through her I too may obtain children." ⁴ So she gave him her servant-woman Bilhah as a wife, and Jacob went in to her. ⁵ And Bilhah conceived and bore Jacob a son. ⁶ Then Rachel said, "God has rendered justice to me and has indeed listened to my voice and has given me a son." Therefore she named him Dan. ⁷ And Rachel's servant-woman Bilhah conceived again and bore Jacob a second son. ⁸ So Rachel said, "With mighty wrestlings I have wrestled with my sister, *and* I have indeed prevailed." And she named him Naphtali.

9 Then Leah saw that she had stopped bearing, so she took her servant-woman Zilpah and gave her to Jacob as a wife. ¹⁰ And Leah's servant-woman Zilpah bore Jacob a son. ¹¹ Then Leah said, "How fortunate!" So she named him Gad. ¹² And Leah's servant-woman Zilpah bore Jacob a second son. ¹³ Then Leah said, "Happy am I! For women will call me happy." So she named him Asher.

14 And in the days of the wheat harvest, Reuben went and found mandrakes in the field and brought them to his mother Leah. Then Rachel said to Leah, "Please give me some of your son's mandrakes." ¹⁵ But she said to her, "Is it a small matter for you to take my husband? And would you take my son's mandrakes also?" So Rachel said, "Therefore he will lie with you tonight in return for your son's mandrakes." ¹⁶ Then Jacob came in from the field in the evening. And Leah went out to meet him and said, "You must come in to me, for I have surely hired you with my son's mandrakes." So he lay with her that night. ¹⁷ And God listened to Leah, and she conceived and bore Jacob a fifth son. ¹⁸ And Leah said, "God has given me my wages because I gave my servant-woman to my husband." So she named him Issachar. ¹⁹ Then Leah conceived again and bore a sixth son to Jacob. ²⁰ And Leah said, "God has gifted me a good gift; this time my husband will honor me because I have borne him six sons." So she named him Zebulun. ²¹ Afterward she bore a daughter and named her Dinah.

22 Then God remembered Rachel, and God listened to her and opened her womb. ²³ So she conceived and bore a son and said, "God has taken away my reproach." ²⁴ And she named him Joseph, saying, "May Yahweh give me another son."

Jacob Names His Wages

25 Now it happened when Rachel had borne Joseph, that Jacob said to Laban, "Send me away, that I may go to my own place and to my own land. ²⁶ Give *me* my wives and my children for whom I have served you, and let me go; for you yourself know my service which I have rendered you." ²⁷ But Laban said to him, "If now I have found favor in your sight, *stay with me*; I have interpreted an omen that Yahweh has blessed me on your account." ²⁸ And he *continued* to say, "Name me your wages, and I will give it." ²⁹ But he said to him, "You yourself know how I have served you and how your livestock have fared with me. ³⁰ For you had little before I came, but it has spread out to a multitude, and Yahweh has blessed you at *every* step of mine. But now, when shall I provide for my own household also?" ³¹ So he said, "What shall I give you?" And Jacob said, "You shall not give me anything. If you will do this *one* thing for you, I will again pasture *and* keep your flock: ³² let me pass through your entire flock today, removing from there every speckled and spotted sheep and every black one among the lambs and the spotted and speckled among the goats; and *such* shall be my wages. ³³ So my righteousness will answer for me later, when you come concerning my wages. Every one that is not speckled and spotted among the goats and black among the lambs, *if found* with me, will be considered stolen." ³⁴ And Laban said, "Behold, let it be according to your word." ³⁵ So he removed on that day the striped and spotted male goats and all the speckled and spotted female goats, every one with white in it, and all the black ones among the sheep, and gave them into the care of his sons. ³⁶ And he put *a distance of* three days' journey between himself and

Jacob, and Jacob was pasturing the rest of Laban's flocks.

37 Then Jacob took fresh rods of poplar and almond and plane trees, and he peeled white stripes in them, exposing the white which *was* in the rods. ³⁸ And he set the rods which he had peeled in front of the flocks in the trough, *that is*, in the watering channels, where the flocks came to drink; and they mated when they came to drink. ³⁹ So the flocks mated by the rods, and the flocks brought forth striped, speckled, and spotted. ⁴⁰ And Jacob separated the lambs, and he made the flocks face toward the striped and all the black in the flock of Laban; and he set his own herds apart and did not set them with Laban's flock. ⁴¹ Now it would be that, whenever the stronger of the flock were mating, Jacob would place the rods in the sight of the flock in the trough, so that they might mate by the rods; ⁴² but when the flock was feeble, he did not put *them* in; so the feebler were Laban's and the stronger Jacob's. ⁴³ So the man spread out exceedingly and had large flocks and female and male servants and camels and donkeys.

Jacob Leaves While Laban Is Gone

31 Then Jacob heard the words of Laban's sons, saying, "Jacob has taken away all that belonged to our father, and from what belonged to our father he has made all this wealth." ² And Jacob saw the face of Laban, and behold, it was not *friendly* toward him as formerly. ³ Then Yahweh said to Jacob, "Return to the land of your fathers and to your kin, and I will be with you." ⁴ So Jacob sent and called Rachel and Leah to his flock in the field, ⁵ and he said to them, "I see your father's face, that it is not *friendly* toward me as formerly, but the God of my father has been with me.

⁶ You also know that I have served your father with all my power. ⁷ Yet your father has cheated me and changed my wages ten times; however, God did not allow him to harm me. ⁸ If he spoke thus, 'The speckled shall be your wages,' then all the flock bore speckled; and if he spoke thus, 'The striped shall be your wages,' then all the flock bore striped. ⁹ Thus God has delivered your father's livestock and given *them* to me. ¹⁰ Now it happened at the time when the flock were mating that I lifted up my eyes and saw in a dream, and behold, the male goats which were mating *were* striped, speckled, and mottled. ¹¹ Then the angel of God said to me in the dream, 'Jacob,' and I said, 'Here I am.' ¹² He said, 'Lift up now your eyes and see *that* all the male goats which are mating are striped, speckled, and mottled; for I have seen all that Laban has been doing to you. ¹³ I am the God *of* Bethel, where you anointed a pillar, where you made a vow to Me; now arise, leave this land, and return to the land of your kin.' " ¹⁴ Then Rachel and Leah said to him, "Do we still have any portion or inheritance in our father's house? ¹⁵ Are we not counted by him as foreigners? For he has sold us and has also entirely consumed our purchase price. ¹⁶ Surely all the riches which God has delivered *over to us* from our father belong to us and our children; now then, do whatever God has said to you."

17 Then Jacob arose and put his children and his wives upon camels; ¹⁸ and he drove away all his livestock and all his possessions which he had accumulated, his acquired livestock which he had accumulated in Paddan-aram, in order to go to the land of Canaan to his father Isaac. ¹⁹ Now Laban had gone to shear his flock. Then Rachel stole the household idols that were her father's. ²⁰ And Jacob deceived Laban the Aramean by not telling him that he was fleeing. ²¹ So he fled with all that he had; and he arose and crossed the River and set his face toward the hill country of Gilead.

Laban Pursues Jacob

22 Then it was told to Laban on the third day that Jacob had fled; ²³ so he took his relatives with him and pursued him *a distance of* seven days' journey, and he overtook him in the hill country of Gilead. ²⁴ And God came to Laban the Aramean in a dream of the night and said to him, "Beware lest you speak to Jacob either good or bad."

25 So Laban caught up with Jacob. Now Jacob had pitched his tent in the hill country, and Laban with his relatives camped in the hill country of Gilead. ²⁶ Then Laban said to Jacob, "What have you done by deceiving me and carrying away my daughters like captives of the sword? ²⁷ Why did you flee secretly and deceive me and not tell me—so that I might have sent you away with gladness and with songs, with tambourine and with lyre— ²⁸ and not allow me to kiss my sons and my daughters? Now you have acted foolishly. ²⁹ It is in my hand to do evil against you, but the God of your father spoke to me last night, saying, 'Beware of speaking either good or evil to Jacob.' ³⁰ So now you have indeed gone away because you longed greatly for your father's house; *but* why did you steal my gods?" ³¹ Then Jacob answered and said to Laban, "Because I was afraid, because I said, 'Lest you take your daughters from me by force.' ³² The one with whom you find your gods shall not live; in the presence of our relatives recognize what is yours among my belongings and take *it* for yourself." But Jacob did not know that Rachel had stolen them.

33 So Laban went into Jacob's tent and into Leah's tent and into the tent of the two maidservants, but he did not find *them.* Then he went out of Leah's tent and entered Rachel's tent. ³⁴ Now Rachel had taken the household idols and put them in the camel's saddle, and she sat on them. And Laban felt through all the tent but did not find *them.* ³⁵ And she said to her father, "Let not my lord be angry that I cannot rise before you, for the manner of women is upon me." So he searched but did not find the household idols.

36 Then Jacob became angry and contended with Laban; and Jacob answered and said to Laban, "What is my transgression? What is my sin that you have hotly pursued me? ³⁷ Though you have felt through all my goods, what have you found of all your household goods? Place *it* here before my relatives and your relatives, that they may decide between us two. ³⁸ These twenty years I *have been* with you; your ewes and your female goats have not miscarried, nor have I eaten the rams of your flocks. ³⁹ That which was torn *of beasts* I did not bring to you; I bore the loss of it myself. You required it of my hand *whether* stolen by day or stolen by night. ⁴⁰ *Thus* I was: by day the heat consumed me and the frost by night, and my sleep fled from my eyes. ⁴¹ These twenty years I have been in your house; I served you fourteen years for your two daughters and six years for your flock, and you changed my wages ten times. ⁴² If the God of my father, the God of Abraham, and the dread of Isaac, had not been for me, surely now you would have sent me away empty. God has seen my affliction and the toil of my hands, so He rendered *the* decision last night."

The Covenant at Mizpah

43 Then Laban answered and said to Jacob, "The daughters are my daughters, and the children are my children, and the flocks are my flocks, and all that you see is mine. But what can I do this day to these daughters of mine or to their children whom they have borne? ⁴⁴ So now come, let us cut a covenant, you and I, and let it be a witness between you and me." ⁴⁵ Then Jacob took a stone and raised it up *as* a pillar. ⁴⁶ And Jacob said to his relatives, "Gather stones." So they took stones and made a heap, and they ate there by the heap. ⁴⁷ And Laban called it Jegar-sahadutha, but Jacob called it Galeed. ⁴⁸ Then Laban said, "This heap is a witness between you and me this day." Therefore it was named Galeed, ⁴⁹ and Mizpah, for he said, "May Yahweh watch between you and me when we are absent one from the other. ⁵⁰ If you afflict my daughters, or if you take wives besides my daughters, *although* no man is with us, see, God is witness between you and me." ⁵¹ And Laban said to Jacob, "Behold this heap and behold the pillar which I have set between you and me. ⁵² This heap is a witness, and the pillar is a witness, that I will not pass by this heap to you *for harm*, and you will not pass by this heap and this pillar to me for harm. ⁵³ The God of Abraham and the God of Nahor, the God of their father, judge between us." So Jacob swore by the dread of his father Isaac. ⁵⁴ Then Jacob offered a sacrifice on the mountain and called his relatives to eat a meal; and they ate the meal and spent the night on the mountain. ⁵⁵ And Laban arose early in the morning and kissed his sons and his daughters and blessed them. Then Laban departed and returned to his place.

Jacob's Fear of Esau

32 Now Jacob went on his way, and the angels of God met him. ² Then Jacob said when he saw them, "This is God's camp." So he named that place Mahanaim.

3 Then Jacob sent messengers before him to his brother Esau in the land of Seir, the country of Edom. ⁴ He also commanded them saying, "Thus you shall say to my lord, to Esau: 'Thus says your servant Jacob, "I have sojourned with Laban and have been delayed until now; ⁵ and I have oxen and donkeys *and* flocks and male and female slaves; and I have sent to tell my lord, that I may find favor in your sight." '"

6 Then the messengers returned to Jacob, saying, "We came to your brother, to Esau, and furthermore he is coming to meet you, and four hundred men are with him." ⁷ Then Jacob was greatly afraid and distressed; and he divided the people who were with him, and the flocks and the herds and the camels, into two camps. ⁸ And he said, "If Esau comes to the one camp and strikes it, then the camp which remains will escape."

9 And Jacob said, "O God of my father Abraham and God of my father Isaac, O Yahweh, who said to me, 'Return to your land and to your kin, and I will prosper you,' ¹⁰ I am unworthy of all the lovingkindness and of all the truth which You have shown to Your slave; for with my staff *only* I crossed this Jordan, and now I have become two camps. ¹¹ Deliver me, I pray, from the hand of my brother, from the hand of Esau; for I fear him, lest he come and strike me down *with* the mothers and the children. ¹² For You said, 'I will surely prosper you and make your seed as the sand of the sea, which is too great to be numbered.' "

13 So he spent the night there. Then he took from what he had with him a present for his brother Esau: ¹⁴ two hundred female goats and twenty male goats, two hundred ewes and twenty rams, [15] thirty milking camels and their colts, forty cows and ten bulls, twenty female donkeys and ten male donkeys. [16] And he gave *them* into the hand of his servants, every flock by itself, and said to his servants, "Pass on before me and put a space between flocks." [17] And he commanded the first one in front, saying, "When my brother Esau meets you and asks you, saying, 'To whom do you belong, and where are you going, and to whom do these *animals* in front of you belong?' [18] then you shall say, '*These* belong to your servant Jacob; it is a present sent to my lord, to Esau. And behold, he also is behind us.'" [19] Then he commanded also the second and the third and all those who followed the flocks, saying, "After this manner you shall speak to Esau when you find him; [20] and you shall say, 'Behold, your servant Jacob also is behind us.'" For he said, "I will appease his face with the present that goes before me. Then afterward I will see his face; perhaps he will lift up my face." [21] So the present passed on before him, while he himself spent that night in the camp.

22 And he arose that same night and took his two wives and his two servant-women and his eleven children and crossed the ford of the Jabbok. [23] And he took them and sent them across the stream. And he sent across whatever he had.

Jacob Wrestles with God

[24] Then Jacob was left alone, and a man wrestled with him until the breaking of dawn. [25] And he saw that he had not prevailed against him, so he touched the socket of his thigh; and so the socket of Jacob's thigh was dislocated while he wrestled with him. [26] Then he said, "Let me go, for the dawn is breaking." But he said, "I will not let you go unless you bless me." [27] So he said to him, "What is your name?" And he said, "Jacob." [28] Then He said, "Your name shall no longer be Jacob, but Israel; for you have striven with God and with men and have prevailed." [29] Then Jacob asked him and said, "Please tell me your name." But he said, "Why is it that you ask my name?" And he blessed him there. [30] So Jacob named the place Peniel, for *he said,* "I have seen God face to face, yet my life has been delivered." [31] And the sun rose upon him just as he crossed over Penuel, and he was limping on his thigh. [32] Therefore, to this day the sons of Israel do not eat the sinew of the hip which is on the socket of the thigh because he touched the socket of Jacob's thigh in the sinew of the hip.

Jacob Meets Esau

33 Then Jacob lifted up his eyes and saw, and behold, Esau was coming, and four hundred men with him. So he divided the children among Leah and Rachel and the two servant-women. [2] And he put the servant-women and their children first, and Leah and her children after *them,* and Rachel and Joseph after *them.* [3] But he himself passed on ahead of them and bowed down to the ground seven times, until he came near to his brother.

4 Then Esau ran to meet him and embraced him and fell on his neck and kissed him, and they wept. [5] And he lifted up his eyes and saw the women and the children and said, "Who are these with you?" And he said, "The children whom God has graciously given your servant." [6] Then the servant-women came near with their children, and they bowed down. [7] Leah likewise came near with her children, and they bowed down; and afterward Joseph came near with Rachel, and they bowed down. [8] And he said, "What do you mean by all these camps which I have met?" And he said, "To find favor in the sight of my lord." [9] But Esau said, "I have plenty, my brother; let what you have be your own." [10] And Jacob said, "No, please, if now I have found favor in your sight, then take my present from my hand, for I see your face as one sees the face of God, and you have received me favorably. [11] Please take my blessing which has been brought to you, because God has dealt graciously with me and because I have everything." Thus he urged him, and he took it.

12 Then Esau said, "Let us take our journey and go, and I will go before you." [13] But he said to him, "My lord knows that the children are weak and that the flocks and herds which are nursing are a care to me. And if they are driven hard one day, all the flocks will die. [14] Please let my lord pass on before his servant, and I will lead on slowly, according to the pace of the cattle that are before me and according to the pace of the children, until I come to my lord at Seir."

15 Then Esau said, "Please let me leave with you some of the people who are with me." But he said, "Why do this? Let me find favor in the sight of my lord." [16] So Esau returned that day on his way to Seir. [17] But Jacob journeyed to Succoth and built for himself a house and made booths for his livestock; therefore the place is named Succoth.

Jacob Camps in Shechem

18 Now Jacob came safely to the city of Shechem, which is in the land of Canaan, when he came from Paddan-aram, and he camped before the city. [19] Then he bought a portion of a field where he had pitched his tent from the hand of the sons of Hamor, Shechem's father, for one hundred qesitah. [20] Then he set up there an altar and called it El-Elohe-Israel.

Simeon and Levi Deceive Shechem

34 Now Dinah the daughter of Leah, whom she had borne to Jacob, went out to see the daughters of the land. [2] Then Shechem the son of Hamor the Hivite, the prince of the land, saw her and took her and lay with her and violated her. [3] And he was deeply attracted to Dinah the daughter of Jacob, and he loved the young woman and spoke to the heart of the young woman. [4] So Shechem spoke to his father Hamor, saying, "Get me this girl as a wife." [5] Now Jacob heard that he had defiled Dinah his daughter; but his sons were with his livestock in the field, so Jacob kept silent until they came in. [6] Then Hamor the father of Shechem went out to Jacob to speak with him. [7] Now the sons of Jacob came in from the field when they heard it; and the men were grieved, and they were very angry because he had done a disgraceful thing in Israel by lying with Jacob's daughter, for such a thing ought not to be done.

8 But Hamor spoke with them, saying, "The soul of my son Shechem longs for your daughter; please give her to him as a wife. [9] And intermarry with us; give your daughters to us and take our daughters for yourselves. [10] Thus you shall live with us, and the land shall be open before you; live and trade in it and take possession of property in it." [11] And Shechem also said to her father and to her brothers, "If I find favor in your sight, then I will give whatever you say to me. [12] Ask me ever so much bridal payment and gift, and I will give according as you say to me; but give me the girl as a wife."

13 But Jacob's sons answered Shechem and his father Hamor with deceit, and *thus* they spoke, because he had defiled Dinah their sister. ¹⁴ And they said to them, "We cannot do this thing, to give our sister to one who is uncircumcised, for that would be a reproach to us. ¹⁵ Only on this *condition* will we consent to you: if you will become like us, in that every male among you be circumcised, ¹⁶ then we will give our daughters to you, and we will take your daughters for ourselves, and we will live with you and become one people. ¹⁷ But if you will not listen to us to be circumcised, then we will take our daughter and go."

18 Now their words seemed good in the sight of Hamor and Shechem, Hamor's son. ¹⁹ So the young man did not delay to do the thing because he was delighted with Jacob's daughter. Now he was more honored than all the household of his father. ²⁰ So Hamor and his son Shechem came to the gate of their city and spoke to the men of their city, saying, ²¹ "These men are peaceful with us; therefore let them live in the land and trade in it, for behold, the land is large enough for them. Let us take their daughters for us as wives and give our daughters to them. ²² Only on this *condition* will the men consent to us to live with us, to become one people: that every male among us be circumcised as they are circumcised. ²³ Will not their livestock and what they acquire and all their cattle be ours? Only let us consent to them, and they will live with us." ²⁴ And all who went out of the gate of his city listened to Hamor and to his son Shechem, and every male was circumcised, all who went out of the gate of his city.

25 Now it happened on the third day, when they were in pain, that two of Jacob's sons, Simeon and Levi, Dinah's brothers, each took his sword and came upon the unsuspecting city and killed every male. ²⁶ And they killed Hamor and his son Shechem with the edge of the sword and took Dinah from Shechem's house and went away. ²⁷ Jacob's sons came upon the slain and plundered the city because they had defiled their sister. ²⁸ They took their flocks and their herds and their donkeys and that which was in the city and that which was in the field; ²⁹ and they captured and plundered all their wealth and all their little ones and their wives, even all that *was* in the houses. ³⁰ Then Jacob said to Simeon and Levi, "You have brought trouble on me by making me odious among the inhabitants of the land, among the Canaanites and the Perizzites; and my men being few in number, they will gather together against me and strike me, and I will be destroyed, I and my household." ³¹ But they said, "Should he treat our sister as a harlot?"

Jacob Goes Up to Bethel

35 Then God said to Jacob, "Arise, go up to Bethel and live there, and make an altar there to God, who appeared to you when you fled from your brother Esau." ² So Jacob said to his household and to all who were with him, "Put away the foreign gods which are among you and cleanse yourselves and change your garments; ³ and let us arise and go up to Bethel, and I will make an altar there to God, who answered me in the day of my distress and has been with me wherever I have gone." ⁴ So they gave to Jacob all the foreign gods which they had and the rings which were in their ears, and Jacob hid them under the oak which was near Shechem.

5 Then they journeyed on, and there was a terror from God upon the cities which were around them, and they did not pursue the sons of Jacob. ⁶ So Jacob came to Luz (that is, Bethel), which is in the land of Canaan, he and all the people who were with him. ⁷ And he built an altar there and called the place El-bethel, because there God had revealed Himself to him when he fled from his brother. ⁸ Then Deborah, Rebekah's nurse, died, and she was buried below Bethel under the oak; it was named Allon-bacuth.

Jacob Is Renamed Israel

9 Then God appeared to Jacob again when he came from Paddan-aram, and He blessed him. ¹⁰ And God said to him,

"Your name is Jacob;
    Your name shall no longer
        be called Jacob,
    But Israel shall be your name."

Thus He called his name Israel. ¹¹ God also said to him,

"I am God Almighty;
    Be fruitful and multiply;
    A nation and an assembly of
        nations shall come from you,
    And kings shall come forth
        from your loins.
¹² "And the land which I gave
        to Abraham and Isaac,
    I will give it to you,
    And I will give the land
        to your seed after you."

¹³ Then God went up from him in the place where He had spoken with him. ¹⁴ And Jacob set up a pillar in the place where He had spoken with him, a pillar of stone, and he poured out a drink offering on it; he also poured oil on it. ¹⁵ So Jacob named the place where God had spoken with him, Bethel.

16 Then they journeyed from Bethel; and there was still some distance to go to Ephrath, and Rachel gave birth, and she suffered severely in her labor.

¹⁷ Now it happened that when she was in severe labor the midwife said to her, "Do not fear, for now you have another son." ¹⁸ Now it happened as her soul was departing (for she died), that she named him Ben-oni; but his father called him Benjamin. ¹⁹ So Rachel died and was buried on the way to Ephrath (that is, Bethlehem). ²⁰ And Jacob set up a pillar over her grave; that is the pillar of Rachel's grave to this day. ²¹ Then Israel journeyed on and pitched his tent beyond the tower of Eder.

The Sons of Jacob

22 Now it happened while Israel was dwelling in that land, that Reuben went and lay with Bilhah his father's concubine, and Israel heard *of it.*

And there were twelve sons of Jacob—²³ the sons of Leah: Reuben, Jacob's firstborn, then Simeon and Levi and Judah and Issachar and Zebulun; ²⁴ the sons of Rachel: Joseph and Benjamin; ²⁵ and the sons of Bilhah, Rachel's servant-woman: Dan and Naphtali; ²⁶ and the sons of Zilpah, Leah's servant-woman: Gad and Asher. These are the sons of Jacob who were born to him in Paddan-aram.

27 And Jacob came to his father Isaac at Mamre of Kiriath-arba (that is, Hebron), where Abraham and Isaac had sojourned.

28 Now the days of Isaac were 180 years. ²⁹ And Isaac breathed his last and died and was gathered to his people, an old man and full of days; and his sons Esau and Jacob buried him.

The Generations of Esau

36 Now these are the generations of Esau (that is, Edom).
2 Esau took his wives from the daughters of Canaan: Adah the daughter of Elon the Hittite, and Oholibamah the

daughter of Anah and the granddaughter of Zibeon the Hivite; ³also Basemath, Ishmael's daughter, the sister of Nebaioth. ⁴And Adah bore Eliphaz to Esau, and Basemath bore Reuel, ⁵and Oholibamah bore Jeush and Jalam and Korah. These are the sons of Esau who were born to him in the land of Canaan.

6 Then Esau took his wives and his sons and his daughters and all his household, and his livestock and all his cattle and all his acquired goods, which he had accumulated in the land of Canaan, and he went to a land away from his brother Jacob. ⁷For their possessions had become too great for them to live together, and the land where they sojourned could not sustain them because of their livestock. ⁸So Esau lived in the hill country of Seir; Esau is Edom.

9 These then are the generations of Esau the father of the Edomites in the hill country of Seir. ¹⁰These are the names of Esau's sons: Eliphaz the son of Esau's wife Adah, Reuel the son of Esau's wife Basemath. ¹¹The sons of Eliphaz were Teman, Omar, Zepho and Gatam and Kenaz. ¹²Timna was a concubine of Esau's son Eliphaz, and she bore Amalek to Eliphaz. These are the sons of Esau's wife Adah. ¹³These are the sons of Reuel: Nahath and Zerah, Shammah and Mizzah. These were the sons of Esau's wife Basemath. ¹⁴These were the sons of Esau's wife Oholibamah, the daughter of Anah and the granddaughter of Zibeon: she bore to Esau, Jeush and Jalam and Korah.

15 These are the chiefs of the sons of Esau. The sons of Eliphaz, the firstborn of Esau, are chief Teman, chief Omar, chief Zepho, chief Kenaz, ¹⁶chief Korah, chief Gatam, chief Amalek. These are the chiefs *descended* from Eliphaz in the land of Edom; these are the sons of Adah. ¹⁷These are the sons of Reuel, Esau's son: chief Nahath, chief Zerah, chief Shammah, chief Mizzah. These are the chiefs *descended* from Reuel in the land of Edom; these are the sons of Esau's wife Basemath. ¹⁸These are the sons of Esau's wife Oholibamah: chief Jeush, chief Jalam, chief Korah. These are the chiefs *descended* from Esau's wife Oholibamah, the daughter of Anah. ¹⁹These are the sons of Esau (that is, Edom), and these are their chiefs.

20 These are the sons of Seir the Horite, the inhabitants of the land: Lotan and Shobal and Zibeon and Anah, ²¹and Dishon and Ezer and Dishan. These are the chiefs *descended* from the Horites, the sons of Seir in the land of Edom. ²²The sons of Lotan were Hori and Hemam; and Lotan's sister was Timna. ²³These are the sons of Shobal: Alvan and Manahath and Ebal, Shepho and Onam. ²⁴These are the sons of Zibeon: Aiah and Anah—he is the Anah who found the hot springs in the wilderness when he was pasturing the donkeys of his father Zibeon. ²⁵These are the children of Anah: Dishon and Oholibamah, the daughter of Anah. ²⁶These are the sons of Dishon: Hemdan and Eshban and Ithran and Cheran. ²⁷These are the sons of Ezer: Bilhan and Zaavan and Akan. ²⁸These are the sons of Dishan: Uz and Aran. ²⁹These are the chiefs of the Horites: chief Lotan, chief Shobal, chief Zibeon, chief Anah, ³⁰chief Dishon, chief Ezer, chief Dishan. These are the chiefs *descended* from the Horites, according to their *various* chiefs in the land of Seir.

31 Now these are the kings who reigned in the land of Edom before *any* king of the sons of Israel reigned. ³²And Bela the son of Beor became king in Edom, and the name of his city was Dinhabah. ³³Then Bela died, and Jobab the son of Zerah of Bozrah became king in his place. [34] Then Jobab died, and Husham of the land of the Temanites became king in his place. [35] Then Husham died, and Hadad the son of Bedad, who struck down Midian in the field of Moab, became king in his place; and the name of his city was Avith. [36] Then Hadad died, and Samlah of Masrekah became king in his place. [37] Then Samlah died, and Shaul of Rehoboth on the River became king in his place. [38] Then Shaul died, and Baal-hanan the son of Achbor became king in his place. [39] Then Baal-hanan the son of Achbor died, and Hadar became king in his place; and the name of his city was Pau; and his wife's name was Mehetabel, the daughter of Matred, daughter of Mezahab.

40 Now these are the names of the chiefs *descended* from Esau, according to their families *and* their places, by their names: chief Timna, chief Alvah, chief Jetheth, [41] chief Oholibamah, chief Elah, chief Pinon, [42] chief Kenaz, chief Teman, chief Mibzar, [43] chief Magdiel, chief Iram. These are the chiefs of Edom (that is, Esau, the father of the Edomites), according to their *places of* habitation in the land of their possession.

The Generations of Jacob

37 Now Jacob lived in the land where his father had sojourned, in the land of Canaan. [2] These are the generations of Jacob.

Joseph, when seventeen years of age, was pasturing the flock with his brothers while he was *still* a youth, along with the sons of Bilhah and the sons of Zilpah, his father's wives. And Joseph brought back an evil report about them to their father. [3] Now Israel loved Joseph more than all his sons because he was the son of his old age; and he made him a varicolored tunic. [4] And his brothers saw that their father loved him more than all his brothers, and *so* they hated him and could not speak to him in peace.

Joseph's Dreams

5 Then Joseph had a dream, and he told it to his brothers; so they hated him even more. [6] And he said to them, "Please listen to this dream which I have had: [7] Indeed, behold, we were binding sheaves in the field, and behold, my sheaf rose up and also stood upright; and behold, your sheaves gathered around and bowed down to my sheaf." [8] Then his brothers said to him, "Are you really going to reign over us? Or are you really going to rule over us?" So they hated him even more for his dreams and for his words.

9 Then he had still another dream and recounted it to his brothers and said, "Behold, I have had still another dream; and behold, the sun and the moon and eleven stars were bowing down to me." [10] And he recounted *it* to his father and to his brothers; and his father rebuked him and said to him, "What is this dream that you have had? Shall I and your mother and your brothers really come to bow ourselves down before you to the ground?" [11] And his brothers were jealous of him, but his father kept the saying *in mind.*

12 Then his brothers went to pasture their father's flock in Shechem. [13] And Israel said to Joseph, "Are not your brothers pasturing *the flock* in Shechem? Come, and I will send you to them." And he said to him, "I will go." [14] Then he said to him, "Go now and see about the welfare of your brothers and the welfare of the flock, and bring word back to me." So he sent him from the valley of Hebron, and he came to Shechem.

15 And a man found him, and behold, he was wandering in the field; and the man asked him, "What are you seeking?" 16 And he said, "I am seeking my brothers; please tell me where they are pasturing *the flock*." 17 Then the man said, "They have journeyed from here; for I heard *them* saying, 'Let us go to Dothan.'" So Joseph went after his brothers and found them at Dothan.

Joseph Sold by His Brothers

18 And they saw him from a distance, and before he came close to them, they plotted against him to put him to death. 19 Then they said to one another, "Here comes this dreamer! 20 So now, come and let us kill him and cast him into one of the pits; and we will say, 'A wild beast devoured him.' Then let us see what will become of his dreams!" 21 But Reuben heard *this* and delivered him out of their hands and said, "Let us not strike down his life." 22 Reuben further said to them, "Shed no blood. Cast him into this pit that is in the wilderness, but do not put forth your hands against him"— that he might deliver him out of their hands to return him to his father. 23 Now it happened, when Joseph reached his brothers, that they stripped Joseph of his tunic, the varicolored tunic that was on him; 24 and they took him and cast him into the pit. Now the pit was empty, without any water in it.

25 And they sat down to eat a meal. Then they lifted up their eyes and saw, and behold, a caravan of Ishmaelites was coming from Gilead, with their camels bearing aromatic gum and balm and myrrh, going to bring *them* down to Egypt. 26 And Judah said to his brothers, "What gain is it that we kill our brother and cover up his blood? 27 Come and let us sell him to the Ishmaelites and not lay our hands on him, for he is our brother,

our *own* flesh." And his brothers listened. 28 Then some Midianite traders passed by, so they pulled *him* up and lifted Joseph out of the pit and sold Joseph to the Ishmaelites for twenty *shekels* of silver. Thus they brought Joseph into Egypt.

29 Then Reuben returned to the pit, and behold, Joseph was not in the pit; so he tore his garments. 30 Then he returned to his brothers and said, "The boy is not *there*; as for me, where am I to go?" 31 So they took Joseph's tunic and slaughtered a male goat and dipped the tunic in the blood; 32 and they sent the varicolored tunic and brought it to their father and said, "We found this; please recognize *it*—whether it is your son's tunic or not." 33 And he recognized it and said, "It is my son's tunic. A wild beast has devoured him; Joseph has surely been torn to pieces!" 34 So Jacob tore his clothes and put sackcloth on his loins and mourned for his son many days. 35 Then all his sons and all his daughters arose to comfort him, but he refused to be comforted. And he said, "Surely I will go down to Sheol in mourning for my son." So his father wept for him. 36 Meanwhile, the Midianites sold him in Egypt to Potiphar, Pharaoh's officer, the captain of the bodyguard.

Judah and Tamar

38 Now it happened at that time that Judah went down from his brothers and turned aside to a certain Adullamite, whose name was Hirah. 2 And Judah saw there a daughter of a certain Canaanite whose name was Shua; and he took her and went in to her. 3 So she conceived and bore a son, and he named him Er. 4 Then she conceived again and bore a son, and she named him Onan. 5 And she bore still another son, and she

named him Shelah; and it was at Chezib that she bore him.

6 Then Judah took a wife for Er his firstborn, and her name *was* Tamar. ⁷ But Er, Judah's firstborn, was evil in the sight of Yahweh, so Yahweh put him to death. ⁸ Then Judah said to Onan, "Go in to your brother's wife, and perform your duty as a brother-in-law to her, and raise a seed for your brother." ⁹ And Onan knew that the seed would not be his; and it happened that when he went in to his brother's wife, he wasted it on the ground in order not to give seed to his brother. ¹⁰ But what he did was displeasing in the sight of Yahweh; so He put him to death also. ¹¹ Then Judah said to his daughter-in-law Tamar, "Live as a widow in your father's house until my son Shelah grows up"; for he thought, "*I am afraid* lest he also die like his brothers." So Tamar went and lived in her father's house.

12 And after a considerable time, Shua's daughter, the wife of Judah, died. Then Judah was comforted, and he went up to his sheepshearers at Timnah, he and his friend Hirah the Adullamite. ¹³ Then it was told to Tamar, "Behold, your father-in-law is going up to Timnah to shear his sheep." ¹⁴ So she removed her widow's garments from herself and covered *herself* with a veil and wrapped herself. And she sat at the entrance of Enaim, which is on the road to Timnah; for she saw that Shelah had grown up, and she had not been given to him as a wife. ¹⁵ Then Judah saw her, and he thought she *was* a harlot, for she had covered her face. ¹⁶ So he turned aside to her by the road and said, "Here now, let me come in to you"; for he did not know that she was his daughter-in-law. And she said, "What will you give me, that you may come in to me?" ¹⁷ He said, therefore, "I will send you a young goat

from the flock." She said, moreover, "Will you give a pledge until you send *it?*" ¹⁸ Then he said, "What pledge shall I give you?" And she said, "Your signet and your cord and your staff that is in your hand." So he gave *them* to her and went in to her, and she conceived by him. ¹⁹ Then she arose and went. And she removed her veil from herself and put on her widow's garments.

20 Then Judah sent the young goat by his friend the Adullamite to take the pledge from the woman's hand, but he did not find her. ²¹ So he asked the men of her place, saying, "Where is the cult prostitute who was by the road at Enaim?" But they said, "There has been no cult prostitute here." ²² So he returned to Judah and said, "I did not find her; and furthermore, the men of the place said, 'There has been no cult prostitute here.'" ²³ Then Judah said, "Let her keep them, lest we become a laughingstock. Behold, I sent this young goat, but you did not find her."

24 Now it happened about three months later that it was told to Judah saying, "Your daughter-in-law Tamar has played the harlot, and behold, she is also with child by harlotry." Then Judah said, "Bring her out and let her be burned!" ²⁵ It was while she was being brought out that she sent to her father-in-law, saying, "I am with child by the man to whom these things belong." And she said, "Please recognize *this* and see, whose signet ring and cords and staff are these?" ²⁶ And Judah recognized *them* and said, "She is more righteous than I, inasmuch as I did not give her to my son Shelah." And he did not know her again.

27 Now it happened at the time she was giving birth, that behold, there were twins in her womb. ²⁸ And it happened, while she was giving birth, one put out a hand, and the midwife took and tied a scarlet *thread* on his hand, saying, "This one came out first." [29] And then it happened, as he drew back his hand, that behold, his brother came out. So she said, "What a breach you have made for yourself!" So he was named Perez. [30] Afterward his brother came out who had the scarlet *thread* on his hand; and he was named Zerah.

Joseph in Potiphar's House

39 Now Joseph was brought down to Egypt; and Potiphar, an Egyptian official of Pharaoh, the captain of the bodyguard, bought him from the Ishmaelites, who had brought him down there. [2] And Yahweh was with Joseph, so he became a successful man. And he was in the house of his master, the Egyptian. [3] Now his master saw that Yahweh was with him and *how* Yahweh caused all that he did to succeed in his hand. [4] So Joseph found favor in his sight and attended on him; and he appointed him overseer over his house, and all that he owned he gave in his hand. [5] Now it happened that from the time he appointed him overseer in his house and over all that he owned, Yahweh blessed the Egyptian's house on account of Joseph; thus the blessing of Yahweh was upon all that he owned, in the house and in the field. [6] So he left everything he owned in Joseph's hand; and with him *there* he did not concern himself with anything except the food which he ate.

Now Joseph was beautiful in form and beautiful in appearance.

[7] And it happened after these events that his master's wife set her eyes on Joseph and said, "Lie with me." [8] But he refused and said to his master's wife, "Behold, with me *here*, my master does not concern himself with anything in

the house, and he has given all that he owns into my hand. [9] There is no one greater in this house than I, and he has withheld nothing from me except you, because you are his wife. How then could I do this great evil and sin against God?" [10] So it happened that as she spoke to Joseph day after day, he did not listen to her to lie beside her *or* be with her.

[11] Now it happened one day that he went into the house to do his work, and none of the men of the household was there inside. [12] Then she seized him by his garment, saying, "Lie with me!" And he left his garment in her hand and fled and went outside. [13] Now it happened, when she saw that he had left his garment in her hand and had fled outside, [14] that she called to the men of her household and spoke to them, saying, "See, he has brought in a Hebrew to us to laugh at us; he came in to me to lie with me, and I screamed. [15] Now it happened that when he heard that I raised my voice and screamed, he left his garment beside me and fled and went outside." [16] And she placed his garment beside her until his master came home. [17] Then she spoke to him with these words, saying, "The Hebrew slave, whom you brought to us, came in to me to laugh at me; [18] and as I raised my voice and screamed, he left his garment beside me and fled outside."

Joseph Is Put into Jail

[19] Now it happened that when his master heard the words of his wife, which she spoke to him, saying, "This is what your slave did to me," his anger burned. [20] So Joseph's master took him and put him into the jail, the place where the king's prisoners were confined; and he was there in the jail. [21] But Yahweh was

with Joseph and extended lovingkindness to him and gave him favor in the sight of the chief jailer. ²² So the chief jailer gave into the hand of Joseph all the prisoners who were in the jail; so that whatever was done there, he was the one who did *it*. ²³ The chief jailer did not supervise anything under Joseph's hand because Yahweh was with him; and whatever he did, Yahweh made to succeed.

Joseph Interprets the Officials' Dreams

40 Now it happened that after these things, the cupbearer and the baker for the king of Egypt offended their lord, the king of Egypt. ² And Pharaoh was furious with his two officials, the chief cupbearer and the chief baker. ³ So he put them in confinement in the house of the captain of the bodyguard, in the jail, the *same* place where Joseph was imprisoned. ⁴ And the captain of the bodyguard appointed Joseph as overseer over them, and he attended to them; and they were in confinement for some time. ⁵ Then the cupbearer and the baker for the king of Egypt, who were confined in jail, both had a dream the same night, each man with his *own* dream *and* each dream with its *own* interpretation. ⁶ Now Joseph came to them in the morning and saw them, and behold, they were dejected. ⁷ So he asked Pharaoh's officials who were with him in confinement in his master's house, saying, "Why are your faces so sad today?" ⁸ Then they said to him, "We have had a dream, and there is no one to interpret it." Then Joseph said to them, "Do not interpretations belong to God? Recount *it* to me, please."

9 So the chief cupbearer recounted his dream to Joseph and said to him, "In my dream, behold, *there was* a vine in front of me; ¹⁰ and on the vine *were* three branches. And as it was budding, its blossoms came out, *and* its clusters produced ripe grapes. ¹¹ Now Pharaoh's cup was in my hand; so I took the grapes and squeezed them into Pharaoh's cup, and I put the cup into Pharaoh's hand." ¹² Then Joseph said to him, "This is the interpretation of it: the three branches are three days; ¹³ within three more days Pharaoh will lift up your head and restore you to your office; and you will put Pharaoh's cup into his hand according to your former custom when you were his cupbearer. ¹⁴ Only remember me when it goes well with you, and please show me lovingkindness by remembering me to Pharaoh and getting me out of this house. ¹⁵ For I was in fact stolen from the land of the Hebrews, and even here I have done nothing that they should have put me into the pit."

16 And the chief baker saw that he had interpreted favorably, so he said to Joseph, "I also *saw* in my dream, and behold, *there were* three baskets of white bread on my head; ¹⁷ and in the top basket *there were* some of all sorts of baked food for Pharaoh, and the birds were eating them out of the basket on my head." ¹⁸ Then Joseph answered and said, "This is its interpretation: the three baskets are three days; ¹⁹ within three more days Pharaoh will lift up your head off of you and will hang you on a tree, and the birds will eat your flesh off of you."

20 Thus it happened on the third day, *which was* Pharaoh's birthday, that he made a feast for all his servants; and he lifted up the head of the chief cupbearer and the head of the chief baker among his servants. ²¹ And he restored the chief cupbearer to his office, and he put the cup into Pharaoh's hand; ²² but he hanged the chief baker, just as Joseph had interpreted to them. ²³ Yet the chief cupbearer did not remember Joseph, but forgot him.

Joseph Interprets Pharaoh's Dream

41 Now it happened at the end of two full years that Pharaoh had a dream, and behold, he was standing by the Nile. ²And behold, from the Nile there came up seven cows, sleek and fat; and they grazed in the reeds. ³Then behold, seven other cows came up after them from the Nile, ugly and thin, and they stood by the *other* cows on the bank of the Nile. ⁴And the ugly and thin cows ate up the seven sleek and fat cows. Then Pharaoh awoke. ⁵He again fell asleep and dreamed a second time; and behold, seven ears of grain came up on a single stalk, plump and good. ⁶And behold, seven ears, thin and scorched by the east wind, sprouted up after them. ⁷And the thin ears swallowed up the seven plump and full ears. Then Pharaoh awoke, and behold, *it was* a dream. ⁸Now it happened that in the morning his spirit was troubled, so he sent and called for all the magicians of Egypt and all its wise men. And Pharaoh recounted to them his dream, but there was no one who could interpret them to Pharaoh.

9 Then the chief cupbearer spoke to Pharaoh, saying, "I would bring to remembrance today my *own* offenses. ¹⁰Pharaoh was furious with his servants, and he put me in confinement in the house of the captain of the bodyguard, *both* me and the chief baker. ¹¹And we had a dream on the same night, he and I; each of us dreamed according to the interpretation of his *own* dream. ¹²Now there *was* with us a Hebrew youth, a slave of the captain of the bodyguard, and we recounted *them* to him, and he interpreted our dreams for us. To each one he interpreted according to his *own* dream. ¹³And just as he interpreted for us, so it happened; he restored me in my office, but he hanged him."

14 Then Pharaoh sent and called for Joseph, and they rushed him out of the pit; and he shaved himself and changed his clothes, and he came to Pharaoh. ¹⁵And Pharaoh said to Joseph, "I have had a dream, but no one can interpret it; yet I have heard it said about you, that you hear a dream *and that* you can interpret it." ¹⁶Joseph then answered Pharaoh, saying, "It is not in me; God will answer *concerning* the welfare of Pharaoh." ¹⁷So Pharaoh spoke to Joseph, "In my dream, behold, I was standing on the bank of the Nile; ¹⁸and behold, seven cows, fat and sleek came up out of the Nile, and they grazed in the reeds. ¹⁹And behold, seven other cows came up after them, poor and very ugly and lean, such as I had never seen in all the land of Egypt, in regard to ugliness; ²⁰and the lean and ugly cows ate up the first seven fat cows. ²¹But they devoured them, and yet it could not be known that they had devoured them. For they were just as ugly as before. Then I awoke. ²²Then I saw also in my dream, and behold, seven ears, full and good, came up on a single stalk; ²³and behold, seven ears, withered, thin, *and* scorched by the east wind, sprouted up after them; ²⁴and the thin ears swallowed the seven good ears. So I told it to the magicians, but there was no one who could declare it to me." **25** Then Joseph said to Pharaoh, "Pharaoh's dreams are one *and the same*; God has declared to Pharaoh what He is about to do. ²⁶The seven good cows are seven years; and the seven good ears are seven years; the dreams are one *and the same*. ²⁷And the seven lean and ugly cows that came up after them are seven years, and the seven lean ears scorched by the east wind will be seven years of famine. ²⁸ It is as I have spoken to Pharaoh: God has shown to Pharaoh what He is about to do. ²⁹ Behold, seven years of great abundance are coming in all the land of Egypt; ³⁰ and after them seven years of famine will arise, and all the abundance will be forgotten in the land of Egypt, and the famine will ravage the land, ³¹ so that the abundance will be unknown in the land because of that subsequent famine; for it *will be* very heavy. ³² Now as for the repeating of the dream to Pharaoh twice, *it means* that the matter is confirmed by God, and God will quickly bring it about. ³³ So now let Pharaoh look for a man understanding and wise, and set him over the land of Egypt. ³⁴ Let Pharaoh take action and appoint overseers over the land, and let him exact a fifth *of the produce* of the land of Egypt in the seven years of abundance. ³⁵ Then let them gather all the food of these good years that are coming, and let them store up the grain for food in the cities under Pharaoh's authority, and let them keep watch over *it.* ³⁶ And let the food be appointed for the land for the seven years of famine which will happen in the land of Egypt, so that the land will not be cut off during the famine."

Joseph Is Set over Egypt

³⁷ And the proposal seemed good to Pharaoh and to all his servants. ³⁸ Then Pharaoh said to his servants, "Can we find a man like this, in whom is a divine spirit?" ³⁹ So Pharaoh said to Joseph, "Since God has made you know all of this, there is no one so understanding and wise as you are. ⁴⁰ You shall be over my house, and according to your command all my people shall do homage; only in the throne I will be greater than you." ⁴¹ And Pharaoh said to Joseph, "See, I have set you over all the land of Egypt." ⁴² Then Pharaoh removed his signet ring from his hand and put it on Joseph's hand and clothed him in garments of fine linen and put the gold necklace around his neck. ⁴³ And he had him ride in his second chariot; and they called out before him, "Bow the knee!" And he set him over all the land of Egypt. ⁴⁴ Moreover, Pharaoh said to Joseph, "*Though* I am Pharaoh, yet without your permission no one shall raise his hand or foot in all the land of Egypt." ⁴⁵ Then Pharaoh named Joseph Zaphenath-paneah; and he gave him Asenath, the daughter of Potiphera priest of On, as a wife. And Joseph went forth over the land of Egypt.

46 Now Joseph was thirty years old when he stood before Pharaoh, king of Egypt. And Joseph went out from the presence of Pharaoh and passed through all the land of Egypt. ⁴⁷ And during the seven years of plenty the land brought forth abundantly. ⁴⁸ So he gathered all the food of *these* seven years which happened in the land of Egypt and placed the food in the cities; he placed in every city the food from its own surrounding fields. ⁴⁹ Thus Joseph stored up grain in great abundance like the sand of the sea, until he stopped measuring *it,* for it was beyond measure.

The Sons of Joseph

50 Now before the year of famine came, two sons were born to Joseph, whom Asenath, the daughter of Potiphera priest of On, bore to him. ⁵¹ And Joseph named the firstborn Manasseh, "For," *he said,* "God has made me forget all my trouble and all my father's household." ⁵² And he named the second Ephraim, "For," *he said,* "God has made me fruitful in the land of my affliction."

53 Then the seven years of plenty which had been in the land of Egypt came to an end, **54** and the seven years of famine began to come, just as Joseph had said. So there was famine in all the lands, but in all the land of Egypt there was bread. **55** Then all the land of Egypt was famished, and the people cried out to Pharaoh for bread; and Pharaoh said to all the Egyptians, "Go to Joseph; whatever he says to you, you shall do." **56** Now the famine was over all the face of the land. And Joseph opened all the storehouses and sold to the Egyptians; and the famine was severe in the land of Egypt. **57** Now all the earth *also* came to Egypt to buy grain from Joseph because the famine was severe in all the earth.

Joseph's Brothers Sent to Egypt

42 Now Jacob saw that there was grain in Egypt, and Jacob said to his sons, "Why are you staring at one another?" **2** Then he said, "Behold, I have heard that there is grain in Egypt; go down there and buy *some* for us from there, so that we may live and not die." **3** So ten brothers of Joseph went down to buy grain from Egypt. **4** But Jacob did not send Joseph's brother Benjamin with his brothers, for he said, "Lest *any* harm befall him." **5** So the sons of Israel came to buy grain among those who were coming, for the famine was in the land of Canaan *also.* **6** Now Joseph was the one in power over the land; he was the one who sold to all the people of the land. And Joseph's brothers came and bowed down to him with *their* faces to the ground. **7** And Joseph saw his brothers and recognized them, but he disguised himself to them and spoke to them harshly. And he said to them, "Where have you come from?" And they said, "From the land of Canaan, to buy food."

8 But Joseph recognized his brothers, although they did not recognize him. **9** And Joseph remembered the dreams which he had about them and said to them, "You are spies; you have come to look at the nakedness of the land." **10** Then they said to him, "No, my lord, but your servants have come to buy food. **11** We are all sons of one man; we are honest men; your servants are not spies." **12** And he said to them, "No, but you have come to look at the nakedness of our land!" **13** So they said, "Your servants are twelve brothers *in all*, the sons of one man in the land of Canaan; and behold, the youngest is with our father today, and one is no more." **14** And Joseph said to them, "It is as I said to you, you are spies; **15** by this you will be tested: by the life of Pharaoh, you shall not go from this place unless your youngest brother comes here! **16** Send one of you that he may get your brother, while you remain confined, that your words may be tested, whether there is truth in you. But if not, by the life of Pharaoh, surely you are spies." **17** Then he put them all together in prison for three days.

18 And Joseph said to them on the third day, "Do this and live, for I fear God: **19** if you are honest men, let one of your brothers be confined in your prison; but as for *the rest of* you, go, bring grain for the famine of your households, **20** and bring your youngest brother to me, so your words may be proven true, and you will not die." And they did so. **21** Then they said to one another, "Surely we are guilty concerning our brother because we saw the distress of his soul when he begged us, yet we would not listen; therefore this distress has come upon us." **22** And Reuben answered them, saying, "Did I not tell you, saying, 'Do not sin against the boy'; yet you would not listen? So also his blood, behold, it is required *of us*." [23] Now they did not know that Joseph was listening, for there was an interpreter between them. [24] And he turned away from them and wept. Then he returned to them and spoke to them. And he took Simeon from them and bound him before their eyes. [25] Then Joseph gave a command to fill their bags with grain and to restore every man's money in his sack and to give them provisions for the journey. And thus it was done for them.

26 So they loaded their donkeys with their grain and went from there. [27] Then one *of them* opened his sack to give his donkey fodder at the lodging place. And he saw his money; and behold, it was in the mouth of his sack. [28] So he said to his brothers, "My money has been returned, and behold, it is even in my sack." And their hearts sank, and they *turned* trembling to one another, saying, "What is this that God has done to us?"

Jacob Is Bereaved

29 Then they came to their father Jacob in the land of Canaan and told him all that had happened to them, saying, [30] "The man, the lord of the land, spoke harshly with us and took us for spies of the country. [31] So we said to him, 'We are honest men; we are not spies. [32] We are twelve brothers, sons of our father; one is no more, and the youngest is with our father today in the land of Canaan.' [33] Then the man, the lord of the land, said to us, 'By this I will know that you are honest men: leave one of your brothers with me and take *grain for* the famine of your households, and go. [34] But bring your youngest brother to me that I may know that you are not spies, but honest men. I will give your brother to you, and you may trade in the land.'" **35** Now it happened that they were

emptying their sacks, and behold, every man's bundle of money *was* in his sack; and they and their father saw their bundles of money, and they feared. [36] And their father Jacob said to them, "You have bereaved me of my children: Joseph is no more, and Simeon is no more, and you would take Benjamin; all these things are against me." [37] Then Reuben spoke to his father, saying, "You may put my two sons to death if I do not bring him *back* to you; put him in my hand, and I will return him to you." [38] But Jacob said, "My son shall not go down with you; for his brother is dead, and he alone remains. If harm should befall him on the journey on which you are going, then you will bring my gray hair down to Sheol in sorrow."

The Brothers Return to Egypt

43 Now the famine was heavy in the land. [2] And it happened when they had finished eating the grain which they had brought from Egypt, that their father said to them, "Go back, buy us a little food." [3] Judah spoke to him, however, saying, "The man solemnly warned us, saying, 'You shall not see my face unless your brother is with you.' [4] If you send our brother with us, we will go down and buy you food. [5] But if you do not send *him*, we will not go down; for the man said to us, 'You will not see my face unless your brother is with you.'" [6] Then Israel said, "Why did you treat me so badly by telling the man whether you still had *another* brother?" [7] But they said, "The man questioned particularly about us and our kin, saying, 'Is your father still alive? Have you *another* brother?' So we told him concerning these things. Could we possibly have known that he would say, 'Bring your brother down'?" [8] Then Judah said to his father Israel, "Send the boy with me, and we will arise and go, that we may live and not die, we as well as you and our little ones. ⁹ I myself will be *the* guarantee for him; from my hand you may require him. If I do not bring him *back* to you and set him before you, then I shall bear the sin before you all *my* days. ¹⁰ For if we had not delayed, surely by now we could have returned twice."

11 Then their father Israel said to them, "If *it must be* so, then do this: take some of the best products of the land in your bags, and bring *them* down to the man as a present, a little balm and a little honey, aromatic gum and myrrh, pistachio nuts and almonds. ¹² Now take double *the* money in your hand, and take back in your hand the money that was put back in the mouth of your sacks; perhaps it was a mistake. ¹³ And take your brother also, and arise, return to the man; ¹⁴ and may God Almighty grant you compassion before the man, so that he will release to you your other brother and Benjamin. And as for me, if I am bereaved of my children, I am bereaved." ¹⁵ So the men took this present, and they took double *the* money in their hand, and Benjamin; and they arose and went down to Egypt and stood before Joseph.

Joseph Sees Benjamin

16 Then Joseph saw Benjamin with them and said to his house steward, "Bring the men into the house, and slay an animal and prepare *it*; for the men are to eat with me at noon." ¹⁷ So the man did as Joseph said and brought the men to Joseph's house. ¹⁸ And the men were afraid because they were brought to Joseph's house; and they said, "*It is* because of the money that was returned in our sacks the first time that we are being brought in, that he may seek occasion against us and fall upon

us and take us for slaves with our donkeys." ¹⁹ So they came near to Joseph's house steward and spoke to him at the entrance of the house, ²⁰ and they said, "Oh, my lord, we indeed came down the first time to buy food, ²¹ and it happened when we came to the lodging place, that we opened our sacks, and behold, each man's money was in the mouth of his sack, our money in full. So we have brought it back in our hand. ²² We have also brought down other money in our hand to buy food; we do not know who put our money in our sacks." ²³ And he said, "Be well, do not be afraid. Your God and the God of your father has given you treasure in your sacks; your money has come to me." Then he brought Simeon out to them. ²⁴ Then the man brought the men into Joseph's house and gave them water, and they washed their feet; and he gave their donkeys fodder. ²⁵ So they prepared the present for Joseph's coming at noon; for they had heard that they were to eat a meal there.

26 Then Joseph came home, and they brought into the house to him the present which was in their hand and bowed to the ground before him. ²⁷ And he asked them about their well-being and said, "Is your old father well, of whom you spoke? Is he still alive?" ²⁸ And they said, "Your servant our father is well; he is still alive." They bowed down and prostrated themselves. ²⁹ Then he lifted his eyes and saw his brother Benjamin, his mother's son. And he said, "Is this your youngest brother, of whom you spoke to me?" And he said, "May God be gracious to you, my son." ³⁰ And Joseph hurried *out* for he was deeply stirred with compassion over his brother, and he sought *a place* to weep; and he entered his chamber and wept there. ³¹ Then he washed his face and came

out; and he restrained himself and said, "Set the meal." ³² So they set *the meal* for him by himself, and for them by themselves, and for the Egyptians who ate with him by themselves, because the Egyptians could not eat bread with the Hebrews, for that is an abomination to the Egyptians. ³³ And they were seated before him, the firstborn according to his birthright and the youngest according to his youth, and the men looked at one another in astonishment. ³⁴ And he took portions to them from his own table, but Benjamin's portion was five times greater than any of theirs. So they feasted and drank freely with him.

The Brothers Fall Before Joseph

44 Then he commanded his house steward, saying, "Fill the men's sacks with food, as much as they can carry, and put each man's money in the mouth of his sack. ² Now put my cup, the silver cup, in the mouth of the sack of the youngest, and his money for the grain." And he did as Joseph had told *him*. ³ As the morning light *broke*, the men were sent away, they with their donkeys. ⁴ Now they had *just* gone out of the city *and* were not far off when Joseph said to his house steward, "Arise, pursue the men; you shall overtake them and say to them, 'Why have you repaid evil for good? ⁵ Is not this the one from which my lord drinks and which he indeed uses to interpret omens? You have done evil in doing this.'"

6 So he overtook them and spoke these words to them. ⁷ And they said to him, "Why does my lord speak such words as these? Far be it from your servants to do such a thing. ⁸ Behold, the money which we found in the mouth of our sacks we have brought back to you from the land of Canaan. How then could we steal silver or gold from your lord's house?

⁹ With whomever of your servants it is found, let him die, and we also will be my lord's slaves." ¹⁰ So he said, "Now let it also be according to your words; he with whom it is found shall be my slave, but *the rest of* you shall be innocent." ¹¹ Then they hurried, each man brought his sack down to the ground, and each man opened his sack. ¹² So he searched, beginning with the oldest and ending with the youngest, and the cup was found in Benjamin's sack. ¹³ Then they tore their clothes, and each man loaded his donkey and returned to the city.

14 Then Judah and his brothers came to Joseph's house, and he was still there. So they fell to the ground before him. ¹⁵ And Joseph said to them, "What is this deed that you have done? Do you not know that such a man as I can indeed interpret omens?" ¹⁶ So Judah said, "What can we say to my lord? What can we speak? And how can we justify ourselves? God has found out the iniquity of your servants; behold, we are my lord's slaves, both we and the one in whose possession the cup has been found." ¹⁷ But he said, "Far be it from me to do this. The man in whose possession the cup has been found, he shall be my slave; but as for you, go up in peace to your father."

Judah Remains Instead of Benjamin

18 Then Judah came near to him and said, "O my lord, may your servant please speak a word in my lord's ears, and do not be angry with your servant; for you are equal to Pharaoh. ¹⁹ My lord asked his servants, saying, 'Have you a father or a brother?' ²⁰ And we said to my lord, 'We have an old father and a little child of *his* old age. Now his brother is dead, so he alone is left of his mother, and his father loves him.' ²¹ Then you said to your servants, 'Bring him down to me that I may set my eyes on him.'

[22] And we said to my lord, 'The boy cannot leave his father; if he should leave his father, his father would die.' [23] You said to your servants, however, 'If your youngest brother does not come down with you, you will not see my face again.' [24] Thus it happened that when we went up to your servant my father, we told him the words of my lord. [25] And our father said, 'Go back, buy us a little food.' [26] But we said, 'We cannot go down. If our youngest brother is with us, then we will go down; for we cannot see the man's face if our youngest brother is not with us.' [27] And your servant my father said to us, 'You know that my wife bore me two sons; [28] and the one went out from me, and I said, "Surely he is torn to pieces," and I have not seen him since. [29] If you take this one also from me and harm befalls him, you will bring my gray hair down to Sheol in evil.' [30] So now, when I come to your servant my father, and the boy is not with us—and his life is bound up in the *boy's* life— [31] so it will be that when he sees that the boy is not *with us*, he will die. Thus your servants will bring the gray hair of your servant our father down to Sheol in sorrow. [32] For your servant became a guarantee for the boy to my father, saying, 'If I do not bring him *back* to you, then I shall bear the sin before my father all *my* days.' [33] So now, please let your servant remain instead of the boy as a slave to my lord, and let the boy go up with his brothers. [34] For how shall I go up to my father if the boy is not with me, lest I see the evil that would overtake my father?"

Joseph Sends for Jacob

45 Then Joseph could not restrain himself before all those who stood by him, and he called out, "Have everyone go out from me." So there was no man with him when Joseph made himself known to his brothers. [2] Then he wept loudly. And the Egyptians heard *it*, and the household of Pharaoh heard *it*. [3] Then Joseph said to his brothers, "I am Joseph! Is my father still alive?" But his brothers could not answer him, for they were terrified at his presence.

4 Then Joseph said to his brothers, "Please come near to me." And they came near. And he said, "I am Joseph, your brother, whom you sold into Egypt. [5] So now do not be grieved or angry with yourselves because you sold me here, for God sent me before you to preserve life. [6] For the famine *has been* in the land these two years, and there are still five years in which there will be neither plowing nor harvesting. [7] So God sent me before you to establish for you a remnant in the earth and to keep you alive for a great *remnant* of survivors. [8] So now, it was not you who sent me here, but God; and He has set me as a father to Pharaoh and lord of all his household and ruler over all the land of Egypt. [9] Hurry and go up to my father, and say to him, 'Thus says your son Joseph, "God has set me as lord of all Egypt; come down to me, do not delay. [10] And you shall live in the land of Goshen, and you shall be near me, you and your children and your children's children and your flocks and your herds and all that you have. [11] There I will also provide for you, for there are still five years of famine *to come*, lest you and your household and all that you have be impoverished."' [12] And behold, your eyes see, and the eyes of my brother Benjamin *see*, that it is my mouth which is speaking to you. [13] So you must tell my father of all my glory in Egypt and all that you have seen; and you must hurry and bring my father down here." [14] Then he fell on his brother Benjamin's neck and wept, and Benjamin wept on his neck. [15] He kissed all his brothers and wept on them, and afterward his brothers talked with him.

16 Now the news was heard in Pharaoh's house, saying, "Joseph's brothers have come." And it was good in the sight of Pharaoh and in the sight of his servants. [17] Then Pharaoh said to Joseph, "Say to your brothers, 'Do this: load your beasts and go to the land of Canaan, [18] and take your father and your households and come to me, and I will give you the best of the land of Egypt, and you will eat the fat of the land.' [19] Now you are commanded, 'Do this: take wagons from the land of Egypt for your little ones and for your wives, and bring your father and come. [20] Now do not concern yourselves with your goods, for the best of all the land of Egypt is yours.'"

21 Then the sons of Israel did so; and Joseph gave them wagons according to the command of Pharaoh, and he gave them provisions for the journey. [22] To each of them he gave changes of garments, but to Benjamin he gave three hundred *pieces of* silver and five changes of garments. [23] Now to his father he sent as follows: ten donkeys loaded with the best things of Egypt and ten female donkeys loaded with grain and bread and sustenance for his father on the journey.

24 So he sent his brothers away, and they departed. And he said to them, "Do not be stirred up on the journey." [25] Then they went up from Egypt, and came to the land of Canaan to their father Jacob. [26] And they told him, saying, "Joseph is still alive, and indeed he is ruler over all the land of Egypt." But his heart was stunned, for he did not believe them. [27] Yet they told him all the words of Joseph that he had spoken to them, and he saw the wagons that Joseph had sent to carry him. Then the spirit of their father Jacob revived. [28] And Israel said, "It is enough! My son Joseph is still alive. I will go and see him before I die."

Jacob Moves to Egypt

46 So Israel set out with all that he had and came to Beersheba and offered sacrifices to the God of his father Isaac. [2] And God spoke to Israel in visions of the night and said, "Jacob, Jacob." And he said, "Here I am." [3] And He said, "I am God, the God of your father; do not be afraid to go down to Egypt, for I will make you a great nation there. [4] I Myself will go down with you to Egypt, and I Myself will also bring you up again; and Joseph will close your eyes with his hand."

5 Then Jacob arose from Beersheba; and the sons of Israel carried their father Jacob and their little ones and their wives in the wagons which Pharaoh had sent to carry him. [6] And they took their livestock and their possessions, which they had accumulated in the land of Canaan, and they came to Egypt, Jacob and all his seed with him: [7] his sons and his grandsons with him, his daughters and his granddaughters, and all his seed he brought with him to Egypt.

8 Now these are the names of the sons of Israel—of Jacob and his sons—who were coming to Egypt: Reuben, Jacob's firstborn. [9] The sons of Reuben: Hanoch and Pallu and Hezron and Carmi. [10] The sons of Simeon: Jemuel and Jamin and Ohad and Jachin and Zohar and Shaul the son of a Canaanite woman. [11] The sons of Levi: Gershon, Kohath, and Merari. [12] The sons of Judah: Er and Onan and Shelah and Perez and Zerah (but Er and Onan died in the land of Canaan). And the sons of Perez were Hezron and Hamul. [13] The sons of Issachar: Tola and Puvvah and Iob and Shimron. [14] The sons of Zebulun: Sered and Elon and Jahleel. ¹⁵ These are the sons of Leah, whom she bore to Jacob in Paddan-aram, with his daughter Dinah; all his sons and his daughters *numbered* thirty-three.

16 The sons of Gad: Ziphion and Haggi, Shuni and Ezbon, Eri and Arodi and Areli. ¹⁷ The sons of Asher: Imnah and Ishvah and Ishvi and Beriah and their sister Serah. And the sons of Beriah: Heber and Malchiel. ¹⁸ These are the sons of Zilpah, whom Laban gave to his daughter Leah; and she bore to Jacob these sixteen persons.

19 The sons of Jacob's wife Rachel: Joseph and Benjamin. ²⁰ Now to Joseph in the land of Egypt were born Manasseh and Ephraim, whom Asenath, the daughter of Potiphera, priest of On, bore to him. ²¹ The sons of Benjamin: Bela and Becher and Ashbel, Gera and Naaman, Ehi and Rosh, Muppim and Huppim and Ard. ²² These are the sons of Rachel, who were born to Jacob; *there were* fourteen persons in all.

23 The sons of Dan: Hushim. ²⁴ The sons of Naphtali: Jahzeel and Guni and Jezer and Shillem. ²⁵ These are the sons of Bilhah, whom Laban gave to his daughter Rachel, and she bore these to Jacob; *there were* seven persons in all. ²⁶ All the persons belonging to Jacob, who came to Egypt, who came out of his loins, excluding the wives of Jacob's sons, *were* sixty-six persons in all, ²⁷ and the sons of Joseph, who were born to him in Egypt were two; all the persons of the house of Jacob, who came to Egypt, *were* seventy.

28 Now he sent Judah before him to Joseph, to point out *the way* before him to Goshen; and they came into the land of Goshen. ²⁹ And Joseph harnessed his chariot and went up to Goshen to meet his father Israel; as soon as he appeared before him, he fell on his neck and wept on his neck a long time. ³⁰ Then Israel said to Joseph, "Now I can die, since I have seen your face, that you are still alive." ³¹ And Joseph said to his brothers and to his father's household, "I will go up and tell Pharaoh and say to him, 'My brothers and my father's household, who *were* in the land of Canaan, have come to me; ³² and the men are shepherds, for they have been keepers of livestock; and they have brought their flocks and their herds and all that they have.' ³³ And it will be when Pharaoh calls you and says, 'What is your occupation?' ³⁴ then you shall say, 'Your servants have been keepers of livestock from our youth and until now, both we and our fathers,' that you may live in the land of Goshen; for every shepherd is an abomination to the Egyptians."

Jacob's Family Settles in Goshen

47 Then Joseph went in and told Pharaoh and said, "My father and my brothers and their flocks and their herds and all that they have, have come out of the land of Canaan; and behold, they are in the land of Goshen." ² And he took five men from among his brothers and set them before Pharaoh. ³ Then Pharaoh said to his brothers, "What is your occupation?" So they said to Pharaoh, "Your servants are shepherds, both we and our fathers." ⁴ And they said to Pharaoh, "We have come to sojourn in the land, for there is no pasture for your servants' flocks, for the famine is heavy in the land of Canaan. So now, please let your servants live in the land of Goshen." ⁵ Then Pharaoh said to Joseph, "Your father and your brothers have come to you. ⁶ The land of Egypt is at your disposal; have your father and your brothers settle in the best of the land, let them settle in the land of Goshen; and if you know any excellent men among them, then put them in charge of my livestock."

7 Then Joseph brought his father Jacob and stood him before Pharaoh; and Jacob blessed Pharaoh. ⁸ And Pharaoh said to Jacob, "How many are the days of the years of your life?" ⁹ So Jacob said to Pharaoh, "The days of the years of my sojourning are 130; few and evil have been the days of the years of my life, and they have not attained to the days of the years that my fathers lived during the days of their sojourning." ¹⁰ And Jacob blessed Pharaoh and went out from the presence of Pharaoh. ¹¹ So Joseph settled his father and his brothers and gave them a possession in the land of Egypt, in the best of the land, in the land of Rameses, as Pharaoh had commanded. ¹² And Joseph provided his father and his brothers and all his father's household with food, according to their little ones.

Joseph and the Famine

13 Now there was no food in all the land because the famine was very heavy, so that the land of Egypt and the land of Canaan languished because of the famine. ¹⁴ And Joseph gathered all the money that was found in the land of Egypt and in the land of Canaan for the grain which they bought, and Joseph brought the money into Pharaoh's house. ¹⁵ Then the money came to an end in the land of Egypt and in the land of Canaan. So all the Egyptians came to Joseph and said, "Give us food, for why should we die in your presence? For *our* money is gone." ¹⁶ Then Joseph said, "Give up your livestock, and I will give you *food* for your livestock, since *your* money is gone." ¹⁷ So they brought their livestock to Joseph, and Joseph gave them food in exchange for the horses and the flocks and the herds and the donkeys; and he fed them with food

in exchange for all their livestock that year. ¹⁸ Then that year came to an end. And they came to him the next year and said to him, "We will not hide from my lord that our money has come to an end, and the livestock are my lord's. There is nothing left for my lord except our bodies and our land. ¹⁹ Why should we die before your eyes, both we and our land? Buy us and our land for food, and we and our land will be slaves to Pharaoh. So give us seed, that we may live and not die, and that the land may not be desolate."

20 So Joseph bought all the land of Egypt for Pharaoh, for every Egyptian sold his field because the famine was severe upon them. Thus the land became Pharaoh's. ²¹ As for the people, he moved them to the cities from one end of Egypt's border to the other end. ²² Only the land of the priests he did not buy, for the priests had an allotment from Pharaoh, and they ate off the allotment which Pharaoh gave them. Therefore, they did not sell their land. ²³ Then Joseph said to the people, "Behold, I have today bought you and your land for Pharaoh; now, *here* is seed for you, and you may sow the land. ²⁴ And it will be, at the harvest you shall give a fifth to Pharaoh, and four-fifths shall be your own for seed of the field and for your food and for those of your households and as food for your little ones." ²⁵ So they said, "You have kept us alive! Let us find favor in the sight of my lord, and we will be Pharaoh's slaves." ²⁶ And Joseph made it a statute concerning the land of Egypt *valid* to this day, that Pharaoh should have the fifth; only the land of the priests did not become Pharaoh's.

27 Now Israel lived in the land of Egypt, in Goshen, and they took possession of property in it and were fruitful and became very numerous. [28] And Jacob lived in the land of Egypt seventeen years; so the days of Jacob, the years of his life, were 147 years.

29 Then the days for Israel to die drew near, and he called his son Joseph and said to him, "Please, if I have found favor in your sight, place now your hand under my thigh and deal with me in lovingkindness and truth. Please do not bury me in Egypt. [30] But I will lie down with my fathers, and you will carry me out of Egypt and bury me in their burial place." And he said, "I will do as you have said." [31] Then he said, "Swear to me." So he swore to him. Then Israel bowed *in worship* at the head of the bed.

Israel Blesses Manasseh and Ephraim

48 Now it happened after these things that Joseph was told, "Behold, your father is sick." So he took his two sons Manasseh and Ephraim with him. [2] Then it was told to Jacob, "Behold, your son Joseph has come to you," so Israel strengthened himself and sat up in the bed. [3] Then Jacob said to Joseph, "God Almighty appeared to me at Luz in the land of Canaan and blessed me, [4] and He said to me, 'Behold, I will make you fruitful and multiply, and I will make you an assembly of peoples, and I will give this land to your seed after you for an everlasting possession.' [5] So now your two sons, who were born to you in the land of Egypt before I came to you in Egypt, are mine; Ephraim and Manasseh shall be mine, as Reuben and Simeon are. [6] But your kin that have been born after them shall be yours; they shall be called by the names of their brothers in their inheritance. [7] Now as for me, when I came from Paddan, Rachel died, to my sorrow, in the land of Canaan on the journey, when there was still some distance to go to Ephrath; and I buried her there on the way to Ephrath (that is, Bethlehem)."

8 Then Israel saw Joseph's sons and said, "Who are these?" [9] And Joseph said to his father, "They are my sons, whom God has given me here." So he said, "Bring them to me, please, that I may bless them." [10] Now the eyes of Israel were *so* dim from age *that* he could not see. Then Joseph brought them close to him, and he kissed them and embraced them. [11] Then Israel said to Joseph, "I never expected to see your face, and behold, God has let me see your seed as well." [12] Then Joseph took them from his knees and bowed with his face to the ground. [13] And Joseph took them both, Ephraim with his right hand toward Israel's left, and Manasseh with his left hand toward Israel's right, and brought them close to him. [14] But Israel stretched out his right hand and laid it on the head of Ephraim, who was the younger, and his left hand on Manasseh's head, crossing his hands, although Manasseh was the firstborn. [15] And he blessed Joseph and said,

"May the God
　　before whom my fathers
　　Abraham and Isaac walked,
The God who has been
　　my shepherd throughout
　　my life to this day,
[16] The angel who has redeemed me
　　from all evil,
Bless *these* boys;
And may my name live on in them,
And the names of my fathers
　　Abraham and Isaac;
And may they grow into
　　a multitude in the midst
　　of the earth."

17 But Joseph saw that his father set his right hand on Ephraim's head, and it was displeasing in his sight; so he took hold of his father's hand to remove it from Ephraim's head to Manasseh's head. [18] And Joseph said to his father, "Not so, my father, for this one is the firstborn. Place your right hand on his head." [19] But his father refused and said, "I know, my son, I know; he also will become a people, and he also will be great. However, his younger brother shall be greater than he, and his seed shall become the fullness of nations." [20] And he blessed them that day, saying,

"By you Israel will pronounce
    blessing, saying,
'May God make you like
    Ephraim and Manasseh!'"

Thus he put Ephraim before Manasseh. [21] Then Israel said to Joseph, "Behold, I am about to die, but God will be with you and will bring you back to the land of your fathers. [22] And I give you one portion more than your brothers, which I took from the hand of the Amorite with my sword and my bow."

Jacob Assembles His Sons

49 Then Jacob summoned his sons and said, "Gather together that I may tell you what will befall you in the last days.

[2] "Assemble together and hear,
        O sons of Jacob;
    And listen to Israel your father.
[3] "Reuben, you are my firstborn;
    My might and the beginning of
        my vigor,
    Preeminent in dignity and
        preeminent in strength.
[4] "Uncontrolled as water, you shall
        not have preeminence,
    Because you went up to
        your father's bed;
    Then you defiled *it*—
        he went up to my couch.
[5] "Simeon and Levi are brothers;
    Their swords are implements
        of violence.

[6] "Let my soul not enter
        into their council;
    Let not my glory be united
        with their assembly;
    Because in their anger
        they killed men,
    And in their self-will
        they hamstrung oxen.
[7] "Cursed be their anger,
        for it is strong;
    And their wrath, for it is cruel.
    I will divide them amongst Jacob,
    And scatter them in Israel.
[8] "Judah, as for you, your brothers
        shall praise you;
    Your hand shall be on the neck of
        your enemies;
    Your father's sons shall bow down
        to you.
[9] "Judah is a lion's whelp;
    From the prey, my son,
        you have gone up.
    He crouches,
        he lies down as a lion,
    And as a lioness,
        who dares rouse him up?
[10] "The scepter shall not depart
        from Judah,
    Nor the ruler's staff
        from between his feet,
    Until Shiloh comes,
    And to him *shall be* the obedience
        of the peoples.
[11] "He ties *his* foal to the vine,
    And his donkey's colt
        to the choice vine;
    He washes his garments in wine,
    And his robes in the blood
        of grapes.
[12] "His eyes are dark from wine,
    And his teeth white from milk.
[13] "Zebulun will dwell
        at the seashore;
    And he *shall be* a shore for ships,
    And his flank *shall be*
        toward Sidon.

14 "Issachar is a strong donkey,
    Lying down between
        the sheepfolds.
¹⁵ "And he saw that a resting place
        was good
    And that the land was pleasant,
    So he bowed his shoulder
        to bear *burdens*,
    And became a slave at forced labor.
16 "Dan shall render justice
        to his people,
    As one of the tribes of Israel.
¹⁷ "Dan shall be a serpent in the way,
    A horned snake in the path,
    That bites the horse's heels,
    So that his rider falls backward.
¹⁸ "For Your salvation I hope,
    O Yahweh.
19 "As for Gad, raiders shall raid him,
    But he will raid *at* their heels.
20 "As for Asher, his food shall be rich,
    And he will yield royal dainties.
21 "Naphtali is a doe let loose,
    He gives beautiful words.
22 "Joseph is a fruitful bough,
    A fruitful bough by a spring;
    Its branches run over a wall.
²³ "And the archers bitterly attacked
        him and shot *at him*,
    And they bore a grudge
        against him;
²⁴ But his bow remained firm,
    And his arms were agile,
    From the hands of
        the Mighty One of Jacob,
    From there is the Shepherd,
        the Stone of Israel,
²⁵ From the God of your father
        who helps you,
    And by the Almighty
        who blesses you
    With blessings of heaven above,
    Blessings of the deep that
        lies beneath,
    Blessings of the breasts and
        of the womb.

²⁶ "The blessings of your father
    Have surpassed the blessings
        of my ancestors
    Up to the utmost bound of
        the everlasting hills;
    May they be on the head of Joseph,
    And on the top of the head of
        the one distinguished among
        his brothers.
27 "Benjamin is a ravenous wolf;
    In the morning he devours the prey,
    And in the evening he divides
        the spoil."

Jacob Breathes His Last

28 All these are the twelve tribes of Israel, and this is what their father spoke to them. So he blessed them. He blessed them, every one with the blessing appropriate to him. ²⁹ Then he commanded them and said to them, "I am about to be gathered to my people; bury me with my fathers in the cave that is in the field of Ephron the Hittite, ³⁰ in the cave that is in the field of Machpelah, which is before Mamre, in the land of Canaan, which Abraham bought along with the field from Ephron the Hittite as a possession for a burial site. ³¹ There they buried Abraham and his wife Sarah, there they buried Isaac and his wife Rebekah, and there I buried Leah— ³² the field and the cave that is in it, purchased from the sons of Heth." ³³ So Jacob finished commanding his sons. And he drew his feet into the bed and breathed his last and was gathered to his people.

50 Then Joseph fell on his father's face and wept over him and kissed him. ² And Joseph commanded his servants the physicians to embalm his father. So the physicians embalmed Israel. ³ Then *the* forty days *to do this* were fulfilled, because in this manner the days of embalming are fulfilled. And the Egyptians wept for him seventy days.

4 Then the days of weeping for him were past, and Joseph spoke to the household of Pharaoh, saying, "If now I have found favor in your sight, please speak in the ears of Pharaoh, saying, ⁵ 'My father made me swear, saying, "Behold, I am about to die; in my grave which I dug for myself in the land of Canaan, there you shall bury me." So now, please let me go up and bury my father; then I will return.'" ⁶ And Pharaoh said, "Go up and bury your father, as he made you swear."

7 So Joseph went up to bury his father, and with him went up all the servants of Pharaoh, the elders of his household, and all the elders of the land of Egypt, ⁸ and all the household of Joseph and his brothers and his father's household; they left only their little ones and their flocks and their herds in the land of Goshen. ⁹ There also went up with him both chariots and horsemen; and it was a very immense camp. ¹⁰ And they came to the threshing floor of Atad, which is beyond the Jordan, and they lamented there with a very great and immense lamentation; and he observed seven days of mourning for his father. ¹¹ Now the inhabitants of the land, the Canaanites, saw the mourning at the threshing floor of Atad, and they said, "This is an immense mourning for the Egyptians." Therefore it was named Abel-mizraim, which is beyond the Jordan.

Jacob's Burial at Machpelah

¹² Thus his sons did for him as he had commanded them. ¹³ Indeed, his sons carried him to the land of Canaan and buried him in the cave of the field of Machpelah before Mamre, which Abraham had bought along with the field for *his* possession *as* a burial site from Ephron the Hittite. ¹⁴ After he had buried his father, Joseph returned to Egypt, he and his brothers, and all who had gone up with him to bury his father.

15 Then Joseph's brothers saw that their father was dead, and they said, "What if Joseph bears a grudge against us and returns back to us all the evil which we dealt against him!" ¹⁶ So they sent *a message* to Joseph, saying, "Your father commanded before he died, saying, ¹⁷ 'Thus you shall say to Joseph, "Please forgive, I beg you, the transgression of your brothers and their sin, for they dealt evil against you."' So now, please forgive the transgression of the slaves of the God of your father." And Joseph wept when they spoke to him. ¹⁸ Then his brothers also came and fell down before him and said, "Behold, we are your slaves." ¹⁹ But Joseph said to them, "Do not be afraid, for am I in God's place? ²⁰ As for you, you meant evil against me, *but* God meant it for good in order to do *what has happened on* this day, to keep many people alive. ²¹ So now, do not be afraid; I will provide for you and your little ones." And he comforted them and spoke to their heart.

The Death of Joseph

22 Now Joseph stayed in Egypt, he and his father's household, and Joseph lived 110 years. ²³ And Joseph saw the third generation of Ephraim's sons; also the sons of Machir, the son of Manasseh, were born on Joseph's knees. ²⁴ And Joseph said to his brothers, "I am about to die, but God will surely take care of you and bring you up from this land to the land which He swore to Abraham, to Isaac, and to Jacob." ²⁵ Then Joseph made the sons of Israel swear, saying, "God will surely take care of you, and you shall carry my bones up from here." ²⁶ So Joseph died at the age of 110 years; and they embalmed him, and he was placed in a coffin in Egypt.

THE NEW TESTAMENT

LEGACY STANDARD BIBLE

THE GOSPEL ACCORDING TO

MATTHEW

CHAPTER 1

The Genealogy of Jesus Christ

THE book of the genealogy of Jesus Christ, the son of David, the son of Abraham:

2 Abraham was the father of Isaac, and Isaac was the father of Jacob, and Jacob was the father of Judah and his brothers.

3 And Judah was the father of Perez and Zerah by Tamar, and Perez was the father of Hezron, and Hezron was the father of Ram.

4 And Ram was the father of Amminadab, and Amminadab was the father of Nahshon, and Nahshon was the father of Salmon.

5 And Salmon was the father of Boaz by Rahab, and Boaz was the father of Obed by Ruth, and Obed was the father of Jesse.

6 And Jesse was the father of David the king.

And David was the father of Solomon by the *wife* of Uriah.

7 And Solomon was the father of Rehoboam, and Rehoboam was the father of Abijah, and Abijah was the father of Asa.

8 And Asa was the father of Jehoshaphat, and Jehoshaphat was the father of Joram, and Joram was the father of Uzziah.

9 And Uzziah was the father of Jotham, and Jotham was the father of Ahaz, and Ahaz was the father of Hezekiah.

10 And Hezekiah was the father of Manasseh, and Manasseh was the father of Amon, and Amon was the father of Josiah.

11 And Josiah was the father of Jeconiah and his brothers, at the time of the deportation to Babylon.

12 And after the deportation to Babylon: Jeconiah was the father of Shealtiel, and Shealtiel was the father of Zerubbabel.

13 And Zerubbabel was the father of Abihud, and Abihud was the father of Eliakim, and Eliakim was the father of Azor.

14 And Azor was the father of Zadok, and Zadok was the father of Achim, and Achim was the father of Eliud.

15 And Eliud was the father of Eleazar, and Eleazar was the father of Matthan, and Matthan was the father of Jacob.

16 And Jacob was the father of Joseph the husband of Mary, by whom Jesus was born, who is called Christ.

17 Therefore all the generations from Abraham to David are fourteen generations; and from David to the deportation to Babylon, fourteen generations; and from the

deportation to Babylon to the Christ, fourteen generations.

The Conception and Birth of Jesus

18 Now the birth of Jesus Christ was as follows: when His mother Mary had been betrothed to Joseph, before they came together she was found to be with child by the Holy Spirit.

19 And Joseph her husband, being a righteous man and not wanting to disgrace her, planned to send her away secretly.

20 But when he had considered this, behold, an angel of the Lord appeared to him in a dream, saying, "Joseph, son of David, do not be afraid to take Mary as your wife; for the One who has been conceived in her is of the Holy Spirit.

21 "And she will bear a Son; and you shall call His name Jesus, for He will save His people from their sins."

22 Now all this took place in order that what was spoken by the Lord through the prophet would be fulfilled, saying,

23 "BEHOLD, THE VIRGIN SHALL BE WITH CHILD AND SHALL BEAR A SON, AND THEY SHALL CALL HIS NAME IMMANUEL," which translated means, "GOD WITH US."

24 And Joseph got up from his sleep and did as the angel of the Lord commanded him, and took *Mary* as his wife,

25 but kept her a virgin until she gave birth to a Son; and he called His name Jesus.

CHAPTER 2

The Visit of the Magi

NOW after Jesus was born in Bethlehem of Judea in the days of Herod the king, behold, magi from the east arrived in Jerusalem, saying,

2 "Where is He who has been born King of the Jews? For we saw His star in the east and have come to worship Him."

3 And when Herod the king heard *this*, he was troubled, and all Jerusalem with him.

4 And gathering together all the chief priests and scribes of the people, he was inquiring of them where the Christ was to be born.

5 And they said to him, "In Bethlehem of Judea; for this is what has been written by the prophet:

6 'AND YOU, BETHLEHEM, LAND OF JUDAH,

ARE BY NO MEANS LEAST AMONG THE LEADERS OF JUDAH;

FOR OUT OF YOU SHALL COME FORTH A LEADER

WHO WILL SHEPHERD MY PEOPLE ISRAEL.' "

7 Then Herod secretly called the magi and carefully determined from them the time the star appeared.

8 And he sent them to Bethlehem and said, "Go and search carefully for the Child; and when you have found *Him*, report to me, so that I too may come and worship Him."

9 Now after hearing the king, they went their way; and behold, the star, which they had seen in the east, was

going on before them until it came and stood over *the place* where the Child was.

10 And when they saw the star, they rejoiced exceedingly with great joy.

11 And after coming into the house they saw the Child with Mary His mother; and they fell to the ground and worshiped Him. Then, opening their treasures, they presented to Him gifts of gold, frankincense, and myrrh.

12 And having been warned in a dream not to return to Herod, the magi departed for their own country by another way.

The Flight to Egypt

13 Now when they had departed, behold, an angel of the Lord *appeared to Joseph in a dream, saying, "Get up! Take the Child and His mother and flee to Egypt, and remain there until I tell you; for Herod is going to search for the Child to destroy Him."

14 So Joseph got up and took the Child and His mother while it was still night, and departed for Egypt.

15 And he remained there until the death of Herod, in order that what had been spoken by the Lord through the prophet would be fulfilled, saying, "Out of Egypt I called My Son."

Herod Slaughters Children

16 Then when Herod saw that he had been tricked by the magi, he became very enraged, and sent and slew all the male children who were in Bethlehem and all its vicinity, from two years old and under,

according to the time which he had carefully determined from the magi.

17 Then what had been spoken through Jeremiah the prophet was fulfilled, saying,

18 "A voice was heard in Ramah,
Weeping and great mourning,
Rachel weeping for her
    children;
And she was refusing to be
    comforted,
Because they were no more."

19 But when Herod died, behold, an angel of the Lord *appeared in a dream to Joseph in Egypt, saying,

20 "Get up, take the Child and His mother, and go into the land of Israel; for those who sought the Child's life are dead."

21 So Joseph got up, took the Child and His mother, and came into the land of Israel.

22 But when he heard that Archelaus was reigning over Judea in place of his father Herod, he was afraid to go there. Then after being warned *by God* in a dream, he departed for the district of Galilee,

23 and came and lived in a city called Nazareth, so that what was spoken through the prophets would be fulfilled: "He shall be called a Nazarene."

CHAPTER 3

The Preaching of John the Baptist

NOW in those days John the Baptist *came, preaching in the wilderness of Judea, saying,

2 "Repent, for the kingdom of heaven is at hand."

3 For this is the one referred to by Isaiah the prophet, saying,

"THE VOICE OF ONE CRYING IN THE
  WILDERNESS,
'MAKE READY THE WAY OF THE LORD,
MAKE HIS PATHS STRAIGHT!'"

4 Now John himself had a garment of camel's hair and a leather belt around his waist; and his food was locusts and wild honey.

5 Then Jerusalem was going out to him, and all Judea, and all the district around the Jordan;

6 and they were being baptized by him in the Jordan River, as they confessed their sins.

7 But when he saw many of the Pharisees and Sadducees coming for his baptism, he said to them, "You brood of vipers, who warned you to flee from the wrath to come?

8 "Therefore bear fruit in keeping with repentance;

9 and do not suppose that you can say to yourselves, 'We have Abraham for our father'; for I say to you that from these stones God is able to raise up children to Abraham.

10 "And the axe is already laid at the root of the trees; therefore every tree that does not bear good fruit is cut down and thrown into the fire.

11 "As for me, I baptize you with water for repentance, but He who is coming after me is mightier than I, and I am not fit to remove His sandals; He will baptize you with the Holy Spirit and fire.

12 "His winnowing fork is in His hand, and He will thoroughly clear His threshing floor; and He will gather His wheat into the barn, but He will burn up the chaff with unquenchable fire."

The Baptism of Jesus

13 Then Jesus *arrived from Galilee at the Jordan coming to John to be baptized by him.

14 But John tried to prevent Him, saying, "I have need to be baptized by You, and do You come to me?"

15 But Jesus answered and said to him, "Permit it at this time; for in this way it is fitting for us to fulfill all righteousness." Then he *permitted Him.

16 And after being baptized, Jesus came up immediately from the water; and behold, the heavens were opened, and he saw the Spirit of God descending like a dove and coming upon Him,

17 and behold, there was a voice out of the heavens saying, "This is My beloved Son, in whom I am well-pleased."

CHAPTER 4

The Temptation of Jesus

THEN Jesus was led up by the Spirit into the wilderness to be tempted by the devil.

2 And after He had fasted forty days and forty nights, He then became hungry.

3 And the tempter came and said to Him, "If You are the Son of God, command that these stones become bread."

4 But He answered and said, "It is written, 'MAN SHALL NOT LIVE ON BREAD ALONE, BUT ON EVERY WORD THAT PROCEEDS OUT OF THE MOUTH OF GOD.'"

5 Then the devil *took Him into the holy city and had Him stand on the pinnacle of the temple,

6 and *said to Him, "If You are the Son of God, throw Yourself down; for it is written,

'HE WILL COMMAND HIS ANGELS
      CONCERNING YOU';

and

'ON *their* HANDS THEY WILL BEAR
      YOU UP,
LEST YOU STRIKE YOUR FOOT
      AGAINST A STONE.'"

7 Jesus said to him, "Again, it is written, 'YOU SHALL NOT PUT THE LORD YOUR GOD TO THE TEST.'"

8 Again, the devil *took Him to a very high mountain and *showed Him all the kingdoms of the world and their glory;

9 and he said to Him, "All these things I will give You, if You fall down and worship me."

10 Then Jesus *said to him, "Go, Satan! For it is written, 'YOU SHALL WORSHIP THE LORD YOUR GOD, AND SERVE HIM ONLY.'"

11 Then the devil *left Him; and behold, angels came and *began to* minister to Him.

Jesus Begins His Ministry

12 Now when *Jesus* heard that John had been taken into custody, He departed into Galilee;

13 and leaving Nazareth, He came and lived in Capernaum, which is by the sea, in the region of Zebulun and Naphtali,

14 in order that what was spoken through Isaiah the prophet would be fulfilled, saying,

15 "THE LAND OF ZEBULUN AND THE
      LAND OF NAPHTALI,
BY THE WAY OF THE SEA, BEYOND
      THE JORDAN, GALILEE OF THE
      GENTILES—
16 THE PEOPLE WHO WERE SITTING
      IN DARKNESS SAW A GREAT
      LIGHT,
AND THOSE WHO WERE SITTING
      IN THE LAND AND SHADOW OF
      DEATH,
UPON THEM A LIGHT DAWNED."

17 From that time Jesus began to preach and say, "Repent, for the kingdom of heaven is at hand."

The First Disciples

18 Now as *Jesus* was walking by the Sea of Galilee, He saw two brothers, Simon who was called Peter, and Andrew his brother, casting a net into the sea; for they were fishermen.

19 And He *said to them, "Follow Me, and I will make you fishers of men."

20 And immediately they left their nets and followed Him.

21 And going on from there He saw two other brothers, James the *son* of Zebedee, and John his brother, in the boat with Zebedee their father, mending their nets; and He called them.

22 And immediately they left the boat and their father, and followed Him.

Ministry in Galilee

23 And Jesus was going throughout all Galilee, teaching in their synagogues and preaching the gospel of the kingdom, and healing every kind of disease and every kind of sickness among the people.

24 And the news about Him spread throughout all Syria; and they brought to Him all who were ill, those suffering with various diseases and pains, demoniacs, epileptics, paralytics; and He healed them.

25 And large crowds followed Him from Galilee and the Decapolis and Jerusalem and Judea and *from* beyond the Jordan.

CHAPTER 5

The Sermon on the Mount; The Beatitudes

NOW when Jesus saw the crowds, He went up on the mountain; and after He sat down, His disciples came to Him.

2 And He opened His mouth and *began to* teach them, saying,

3 "Blessed are the poor in spirit, for theirs is the kingdom of heaven.

4 "Blessed are those who mourn, for they shall be comforted.

5 "Blessed are the lowly, for they shall inherit the earth.

6 "Blessed are those who hunger and thirst for righteousness, for they shall be satisfied.

7 "Blessed are the merciful, for they shall receive mercy.

8 "Blessed are the pure in heart, for they shall see God.

9 "Blessed are the peacemakers, for they shall be called sons of God.

10 "Blessed are those who have been persecuted for the sake of righteousness, for theirs is the kingdom of heaven.

11 "Blessed are you when *people* insult you and persecute you, and falsely say all kinds of evil against you because of Me.

12 "Rejoice and be glad, for your reward in heaven is great; for in the same way they persecuted the prophets who were before you.

Salt and Light

13 "You are the salt of the earth; but if the salt has become tasteless, how will it be made salty *again*? It is no longer good for anything, except to be thrown out to be trampled under foot by men.

14 "You are the light of the world. A city set on a hill cannot be hidden;

15 nor does *anyone* light a lamp and put it under a basket, but on the lampstand, and it gives light to all who are in the house.

16 "Let your light shine before men in such a way that they may see your good works, and glorify your Father who is in heaven.

17 "Do not think that I came to abolish the Law or the Prophets;

I did not come to abolish but to fulfill.

18 "For truly I say to you, until heaven and earth pass away, not the smallest letter or stroke shall pass from the Law until all is accomplished.

19 "Whoever then annuls one of the least of these commandments, and teaches others *to do* the same, shall be called least in the kingdom of heaven; but whoever does and teaches *them*, he shall be called great in the kingdom of heaven.

20 "For I say to you that unless your righteousness surpasses *that* of the scribes and Pharisees, you will not enter the kingdom of heaven.

Personal Relationships

21 "You have heard that the ancients were told, 'YOU SHALL NOT MURDER' and 'Whoever murders shall be guilty before the court.'

22 "But I say to you that everyone who is angry with his brother shall be guilty before the court; and whoever says to his brother, 'Raca,' shall be guilty before the Sanhedrin; and whoever says, 'You fool,' shall be guilty *enough to go* into the fiery hell.

23 "Therefore if you are presenting your offering at the altar, and there remember that your brother has something against you,

24 leave your offering there before the altar and go; first be reconciled to your brother, and then come and present your offering.

25 "Make friends quickly with your opponent at law while you are with him on the way, so that your opponent may not hand you over to the judge, and the judge to the officer, and you be thrown into prison.

26 "Truly I say to you, you will not come out of there until you have paid up the last [1]quadrans.

27 "You have heard that it was said, 'YOU SHALL NOT COMMIT ADULTERY';

28 but I say to you that everyone who looks at a woman to lust for her has already committed adultery with her in his heart.

29 "But if your right eye makes you stumble, tear it out and throw it from you; for it is better for you to lose one of the parts of your body, than for your whole body to be thrown into hell.

30 "And if your right hand makes you stumble, cut it off and throw it from you; for it is better for you to lose one of the parts of your body, than for your whole body to go into hell.

31 "Now it was said, 'WHOEVER SENDS HIS WIFE AWAY, LET HIM GIVE HER A CERTIFICATE OF DIVORCE';

32 but I say to you that everyone who divorces his wife, except for the reason of sexual immorality, makes her commit adultery; and whoever marries a divorced woman commits adultery.

33 "Again, you have heard that the ancients were told, 'YOU SHALL NOT

---

[1] A Roman copper coin, approx. 1/64 of a laborer's daily wage

MAKE FALSE VOWS, BUT SHALL FULFILL YOUR VOWS TO THE LORD.'

34 "But I say to you, make no oath at all, either by heaven, for it is the throne of God,

35 or by the earth, for it is the footstool of His feet, or by Jerusalem, for it is THE CITY OF THE GREAT KING.

36 "Nor shall you make an oath by your head, for you cannot make one hair white or black.

37 "But let your statement be, 'Yes, yes' or 'No, no'; anything beyond these is of the evil one.

38 "You have heard that it was said, 'AN EYE FOR AN EYE, AND A TOOTH FOR A TOOTH.'

39 "But I say to you, do not resist an evil person; but whoever slaps you on your right cheek, turn the other to him also.

40 "And if anyone wants to sue you and take your tunic, let him have your garment also.

41 "And whoever forces you to go one mile, go with him two.

42 "Give to him who asks of you, and do not turn away from him who wants to borrow from you.

43 "You have heard that it was said, 'YOU SHALL LOVE YOUR NEIGHBOR and hate your enemy.'

44 "But I say to you, love your enemies and pray for those who persecute you,

45 so that you may be sons of your Father who is in heaven; for He causes His sun to rise on *the* evil and *the* good, and sends rain on *the* righteous and *the* unrighteous.

46 "For if you love those who love you, what reward do you have? Do not even the tax collectors do the same?

47 "And if you greet only your brothers, what more are you doing *than others*? Do not even the Gentiles do the same?

48 "Therefore you are to be perfect, as your heavenly Father is perfect.

CHAPTER 6

Giving to the Poor and Prayer

"BEWARE of doing your righteousness before men to be noticed by them; otherwise you have no reward with your Father who is in heaven.

2 "Therefore, when you give to the poor, do not sound a trumpet before you, as the hypocrites do in the synagogues and in the streets, so that they may be glorified by men. Truly I say to you, they have their reward in full.

3 "But when you give to the poor, do not let your left hand know what your right hand is doing,

4 so that your giving will be in secret; and your Father who sees *what is done* in secret will reward you.

5 "And when you pray, you are not to be like the hypocrites; for they love to stand and pray in the synagogues and on the street corners so that they may be seen by men. Truly I say to you, they have their reward in full.

6 "But you, when you pray, go into your inner room, and when you have shut your door, pray to your Father who is in secret, and your Father who sees *what is done* in secret will reward you.

7 "And when you are praying, do not use meaningless repetition as the Gentiles do, for they suppose that they will be heard for their many words.

8 "Therefore, do not be like them; for your Father knows what you need before you ask Him.

9 "Pray, then, in this way:
'Our Father who is in heaven,
Hallowed be Your name.
10 'Your kingdom come.
Your will be done,
On earth as it is in heaven.
11 'Give us this day our daily bread.
12 'And forgive us our debts, as we
also have forgiven our
debtors.
13 'And do not lead us into
temptation, but deliver us
from the evil one. [For Yours
is the kingdom and the
power and the glory forever.
Amen.']

14 "For if you forgive others for their transgressions, your heavenly Father will also forgive you.

15 "But if you do not forgive others, then your Father will not forgive your transgressions.

Fasting

16 "Now whenever you fast, do not put on a gloomy face as the hypocrites do, for they neglect their appearance so that they will be noticed by men when they are fasting. Truly I say to you, they have their reward in full.

17 "But you, when you fast, anoint your head and wash your face

18 so that your fasting will not be noticed by men, but by your Father who is in secret; and your Father who sees *what is done* in secret will reward you.

Treasures in Heaven

19 "Do not store up for yourselves treasures on earth, where moth and rust destroy, and where thieves break in and steal.

20 "But store up for yourselves treasures in heaven, where neither moth nor rust destroys, and where thieves do not break in or steal;

21 for where your treasure is, there your heart will be also.

22 "The eye is the lamp of the body; so then if your eye is clear, your whole body will be full of light.

23 "But if your eye is bad, your whole body will be full of darkness. If then the light that is in you is darkness, how great is the darkness!

24 "No one can serve two masters; for either he will hate the one and love the other, or he will be devoted to one and despise the other. You cannot serve God and wealth.

Do Not Worry

25 "For this reason I say to you, do not be worried about your life,

as to what you will eat or what you will drink; nor for your body, *as to* what you will put on. Is not life more than food, and the body more than clothing?

26 "Look at the birds of the air, that they do not sow, nor reap nor gather into barns, and *yet* your heavenly Father feeds them. Are you not worth much more than they?

27 "And which of you by worrying can add a single ¹cubit to his life span?

28 "And why are you worried about clothing? Observe how the lilies of the field grow; they do not toil nor do they spin,

29 yet I say to you that not even Solomon in all his glory clothed himself like one of these.

30 "But if God so clothes the grass of the field, which is *alive* today and tomorrow is thrown into the furnace, *will He* not much more *clothe* you? You of little faith!

31 "Do not worry then, saying, 'What will we eat?' or 'What will we drink?' or 'What will we wear for clothing?'

32 "For all these things the Gentiles eagerly seek; for your heavenly Father knows that you need all these things.

33 "But seek first His kingdom and His righteousness, and all these things will be added to you.

34 "So do not worry about tomorrow; for tomorrow will worry about itself. Each day has enough trouble of its own.

CHAPTER 7

Judging Others

"DO not judge, so that you will not be judged.

2 "For with what judgment you judge, you will be judged; and with what measure you measure, it will be measured to you.

3 "And why do you look at the speck that is in your brother's eye, but do not notice the log that is in your own eye?

4 "Or how can you say to your brother, 'Let me take the speck out of your eye,' and behold, the log is in your own eye?

5 "You hypocrite, first take the log out of your own eye, and then you will see clearly to take the speck out of your brother's eye.

6 "Do not give what is holy to dogs, and do not throw your pearls before swine, lest they trample them under their feet, and turn and tear you to pieces.

Ask, and It Will Be Given

7 "Ask, and it will be given to you; seek, and you will find; knock, and it will be opened to you.

8 "For everyone who asks receives, and he who seeks finds, and to him who knocks it will be opened.

¹ A cubit was approx. 18 in. or 45 cm

9 "Or what man is there among you who, when his son asks for a loaf, will give him a stone?

10 "Or if he asks for a fish, he will not give him a snake, will he?

11 "If you then, being evil, know how to give good gifts to your children, how much more will your Father who is in heaven give what is good to those who ask Him!

12 "Therefore, in all things, whatever you want people to do for you, so do for them, for this is the Law and the Prophets.

The Narrow Gate

13 "Enter through the narrow gate; for the gate is wide and the way is broad that leads to destruction, and there are many who enter through it.

14 "For the gate is narrow and the way is constricted that leads to life, and there are few who find it.

A Tree and Its Fruit

15 "Beware of the false prophets, who come to you in sheep's clothing, but inwardly are ravenous wolves.

16 "You will know them by their fruits. Are grapes gathered from thorn bushes or figs from thistles?

17 "Even so, every good tree bears good fruit, but the bad tree bears bad fruit.

18 "A good tree cannot bear bad fruit, nor can a bad tree bear good fruit.

19 "Every tree that does not bear good fruit is cut down and thrown into the fire.

20 "So then, you will know them by their fruits.

21 "Not everyone who says to Me, 'Lord, Lord,' will enter the kingdom of heaven, but he who does the will of My Father who is in heaven *will enter.*

22 "Many will say to Me on that day, 'Lord, Lord, in Your name did we not prophesy, and in Your name cast out demons, and in Your name do many miracles?'

23 "And then I will declare to them, 'I never knew you; DEPART FROM ME, YOU WHO PRACTICE LAWLESSNESS.'

Build Your House on the Rock

24 "Therefore everyone who hears these words of Mine and does them, may be compared to a wise man who built his house on the rock.

25 "And the rain descended, and the rivers came, and the winds blew and fell against that house; and *yet* it did not fall, for it had been founded on the rock.

26 "And everyone hearing these words of Mine and not doing them, may be compared to a foolish man who built his house on the sand.

27 "And the rain descended, and the rivers came, and the winds blew and slammed against that house; and it fell—and great was its fall."

28 Now it happened that when Jesus had finished these words, the crowds were astonished at His teaching;

29 for He was teaching them as *one* having authority, and not as their scribes.

CHAPTER 8

Jesus Cleanses a Leper

NOW when Jesus came down from the mountain, large crowds followed Him.

2 And behold, a leper came to Him and was bowing down before Him, and said, "Lord, if You are willing, You can make me clean."

3 And Jesus stretched out His hand and touched him, saying, "I am willing; be cleansed." And immediately his leprosy was cleansed.

4 And Jesus *said to him, "See that you tell no one; but go, show yourself to the priest and present the offering that Moses commanded, as a testimony to them."

The Centurion's Faith

5 And when Jesus entered Capernaum, a centurion came to Him, pleading *with* Him,

6 and saying, "Lord, my servant is lying paralyzed at home, fearfully tormented."

7 And Jesus *said to him, "I will come and heal him."

8 But the centurion said, "Lord, I am not good enough for You to come under my roof, but just say the word, and my servant will be healed.

9 "For I also am a man under authority, with soldiers under me; and I say to this man, 'Go!' and he goes, and to another, 'Come!' and he comes, and to my slave, 'Do this!' and he does *it.*"

10 Now when Jesus heard *this*, He marveled and said to those who were following, "Truly I say to you, I have not found such great faith with anyone in Israel.

11 "And I say to you that many will come from east and west, and recline *at the table* with Abraham, Isaac, and Jacob in the kingdom of heaven;

12 but the sons of the kingdom will be cast out into the outer darkness; in that place there will be weeping and gnashing of teeth."

13 And Jesus said to the centurion, "Go; it shall be done for you as you have believed." And the servant was healed that *very* moment.

Peter's Mother-in-Law and Many Others Healed

14 When Jesus came into Peter's home, He saw his mother-in-law lying sick in bed with a fever.

15 And He touched her hand, and the fever left her; and she got up and *began* waiting on Him.

16 Now when evening came, they brought to Him many who were demon-possessed; and He cast out the spirits with a word, and healed all who were ill

17 in order to fulfill what was spoken through Isaiah the prophet, saying, "HE HIMSELF TOOK OUR INFIRMITIES AND CARRIED AWAY OUR DISEASES."

The Cost of Following Jesus

18 Now when Jesus saw a crowd around Him, He gave orders to depart to the other side *of the sea.*

19 Then a scribe came and said to Him, "Teacher, I will follow You wherever You go."

20 And Jesus *said to him, "The foxes have holes and the birds of the air *have* nests, but the Son of Man has nowhere to lay His head."

21 And another of the disciples said to Him, "Lord, permit me first to go and bury my father."

22 But Jesus *said to him, "Follow Me, and allow the dead to bury their own dead."

Jesus Calms a Storm

23 And when He got into the boat, His disciples followed Him.

24 And behold, there arose a great storm on the sea, so that the boat was being covered with the waves; but Jesus Himself was sleeping.

25 And they came to *Him* and got Him up, saying, "Save *us*, Lord; we are perishing!"

26 And He *said to them, "Why are you *so* cowardly, you men of little faith?" Then He got up and rebuked the winds and the sea, and it became perfectly calm.

27 And the men marveled, and said, "What kind of a man is this, that even the winds and the sea obey Him?"

Jesus Saves Men from Demons

28 And when He came to the other side, into the region of the Gadarenes, two men who were demon-possessed met Him as they were coming out of the tombs. *They* were so extremely violent that no one could pass by that way.

29 And behold, they cried out, saying, "What do we have to do with You, Son of God? Have You come here to torment us before the time?"

30 Now there was a herd of many swine feeding at a distance from them.

31 And the demons *began to* plead with Him, saying, "If You *are going to* cast us out, send us into the herd of swine."

32 And He said to them, "Go!" And coming out, they went into the swine; and behold, the whole herd rushed down the steep bank into the sea and perished in the waters.

33 Now the herdsmen ran away, and went to the city and reported everything, including what had happened to the demoniacs.

34 And behold, the whole city came out to meet Jesus; and when they saw Him, they pleaded with Him to leave their region.

CHAPTER 9

Jesus Heals a Paralytic

AND getting into a boat, Jesus crossed over *the sea* and came to His own city.

2 And behold, they brought to Him a paralytic lying on a bed. Seeing their faith, Jesus said to the paralytic, "Take courage, son; your sins are forgiven."

3 And behold, some of the scribes said to themselves, "This man blasphemes."

4 And Jesus knowing their thoughts said, "Why are you thinking evil in your hearts?

5 "For which is easier, to say, 'Your sins are forgiven,' or to say, 'Get up and walk'?

6 "But so that you may know that the Son of Man has authority on earth to forgive sins"—then He *said to the paralytic, "Get up, pick up your bed and go home."

7 And he got up and went home.

8 But when the crowds saw *this*, they were afraid, and glorified God, who had given such authority to men.

Matthew and Sinners Called

9 And as Jesus went on from there, He saw a man called Matthew, sitting in the tax office; and He *said to him, "Follow Me!" And he stood up and followed Him.

10 Then it happened that as Jesus was reclining *at the table* in the house, behold, many tax collectors and sinners came and were dining with Jesus and His disciples.

11 And when the Pharisees saw *this*, they said to His disciples, "Why is your Teacher eating with the tax collectors and sinners?"

12 But when Jesus heard *this*, He said, "*It is* not those who are healthy who need a physician, but those who are sick.

13 "But go and learn what this means: 'I DESIRE COMPASSION, AND NOT SACRIFICE,' for I did not come to call the righteous, but sinners."

A Question About Fasting

14 Then the disciples of John *came to Him, asking, "Why do we and the Pharisees fast, but Your disciples do not fast?"

15 And Jesus said to them, "Can the attendants of the bridegroom mourn as long as the bridegroom is with them? But the days will come when the bridegroom is taken away from them, and then they will fast.

16 "But no one puts a patch of unshrunk cloth on an old garment; for the patch pulls away from the garment, and a worse tear results.

17 "Nor do *people* put new wine into old wineskins; otherwise the wineskins burst, and the wine pours out and the wineskins are ruined; but they put new wine into fresh wineskins, and both are preserved."

Miracles of Healing

18 While He was saying these things to them, behold, a *synagogue* official came and was bowing down before Him, and said, "My daughter has just died; but come and lay Your hand on her, and she will live."

19 And Jesus got up and *began to* follow him, and *so did* His disciples.

20 And behold, a woman who had been suffering from a hemorrhage for twelve years, came up behind Him and touched the fringe of His garment;

21 for she was saying to herself, "If I only touch His garment, I will be saved *from this*."

22 But Jesus turning and seeing her said, "Daughter, take courage; your faith has saved you." At once the woman was saved *from her hemorrhage.*

23 And when Jesus came into the official's house, and saw the flute-players and the crowd in noisy disorder,

24 He was saying, "Leave; for the girl has not died, but is asleep." And they *began* laughing at Him.

25 But when the crowd had been sent out, coming in, He took her by the hand, and the girl got up.

26 And this news spread throughout all that land.

27 And as Jesus went on from there, two blind men followed Him, crying out, "Have mercy on us, Son of David!"

28 And when He entered the house, the blind men came up to Him, and Jesus *said to them, "Do you believe that I am able to do this?" They *said to Him, "Yes, Lord."

29 Then He touched their eyes, saying, "It shall be done to you according to your faith."

30 And their eyes were opened. And Jesus sternly warned them, saying, "See that no one knows *about this!*"

31 But they went out and spread the news about Him throughout all that land.

32 Now as they were going out, behold, a mute, demon-possessed man was brought to Him.

33 And after the demon was cast out, the mute man spoke; and the crowds marveled, saying, "Nothing like this has ever been seen in Israel."

34 But the Pharisees were saying, "He casts out the demons by the ruler of the demons."

35 And Jesus was going through all the cities and villages, teaching in their synagogues, and preaching the gospel of the kingdom, and healing every kind of disease and every kind of sickness.

36 And seeing the crowds, He felt compassion for them, because they were distressed and downcast like sheep without a shepherd.

37 Then He *said to His disciples, "The harvest is plentiful, but the workers are few.

38 "Therefore pray earnestly to the Lord of the harvest to send out workers into His harvest."

CHAPTER 10

Jesus Appoints the Twelve

AND summoning His twelve disciples, *Jesus* gave them authority over unclean spirits, to cast them out, and to heal every kind of disease and every kind of sickness.

2 Now the names of the twelve apostles are these: The first, Simon, who is called Peter, and Andrew his brother; and James the son of Zebedee, and John his brother;

3 Philip and Bartholomew; Thomas and Matthew the tax collector; James the son of Alphaeus, and Thaddaeus;

4 Simon the Zealot, and Judas Iscariot, the one who betrayed Him.

The Twelve Disciples Sent Out

5 These twelve Jesus sent out after instructing them, saying, "Do not go in the way of the Gentiles, and do not enter *any* city of the Samaritans;

6 but rather go to the lost sheep of the house of Israel.

7 "And as you go, preach, saying, 'The kingdom of heaven is at hand.'

8 "Heal *the* sick, raise *the* dead, cleanse *the* lepers, cast out demons. Freely you received, freely give.

9 "Do not acquire gold, or silver, or copper for your money belts,

10 or a bag for *your* journey, or even two tunics, or sandals, or a staff; for the worker is worthy of his support.

11 "And whatever city or village you enter, inquire who is worthy in it, and stay there until you leave.

12 "Now as you enter the house, give it your greeting.

13 "And if the house is worthy, let your peace come upon it. But if it is not worthy, let your peace return to you.

14 "And whoever does not receive you, nor heed your words, as you leave that house or that city, shake the dust off your feet.

15 "Truly I say to you, it will be more tolerable for the land of Sodom and Gomorrah in the day of judgment than for that city.

The Promise of Persecution

16 "Behold, I send you out as sheep in the midst of wolves; so be shrewd as serpents and innocent as doves.

17 "But beware of men, for they will deliver you over to the courts and flog you in their synagogues;

18 and you will even be brought before governors and kings for My sake, as a testimony to them and to the Gentiles.

19 "But when they deliver you over, do not worry about how or what you are to say; for it will be given to you in that hour what you are to say.

20 "For it is not you who speak, but the Spirit of your Father who speaks in you.

21 "And brother will betray brother to death, and a father *his* child; and children will rise up against parents and cause them to be put to death.

22 "And you will be hated by all because of My name, but it is the one who has endured to the end who will be saved.

23 "But whenever they persecute you in this city, flee to the next; for truly I say to you, you will not finish *going through* the cities of Israel until the Son of Man comes.

The Meaning of Discipleship

24 "A disciple is not above his teacher, nor a slave above his master.

25 "It is enough for the disciple that he become like his teacher, and the

slave like his master. If they have called the head of the house Beelzebul, how much more the members of his household!

26 "Therefore do not fear them, for there is nothing concealed that will not be revealed, and hidden that will not be known.

27 "What I tell you in the darkness, speak in the light; and what you hear *whispered* in *your* ear, proclaim upon the housetops.

28 "And do not fear those who kill the body but are unable to kill the soul; but rather fear Him who is able to destroy both soul and body in hell.

29 "Are not two sparrows sold for an ¹assarion? And *yet* not one of them will fall to the ground apart from your Father.

30 "But the very hairs of your head are all numbered.

31 "So do not fear; you are more valuable than many sparrows.

32 "Therefore everyone who confesses Me before men, I will also confess him before My Father who is in heaven.

33 "But whoever denies Me before men, I will also deny him before My Father who is in heaven.

34 "Do not think that I came to bring peace on the earth; I did not come to bring peace, but a sword.

35 "For I came to SET A MAN AGAINST HIS FATHER, AND A DAUGHTER AGAINST HER MOTHER, AND A DAUGHTER-IN-LAW AGAINST HER MOTHER-IN-LAW;

36 and A MAN'S ENEMIES WILL BE THE MEMBERS OF HIS HOUSEHOLD.

37 "He who loves father or mother more than Me is not worthy of Me; and he who loves son or daughter more than Me is not worthy of Me.

38 "And he who does not take his cross and follow after Me is not worthy of Me.

39 "He who has found his life will lose it, and he who has lost his life for My sake will find it.

The Reward of Service

40 "He who receives you receives Me, and he who receives Me receives Him who sent Me.

41 "He who receives a prophet in the name of a prophet shall receive a prophet's reward; and he who receives a righteous man in the name of a righteous man shall receive a righteous man's reward.

42 "And whoever in the name of a disciple gives to one of these little ones even a cup of cold water to drink, truly I say to you, he shall not lose his reward."

CHAPTER 11

Questions from John the Baptist

NOW it happened that when Jesus had finished giving instructions to His twelve disciples, He departed from there to teach and preach in their cities.

¹ A Roman copper coin, approx. 1/16 of a laborer's daily wage

2 Now when John in prison heard of the works of Christ, he sent *word* by his disciples

3 and said to Him, "Are You the One who is to come, or shall we look for someone else?"

4 And Jesus answered and said to them, "Go and report to John what you hear and see:

5 *the* BLIND RECEIVE SIGHT and *the* lame walk, *the* lepers are cleansed and *the* deaf hear, *the* dead are raised up, and *the* POOR HAVE THE GOSPEL PREACHED TO THEM.

6 "And blessed is he who does not take offense at Me."

Jesus' Tribute to John the Baptist

7 Now as these men were going *away*, Jesus began to speak to the crowds about John, "What did you go out into the wilderness to see? A reed shaken by the wind?

8 "But what did you go out to see? A man dressed in soft *clothing*? Behold, those who wear soft *clothing* are in kings' palaces!

9 "But what did you go out to see? A prophet? Yes, I tell you, and one who is more than a prophet.

10 "This is the one about whom it is written,

'BEHOLD, I SEND MY MESSENGER AHEAD OF YOU,
WHO WILL PREPARE YOUR WAY BEFORE YOU.'

11 "Truly I say to you, among those born of women there has not arisen *anyone* greater than John the Baptist! Yet the one who is least in the kingdom of heaven is greater than he.

12 "And from the days of John the Baptist until now the kingdom of heaven suffers violence, and violent men take it by force.

13 "For all the prophets and the Law prophesied until John.

14 "And if you are willing to accept *it*, John himself is Elijah who was to come.

15 "He who has ears to hear, let him hear.

16 "But to what shall I compare this generation? It is like children sitting in the marketplaces, who call out to the other *children*,

17 and say, 'We played the flute for you, and you did not dance; we sang a dirge, and you did not mourn.'

18 "For John came neither eating nor drinking, and they say, 'He has a demon!'

19 "The Son of Man came eating and drinking, and they say, 'Behold, a gluttonous man and a drunkard, a friend of tax collectors and sinners!' Yet wisdom is vindicated by her deeds."

Woe to Unrepentant Cities

20 Then He began to denounce the cities in which most of His miracles were done, because they did not repent.

21 "Woe to you, Chorazin! Woe to you, Bethsaida! For if the miracles had occurred in Tyre and Sidon which occurred in you, they would have repented long ago in sackcloth and ashes.

22 "Nevertheless I say to you, it will be more tolerable for Tyre and Sidon in the day of judgment than for you.

23 "And Capernaum, will you be exalted to heaven? You will descend to Hades; for if the miracles had occurred in Sodom which occurred in you, it would have remained to this day.

24 "Nevertheless I say to you that it will be more tolerable for the land of Sodom in the day of judgment, than for you."

Come to Me

25 At that time Jesus said, "I praise You, Father, Lord of heaven and earth, that You have hidden these things from *the* wise and intelligent and have revealed them to infants.

26 "Yes, Father, for this way was well-pleasing in Your sight.

27 "All things have been handed over to Me by My Father; and no one knows the Son except the Father; nor does anyone know the Father except the Son, and anyone to whom the Son wills to reveal *Him*.

28 "Come to Me, all who are weary and heavy-laden, and I will give you rest.

29 "Take My yoke upon you and learn from Me, for I am gentle and humble in heart, and YOU WILL FIND REST FOR YOUR SOULS.

30 "For My yoke is easy and My burden is light."

CHAPTER 12

Lord of the Sabbath

AT that time Jesus went through the grainfields on the Sabbath, and His disciples became hungry and began to pick the heads of grain and eat.

2 But when the Pharisees saw *this*, they said to Him, "Look, Your disciples do what is not lawful to do on a Sabbath."

3 But He said to them, "Have you not read what David did when he became hungry, he and his companions,

4 how he entered the house of God, and they ate the consecrated bread, which was not lawful for him to eat nor for those with him, but for the priests alone?

5 "Or have you not read in the Law, that on the Sabbath the priests in the temple break the Sabbath and are innocent?

6 "But I say to you that something greater than the temple is here.

7 "But if you had known what this means, 'I DESIRE COMPASSION, AND NOT A SACRIFICE,' you would not have condemned the innocent.

8 "For the Son of Man is Lord of the Sabbath."

Jesus Heals a Man on the Sabbath

9 And departing from there, He went into their synagogue.

10 And behold, a man *was there* whose hand was withered. And they questioned Jesus, saying, "Is it lawful to heal on the Sabbath?"—so that they might accuse Him.

11 And He said to them, "What man is there among you who has a sheep, and if it falls into a pit on the Sabbath, will not take hold of it and lift it out?

12 "How much more valuable then is a man than a sheep! So then, it is lawful to do good on the Sabbath."

13 Then He *said to the man, "Stretch out your hand!" He stretched it out, and it was restored to normal, like the other.

14 But going out, the Pharisees took counsel together against Him, *as to* how they might destroy Him.

15 But Jesus, aware *of this*, withdrew from there. Many followed Him, and He healed them all,

16 and warned them not to make Him known,

17 in order that what was spoken through Isaiah the prophet would be fulfilled, saying,

18 "BEHOLD, MY SERVANT WHOM I
      HAVE CHOSEN;
   MY BELOVED IN WHOM MY SOUL
      IS WELL-PLEASED;
   I WILL PUT MY SPIRIT UPON HIM,
   AND HE SHALL PROCLAIM JUSTICE
      TO THE GENTILES.

19 "HE WILL NOT QUARREL, NOR CRY
      OUT;
   NOR WILL ANYONE HEAR HIS
      VOICE IN THE STREETS.

20 "A BATTERED REED HE WILL NOT
      BREAK OFF,
   AND A SMOLDERING WICK HE WILL
      NOT PUT OUT,
   UNTIL HE LEADS JUSTICE TO
      VICTORY.

21 "AND IN HIS NAME THE GENTILES
      WILL HOPE."

A Kingdom Divided

22 Then a demon-possessed man *who was* blind and mute was brought to Jesus, and He healed him, so that the mute man spoke and saw.

23 And all the crowds were astounded, and were saying, "Can this man *really* be the Son of David?"

24 But when the Pharisees heard *this*, they said, "This man does not cast out demons except by Beelzebul the ruler of the demons."

25 And knowing their thoughts He said to them, "Any kingdom divided against itself is laid waste; and any city or house divided against itself will not stand.

26 "And if Satan casts out Satan, he is divided against himself; how then will his kingdom stand?

27 "And if I by Beelzebul cast out demons, by whom do your sons cast *them* out? For this reason they will be your judges.

28 "But if I cast out demons by the Spirit of God, then the kingdom of God has come upon you.

29 "Or how can anyone enter the strong man's house and carry off his property, unless he first binds the strong man? And then he will plunder his house.

Blasphemy Against the Holy Spirit

30 "He who is not with Me is against Me; and he who does not gather with Me scatters.

31 "Therefore I say to you, any sin and blasphemy shall be forgiven people, but the blasphemy against the Spirit shall not be forgiven.

32 "And whoever speaks a word against the Son of Man, it shall be forgiven him; but whoever speaks against the Holy Spirit, it shall not be forgiven him, either in this age or in the *age* to come.

The Heart Is Revealed by Words

33 "Either make the tree good and its fruit good, or make the tree bad and its fruit bad; for the tree is known by its fruit.

34 "You brood of vipers, how can you, being evil, speak what is good? For the mouth speaks out of that which fills the heart.

35 "The good man brings out of *his* good treasure what is good; and the evil man brings out of *his* evil treasure what is evil.

36 "But I tell you that every careless word that people speak, they shall give an accounting for it in the day of judgment.

37 "For by your words you will be justified, and by your words you will be condemned."

The Sign of Jonah

38 Then some of the scribes and Pharisees answered and said to Him, "Teacher, we want to see a sign from You."

39 But He answered and said to them, "An evil and adulterous generation eagerly seeks for a sign; and *yet* no sign will be given to it but the sign of Jonah the prophet;

40 for just as JONAH WAS THREE DAYS AND THREE NIGHTS IN THE BELLY OF THE SEA MONSTER, so will the Son of Man be three days and three nights in the heart of the earth.

41 "The men of Nineveh will stand up with this generation at the judgment, and will condemn it because they repented at the preaching of Jonah; and behold, something greater than Jonah is here.

42 "The Queen of the South will rise up with this generation at the judgment and will condemn it, because she came from the ends of the earth to hear the wisdom of Solomon; and behold, something greater than Solomon is here.

43 "Now when the unclean spirit goes out of a man, it passes through waterless places seeking rest, and does not find *it*.

44 "Then it says, 'I will return to my house from which I came'; and when it comes, it finds *it* unoccupied, swept, and put in order.

45 "Then it goes and takes along with it seven other spirits more wicked than itself, and they go in and live there; and the last state of that man becomes worse than the first. That is the way it will also be with this evil generation."

Jesus' Mother and Brothers

46 While He was still speaking to the crowds, behold, His mother and brothers were standing outside, seeking to speak to Him.

47 Now someone said to Him, "Behold, Your mother and Your brothers are standing outside seeking to speak to You."

48 But Jesus answered the one who was telling Him and said, "Who is My mother and who are My brothers?"

49 And stretching out His hand toward His disciples, He said, "Behold My mother and My brothers!

50 "For whoever does the will of My Father who is in heaven, he is My brother and sister and mother."

CHAPTER 13

The Parable of the Sower

ON that day Jesus went out of the house and was sitting by the sea.

2 And large crowds gathered to Him, so He got into a boat and sat down, and the whole crowd was standing on the beach.

3 And He spoke many things to them in parables, saying, "Behold, the sower went out to sow;

4 and as he sowed, some *seeds* fell beside the road, and the birds came and ate them up.

5 "And others fell on the rocky places, where they did not have much soil; and immediately they sprang up, because they had no depth of soil.

6 "But when the sun had risen, they were scorched; and because they had no root, they withered away.

7 "And others fell among the thorns, and the thorns came up and choked them out.

8 "And others fell on the good soil and were yielding a crop, some a hundredfold, some sixty, and some thirty.

9 "He who has ears, let him hear."

The Purpose of the Parables

10 And the disciples came and said to Him, "Why do You speak to them in parables?"

11 And Jesus answered and said to them, "To you it has been given to know the mysteries of the kingdom of heaven, but to them it has not been given.

12 "For whoever has, to him *more* shall be given, and he will have an abundance; but whoever does not have, even what he has shall be taken away from him.

13 "Therefore I speak to them in parables; because while seeing they do not see, and while hearing they do not hear, nor do they understand.

14 "And in them the prophecy of Isaiah is being fulfilled, which says,

'YOU WILL KEEP ON HEARING, BUT
    WILL NOT UNDERSTAND;
YOU WILL KEEP ON SEEING, BUT
    WILL NOT PERCEIVE;
15 FOR THE HEART OF THIS PEOPLE
    HAS BECOME DULL,
AND WITH THEIR EARS THEY
    SCARCELY HEAR,
AND THEY HAVE CLOSED THEIR
    EYES,
LEST THEY WOULD SEE WITH
    THEIR EYES,

Hear with their ears,
And understand with their
     heart and return,
And I would heal them.'

16 "But blessed are your eyes, because they see; and your ears, because they hear.

17 "For truly I say to you that many prophets and righteous men desired to see what you see, and did not see *it*, and to hear what you hear, and did not hear *it*.

The Parable of the Sower Explained

18 "Hear then the parable of the sower.

19 "When anyone hears the word of the kingdom and does not understand it, the evil one comes and snatches away what has been sown in his heart. This is the one on whom seed was sown beside the road.

20 "And the one on whom seed was sown on the rocky places, this is the man who hears the word and immediately receives it with joy;

21 yet he has no root in himself, but is *only* temporary, and when affliction or persecution arises because of the word, immediately he falls away.

22 "And the one on whom seed was sown among the thorns, this is the one who hears the word, and the worry of the world and the deceitfulness of wealth choke the word, and it becomes unfruitful.

23 "And the one on whom seed was sown on the good soil, this is the man who hears the word and understands it; who indeed bears fruit and brings forth, some a hundredfold, some sixty, and some thirty."

The Parable of Tares Among Wheat

24 He presented another parable to them, saying, "The kingdom of heaven may be compared to a man who sowed good seed in his field.

25 "But while his men were sleeping, his enemy came and sowed tares among the wheat, and went away.

26 "But when the wheat sprouted and bore grain, then the tares became evident also.

27 "The slaves of the landowner came and said to him, 'Sir, did you not sow good seed in your field? How then does it have tares?'

28 "And he said to them, 'An enemy has done this!' The slaves *said to him, 'Do you want us, then, to go and gather them up?'

29 "But he *said, 'No; for while you are gathering up the tares, you may uproot the wheat with them.

30 'Allow both to grow together until the harvest; and in the time of the harvest I will say to the reapers, "First gather up the tares and bind them in bundles to burn them up; but gather the wheat into my barn." ' "

The Parables of the Mustard Seed and Leaven

31 He presented another parable to them, saying, "The kingdom of heaven is like a mustard seed, which a man took and sowed in his field;

32 and this is the smallest of all seeds, but when it is fully grown, it is

the largest of the garden plants and becomes a tree, so that THE BIRDS OF THE AIR come and NEST IN ITS BRANCHES."

33 He spoke another parable to them, "The kingdom of heaven is like leaven, which a woman took and hid in [1]three sata of flour until it was all leavened."

34 All these things Jesus spoke to the crowds in parables, and He was not speaking to them without a parable

35 so that what was spoken through the prophet would be fulfilled, saying,

> "I WILL OPEN MY MOUTH IN
>   PARABLES;
> I WILL UTTER THINGS HIDDEN
>   SINCE THE FOUNDATION OF
>   THE WORLD."

The Parable of Tares Explained

36 Then He left the crowds and went into the house. And His disciples came to Him and said, "Explain to us the parable of the tares of the field."

37 And He answered and said, "The one who sows the good seed is the Son of Man,

38 and the field is the world; and *as for* the good seed, these are the sons of the kingdom; and the tares are the sons of the evil one;

39 and the enemy who sowed them is the devil, and the harvest is the end of the age; and the reapers are angels.

40 "So just as the tares are gathered up and burned with fire, so shall it be at the end of the age.

41 "The Son of Man will send forth His angels, and they will gather out of His kingdom all stumbling blocks, and those who commit lawlessness,

42 and will throw them into the fiery furnace; in that place there will be weeping and gnashing of teeth.

43 "Then THE RIGHTEOUS WILL SHINE FORTH AS THE SUN in the kingdom of their Father. He who has ears, let him hear.

A Hidden Treasure

44 "The kingdom of heaven is like a treasure hidden in the field, which a man found and hid *again*; and from joy over it he goes and sells all that he has and buys that field.

A Costly Pearl

45 "Again, the kingdom of heaven is like a merchant seeking fine pearls,

46 and upon finding one pearl of great value, he went and sold all that he had and bought it.

A Dragnet

47 "Again, the kingdom of heaven is like a dragnet cast into the sea, and gathering *fish* of every kind;

48 and when it was filled, they drew it up on the beach; and they sat down and gathered the good *fish* into containers, but the bad they threw away.

49 "So it will be at the end of the age; the angels will come forth and take out the wicked from among the righteous,

50 and will throw them into the fiery furnace; in that place there will be weeping and gnashing of teeth.

---

[1] Approx. 48 lb. or 39 l, a saton was approx. 16 lb. or 13 l

51 "Have you understood all these things?" They *said to Him, "Yes."

52 And He said to them, "Therefore every scribe who has become a disciple of the kingdom of heaven is like a head of a household, who brings out of his treasure things new and old."

Jesus Rejected at Nazareth

53 Now it happened that when Jesus had finished these parables, He departed from there.

54 And He came to His hometown and *began* teaching them in their synagogue, so that they were astonished, and said, "Where *did* this man *get* this wisdom and *these* miraculous powers?

55 "Is not this the carpenter's son? Is not His mother called Mary, and His brothers, James and Joseph and Simon and Judas?

56 "And His sisters, are they not all with us? Where then *did* this man *get* all these things?"

57 And they were taking offense at Him. But Jesus said to them, "A prophet is not without honor except in his hometown and in his *own* household."

58 And He did not do many miracles there because of their unbelief.

CHAPTER 14

John the Baptist Beheaded

AT that time Herod the tetrarch heard the news about Jesus,

2 and said to his servants, "This is John the Baptist; he has risen from the dead, and that is why miraculous powers are at work in him."

3 For when Herod had John arrested, he bound him and put him in prison because of Herodias, the wife of his brother Philip.

4 For John had been saying to him, "It is not lawful for you to have her."

5 And although Herod wanted to put him to death, he feared the crowd, because they were regarding John as a prophet.

6 But when Herod's birthday came, the daughter of Herodias danced before *them* and pleased Herod,

7 so *much* that he promised with an oath to give her whatever she asked.

8 Now having been prompted by her mother, she *said, "Give me here on a platter the head of John the Baptist."

9 And although he was grieved, the king commanded *it* to be given because of his oaths, and because of his dinner guests.

10 And he sent and had John beheaded in the prison.

11 And his head was brought on a platter and given to the girl, and she brought it to her mother.

12 And his disciples came and took away the body and buried it; and they went and reported to Jesus.

Jesus Feeds Five Thousand

13 Now when Jesus heard *about John*, He withdrew from there in a boat to a desolate place by Himself; and when the crowds heard *of this*, they followed Him on foot from the cities.

14 And when He went ashore, He saw a large crowd, and felt compassion for them and healed their sick.

15 Now when it was evening, the disciples came to Him and said, "This place is desolate and the hour is already late; so send the crowds away, that they may go into the villages and buy food for themselves."

16 But Jesus said to them, "They do not need to go away; you give them *something* to eat!"

17 But they *said to Him, "We have here only five loaves and two fish."

18 And He said, "Bring them here to Me."

19 And ordering the crowds to sit down on the grass, He took the five loaves and the two fish, and looking up toward heaven, He blessed *the food.* And breaking the loaves, He gave them to the disciples, and the disciples *gave them* to the crowds,

20 and they all ate and were satisfied. They picked up what was left over of the broken pieces, twelve full baskets.

21 And there were about five thousand men who ate, besides women and children.

Jesus Walks on the Sea

22 Immediately He made the disciples get into the boat and go ahead of Him to the other side, while He sent the crowds away.

23 And after He had sent the crowds away, He went up on the mountain by Himself to pray; and when it was evening, He was there alone.

24 But the boat was already many ¹stadia away from the land, being battered by the waves; for the wind was against *them.*

25 And in the fourth watch of the night He came to them, walking on the sea.

26 Now when the disciples saw Him walking on the sea, they were terrified, and said, "It is a ghost!" And they cried out in fear.

27 But immediately Jesus spoke to them, saying, "Take courage, it is I; do not be afraid."

28 And Peter answered and said to Him, "Lord, if it is You, command me to come to You on the water."

29 And He said, "Come!" And getting out of the boat, Peter walked on the water and came toward Jesus.

30 But seeing the wind, he became frightened, and beginning to sink, he cried out, saying, "Lord, save me!"

31 And immediately Jesus stretched out His hand and took hold of him, and *said to him, "You of little faith, why did you doubt?"

32 And when they got into the boat, the wind stopped.

33 And those who were in the boat worshiped Him, saying, "You are truly God's Son!"

34 And when they had crossed over, they came to land at Gennesaret.

¹ A stadion was approx. 607 ft. or 185 m

35 And when the men of that place recognized Him, they sent *word* into all that surrounding district and brought to Him all who were sick;

36 and they were pleading *with* Him that they might just touch the fringe of His garment; and as many as touched *it* were cured.

CHAPTER 15

God's Commandments, Man's Traditions

THEN some Pharisees and scribes *came to Jesus from Jerusalem and said,

2 "Why do Your disciples break the tradition of the elders? For they do not wash their hands when they eat bread."

3 And He answered and said to them, "Why do you yourselves transgress the commandment of God for the sake of your tradition?

4 "For God said, 'HONOR YOUR FATHER AND MOTHER,' and, 'HE WHO SPEAKS EVIL OF FATHER OR MOTHER IS TO BE PUT TO DEATH.'

5 "But you say, 'Whoever says to *his* father or mother, "Whatever you might benefit from me is given *to God*,"

6 he need not honor his father.' And *by this* you invalidated the word of God for the sake of your tradition.

7 "You hypocrites, rightly did Isaiah prophesy of you:

8 'THIS PEOPLE HONORS ME WITH THEIR LIPS,
BUT THEIR HEART IS FAR AWAY FROM ME.

9 'BUT IN VAIN DO THEY WORSHIP ME,
TEACHING AS DOCTRINES THE COMMANDS OF MEN.' "

10 After Jesus called the crowd to Him, He said to them, "Hear and understand.

11 "*It is* not what enters into the mouth *that* defiles the man, but what proceeds out of the mouth, this defiles the man."

12 Then the disciples *came and *said to Him, "Do You know that the Pharisees were offended when they heard this statement?"

13 But He answered and said, "Every plant which My heavenly Father did not plant shall be uprooted.

14 "Let them alone; they are blind guides of the blind. And if a blind man guides a blind man, both will fall into a pit."

The Heart of Man

15 Now Peter answered and said to Him, "Explain the parable to us."

16 And Jesus said, "Are you still lacking in understanding also?

17 "Do you not understand that everything that goes into the mouth passes into the stomach, and goes into the sewer?

18 "But the things that proceed out of the mouth come from the heart, and those defile the man.

19 "For out of the heart come evil thoughts, murders, adulteries, sexual immoralities, thefts, false witness, slanders.

20 "These are the things which defile the man; but to eat with

unwashed hands does not defile the man."

The Canaanite Woman

21 And going away from there, Jesus withdrew into the district of Tyre and Sidon.

22 And behold, a Canaanite woman from that region came out and *began to* cry out, saying, "Have mercy on me, Lord, Son of David; my daughter is cruelly demon-possessed."

23 But He did not answer her a word. And His disciples came and were pleading with Him, saying, "Send her away, because she keeps shouting at us."

24 But He answered and said, "I was not sent except to the lost sheep of the house of Israel."

25 But she came and was bowing down before Him, saying, "Lord, help me!"

26 And He answered and said, "It is not good to take the children's bread and throw it to the dogs."

27 But she said, "Yes, Lord; but even the dogs feed on the crumbs which fall from their masters' table."

28 Then Jesus answered and said to her, "O woman, your faith is great; it shall be done for you as you wish." And her daughter was healed at once.

Jesus Heals the Crowds

29 And departing from there, Jesus went along by the Sea of Galilee, and having gone up on the mountain, He was sitting there.

30 And large crowds came to Him, bringing with them *those who were* lame, crippled, blind, mute, and many others, and they laid them down at His feet; and He healed them.

31 So the crowd marveled as they saw the mute speaking, the crippled restored, and the lame walking, and the blind seeing; and they glorified the God of Israel.

Jesus Feeds Four Thousand

32 And Jesus called His disciples to Him, and said, "I feel compassion for the crowd, because they have remained with Me now three days and have nothing to eat; and I do not want to send them away hungry, lest they faint on the way."

33 And the disciples *said to Him, "Where would we get so many loaves in *this* desolate place to satisfy such a large crowd?"

34 And Jesus *said to them, "How many loaves do you have?" And they said, "Seven, and a few small fish."

35 And He directed the crowd to sit down on the ground;

36 and He took the seven loaves and the fish; and giving thanks, He broke them and kept giving them to the disciples, and the disciples *gave them* to the crowds.

37 And they all ate and were satisfied, and they picked up what was left over of the broken pieces, seven *large* baskets full.

38 And those who ate were four thousand men, besides women and children.

39 And sending away the crowds, Jesus got into the boat and came to the region of Magadan.

CHAPTER 16

The Pharisees and Sadducees Test Jesus

AND the Pharisees and Sadducees came, and testing Him, they asked Him to show them a sign from heaven.

2 But He replied to them, "When it is evening, you say, '*It will be* fair weather, for the sky is red.'

3 "And in the morning, '*There will be* a storm today, for the sky is red and threatening.' Do you know how to discern the appearance of the sky, but cannot *discern* the signs of the times?

4 "An evil and adulterous generation eagerly seeks for a sign; and a sign will not be given it, except the sign of Jonah." And He left them and went away.

5 And coming to the other side *of the sea,* the disciples had forgotten to bring bread.

6 And Jesus said to them, "Watch out and beware of the leaven of the Pharisees and Sadducees."

7 Now they *began to* discuss *this* among themselves, saying, "*He said that* because we did not bring bread."

8 But Jesus, aware of this, said, "You men of little faith, why do you discuss among yourselves that you have no bread?

9 "Do you not yet understand or remember the five loaves of the five thousand, and how many baskets *full* you picked up?

10 "Or the seven loaves of the four thousand, and how many *large* baskets *full* you picked up?

11 "How is it that you do not understand that I did not speak to you concerning bread? But beware of the leaven of the Pharisees and Sadducees."

12 Then they understood that He did not say to beware of the leaven of bread, but of the teaching of the Pharisees and Sadducees.

Peter Confesses Jesus Is the Christ

13 Now when Jesus came into the district of Caesarea Philippi, He was asking His disciples, saying, "Who do people say that the Son of Man is?"

14 And they said, "Some *say* John the Baptist; and others, Elijah; but still others, Jeremiah, or one of the prophets."

15 He *said to them, "But who do you say that I am?"

16 And Simon Peter answered and said, "You are the Christ, the Son of the living God."

17 And Jesus answered and said to him, "Blessed are you, Simon Bar-Jonah, because flesh and blood did not reveal *this* to you, but My Father who is in heaven.

18 "And I also say to you that you are Peter, and upon this rock I will build My church; and the gates of Hades will not overpower it.

19 "I will give you the keys of the kingdom of heaven; and whatever you bind on earth shall have been bound in heaven, and whatever you loose on earth shall have been loosed in heaven."

20 Then He warned the disciples that they should tell no one that He was the Christ.

Jesus Foretells His Death and Resurrection

21 From that time Jesus began to show His disciples that He must go to Jerusalem, and suffer many things from the elders and chief priests and scribes, and be killed, and be raised up on the third day.

22 And Peter took Him aside and began to rebuke Him, saying, "God forbid *it*, Lord! This shall never happen to You."

23 But He turned and said to Peter, "Get behind Me, Satan! You are a stumbling block to Me; for you are not setting your mind on God's interests, but man's."

Take Up Your Cross

24 Then Jesus said to His disciples, "If anyone wishes to come after Me, let him deny himself, and take up his cross and follow Me.

25 "For whoever wishes to save his life will lose it; but whoever loses his life for My sake will find it.

26 "For what will it profit a man if he gains the whole world and forfeits his soul? Or what will a man give in exchange for his soul?

27 "For the Son of Man is going to come in the glory of His Father with His angels, and WILL THEN REPAY EACH ONE ACCORDING TO HIS DEEDS.

28 "Truly I say to you, there are some of those who are standing here who will not taste death until they see the Son of Man coming in His kingdom."

CHAPTER 17

The Transfiguration

AND six days later Jesus *brought with Him Peter and James and John his brother, and *led them up on a high mountain by themselves.

2 And He was transfigured before them; and His face shone like the sun, and His garments became as white as light.

3 And behold, Moses and Elijah appeared to them, talking with Him.

4 And Peter answered and said to Jesus, "Lord, it is good for us to be here; if You wish, I will make three booths here, one for You, and one for Moses, and one for Elijah."

5 While he was still speaking, behold, a bright cloud overshadowed them, and behold, a voice out of the cloud said, "This is My beloved Son, with whom I am well-pleased; listen to Him!"

6 And when the disciples heard *this*, they fell on their faces and were terrified.

7 And Jesus came to *them* and

touched them and said, "Get up, and do not be afraid."

8 And lifting up their eyes, they saw no one except Jesus Himself alone.

9 And as they were coming down from the mountain, Jesus commanded them, saying, "Tell the vision to no one until the Son of Man has risen from the dead."

10 And His disciples asked Him, saying, "Why then do the scribes say that Elijah must come first?"

11 And He answered and said, "Elijah is coming and will restore all things;

12 but I say to you that Elijah already came, and they did not recognize him, but did to him whatever they wished. So also the Son of Man is going to suffer at their hands."

13 Then the disciples understood that He had spoken to them about John the Baptist.

Jesus Casts Out a Demon

14 And when they came to the crowd, a man came up to Jesus, falling on his knees before Him and saying,

15 "Lord, have mercy on my son, for he has seizures and suffers terribly; for he often falls into the fire and often into the water.

16 "And I brought him to Your disciples, and they could not cure him."

17 And Jesus answered and said, "O you unbelieving and perverse generation, how long shall I be with you? How long shall I put up with you? Bring him here to Me."

18 And Jesus rebuked him, and the demon came out of him, and the boy was cured at once.

19 Then the disciples came to Jesus privately and said, "Why could we not cast it out?"

20 And He *said to them, "Because of your little faith; for truly I say to you, if you have faith the size of a mustard seed, you will say to this mountain, 'Move from here to there,' and it will move; and nothing will be impossible to you.

21 ["But this kind does not go out except by prayer and fasting."]

22 And while they were gathering together in Galilee, Jesus said to them, "The Son of Man is going to be delivered into the hands of men;

23 and they will kill Him, and He will be raised on the third day." And they were deeply grieved.

The Temple Tax

24 Now when they came to Capernaum, those who collected the [1]two-drachma *tax* came to Peter and said, "Does your teacher not pay the [1]two-drachma *tax*?"

25 He *said, "Yes." And when he came into the house, Jesus spoke to him first, saying, "What do you think, Simon? From whom do the kings of the earth collect tolls or taxes, from their sons or from strangers?"

26 And when Peter said, "From

---

[1] A Gr silver coin, approx. a laborer's daily wage

strangers," Jesus said to him, "Then the sons are exempt.

27 "However, so that we do not offend them, go to the sea and throw in a hook, and take the first fish that comes up; and when you open its mouth, you will find a ¹stater. Take that and give it to them for Me and you."

CHAPTER 18

Who Is Greatest in Heaven?

AT that time the disciples came to Jesus and said, "Who then is greatest in the kingdom of heaven?"

2 And He called a child to Himself and set him before them,

3 and said, "Truly I say to you, unless you are converted and become like children, you will never enter the kingdom of heaven.

4 "Whoever therefore will humble himself as this child, he is the greatest in the kingdom of heaven.

5 "And whoever receives one such child in My name receives Me;

6 but whoever causes one of these little ones who believe in Me to stumble, it is better for him that a heavy millstone be hung around his neck, and that he be drowned in the depth of the sea.

Stumbling Blocks

7 "Woe to the world because of *its* stumbling blocks! For it is inevitable that stumbling blocks come;

nevertheless, woe to that man through whom the stumbling block comes!

8 "And if your hand or your foot causes you to stumble, cut it off and throw it from you; it is better for you to enter life crippled or lame, than, having two hands or two feet, to be cast into the eternal fire.

9 "And if your eye causes you to stumble, tear it out and throw it from you. It is better for you to enter life with one eye, than, having two eyes, to be cast into the fiery hell.

10 "See that you do not despise one of these little ones, for I say to you that their angels in heaven continually see the face of My Father who is in heaven.

11 ["For the Son of Man has come to save that which was lost.]

The Parable of the Lost Sheep

12 "What do you think? If any man has one hundred sheep, and one of them has gone astray, does he not leave the ninety-nine on the mountains and go and search for the one that is straying?

13 "And if it turns out that he finds it, truly I say to you, he rejoices over it more than over the ninety-nine which have not gone astray.

14 "In this way, it is not the will of your Father who is in heaven that one of these little ones perish.

If Your Brother Sins

15 "Now if your brother sins, go and show him his fault, between you and

¹ Lit *standard coin*, approx. 4 days of a laborer's wages

him alone; if he listens to you, you have won your brother.

16 "But if he does not listen *to you*, take one or two more with you, so that BY THE MOUTH OF TWO OR THREE WITNESSES EVERY FACT MAY BE CONFIRMED.

17 "And if he refuses to listen to them, tell it to the church; and if he refuses to listen even to the church, let him be to you as the Gentile and the tax collector.

18 "Truly I say to you, whatever you bind on earth shall have been bound in heaven; and whatever you loose on earth shall have been loosed in heaven.

19 "Again I say to you, that if two of you agree on earth about anything that they may ask, it shall be done for them by My Father who is in heaven.

20 "For where two or three have gathered together in My name, I am there in their midst."

Forgiveness

21 Then Peter came and said to Him, "Lord, how often shall my brother sin against me and I forgive him? Up to seven times?"

22 Jesus *said to him, "I do not say to you, up to seven times, but up to seventy times seven.

23 "For this reason the kingdom of heaven may be compared to a king who wished to settle accounts with his slaves.

24 "When he had begun to settle *them*, one who owed him ten thousand [1]talents was brought to him.

25 "But since he did not have *the means* to repay, his lord commanded him to be sold, along with his wife and children and all that he had, and repayment to be made.

26 "Therefore, the slave fell *to the ground* and was prostrating himself before him, saying, 'Have patience with me and I will repay you everything.'

27 "And feeling compassion, the lord of that slave released him and forgave him the debt.

28 "But that slave went out and found one of his fellow slaves who owed him one hundred [2]denarii; and he seized him and *began to* choke *him*, saying, 'Pay back what you owe.'

29 "So, his fellow slave fell *to the ground* and was pleading with him, saying, 'Have patience with me and I will repay you.'

30 "But he was unwilling and went and threw him in prison until he should pay back what was owed.

31 "So, when his fellow slaves saw what had happened, they were deeply grieved and came and reported to their lord all that had happened.

32 "Then summoning him, his lord *said to him, 'You wicked slave, I forgave you all that debt because you pleaded with me.

[1] A talent was approx. worth more than 15 years of a laborer's wages   [2] A Roman silver coin, approx. a laborer's daily wage

33 'Should you not also have had mercy on your fellow slave, in the same way that I had mercy on you?'

34 "And his lord, moved with anger, handed him over to the torturers until he should repay all that was owed him.

35 "My heavenly Father will also do the same to you, if each of you does not forgive his brother from your hearts."

CHAPTER 19

Teaching About Divorce

NOW it happened that when Jesus had finished these words, He departed from Galilee and came into the region of Judea beyond the Jordan;

2 and large crowds followed Him, and He healed them there.

3 And *some* Pharisees came to Jesus, testing Him and saying, "Is it lawful *for a man* to divorce his wife for any reason at all?"

4 And He answered and said, "Have you not read that He who created *them* from the beginning MADE THEM MALE AND FEMALE,

5 and said, 'FOR THIS REASON A MAN SHALL LEAVE HIS FATHER AND MOTHER AND BE JOINED TO HIS WIFE, AND THE TWO SHALL BECOME ONE FLESH'?

6 "So they are no longer two, but one flesh. What therefore God has joined together, let no man separate."

7 They *said to Him, "Why then did Moses command to GIVE HER A CERTIFICATE OF DIVORCE AND SEND *her* AWAY?"

8 He *said to them, "Because of your hardness of heart Moses permitted you to divorce your wives; but from the beginning it has not been this way.

9 "And I say to you, whoever divorces his wife, except for sexual immorality, and marries another woman commits adultery."

10 The disciples *said to Him, "If the relationship of the man with his wife is like this, it is better not to marry."

11 But He said to them, "Not all men *can* accept this statement, but *only* those to whom it has been given.

12 "For there are eunuchs who were born that way from their mother's womb; and there are eunuchs who were made eunuchs by men; and there are *also* eunuchs who made themselves eunuchs for the sake of the kingdom of heaven. He who is able to accept *this*, let him accept *it*."

Jesus Blesses Children

13 Then *some* children were brought to Him so that He might lay His hands on them and pray; and the disciples rebuked them.

14 But Jesus said, "Let the children alone, and do not hinder them from coming to Me; for the kingdom of heaven belongs to such as these."

15 And after laying His hands on them, He departed from there.

The Rich Young Ruler

16 And behold, someone came to Him and said, "Teacher, what good

thing shall I do that I may have eternal life?"

17 And He said to him, "Why are you asking Me about what is good? There is *only* One who is good; but if you wish to enter into life, keep the commandments."

18 *Then* he *said to Him, "Which ones?" And Jesus said, "YOU SHALL NOT MURDER; YOU SHALL NOT COMMIT ADULTERY; YOU SHALL NOT STEAL; YOU SHALL NOT BEAR FALSE WITNESS;

19 HONOR YOUR FATHER AND MOTHER; and YOU SHALL LOVE YOUR NEIGHBOR AS YOURSELF."

20 The young man *said to Him, "All these things I have kept; what am I still lacking?"

21 Jesus said to him, "If you wish to be complete, go *and* sell your possessions and give to the poor, and you will have treasure in heaven; and come, follow Me."

22 But when the young man heard this statement, he went away grieving; for he was one who owned much property.

23 And Jesus said to His disciples, "Truly I say to you, it is hard for a rich man to enter the kingdom of heaven.

24 "And again I say to you, it is easier for a camel to go through the eye of a needle, than for a rich man to enter the kingdom of God."

25 And when the disciples heard *this*, they were very astonished and said, "Then who can be saved?"

26 And looking at *them* Jesus said to them, "With people this is impossible, but with God all things are possible."

Many Who Are First Will Be Last

27 Then Peter answered and said to Him, "Behold, we have left everything and followed You; what then will there be for us?"

28 And Jesus said to them, "Truly I say to you, that you who have followed Me, in the regeneration when the Son of Man will sit on His glorious throne, you also shall sit upon twelve thrones, judging the twelve tribes of Israel.

29 "And everyone who has left houses or brothers or sisters or father or mother or children or farms for My name's sake, will receive one hundred times as much, and will inherit eternal life.

30 "But many *who are* first will be last; and *the* last, first.

CHAPTER 20

Laborers in the Vineyard

"FOR the kingdom of heaven is like a landowner who went out early in the morning to hire laborers for his vineyard.

2 "Now when he had agreed with the laborers for a ¹denarius for the day, he sent them into his vineyard.

3 "And he went out about the third

¹ A Roman silver coin, approx. a laborer's daily wage

hour and saw others standing idle in the marketplace;

4 and to those he said, 'You also go into the vineyard, and whatever is right I will give you.' And *so* they went.

5 "Again he went out about the sixth and the ninth hour, and did the same thing.

6 "And about the eleventh *hour* he went out and found others standing *around*; and he *said to them, 'Why have you been standing here idle all day long?'

7 "They *said to him, 'Because no one hired us.' He *said to them, 'You go into the vineyard too.'

8 "Now when evening came, the owner of the vineyard *said to his foreman, 'Call the laborers and pay them their wages, beginning with the last *group* to the first.'

9 "And when those *hired* about the eleventh hour came, each one received a denarius.

10 "And when those *hired* first came, they supposed that they would receive more; but each of them also received a denarius.

11 "Now when they received it, they were grumbling at the landowner,

12 saying, 'These last men have worked *only* one hour, and you have made them equal to us who have borne the burden of the day and the scorching heat.'

13 "But he answered and said to one of them, 'Friend, I am doing you no wrong; did you not agree with me for a denarius?

14 'Take what is yours and go, but I wish to give to this last man the same as to you.

15 'Is it not lawful for me to do what I wish with what is my own? Or is your eye envious because I am generous?'

16 "So the last shall be first, and the first last."

Jesus Again Foretells His Death and Resurrection

17 And as Jesus was about to go up to Jerusalem, He took the twelve *disciples* aside by themselves, and on the way He said to them,

18 "Behold, we are going up to Jerusalem; and the Son of Man will be betrayed to the chief priests and scribes, and they will condemn Him to death,

19 and will deliver Him over to the Gentiles to mock and flog and crucify *Him*, and on the third day He will be raised up."

A Request for Status

20 Then the mother of the sons of Zebedee came to Him with her sons, bowing down and making a request of Him.

21 And He said to her, "What do you wish?" She *said to Him, "Command that in Your kingdom these two sons of mine may sit one on Your right and one on Your left."

22 But Jesus answered and said, "You do not know what you are asking. Are you able to drink the cup that I am about to drink?" They *said to Him, "We are able."

23 He *said to them, "My cup you shall drink; but to sit on My right and on *My* left, this is not Mine to give, but it is for those for whom it has been prepared by My Father."

24 And hearing *this*, the ten became indignant with the two brothers.

25 But Jesus called them to Himself and said, "You know that the rulers of the Gentiles lord it over them, and *their* great men exercise authority over them.

26 "It is not this way among you, but whoever wishes to become great among you shall be your servant,

27 and whoever wishes to be first among you shall be your slave;

28 just as the Son of Man did not come to be served, but to serve, and to give His life a ransom for many."

Sight for the Blind

29 And as they were leaving Jericho, a large crowd followed Him.

30 And behold, two blind men sitting by the road, hearing that Jesus *was passing by, cried out, saying, "Lord, have mercy on us, Son of David!"

31 But the crowd sternly told them to be quiet, but they cried out all the more, saying, "Lord, Son of David, have mercy on us!"

32 And Jesus stopped and called them, and said, "What do you want Me to do for you?"

33 They *said to Him, "Lord, that our eyes be opened."

34 And moved with compassion, Jesus touched their eyes; and immediately they regained their sight and followed Him.

CHAPTER 21

The Triumphal Entry

AND when they had approached Jerusalem and came to Bethphage, at the Mount of Olives, then Jesus sent two disciples,

2 saying to them, "Go into the village opposite you, and immediately you will find a donkey tied *there* and a colt with her; untie them and bring them to Me.

3 "And if anyone says anything to you, you shall say, 'The Lord has need of them,' and immediately he will send them."

4 And this took place in order that what was spoken through the prophet would be fulfilled, saying,

5 "SAY TO THE DAUGHTER OF ZION,
  'BEHOLD YOUR KING IS COMING
      TO YOU,
  LOWLY, AND MOUNTED ON A
      DONKEY,
  AND ON A COLT, THE FOAL OF A
      PACK ANIMAL.'"

6 And the disciples went and did just as Jesus had instructed them,

7 and brought the donkey and the colt, and laid their garments on them; and He sat on the garments.

8 And most of the crowd spread their garments in the road, and others were cutting branches from the trees and spreading them in the road.

9 And the crowds going ahead of

Him, and those who followed, were crying out, saying,

> "Hosanna to the Son of David;
> BLESSED IS HE WHO COMES IN THE NAME OF THE LORD;
> Hosanna in the highest!"

10 And when He had entered Jerusalem, all the city was stirred, saying, "Who is this?"

11 And the crowds were saying, "This is the prophet Jesus, from Nazareth in Galilee."

Cleansing the Temple

12 And Jesus entered the temple and drove out all those who were buying and selling in the temple, and overturned the tables of the money changers and the seats of those who were selling doves.

13 And He *said to them, "It is written, 'MY HOUSE SHALL BE CALLED A HOUSE OF PRAYER'; but you are making it a ROBBERS' DEN."

14 And the blind and the lame came to Him in the temple, and He healed them.

15 But when the chief priests and the scribes saw the marvelous things which He had done, and the children who were shouting in the temple, saying, "Hosanna to the Son of David," they became indignant

16 and said to Him, "Do You hear what these *children* are saying?" And Jesus *said to them, "Yes; have you never read, 'OUT OF THE MOUTH OF INFANTS AND NURSING BABIES YOU HAVE PREPARED PRAISE FOR YOURSELF'?"

17 And He left them and went out of the city to Bethany, and spent the night there.

The Barren Fig Tree

18 Now in the morning, when He was returning to the city, He became hungry.

19 And seeing a lone fig tree by the road, He came to it and found nothing on it except leaves only; and He *said to it, "No longer shall there ever be *any* fruit from you." And at once the fig tree withered.

20 And seeing *this*, the disciples marveled, saying, "How did the fig tree wither *all* at once?"

21 And Jesus answered and said to them, "Truly I say to you, if you have faith and do not doubt, you will not only do what was done to the fig tree, but even if you say to this mountain, 'Be taken up and cast into the sea,' it will happen.

22 "And all things you ask in prayer, believing, you will receive."

The Authority of Jesus Challenged

23 And when He entered the temple, the chief priests and the elders of the people came to Him while He was teaching, and said, "By what authority are You doing these things, and who gave You this authority?"

24 And Jesus answered and said to them, "I will also ask you one thing, which if you tell Me, I will also tell you by what authority I do these things.

25 "The baptism of John was from what *source*, from heaven or from

men?" And they *began* reasoning among themselves, saying, "If we say, 'From heaven,' He will say to us, 'Then why did you not believe him?'

26 "But if we say, 'From men,' we fear the crowd; for they all regard John as a prophet."

27 And they answered Jesus and said, "We do not know." He also said to them, "Neither will I tell you by what authority I do these things.

The Parable of Two Sons

28 "But what do you think? A man had two sons, and he came to the first and said, 'Son, go work today in the vineyard.'

29 "And he answered and said, 'I will not'; but afterward he regretted it and went.

30 "And the man came to the second and said the same thing; and he answered and said, 'I *will*, sir'; but he did not go.

31 "Which of the two did the will of his father?" They *said, "The first." Jesus *said to them, "Truly I say to you that the tax collectors and prostitutes will get into the kingdom of God before you.

32 "For John came to you in the way of righteousness and you did not believe him; but the tax collectors and prostitutes did believe him; and you, seeing *this*, did not even regret afterward so as to believe him.

The Parable of the Vine-Growers

33 "Listen to another parable. There was a landowner who PLANTED A VINEYARD AND PUT A WALL AROUND IT AND DUG A WINE PRESS IN IT, AND BUILT A TOWER, and rented it out to vine-growers and went on a journey.

34 "Now when the harvest time approached, he sent his slaves to the vine-growers to receive his fruit.

35 "And the vine-growers took his slaves and beat one, and killed another, and stoned a third.

36 "Again he sent another group of slaves larger than the first; and they did the same thing to them.

37 "But afterward he sent his son to them, saying, 'They will respect my son.'

38 "But when the vine-growers saw the son, they said among themselves, 'This is the heir; come, let us kill him and seize his inheritance.'

39 "And they took him, and threw him out of the vineyard and killed him.

40 "Therefore when the owner of the vineyard comes, what will he do to those vine-growers?"

41 They *said to Him, "He will bring those wretches to a wretched end, and will rent out the vineyard to other vine-growers who will pay him the proceeds at the *proper* seasons."

42 Jesus *said to them, "Did you never read in the Scriptures,

'THE STONE WHICH THE BUILDERS REJECTED,

THIS HAS BECOME THE CHIEF CORNER *stone*;

This came about from the
Lord,
And it is marvelous in our
eyes'?

43 "Therefore I say to you, the kingdom of God will be taken away from you and given to a nation, producing the fruit of it.

44 "And he who falls on this stone will be broken to pieces; but on whomever it falls, it will scatter him like dust."

45 And when the chief priests and the Pharisees heard His parables, they understood that He *was speaking about them.

46 And although they were seeking to seize Him, they feared the crowds, because they were regarding Him to be a prophet.

CHAPTER 22

The Parable of the Wedding Feast

AND Jesus answered and spoke to them again in parables, saying,

2 "The kingdom of heaven may be compared to a king who gave a wedding feast for his son.

3 "And he sent out his slaves to call those who had been called to the wedding feast, and they were unwilling to come.

4 "Again he sent out other slaves saying, 'Tell those who have been called, "Behold, I have prepared my dinner; my oxen and my fattened livestock are *all* butchered and everything is ready; come to the wedding feast."'

5 "But they paid no attention and went their way, one to his own farm, another to his business,

6 and the rest seized his slaves and mistreated them and killed them.

7 "But the king was enraged, and he sent his armies and destroyed those murderers and set their city on fire.

8 "Then he *said to his slaves, 'The wedding is ready, but those who were called were not worthy.

9 'Go therefore to the main highways, and as many as you find *there*, call to the wedding feast.'

10 "And those slaves went out into the streets and gathered together all they found, both evil and good; and the wedding hall was filled with dinner guests.

11 "But when the king came in to look over the dinner guests, he saw a man there who was not dressed in wedding clothes,

12 and he *said to him, 'Friend, how did you come in here without wedding clothes?' And the man was speechless.

13 "Then the king said to the servants, 'Bind him hand and foot, and throw him into the outer darkness; in that place there will be weeping and gnashing of teeth.'

14 "For many are called, but few *are* chosen."

Taxes to Caesar

15 Then the Pharisees went and took counsel together about how they might trap Him in what He said.

16 And they *sent their disciples to Him, along with the Herodians, saying, "Teacher, we know that You are truthful and teach the way of God in truth, and defer to no one; for You are not partial to any.

17 "Therefore, tell us, what do You think? Is it lawful to give a tax to Caesar, or not?"

18 But Jesus, knowing their wickedness, said, "Why are you testing Me, you hypocrites?

19 "Show Me the coin *used* for the tax." And they brought Him a denarius.

20 And He *said to them, "Whose likeness and inscription is this?"

21 They *said to Him, "Caesar's." Then He *said to them, "Therefore, render to Caesar the things that are Caesar's; and to God the things that are God's."

22 And hearing *this*, they marveled, and leaving Him, they went away.

The Sadducees and the Resurrection

23 On that day *some* Sadducees (who say there is no resurrection) came to Jesus and asked Him a question,

24 saying, "Teacher, Moses said, 'IF A MAN DIES HAVING NO CHILDREN, HIS BROTHER AS NEXT OF KIN SHALL MARRY HIS WIFE AND RAISE UP A SEED FOR HIS BROTHER.'

25 "Now there were seven brothers with us; and the first married and died, and having no seed, he left his wife to his brother;

26 so also the second, and the third, down to the seventh.

27 "And last of all, the woman died.

28 "In the resurrection, therefore, whose wife of the seven will she be? For they all had *married* her."

29 But Jesus answered and said to them, "You are mistaken, not understanding the Scriptures nor the power of God.

30 "For in the resurrection they neither marry nor are given in marriage, but are like angels in heaven.

31 "But regarding the resurrection of the dead, have you not read what was spoken to you by God, saying,

32 'I AM THE GOD OF ABRAHAM, AND THE GOD OF ISAAC, AND THE GOD OF JACOB'? He is not the God of the dead but of the living."

33 And when the crowds heard *this*, they were astonished at His teaching.

The Foremost Commandment

34 But when the Pharisees heard that Jesus had silenced the Sadducees, they gathered themselves together.

35 And one of them, a scholar of the Law, asked *Him* a question, testing Him,

36 "Teacher, which is the great commandment in the Law?"

37 And He said to him, " 'YOU SHALL LOVE THE LORD YOUR GOD WITH ALL YOUR HEART, AND WITH ALL YOUR SOUL, AND WITH ALL YOUR MIND.'

38 "This is the great and foremost commandment.

39 "And the second is like it, 'YOU SHALL LOVE YOUR NEIGHBOR AS YOURSELF.'

40 "On these two command-ments hang the whole Law and the Prophets."

41 Now while the Pharisees were gathered together, Jesus asked them a question,

42 saying, "What do you think about the Christ, whose son is He?" They *said to Him, "*The son* of David."

43 He *said to them, "Then how does David in the Spirit call Him 'Lord,' saying,

44 'THE LORD SAID TO MY LORD,
    "SIT AT MY RIGHT HAND,
    UNTIL I PUT YOUR ENEMIES
        BENEATH YOUR FEET" '?

45 "Therefore, if David calls Him 'Lord,' how is He his son?"

46 And no one was able to answer Him a word, nor did anyone dare from that day on to ask Him another question.

CHAPTER 23

The Scribes and Pharisees Denounced

THEN Jesus spoke to the crowds and to His disciples,

2 saying: "The scribes and the Pharisees have seated themselves in the chair of Moses;

3 therefore all that they tell you, do and keep, but do not do accord-ing to their deeds; for they say *things* and do not do *them*.

4 "And they tie up heavy burdens and lay them on men's shoulders, but they themselves are unwilling to move them with *so much as* a finger.

5 "But they do all their deeds to be noticed by men; for they broaden their phylacteries and lengthen the tassels *of their garments*.

6 "And they love the place of hon-or at banquets and the best seats in the synagogues,

7 and respectful greetings in the marketplaces, and being called Rabbi by men.

8 "But do not be called Rabbi; for One is your Teacher, and you are all brothers.

9 "And do not call *anyone* on earth your father; for One is your Father, He who is in heaven.

10 "Do not be called instructors; for One is your Instructor, *that is*, Christ.

11 "But the greatest among you shall be your servant.

12 "And whoever exalts himself shall be humbled; and whoever humbles himself shall be exalted.

Woes to the Scribes and Pharisees

13 "But woe to you, scribes and Pharisees, hypocrites, because you shut off the kingdom of heaven from people; for you do not enter in your-selves, nor do you allow those who are entering to go in.

14 ["Woe to you, scribes and Phar-isees, hypocrites, because you de-vour widows' houses, and for a pretense you make long prayers; therefore you will receive greater condemnation.]

15 "Woe to you, scribes and Phari-sees, hypocrites, because you travel

around on sea and land to make one proselyte; and when he becomes one, you make him twice as much a son of hell as yourselves.

16 "Woe to you, blind guides, who say, 'Whoever swears by the sanctuary, *that* is nothing; but whoever swears by the gold of the sanctuary is obligated.'

17 "You fools and blind men! For which is more important, the gold or the sanctuary that sanctified the gold?

18 "And, 'Whoever swears by the altar, *that* is nothing, but whoever swears by the offering on it, he is obligated.'

19 "You blind men, which is more important, the offering, or the altar that sanctifies the offering?

20 "Therefore, whoever swears by the altar, swears *both* by the altar and by everything on it.

21 "And whoever swears by the sanctuary, swears *both* by the sanctuary and by Him who dwells within it.

22 "And whoever swears by heaven, swears *both* by the throne of God and by Him who sits upon it.

23 "Woe to you, scribes and Pharisees, hypocrites! For you tithe mint and dill and cumin, and have neglected the weightier provisions of the Law: justice and mercy and faithfulness; but these are the things you should have done without neglecting the others.

24 "You blind guides, who strain out a gnat but swallow a camel!

25 "Woe to you, scribes and Pharisees, hypocrites! For you clean the outside of the cup and of the dish, but inside they are full of robbery and self-indulgence.

26 "You blind Pharisee, first clean the inside of the cup and of the dish, so that the outside of it may become clean also.

27 "Woe to you, scribes and Pharisees, hypocrites! For you are like whitewashed tombs which on the outside appear beautiful, but inside they are full of dead men's bones and all uncleanness.

28 "In this way, you also outwardly appear righteous to men, but inwardly you are full of hypocrisy and lawlessness.

29 "Woe to you, scribes and Pharisees, hypocrites! For you build the tombs of the prophets and adorn the monuments of the righteous,

30 and say, 'If we had been *living* in the days of our fathers, we would not have been partners with them in *shedding* the blood of the prophets.'

31 "So you bear witness against yourselves, that you are sons of those who murdered the prophets.

32 "Fill up, then, the measure *of the guilt* of your fathers.

33 "You serpents, you brood of vipers, how will you escape the sentence of hell?

34 "On account of this, behold, I am sending you prophets and wise men and scribes; some of them you will kill and crucify, and some of them

you will flog in your synagogues, and persecute from city to city,

35 so that upon you may fall *the guilt of* all the righteous blood shed on earth, from the blood of righteous Abel to the blood of Zechariah, the son of Berechiah, whom you murdered between the sanctuary and the altar.

36 "Truly I say to you, all these things will come upon this generation.

Lament over Jerusalem

37 "Jerusalem, Jerusalem, who kills the prophets and stones those who are sent to her! How often I wanted to gather your children together, the way a hen gathers her chicks under her wings, and you did not want *it.*

38 "Behold, your house is being left to you desolate!

39 "For I say to you, from now on you will not see Me until you say, 'BLESSED IS HE WHO COMES IN THE NAME OF THE LORD!' "

CHAPTER 24

Signs of Christ's Return

AND coming out from the temple, Jesus was going along, and His disciples came up to point out the temple buildings to Him.

2 And He answered and said to them, "Do you not see all these things? Truly I say to you, not one stone here will be left upon another, which will not be torn down."

3 Now as He was sitting on the Mount of Olives, the disciples came to Him privately, saying, "Tell us, when will these things happen, and what *will be* the sign of Your coming and of the end of the age?"

4 And Jesus answered and said to them, "See to it that no one deceives you.

5 "For many will come in My name, saying, 'I am the Christ,' and will deceive many.

6 "And you are going to hear of wars and rumors of wars. See that you are not alarmed, for *those things* must take place, but *that* is not yet the end.

7 "For nation will rise against nation, and kingdom against kingdom, and in various places there will be famines and earthquakes.

8 "But all these things are *merely* the beginning of birth pains.

9 "Then they will deliver you to tribulation, and will kill you, and you will be hated by all nations because of My name.

10 "And at that time many will fall away and will betray one another and hate one another.

11 "Many false prophets will arise and will deceive many.

12 "And because lawlessness is multiplied, most people's love will grow cold.

13 "But the one who endures to the end, he will be saved.

14 "And this gospel of the kingdom shall be proclaimed in the whole world as a witness to all

the nations, and then the end will come.

Abomination of Desolation and the Tribulation

15 "Therefore when you see the ABOMINATION OF DESOLATION which was spoken of through Daniel the prophet, standing in the holy place (let the reader understand),

16 then those who are in Judea must flee to the mountains.

17 "Whoever is on the housetop must not go down to get the things out that are in his house.

18 "And whoever is in the field must not turn back to get his garment.

19 "But woe to those who are pregnant and to those who are nursing babies in those days!

20 "But pray that your flight will not be in the winter, or on a Sabbath.

21 "For then there will be a great tribulation, such as has not occurred since the beginning of the world until now, nor ever will.

22 "And unless those days had been cut short, no life would have been saved; but for the sake of the elect those days will be cut short.

23 "Then if anyone says to you, 'Behold, here is the Christ,' or 'There *He is*,' do not believe *him*.

24 "For false christs and false prophets will arise and will show great signs and wonders, so as to deceive, if possible, even the elect.

25 "Behold, I have told you in advance.

26 "Therefore, if they say to you,

'Behold, He is in the wilderness,' do not go out, *or*, 'Behold, He is in the inner rooms,' do not believe *them*.

27 "For just as the lightning comes from the east and appears even to the west, so will the coming of the Son of Man be.

28 "Wherever the corpse is, there the vultures will gather.

The Coming of the Son of Man

29 "But immediately after the tribulation of those days THE SUN WILL BE DARKENED, AND THE MOON WILL NOT GIVE ITS LIGHT, AND THE STARS WILL FALL from the sky, and the POWERS OF THE HEAVENS will be shaken.

30 "And then the sign of the Son of Man will appear in the sky, and then all the tribes of the earth will mourn, and they will see the SON OF MAN COMING ON THE CLOUDS OF THE SKY with power and great glory.

31 "And He will send forth His angels with A GREAT TRUMPET and THEY WILL GATHER TOGETHER His elect from the four winds, from one end of the sky to the other.

The Parable of the Fig Tree

32 "Now learn the parable from the fig tree: when its branch has already become tender and puts forth its leaves, you know that summer is near;

33 so, you too, when you see all these things, recognize that He is near, *right* at the door.

34 "Truly I say to you, this generation

will not pass away until all these things take place.

35 "Heaven and earth will pass away, but My words will not pass away.

36 "But of that day and hour no one knows, not even the angels of heaven, nor the Son, but the Father alone.

37 "For just as the days of Noah were, so the coming of the Son of Man will be.

38 "For as in those days before the flood they were eating and drinking, marrying and giving in marriage, until the day that Noah entered the ark,

39 and they did not understand until the flood came and took them all away; so will the coming of the Son of Man be.

40 "Then there will be two in the field; one will be taken, and one will be left.

41 "Two women *will be* grinding *grain* at the mill; one will be taken and one will be left.

Be Ready for His Coming

42 "Therefore stay awake, for you do not know which day your Lord is coming.

43 "But be sure of this, that if the head of the house had known at what time of the night the thief was coming, he would have stayed awake and would not have allowed his house to be broken into.

44 "For this reason you also must be ready; for the Son of Man is coming at an hour when you do not think *He will*.

45 "Who then is the faithful and prudent slave whom his master put in charge of his household to give them their food at the proper time?

46 "Blessed is that slave whom his master finds so doing when he comes.

47 "Truly I say to you that he will put him in charge of all his possessions.

48 "But if that evil slave says in his heart, 'My master is not coming for a long time,'

49 and begins to beat his fellow slaves and eat and drink with drunkards;

50 the master of that slave will come on a day when he does not expect *him* and at an hour which he does not know,

51 and will cut him in pieces and assign him a place with the hypocrites; in that place there will be weeping and gnashing of teeth.

CHAPTER 25

The Parable of Ten Virgins

"THEN the kingdom of heaven may be compared to ten virgins, who took their lamps and went out to meet the bridegroom.

2 "Now five of them were foolish, and five were prudent.

3 "For when the foolish took their lamps, they took no oil with them,

4 but the prudent took oil in flasks along with their lamps.

5 "Now while the bridegroom was

delaying, they all got drowsy and *began to* sleep.

6 "But at midnight there was a shout, 'Behold, the bridegroom! Come out to meet him.'

7 "Then all those virgins rose and trimmed their lamps.

8 "And the foolish said to the prudent, 'Give us some of your oil, for our lamps are going out.'

9 "But the prudent answered, saying, 'No, there will not be enough for us and you *too*; go instead to the dealers and buy *some* for yourselves.'

10 "And while they were going away to make the purchase, the bridegroom came, and those who were ready went in with him to the wedding feast; and the door was shut.

11 "And later the other virgins also *came, saying, 'Lord, lord, open up for us.'

12 "But he answered and said, 'Truly I say to you, I do not know you.'

13 "Therefore, stay awake, for you do not know the day nor the hour.

The Parable of the Talents

14 "For *it is* just like a man *about* to go on a journey, who called his own slaves and handed over his possessions to them.

15 "And to one he gave five talents, to another, two, and to another, one, each according to his own ability; and he went on his journey.

16 "Immediately the one who had received the five talents went and traded with them, and gained five more talents.

17 "In the same manner the one who *had received* the two *talents* gained two more.

18 "But he who received the one *talent* went away, and dug *a hole* in the ground and hid his master's money.

19 "Now after a long time the master of those slaves *came and *settled accounts with them.

20 "And the one who had received the five talents came up and brought five more talents, saying, 'Master, you handed five talents over to me. See, I have gained five more talents.'

21 "His master said to him, 'Well done, good and faithful slave. You were faithful with a few things, I will put you in charge of many things; enter into the joy of your master.'

22 "Also the one who *had received* the two talents came up and said, 'Master, you handed two talents over to me. See, I have gained two more talents.'

23 "His master said to him, 'Well done, good and faithful slave. You were faithful with a few things, I will put you in charge of many things; enter into the joy of your master.'

24 "And the one also who had received the one talent came up and said, 'Master, I knew you to be a hard man, reaping where you did not sow and gathering where you scattered no *seed*.

25 'And I was afraid, and went away and hid your talent in the ground. See, you have what is yours.'

26 "But his master answered and said to him, 'You wicked, lazy slave, you knew that I reap where I did not sow and gather where I scattered no *seed*.

27 'Therefore, you ought to have put my money in the bank, and on my arrival I would have received my *money* back with interest.

28 'Therefore take away the talent from him, and give it to the one who has the ten talents.'

29 "For to everyone who has, *more* shall be given, and he will have an abundance; but from the one who does not have, even what he does have shall be taken away.

30 "And throw out the worthless slave into the outer darkness; in that place there will be weeping and gnashing of teeth.

The Final Judgment

31 "But when the Son of Man comes in His glory, and all the angels with Him, then He will sit on His glorious throne.

32 "And all the nations will be gathered before Him; and He will separate them from one another, as the shepherd separates the sheep from the goats;

33 and He will put the sheep on His right, and the goats on the left.

34 "Then the King will say to those on His right, 'Come, you who are blessed of My Father, inherit the kingdom, which has been prepared for you from the foundation of the world.

35 'For I was hungry, and you gave Me *something* to eat; I was thirsty, and you gave Me *something* to drink; I was a stranger, and you invited Me in;

36 naked, and you clothed Me; I was sick, and you visited Me; I was in prison, and you came to Me.'

37 "Then the righteous will answer Him, saying, 'Lord, when did we see You hungry, and feed You, or thirsty, and give You *something* to drink?

38 'And when did we see You a stranger, and invite You in, or naked, and clothe You?

39 'And when did we see You sick, or in prison, and come to You?'

40 "And the King will answer and say to them, 'Truly I say to you, to the extent that you did it to one of these brothers of Mine, *even* the least *of them*, you did it to Me.'

41 "Then He will also say to those on His left, 'Depart from Me, accursed ones, into the eternal fire which has been prepared for the devil and his angels;

42 for I was hungry, and you gave Me *nothing* to eat; I was thirsty, and you gave Me nothing to drink;

43 I was a stranger, and you did not invite Me in; naked, and you did not clothe Me; sick, and in prison, and you did not visit Me.'

44 "Then they themselves also will answer, saying, 'Lord, when did we see You hungry, or thirsty, or a stranger, or naked, or sick, or in prison, and did not take care of You?'

45 "Then He will answer them, saying, 'Truly I say to you, to the extent that you did not do it to one of the least of these, you did not do it to Me.'

46 "And these will go away into eternal punishment, but the righteous into eternal life."

CHAPTER 26

The Plot to Kill Jesus

NOW it happened that when Jesus had finished all these words, He said to His disciples,

2 "You know that after two days the Passover is coming, and the Son of Man is *to be* delivered over for crucifixion."

3 Then the chief priests and the elders of the people were gathered together in the court of the high priest, named Caiaphas;

4 and they plotted together to seize Jesus by stealth and kill Him.

5 But they were saying, "Not during the festival, lest a riot occur among the people."

The Costly Perfume

6 Now when Jesus was in Bethany, at the home of Simon the leper,

7 a woman came to Him with an alabaster jar of very costly perfume, and she poured it on His head as He reclined *at the table*.

8 But when the disciples saw *this*, they were indignant, saying, "Why this waste?

9 "For this *perfume* might have been sold for a high price and *the money* given to the poor."

10 But Jesus, aware of this, said to them, "Why do you bother the woman? For she has done a good work to Me.

11 "For you always have the poor with you; but you do not always have Me.

12 "For when she poured this perfume on My body, she did it to prepare Me for burial.

13 "Truly I say to you, wherever this gospel is proclaimed in the whole world, what this woman has done will also be spoken of in memory of her."

Judas Looks to Betray Jesus

14 Then one of the twelve, named Judas Iscariot, went to the chief priests

15 and said, "What are you willing to give me to deliver Him to you?" And they weighed out [1]thirty pieces of silver to him.

16 And from then on he *began* looking for a good opportunity to betray Jesus.

The Passover Meal

17 Now on the first *day* of Unleavened Bread the disciples came to Jesus, saying, "Where do You want us to prepare for You to eat the Passover?"

---

[1] Silver shekels, approx. 120 days of a laborer's wages

18 And He said, "Go into the city to a certain man, and say to him, 'The Teacher says, "My time is near; I am keeping the Passover at your house with My disciples." ' "

19 And the disciples did as Jesus had directed them; and they prepared the Passover.

20 Now when evening came, Jesus was reclining *at the table* with the twelve disciples.

21 And as they were eating, He said, "Truly I say to you that one of you will betray Me."

22 And being deeply grieved, they each one began to say to Him, "Surely not I, Lord?"

23 And He answered and said, "He who dipped his hand with Me in the bowl is the one who will betray Me.

24 "The Son of Man is going, just as it is written of Him; but woe to that man by whom the Son of Man is betrayed! It would have been good for that man if he had not been born."

25 And Judas, who was betraying Him, answered and said, "Surely not I, Rabbi?" Jesus *said to him, "You yourself said *it*."

The Lord's Supper

26 Now while they were eating, Jesus took *some* bread, and after a blessing, He broke *it*. And giving *it* to the disciples, He said, "Take, eat; this is My body."

27 And when He had taken a cup and given thanks, He gave *it* to them, saying, "Drink from it, all of you;

28 for this is My blood of the covenant, which is poured out for many for forgiveness of sins.

29 "But I say to you, I will not drink of this fruit of the vine from now on until that day when I drink it new with you in My Father's kingdom."

30 And after singing a hymn, they went out to the Mount of Olives.

31 Then Jesus *said to them, "You will all fall away because of Me this night, for it is written, 'I WILL STRIKE DOWN THE SHEPHERD, AND THE SHEEP OF THE FLOCK SHALL BE SCATTERED.'

32 "But after I have been raised, I will go ahead of you to Galilee."

33 But Peter answered and said to Him, "*Even* though all may fall away because of You, I will never fall away."

34 Jesus said to him, "Truly I say to you that this *very* night, before a rooster crows, you will deny Me three times."

35 Peter *said to Him, "Even if I have to die with You, I will not deny You." All the disciples said the same thing too.

Jesus Prays in Gethsemane

36 Then Jesus *came with them to a place called Gethsemane, and *said to His disciples, "Sit here while I go over there and pray."

37 And He took with Him Peter and the two sons of Zebedee, and began to be grieved and distressed.

38 Then He *said to them, "My soul is deeply grieved, to the point of death; remain here and keep watch with Me."

39 And He went a little beyond *them*, and fell on His face and prayed, saying, "My Father, if it is possible, let this cup pass from Me; yet not as I will, but as You will."

40 And He *came to the disciples and *found them sleeping, and *said to Peter, "So, you *men* could not keep watch with Me for one hour?

41 "Keep watching and praying that you may not enter into temptation; the spirit is willing, but the flesh is weak."

42 He went away again a second time and prayed, saying, "My Father, if this cannot pass away unless I drink it, Your will be done."

43 And again He came and found them sleeping, for their eyes were heavy.

44 And He left them again, and went away and prayed a third time, saying the same thing once more.

45 Then He *came to the disciples and *said to them, "Are you still sleeping and resting? Behold, the hour is at hand and the Son of Man is being betrayed into the hands of sinners.

46 "Get up, let us go; behold, the one who betrays Me is at hand!"

The Betrayal and Arrest of Jesus

47 And while He was still speaking, behold, Judas, one of the twelve, came up, and with him *was* a large crowd with swords and clubs, *who came* from the chief priests and elders of the people.

48 Now he who was betraying Him gave them a sign, saying, "Whomever I kiss, He is the one; seize Him."

49 And immediately Judas went to Jesus and said, "Greetings, Rabbi!" and kissed Him.

50 And Jesus said to him, "Friend, *do* what you have come for." Then they came and laid hands on Jesus and seized Him.

51 And behold, one of those who were with Jesus stretched out his hand and drew out his sword and struck the slave of the high priest and cut off his ear.

52 Then Jesus *said to him, "Put your sword back into its place; for all those who take up the sword shall perish by the sword.

53 "Or do you think that I cannot appeal to My Father, and He will at once put at My disposal more than twelve legions of angels?

54 "Therefore, how will the Scriptures be fulfilled, *which say* that it must happen this way?"

55 At that time Jesus said to the crowds, "Have you come out with swords and clubs to arrest Me as *you would* against a robber? Every day I used to sit in the temple teaching and you did not seize Me.

56 "But all this has taken place in order that the Scriptures of the prophets would be fulfilled." Then all the disciples left Him and fled.

Jesus Before Caiaphas

57 Now those who had seized Jesus led Him away to Caiaphas, the high priest, where the scribes and the elders were gathered together.

58 But Peter was following Him at a distance as far as the courtyard of the high priest, and entered in, and sat down with the officers to see the outcome.

59 Now the chief priests and the whole Sanhedrin kept trying to obtain false testimony against Jesus, so that they might put Him to death.

60 And they did not find *any*, even though many false witnesses came forward. But later on two came forward,

61 and said, "This man stated, 'I am able to destroy the sanctuary of God and to rebuild it in three days.' "

62 And the high priest stood up and said to Him, "Do You not answer? What are these men testifying against You?"

63 But Jesus kept silent. And the high priest said to Him, "I put You under oath by the living God, that You tell us whether You are the Christ, the Son of God."

64 Jesus *said to him, "You yourself said *it*; nevertheless I tell you, hereafter you will see THE SON OF MAN SITTING AT THE RIGHT HAND OF POWER and COMING ON THE CLOUDS OF HEAVEN."

65 Then the high priest tore his garments and said, "He has blasphemed! What further need do we have of witnesses? Behold, you have now heard the blasphemy;

66 what do you think?" They answered and said, "He deserves death!"

67 Then they spat in His face and beat Him with their fists; and others slapped *Him*,

68 and said, "Prophesy to us, O Christ; who is the one who hit You?"

Peter's Denials

69 Now Peter was sitting outside in the courtyard, and a servant-girl came to him and said, "You too were with Jesus the Galilean."

70 But he denied *it* before them all, saying, "I do not know what you are talking about."

71 And when he had gone out to the gateway, another *servant-girl* saw him and *said to those who were there, "This man was with Jesus of Nazareth."

72 And again he denied *it* with an oath, "I do not know the man."

73 A little later the bystanders came up and said to Peter, "Surely you too are *one* of them; for even the way you talk gives you away."

74 Then he began to curse and swear, "I do not know the man!" And immediately a rooster crowed.

75 And Peter remembered the word which Jesus had said, "Before a rooster crows, you will deny Me three times." And he went out and cried bitterly.

CHAPTER 27

Judas' Remorse

NOW when morning came, all the chief priests and the elders of the people took counsel together against Jesus to put Him to death;

2 and they bound Him, and led Him away and delivered Him to Pilate the governor.

3 Then when Judas, who had betrayed Him, saw that He had been condemned, he felt remorse and returned the thirty pieces of silver to the chief priests and elders,

4 saying, "I have sinned by betraying innocent blood." But they said, "What is that to us? See to that yourself!"

5 And he threw the pieces of silver into the sanctuary and departed; and he went away and hanged himself.

6 And the chief priests took the pieces of silver and said, "It is not lawful to put them into the temple treasury, since it is the price of blood."

7 And taking counsel together, they bought with the money the Potter's Field as a burial place for strangers.

8 For this reason that field has been called the Field of Blood to this day.

9 Then that which was spoken through Jeremiah the prophet was fulfilled, saying, "AND THEY TOOK THE THIRTY PIECES OF SILVER, THE PRICE OF THE ONE WHOSE PRICE HAD BEEN SET by the sons of Israel;

10 AND THEY GAVE THEM FOR THE POTTER'S FIELD, AS THE LORD DIRECTED ME."

Jesus Before Pilate

11 Now Jesus stood before the governor, and the governor questioned Him, saying, "Are You the King of the Jews?" And Jesus said to him, "You yourself say it."

12 And while He was being accused by the chief priests and elders, He did not answer.

13 Then Pilate *said to Him, "Do You not hear how many things they testify against You?"

14 And He did not answer him with regard to even a single charge, so the governor marveled greatly.

15 Now at the feast the governor was accustomed to release for the crowd any one prisoner whom they wanted.

16 And at that time they were holding a notorious prisoner, called Barabbas.

17 So when the people gathered together, Pilate said to them, "Whom do you want me to release for you? Barabbas, or Jesus who is called Christ?"

18 For he knew that because of envy they had delivered Him over.

19 Now while he was sitting on the judgment seat, his wife sent him a message, saying, "Have nothing to do with that righteous Man; for last night I suffered greatly in a dream because of Him."

20 But the chief priests and the elders persuaded the crowds to ask for Barabbas and to put Jesus to death.

21 But the governor answered and said to them, "Which of the two do you want me to release for you?" And they said, "Barabbas."

22 Pilate *said to them, "Then, what shall I do with Jesus who is called Christ?" They all *said, "Let Him be crucified!"

23 And he said, "Why, what evil did He do?" But they were crying out all the more, saying, "Let Him be crucified!"

24 Now when Pilate saw that he was accomplishing nothing, but rather that a riot was starting, he took water and washed his hands in front of the crowd, saying, "I am innocent of this man's blood; see to that yourselves."

25 And all the people answered and said, "His blood be on us and on our children!"

26 Then he released Barabbas for them; but after having Jesus scourged, he delivered Him over to be crucified.

Jesus Is Mocked

27 Then when the soldiers of the governor took Jesus into the Praetorium, they gathered the whole Roman cohort around Him.

28 And they stripped Him and put a scarlet robe on Him.

29 And after twisting together a crown of thorns, they put it on His head, and a reed in His right hand; and they knelt down before Him and mocked Him, saying, "Hail, King of the Jews!"

30 And they spat on Him, and took the reed and began to beat Him on the head.

31 When they had mocked Him, they took the scarlet robe off Him and put His own garments back on Him, and led Him away to crucify Him.

32 And as they were coming out, they found a man of Cyrene named Simon, whom they pressed into service to bear His cross.

The Crucifixion

33 And when they came to a place called Golgotha, which means Place of a Skull,

34 they gave Him wine to drink mixed with gall; and after tasting it, He did not want to drink.

35 And when they had crucified Him, they divided up His garments among themselves by casting lots.

36 And sitting down, they began to keep watch over Him there.

37 And above His head they put up the charge against Him which read, "THIS IS JESUS THE KING OF THE JEWS."

38 At that time two robbers *were crucified with Him, one on the right and one on the left.

39 And those passing by were blaspheming Him, shaking their heads

40 and saying, "You who are going to destroy the sanctuary and rebuild it in three days, save Yourself! If You are the Son of God, come down from the cross."

41 In the same way the chief priests also, along with the scribes and elders, were mocking Him and saying,

42 "He saved others; He cannot save Himself. He is the King of Israel;

let Him now come down from the cross, and we will believe in Him.

43 "HE TRUSTS IN GOD; LET GOD RESCUE *Him* now, IF HE DELIGHTS IN HIM; for He said, 'I am the Son of God.'"

44 And the robbers who had been crucified with Him were also insulting Him with the same words.

45 Now from the sixth hour darkness fell upon all the land until the ninth hour.

46 And about the ninth hour Jesus cried out with a loud voice, saying, "ELI, ELI, LAMA SABACHTHANI?" that is, "MY GOD, MY GOD, WHY HAVE YOU FORSAKEN ME?"

47 And some of those who were standing there, when they heard it, *began* saying, "This man is calling for Elijah."

48 And immediately one of them ran, and taking a sponge, he filled it with sour wine and put it on a reed, and gave Him a drink.

49 But the rest *of them* were saying, "Let us see whether Elijah will come to save Him."

50 And Jesus cried out again with a loud voice, and yielded up His spirit.

51 And behold, the veil of the sanctuary was torn in two from top to bottom; and the earth shook and the rocks were split.

52 And the tombs were opened, and many bodies of the saints who had fallen asleep were raised;

53 and coming out of the tombs after His resurrection they entered the holy city and appeared to many.

54 Now the centurion, and those who were with him keeping guard over Jesus, when they saw the earthquake and the things that were happening, became very frightened and said, "Truly this was God's Son!"

55 And many women were there looking on from a distance, who had followed Jesus from Galilee while ministering to Him.

56 Among them was Mary Magdalene, and Mary the mother of James and Joseph, and the mother of the sons of Zebedee.

Jesus Is Buried

57 Now when it was evening, there came a rich man from Arimathea, named Joseph, who himself had also become a disciple of Jesus.

58 This man went to Pilate and asked for the body of Jesus. Then Pilate ordered it to be given *to him*.

59 And Joseph took the body and wrapped it in a clean linen cloth,

60 and laid it in his own new tomb, which he had hewn out in the rock; and he rolled a large stone against the entrance of the tomb and went away.

61 And Mary Magdalene was there, and the other Mary, sitting opposite the grave.

62 Now on the next day, the day after the Preparation, the chief priests and the Pharisees gathered together with Pilate,

63 and said, "Sir, we remember that when He was still alive that deceiver

said, 'After three days I *am to* rise again.'

64 "Therefore, order for the grave to be made secure until the third day, lest His disciples come and steal Him away and say to the people, 'He has risen from the dead,' and the last deception will be worse than the first."

65 Pilate said to them, "You have a guard; go, make it *as* secure as you know how."

66 And they went and made the grave secure, and along with the guard they set a seal on the stone.

CHAPTER 28

Jesus Is Risen!

NOW after the Sabbath, as it began to dawn toward the first *day* of the week, Mary Magdalene and the other Mary came to look at the grave.

2 And behold, there was a great earthquake, for an angel of the Lord descended from heaven and came and rolled away the stone and sat upon it.

3 And his appearance was like lightning, and his clothing as white as snow.

4 And the guards quaked from fear of him and became like dead men.

5 And the angel answered and said to the women, "Do not be afraid; for I know that you are looking for Jesus who has been crucified.

6 "He is not here, for He has risen, just as He said. Come, see the place where He was lying.

7 "And go quickly and tell His disciples that He has risen from the dead; and behold, He is going ahead of you into Galilee, there you will see Him; behold, I have told you."

8 And they left the tomb quickly with fear and great joy and ran to report it to His disciples.

9 And behold, Jesus met them and said, "Greetings!" And they came up and took hold of His feet and worshiped Him.

10 Then Jesus *said to them, "Do not be afraid; go and report to My brothers to leave for Galilee, and there they will see Me."

11 Now while they were on their way, behold, some of the guard came into the city and reported to the chief priests all that had happened.

12 And when they had assembled with the elders and took counsel together, they gave a large sum of money to the soldiers,

13 and said, "You are to say, 'His disciples came by night and stole Him away while we were asleep.'

14 "And if this is heard before the governor, we will win him over and keep you out of trouble."

15 And they took the money and did as they had been instructed; and this story was widely spread among the Jews, *and is* to this day.

The Great Commission

16 But the eleven disciples proceeded to Galilee, to the mountain which Jesus had designated.

17 And when they saw Him, they worshiped *Him*; but some doubted.

18 And Jesus came up and spoke to them, saying, "All authority has been given to Me in heaven and on earth.

19 "Go therefore and make disciples of all the nations, baptizing them in the name of the Father and the Son and the Holy Spirit,

20 teaching them to keep all that I commanded you; and behold, I am with you always, even to the end of the age."

THE GOSPEL ACCORDING TO
MARK

CHAPTER 1

The Preaching of
John the Baptist

THE beginning of the gospel of Jesus Christ, the Son of God.

2 As it is written in Isaiah the prophet:

"BEHOLD, I SEND MY MESSENGER
    AHEAD OF YOU,
WHO WILL PREPARE YOUR WAY;

3 THE VOICE OF ONE CRYING IN THE
    WILDERNESS,
'MAKE READY THE WAY OF THE
    LORD,
MAKE HIS PATHS STRAIGHT.'"

4 John the Baptist appeared in the wilderness preaching a baptism of repentance for the forgiveness of sins.

5 And all the region of Judea was going out to him, and all the people of Jerusalem; and they were being baptized by him in the Jordan River, confessing their sins.

6 And John was clothed with camel's hair and *wore* a leather belt around his waist and was eating locusts and wild honey.

7 And he was preaching, saying, "After me One is coming who is mightier than I, and I am not fit to stoop down and untie the strap of His sandals.

8 "I baptized you with water; but He will baptize you with the Holy Spirit."

The Baptism of Jesus

9 Now it happened that in those days Jesus came from Nazareth in Galilee and was baptized by John in the Jordan.

10 And immediately coming up out of the water, He saw the heavens opening, and the Spirit like a dove descending upon Him;

11 and a voice came out of the heavens: "You are My beloved Son, in You I am well-pleased."

12 And immediately the Spirit *drove Him *to go* out into the wilderness.

13 And He was in the wilderness forty days being tempted by Satan; and He was with the wild beasts, and the angels were ministering to Him.

Jesus Preaches in Galilee

14 Now after John had been delivered up *into custody*, Jesus came into Galilee, preaching the gospel of God,

15 and saying, "The time is fulfilled, and the kingdom of God is at hand; repent and believe in the gospel."

16 As He was going along by the Sea of Galilee, He saw Simon and Andrew, the brother of Simon, casting a net in the sea; for they were fishermen.

17 And Jesus said to them, "Follow Me, and I will make you become fishers of men."

18 And immediately they left their nets and followed Him.

19 And going on a little farther, He saw James the son of Zebedee, and John his brother, who were also in the boat mending the nets.

20 And immediately He called them; and they left their father Zebedee in the boat with the hired servants, and went away to follow Him.

21 And they *went into Capernaum; and immediately on the Sabbath He entered the synagogue and *began to* teach.

22 And they were astonished at His teaching; for He was teaching them as *one* having authority, and not as the scribes.

23 And immediately there was a man in their synagogue with an unclean spirit; and he cried out,

24 saying, "What do we have to do with you, Jesus the Nazarene? Have You come to destroy us? I know who You are—the Holy One of God!"

25 And Jesus rebuked him, saying, "Be quiet, and come out of him!"

26 And throwing him into convulsions, the unclean spirit cried out with a loud voice and came out of him.

27 And they were all amazed, so that they were arguing among themselves, saying, "What is this? A new teaching with authority! He commands even the unclean spirits, and they obey Him."

28 And immediately the news about Him spread everywhere into all the surrounding district of Galilee.

Simon's Mother-in-Law and Many Others Healed

29 And immediately after they came out of the synagogue, they came into the house of Simon and Andrew, with James and John.

30 Now Simon's mother-in-law was lying sick with a fever; and immediately they *spoke to Jesus about her.

31 And He came to her and raised her up, taking her by the hand, and the fever left her, and she *began* waiting on them.

32 Now when evening came, after the sun had set, they *began* bringing to Him all who were ill and those who were demon-possessed.

33 And the whole city had gathered at the door.

34 And He healed many who were ill with various diseases, and cast out many demons; and He was not permitting the demons to speak, because they knew who He was.

35 And in the early morning, while it was still dark, Jesus rose up, went out of *the house*, and went away to a desolate place, and was praying there.

36 And Simon and his companions searched for Him;

37 and they found Him, and *said to Him, "Everyone is looking for You."

38 And He *said to them, "Let us go elsewhere, to the towns nearby, so that I may preach there also; for that is what I came out for."

39 And He went, preaching in their synagogues throughout all Galilee and casting out the demons.

40 And a leper *came to Jesus, pleading with Him and falling on his knees before Him, and saying, "If You are willing, You can make me clean."

41 And moved with compassion, He stretched out His hand and touched him, and *said to him, "I am willing; be cleansed."

42 And immediately the leprosy left him and he was cleansed.

43 And He sternly warned him and immediately sent him away,

44 and He *said to him, "See that you say nothing to anyone; but go, show yourself to the priest and offer for your cleansing what Moses commanded, as a testimony to them."

45 But he went out and began to proclaim it freely and to spread the news around, to such an extent that Jesus could no longer publicly enter a city, but stayed out in desolate areas; and they were coming to Him from everywhere.

CHAPTER 2

Jesus Heals a Paralytic

AND when He had come back to Capernaum several days afterward, it was heard that He was at home.

2 And many were gathered together, so that there was no longer room, not even near the door; and He was speaking the word to them.

3 And they *came, bringing to Him a paralytic, carried by four men.

4 And being unable to bring *him* to Jesus because of the crowd, they removed the roof *over* where He was; and when they had dug an opening, they let down the mat where the paralytic was lying.

5 And Jesus seeing their faith *said to the paralytic, "Child, your sins are forgiven."

6 But some of the scribes were sitting there and reasoning in their hearts,

7 "Why does this man speak that way? He is blaspheming; who can forgive sins but God alone?"

8 Immediately Jesus, aware in His spirit that they were reasoning that way within themselves, *said to them, "Why are you reasoning about these things in your hearts?

9 "Which is easier, to say to the paralytic, 'Your sins are forgiven'; or to say, 'Get up, and pick up your mat and walk'?

10 "But so that you may know that the Son of Man has authority on earth to forgive sins"—He *said to the paralytic,

11 "I say to you, get up, pick up your mat, and go to your home."

12 And he got up and immediately picked up the mat and went out before everyone, so that they were all amazed and were glorifying God, saying, "We have never seen anything like this."

13 And He went out again by the seashore; and the entire crowd was coming to Him, and He was teaching them.

Levi and Sinners Called

14 And as He passed by, He saw Levi the *son* of Alphaeus sitting in the tax office, and He *said to him, "Follow Me!" And He stood up and followed Him.

15 And it *happened that as He was reclining *at the table* in his house, many tax collectors and sinners were reclining with Jesus and His disciples. For there were many of them, and they were following Him.

16 And when the scribes of the Pharisees saw that He was eating with the sinners and tax collectors, they were saying to His disciples, "He is eating and drinking with tax collectors and sinners!"

17 And hearing *this*, Jesus *said to them, "Those who are healthy do not have need for a physician, but *only* those who are sick; I did not come to call the righteous, but sinners."

18 And John's disciples and the Pharisees were fasting; and they *came and *said to Him, "Why do John's disciples and the disciples of the Pharisees fast, but Your disciples do not fast?"

19 And Jesus said to them, "Can the attendants of the bridegroom fast when the bridegroom is with them? So long as they have the bridegroom with them, they cannot fast.

20 "But the days will come when the bridegroom is taken away from them, and then they will fast in that day.

21 "No one sews a piece of unshrunk cloth on an old garment; otherwise that patch pulls away from it, the new from the old, and a worse tear results.

22 "And no one puts new wine into old wineskins; otherwise the wine will burst the skins, and the wine is lost and the skins *as well*; but *one puts* new wine into fresh wineskins."

Lord of the Sabbath

23 And it happened that He was passing through the grainfields on the Sabbath, and His disciples began to make their way along while picking the heads *of grain*.

24 And the Pharisees were saying to Him, "Look, why are they doing what is not lawful on the Sabbath?"

25 And He *said to them, "Have you never read what David did when he was in need and he and his companions became hungry;

26 how he entered the house of God around the time of Abiathar the high priest, and ate the consecrated bread, which is not lawful for *anyone* to eat except the priests, and he also gave it to those who were with him?"

27 And Jesus was saying to them, "The Sabbath was made for man, and not man for the Sabbath.

28 "Consequently the Son of Man is Lord even of the Sabbath."

CHAPTER 3

Jesus Heals a Man on the Sabbath

AND He entered again into a synagogue; and a man was there with a withered hand.

2 And they were watching Him to see if He would heal him on the Sabbath, so that they might accuse Him.

3 And He *said to the man with the withered hand, "Get up and come forward!"

4 And He *said to them, "Is it lawful to do good or to do harm on the Sabbath, to save a life or to kill?" But they kept silent.

5 And after looking around at them with anger, grieved at their hardness of heart, He *said to the man, "Stretch out your hand." And he stretched it out, and his hand was restored.

6 And the Pharisees went out and immediately *began* taking counsel together with the Herodians against Him, *as to* how they might destroy Him.

7 And Jesus withdrew to the sea with His disciples; and a great multitude from Galilee followed; and from Judea,

8 and from Jerusalem, and from Idumea, and beyond the Jordan, and the vicinity of Tyre and Sidon, a great number of people heard of all that He was doing and came to Him.

9 And He told His disciples that a boat should stand ready for Him because of the crowd, so that they would not crowd Him;

10 for He had healed many, with the result that all those who had afflictions pressed around Him in order to touch Him.

11 And whenever the unclean spirits were seeing Him, they would fall down before Him and cry out, saying, "You are the Son of God!"

12 And He earnestly warned them not to tell who He was.

Jesus Appoints the Twelve

13 And He *went up on the mountain and *summoned those whom He Himself wanted, and they came to Him.

14 And He appointed twelve (whom He also named apostles) to be with Him and to send them out to preach,

15 and to have authority to cast out the demons.

16 And He appointed the twelve: Simon (to whom He gave the name Peter),

17 and James, the *son* of Zebedee, and John the brother of James (to them He gave the name Boanerges, which means, "Sons of Thunder");

18 and Andrew, and Philip, and Bartholomew, and Matthew, and Thomas, and James the son of Alphaeus, and Thaddaeus, and Simon the Zealot;

19 and Judas Iscariot, who also betrayed Him.

20 And He *came home, and the crowd *gathered again, so that they could not even eat a meal.

21 And when His own people heard *this*, they went out to take custody of Him; for they were saying, "He has lost His senses."

22 And the scribes who came down from Jerusalem were saying, "He is possessed by Beelzebul," and "He

casts out the demons by the ruler of the demons."

23 And He called them to Himself and *began* speaking to them in parables, "How can Satan cast out Satan?

24 "And if a kingdom is divided against itself, that kingdom cannot stand.

25 "And if a house is divided against itself, that house will not be able to stand.

26 "And if Satan has risen up against himself and is divided, he cannot stand, but he is finished!

27 "But no one can enter the strong man's house and plunder his property unless he first binds the strong man, and then he will plunder his house.

28 "Truly I say to you, all sins shall be forgiven the sons of men, and whatever blasphemies they utter;

29 but whoever blasphemes against the Holy Spirit never has forgiveness, but is guilty of an eternal sin"—

30 because they were saying, "He has an unclean spirit."

31 Then His mother and His brothers *arrived, and standing outside they sent *word* to Him, calling Him.

32 And a crowd was sitting around Him, and they *said to Him, "Behold, Your mother and Your brothers are outside looking for You."

33 And answering them, He *said, "Who are My mother and My brothers?"

34 And looking about at those who were sitting around Him, He *said, "Behold My mother and My brothers!

35 "For whoever does the will of God, he is My brother and sister and mother."

CHAPTER 4

The Parable of the Sower

AND He began to teach again by the sea. And such a very large crowd gathered to Him that He got into a boat in the sea and sat down; and the whole crowd was by the sea on the land.

2 And He was teaching them many things in parables, and was saying to them in His teaching,

3 "Listen *to this*! Behold, the sower went out to sow;

4 and it happened that as he was sowing, some *seed* fell beside the road, and the birds came and ate it up.

5 "And other *seed* fell on the rocky *ground* where it did not have much soil; and immediately it sprang up because it had no depth of soil.

6 "And after the sun rose, it was scorched; and because it had no root, it withered away.

7 "And other *seed* fell among the thorns, and the thorns came up and choked it, and it yielded no crop.

8 "And other *seeds* fell into the good soil, and as they grew up and increased, they were yielding a crop and produced thirty, sixty, and a hundredfold."

9 And He was saying, "He who has ears to hear, let him hear."

10 And when He was alone, His followers, along with the twelve, *began* asking Him *about* the parables.

11 And He was saying to them, "To you has been given the mystery of the kingdom of God, but to those who are outside, everything comes in parables,

12 so that WHILE SEEING, THEY MAY SEE AND NOT PERCEIVE, AND WHILE HEARING, THEY MAY HEAR AND NOT UNDERSTAND, LEST THEY RETURN AND BE FORGIVEN."

The Parable of the Sower Explained

13 And He *said to them, "Do you not understand this parable? How will you understand all the parables?

14 "The sower sows the word.

15 "And these are the ones who are beside the road where the word is sown: when they hear, immediately Satan comes and takes away the word which has been sown in them.

16 "And in a similar way, these are the ones being sown on the rocky *places*: those who, when hearing the word, immediately receive it with joy;

17 and they have no root in themselves, but are *only* temporary; then, when affliction or persecution arises because of the word, immediately they fall away.

18 "And others are those being sown among the thorns; these are the ones who have heard the word,

19 but the worries of the world, and the deceitfulness of riches, and the desires for anything else enter in and choke the word, and it becomes unfruitful.

20 "And those are the ones which were sown on the good soil: they who hear the word and accept it and are bearing fruit, thirty, sixty, and a hundredfold."

21 And He was saying to them, "Is a lamp brought to be put under a basket or under a bed? Is it not to be put on the lampstand?

22 "For nothing is hidden, except to be revealed; nor has *anything* been secret, but that it would come to light.

23 "If anyone has ears to hear, let him hear."

24 And He was saying to them, "Beware what you listen to. By your standard of measure it will be measured to you, and more will be given to you.

25 "For whoever has, to him *more* shall be given; and whoever does not have, even what he has shall be taken away from him."

The Parable of the Seed

26 And He was saying, "The kingdom of God is like a man who casts seed upon the soil;

27 and he sleeps and rises, night and day, and the seed sprouts and grows— how, he himself does not know.

28 "The soil produces crops by itself; first the blade, then the head, then the mature grain in the head.

29 "But when the grain is ripe, he immediately puts in the sickle, because the harvest has come."

The Parable of the Mustard Seed

30 And He was saying, "How shall we compare the kingdom of God, or by what parable shall we present it?

31 "*It is* like a mustard seed, which,

when sown upon the soil, though it is smallest of all the seeds that are upon the soil,

32 yet when it is sown, it grows up and becomes largest of all the garden plants and forms large branches; so that THE BIRDS OF THE AIR can NEST UNDER ITS SHADE."

33 And with many such parables He was speaking the word to them, as they were able to hear *it*;

34 and He was not speaking to them without a parable; but He was explaining everything privately to His own disciples.

Jesus Calms a Storm

35 And on that day, when evening came, He *said to them, "Let us go over to the other side."

36 And leaving the crowd, they *took Him along with them in the boat, just as He was; and other boats were with Him.

37 And a great windstorm *arose, and the waves were breaking into the boat so that the boat was already filling up.

38 And Jesus Himself was in the stern, sleeping on the cushion; and they *got Him up and *said to Him, "Teacher, do You not care that we are perishing?"

39 And He woke up and rebuked the wind and said to the sea, "Silence! Be still." And the wind died down and it became perfectly calm.

40 And He said to them, "Why are you *so* cowardly? Do you still have no faith?"

41 And they became very afraid and were saying to one another, "Who then is this, that even the wind and the sea obey Him?"

CHAPTER 5

Jesus Saves a Man with Many Demons

THEN they came to the other side of the sea, into the region of the Gerasenes.

2 And when He got out of the boat, immediately a man from the tombs with an unclean spirit met Him,

3 who had his dwelling among the tombs. And no one was able to bind him anymore, even with a chain;

4 because he had often been bound with shackles and chains, and the chains had been torn apart by him and the shackles broken in pieces, and no one was strong enough to subdue him.

5 And constantly, night and day, among the tombs and in the mountains, he was crying out and gashing himself with stones.

6 And seeing Jesus from a distance, he ran up and bowed down before Him;

7 and crying out with a loud voice, he *said, "What do I have to do with You, Jesus, Son of the Most High God? I implore You by God, do not torment me!"

8 For He had been saying to him, "Come out of the man, you unclean spirit!"

9 And He was asking him, "What

is your name?" And he *said to Him, "My name is Legion; for we are many."

10 And he *began* pleading with Him earnestly not to send them out of the region.

11 Now there was a large herd of swine feeding nearby on the mountain.

12 *And the demons* pleaded with Him, saying, "Send us into the swine so that we may enter them."

13 And Jesus gave them permission. And coming out, the unclean spirits entered the swine; and the herd rushed down the steep bank into the sea, about two thousand *of them*; and they were drowned in the sea.

14 And their herdsmen ran away and reported it in the city and in the countryside. And *the people* came to see what it was that had happened.

15 And they *came to Jesus and *observed the demon-possessed man sitting down, clothed and in his right mind, the very man who had the "legion"; and they became frightened.

16 And those who had seen it recounted to them how *this* had happened to the demon-possessed man, and *all* about the swine.

17 And they began to plead with Him to leave their region.

18 And as He was getting into the boat, the man who had been demon-possessed was pleading with Him that he might accompany Him.

19 And He did not let him, but He *said to him, "Go home to your people and report to them what great things the Lord has done for you, and *how* He had mercy on you."

20 And he went away and began to preach in the Decapolis what great things Jesus had done for him; and everyone was marveling.

*Jesus Heals a Woman and
Jairus' Daughter*

21 And when Jesus had crossed over again in the boat to the other side, a large crowd gathered around Him; and so He stayed by the seashore.

22 And one of the synagogue officials named Jairus *came up, and on seeing Him, *fell at His feet

23 and *pleaded with Him earnestly, saying, "My little daughter is at the point of death; *please come*, that by coming, You may lay Your hands on her, so that she will be saved and live."

24 And He went off with him; and a large crowd was following Him and pressing in on Him.

25 And a woman—who had a hemorrhage for twelve years

26 and had endured much at the hands of many physicians, and had spent all that she had and was not helped at all, but rather had grown worse—

27 after hearing about Jesus, she came up in the crowd behind *Him* and touched His garment.

28 For she was saying, "If I just touch His garments, I will be saved *from this*."

29 And immediately the flow of her blood was dried up; and she knew

within her body that she had been healed of her affliction.

30 And immediately Jesus, perceiving in Himself that the power *proceeding* from Him had gone forth, turned around in the crowd and was saying, "Who touched My garments?"

31 And His disciples were saying to Him, "You see the crowd pressing in on You, and You say, 'Who touched Me?'"

32 And He was looking around to see the woman who had done this.

33 But the woman fearing and trembling, aware of what had happened to her, came and fell down before Him and told Him the whole truth.

34 And He said to her, "Daughter, your faith has saved you; go in peace and be healed of your affliction."

35 While He was still speaking, they *came from the *house of* the synagogue official, saying, "Your daughter has died; why trouble the Teacher anymore?"

36 But Jesus, overhearing what had been spoken, *said to the synagogue official, "Do not be afraid, only believe."

37 And He allowed no one to accompany Him, except Peter and James and John the brother of James.

38 And they *came to the house of the synagogue official; and He *saw a commotion, and *people* loudly crying and wailing.

39 And entering in, He *said to them, "Why are you making a commotion and crying? The child has not died, but is asleep."

40 And they *began* laughing at Him. But putting them all out, He *took along the child's father and mother and His own companions, and *entered *the room* where the child was.

41 And taking the child by the hand, He *said to her, "Talitha kum!" (which translated means, "Little girl, I say to you, arise!").

42 And immediately the little girl stood up and *began to* walk, for she was twelve years old. And immediately they were completely astounded.

43 And He gave them strict orders that no one should know about this, and He said that *some food* should be given to her to eat.

CHAPTER 6

Jesus Rejected at Nazareth

AND Jesus went out from there and *came into His hometown; and His disciples *followed Him.

2 And when the Sabbath came, He began to teach in the synagogue; and many listeners were astonished, saying, "Where did this man *get* these things, and what is *this* wisdom given to this man, and such miracles as these performed by His hands?

3 "Is this man not the carpenter, the son of Mary, and brother of James and Joses and Judas and Simon? Are not His sisters here with us?" And they were taking offense at Him.

4 And Jesus was saying to them, "A prophet is not without honor except

in his hometown and among his *own* relatives and in his *own* household."

5 And He could do no miracle there except that He laid His hands on a few sick people and healed them.

6 And He was marveling at their unbelief.

And He was going around the villages teaching.

The Twelve Sent Out

7 And He *summoned the twelve and began to send them out in pairs, and was giving them authority over the unclean spirits;

8 and He instructed them that they should take nothing for *their* journey, except a staff only—no bread, no bag, no money in their belt—

9 but *to* wear sandals; and *He added*, "Do not put on two tunics."

10 And He was saying to them, "Wherever you enter a house, stay there until you leave town.

11 "And any place that does not receive you or listen to you, as you go out from there, shake the dust off the soles of your feet for a testimony against them."

12 And they went out and preached that *men* should repent.

13 And they were casting out many demons and were anointing with oil many sick people and healing them.

The Death of John the Baptist

14 And King Herod heard *it*, for His name had become well known; and *people* were saying, "John the Baptist has risen from the dead, and that is why these miraculous powers are at work in Him."

15 But others were saying, "He is Elijah." And others were saying, "*He is* a prophet, like one of the prophets *of old*."

16 But when Herod heard *it*, he kept saying, "John, whom I beheaded, has risen!"

17 For Herod himself had sent and had John arrested and bound in prison on account of Herodias, the wife of his brother Philip, because he had married her.

18 For John had been saying to Herod, "It is not lawful for you to have your brother's wife."

19 Now Herodias was holding a grudge against him and was wanting to put him to death and was not able;

20 for Herod was afraid of John, knowing that he was a righteous and holy man, and he was keeping him safe. And when he heard him, he was very perplexed; but he used to enjoy listening to him.

21 And a strategic day came when Herod on his birthday gave a banquet for his great men and military commanders and the leading men of Galilee;

22 and when the daughter of Herodias herself came in and danced, she pleased Herod and his dinner guests; and the king said to the girl, "Ask me for whatever you want and I will give it to you."

23 And he swore to her, "Whatever you ask of me, I will give it to you; up to half of my kingdom."

24 And she went out and said to her mother, "What shall I ask for?" And she said, "The head of John the Baptist."

25 And immediately she came in a hurry to the king and asked, saying, "I want you to give me at once the head of John the Baptist on a platter."

26 And although the king was very sorry, *yet* because of his oaths and because of his dinner guests, he did not want to refuse her.

27 And immediately the king sent an executioner and commanded *him* to bring *back* his head. And he went and beheaded him in the prison,

28 and brought his head on a platter, and gave it to the girl; and the girl gave it to her mother.

29 And when his disciples heard *this*, they came and took away his body and laid it in a tomb.

30 And the apostles *gathered together with Jesus; and they reported to Him all that they had done and taught.

31 And He *said to them, "Come away by yourselves to a desolate place and rest a while." (For there were many *people* coming and going, and they did not even have time to eat.)

32 And they went away in the boat to a desolate place by themselves.

Jesus Feeds Five Thousand

33 And *the people* saw them going, and many recognized *them* and ran there together on foot from all the cities, and got there ahead of them.

34 And when Jesus went ashore, He saw a large crowd, and He felt compassion for them because they were like sheep without a shepherd; and He began to teach them many things.

35 And when it was already quite late, His disciples came to Him and *began* saying, "This place is desolate and it is already quite late;

36 send them away so that they may go into the surrounding countryside and villages and buy themselves something to eat."

37 But He answered and said to them, "You give them *something* to eat!" And they *said to Him, "Shall we go and spend two hundred [1]denarii on bread and give them *something* to eat?"

38 And He *said to them, "How many loaves do you have? Go look!" And when they found out, they *said, "Five, and two fish."

39 And He commanded them all to sit down by groups on the green grass.

40 And they sat down in groups of hundreds and of fifties.

41 And He took the five loaves and the two fish, and looking up toward heaven, He blessed *the food* and broke the loaves. And He kept giving *them* to the disciples to set before them, and He divided up the two fish among them all.

42 And they all ate and were satisfied,

[1] A Roman silver coin, approx. a laborer's daily wage

43 and they picked up twelve full baskets of the broken pieces, and also of the fish.

44 And there were five thousand men who ate the loaves.

Jesus Walks on the Sea

45 And immediately Jesus made His disciples get into the boat and go ahead of *Him* to the other side to Bethsaida, while He Himself was sending the crowd away.

46 And after bidding them farewell, He left for the mountain to pray.

47 And when it was evening, the boat was in the middle of the sea, and He was alone on the land.

48 And seeing them straining at the oars, for the wind was against them, at about the fourth watch of the night He *came to them, walking on the sea; and He was intending to pass by them.

49 But when they saw Him walking on the sea, they thought that it was a ghost, and cried out;

50 for they all saw Him and were terrified. But immediately He spoke with them and *said to them, "Take courage; it is I, do not be afraid."

51 Then He got into the boat with them, and the wind stopped; and they were utterly amazed,

52 for they had not gained any insight about the loaves, but their heart was hardened.

Many Healed at Gennesaret

53 And when they had crossed over they came to land at Gennesaret, and moored to the shore.

54 And when they got out of the boat, immediately *the people* recognized Him,

55 and ran about that whole region and began to carry here and there on their mats those who were sick, to the place they heard He was.

56 And wherever He was entering villages, or cities, or countryside, they were laying the sick in the marketplaces, and pleading with Him that they might just touch the fringe of His garment; and as many as touched it were being saved *from their sicknesses.*

CHAPTER 7

God's Commandments, Man's Traditions

AND the Pharisees and some of the scribes *gathered around Him when they had come from Jerusalem,

2 and had seen that some of His disciples were eating their bread with defiled hands, that is, unwashed.

3 (For the Pharisees and all the Jews do not eat unless they carefully wash their hands, *thus* observing the tradition of the elders;

4 and *when they come* from the marketplace, they do not eat unless they wash themselves; and there are many other things which they have received in order to observe, such as the washing of cups and pitchers and copper pots.)

5 And the Pharisees and the scribes *asked Him, "Why do Your disciples not walk according to the

tradition of the elders, but eat their bread with defiled hands?"

6 And He said to them, "Rightly did Isaiah prophesy of you hypocrites, as it is written:

'THIS PEOPLE HONORS ME WITH
   THEIR LIPS,
BUT THEIR HEART IS FAR AWAY
   FROM ME.
7 'BUT IN VAIN DO THEY WORSHIP
   ME,
TEACHING AS DOCTRINES THE
   COMMANDS OF MEN.'

8 "Leaving the commandment of God, you hold to the tradition of men."

9 And He was also saying to them, "You are good at setting aside the commandment of God in order to keep your tradition.

10 "For Moses said, 'HONOR YOUR FATHER AND YOUR MOTHER'; and, 'HE WHO SPEAKS EVIL OF FATHER OR MOTHER, IS TO BE PUT TO DEATH';

11 but you say, 'If a man says to *his* father or *his* mother, whatever you might benefit from me is Corban (that is to say, given *to God*),'

12 you no longer leave him to do anything for *his* father or *his* mother;

13 *thus* invalidating the word of God by your tradition which you have handed down; and you do many things such as that."

The Heart of Man

14 And after He called the crowd to Him again, He *began* saying to them, "Listen to Me, all of you, and understand:

15 there is nothing outside the man which can defile him if it goes into him; but the things which proceed out of the man are what defile the man.

16 ["And if anyone has ears to hear, let him hear."]

17 And when He had left the crowd *and* entered the house, His disciples were asking Him about the parable.

18 And He *said to them, "Are you lacking understanding in this way as well? Do you not perceive that whatever goes into the man from outside cannot defile him,

19 because it does not go into his heart, but into his stomach, and goes to the sewer?" (*Thus He* declared all foods clean.)

20 And He was saying, "That which proceeds out of the man, that is what defiles the man.

21 "For from within, out of the heart of men, proceed the evil thoughts, sexual immoralities, thefts, murders, adulteries,

22 coveting, wickedness, deceit, sensuality, envy, slander, pride *and* foolishness.

23 "All these evil things proceed from within and defile the man."

A Gentile Woman's Faith

24 Now Jesus stood up and went away from there to the region of Tyre. And when He had entered a house, He was wanting no one to know *of it*; yet He could not escape notice.

25 But after hearing of Him, a woman whose little daughter had an

unclean spirit immediately came and fell at His feet.

26 Now the woman was a Greek, of Syrophoenician descent. And she kept asking Him to cast the demon out of her daughter.

27 And He was saying to her, "Let the children be satisfied first, for it is not good to take the children's bread and throw it to the dogs."

28 But she answered and *said to Him, "Yes, Lord, *but* even the dogs under the table feed on the children's crumbs."

29 And He said to her, "Because of this answer go; the demon has gone out of your daughter."

30 And going back to her home, she found the child lying on the bed, the demon having left.

The Deaf Hear, the Mute Speak

31 And again He went out from the region of Tyre, and came through Sidon to the Sea of Galilee, within the region of the Decapolis.

32 And they *brought to Him one who was deaf and spoke with difficulty, and they *pleaded with Him to lay His hand on him.

33 And Jesus took him aside from the crowd, by himself, and put His fingers into his ears, and after spitting, He touched his tongue;

34 and looking up to heaven with a sigh, He *said to him, "Ephphatha!" that is, "Be opened!"

35 And his ears were opened, and the impediment of his tongue was removed, and he *began* speaking plainly.

36 And He gave them orders not to tell anyone; but the more He was ordering them, the more widely they continued to proclaim it.

37 And they were utterly astonished, saying, "He has done all things well; He makes even the deaf to hear and the mute to speak."

CHAPTER 8

Jesus Feeds Four Thousand

IN those days, when there was again a large crowd and they had nothing to eat, Jesus called His disciples and *said to them,

2 "I feel compassion for the crowd because they have remained with Me now three days and have nothing to eat.

3 "And if I send them away hungry to their homes, they will faint on the way; and some of them have come from a great distance."

4 And His disciples answered Him, "Where will anyone be able *to find enough* bread here in *this* desolate place to satisfy these people?"

5 And He was asking them, "How many loaves do you have?" And they said, "Seven."

6 And He *directed the crowd to sit down on the ground; and taking the seven loaves, He gave thanks and broke them. And He kept giving them to His disciples to serve to them, and they served them to the crowd.

7 And they also had a few small

fish; and after He blessed them, He ordered these to be served as well.

8 And they ate and were satisfied; and they picked up seven *large* baskets full of what was left over of the broken pieces.

9 Now about four thousand were *there*, and He sent them away.

10 And immediately He entered the boat with His disciples and came to the district of Dalmanutha.

11 And the Pharisees came out and began to argue with Him, seeking from Him a sign from heaven, testing Him.

12 And sighing deeply in His spirit, He *said, "Why does this generation seek a sign? Truly I say to you, no sign will be given to this generation."

13 And leaving them, He again embarked and went away to the other side.

14 And they had forgotten to take bread, and did not have more than one loaf in the boat with them.

15 And He was giving orders to them, saying, "Watch out! Beware of the leaven of the Pharisees and the leaven of Herod."

16 And they *began to* discuss with one another *the fact* that they had no bread.

17 And Jesus, aware of this, *said to them, "Why do you discuss *the fact* that you have no bread? Do you not yet perceive or understand? Do you have a hardened heart?

18 "HAVING EYES, DO YOU NOT SEE? AND HAVING EARS, DO YOU NOT HEAR? And do you not remember,

19 when I broke the five loaves for the five thousand, how many baskets full of broken pieces you picked up?" They *said to Him, "Twelve."

20 "When *I broke* the seven for the four thousand, how many *large* baskets full of broken pieces did you pick up?" And they *said to Him, "Seven."

21 And He was saying to them, "Do you not yet understand?"

22 And they *came to Bethsaida. And they *brought a blind man to Jesus and *pleaded with Him to touch him.

23 And taking the blind man by the hand, He brought him out of the village; and after spitting on his eyes and laying His hands on him, He was asking him, "Do you see anything?"

24 And he looked up and was saying, "I see men, for I see *them* like trees, walking around."

25 Then again He laid His hands on his eyes; and he looked intently and was restored, and *began to* see everything clearly.

26 And He sent him to his home, saying, "Do not even enter the village."

Peter Confesses Jesus Is the Christ

27 And Jesus went out, along with His disciples, to the villages of Caesarea Philippi; and on the way He was asking His disciples, saying to them, "Who do people say that I am?"

28 And they told Him, saying, "John the Baptist; and others *say* Elijah; but others, one of the prophets."

29 And He *continued* asking them, "But who do you say that I am?" Peter

*answered and *said to Him, "You are the Christ."

30 And He warned them to tell no one about Him.

31 And He began to teach them that the Son of Man must suffer many things and be rejected by the elders and the chief priests and the scribes, and be killed, and after three days rise again.

32 And He was stating the matter openly. And Peter took Him aside and began to rebuke Him.

33 But turning around and seeing His disciples, He rebuked Peter and *said, "Get behind Me, Satan! For you are not setting your mind on God's interests, but man's."

Take Up Your Cross

34 And He summoned the crowd with His disciples, and said to them, "If anyone wishes to come after Me, he must deny himself, and take up his cross and follow Me.

35 "For whoever wishes to save his life will lose it, but whoever loses his life for My sake and the gospel's will save it.

36 "For what does it profit a man to gain the whole world, and forfeit his soul?

37 "For what will a man give in exchange for his soul?

38 "For whoever is ashamed of Me and My words in this adulterous and sinful generation, the Son of Man will also be ashamed of him when He comes in the glory of His Father with the holy angels."

CHAPTER 9

The Transfiguration

AND Jesus was saying to them, "Truly I say to you, there are some of those who are standing here who will not taste death until they see the kingdom of God having come in power."

2 And six days later, Jesus *took with Him Peter and James and John, and *brought them up on a high mountain alone by themselves. And He was transfigured before them;

3 and His garments were shining intensely white, as no launderer on earth can whiten them.

4 And Elijah appeared to them along with Moses and they were conversing with Jesus.

5 And Peter answered and *said to Jesus, "Rabbi, it is good for us to be here; let us make three booths, one for You, and one for Moses, and one for Elijah."

6 For he did not know what to answer; for they became terrified.

7 Then a cloud formed, overshadowing them, and a voice came out of the cloud, "This is My beloved Son, listen to Him!"

8 And all at once when they looked around, they saw no one with them anymore, except Jesus alone.

9 And as they were coming down from the mountain, He gave them orders not to recount to anyone what they had seen, until the Son of Man rose from the dead.

10 And they seized upon that statement, arguing with one another what rising from the dead meant.

11 And they *began* asking Him, saying, "*Why is it* that the scribes say that Elijah must come first?"

12 And He said to them, "Elijah does first come and restore all things. And *yet* how is it written of the Son of Man that He will suffer many things and be treated with contempt?

13 "But I say to you that Elijah has indeed come, and they did to him whatever they wished, just as it is written of him."

I Believe, Help My Unbelief

14 And when they came *back* to the disciples, they saw a large crowd around them, and scribes arguing with them.

15 And immediately, when the entire crowd saw Him, they were amazed. And as they ran up, they were greeting Him.

16 And He asked them, "What are you arguing with them?"

17 And one of the crowd answered Him, "Teacher, I brought You my son, possessed with a spirit which makes him mute;

18 and whenever it seizes him, it slams him *to the ground* and he foams *at the mouth*, and grinds his teeth and becomes rigid. I told Your disciples to cast it out, and they could not *do it*."

19 And He *answered them and *said, "O unbelieving generation, how long shall I be with you? How long shall I put up with you? Bring him to Me!"

20 And they brought the boy to Him. When he saw Him, immediately the spirit threw him into a convulsion, and falling to the ground, he *began* rolling around, foaming *at the mouth*.

21 And He asked his father, "How long has this been happening to him?" And he said, "From childhood.

22 "And it has often thrown him both into the fire and into the water to destroy him. But if You can do anything, take pity on us and help us!"

23 And Jesus said to him, " 'If You can?' All things are possible to him who believes."

24 Immediately the boy's father cried out and was saying, "I do believe; help my unbelief."

25 Now when Jesus saw that a crowd was rapidly gathering, He rebuked the unclean spirit, saying to it, "You mute and deaf spirit, I command you, come out of him and do not enter him again."

26 And after crying out and throwing him into terrible convulsions, it came out; and *the boy* became so much like a corpse that most *of them* said, "He is dead!"

27 But Jesus took him by the hand and raised him; and he stood up.

28 And when He came into the house, His disciples *began* questioning Him privately, "Why could we not cast it out?"

29 And He said to them, "This kind cannot come out by anything but prayer."

Jesus Foretells His Death and Resurrection

30 From there they went out and were going through Galilee, and He was not wanting anyone to know *about it.*

31 For He was teaching His disciples and telling them, "The Son of Man is to be delivered into the hands of men, and they will kill Him; and when He has been killed, He will rise again three days later."

32 But they did not understand *this* statement, and they were afraid to ask Him.

33 And they came to Capernaum; and when He was in the house, He *began to* question them, "What were you discussing on the way?"

34 But they kept silent, for on the way they had discussed with one another which *of them was* the greatest.

35 And sitting down, He called the twelve and *said to them, "If anyone wants to be first, he shall be last of all and servant of all."

36 And taking a child, He set him before them. And taking him in His arms, He said to them,

37 "Whoever receives one child like this in My name receives Me; and whoever receives Me does not receive Me, but Him who sent Me."

Warnings About Discipleship

38 John said to Him, "Teacher, we saw someone casting out demons in Your name, and we tried to hinder him because he was not following us."

39 But Jesus said, "Do not hinder him, for there is no one who will perform a miracle in My name, and be able soon afterward to speak evil of Me.

40 "For he who is not against us is for us.

41 "For whoever gives you a cup of water to drink in *My* name because you are of Christ, truly I say to you, he will not lose his reward.

42 "And whoever causes one of these little ones who believe to stumble, it would be better for him if, with a heavy millstone hung around his neck, he had been cast into the sea.

43 "And if your hand causes you to stumble, cut it off; it is better for you to enter life crippled, than, having your two hands, to go into hell, into the unquenchable fire,

44 [and where THEIR WORM DOES NOT DIE, AND THE FIRE IS NOT QUENCHED.]

45 "And if your foot causes you to stumble, cut it off; it is better for you to enter life lame, than, having your two feet, to be cast into hell,

46 [and where THEIR WORM DOES NOT DIE, AND THE FIRE IS NOT QUENCHED.]

47 "And if your eye causes you to stumble, gouge it out; it is better for you to enter the kingdom of God with one eye, than, having two eyes, to be cast into hell,

48 where THEIR WORM DOES NOT DIE, AND THE FIRE IS NOT QUENCHED.

49 "For everyone will be salted with fire.

50 "Salt is good; but if the salt becomes unsalty, with what will you make it salty *again*? Have salt in yourselves, and be at peace with one another."

CHAPTER 10

Teaching About Divorce

AND standing up, He *went from there to the region of Judea and beyond the Jordan; crowds *gathered around Him again, and, according to His custom, He once more *began to* teach them.

2 And *some* Pharisees came up to Jesus, testing Him, and *began to* question Him whether it was lawful for a man to divorce a wife.

3 And He answered and said to them, "What did Moses command you?"

4 And they said, "Moses permitted *a man* TO WRITE A CERTIFICATE OF DIVORCE AND SEND *her* AWAY."

5 But Jesus said to them, "Because of your hardness of heart he wrote for you this commandment.

6 "But from the beginning of creation, *God* MADE THEM MALE AND FEMALE.

7 "FOR THIS REASON A MAN SHALL LEAVE HIS FATHER AND MOTHER,

8 AND THE TWO SHALL BECOME ONE FLESH; so they are no longer two, but one flesh.

9 "What therefore God has joined together, let no man separate."

10 And in the house the disciples *began* questioning Him about this again.

11 And He *said to them, "Whoever divorces his wife and marries another woman commits adultery against her;

12 and if she herself divorces her husband and marries another man, she is committing adultery."

Jesus Blesses Little Children

13 And they were bringing children to Him so that He might touch them; but the disciples rebuked them.

14 But when Jesus saw this, He was indignant and said to them, "Permit the children to come to Me; do not hinder them; for the kingdom of God belongs to such as these.

15 "Truly I say to you, whoever does not receive the kingdom of God like a child will not enter it *at all.*"

16 And He took them in His arms and *began* blessing them, laying His hands on them.

The Rich Young Ruler

17 And as He was setting out on a journey, a man ran up to Him and knelt before Him, and *began* asking Him, "Good Teacher, what shall I do to inherit eternal life?"

18 And Jesus said to him, "Why do you call Me good? No one is good except God alone.

19 "You know the commandments, 'DO NOT MURDER, DO NOT COMMIT ADULTERY, DO NOT STEAL, DO NOT BEAR FALSE WITNESS, Do not defraud, HONOR YOUR FATHER AND MOTHER.'"

20 And he said to Him, "Teacher, I have kept all these things from my youth up."

21 And looking at him, Jesus loved him and said to him, "One thing you lack: go and sell all you possess and give to the poor, and you will have

treasure in heaven; and come, follow Me."

22 But at these words he was saddened, and he went away grieving, for he was one who owned much property.

23 And Jesus, looking around, *said to His disciples, "How hard it will be for those who are wealthy to enter the kingdom of God!"

24 And the disciples were amazed at His words. But Jesus *answered again and *said to them, "Children, how hard it is to enter the kingdom of God!

25 "It is easier for a camel to go through the eye of a needle than for a rich man to enter the kingdom of God."

26 And they were even more astonished, saying to Him, "Then who can be saved?"

27 Looking at them, Jesus *said, "With people it is impossible, but not with God; for all things are possible with God."

28 Peter began to say to Him, "Behold, we have left everything and followed You."

29 Jesus said, "Truly I say to you, there is no one who has left house or brothers or sisters or mother or father or children or farms, for My sake and for the gospel's sake,

30 except *one who* will receive one hundred times as much now in the present age—houses and brothers and sisters and mothers and children and farms, *along* with persecutions—and in the age to come, eternal life.

31 "But many *who are* first will be last, and the last, first."

Jesus Again Foretells His Death and Resurrection

32 And they were on the road going up to Jerusalem, and Jesus was walking on ahead of them; and they were amazed, and those who followed were fearful. And again He took the twelve aside and began to tell them what was going to happen to Him:

33 "Behold, we are going up to Jerusalem, and the Son of Man will be betrayed to the chief priests and the scribes; and they will condemn Him to death and will deliver Him over to the Gentiles.

34 "And they will mock Him and spit on Him, and flog Him and kill *Him*, and three days later He will rise again."

A Request for Status

35 Then James and John, the two sons of Zebedee, *came up to Jesus, saying to Him, "Teacher, we want You to do for us whatever we ask of You."

36 And He said to them, "What do you want Me to do for you?"

37 And they said to Him, "Grant that we may sit, one on Your right and one on *Your* left, in Your glory."

38 But Jesus said to them, "You do not know what you are asking. Are you able to drink the cup that I drink, or to be baptized with the baptism with which I am baptized?"

39 And they said to Him, "We are able." And Jesus said to them, "The cup that I drink you shall drink; and

you shall be baptized with the baptism with which I am baptized.

40 "But to sit on My right or on *My* left, *this* is not Mine to give; but it is for those for whom it has been prepared."

41 And hearing *this*, the ten began to feel indignant with James and John.

42 And calling them to Himself, Jesus *said to them, "You know that those who are recognized as rulers of the Gentiles lord it over them; and their great men exercise authority over them.

43 "But it is not this way among you, but whoever wishes to become great among you shall be your servant;

44 and whoever wishes to be first among you shall be slave of all.

45 "For even the Son of Man did not come to be served, but to serve, and to give His life a ransom for many."

Bartimaeus Regains His Sight

46 Then they *came to Jericho. And as He was leaving Jericho with His disciples and a large crowd, a blind beggar *named* Bartimaeus, the son of Timaeus, was sitting by the road.

47 And when he heard that it was Jesus the Nazarene, he began to cry out and say, "Jesus, Son of David, have mercy on me!"

48 And many were sternly telling him to be quiet, but he kept crying out all the more, "Son of David, have mercy on me!"

49 And Jesus stopped and said, "Call him *here*." So they *called the blind man, saying to him, "Take courage, get up! He is calling for you."

50 And throwing off his *outer* garment, he jumped up and came to Jesus.

51 And Jesus answered him and said, "What do you want Me to do for you?" And the blind man said to Him, "Rabboni, *I want* to regain my sight!"

52 And Jesus said to him, "Go; your faith has saved you." Immediately he regained his sight and *began* following Him on the road.

CHAPTER 11

The Triumphal Entry

AND as they *approached Jerusalem, at Bethphage and Bethany, near the Mount of Olives, He *sent two of His disciples,

2 and *said to them, "Go into the village opposite you, and immediately as you enter it, you will find a colt tied *there*, on which no one yet has ever sat; untie it and bring it *here*.

3 "And if anyone says to you, 'Why are you doing this?' you say, 'The Lord has need of it'; and immediately he will send it back here."

4 And they went away and found a colt tied at the door, outside in the street; and they *untied it.

5 And some of the bystanders were saying to them, "What are you doing, untying the colt?"

6 And they spoke to them just as Jesus had told *them*, and they gave them permission.

7 And they *brought the colt to Jesus and put their garments on it; and He sat on it.

8 And many spread their garments in the road, and others *spread* leafy branches, having cut *them* from the fields.

9 And those who went in front and those who followed were shouting:

"Hosanna!

Blessed is He who comes in the name of the Lord;

10 Blessed *is* the coming kingdom of our father David;

Hosanna in the highest!"

11 And Jesus entered Jerusalem *and came* into the temple; and after looking around at everything, He left for Bethany with the twelve, since it was already late.

The Barren Fig Tree

12 And on the next day, when they had left Bethany, He became hungry.

13 And seeing at a distance a fig tree that had leaves, He went *to see* if perhaps He would find anything on it; and when He came to it, He found nothing but leaves, for it was not the season for figs.

14 And He answered and said to it, "May no one ever eat fruit from you again!" And His disciples were listening.

Jesus Drives Merchants from the Temple

15 Then they *came to Jerusalem. And He entered the temple and began to drive out those who were buying and selling in the temple, and overturned the tables of the money changers and the seats of those who were selling doves;

16 and He was not permitting anyone to carry merchandise through the temple.

17 And He *began to* teach and say to them, "Is it not written, 'My house shall be called a house of prayer for all the nations'? But you have made it a robbers' den."

18 And the chief priests and the scribes heard *this*, and *began* seeking how to destroy Him; for they were afraid of Him, for the whole crowd was astonished at His teaching.

19 And when evening came, they were going out of the city.

20 And as they were passing by in the morning, they saw the fig tree withered from the roots.

21 And being reminded, Peter *said to Him, "Rabbi, look, the fig tree which You cursed has withered."

22 And Jesus answered and *said to them, "Have faith in God.

23 "Truly I say to you, whoever says to this mountain, 'Be taken up and cast into the sea,' and does not doubt in his heart, but believes that what he says is going to happen, it will be *granted* him.

24 "For this reason I say to you, all things for which you pray and ask, believe that you have received them, and they will be *granted* to you.

25 "And whenever you stand praying, forgive, if you have anything against anyone, so that your Father who is in heaven will also forgive you your transgressions.

26 ["But if you do not forgive, neither will your Father who is in heaven forgive your transgressions."]

The Authority of Jesus Challenged

27 Then they *came again to Jerusalem. And as He was walking in the temple, the chief priests and the scribes and the elders *came to Him,

28 and *began* saying to Him, "By what authority are You doing these things, or who gave You this authority to do these things?"

29 And Jesus said to them, "I will ask you one question, and you answer Me, and *then* I will tell you by what authority I do these things.

30 "Was the baptism of John from heaven, or from men? Answer Me."

31 And they *began* reasoning among themselves, saying, "If we say, 'From heaven,' He will say, 'Then why did you not believe him?'

32 "But if we say, 'From men'?"— they were afraid of the crowd, for everyone was regarding John to have been a real prophet.

33 And answering Jesus, they *said, "We do not know." And Jesus *said to them, "Neither will I tell you by what authority I do these things."

CHAPTER 12

The Parable of the Vine-Growers

AND He began to speak to them in parables: "A man PLANTED A VINEYARD AND PUT A WALL AROUND IT, AND DUG A VAT UNDER THE WINE PRESS AND BUILT A TOWER, and rented it out to vine-growers and went on a journey.

2 "And at the *harvest* time he sent a slave to the vine-growers, in order to receive *some* of the fruit of the vineyard from the vine-growers.

3 "And they took him, and beat him and sent him away empty-handed.

4 "And again he sent them another slave, and they wounded him in the head, and treated him shamefully.

5 "And he sent another, and that one they killed; and *so with* many others, beating some and killing others.

6 "He had one more, a beloved son; he sent him last *of all* to them, saying, 'They will respect my son.'

7 "But those vine-growers said to one another, 'This is the heir; come, let us kill him, and the inheritance will be ours!'

8 "And they took him, and killed him and threw him out of the vineyard.

9 "What will the owner of the vineyard do? He will come and destroy the vine-growers, and will give the vineyard to others.

10 "Have you not even read this Scripture:
'THE STONE WHICH THE BUILDERS REJECTED,
THIS HAS BECOME THE CHIEF CORNER *stone*;

11 THIS CAME ABOUT FROM THE LORD,
AND IT IS MARVELOUS IN OUR EYES'?"

12 And they were seeking to seize Him, and *yet* they feared the crowd, for they understood that He spoke

the parable against them. And *so* they left Him and went away.

Taxes to Caesar

13 Then they *sent some of the Pharisees and Herodians to Him in order to trap Him in a statement.

14 And they *came and *said to Him, "Teacher, we know that You are truthful and defer to no one; for You are not partial to any, but teach the way of God in truth. Is it lawful to pay a tax to Caesar, or not?

15 "Shall we pay or shall we not pay?" But He, knowing their hypocrisy, said to them, "Why are you testing Me? Bring Me a ¹denarius to look at."

16 And they brought *one*. And He *said to them, "Whose likeness and inscription is this?" And they said to Him, "Caesar's."

17 And Jesus said to them, "Render to Caesar the things that are Caesar's, and to God the things that are God's." And they were amazed at Him.

The Sadducees and the Resurrection

18 Then *some* Sadducees (who say that there is no resurrection) *came to Jesus, and *began* questioning Him, saying,

19 "Teacher, Moses wrote for us that IF A MAN'S BROTHER DIES and leaves behind a wife AND LEAVES NO CHILD, HIS BROTHER SHOULD MARRY THE WIFE AND RAISE UP A SEED FOR HIS BROTHER.

20 "There were seven brothers; and the first married a wife, and died leaving no seed.

21 "And the second one married her, and died leaving behind no seed; and the third likewise;

22 and *so* all seven left no seed. Last of all the woman died also.

23 "In the resurrection, when they rise again, whose wife will she be? For all seven had married her."

24 Jesus said to them, "Is this not the reason you are mistaken, that you do not understand the Scriptures nor the power of God?

25 "For when they rise from the dead, they neither marry nor are given in marriage, but are like angels in heaven.

26 "But regarding the fact that the dead are raised, have you not read in the book of Moses, in the *passage* about *the burning* bush, how God spoke to him, saying, 'I AM THE GOD OF ABRAHAM, AND THE GOD OF ISAAC, AND THE GOD OF JACOB'?

27 "He is not the God of the dead, but of the living; you are greatly mistaken."

The Foremost Commandment

28 And when one of the scribes came and heard them arguing, he recognized that He had answered them well and asked Him, "What commandment is the foremost of all?"

29 Jesus answered, "The foremost is, 'HEAR, O ISRAEL! THE LORD OUR GOD IS ONE LORD;

30 AND YOU SHALL LOVE THE LORD YOUR GOD WITH ALL YOUR HEART,

---

¹ A Roman silver coin, approx. a laborer's daily wage

AND WITH ALL YOUR SOUL, AND WITH ALL YOUR MIND, AND WITH ALL YOUR STRENGTH.'

31 "The second is this, 'YOU SHALL LOVE YOUR NEIGHBOR AS YOURSELF.' There is no other commandment greater than these."

32 And the scribe said to Him, "Right, Teacher; You have truly stated that HE IS ONE, AND THERE IS NO ONE ELSE BESIDES HIM;

33 AND TO LOVE HIM WITH ALL THE HEART AND WITH ALL THE UNDERSTANDING AND WITH ALL THE STRENGTH, AND TO LOVE ONE'S NEIGHBOR AS HIMSELF, is much more than all burnt offerings and sacrifices."

34 And when Jesus saw that he had answered thoughtfully, He said to him, "You are not far from the kingdom of God." After that, no one would dare to ask Him any more questions.

35 And Jesus *began to* say, as He taught in the temple, "How *is it that* the scribes say that the Christ is the son of David?

36 "David himself said in the Holy Spirit,

'THE LORD SAID TO MY LORD,

"SIT AT MY RIGHT HAND,

UNTIL I PUT YOUR ENEMIES

BENEATH YOUR FEET." '

37 "David himself calls Him 'Lord'; so in what sense is He his son?" And the large crowd enjoyed listening to Him.

38 And in His teaching He was saying: "Beware of the scribes who want to walk around in long robes, and *want* respectful greetings in the marketplaces,

39 and best seats in the synagogues and places of honor at banquets,

40 who devour widows' houses, and for appearance's sake offer long prayers; these will receive greater condemnation."

The Widow's Offering

41 And He sat down opposite the treasury, and *began* observing how the crowd was putting money into the treasury; and many rich people were putting in large sums.

42 And a poor widow came and put in two [1]lepta, which amount to a [2]quadrans.

43 And calling His disciples to Him, He said to them, "Truly I say to you, this poor widow put in more than all those putting *money* into the treasury;

44 for they all put in out of their surplus, but she, out of her poverty, put in all she owned, all she had to live on."

CHAPTER 13

Signs of Christ's Return

AND as He was going out of the temple, one of His disciples *said to

---

[1] Smallest Greek copper coin, approx. 1/128 of a laborer's daily wage   [2] A Roman copper coin, approx. 1/64 of a laborer's daily wage

Him, "Teacher, behold what wonderful stones and what wonderful buildings!"

2 And Jesus said to him, "Do you see these great buildings? Not one stone will be left upon another which will not be torn down."

3 And as He was sitting on the Mount of Olives opposite the temple, Peter and James and John and Andrew were questioning Him privately,

4 "Tell us, when will these things be, and what *will be* the sign when all these things are going to be fulfilled?"

5 And Jesus began to say to them, "See to it that no one deceives you.

6 "Many will come in My name, saying, 'I am *He!*' and will mislead many.

7 "And when you hear of wars and rumors of wars, do not be alarmed; *those things* must take place; but *that is* not yet the end.

8 "For nation will rise up against nation, and kingdom against kingdom; there will be earthquakes in various places; there will *also* be famines. These things are *merely* the beginning of birth pains.

9 "But see to yourselves; for they will deliver you to *the* courts, and you will be beaten in *the* synagogues, and you will stand before governors and kings for My sake, as a witness to them.

10 "And the gospel must first be proclaimed to all the nations.

11 "And when they lead you away, delivering you up, do not worry beforehand about what you are to say, but say whatever is given to you in that hour; for it is not you who speak, but *it is* the Holy Spirit.

12 "And brother will betray brother to death, and a father *his* child; and children will rise up against parents and have them put to death.

13 "And you will be hated by all because of My name, but the one who endures to the end, he will be saved.

The Abomination of Desolation and the Tribulation

14 "But when you see the ABOMINATION OF DESOLATION standing where it should not be (let the reader understand), then those who are in Judea must flee to the mountains.

15 "And the one who is on the housetop must not go down, or go in to get anything out of his house;

16 and the one who is in the field must not turn back to get his garment.

17 "But woe to those who are pregnant and to those who are nursing babies in those days!

18 "But pray that it may not happen in the winter.

19 "For those days will be a *time of* tribulation such as has not occurred since the beginning of the creation which God created until now, and never will.

20 "And unless the Lord had shortened *those* days, no life would have been saved; but for the sake of the elect, whom He chose, He shortened the days.

21 "And then if anyone says to you, 'Behold, here is the Christ'; or, 'Behold, *He is* there'; do not believe *him*;

22 for false christs and false prophets will arise, and will show signs and wonders, in order to lead astray, if possible, the elect.

23 "But as for you, see! I have told you everything in advance.

The Coming of the Son of Man

24 "But in those days, after that tribulation, THE SUN WILL BE DARKENED AND THE MOON WILL NOT GIVE ITS LIGHT,

25 AND THE STARS WILL BE FALLING from heaven, AND THE POWERS THAT ARE IN THE HEAVENS will be shaken.

26 "And then they will see THE SON OF MAN COMING IN CLOUDS with great power and glory.

27 "And then He will send forth the angels, and will gather together His elect from the four winds, from the farthest end of the earth to the farthest end of heaven.

The Parable of the Fig Tree

28 "Now learn the parable from the fig tree: when its branch has already become tender and puts forth its leaves, you know that summer is near.

29 "Even so, you too, when you see these things happening, recognize that He is near, *right* at the door.

30 "Truly I say to you, this generation will not pass away until all these things take place.

31 "Heaven and earth will pass away, but My words will not pass away.

32 "But of that day or hour no one knows, not even the angels in heaven, nor the Son, but the Father *alone*.

33 "See to it, keep on the alert; for you do not know when the *appointed* time will come.

34 "*It is* like a man away on a journey, *who*, leaving his house and giving authority to his slaves—each one his task, also commanded the doorkeeper to stay awake.

35 "Therefore, stay awake—for you do not know when the master of the house is coming, whether in the evening, at midnight, or when the rooster crows, or in the morning—

36 lest he come suddenly and find you sleeping.

37 "And what I say to you I say to all, 'Stay awake!' "

CHAPTER 14

The Plot to Kill Jesus

NOW the Passover and Unleavened Bread were two days away; and the chief priests and the scribes were seeking how, after seizing Him in secret, they might kill *Him*;

2 for they were saying, "Not during the festival, lest there be a riot of the people."

The Costly Perfume

3 And while He was in Bethany at the home of Simon the leper, and reclining *at the table*, there came a woman with an alabaster jar of perfume of very costly pure nard; *and* she broke the jar and poured it over His head.

4 But some were indignantly *remarking* to one another, "Why has this perfume been wasted?

5 "For this perfume might have been sold for over three hundred denarii and given to the poor." And they were scolding her.

6 But Jesus said, "Let her alone; why do you bother her? She did a good work to Me.

7 "For you always have the poor with you, and whenever you wish you can do good to them; but you do not always have Me.

8 "She has done what she could; she anointed My body beforehand for the burial.

9 "And truly I say to you, wherever the gospel is proclaimed in the whole world, what this woman did will also be spoken of in memory of her."

10 Then Judas Iscariot, who was one of the twelve, went away to the chief priests in order to betray Him to them.

11 And when they heard *this*, they were glad and promised to give him money. And he *began* seeking how to betray Him at an opportune time.

The Passover Meal

12 And on the first day of Unleavened Bread, when the Passover lamb was being sacrificed, His disciples *said to Him, "Where do You want us to go and prepare for You to eat the Passover?"

13 And He *sent two of His disciples and *said to them, "Go into the city, and a man will meet you carrying a pitcher of water; follow him;

14 and wherever he enters, say to the owner of the house, 'The Teacher says, "Where is My guest room in which I may eat the Passover with My disciples?"'

15 "And he himself will show you a large upper room furnished *and* ready; prepare for us there."

16 And the disciples went out and came to the city, and found *it* just as He had told them; and they prepared the Passover.

17 And when it was evening He *came with the twelve.

18 And as they were reclining *at the table* and eating, Jesus said, "Truly I say to you that one of you will betray Me—the one who is eating with Me."

19 They began to be grieved and to say to Him one by one, "Surely not I?"

20 And He said to them, "*It is* one of the twelve, the one who dips with Me in the bowl.

21 "For the Son of Man *is to* go just as it is written of Him; but woe to that man by whom the Son of Man is betrayed! *It would have been* good for that man if he had not been born."

The Lord's Supper

22 And while they were eating, He took *some* bread, and after a blessing, He broke *it*, and gave *it* to them, and said, "Take *it*; this is My body."

23 And when He had taken a cup *and* given thanks, He gave *it* to them, and they all drank from it.

24 And He said to them, "This is My blood of the covenant, which is poured out for many.

25 "Truly I say to you, I will never again drink of the fruit of the vine until that day when I drink it new in the kingdom of God."

26 And after singing a hymn, they went out to the Mount of Olives.

27 And Jesus *said to them, "You will all fall away, because it is written, 'I WILL STRIKE DOWN THE SHEPHERD, AND THE SHEEP SHALL BE SCATTERED.'

28 "But after I have been raised, I will go ahead of you to Galilee."

29 But Peter said to Him, "Even though all may fall away, yet I will not."

30 And Jesus *said to him, "Truly I say to you, that today, this very night, before a rooster crows twice, you yourself will deny Me three times."

31 But Peter kept saying insistently, "If I have to die with You, I will not deny You!" And they all were saying the same thing also.

Jesus Prays in Gethsemane

32 Then they *came to a place named Gethsemane; and He *said to His disciples, "Sit here until I have prayed."

33 And He *took with Him Peter and James and John, and began to be very distressed and troubled.

34 And He *said to them, "My soul is deeply grieved to the point of death; remain here and keep watch."

35 And He went a little beyond them, and fell to the ground and began to pray that if it were possible, the hour might pass from Him.

36 And He was saying, "Abba! Father! All things are possible for You; remove this cup from Me; yet not what I will, but what You will."

37 And He *came and *found them sleeping, and *said to Peter, "Simon, are you sleeping? Could you not keep watch for one hour?

38 "Keep watching and praying that you may not come into temptation; the spirit is willing, but the flesh is weak."

39 And again He went away and prayed, saying the same words.

40 And again He came and found them sleeping, for their eyes were very heavy; and they did not know what to answer Him.

41 And He *came the third time, and *said to them, "Are you still sleeping and resting? It is enough; the hour has come; behold, the Son of Man is being betrayed into the hands of sinners.

42 "Get up, let us go; behold, the one who betrays Me is at hand!"

The Betrayal and Arrest of Jesus

43 And immediately while He was still speaking, Judas, one of the twelve, *came up, and with him was a crowd with swords and clubs, who were from the chief priests and the scribes and the elders.

44 Now he who was betraying Him had given them a signal, saying, "Whomever I kiss, He is the one; seize Him and lead Him away under guard."

45 And after coming, Judas, having immediately gone to Him, *said, "Rabbi!" and kissed Him.

46 And they laid hands on Him and seized Him.

47 But one of those who stood by drew his sword, and struck the slave of the high priest and cut off his ear.

48 And Jesus answered and said to them, "Have you come out with swords and clubs to arrest Me, as *you would* against a robber?

49 "Every day I was with you in the temple teaching, and you did not seize Me; but *this has taken place* in order that the Scriptures would be fulfilled."

50 And they all left Him and fled.

51 And a young man was following Him, wearing *nothing but* a linen sheet over *his* naked *body*; and they *seized him.

52 But he pulled free of the linen sheet and escaped naked.

Jesus Before His Accusers

53 Then they led Jesus away to the high priest; and all the chief priests and the elders and the scribes *gathered together.

54 And Peter followed Him at a distance, right into the courtyard of the high priest; and he was sitting with the officers and warming himself at the fire.

55 Now the chief priests and the whole Sanhedrin were seeking to obtain testimony against Jesus to put Him to death, and they were not finding any.

56 For many were giving false testimony against Him, but their testimony was not consistent.

57 And some, standing up, were giving false testimony against Him, saying,

58 "We ourselves heard Him say, 'I will destroy this sanctuary made with hands, and in three days I will build another made without hands.'"

59 And not even in this way was their testimony consistent.

60 And the high priest stood up in *their* midst and questioned Jesus, saying, "You answer nothing? What are these men testifying against You?"

61 But He kept silent and did not answer. Again the high priest was questioning Him and *said to Him, "Are You the Christ, the Son of the Blessed *One*?"

62 And Jesus said, "I am; and you shall see THE SON OF MAN SITTING AT THE RIGHT HAND OF THE POWER, and COMING WITH THE CLOUDS OF HEAVEN."

63 And tearing his tunics, the high priest *said, "What further need do we have of witnesses?

64 "You have heard the blasphemy; how does it seem to you?" And they all condemned Him to be deserving of death.

65 And some began to spit at Him, and to blindfold Him, and to beat Him with their fists, and to say to Him, "Prophesy!" And the officers received Him with slaps *in the face.*

Peter's Denials

66 And as Peter was below in the courtyard, one of the servant-girls of the high priest *came,

67 and seeing Peter warming himself, she looked at him and *said, "You also were with the Nazarene, Jesus."

68 But he denied *it*, saying, "I neither know nor understand what you are talking about." And he went out into the entryway.

69 And when the servant-girl saw him, she began once more to say to the bystanders, "This is *one* of them!"

70 But again he was denying it. And after a little while the bystanders were again saying to Peter, "Surely you are *one* of them, for you are also a Galilean."

71 But he began to curse and swear, "I do not know this man you are talking about!"

72 And immediately a rooster crowed a second time. And Peter remembered how Jesus had said the statement to him, "Before a rooster crows twice, you will deny Me three times." And throwing himself down, he *began to* cry.

CHAPTER 15

Jesus Before Pilate

AND early in the morning the chief priests with the elders and scribes and the whole Sanhedrin, immediately held council; and binding Jesus, led Him away and delivered *Him* to Pilate.

2 And Pilate questioned Him, "Are You the King of the Jews?" And He answered him and *said, "You yourself say *it*."

3 And the chief priests *began to* accuse Him of many things.

4 Then Pilate was questioning Him again, saying, "You answer nothing? See how many accusations they bring against You!"

5 But Jesus made no further answer; so Pilate marveled.

6 Now at the feast he used to release for them *any* one prisoner whom they requested.

7 And the man named Barabbas had been imprisoned with the insurrectionists who had committed murder in the insurrection.

8 And the crowd went up and began asking him *to do* as he had been accustomed to do for them.

9 And Pilate answered them, saying, "Do you want me to release for you the King of the Jews?"

10 For he was aware that the chief priests had delivered Him over because of envy.

11 But the chief priests stirred up the crowd *to ask* him to release Barabbas for them instead.

12 And answering again, Pilate was saying to them, "Then what shall I do with Him whom you call the King of the Jews?"

13 And they shouted again, "Crucify Him!"

14 But Pilate was saying to them, "Why? What evil did He do?" But they shouted all the more, "Crucify Him!"

15 And wishing to satisfy the crowd, Pilate released Barabbas for them, and after having Jesus scourged, he delivered Him over to be crucified.

Jesus Is Mocked

16 So the soldiers took Him away into the palace (that is, the Praetorium), and they *called together the whole *Roman* cohort.

17 And they *dressed Him up in purple, and after twisting a crown of thorns, they *put it on Him;

18 and they began to greet Him, "Hail, King of the Jews!"

19 And they kept beating His head with a reed, and spitting on Him; and kneeling, they were bowing down before Him.

20 And after they had mocked Him, they took the purple robe off Him and put His *own* garments on Him. And they *led Him out to crucify Him.

21 And they *pressed into service a passer-by coming from the countryside, Simon of Cyrene (the father of Alexander and Rufus), to carry His cross.

The Crucifixion

22 Then they *brought Him to the place Golgotha, which is translated, Place of a Skull.

23 And they tried to give Him wine mixed with myrrh; but He did not take it.

24 And they *crucified Him, and *divided up His garments among themselves, casting lots for them *to decide* who should take what.

25 Now it was the third hour, and they crucified Him.

26 And the inscription of the charge against Him read, "THE KING OF THE JEWS."

27 And they *crucified two robbers with Him, one on His right and one on His left.

28 [And the Scripture was fulfilled which says, "And He was numbered with transgressors."]

29 And those passing by were blaspheming Him, shaking their heads, and saying, "Ha! You who *are going to* destroy the sanctuary and rebuild it in three days,

30 save Yourself by coming down from the cross!"

31 In the same way, mocking *Him* to one another, the chief priests also, along with the scribes, were saying, "He saved others; He cannot save Himself.

32 "Let *this* Christ, the King of Israel, now come down from the cross, so that we may see and believe!" Those who were crucified with Him were also insulting Him.

33 And when the sixth hour came, darkness fell over the whole land until the ninth hour.

34 And at the ninth hour Jesus cried out with a loud voice, "Eloi, Eloi, lama sabachthani?" which is translated, "My God, My God, why have You forsaken Me?"

35 And when some of the bystanders heard it, they *began* saying, "Look, He is calling for Elijah."

36 And someone ran and filled a sponge with sour wine, put it on a reed, and gave Him a drink, saying, "Let us see whether Elijah will come to take Him down."

37 And Jesus, uttering a loud cry, breathed His last.

38 And the veil of the sanctuary was torn in two from top to bottom.

39 And when the centurion, who was standing right in front of Him, saw the way He breathed His last, he said, "Truly this man was God's Son!"

40 And there were also *some* women looking on from a distance, among whom *were* Mary Magdalene, and Mary the mother of James the Less and Joses, and Salome,

41 who, when He was in Galilee, were following Him and serving Him; and *there were* many other women who came up with Him to Jerusalem.

Jesus Is Buried

42 And when evening had already come, because it was Preparation day, that is, the day before the Sabbath,

43 Joseph of Arimathea came, a prominent Council member, who himself was waiting for the kingdom of God; and he gathered up courage and went in before Pilate, and asked for the body of Jesus.

44 And Pilate wondered if He had died by this time, and summoning the centurion, he questioned him as to whether He already died.

45 And ascertaining this from the centurion, he granted the body to Joseph.

46 And when Joseph had bought a linen cloth and took Him down, he wrapped Him in the linen cloth and laid Him in a tomb which had been hewn out in the rock. And he rolled a stone against the entrance of the tomb.

47 And Mary Magdalene and Mary the *mother* of Joses were looking on *to see* where He had been laid.

CHAPTER 16

Jesus Is Risen!

AND when the Sabbath passed, Mary Magdalene, and Mary the *mother* of James, and Salome, bought spices, so that they might come and anoint Him.

2 And very early on the first day of the week, they *came to the tomb when the sun had risen.

3 And they were saying to one another, "Who will roll away the stone for us from the entrance of the tomb?"

4 And looking up, they *saw that the stone had been rolled away, although it was very large.

5 And entering the tomb, they saw a young man sitting on the right side, wearing a white robe; and they were amazed.

6 And he *said to them, "Do not be amazed; you are looking for Jesus the Nazarene, who has been crucified. He has risen; He is not here; behold, the place where they laid Him.

7 "But go, tell His disciples and Peter, 'He is going ahead of you to Galilee; there you will see Him, just as He told you.'"

8 And they went out and fled from the tomb, for trembling and astonishment were gripping them; and

they said nothing to anyone, for they were afraid.

9 [Now after He had risen early on the first day of the week, He first appeared to Mary Magdalene, from whom He had cast out seven demons.

10 She went and reported to those who had been with Him, while they were mourning and crying.

11 And when they heard that He was alive and had been seen by her, they refused to believe it.

12 After that, He appeared in a different form to two of them while they were walking along on their way to the countryside.

13 And they went away and reported it to the others, but they did not believe them either.

The Great Commission

14 Afterward He appeared to the eleven themselves as they were reclining *at the table*; and He reproached them for their unbelief and hardness of heart, because they had not believed those who had seen Him after He had risen.

15 And He said to them, "Go into all the world and preach the gospel to all creation.

16 "He who has believed and has been baptized shall be saved; but he who has disbelieved shall be condemned.

17 "And these signs will accompany those who have believed: in My name they will cast out demons, they will speak with new tongues;

18 and they will pick up serpents, and if they drink any deadly *poison*, it will not hurt them; they will lay hands on the sick, and they will recover."

19 So then, the Lord Jesus, after He had spoken to them, was taken up into heaven and sat down at the right hand of God.

20 And they went out and preached everywhere, while the Lord worked with them, and confirmed the word by the signs that followed.]

[*And they promptly reported all these instructions to Peter and his companions. And after that, Jesus Himself sent out through them from east to west the sacred and imperishable preaching of eternal salvation.*]

THE GOSPEL ACCORDING TO

LUKE

CHAPTER 1

Luke's Account of Things Fulfilled

INASMUCH as many have undertaken to compile an account of the things that have been fulfilled among us,

2 just as those, who from the beginning were eyewitnesses and servants of the word, handed *them* down to us,

3 it seemed fitting for me as well, having investigated everything carefully from the beginning, to write *it* out for you in orderly sequence, most excellent Theophilus,

4 so that you may know the certainty about the things you have been taught.

John the Baptist's Birth Foretold

5 In the days of Herod, king of Judea, there was a priest named Zechariah, of the division of Abijah, and he had a wife from the daughters of Aaron, and her name was Elizabeth.

6 And they were both righteous in the sight of God, walking blamelessly in all the commandments and righteous requirements of the Lord.

7 But they had no child, because Elizabeth was barren, and they were both advanced in years.

8 Now it happened that while he was performing his priestly service before God in the order of his division,

9 according to the custom of the priestly office, he was chosen by lot to enter the sanctuary of the Lord and burn incense.

10 And the whole multitude of the people were praying outside at the hour of the incense offering.

11 And an angel of the Lord appeared to him, standing to the right of the altar of incense.

12 And Zechariah was troubled when he saw *the angel*, and fear fell upon him.

13 But the angel said to him, "Do not be afraid, Zechariah, for your prayer has been heard, and your wife Elizabeth will bear you a son, and you will call his name John.

14 "And you will have joy and gladness, and many will rejoice at his birth.

15 "For he will be great in the sight of the Lord; and HE WILL NOT DRINK ANY WINE OR STRONG DRINK, and he will be filled with the Holy Spirit while yet in his mother's womb.

16 "And he will turn many of the sons of Israel back to the Lord their God.

17 "And he will go before Him in the spirit and power of Elijah, TO TURN THE HEARTS OF THE FATHERS BACK TO THE CHILDREN, and the disobedient

to the attitude of the righteous, to make ready a people prepared for the Lord."

18 And Zechariah said to the angel, "How will I know this? For I am an old man and my wife is advanced in years."

19 And the angel answered and said to him, "I am Gabriel, who stands before God, and I was sent to speak to you and to bring you this good news.

20 "And behold, you shall be silent and unable to speak until the day when these things take place, because you did not believe my words, which will be fulfilled in their proper time."

21 And the people were waiting for Zechariah, and were wondering at his delay in the sanctuary.

22 But when he came out, he was unable to speak to them, and they realized that he had seen a vision in the sanctuary. And he kept making signs to them, and remained mute.

23 And it happened that when the days of his priestly service were fulfilled, he went back home.

24 After these days Elizabeth his wife conceived, and she kept herself in seclusion for five months, saying,

25 "This is the way the Lord has dealt with me in the days when He looked upon *me* to take away my disgrace among men."

Jesus' Birth Foretold

26 Now in the sixth month the angel Gabriel was sent from God to a city in Galilee called Nazareth,

27 to a virgin betrothed to a man whose name was Joseph, of the house of David, and the virgin's name was Mary.

28 And coming in, he said to her, "Greetings, favored one! The Lord *is* with you."

29 But she was very perplexed at *this* statement, and was pondering what kind of greeting this was.

30 And the angel said to her, "Do not be afraid, Mary, for you have found favor with God.

31 "And behold, you will conceive in *your* womb and bear a son, and you shall name Him Jesus.

32 "He will be great and will be called the Son of the Most High, and the Lord God will give Him the throne of His father David,

33 and He will reign over the house of Jacob forever, and there will be no end of His kingdom."

34 But Mary said to the angel, "How will this be, since I am a virgin?"

35 The angel answered and said to her, "The Holy Spirit will come upon you, and the power of the Most High will overshadow you; and for that reason the holy Child shall be called the Son of God.

36 "And behold, your relative Elizabeth has also conceived a son in her old age; and this is the sixth month for her who was called barren.

37 "For nothing will be impossible with God."

38 And Mary said, "Behold, the slave of the Lord; may it be done to me according to your word." And the angel departed from her.

Mary Visits Elizabeth

39 Now at this time Mary arose and went in a hurry to the hill country, to a city of Judah,

40 and entered the house of Zechariah and greeted Elizabeth.

41 And it happened that when Elizabeth heard Mary's greeting, the baby leaped in her womb, and Elizabeth was filled with the Holy Spirit.

42 And she cried out with a loud voice and said, "Blessed *are* you among women, and blessed *is* the fruit of your womb!

43 "And how has it *happened* to me, that the mother of my Lord would come to me?

44 "For behold, when the sound of your greeting reached my ears, the baby leaped in my womb for joy.

45 "And blessed *is* she who believed that there would be a fulfillment of what had been spoken to her by the Lord."

Mary Magnifies the Lord

46 And Mary said:
"My soul magnifies the Lord,

47 And my spirit has rejoiced in God my Savior.

48 "For He has looked upon
    the humble state of His
    slave,
For behold, from this time on,
    all generations will count
    me blessed.

49 "For the Mighty One has done
    great things for me,
And holy is His name.

50 "AND HIS MERCY IS UPON
    GENERATION AFTER
    GENERATION
TOWARD THOSE WHO FEAR HIM.

51 "He has done a mighty deed
    with His arm;
He has scattered *those who were*
    proud in the thoughts of
    their heart.

52 "He has brought down rulers
    from *their* thrones,
And has exalted those who were
    humble.

53 "HE HAS FILLED THE HUNGRY
    WITH GOOD THINGS,
And sent away the rich
    empty-handed.

54 "He has given help to Israel His
    servant,
In remembrance of His mercy,

55 As He spoke to our fathers,
To Abraham and his seed forever."

56 And Mary stayed with her about three months, and *then* returned to her home.

John the Baptist Is Born

57 Now the time was fulfilled for Elizabeth to give birth, and she gave birth to a son.

58 And her neighbors and her relatives heard that the Lord had magnified His great mercy toward her, and they were rejoicing with her.

59 And it happened that on the eighth day they came to circumcise the child, and they were going to call him Zechariah, after the name of his father.

60 But his mother answered and said, "No, but he shall be called John."

61 And they said to her, "There is no one among your relatives who is called by this name."

62 And they were making signs to his father, as to what he wanted him called.

63 And he asked for a tablet and wrote as follows, "His name is John." And they all marveled.

64 And at once his mouth was opened and his tongue *loosed*, and he *began to* speak, blessing God.

65 And fear came on all those living around them, and all these matters were being talked about in all the hill country of Judea.

66 And all who heard *these things* put *them* in their heart, saying, "What then will this child be?" For the hand of the Lord was indeed with him.

Zechariah's Prophecy

67 And his father Zechariah was filled with the Holy Spirit, and prophesied, saying:

68 "Blessed *be* the Lord God of Israel,
For He visited and accomplished
redemption for His people,

69 And raised up a horn of
salvation for us
In the house of David His
servant—

70 As He spoke by the mouth of His
holy prophets from of old—

71 Salvation FROM OUR ENEMIES,
And FROM THE HAND OF ALL WHO
HATE US,

72 To show mercy toward our fathers,
And to remember His holy
covenant,

73 The oath which He swore to
Abraham our father,

74 To grant us that we, being
rescued from the hand of
our enemies,
Might serve Him without fear,

75 In holiness and righteousness
before Him all our days.

76 "And you, child, will be called the
prophet of the Most High,
For you will go ON BEFORE THE
LORD TO MAKE READY HIS
WAYS,

77 To give to His people *the*
knowledge of salvation
By the forgiveness of their sins,

78 Because of the tender mercy of
our God,
With which the Sunrise from on
high will visit us,

79 TO SHINE UPON THOSE WHO SIT IN
DARKNESS AND THE SHADOW
OF DEATH,
To direct our feet into the way
of peace."

80 And the child continued to grow and to become strong in spirit, and he lived in the desolate regions until the day of his public appearance to Israel.

CHAPTER 2

Jesus Is Born in Bethlehem

NOW it happened that in those days a decree went out from Caesar Augustus for a census to be taken of all the inhabited earth.

2 This was the first census taken while Quirinius was governor of Syria.

3 And everyone was going to be registered for the census, each to his own city.

4 And Joseph also went up from Galilee, from the city of Nazareth, to Judea, to the city of David, which is called Bethlehem, because he was of the house and family of David,

5 in order to register along with Mary, who was betrothed to him, *and* was with child.

6 Now it happened that while they were there, the days were fulfilled for her to give birth.

7 And she gave birth to her first-born son; and she wrapped Him in cloths, and laid Him in a manger, because there was no place for them in the guest room.

8 In the same region there were *some* shepherds staying out in the fields and keeping watch over their flock by night.

9 And an angel of the Lord stood before them, and the glory of the Lord shone around them; and they were terribly frightened.

10 But the angel said to them, "Do not be afraid; for behold, I bring you good news of great joy which will be for all the people.

11 For today in the city of David there has been born for you a Savior, who is Christ the Lord.

12 "And this *will be* the sign for you: you will find a baby wrapped in cloths and lying in a manger."

13 And suddenly there appeared with the angel a multitude of the heavenly host praising God and saying,

14 "Glory to God in the highest,
And on earth peace among men
    with whom He is pleased."

15 And it happened that when the angels had gone away from them into heaven, the shepherds *began* saying to one another, "Let us go to Bethlehem then, and see this thing that has happened which the Lord has made known to us."

16 So they went in a hurry and found their way to Mary and Joseph, and the baby lying in the manger.

17 And when they had seen this, they made known the statement which had been told them about this Child.

18 And all who heard it marveled at the things which were told them by the shepherds.

19 But Mary was treasuring all these things, pondering them in her heart.

20 And the shepherds went back, glorifying and praising God for all that they had heard and seen, just as was told them.

Jesus Presented at the Temple

21 And when eight days were fulfilled so that *they* could circumcise Him, His name was called Jesus, the name given by the angel before He was conceived in the womb.

22 And when the days for their cleansing according to the Law of Moses were fulfilled, they brought Him up to Jerusalem to present Him to the Lord

23 (as it is written in the Law of the Lord, "EVERY *firstborn* MALE THAT OPENS THE WOMB SHALL BE CALLED HOLY TO THE LORD"),

24 and to offer a sacrifice according to what was said in the Law of the Lord, "A PAIR OF TURTLEDOVES OR TWO YOUNG PIGEONS."

25 And behold, there was a man in Jerusalem whose name was Simeon, and this man was righteous and devout, waiting for the comfort of Israel, and the Holy Spirit was upon him.

26 And it had been revealed to him by the Holy Spirit that he would not see death before he had seen the Lord's Christ.

27 And he came in the Spirit into the temple, and when the parents brought in the child Jesus to carry out for Him the custom of the Law,

28 then he took Him into his arms and blessed God, and said,

29 "Now Master, You are releasing Your slave in peace,
According to Your word.

30 For my eyes have seen Your salvation,

31 Which You prepared in the presence of all peoples,

32 A LIGHT FOR REVELATION TO THE GENTILES,
And for the glory of Your people Israel."

33 And His father and mother were marveling at the things which were being said about Him.

34 And Simeon blessed them and said to Mary His mother, "Behold, this *Child* is appointed for the fall and rise of many in Israel, and for a sign to be opposed—

35 and a sword will pierce through your own soul as well—that the thoughts from many hearts may be revealed."

36 And there was a prophetess, Anna the daughter of Phanuel, of the tribe of Asher. She was advanced in years having lived with *her* husband seven years from *when she was* a virgin,

37 and then as a widow to the age of eighty-four. She never left the temple, serving night and day with fastings and prayers.

38 And at that very moment she came up and *began* giving thanks to God, and continued to speak of Him to all those who were waiting for the redemption of Jerusalem.

The Return to Nazareth

39 And when they had finished everything according to the Law of the Lord, they returned to Galilee, to their own city of Nazareth.

40 Now the Child continued to grow and become strong, being filled with wisdom; and the grace of God was upon Him.

The Boy Jesus in the Temple

41 And His parents would go to Jerusalem every year at the Feast of the Passover.

42 And when He became twelve years *old*, they went up *there* according to the custom of the Feast;

43 and as they were returning, after finishing the days *of the Feast*, the boy Jesus stayed behind in Jerusalem. But His parents did not know.

44 But supposing Him to be in the caravan, they went a day's journey, and

they *began* searching for Him among their relatives and acquaintances.

45 When they did not find Him, they returned to Jerusalem searching for Him.

46 And it happened that after three days they found Him in the temple, sitting in the midst of the teachers, both listening to them and asking them questions.

47 And all who heard Him were astounded at His understanding and His answers.

48 When they saw Him, they were astonished, and His mother said to Him, "Child, why have You treated us this way? Behold, Your father and I have been anxiously searching for You."

49 And He said to them, "Why is it that you were searching for Me? Did you not know that I had to be in My Father's *house*?"

50 But they did not understand the statement which He had spoken to them.

51 And He went down with them and came to Nazareth, and He continued in subjection to them, and His mother was treasuring all *these* things in her heart.

52 And Jesus was advancing in wisdom and stature, and in favor with God and men.

CHAPTER 3

The Preaching of John the Baptist

NOW in the fifteenth year of the reign of Tiberius Caesar, when Pontius Pilate was governor of Judea, and Herod was tetrarch of Galilee, and his brother Philip was tetrarch of the region of Ituraea and Trachonitis, and Lysanias was tetrarch of Abilene,

2 during the high priesthood of Annas and Caiaphas, the word of God came to John, the son of Zechariah, in the wilderness.

3 And he came into all the district around the Jordan, preaching a baptism of repentance for the forgiveness of sins;

4 as it is written in the book of the words of Isaiah the prophet,

"THE VOICE OF ONE CRYING IN THE
    WILDERNESS,
'MAKE READY THE WAY OF
    THE LORD,
MAKE HIS PATHS STRAIGHT.
5 'EVERY RAVINE WILL BE FILLED,
AND EVERY MOUNTAIN AND HILL
    WILL BE BROUGHT LOW;
THE CROOKED WILL BE STRAIGHT,
AND THE ROUGH ROADS SMOOTH.
6 AND ALL FLESH WILL SEE THE
    SALVATION OF GOD.'"

7 So he was saying to the crowds who were going out to be baptized by him, "You brood of vipers, who warned you to flee from the wrath to come?

8 "Therefore bear fruits in keeping with repentance, and do not begin to say to yourselves, 'We have Abraham for our father,' for I say to you that from these stones God is able to raise up children to Abraham.

9 "But indeed the axe is already laid at the root of the trees; therefore,

every tree that does not bear good fruit is cut down and thrown into the fire."

10 And the crowds were questioning him, saying, "Then what should we do?"

11 And he would answer and say to them, "The man who has two tunics is to share with him who has none; and he who has food is to do likewise."

12 And tax collectors also came to be baptized, and they said to him, "Teacher, what should we do?"

13 And he said to them, "Collect no more than what you have been ordered to."

14 And soldiers were also questioning him, saying, "What should we also do?" And he said to them, "Do not take money from anyone by force, or extort *anyone*, and be content with your wages."

15 Now while the people were in a state of expectation and all were reasoning in their hearts about John, as to whether he was the Christ,

16 John answered, saying to them all, "As for me, I baptize you with water, but One is coming who is mightier than I, and I am not fit to untie the strap of His sandals; He will baptize you with the Holy Spirit and fire.

17 "His winnowing fork is in His hand to thoroughly clear His threshing floor and to gather the wheat into His barn, but He will burn up the chaff with unquenchable fire."

18 So with many other exhortations he proclaimed the gospel to the people.

19 But when Herod the tetrarch was reproved by him because of Herodias, his brother's wife, and because of all the wicked things which Herod had done,

20 Herod also added this to them all: he locked John up in prison.

The Baptism of Jesus

21 Now it happened that when all the people were being baptized, Jesus was also baptized, and while He was praying, heaven was opened,

22 and the Holy Spirit descended upon Him in bodily form like a dove, and a voice came out of heaven, "You are My beloved Son, in You I am well-pleased."

The Genealogy of Jesus

23 When He began His ministry, Jesus Himself was about thirty years of age, being, as was supposed, the son of Joseph, the son of Eli,

24 the son of Matthat, the son of Levi, the son of Melchi, the son of Jannai, the son of Joseph,

25 the son of Mattathias, the son of Amos, the son of Nahum, the son of Hesli, the son of Naggai,

26 the son of Maath, the son of Mattathias, the son of Semein, the son of Josech, the son of Joda,

27 the son of Joanan, the son of Rhesa, the son of Zerubbabel, the son of Shealtiel, the son of Neri,

28 the son of Melchi, the son of Addi, the son of Cosam, the son of Elmadam, the son of Er,

29 the son of Joshua, the son of

Eliezer, the son of Jorim, the son of Matthat, the son of Levi,

30 the son of Simeon, the son of Judah, the son of Joseph, the son of Jonam, the son of Eliakim,

31 the son of Melea, the son of Menna, the son of Mattatha, the son of Nathan, the son of David,

32 the son of Jesse, the son of Obed, the son of Boaz, the son of Salmon, the son of Nahshon,

33 the son of Amminadab, the son of Admin, the son of Ram, the son of Hezron, the son of Perez, the son of Judah,

34 the son of Jacob, the son of Isaac, the son of Abraham, the son of Terah, the son of Nahor,

35 the son of Serug, the son of Reu, the son of Peleg, the son of Heber, the son of Shelah,

36 the son of Cainan, the son of Arphaxad, the son of Shem, the son of Noah, the son of Lamech,

37 the son of Methuselah, the son of Enoch, the son of Jared, the son of Mahalaleel, the son of Cainan,

38 the son of Enosh, the son of Seth, the son of Adam, the son of God.

CHAPTER 4

The Temptation of Jesus

NOW Jesus, full of the Holy Spirit, returned from the Jordan and was being led around by the Spirit in the wilderness

2 for forty days, being tempted by the devil. And He ate nothing during those days, and when they had finished, He was hungry.

3 And the devil said to Him, "If You are the Son of God, tell this stone to become bread."

4 And Jesus answered him, "It is written, 'MAN SHALL NOT LIVE ON BREAD ALONE.'"

5 And he led Him up and showed Him all the kingdoms of the world in a moment of time.

6 And the devil said to Him, "I will give You all this dominion and its glory, for it has been handed over to me, and I give it to whomever I wish.

7 "Therefore if You worship before me, it shall all be Yours."

8 And Jesus answered and said to him, "It is written, 'YOU SHALL WORSHIP THE LORD YOUR GOD AND SERVE HIM ONLY.'"

9 And he led Him to Jerusalem and had Him stand on the pinnacle of the temple, and said to Him, "If You are the Son of God, throw Yourself down from here,

10 for it is written,

'HE WILL COMMAND HIS ANGELS
      CONCERNING YOU TO GUARD
      YOU,'

11 and,

'ON *their* HANDS THEY WILL BEAR
      YOU UP,

LEST YOU STRIKE YOUR FOOT
      AGAINST A STONE.'"

12 And Jesus answered and said to him, "It is said, 'YOU SHALL NOT PUT THE LORD YOUR GOD TO THE TEST.'"

13 And when the devil had finished

every temptation, he left Him until an opportune time.

Jesus Begins His Ministry

14 And Jesus returned to Galilee in the power of the Spirit, and news about Him spread through all the surrounding district.

15 And He was teaching in their synagogues, being glorified by all.

Jesus Rejected at Nazareth

16 And He came to Nazareth, where He had been brought up, and, as was His custom, He entered the synagogue on the Sabbath and stood up to read.

17 And the scroll of the prophet Isaiah was handed to Him. And He opened the scroll and found the place where it was written,

18 "THE SPIRIT OF THE LORD IS
  UPON ME,
BECAUSE HE ANOINTED ME TO
  PREACH THE GOSPEL TO THE
  POOR.
HE HAS SENT ME TO PROCLAIM
  RELEASE TO THE CAPTIVES,
AND RECOVERY OF SIGHT TO THE
  BLIND,
TO SET FREE THOSE WHO ARE
  OPPRESSED,
19 TO PROCLAIM THE FAVORABLE
  YEAR OF THE LORD."

20 And He closed the scroll, gave it back to the attendant and sat down, and the eyes of all in the synagogue were fixed on Him.

21 And He began to say to them, "Today this Scripture has been fulfilled in your hearing."

22 And all were speaking well of Him and marveling at the gracious words which were coming forth from His lips, and they were saying, "Is this not Joseph's son?"

23 And He said to them, "No doubt you will quote this proverb to Me, 'Physician, heal yourself! Whatever we heard took place at Capernaum, do also here in your hometown as well.'"

24 And He said, "Truly I say to you, no prophet is welcome in his hometown.

25 "But I say to you in truth, there were many widows in Israel in the days of Elijah, when the sky was shut up for three years and six months, when a great famine came over all the land,

26 and yet Elijah was sent to none of them, but only to Zarephath, *in the land* of Sidon, to a woman who was a widow.

27 "And there were many lepers in Israel in the time of Elisha the prophet, and none of them was cleansed, but only Naaman the Syrian."

28 And all *the people* in the synagogue were filled with rage as they heard these things,

29 and they stood up and drove Him out of the city, and led Him to the edge of the hill on which their city had been built, in order to throw Him down the cliff.

30 But passing through their midst, He went on His way.

Jesus Casts Out an Unclean Demon

31 And He came down to Capernaum, a city of Galilee, and He was teaching them on the Sabbath;

32 and they were amazed at His teaching, for His message was with authority.

33 And in the synagogue there was a man possessed by the spirit of an unclean demon, and he cried out with a loud voice,

34 "Let us alone! What do we have to do with You, Jesus the Nazarene? Have You come to destroy us? I know who You are—the Holy One of God!"

35 But Jesus rebuked it, saying, "Be quiet and come out of him!" And when the demon had thrown him down in the midst *of the people*, it came out of him without doing him any harm.

36 And amazement came upon them all, and they were talking with one another saying, "What is this message? For with authority and power He commands the unclean spirits and they come out."

37 And the report about Him was spreading into every place in the surrounding district.

*Peter's Mother-in-Law and
Many Others Healed*

38 Then He stood up and *left* the synagogue, and entered Simon's home. Now Simon's mother-in-law was suffering from a high fever, and they asked Him to help her.

39 And standing over her, He rebuked the fever, and it left her. Immediately she stood up and *began* waiting on them.

40 And while the sun was setting, all those who had any *who were* sick with various diseases brought them to Him, and laying His hands on each one of them, He was healing them.

41 And demons also were coming out of many, shouting and saying, "You are the Son of God!" But rebuking *them*, He was not allowing them to speak, because they knew Him to be the Christ.

42 When day came, Jesus left and went to a secluded place; and the crowds were eagerly seeking for Him, and came to Him and tried to keep Him from going away from them.

43 But He said to them, "I must proclaim the good news of the kingdom of God to the other cities also, for I was sent for this purpose."

44 So He kept on preaching in the synagogues of Judea.

CHAPTER 5

The First Disciples

NOW it happened that while the crowd was pressing around Him and listening to the word of God, He was standing at the edge of the lake of Gennesaret;

2 and He saw two boats lying at the edge of the lake, and the fishermen, having gotten out of them, were washing their nets.

3 And He got into one of the boats, which was Simon's, and asked him to put out a little way from the land. And He sat down and *began* teaching the crowds from the boat.

4 And when He had finished speaking, He said to Simon, "Put out into

the deep water and let down your nets for a catch."

5 Simon answered and said, "Master, we labored all night and caught nothing, but at Your word, I will let down the nets."

6 And when they had done this, they enclosed a great quantity of fish. And their nets *began to* break;

7 so they signaled to their partners in the other boat for them to come and help them. And they came and filled both of the boats, so that they began to sink.

8 But when Simon Peter saw *this*, he fell down at Jesus' knees, saying, "Go away from me Lord, for I am a sinful man!"

9 For amazement had seized him and all his companions because of the catch of fish which they had taken,

10 and James and John, sons of Zebedee, who were partners with Simon, *were* also likewise *amazed*. And Jesus said to Simon, "Do not fear, from now on you will be catching men."

11 And when they had brought their boats to land, they left everything and followed Him.

Jesus Heals a Leper

12 And it happened that while He was in one of the cities, behold, *there was* a man covered with leprosy; and when he saw Jesus, he fell on his face and begged Him, saying, "Lord, if You are willing, You can make me clean."

13 And He stretched out His hand and touched him, saying, "I am willing; be cleansed." And immediately the leprosy left him.

14 And He directed him to tell no one, "But go and show yourself to the priest and make an offering for your cleansing, just as Moses commanded, as a testimony to them."

15 But the news about Him was spreading even farther, and large crowds were gathering to hear *Him* and to be healed of their sicknesses.

16 But He Himself would *often* slip away to the desolate regions and pray.

Jesus Heals a Paralytic

17 And it happened that one day He was teaching; and there were *some* Pharisees and teachers of the law sitting *there*, who had come from every village of Galilee and Judea and *from* Jerusalem, and the power of the Lord was *present* for Him to perform healing.

18 And behold, *some* men *were* carrying on a stretcher a man who was paralyzed; and they were trying to bring him in and to set him down before Him.

19 But not finding any *way* to bring him in because of the crowd, they went up on the roof and let him down through the tiles with his stretcher, into the middle *of the crowd*, in front of Jesus.

20 And seeing their faith, He said, "Friend, your sins are forgiven you."

21 The scribes and the Pharisees began to reason, saying, "Who is this who speaks blasphemies? Who can forgive sins, but God alone?"

22 But Jesus, knowing their reasonings, answered and said to them, "Why are you reasoning in your hearts?

23 "Which is easier, to say, 'Your sins have been forgiven you,' or to say, 'Get up and walk'?

24 "But, so that you may know that the Son of Man has authority on earth to forgive sins,"—He said to the paralytic—"I say to you, get up, and, picking up your stretcher, go home."

25 And immediately he rose up before them, and picked up what he had been lying on, and went home glorifying God.

26 And astonishment seized them all and they *began* glorifying God; and they were filled with fear, saying, "We have seen remarkable things today."

Levi and Sinners Called

27 And after that He went out and noticed a tax collector named Levi sitting in the tax office, and He said to him, "Follow Me."

28 And he left everything behind, and rose up and *began to* follow Him.

29 And Levi gave a big reception for Him in his house; and there was a great crowd of tax collectors and other *people* who were reclining *at the table* with them.

30 And the Pharisees and their scribes *began* grumbling at His disciples, saying, "Why do you eat and drink with the tax collectors and sinners?"

31 And Jesus answered and said to them, "*It is* not those who are well who need a physician, but those who are sick.

32 "I have not come to call the righteous but sinners to repentance."

33 And they said to Him, "The disciples of John often fast and offer prayers, the *disciples* of the Pharisees also do likewise, but Yours eat and drink."

34 And Jesus said to them, "Can you make the attendants of the bridegroom fast while the bridegroom is with them?

35 "But *the* days will come; and when the bridegroom is taken away from them, then they will fast in those days."

36 And He was also telling them a parable: "No one tears a piece of cloth from a new garment and puts it on an old garment; otherwise he will both tear the new and the piece from the new will not match the old.

37 "And no one puts new wine into old wineskins; otherwise the new wine will burst the skins and it will be spilled out, and the skins will be ruined.

38 "But new wine must be put into fresh wineskins.

39 "And no one, after drinking old *wine* wishes for new; for he says, 'The old is good enough.'"

CHAPTER 6

Lord of the Sabbath

NOW it happened that on a Sabbath He was passing through *some* grainfields, and His disciples were picking and eating the heads of grain, rubbing them in their hands.

2 But some of the Pharisees said, "Why do you do what is not lawful on the Sabbath?"

3 And Jesus answered and said to them, "Have you never read what David did when he was hungry, he and those who were with him,

4 how he entered the house of God, and took and ate the consecrated bread which is not lawful for any to eat except the priests alone, and gave it to his companions?"

5 And He was saying to them, "The Son of Man is Lord of the Sabbath."

Jesus Heals a Man on the Sabbath

6 Now it happened that on another Sabbath He entered the synagogue and was teaching, and there was a man there whose right hand was withered.

7 And the scribes and the Pharisees were watching Him closely *to see* if He heals on the Sabbath, so that they might find *reason* to accuse Him.

8 But He knew what they were thinking, and He said to the man with the withered hand, "Get up and come forward!" And he stood up and came forward.

9 And Jesus said to them, "I ask you, is it lawful to do good or to do harm on the Sabbath, to save a life or to destroy it?"

10 And after looking around at them all, He said to him, "Stretch out your hand!" And he did *so*, and his hand was restored.

11 But they themselves were filled with rage, and were discussing together what they might do to Jesus.

Jesus Appoints the Twelve

12 Now it happened that at this time He went off to the mountain to pray, and He was spending the whole night in prayer to God.

13 And when day came, He called His disciples to Him and chose twelve of them, whom He also named as apostles:

14 Simon, whom He also named Peter, and Andrew his brother; and James and John; and Philip and Bartholomew;

15 and Matthew and Thomas; James *the son* of Alphaeus, and Simon who was called the Zealot;

16 Judas *the son* of James, and Judas Iscariot, who became a traitor.

17 And Jesus came down with them and stood on a level place; and *there was* a large crowd of His disciples, and a great multitude of people from all Judea and Jerusalem and the coastal region of Tyre and Sidon,

18 who had come to hear Him and to be healed of their diseases; and those who were troubled with unclean spirits were being cured.

19 And all the crowd was trying to touch Him, for power was coming from Him and healing *them* all.

The Beatitudes

20 And turning His gaze toward His disciples, He *began to* say, "Blessed *are* the poor, for yours is the kingdom of God.

21 "Blessed *are* those who hunger now, for you shall be satisfied. Blessed *are* those who cry now, for you shall laugh.

22 "Blessed are you when men hate you, and exclude you, and insult you, and scorn your name as evil, for the sake of the Son of Man.

23 "Be glad in that day and leap *for joy,* for behold, your reward is great in heaven. For their fathers were doing the same things to the prophets.

Jesus Pronounces Woes

24 "But woe to you who are rich, for you are receiving your comfort in full.

25 "Woe to you who are well-fed now, for you shall be hungry. Woe *to you* who laugh now, for you shall mourn and cry.

26 "Woe *to you* when all men speak well of you, for their fathers were doing the same things to the false prophets.

Love Your Enemies

27 "But I say to you who hear, love your enemies, do good to those who hate you,

28 bless those who curse you, pray for those who disparage you.

29 "Whoever hits you on the cheek, offer him the other also; and whoever takes away your garment, do not withhold your tunic from him either.

30 "Give to everyone who asks of you, and whoever takes away what is yours, do not demand it back.

31 "And treat others the same way you want them to treat you.

32 "And if you love those who love you, what credit is *that* to you? For even sinners love those who love them.

33 "And if you do good to those who do good to you, what credit is *that* to you? For even sinners do the same.

34 "And if you lend to those from whom you expect to receive, what credit is *that* to you? Even sinners lend to sinners in order to receive back the same *amount.*

35 "But love your enemies, and do good, and lend, expecting nothing in return; and your reward will be great, and you will be sons of the Most High; for He Himself is kind to the ungrateful and evil.

36 "Be merciful, just as your Father is merciful.

Do Not Judge

37 "And do not judge, and you will not be judged; and do not condemn, and you will not be condemned; pardon, and you will be pardoned.

38 "Give, and it will be given to you. They will pour into your lap a good measure—pressed down, shaken together, running over. For by your standard of measure it will be measured to you in return."

39 And He also spoke a parable to them: "Can a blind man guide a blind man? Will they not both fall into a pit?

40 "A student is not above his teacher; but everyone, after he has been fully trained, will be like his teacher.

41 "And why do you look at the

speck that is in your brother's eye, but do not notice the log that is in your own eye?

42 "How can you say to your brother, 'Brother, let me take out the speck that is in your eye,' when you yourself do not see the log that is in your own eye? You hypocrite, first take the log out of your own eye, and then you will see clearly to take out the speck that is in your brother's eye.

43 "For there is no good tree which produces bad fruit, nor, on the other hand, a bad tree which produces good fruit.

44 "For each tree is known by its own fruit. For men do not gather figs from thorns, nor do they pick grapes from a bramble bush.

45 "The good man out of the good treasure of his heart brings forth what is good; and the evil *man* out of the evil *treasure* brings forth what is evil. For his mouth speaks from the abundance of his heart.

Build Your House on the Rock

46 "Now why do you call Me, 'Lord, Lord,' and do not do what I say?

47 "Everyone who comes to Me and hears My words and does them, I will show you whom he is like:

48 he is like a man building a house, who dug and went deep, and laid a foundation on the rock; and when a flood occurred, the river burst against that house and could not shake it, because it had been well built.

49 "But the one who heard and did not do *accordingly*, is like a man who built a house on the ground without any foundation; and the river burst against it and immediately it collapsed, and the ruin of that house was great."

CHAPTER 7

The Centurion's Faith

WHEN He had completed all His words in the hearing of the people, He went to Capernaum.

2 And a centurion's slave, who was highly regarded by him, was sick and about to die.

3 Now when he heard about Jesus, he sent some Jewish elders asking Him to come and save the life of his slave.

4 And when they came to Jesus, they were earnestly pleading with Him, saying, "He is worthy for You to grant this to him;

5 for he loves our nation and it was he who built us our synagogue."

6 Now Jesus was going on His way with them; and when He was not far from the house, the centurion sent friends, saying to Him, "Lord, do not trouble Yourself further, for I am not good enough for You to come under my roof.

7 "For this reason I did not even consider myself worthy to come to You, but *just* say the word, and my servant will be healed.

8 "For I also am a man placed under authority, with soldiers under me; and I say to this one, 'Go!' and he goes, and to another, 'Come!' and he comes, and to my slave, 'Do this!' and he does it."

9 Now when Jesus heard this, He marveled at him. And He turned to the crowd that was following Him and said, "I say to you, not even in Israel have I found such great faith."

10 And when those who had been sent returned to the house, they found the slave in good health.

11 And it happened that soon afterwards He went to a city called Nain, and His disciples were going along with Him, accompanied by a large crowd.

12 Now as He approached the gate of the city, behold, a dead man was being carried out, the only son of his mother, and she was a widow. And a sizeable crowd from the city was with her.

13 And when the Lord saw her, He felt compassion for her and said to her, "Do not cry."

14 And He came up and touched the coffin, and the bearers came to a halt. And He said, "Young man, I say to you, arise!"

15 And the dead man sat up and began to speak. And *Jesus* gave him back to his mother.

16 And fear gripped them all, and they *began* glorifying God, saying, "A great prophet has arisen among us!" and, "God has visited His people!"

17 And this report concerning Him went out all over Judea and in all the surrounding district.

Questions from John the Baptist

18 And the disciples of John reported to him about all these things.

19 Summoning two of his disciples, John sent them to the Lord, saying, "Are You the One who is to come, or should we look for someone else?"

20 When the men came to Him, they said, "John the Baptist has sent us to You, saying, 'Are You the One who is to come, or should we look for someone else?'"

21 At that very time He cured many *people* of diseases and afflictions and evil spirits, and He granted sight to many *who were* blind.

22 And He answered and said to them, "Go and report to John what you have seen and heard: *the* BLIND RECEIVE SIGHT, *the* lame walk, *the* lepers are cleansed, and *the* deaf hear, *the* dead are raised up, *the* POOR HAVE THE GOSPEL PREACHED TO THEM.

23 "Blessed is he who does not take offense at Me."

24 And when the messengers of John had left, He began to speak to the crowds about John, "What did you go out into the wilderness to behold? A reed shaken by the wind?

25 "But what did you go out to see? A man dressed in soft garments? Behold, those who are splendidly clothed and live in luxury are *found* in royal palaces!

26 "But what did you go out to see? A prophet? Yes, I say to you, and even more than a prophet.

27 "This is *the one* about whom it is written,

'BEHOLD, I SEND MY MESSENGER AHEAD OF YOU,
WHO WILL PREPARE YOUR WAY BEFORE YOU.'

28 "I say to you, among those born of women there is no one greater than John; yet he who is least in the kingdom of God is greater than he."

29 And when all the people and the tax collectors heard *this*, they acknowledged God's justice, having been baptized with the baptism of John.

30 But the Pharisees and the scholars of the Law rejected God's purpose for themselves, not having been baptized by John.

31 "To what then shall I compare the men of this generation, and what are they like?

32 "They are like children, sitting in the marketplace and calling to one another, who say, 'We played the flute for you, and you did not dance; we sang a dirge, and you did not cry.'

33 "For John the Baptist has come eating no bread and drinking no wine, and you say, 'He has a demon!'

34 "The Son of Man has come eating and drinking, and you say, 'Behold, a gluttonous man and a drunkard, a friend of tax collectors and sinners!'

35 "Yet wisdom is vindicated by all her children."

36 Now one of the Pharisees was asking Him to eat with him, and He entered the Pharisee's house and reclined *at the table.*

37 And behold, there was a woman in the city who was a sinner. And when she learned that He was reclining *at the table* in the Pharisee's house, she brought an alabaster jar of perfume.

38 And standing behind *Him* at His feet, crying, she began to wet His feet with her tears. And she kept wiping them with the hair of her head, and kissing His feet and anointing them with the perfume.

39 Now when the Pharisee, who had invited Him, saw this, he said to himself, saying, "If this man were a prophet He would know who and what sort of person this woman is who is touching Him, that she is a sinner."

The Parable of Two Debtors

40 And Jesus answered and said to him, "Simon, I have something to say to you." And he replied, "Say it, Teacher."

41 "A moneylender had two debtors: one owed five hundred [1]denarii, and the other fifty.

42 "When they were unable to repay, he graciously forgave them both. So which of them will love him more?"

43 Simon answered and said, "I suppose the one whom he graciously forgave more." And He said to him, "You have judged correctly."

44 And turning toward the woman, He said to Simon, "Do you see this woman? I entered your house; you gave Me no water for My feet, but she has wet My feet with her tears and wiped them with her hair.

45 "You gave Me no kiss; but she, since the time I came in, has not ceased to kiss My feet.

[1] A Roman silver coin, approx. a laborer's daily wage

46 "You did not anoint My head with oil, but she anointed My feet with perfume.

47 "For this reason I say to you, her sins, which are many, have been forgiven, for she loved much. But he who is forgiven little, loves little."

48 Then He said to her, "Your sins have been forgiven."

49 And those who were reclining *at the table* with Him began to say to themselves, "Who is this *man* who even forgives sins?"

50 And He said to the woman, "Your faith has saved you; go in peace."

CHAPTER 8

*Many Women Contribute
to Jesus' Ministry*

AND it happened that soon afterward He was going around from one city and village to another, preaching and proclaiming the good news of the kingdom of God. The twelve were with Him,

2 and *also* some women who had been healed of evil spirits and sicknesses: Mary who was called Magdalene, from whom seven demons had gone out,

3 and Joanna the wife of Chuza, Herod's manager, and Susanna, and many others who were ministering to them from their possessions.

The Parable of the Sower

4 Now when a large crowd was coming together, and those from the various cities were journeying to Him, He spoke by way of a parable:

5 "The sower went out to sow his seed. And as he sowed, some fell beside the road, and it was trampled under foot and the birds of the air ate it up.

6 "And other *seed* fell on rock and as soon as it grew up, it withered away, because it had no moisture.

7 "And other *seed* fell among the thorns, and when the thorns grew up with it, they choked it out.

8 "And other *seed* fell into the good soil; and growing up, it produced a crop one hundred times as great." As He said these things, He would call out, "He who has ears to hear, let him hear."

The Parable of the Sower Explained

9 And His disciples *began* questioning Him as to what this parable meant.

10 And He said, "To you it has been granted to know the mysteries of the kingdom of God, but to the rest *it is* in parables, so that SEEING THEY MAY NOT SEE, AND HEARING THEY MAY NOT UNDERSTAND.

11 "Now the parable is this: the seed is the word of God.

12 "And those beside the road are those who have heard; then the devil comes and takes away the word from their heart, so that they will not believe and be saved.

13 "And those on the rock are those who, when they hear, receive the word with joy, and these have no

root; they believe for a while, and in time of temptation fall away.

14 "And the *seed* which fell among the thorns, these are the ones who have heard, and as they go on their way they are choked with worries and riches and pleasures of life, and do not bear ripe fruit.

15 "But the *seed* in the good soil, these are the ones who have heard the word in an honest and good heart, and hold it fast, and bear fruit with perseverance.

A Lampstand and the Light

16 "Now no one after lighting a lamp covers it with a container or puts it under a bed, but he puts it on a lampstand, so that those who come in may see the light.

17 "For nothing is hidden that will not become evident, nor *anything* secret that will not be known and come to light.

18 "So beware how you listen, for whoever has, to him *more* shall be given; and whoever does not have, even what he thinks he has shall be taken away from him."

Jesus' Mother and Brothers

19 And His mother and brothers came to Him, and they were unable to get to Him because of the crowd.

20 And it was reported to Him, "Your mother and Your brothers are standing outside, wishing to see You."

21 But He answered and said to them, "My mother and My brothers are these who hear the word of God and do it."

Jesus Calms a Storm

22 Now it happened that on one of *those* days He and His disciples got into a boat, and He said to them, "Let us go over to the other side of the lake." So they set sail.

23 But as they were sailing along, He fell asleep, and a windstorm descended on the lake, and they *began to* be swamped and in danger.

24 And they came to Him and woke Him up, saying, "Master, Master, we are perishing!" And He woke up and rebuked the wind and the surging waves, and they stopped, and it became calm.

25 And He said to them, "Where is your faith?" They were fearful and marveled, saying to one another, "Who then is this, that He commands even the winds and the water, and they obey Him?"

Jesus Saves a Man from Many Demons

26 Then they sailed to the region of the Gerasenes, which is opposite Galilee.

27 And when He came out onto the land, a man from the city met Him, one who was possessed with demons and had not put on any garment for a long time, and was not living in a house, but in the tombs.

28 Now seeing Jesus, he cried out and fell before Him, and said in a loud voice, "What do I have to do with You, Jesus, Son of the Most High God? I beg You, do not torment me."

29 For He had commanded the unclean spirit to come out of the man.

For it had seized him many times, and he was bound with chains and shackles, being kept under guard. And *yet* breaking his bonds, he was driven by the demon into the desolate regions.

30 And Jesus asked him, "What is your name?" And he said, "Legion," for many demons had entered him.

31 And they were pleading with Him not to command them to go away into the abyss.

32 Now there was a herd of many swine feeding there on the mountain, and *the demons* pleaded with Him to permit them to enter the swine. And He gave them permission.

33 And when the demons came out of the man, they entered the swine, and the herd rushed down the steep bank into the lake and was drowned.

34 And when the herdsmen saw what had happened, they ran away and reported it in the city and in the countryside.

35 And *the people* went out to see what had happened, and they came to Jesus, and found the man from whom the demons had gone out, sitting down at the feet of Jesus, clothed and in his right mind. And they were afraid.

36 And those who had seen *it* reported to them how the man who was demon-possessed had been saved.

37 And all the people of the country of the Gerasenes and the surrounding district asked Him to leave them, for they were gripped with great fear. And He got into a boat and returned.

38 But the man from whom the demons had gone out was begging Him that he might accompany Him. But He sent him away, saying,

39 "Return to your house and recount what great things God has done for you." So he went away, proclaiming throughout the whole city what great things Jesus had done for him.

Jesus Heals a Woman and Jairus' Daughter

40 And as Jesus returned, the crowd welcomed Him, for they had all been waiting for Him.

41 And behold, there came a man named Jairus, and he was an official of the synagogue. And falling at Jesus' feet, he *began to* plead with Him to come to his house,

42 for he had an only daughter, about twelve years old, and she was dying. But as He went, the crowds were pressing against Him.

43 And a woman who had a hemorrhage for twelve years, and could not be healed by anyone,

44 came up behind Him and touched the fringe of His garment, and immediately her hemorrhage stopped.

45 And Jesus said, "Who is the one who touched Me?" And while they were all denying it, Peter said, "Master, the crowds are surrounding and pressing in on You."

46 But Jesus said, "Someone did touch Me, for I knew that power had gone out of Me."

47 And when the woman saw that she had not escaped notice, she came trembling. And falling down before Him, she declared in the presence of

all the people the reason why she had touched Him and how she had been immediately healed.

48 And He said to her, "Daughter, your faith has saved you; go in peace."

49 While He was still speaking, someone *came from *the house of the synagogue official, saying, "Your daughter has died; do not trouble the Teacher anymore."

50 But when Jesus heard *this*, He answered him, "Do not be afraid *any longer*; only believe, and she will be saved."

51 So when He came to the house, He did not allow anyone to enter with Him, except Peter and John and James, and the girl's father and mother.

52 Now they were all crying and lamenting for her, but He said, "Stop crying, for she has not died, but is asleep."

53 And they *began* laughing at Him, knowing that she had died.

54 He, however, took her by the hand and called, saying, "Child, arise!"

55 And her spirit returned, and she stood up immediately. And He gave orders for *something* to be given her to eat.

56 And her parents were astounded, but He directed them to tell no one what had happened.

CHAPTER 9

The Twelve Disciples Sent Out

AND calling the twelve together, He gave them power and authority over all the demons and to heal diseases.

2 And He sent them out to preach the kingdom of God and to heal the sick.

3 And He said to them, "Take nothing for *your* journey, neither a staff, nor a bag, nor bread, nor money; nor have two tunics apiece.

4 "And whatever house you enter, stay there until you leave that city.

5 "And as for those who do not receive you, as you go out from that city, shake the dust off your feet as a testimony against them."

6 And departing, they were going throughout the villages, proclaiming the gospel and healing everywhere.

7 Now Herod the tetrarch heard of all that was happening, and he was greatly perplexed, because it was said by some that John had risen from the dead,

8 and by some that Elijah had appeared, and by others that one of the prophets of old had risen again.

9 And Herod said, "I myself had John beheaded, but who is this man about whom I hear such things?" And he kept trying to see Him.

10 And when the apostles returned, they recounted to Him all that they had done. Taking them with Him, He slipped away by Himself to a city called Bethsaida.

11 But when the crowds became aware of this, they followed Him; and welcoming them, He *began* speaking to them about the kingdom of God

and curing those who had need of healing.

Jesus Feeds Five Thousand

12 Now the day was ending, and the twelve came and said to Him, "Send the crowd away, that they may go into the surrounding villages and countryside and obtain lodging and find provisions, for here we are in a desolate place."

13 But He said to them, "You give them *something* to eat!" And they said, "We have no more than five loaves and two fish, unless perhaps we go and buy food for all these people."

14 (For there were about five thousand men.) And He said to His disciples, "Have them sit down in groups of about fifty each."

15 And they did so, and had them all sit down.

16 Then He took the five loaves and the two fish, and looking up to heaven, He blessed them. And He broke *them* and kept giving *them* to the disciples to set before the crowd.

17 And they all ate and were satisfied; and the broken pieces which they had left over were picked up, twelve baskets *full*.

Peter Confesses Jesus Is the Christ

18 And it happened that while He was praying alone, the disciples were with Him, and He questioned them, saying, "Who do the crowds say that I am?"

19 And they answered and said, "John the Baptist, and others *say* Elijah, but others, that one of the prophets of old has risen again."

20 And He said to them, "But who do you say that I am?" And Peter answered and said, "The Christ of God."

21 But He warned them and directed *them* not to tell this to anyone,

22 saying, "The Son of Man must suffer many things and be rejected by the elders and chief priests and scribes, and be killed and be raised up on the third day."

Take Up Your Cross

23 And He was saying to *them* all, "If anyone wishes to come after Me, let him deny himself, and take up his cross daily and follow Me.

24 "For whoever wishes to save his life will lose it, but whoever loses his life for My sake, he is the one who will save it.

25 "For what is a man profited if he gains the whole world, and loses or forfeits himself?

26 "For whoever is ashamed of Me and My words, the Son of Man will be ashamed of him when He comes in His glory, and *the glory* of the Father and of the holy angels.

27 "But I say to you truthfully, there are some of those standing here who will not taste death until they see the kingdom of God."

The Transfiguration

28 Now it happened some eight days after these words, that taking along Peter and John and James, He went up on the mountain to pray.

29 And it happened that while He was praying, the appearance of His

face became different, and His clothing *became* white *and* gleaming.

30 And behold, two men were talking with Him, and they were Moses and Elijah,

31 who, appearing in glory, were speaking of His departure which He was about to fulfill at Jerusalem.

32 Now Peter and his companions had been overcome with sleep, but when they were fully awake, they saw His glory and the two men standing with Him.

33 And it happened that as they were leaving Him, Peter said to Jesus, "Master, it is good for us to be here; let us make three booths: one for You, and one for Moses, and one for Elijah"—not realizing what he was saying.

34 While he was saying this, a cloud formed and *began to* overshadow them; and they were afraid as they entered the cloud.

35 Then a voice came out of the cloud, saying, "This is My Son, *My* Chosen One; listen to Him!"

36 And when the voice had spoken, Jesus was found alone. And they kept silent, and reported to no one in those days any of the things which they had seen.

Jesus Casts Out a Demon

37 Now it happened on the next day, that when they came down from the mountain, a large crowd met Him.

38 And behold, a man from the crowd shouted, saying, "Teacher, I beg You to look at my son, for he is my only *one*,

39 and behold, a spirit seizes him, and he suddenly screams, and it throws him into a convulsion with foaming *at the mouth*, and only with difficulty does it leave him, mauling him *as it leaves*.

40 "And I begged Your disciples to cast it out, and they could not."

41 And Jesus answered and said, "You unbelieving and perverse generation, how long shall I be with you and put up with you? Bring your son here."

42 Now while he was still approaching, the demon slammed him *to the ground* and threw him into a convulsion. But Jesus rebuked the unclean spirit and healed the boy and gave him back to his father.

43 And they were all astonished at the majesty of God.

Jesus Foretells His Death and Resurrection

But while everyone was marveling at all that He was doing, He said to His disciples,

44 "Put these words into your ears; for the Son of Man is going to be delivered into the hands of men."

45 But they did not understand this statement, and it was concealed from them so that they would not perceive it, and they were afraid to ask Him about this statement.

Who Is the Greatest?

46 Now an argument started among them as to which of them might be the greatest.

47 But Jesus, knowing what they were thinking in their heart, took a child and stood him by His side,

48 and said to them, "Whoever

receives this child in My name receives Me, and whoever receives Me receives Him who sent Me; for the one who is least among all of you, this is the one who is great."

49 And John answered and said, "Master, we saw someone casting out demons in Your name, and we tried to hinder him because he does not follow along with us."

50 But Jesus said to him, "Do not hinder *him*, for he who is not against you is for you."

51 Now it happened that when the days for Him to be taken up were soon to be fulfilled, He set His face to go to Jerusalem;

52 and He sent messengers on ahead of Him, and they went and entered a village of the Samaritans to make arrangements for Him.

53 But they did not receive Him, because He was journeying with His face toward Jerusalem.

54 And when His disciples James and John saw *this*, they said, "Lord, do You want us to command fire to come down from heaven and consume them?"

55 But He turned and rebuked them, [and said, "You do not know what kind of spirit you are of,

56 for the Son of Man did not come to destroy men's lives, but to save them."] And they went on to another village.

The Cost of Following Jesus

57 And as they were going along the road, someone said to Him, "I will follow You wherever You go."

58 And Jesus said to him, "The foxes have holes and the birds of the air *have* nests, but the Son of Man has nowhere to lay His head."

59 And He said to another, "Follow Me." But he said, "Lord, permit me first to go and bury my father."

60 But He said to him, "Allow the dead to bury their own dead; but as for you, go and proclaim everywhere the kingdom of God."

61 Another also said, "I will follow You, Lord, but first permit me to say farewell to those at home."

62 But Jesus said to him, "No one, after putting his hand to the plow and looking back, is fit for the kingdom of God."

CHAPTER 10

The Seventy Sent Out

NOW after this the Lord appointed seventy others, and sent them in pairs ahead of Him to every city and place where He Himself was going to come.

2 And He was saying to them, "The harvest is plentiful, but the laborers are few; therefore pray earnestly to the Lord of the harvest to send out laborers into His harvest.

3 "Go! Behold, I send you out as lambs in the midst of wolves.

4 "Carry no money belt, no bag, no sandals, and greet no one on the way.

5 "Whatever house you enter, first say, 'Peace be to this house.'

6 "And if a man of peace is there, your peace will rest on him, but if not, it will return to you.

7 "Stay in that house, eating and

drinking what they give you; for the laborer is worthy of his wages. Do not keep moving from house to house.

8 "And whatever city you enter and they receive you, eat what is set before you;

9 and heal those in it who are sick, and say to them, 'The kingdom of God has come near to you.'

10 "But in whatever city you enter and they do not receive you, go out into its streets and say,

11 'Even the dust of your city which clings to our feet we wipe off against you; yet know this, that the kingdom of God is at hand.'

12 "I say to you, it will be more tolerable in that day for Sodom than for that city.

13 "Woe to you, Chorazin! Woe to you, Bethsaida! For if the miracles had been performed in Tyre and Sidon which occurred in you, they would have repented long ago, sitting in sackcloth and ashes.

14 "But it will be more tolerable for Tyre and Sidon in the judgment than for you.

15 "And you, Capernaum, will you be exalted to heaven? You will be brought down to Hades!

16 "The one who listens to you listens to Me, and the one who rejects you rejects Me. And he who rejects Me rejects the One who sent Me."

The Joyful Results

17 Now the seventy returned with joy, saying, "Lord, even the demons are subject to us in Your name."

18 And He said to them, "I was watching Satan fall from heaven like lightning.

19 "Behold, I have given you authority to tread on serpents and scorpions, and over all the power of the enemy, and nothing will injure you.

20 "Nevertheless do not rejoice in this, that the spirits are subject to you, but rejoice that your names are recorded in heaven."

21 At that very time He rejoiced greatly in the Holy Spirit, and said, "I praise You, O Father, Lord of heaven and earth, that You have hidden these things from *the* wise and intelligent and have revealed them to infants. Yes, Father, for this way was well-pleasing in Your sight.

22 "All things have been handed over to Me by My Father, and no one knows who the Son is except the Father, and who the Father is except the Son, and anyone to whom the Son wills to reveal *Him*."

23 And turning to the disciples, He said privately, "Blessed *are* the eyes which see the things you see,

24 for I say to you, that many prophets and kings wished to see the things which you see, and did not see *them*, and to hear the things which you hear, and did not hear *them*."

The Good Samaritan

25 And behold, a scholar of the Law stood up and was putting Him to the test, saying, "Teacher, what shall I do to inherit eternal life?"

26 And He said to him, "What is

written in the Law? How do you read *it*?"

27 And he answered and said, "You SHALL LOVE THE LORD YOUR GOD WITH ALL YOUR HEART, AND WITH ALL YOUR SOUL, AND WITH ALL YOUR STRENGTH, AND WITH ALL YOUR MIND; AND YOUR NEIGHBOR AS YOURSELF."

28 And He said to him, "You have answered correctly; DO THIS AND YOU WILL LIVE."

29 But wishing to justify himself, he said to Jesus, "And who is my neighbor?"

30 Jesus replied and said, "A man was going down from Jerusalem to Jericho, and fell among robbers, and they stripped him and beat him, and went away leaving him half dead.

31 "And a priest happened to be going down on that road, and when he saw him, he passed by on the other side.

32 "Likewise a Levite also, when he came to the place and saw him, passed by on the other side.

33 "But a Samaritan, who was on a journey, came upon him, and when he saw him, he felt compassion.

34 And he came to him and bandaged up his wounds, pouring oil and wine on *them*, and he put him on his own animal, and brought him to an inn and took care of him.

35 "And on the next day he took out two denarii and gave them to the innkeeper and said, 'Take care of him, and whatever more you spend, when I return I will repay you.'

36 "Which of these three do you think proved to be a neighbor to the man who fell into the robbers' *hands*?"

37 And he said, "The one who showed mercy toward him." Then Jesus said to him, "Go and do the same."

Martha and Mary

38 Now as they were traveling along, He entered a village; and a woman named Martha welcomed Him into her home.

39 And she had a sister called Mary, who was also seated at the Lord's feet, listening to His word.

40 But Martha was distracted with all her preparations; and she came up *to Him* and said, "Lord, do You not care that my sister has left me to do all the preparations alone? Then tell her to help me."

41 But the Lord answered and said to her, "Martha, Martha, you are worried and bothered about so many things,

42 but *only* one thing is necessary, for Mary has chosen the good part, which shall not be taken away from her."

CHAPTER 11

The Lord's Prayer

AND it happened that while Jesus was praying in a certain place, after He had finished, one of His disciples said to Him, "Lord, teach us to pray just as John also taught his disciples."

2 And He said to them, "When you pray, say:

'Father, hallowed be Your name.
Your kingdom come.

3 'Give us each day our daily bread.

4 'And forgive us our sins,
For we ourselves also forgive
everyone who is indebted
to us.
And lead us not into
temptation.' "

5 Then He said to them, "Which of you has a friend and will go to him at midnight and say to him, 'Friend, lend me three loaves,

6 for a friend of mine has come to me from a journey, and I have nothing to set before him';

7 and from inside he answers and says, 'Do not bother me; the door has already been shut and my children and I are in bed; I cannot rise up and give you *anything.*'

8 "I tell you, even though he will not arise and give him *anything* because he is his friend, yet because of his persistence he will get up and give him as much as he needs.

9 "So I say to you, ask, and it will be given to you; seek, and you will find; knock, and it will be opened to you.

10 "For everyone who asks, receives; and he who seeks, finds; and to him who knocks, it will be opened.

11 "But what father among you, *if* his son asks for a fish, will give him a snake instead of a fish?

12 "Or, *if his son* asks for an egg, will give him a scorpion?

13 "If you then, being evil, know how to give good gifts to your children, how much more will *your* heavenly Father give the Holy Spirit to those who ask Him?"

A Kingdom Divided

14 And He was casting out a demon, and it was mute. Now it happened that when the demon had gone out, the mute man spoke, and the crowds marveled.

15 But some of them said, "He casts out demons by Beelzebul, the ruler of the demons."

16 And others, testing *Him*, were seeking from Him a sign from heaven.

17 But He knew their thoughts and said to them, "Any kingdom divided against itself is laid waste, and a house *divided* against itself falls.

18 "But if Satan also is divided against himself, how will his kingdom stand? For you say that I cast out demons by Beelzebul.

19 "And if I by Beelzebul cast out demons, by whom do your sons cast them out? For this reason, they will be your judges.

20 "But if I cast out demons by the finger of God, then the kingdom of God has come upon you.

21 "When a strong *man*, fully armed, guards his own house, his possessions are undisturbed.

22 "But when someone stronger than he attacks him and overpowers him, he takes away from him all his armor on which he had relied and distributes his plunder.

23 "He who is not with Me is against

Me and he who does not gather with Me, scatters.

24 "When the unclean spirit goes out of a man, it passes through waterless places seeking rest, and not finding any, it says, 'I will return to my house from which I came.'

25 "And when it comes, it finds it swept and put in order.

26 "Then it goes and takes along seven other spirits more evil than itself, and they go in and live there, and the last state of that man becomes worse than the first."

27 Now it happened that while Jesus was saying these things, one of the women in the crowd raised her voice and said to Him, "Blessed is the womb that bore You and the breasts at which You nursed."

28 But He said, "On the contrary, blessed are those who hear the word of God and keep it."

The Sign of Jonah

29 Now as the crowds were increasing, He began to say, "This generation is a wicked generation; it seeks a sign, and *yet* no sign will be given to it but the sign of Jonah.

30 "For just as Jonah became a sign to the Ninevites, so will the Son of Man be to this generation.

31 "The Queen of the South will rise up at the judgment with the men of this generation and condemn them, because she came from the ends of the earth to hear the wisdom of Solomon. And behold, something greater than Solomon is here.

32 "The men of Nineveh will stand up at the judgment with this generation and condemn it, because they repented at the preaching of Jonah. And behold, something greater than Jonah is here.

33 "No one, after lighting a lamp, puts it away in a cellar nor under a basket, but on the lampstand, so that those who enter may see the light.

34 "The eye is the lamp of your body; when your eye is clear, your whole body also is full of light, but when it is bad, your body also is full of darkness.

35 "Therefore watch out that the light in you is not darkness.

36 "If therefore your whole body is full of light, with no dark part in it, it will be wholly illumined, as when the lamp illumines you with its rays."

Woes to the Pharisees and Lawyers

37 Now when He had spoken, a Pharisee *asked Him to have a meal with him. And He went in and reclined *at the table*.

38 But when the Pharisee saw it, he marveled that He had not first ceremonially washed before the meal.

39 But the Lord said to him, "Now you Pharisees clean the outside of the cup and of the platter, but inside of you, you are full of robbery and wickedness.

40 "You foolish ones, did not He who made the outside make the inside also?

41 "But give that which is within as

charity, and then all things are clean for you.

42 "But woe to you Pharisees! For you pay tithe of mint and rue and every *kind of* garden herb, and *yet* disregard justice and the love of God, but these are the things you should have done without neglecting the others.

43 "Woe to you Pharisees! For you love the best seat in the synagogues and the respectful greetings in the marketplaces.

44 "Woe to you! For you are like concealed tombs, and the people who walk over *them* are unaware *of it*."

45 Now one of the scholars of the Law answered and said to Him, "Teacher, when You say these things, You insult us too."

46 But He said, "Woe to you scholars of the Law as well! For you weigh men down with burdens hard to bear, and you yourselves will not even touch the burdens with one of your fingers.

47 "Woe to you! For you build the tombs of the prophets, but your fathers killed them.

48 "So you are witnesses and approve the deeds of your fathers; because it was they who killed them, and you build *their tombs*.

49 "For this reason also the wisdom of God said, 'I will send to them prophets and apostles, and *some* of them they will kill and *some* they will persecute,

50 so that the blood of all the prophets, shed since the foundation of the world, may be charged against this generation,

51 from the blood of Abel to the blood of Zechariah, who was killed between the altar and the house *of God*; yes, I tell you, it shall be charged against this generation.'

52 "Woe to you, scholars of the Law! For you have taken away the key of knowledge; you yourselves did not enter, and you hindered those who were entering."

53 And when He left there, the scribes and the Pharisees began to be very hostile and to question Him closely on many subjects,

54 plotting to catch Him in something He might say.

CHAPTER 12

Fear Only God

AT this time, after so many thousands of the crowd had gathered together that they were trampling on one another, He began saying to His disciples first, "Be on your guard for the leaven of the Pharisees, which is hypocrisy.

2 "But there is nothing covered up that will not be revealed, and hidden that will not be known.

3 "Accordingly, whatever you have said in the dark will be heard in the light, and what you have whispered in the inner rooms will be proclaimed upon the housetops.

4 "But I say to you, My friends, do not fear those who kill the body and after that have no more that they can do.

5 "But I will show you whom to fear: fear the One who, after He has killed, has authority to cast into hell; yes, I tell you, fear Him!

6 "Are not five sparrows sold for two [1]assaria? *Yet* not one of them is forgotten before God.

7 "Indeed, the *very* hairs of your head are all numbered. Do not fear; you are more valuable than many sparrows.

Blasphemy Against the Holy Spirit

8 "And I say to you, everyone who confesses Me before men, the Son of Man will confess him also before the angels of God,

9 but he who denies Me before men will be denied before the angels of God.

10 "And everyone who speaks a word against the Son of Man, it will be forgiven him, but he who blasphemes against the Holy Spirit, it will not be forgiven him.

11 "Now when they bring you before the synagogues and the rulers and the authorities, do not worry about how or what you are to speak in your defense, or what you are to say,

12 for the Holy Spirit will teach you in that very hour what you ought to say."

The Parable of the Rich Fool

13 And someone from the crowd said to Him, "Teacher, tell my brother to divide the *family* inheritance with me."

14 But He said to him, "Man, who appointed Me a judge or arbitrator over you?"

15 Then He said to them, "Watch out and be on your guard against every form of greed, for not *even* when one has an abundance does his life consist of his possessions."

16 And He told them a parable, saying, "The land of a rich man was very productive.

17 "And he *began* reasoning to himself, saying, 'What shall I do, since I have no place to store my crops?'

18 "Then he said, 'This is what I will do: I will tear down my barns and build larger ones, and there I will store all my grain and my goods.

19 'And I will say to my soul, "Soul, you have many goods laid up for many years *to come*; take your ease, eat, drink *and* be merry." '

20 "But God said to him, 'You fool! This *very* night your soul is required of you; and *now* who will own what you prepared?'

21 "So is the one who stores up treasure for himself, and is not rich toward God."

Do Not Worry

22 And He said to His disciples, "For this reason I say to you, do not worry about *your* life, *as to* what you will eat; nor for your body, *as to* what you will put on.

---

[1] A Roman copper coin, approx. 1/16 of a laborer's daily wage

23 "For life is more than food, and the body more than clothing.

24 "Consider the ravens, for they neither sow nor reap; they have no storeroom nor barn, and *yet* God feeds them; how much more valuable you are than the birds!

25 "And which of you by worrying can add a *single* ¹cubit to his life span?

26 "Therefore, if you cannot do even a very little thing, why do you worry about other matters?

27 "Consider the lilies, how they grow: they neither toil nor spin, but I tell you, not even Solomon in all his glory clothed himself like one of these.

28 "But if God so clothes the grass in the field, which is *alive* today and tomorrow is thrown into the furnace, how much more *will He clothe* you? You of little faith!

29 "And do not seek what you will eat and what you will drink, and do not keep worrying.

30 "For all these things the nations of the world eagerly seek, but your Father knows that you need these things.

31 "But seek His kingdom, and these things will be added to you.

32 "Do not fear, little flock, for your Father is well pleased to give you the kingdom.

33 "Sell your possessions and give *it* as charity; make yourselves money belts which do not wear out, an unfailing treasure in heaven, where no thief comes near nor moth destroys.

34 "For where your treasure is, there your heart will be also.

Be Ready for His Coming

35 "GIRD UP YOUR LOINS, and *keep* your lamps lit.

36 "And be like men who are waiting for their master when he returns from the wedding feast, so that they may immediately open *the door* to him when he comes and knocks.

37 "Blessed are those slaves whom the master will find awake when he comes; truly I say to you, that he will gird himself *to serve*, and have them recline *at the table*, and will come up and wait on them.

38 "Whether he comes in the second watch, or even in the third, and finds *them* so, blessed are those *slaves*.

39 "But be sure of this, that if the head of the house had known at what hour the thief was coming, he would not have allowed his house to be broken into.

40 "You too, be ready, for the Son of Man is coming at an hour that you do not expect."

41 Now Peter said, "Lord, are You addressing this parable to us, or to everyone *else* as well?"

42 And the Lord said, "Who then is the faithful and prudent steward, whom his master will put in charge of his servants, to give them their rations at the proper time?

43 "Blessed is that slave whom his master finds so doing when he comes.

¹ A cubit was approx. 18 in. or 45 cm

44 "Truly I say to you that he will put him in charge of all his possessions.

45 "But if that slave says in his heart, 'My master will be a long time in coming,' and begins to beat the male and female servants, and to eat and drink and get drunk,

46 the master of that slave will come on a day when he does not expect and at an hour he does not know, and will cut him in pieces, and assign him a place with the unbelievers.

47 "And that slave who knew his master's will and did not get ready or act in accord with his will, will receive many beatings,

48 but the one who did not know it, and committed deeds worthy of a beating, will receive but a few. From everyone who has been given much, much will be required, and to whom they entrusted much, of him they will ask all the more.

Not Peace, but Division

49 "I have come to cast fire upon the earth, and how I wish it were already kindled!

50 "But I have a baptism to undergo, and how distressed I am until it is finished!

51 "Do you think that I came to grant peace on earth? I tell you, no, but rather division;

52 for from now on five *members* in one household will be divided, three against two and two against three.

53 "They will be divided, father against son and son against father, mother against daughter and daughter against mother, mother-in-law against her daughter-in-law and daughter-in-law against mother-in-law."

54 And He was also saying to the crowds, "When you see a cloud rising in the west, immediately you say, 'A shower is coming,' and so it happens.

55 "And when *you see* a south wind blowing, you say, 'It will be a hot day,' and it happens.

56 "You hypocrites! You know how to examine the appearance of the earth and the sky, but why do you not examine this present time?

57 "And why do you not even judge for yourselves what is right?

58 "For while you are going with your opponent to appear before the magistrate, on *your* way *there* make an effort to settle with him, so that he may not drag you before the judge, and the judge turn you over to the officer, and the officer throw you into prison.

59 "I say to you, you will not get out of there until you have paid the last ¹lepton."

CHAPTER 13

Repent or Perish

NOW at that same time there were some present who were reporting to Him about the Galileans whose

¹ Smallest Greek copper coin, approx. 1/128 of a laborer's daily wage

blood Pilate had mixed with their sacrifices.

2 And Jesus answered and said to them, "Do you think that these Galileans were *greater* sinners than all *other* Galileans because they suffered these things?

3 "I tell you, no, but unless you repent, you will all likewise perish.

4 "Or do you think that those eighteen on whom the tower in Siloam fell and killed them were *worse* offenders than all the men who live in Jerusalem?

5 "I tell you, no, but unless you repent, you will all likewise perish."

The Parable of the Barren Fig Tree

6 And He was telling this parable: "A man had a fig tree which had been planted in his vineyard; and he came seeking fruit on it and did not find any.

7 "And he said to the vineyard-keeper, 'Behold, for three years I have come seeking fruit on this fig tree without finding any. Cut it down! Why does it even use up the ground?'

8 "And he answered and said to him, 'Let it alone, sir, for this year too, until I dig around it and put in manure,

9 and if it bears fruit next year, *fine*, but if not, cut it down.'"

A Woman Healed on the Sabbath

10 And He was teaching in one of the synagogues on the Sabbath.

11 And behold, there was a woman who for eighteen years had a sickness caused by a spirit, and she was bent double, and could not straighten up at all.

12 But when Jesus saw her, He called her over and said to her, "Woman, you are freed from your sickness."

13 And He laid His hands on her, and immediately she was made erect again and *began* glorifying God.

14 But the synagogue official, indignant because Jesus healed on the Sabbath, answered and was saying to the crowd, "There are six days in which work should be done; so come during them and get healed, and not on the Sabbath day."

15 But the Lord answered him and said, "You hypocrites, does not each of you on the Sabbath release his ox or his donkey from the stall and lead it away to water *it*?

16 "And this woman, being a daughter of Abraham, whom Satan has bound for—behold—eighteen years, should she not have been released from this bond on the Sabbath day?"

17 And as He said this, all His opponents were being put to shame; and the entire crowd was rejoicing over all the glorious things being done by Him.

The Parables of the Mustard Seed and the Leaven

18 Therefore, He was saying, "What is the kingdom of God like, and to what shall I compare it?

19 "It is like a mustard seed, which a man took and threw into his own garden, and it grew and became a tree, and THE BIRDS OF THE AIR NESTED IN ITS BRANCHES."

20 And again He said, "To what shall I compare the kingdom of God?

21 "It is like leaven, which a woman took and hid in ¹three sata of flour until it was all leavened."

The Narrow Door

22 And He was passing through from one city and village to another, teaching, and proceeding on His way to Jerusalem.

23 And someone said to Him, "Lord, are there *just* a few who are being saved?" And He said to them,

24 "Strive to enter through the narrow door, for many, I tell you, will seek to enter and will not be able.

25 "Once the head of the house gets up and shuts the door, and you begin to stand outside and knock on the door, saying, 'Lord, open up to us!' then He will answer and say to you, 'I do not know where you are from.'

26 "Then you will begin to say, 'We ate and drank in Your presence, and You taught in our streets'.

27 And He will say, 'I tell you, I do not know where you are from; DE-PART FROM ME, ALL YOU WORKERS OF UNRIGHTEOUSNESS.'

28 "In that place there will be weeping and gnashing of teeth when you see Abraham and Isaac and Jacob and all the prophets in the kingdom of God, but yourselves being cast out.

29 "And they will come from east and west and from north and south, and will recline *at the table* in the kingdom of God.

30 "And behold, *some* are last who will be first and *some* are first who will be last."

Lament over Jerusalem

31 Just at that time some Pharisees approached, saying to Him, "Leave and go from here, for Herod wants to kill You."

32 And He said to them, "Go and tell that fox, 'Behold, I cast out demons and perform cures today and tomorrow, and on the third *day* I finish.'

33 "Nevertheless I must journey on today and tomorrow and the next *day*, for it is not possible that a prophet would perish outside of Jerusalem.

34 "O Jerusalem, Jerusalem, *the city* that kills the prophets and stones those sent to her! How often I wanted to gather your children together, just as a hen *gathers* her brood under her wings, and you did not want *it*!

35 "Behold, your house is left to you *desolate*, and I say to you, you will not see Me until *the time* comes when you say, 'BLESSED IS HE WHO COMES IN THE NAME OF THE LORD!'"

CHAPTER 14

Jesus Heals on the Sabbath

AND it happened that when He went into the house of one of the leaders

---

¹ Approx. 48 lb. or 39 l, a saton was approx. 16 lb. or 13 l

of the Pharisees on *the* Sabbath to eat bread, they were watching Him closely.

2 And behold, in front of Him was a man suffering from dropsy.

3 And Jesus answered and spoke to the scholars of the Law and Pharisees, saying, "Is it lawful to heal on the Sabbath, or not?"

4 But they were silent. And He took hold of him, healed him, and sent him away.

5 And He said to them, "Which one of you will have a son or an ox fall into a well, and will not immediately pull him out on a Sabbath day?"

6 And they could make no reply to this.

The Parable of the Wedding Feast

7 And He was telling a parable to the invited guests when He noticed how they were picking out the places of honor *at the table,* saying to them,

8 "When you are invited by someone to a wedding feast, do not recline at the place of honor, lest someone more highly regarded than you be invited by him,

9 and he who invited you both will come and say to you, 'Give *your* place to this man,' and then in shame you proceed to occupy the last place.

10 "But when you are invited, go and recline at the last place, so that when the one who has invited you comes, he may say to you, 'Friend, move up higher'; then you will have honor in the sight of all who recline at the table with you.

11 "For everyone who exalts himself will be humbled, and he who humbles himself will be exalted."

12 And He also went on to say to the one who had invited Him, "When you give a luncheon or a dinner, do not invite your friends or your brothers or your relatives or rich neighbors, lest they also invite you in return and *that* will be your repayment.

13 "But when you give a reception, invite the poor, *the* crippled, *the* lame, *the* blind,

14 and you will be blessed, since they do not have *the means* to repay you; for it will be repaid to you at the resurrection of the righteous."

15 But when one of those who were reclining *at the table* with Him heard this, he said to Him, "Blessed is everyone who will eat bread in the kingdom of God!"

The Parable of the Dinner

16 And He said to him, "A man was giving a big dinner, and he invited many.

17 And at the dinner hour he sent his slave to say to those who had been invited, 'Come, for everything is ready now.'

18 "But they all alike began to make excuses. The first one said to him, 'I have bought a piece of land and I need to go out and look at it. I ask you, consider me excused.'

19 "And another one said, 'I have bought five yoke of oxen, and I am going to try them out. I ask you, consider me excused.'

20 "And another one said, 'I have married a wife, and for that reason I cannot come.'

21 "And when the slave came *back*, he reported these things to his master. Then the head of the household became angry and said to his slave, 'Go out at once into the streets and lanes of the city and bring in here the poor and crippled and blind and lame.'

22 "And the slave said, 'Master, what you commanded has been done, and still there is room.'

23 "And the master said to the slave, 'Go out into the highways and along the fences, and compel *them* to come in, so that my house may be filled.

24 'For I tell you, none of those men who were invited shall taste of my dinner.'"

The Cost of Discipleship

25 Now many crowds were going along with Him, and He turned and said to them,

26 "If anyone comes to Me, and does not hate his own father and mother and wife and children and brothers and sisters, yes, and even his own life, he cannot be My disciple.

27 "Whoever does not carry his own cross and come after Me cannot be My disciple.

28 "For which one of you, when he wants to build a tower, does not first sit down and calculate the cost to see if he has enough to complete it?

29 "Lest, when he has laid a foundation and is not able to finish, all who observe it begin to ridicule him,

30 saying, 'This man began to build and was not able to finish.'

31 "Or what king, when he sets out to meet another king in battle, will not first sit down and consider whether he is strong enough with ten thousand *men* to encounter the one coming against him with twenty thousand?

32 "Or else, while the other is still far away, he sends a delegation and asks for terms of peace.

33 "So then, none of you can be My disciple who does not give up all his own possessions.

34 "Therefore, salt is good, but if even salt has become tasteless, with what will it be seasoned?

35 "It is useless either for the soil or for the manure pile; it is thrown out. He who has ears to hear, let him hear."

CHAPTER 15

The Parable of the Lost Sheep

NOW all the tax collectors and the sinners were coming near Him to listen to Him.

2 And both the Pharisees and the scribes were grumbling, saying, "This man receives sinners and eats with them."

3 So He told them this parable, saying,

4 "What man among you, if he has one hundred sheep and has lost one of them, does not leave the ninety-nine in the open pasture and go after the one which is lost until he finds it?

5 "And when he has found it, he lays it on his shoulders, rejoicing.

6 "And when he comes home, he calls together his friends and his neighbors, saying to them, 'Rejoice with me, for I have found my sheep which was lost!'

7 "I tell you that in the same way, there will be *more* joy in heaven over one sinner who repents than over ninety-nine righteous persons who need no repentance.

The Parable of the Lost Drachma

8 "Or what woman, if she has ten ¹drachmas and loses one drachma, does not light a lamp and sweep the house and search carefully until she finds it?

9 "And when she has found it, she calls together her friends and neighbors, saying, 'Rejoice with me, for I have found the drachma which I had lost!'

10 "In the same way, I tell you, there is joy in the presence of the angels of God over one sinner who repents."

The Parable of the Prodigal Son

11 And He said, "A man had two sons.

12 "And the younger of them said to his father, 'Father, give me the share of the estate that falls *to me*.' So he divided his wealth between them.

13 "And not many days later, the younger son gathered everything together and went on a journey into a distant country, and there he squandered his estate living recklessly.

14 "Now when he had spent everything, a severe famine occurred in that country, and he began to be impoverished.

15 "So he went and hired himself out to one of the citizens of that country, and he sent him into his fields to feed swine.

16 "And he was desiring to be fed with the pods that the swine were eating, and no one was giving *anything* to him.

17 "But when he came to himself, he said, 'How many of my father's hired men have more than enough bread, but I am dying here with hunger!

18 'I will rise up and go to my father, and will say to him, "Father, I have sinned against heaven, and before you.

19 I am no longer worthy to be called your son; make me as one of your hired men."'

20 "So he rose up and came to his father. But while he was still a long way off, his father saw him and felt compassion, and ran and embraced him and kissed him.

21 "And the son said to him, 'Father, I have sinned against heaven and before you. I am no longer worthy to be called your son.'

22 "But the father said to his slaves, 'Quickly bring out the best robe and put it on him, and put a ring on his hand and sandals on his feet,

23 and bring the fattened calf,

---

¹ A Greek silver coin, approx. a laborer's daily wage

slaughter it, and let us eat and celebrate,

24 for this son of mine was dead and has come to life again; he was lost and has been found.' And they began to celebrate.

25 "Now his older son was in the field, and when he came and approached the house, he heard music and dancing.

26 "And summoning one of the servants, he *began* inquiring what these things could be.

27 "And he said to him, 'Your brother has come, and your father has killed the fattened calf because he has received him back safe and sound.'

28 "But he became angry and was not wanting to go in, and his father came out and *began* pleading with him.

29 "But he answered and said to his father, 'Look! For so many years I have been serving you and never have I neglected a command of yours. And *yet* never have you given me a young goat, so that I might celebrate with my friends.

30 But when this son of yours came, who has devoured your wealth with prostitutes, you killed the fattened calf for him.'

31 "And he said to him, 'Child, you are always with me, and all that is mine is yours.

32 But we had to celebrate and rejoice, for this brother of yours was dead and is alive, and *was* lost and has been found.'"

CHAPTER 16

The Parable of the Unrighteous Steward

NOW He was also saying to the disciples, "There was a rich man who had a steward, and this *steward* was reported to him as squandering his possessions.

2 "And he called for him and said to him, 'What is this I hear about you? Give an accounting of your stewardship, for you can no longer be steward.'

3 "And the steward said to himself, 'What shall I do, since my master is taking the stewardship away from me? I am not strong enough to dig; I am ashamed to beg.

4 'I know what I shall do, so that when I am removed from the stewardship people will take me into their homes.'

5 "And he summoned each one of his master's debtors, and he *began* saying to the first, 'How much do you owe my master?'

6 "And he said, 'One hundred ¹baths of oil.' And he said to him, 'Take your bill, and sit down quickly and write fifty.'

7 "Then he said to another, 'And how much do you owe?' And he said, 'One hundred ²kors of wheat.' He *said to him, 'Take your bill, and write eighty.'

8 "And his master praised the unrighteous steward because he had acted shrewdly, for the sons of this

---

¹ A bath was approx. 6 gal. or 23 l ² A kor was approx. 6.5 bu. or 230 l

age are more shrewd in relation to their own kind than the sons of light.

9 "And I say to you, make friends for yourselves from the wealth of unrighteousness, so that when it fails, they will take you into the eternal dwellings.

10 "He who is faithful in a very little thing is faithful also in much, and he who is unrighteous in a very little thing is unrighteous also in much.

11 "Therefore if you have not been faithful in the *use of* unrighteous wealth, who will entrust the true *riches* to you?

12 "And if you have not been faithful in *the use of* that which is another's, who will give you that which is your own?

13 "No servant can serve two masters; for either he will hate the one and love the other, or else he will be devoted to one and despise the other. You cannot serve God and wealth."

14 Now the Pharisees, who were lovers of money, were listening to all these things and were scoffing at Him.

15 And He said to them, "You are those who justify yourselves in the sight of men, but God knows your hearts, for that which is highly esteemed among men is detestable in the sight of God.

16 "The Law and the Prophets were until John; since that time the good news of the kingdom of God is proclaimed, and everyone is forcing his way into it.

17 "But it is easier for heaven and earth to pass away than for one stroke of a letter of the Law to fail.

18 "Everyone who divorces his wife and marries another commits adultery, and he who marries a woman who is divorced from a husband commits adultery.

The Rich Man and Lazarus

19 "Now there was a rich man, and he habitually dressed in purple and fine linen, joyously living in splendor every day.

20 "But a poor man named Lazarus was laid at his gate, covered with sores,

21 and desiring to be fed with the *crumbs* which were falling from the rich man's table; besides, even the dogs were coming and licking his sores.

22 "Now it happened that the poor man died and was carried away by the angels to Abraham's bosom, and the rich man also died and was buried.

23 "And in Hades he lifted up his eyes, being in torment, and *saw Abraham far away and Lazarus in his bosom.

24 "And he cried out and said, 'Father Abraham, have mercy on me, and send Lazarus so that he may dip the tip of his finger in water and cool off my tongue, for I am in agony in this flame.'

25 "But Abraham said, 'Child, remember that during your life you received your good things, and likewise Lazarus bad things. But now he is being comforted here, and you are in agony.

26 'And besides all this, between us and you there is a great chasm fixed,

so that those who wish to come over from here to you are not able, and none may cross over from there to us.'

27 "And he said, 'Then I am asking you, father, that you send him to my father's house—

28 for I have five brothers—in order that he may warn them, so that they will not also come to this place of torment.'

29 "But Abraham *said, 'They have Moses and the Prophets; let them hear them.'

30 "But he said, 'No, father Abraham, but if someone goes to them from the dead, they will repent!'

31 "But he said to him, 'If they do not listen to Moses and the Prophets, they will not be persuaded even if someone rises from the dead.'"

CHAPTER 17

Do All Which Jesus Commands

NOW He said to His disciples, "It is inevitable that stumbling blocks come, but woe to him through whom they come!

2 "It would be better for him if a millstone were hung around his neck and he were thrown into the sea, than that he would cause one of these little ones to stumble.

3 "Be on your guard! If your brother sins, rebuke him; and if he repents, forgive him.

4 "And if he sins against you seven times a day, and returns to you seven times, saying, 'I repent,' forgive him."

5 And the apostles said to the Lord, "Increase our faith!"

6 And the Lord said, "If you have faith like a mustard seed, you would say to this mulberry tree, 'Be uprooted and be planted in the sea'; and it would obey you.

7 "But which of you, having a slave plowing or tending sheep, will say to him when he has come in from the field, 'Come immediately and sit down to eat'?

8 "But will he not say to him, 'Prepare something for me to eat, and, clothing yourself *properly*, serve me while I eat and drink; and afterward you may eat and drink'?

9 "Is he grateful to the slave because he did the things which were commanded?

10 "In this way, you also, when you do all the things which are commanded of you, say, 'We are unworthy slaves; we have done *only* that which we ought to have done.'"

Jesus Cleanses Ten Lepers

11 And it happened that while He was on the way to Jerusalem, He was passing through Samaria and Galilee.

12 And as He entered a village, ten leprous men who stood at a distance met Him.

13 And they raised their voices, saying, "Jesus, Master, have mercy on us!"

14 When He saw them, He said to them, "Go and show yourselves to the priests." And it happened that as they were going, they were cleansed.

15 Now one of them, when he saw

that he had been healed, turned back, glorifying God with a loud voice,

16 and he fell on his face at His feet, giving thanks to Him. And he was a Samaritan.

17 Then Jesus answered and said, "Were there not ten cleansed? But the nine—where are they?

18 "Was there no one found who turned back to give glory to God, except this foreigner?"

19 And He said to him, "Stand up and go; your faith has saved you."

20 Now having been questioned by the Pharisees as to when the kingdom of God was coming, He answered them and said, "The kingdom of God is not coming with *signs to be* observed,

21 nor will they say, 'Look, here!' or, 'There!' For behold, the kingdom of God is in your midst."

The Coming of the Son of Man

22 And He said to the disciples, "The days will come when you will long to see one of the days of the Son of Man, and you will not see it.

23 "And they will say to you, 'Look there! Look here!' Do not go away, and do not run after *them.*

24 "For just like the lightning, when it flashes out of one part of the sky, shines to the other part of the sky, so will the Son of Man be in His day.

25 "But first He must suffer many things and be rejected by this generation.

26 "And just as it was in the days of Noah, so it will be also in the days of the Son of Man:

27 they were eating, they were drinking, they were marrying, they were being given in marriage, until the day that Noah entered the ark, and the flood came and destroyed them all.

28 "It was the same as in the days of Lot—they were eating, they were drinking, they were buying, they were selling, they were planting, they were building;

29 but on the day that Lot went out from Sodom it rained fire and brimstone from heaven and destroyed them all.

30 "It will be just the same on the day that the Son of Man is revealed.

31 "On that day, the one who is on the housetop and whose goods are in the house must not go down to take them out, and likewise the one who is in the field must not turn back.

32 "Remember Lot's wife.

33 "Whoever seeks to keep his life will lose it, and whoever loses *his life* will preserve it.

34 "I tell you, on that night there will be two in one bed; one will be taken and the other will be left.

35 "There will be two women grinding *grain* at the same place; one will be taken and the other will be left.

36 ["Two men will be in the field; one will be taken and the other will be left."]

37 And answering they *said to Him, "Where, Lord?" And He said to them, "Where the body *is,* there also the vultures will be gathered."

CHAPTER 18

The Parables on Prayer

NOW He was telling them a parable to show that at all times they ought to pray and not to lose heart,

2 saying, "In a certain city there was a certain judge who did not fear God and did not respect man.

3 "Now there was a widow in that city, and she kept coming to him, saying, 'Give me justice from my opponent.'

4 "And for a while he was unwilling; but afterward he said to himself, 'Even though I do not fear God nor respect man,

5 yet because this widow is bothering me, I will give her justice, lest by continually coming she wears me out.'"

6 And the Lord said, "Hear what the unjust judge *said.

7 Now, will God not bring about justice for His elect who cry to Him day and night, and will He delay long over them?

8 "I tell you that He will bring about justice for them quickly. However, when the Son of Man comes, will He find that faith on the earth?"

9 And He also told this parable to some people who trusted in themselves that they were righteous, and viewed others with contempt:

10 "Two men went up into the temple to pray, one a Pharisee and the other a tax collector.

11 "The Pharisee stood and was praying these things to himself: 'God, I thank You that I am not like other people: swindlers, unjust, adulterers, or even like this tax collector.

12 'I fast twice a week; I pay tithes of all that I get.'

13 "But the tax collector, standing some distance away, was even unwilling to lift up his eyes to heaven, but was beating his chest, saying, 'God, be merciful to me, the sinner!'

14 "I tell you, this man went down to his house justified rather than the other, for everyone who exalts himself will be humbled, but he who humbles himself will be exalted."

15 And they were bringing even their babies to Him so that He would touch them, but when the disciples saw it, they were rebuking them.

16 But Jesus called for them, saying, "Permit the children to come to Me, and do not hinder them, for the kingdom of God belongs to such as these.

17 "Truly I say to you, whoever does not receive the kingdom of God like a child will never enter it."

The Rich Young Ruler

18 And a ruler questioned Him, saying, "Good Teacher, what shall I do to inherit eternal life?"

19 And Jesus said to him, "Why do you call Me good? No one is good except God alone.

20 "You know the commandments, 'DO NOT COMMIT ADULTERY, DO NOT MURDER, DO NOT STEAL, DO NOT BEAR

FALSE WITNESS, HONOR YOUR FATHER AND MOTHER.'"

21 And he said, "All these things I have kept from *my* youth."

22 And when Jesus heard *this*, He said to him, "One thing you still lack: sell all that you possess and distribute it to the poor, and you shall have treasure in heaven. And come, follow Me."

23 But when he heard these things, he became very sad, for he was extremely rich.

24 And Jesus looked at him and said, "How hard it is for those who are wealthy to enter the kingdom of God!

25 "For it is easier for a camel to go through the eye of a needle than for a rich man to enter the kingdom of God."

26 And those who heard it said, "Then who can be saved?"

27 But He said, "The things that are impossible with people are possible with God."

28 And Peter said, "Behold, we have left *all that is* our own and followed You."

29 And He said to them, "Truly I say to you, there is no one who has left house or wife or brothers or parents or children, for the sake of the kingdom of God,

30 who will not receive many times more at this time and in the age to come, eternal life."

31 But when He took the twelve aside, He said to them, "Behold, we are going up to Jerusalem, and all things which are written through the prophets about the Son of Man will be completed.

32 "For He will be delivered over to the Gentiles, and will be mocked and mistreated and spit upon,

33 and after they have flogged Him, they will kill Him, and the third day He will rise again."

34 But the disciples understood none of these things, and this statement was hidden from them, and they did not comprehend the things that were said.

Bartimaeus Regains His Sight

35 Now it happened that as Jesus was approaching Jericho, a blind man was sitting by the road begging.

36 Now hearing a crowd going by, he *began to* inquire what this was.

37 They reported to him, "Jesus of Nazareth is passing by."

38 And he called out, saying, "Jesus, Son of David, have mercy on me!"

39 And those who went ahead were rebuking him so that he would be quiet, but he kept crying out all the more, "Son of David, have mercy on me!"

40 And Jesus stopped and commanded that he be brought to Him, and when he came near, He questioned him,

41 "What do you want Me to do for you?" And he said, "Lord, *I want* to regain my sight!"

42 And Jesus said to him, "Receive your sight; your faith has saved you."

43 Immediately he regained his sight and *began* following Him, glorifying

God. And when all the people saw it, they gave praise to God.

CHAPTER 19

Zaccheus Is Saved

AND He entered Jericho and was passing through.

2 And behold, there was a man called by the name of Zaccheus; he was a chief tax collector and he was rich.

3 And Zaccheus was trying to see who Jesus was, and was unable because of the crowd, for he was small in stature.

4 So he ran on before and climbed up into a sycamore tree in order to see Him, for He was about to pass through that way.

5 And when Jesus came to the place, He looked up and said to him, "Zaccheus, hurry and come down, for today I must stay at your house."

6 And he hurried and came down and received Him gladly.

7 And when they saw it, they all *began to* grumble, saying, "He has gone to be the guest of a man who is a sinner."

8 But Zaccheus stopped and said to the Lord, "Behold, half of my possessions, Lord, I will give to the poor, and if I have extorted anyone of anything, I will give back four times as much."

9 And Jesus said to him, "Today salvation has come to this house, because he, too, is a son of Abraham.

10 "For the Son of Man has come to seek and to save the lost."

The Parable of the Ten Minas

11 Now while they were listening to these things, Jesus went on to tell a parable, because He was near Jerusalem, and they thought that the kingdom of God was going to appear immediately.

12 So He said, "A nobleman went to a distant country to receive a kingdom for himself, and *then* return.

13 "And he called ten of his slaves, and gave them ten [1]minas and said to them, 'Engage in business until I come *back*.'

14 "But his citizens hated him and sent a delegation after him, saying, 'We do not want this man to reign over us.'

15 "And it happened that when he returned, after receiving the kingdom, he ordered that these slaves, to whom he had given the money, be called to him so that he might know how much they had made in business.

16 "So the first appeared, saying, 'Master, your mina has made ten minas more.'

17 "And he said to him, 'Well done, good slave, because you have been faithful in a very little thing, you are to be in authority over ten cities.'

18 "Then the second came, saying, 'Your mina, master, has made five minas.'

19 "And he said to him also, 'And you are to be over five cities.'

---

[1] Gr monetary unit worth approx. 100 days of a laborer's wages

20 "Then another came, saying, 'Master, here is your mina, which I kept put away in a cloth;

21 for I was afraid of you, because you are a strict man; you take up what you did not lay down and reap what you did not sow.'

22 "He *said to him, 'From your own mouth I will judge you, you worthless slave. Did you know that I am a strict man, taking up what I did not lay down and reaping what I did not sow?

23 'Then why did you not put my money in the bank, and having come, I would have collected it with interest?'

24 "Then he said to the bystanders, 'Take the mina away from him and give it to the one who has the ten minas.'

25 "And they said to him, 'Master, he has ten minas *already.*'

26 'I tell you that to everyone who has, more shall be given, but from the one who does not have, even what he does have shall be taken away.

27 'But these enemies of mine, who did not want me to reign over them, bring them here and slay them in my presence.'"

The Triumphal Entry

28 And after He had said these things, He was going on ahead, going up to Jerusalem.

29 And it happened that when He approached Bethphage and Bethany, near the mount called "of Olives," He sent two of the disciples,

30 saying, "Go into the village ahead of *you*; in which, as you enter, you will find a colt tied, on which no one yet has ever sat; untie it and bring it *here.*

31 "And if anyone asks you, 'Why are you untying it?' you shall say this: 'Because the Lord has need of it.'"

32 So when those who were sent departed, they found it just as He had told them.

33 And as they were untying the colt, its owners said to them, "Why are you untying the colt?"

34 And they said, "The Lord has need of it."

35 And they brought it to Jesus, and after they threw their garments on the colt, they put Jesus *on it.*

36 And as He was going, they were spreading their garments on the road.

37 Now as soon as He was approaching, near the descent of the Mount of Olives, the whole multitude of the disciples began to praise God, rejoicing with a loud voice for all the miracles which they had seen,

38 saying,

"BLESSED IS THE KING WHO COMES
    IN THE NAME OF THE LORD.
Peace in heaven and glory in the
    highest!"

39 And some of the Pharisees in the crowd said to Him, "Teacher, rebuke Your disciples."

40 But Jesus answered and said, "I tell you, if these were silent, the stones will cry out!"

Lament over Jerusalem

41 And as He approached *Jerusalem* and saw the city, He cried over it,

42 saying, "If you knew in this day,

even you, the things which make for peace! But now they have been hidden from your eyes.

43 "For the days will come upon you when your enemies will throw up a barricade against you, and surround you and hem you in on every side,

44 and they will level you to the ground and your children within you, and they will not leave in you one stone upon another, because you did not recognize the time of your visitation."

Jesus Drives Merchants from the Temple

45 And Jesus entered the temple and began to drive out those who were selling,

46 saying to them, "It is written, 'AND MY HOUSE SHALL BE A HOUSE OF PRAYER,' but you have made it a ROBBERS' DEN."

47 And He was teaching daily in the temple, but the chief priests and the scribes and the leading men among the people were trying to destroy Him,

48 and they could not find anything that they might do, for all the people hung upon every word He said.

CHAPTER 20

The Authority of Jesus Challenged

AND it happened that on one of the days while He was teaching the people in the temple and proclaiming the gospel, the chief priests and the scribes with the elders came up to *Him*,

2 and they spoke, saying to Him, "Tell us by what authority You are doing these things, or who is the one who gave You this authority?"

3 And Jesus answered and said to them, "I will also ask you a question, and you tell Me:

4 "Was the baptism of John from heaven or from men?"

5 And they reasoned among themselves, saying, "If we say, 'From heaven,' He will say, 'Why did you not believe him?'

6 "But if we say, 'From men,' all the people will stone us to death, for they are convinced that John was a prophet."

7 So they answered that they did not know where *it* came from.

8 And Jesus said to them, "Neither will I tell you by what authority I do these things."

The Parable of the Vine-Growers

9 And He began to tell the people this parable: "A man planted a vineyard and rented it out to vine-growers, and went on a journey for a long time.

10 "And at the *harvest* time he sent a slave to the vine-growers, so that they would give him *some* of the fruit of the vineyard. But the vine-growers sent him away empty-handed having beaten him.

11 "And he proceeded to send another slave; and when they beat him also and treated him shamefully, they sent him away empty-handed.

12 "And he proceeded to send a

third; and this one also they wounded and cast out.

13 "Now the owner of the vineyard said, 'What shall I do? I will send my beloved son; perhaps they will respect him.'

14 "But when the vine-growers saw him, they were reasoning with one another, saying, 'This is the heir; let us kill him so that the inheritance will be ours.'

15 "So they threw him out of the vineyard and killed him. What, then, will the owner of the vineyard do to them?

16 "He will come and destroy these vine-growers and will give the vineyard to others." When they heard *this*, they said, "May it never be!"

17 But when Jesus looked at them, He said, "What then is this that is written:

'THE STONE WHICH THE BUILDERS
    REJECTED,
THIS HAS BECOME THE CHIEF
    CORNER *stone*'?

18 "Everyone who falls on that stone will be broken to pieces, but on whomever it falls, it will scatter him like dust."

Taxes to Caesar

19 And the scribes and the chief priests tried to lay hands on Him that very hour, but they feared the people. For they understood that He spoke this parable against them.

20 So they watched Him, and sent spies who pretended to be righteous, so that they might catch Him in some statement, in order to deliver Him to the rule and the authority of the governor.

21 And they questioned Him, saying, "Teacher, we know that You speak and teach correctly, and You are not partial to any, but teach the way of God in truth.

22 "Is it lawful for us to pay taxes to Caesar, or not?"

23 But He perceived their craftiness and said to them,

24 "Show Me a ¹denarius. Whose likeness and inscription does it have?" They said, "Caesar's."

25 And He said to them, "Then render to Caesar the things that are Caesar's, and to God the things that are God's."

26 And they were unable to catch Him in a word in the presence of the people; and marveling at His answer, they became silent.

The Sadducees Ask About the Resurrection

27 Now some of the Sadducees (who say that there is no resurrection) came to Him,

28 and they questioned Him, saying, "Teacher, Moses wrote for us that IF A MAN'S BROTHER DIES, having a wife, AND HE IS CHILDLESS, HIS BROTHER SHOULD MARRY THE WIFE AND RAISE UP SEED FOR HIS BROTHER.

29 "Now there were seven brothers;

¹ A Roman silver coin, approx. a laborer's daily wage

and the first married a wife and died childless,

30 and the second

31 and the third married her; and in the same way, all seven died, leaving no children.

32 "Finally the woman died also.

33 "Therefore, this woman—in the resurrection—whose wife will she be? For all seven had her as a wife."

34 And Jesus said to them, "The sons of this age marry and are given in marriage,

35 but those who are considered worthy to attain to that age and the resurrection from the dead, neither marry nor are given in marriage.

36 For they cannot even die anymore, because they are like angels and are sons of God, being sons of the resurrection.

37 "But that the dead are raised, even Moses showed in the *passage about the burning* bush, where he calls the Lord THE GOD OF ABRAHAM, AND THE GOD OF ISAAC, AND THE GOD OF JACOB.

38 "Now He is not the God of the dead but of the living; for all live to Him."

39 And some of the scribes answered and said, "Teacher, You have spoken well."

40 For they did not dare to question Him any longer about anything.

41 Then He said to them, "How *is it that* they say the Christ is David's son?

42 "For David himself says in the book of Psalms,

'THE LORD SAID TO MY LORD,
"SIT AT MY RIGHT HAND,

43 UNTIL I PUT YOUR ENEMIES
AS A FOOTSTOOL FOR YOUR FEET." '

44 "Therefore David calls Him 'Lord,' so how is He his son?"

45 And while all the people were listening, He said to the disciples,

46 "Beware of the scribes, who want to walk around in long robes, and love greetings in the marketplaces, and best seats in the synagogues and places of honor at banquets,

47 who devour widows' houses, and for appearance's sake offer long prayers. These will receive greater condemnation."

CHAPTER 21

The Widow's Offering

AND He looked up and saw the rich putting their gifts into the treasury.

2 And He saw a poor widow putting in two [1]lepta.

3 And He said, "Truly I say to you, this poor widow put in more than all *of them.*

4 For they all put in their gifts out of their abundance; but she, out of what she lacked, put in all that she had for living."

5 And while some were talking about the temple, that it had been

---

[1] Smallest Greek copper coin, approx. 1/128 of a laborer's daily wage

adorned with beautiful stones and dedicated gifts, He said,

6 "*As for* these things which you are looking at, the days will come in which there will not be left one stone upon another which will not be torn down."

7 So they questioned Him, saying, "Teacher, when therefore will these things happen? And what *will be* the sign when these things are about to take place?"

8 And He said, "See to it that you are not deceived; for many will come in My name, saying, 'I am *He*,' and, 'The time is at hand.' Do not go after them.

9 "And when you hear of wars and disturbances, do not be terrified; for these things must take place first, but the end *does* not *follow* immediately."

Signs of Christ's Return

10 Then He continued saying to them, "Nation will rise against nation and kingdom against kingdom,

11 and there will be great earthquakes, and in various places famines and plagues; and there will be terrors and great signs from heaven.

12 "But before all these things, they will lay their hands on you and will persecute you, delivering you to the synagogues and prisons, bringing you before kings and governors for My name's sake.

13 "It will result in an opportunity for your testimony.

14 "So set in your hearts not to prepare beforehand to defend yourselves;

15 for I will give you a mouth and wisdom which none of your opponents will be able to resist or refute.

16 "But you will be betrayed even by parents and brothers and relatives and friends, and they will put *some* of you to death,

17 and you will be hated by all because of My name.

18 "Yet not a hair of your head will perish.

19 "By your perseverance you will gain your lives.

20 "But when you see Jerusalem surrounded by armies, then know that its desolation is at hand.

21 "Then those who are in Judea must flee to the mountains, and those who are in the midst of the city must leave, and those who are in the countryside must not enter the city;

22 because these are days of vengeance, so that all things which are written will be fulfilled.

23 "Woe to those who are pregnant and to those who are nursing babies in those days; for there will be great distress upon the land and wrath against this people,

24 and they will fall by the edge of the sword, and will be led captive into all the nations, and Jerusalem will be trampled under foot by the Gentiles until the times of the Gentiles are fulfilled.

When Christ Returns

25 "And there will be signs in sun and moon and stars, and on the earth anguish among nations, in

perplexity at the roaring of the sea and the waves,

26 men fainting from fear and the expectation of the things which are coming upon the world; for the POWERS OF THE HEAVENS will be shaken.

27 "And then they will see THE SON OF MAN COMING IN A CLOUD with power and great glory.

28 "But when these things begin to take place, straighten up and lift up your heads, because your redemption is drawing near."

The Parable of the Fig Tree

29 Then He told them a parable: "Behold the fig tree and all the trees;

30 as soon as they put forth *leaves* and you see it for yourselves, know that summer is now near.

31 "So you also, when you see these things happening, know that the kingdom of God is near.

32 "Truly I say to you, this generation will not pass away until all things take place.

33 "Heaven and earth will pass away, but My words will never pass away.

34 "But be on guard, so that your hearts will not be overcome with dissipation and drunkenness and the worries of life, and that day will not come on you suddenly like a trap;

35 for it will come upon all those who inhabit the face of all the earth.

36 "But keep on the alert at all times, praying earnestly that you may have strength to escape all these things that are about to take place, and to stand before the Son of Man."

37 Now during the day He was teaching in the temple, but during the night He would go out and spend it on the mount called "of Olives."

38 And all the people would get up early in the morning *to come* to Him in the temple to listen to Him.

CHAPTER 22

The Plot to Kill Jesus

NOW the Feast of Unleavened Bread, which is called the Passover, was drawing near.

2 And the chief priests and the scribes were seeking how they might put Him to death; for they were afraid of the people.

3 And Satan entered into Judas who was called Iscariot, who belonged to the number of the twelve.

4 And he went away and discussed with the chief priests and officers how he might betray Him to them.

5 And they were glad and agreed to give him money.

6 So he consented, and *began* seeking a good opportunity to betray Him to them apart from the crowd.

The Passover Meal

7 Then came the *first* day of Unleavened Bread on which the Passover lamb had to be sacrificed.

8 And *Jesus* sent Peter and John, saying, "Go and prepare the Passover for us, so that we may eat it."

9 And they said to Him, "Where do You want us to prepare it?"

10 And He said to them, "Behold, after you have entered the city, a man will meet you carrying a pitcher of water; follow him into the house that he enters.

11 "And you shall say to the owner of the house, 'The Teacher says to you, "Where is the guest room in which I may eat the Passover with My disciples?"'

12 "And he will show you a large, furnished upper room; prepare it there."

13 And they left and found *everything* just as He had told them; and they prepared the Passover.

The Lord's Supper

14 And when the hour had come, He reclined *at the table*, and the apostles with Him.

15 And He said to them, "I have earnestly desired to eat this Passover with you before I suffer;

16 for I say to you, I shall never again eat it until it is fulfilled in the kingdom of God."

17 And when He had taken a cup *and* given thanks, He said, "Take this and share it among yourselves.

18 For I say to you, I will not drink of the fruit of the vine from now on until the kingdom of God comes."

19 And when He had taken *some* bread *and* given thanks, He broke it and gave it to them, saying, "This is My body which is given for you. Do this in remembrance of Me."

20 And in the same way *He took* the cup after they had eaten, saying, "This cup which is poured out for you is the new covenant in My blood.

21 "But behold, the hand of the one betraying Me is with Me on the table.

22 "For indeed, the Son of Man is going as it has been determined; but woe to that man by whom He is betrayed!"

23 And they began to argue among themselves which one of them it might be who was going to do this thing.

Who Is Greatest?

24 And there arose also a dispute among them *as to* which one of them was regarded to be greatest.

25 And He said to them, "The kings of the Gentiles lord it over them, and those who have authority over them are called 'Benefactors.'

26 "But not so with you; rather the one who is the greatest among you must become like the youngest, and the leader like the servant.

27 "For who is greater, the one who reclines *at the table* or the one who serves? Is it not the one who reclines? But I am among you as the one who serves.

28 "Now you are those who have stood by Me in My trials,

29 and I grant you a kingdom, just as My Father granted *one* to Me,

30 that you may eat and drink at My table in My kingdom, and you will sit on thrones judging the twelve tribes of Israel.

31 "Simon, Simon, behold, Satan has demanded to sift *all of* you like wheat.

32 But I have prayed earnestly for you, that your faith may not fail; and you, once you have returned, strengthen your brothers."

33 But he said to Him, "Lord, with You I am ready to go both to prison and to death!"

34 And He said, "I say to you, Peter, the rooster will not crow today until you have denied three times that you know Me."

35 And He said to them, "When I sent you out without money belt and bag and sandals, did you lack anything?" They said, "Not a thing."

36 And He said to them, "But now, whoever has a money belt is to take it along, likewise also a bag, and whoever has no sword should sell his garment and buy one.

37 "For I tell you that this which is written must be completed in Me, 'AND HE WAS NUMBERED WITH TRANSGRESSORS;' for that which refers to Me has its completion."

38 And they said, "Lord, look, here are two swords." And He said to them, "It is enough."

Jesus Prays in Gethsemane

39 And He came out and went as was His custom to the Mount of Olives; and the disciples also followed Him.

40 Now when He arrived at the place, He said to them, "Pray that you may not enter into temptation."

41 And He withdrew from them about a stone's throw, and He knelt down and began to pray,

42 saying, "Father, if You are willing, remove this cup from Me, yet not My will, but Yours be done."

43 Now an angel from heaven appeared to Him, strengthening Him.

44 And being in agony He was praying very fervently, and His sweat became like drops of blood, falling down upon the ground.

45 And when He rose from prayer, He came to the disciples and found them sleeping from sorrow,

46 and said to them, "Why are you sleeping? Rise up and pray that you may not enter into temptation."

The Betrayal and Arrest of Jesus

47 While He was still speaking, behold, a crowd *came*, and the one called Judas, one of the twelve, was coming ahead of them, and he approached Jesus to kiss Him.

48 But Jesus said to him, "Judas, are you betraying the Son of Man with a kiss?"

49 And when those around Him saw what was going to happen, they said, "Lord, shall we strike with the sword?"

50 And one of them struck the slave of the high priest and cut off his right ear.

51 But Jesus answered and said, "Stop! No more of this." And He touched his ear and healed him.

52 Then Jesus said to the chief priests and officers of the temple and elders who had come against Him, "Have you come out with swords and clubs as against a robber?

53 "While I was with you daily in the temple, you did not stretch out your hands against Me, but this hour and the authority of darkness are yours."

54 Now having arrested Him, they led Him *away* and brought Him to the house of the high priest, but Peter was following at a distance.

55 And after they had kindled a fire in the middle of the courtyard and had sat down together, Peter was sitting among them.

56 And a servant-girl, seeing him as he sat in the firelight and looking intently at him, said, "This man was with Him too."

57 But he denied *it*, saying, "Woman, I do not know Him."

58 A little later, another saw him and said, "You are *one* of them too!" But Peter said, "Man, I am not!"

59 And after about an hour had passed, another man *began to* insist, saying, "Certainly this man was with Him too, for he also is a Galilean."

60 But Peter said, "Man, I do not know what you are talking about." Immediately, while he was still speaking, a rooster crowed.

61 And the Lord turned and looked at Peter. And Peter remembered the word of the Lord, how He had told him, "Before a rooster crows today, you will deny Me three times."

62 And he went out and cried bitterly.

63 Now the men who were holding Jesus in custody were mocking Him while they beat Him,

64 and they blindfolded Him and were asking Him, saying, "Prophesy, who is the one who hit You?"

65 And they were saying many other things against Him, blaspheming.

Jesus Before the Sanhedrin

66 And as the day came, the Council of elders of the people assembled, both chief priests and scribes, and they led Him away to their Sanhedrin, saying,

67 "If You are the Christ, tell us." But He said to them, "If I tell you, you will not believe,

68 and if I ask a question, you will not answer.

69 "But from now on THE SON OF MAN WILL BE SEATED AT THE RIGHT HAND of the power OF GOD."

70 And they all said, "Are You the Son of God, then?" And He said to them, "You yourselves say that I am."

71 Then they said, "What further need do we have of testimony? For we have heard it ourselves from His own mouth."

CHAPTER 23

Jesus Before Pilate

THEN their whole assembly rose up and brought Him before Pilate.

2 And they began to accuse Him, saying, "We found this man misleading our nation and forbidding to pay

taxes to Caesar, and saying that He Himself is Christ, a King."

3 So Pilate asked Him, saying, "Are You the King of the Jews?" And He answered him and said, "You yourself say *it*."

4 Then Pilate said to the chief priests and the crowds, "I find no guilt in this man."

5 But they kept on insisting, saying, "He stirs up the people, teaching all over Judea, starting from Galilee even as far as this place."

6 Now when Pilate heard *this*, he asked whether the man was a Galilean.

7 And when he learned that He belonged to Herod's jurisdiction, he sent Him to Herod, who himself also was in Jerusalem in those days.

Jesus Before Herod

8 Now when Herod saw Jesus, he rejoiced greatly; for he had wanted to see Him for a long time, because he had been hearing about Him and was hoping to see some sign performed by Him.

9 And he questioned Him at some length, but He answered him nothing.

10 And the chief priests and the scribes were standing there, vehemently accusing Him.

11 And Herod with his soldiers, after treating Him with contempt and mocking Him, dressed Him in a bright robe and sent Him back to Pilate.

12 Now Herod and Pilate became friends with one another that very day; for before they had been at enmity with each other.

Pilate Grants the Crowd's Request

13 And Pilate summoned the chief priests and the rulers and the people,

14 and said to them, "You brought this man to me as one who incites the people to rebellion, and behold, having examined Him before you, I have found in this man no guilt of what you are accusing Him.

15 "No, nor has Herod, for he sent Him back to us; and behold, nothing deserving death has been done by Him.

16 "Therefore I will punish Him and release Him."

17 [Now he was obliged to release to them at the feast one prisoner.]

18 But they cried out all together, saying, "Away with this man, and release for us Barabbas!"

19 (He had been thrown into prison for an insurrection made in the city and for murder.)

20 But again Pilate addressed them, wanting to release Jesus,

21 but they kept on calling out, saying, "Crucify, crucify Him!"

22 And he said to them a third time, "Why, what evil has this man done? I have found in Him no guilt *worthy of* death; therefore I will punish Him and release Him."

23 But they were insistent, with loud voices asking that He be crucified. And their voices were prevailing.

24 And Pilate pronounced sentence that their demand be granted.

25 And he released the man they

were asking for who had been thrown into prison for insurrection and murder, but he delivered Jesus to their will.

Simon Carries the Cross

26 And when they led Him away, they took hold of a man, Simon of Cyrene, coming in from the country, and placed on him the cross to carry behind Jesus.

27 And following Him was a large multitude of the people, and of women who were mourning and lamenting Him.

28 But Jesus, turning to them, said, "Daughters of Jerusalem, stop crying for Me, but cry for yourselves and for your children.

29 "For behold, the days are coming when they will say, 'Blessed are the barren, and the wombs that never bore, and the breasts that never nursed.'

30 "Then they will begin TO SAY TO THE MOUNTAINS, 'FALL ON US,' AND TO THE HILLS, 'COVER US.'

31 "For if they do these things when the tree is green, what will happen when it is dry?"

32 Now two others also, who were criminals, were being led away to be put to death with Him.

The Crucifixion

33 And when they came to the place called The Skull, there they crucified Him and the criminals, one on the right and the other on the left.

34 But Jesus was saying, "Father, forgive them; for they do not know what they are doing." AND THEY CAST LOTS, DIVIDING UP HIS GARMENTS AMONG THEMSELVES.

35 And the people stood by, looking on. And even the rulers were scoffing at Him, saying, "He saved others; let Him save Himself if this is the Christ of God, His Chosen One."

36 And the soldiers also mocked Him, coming up to Him, offering Him sour wine,

37 and saying, "If You are the King of the Jews, save Yourself!"

38 Now there was also an inscription above Him, "THIS IS THE KING OF THE JEWS."

39 And one of the criminals hanging *there* was blaspheming Him, saying, "Are You not the Christ? Save Yourself and us!"

40 But the other answered, and rebuking him said, "Do you not even fear God, since you are under the same sentence of condemnation?

41 "And we indeed *are suffering* justly, for we are receiving what we deserve for what we have done; but this man has done nothing wrong."

42 And he was saying, "Jesus, remember me when You come in Your kingdom!"

43 And He said to him, "Truly I say to you, today you shall be with Me in Paradise."

44 And it was now about the sixth hour, and darkness fell over the whole land until the ninth hour,

45 because the sun was obscured. And the veil of the sanctuary was torn in two.

46 And Jesus, crying out with a loud

voice, said, "Father, INTO YOUR HANDS I COMMIT MY SPIRIT." Having said this, He breathed His last.

47 Now when the centurion saw what had happened, he *began* praising God, saying, "Certainly this man was righteous."

48 And all the crowds who came together for this spectacle, when they observed what had happened, were returning, beating their chests.

49 And all His acquaintances and the women who accompanied Him from Galilee were standing at a distance, watching these things.

Jesus Is Buried

50 And behold, a man named Joseph, who was a Council member, a good and righteous man

51 (he had not consented to their counsel and action), *a man* from Arimathea, a city of the Jews, who was waiting for the kingdom of God;

52 this man went to Pilate and asked for the body of Jesus.

53 And he took it down and wrapped it in a linen cloth, and laid Him in a tomb cut into the rock, where no one had ever lain.

54 It was Preparation day, and the Sabbath was about to begin.

55 Now the women, who had come with Him from Galilee, followed and beheld the tomb and how His body was laid.

56 Then after they returned, they prepared spices and perfumes.

And on the Sabbath they rested according to the commandment.

CHAPTER 24

Jesus Is Risen!

NOW on the first day of the week, at early dawn, they came to the tomb bringing the spices which they had prepared.

2 And they found the stone rolled away from the tomb,

3 but when they entered, they did not find the body of the Lord Jesus.

4 And it happened that while they were perplexed about this, behold, two men suddenly stood near them in dazzling clothing,

5 and when *the women* were terrified and bowed their faces to the ground, *the men* said to them, "Why do you seek the living One among the dead?

6 "He is not here, but He has risen. Remember how He spoke to you while He was still in Galilee,

7 saying that the Son of Man must be delivered into the hands of sinful men, and be crucified, and the third day rise again."

8 And they remembered His words,

9 and when they returned from the tomb, they reported all these things to the eleven and to all the rest.

10 Now Mary Magdalene and Joanna and Mary the *mother* of James and the rest of the women with them were *there*; they were telling these things to the apostles.

11 But these words appeared to them as nonsense, and they were not believing them.

12 But Peter stood up and ran to the tomb; and stooping to look in, he

*saw the linen wrappings only. And he went away by himself, marveling at what had happened.

The Road to Emmaus

13 And behold, two of them were going that same day to a village named Emmaus, which was [1]sixty stadia from Jerusalem.

14 And they were conversing with each other about all these things which had happened.

15 And it happened that while they were conversing and debating, Jesus Himself approached and was going with them.

16 But their eyes were prevented from recognizing Him.

17 And He said to them, "What are these words that you are discussing with one another as you are walking?" And they stood still, looking sad.

18 And one *of them*, named Cleopas, answered and said to Him, "Are You the only one visiting Jerusalem and unaware of the things which have happened here in these days?"

19 And He said to them, "What things?" And they said to Him, "The things about Jesus the Nazarene, who was a mighty prophet in deed and word in the sight of God and all the people,

20 and how the chief priests and our rulers delivered Him to the sentence of death, and crucified Him.

21 "But we were hoping that it was He who was going to redeem Israel. Indeed, besides all this, it is the third day since these things happened.

22 "But also some women among us astounded us. When they were at the tomb early in the morning,

23 and not finding His body, they came, saying that they had also seen a vision of angels who said that He was alive.

24 "Some of those who were with us went to the tomb and found it just exactly as the women also said, but Him they did not see."

25 And He said to them, "O foolish ones and slow of heart to believe in all that the prophets have spoken!

26 "Was it not necessary for the Christ to suffer these things and to enter into His glory?"

27 Then beginning with Moses and with all the prophets, He interpreted to them the things concerning Himself in all the Scriptures.

28 And they approached the village where they were going, and He acted as though He were going farther.

29 But they urged Him strongly, saying, "Stay with us, for it is toward evening, and the day is now nearly over." So He went in to stay with them.

30 And it happened that when He had reclined *at the table* with them, He took the bread and blessed *it*, and after breaking *it*, He was giving *it* to them.

31 Then their eyes were opened and

---

[1] Approx. 7 mi. or 11 km, a stadion was approx. 607 ft. or 185 m

they recognized Him. And He vanished from their sight.

32 And they said to one another, "Were not our hearts burning within us while He was speaking to us on the road, while He was opening the Scriptures to us?"

33 And they stood up that very hour and returned to Jerusalem, and found gathered together the eleven and those with them,

34 who were saying, "The Lord has really risen and has appeared to Simon."

35 And they were relating their experiences on the road and how He was recognized by them in the breaking of the bread.

Jesus Appears to His Disciples

36 Now while they were telling these things, He Himself stood in their midst and *said to them, "Peace to you."

37 But being startled and frightened, they were thinking that they were seeing a spirit.

38 And He said to them, "Why are you troubled, and why do doubts arise in your hearts?

39 "See My hands and My feet, that it is I Myself; touch Me and see, for a spirit does not have flesh and bones as you see that I have."

40 And when He had said this, He showed them His hands and His feet.

41 And while they still were not believing because of their joy and were *still* marveling, He said to them, "Have you anything here to eat?"

42 They gave Him a piece of a broiled fish,

43 and He took it and ate *it* before them.

44 Now He said to them, "These are My words which I spoke to you while I was still with you, that all things which are written about Me in the Law of Moses and the Prophets and the Psalms must be fulfilled."

45 Then He opened their minds to understand the Scriptures,

46 and He said to them, "Thus it is written, that the Christ would suffer and rise again from the dead the third day,

47 and that repentance for forgiveness of sins would be proclaimed in His name to all the nations, beginning from Jerusalem.

48 "You are witnesses of these things.

49 "And behold, I am sending the promise of My Father upon you, but you are to stay in the city until you are clothed with power from on high."

The Ascension

50 And He led them out as far as Bethany, and lifting up His hands, He blessed them.

51 And it happened that while He was blessing them, He parted from them and was carried up into heaven.

52 And they, after worshiping Him, returned to Jerusalem with great joy,

53 and were continually in the temple blessing God.

THE GOSPEL ACCORDING TO
JOHN

CHAPTER 1

The Deity of Jesus Christ

IN the beginning was the Word, and the Word was with God, and the Word was God.

2 He was in the beginning with God.

3 All things came into being through Him, and apart from Him nothing came into being that has come into being.

4 In Him was life, and the life was the Light of men.

5 And the Light shines in the darkness, and the darkness did not overtake it.

The Witness of John the Baptist

6 There was a man having been sent from God, whose name was John.

7 He came as a witness, to bear witness about the Light, so that all might believe through him.

8 He was not the Light, but *he came* to bear witness about the Light.

9 There was the true Light which, coming into the world, enlightens everyone.

10 He was in the world, and the world was made through Him, and the world did not know Him.

11 He came to what was His own, and those who were His own did not receive Him.

12 But as many as received Him, to them He gave the right to become children of God, *even* to those who believe in His name,

13 who were born, not of blood nor of the will of the flesh nor of the will of man, but of God.

The Word Became Flesh

14 And the Word became flesh, and dwelt among us, and we beheld His glory, glory as of the only begotten from the Father, full of grace and truth.

15 John *bore witness about Him and cried out, saying, "This was He of whom I said, 'He who comes after me has been ahead of me, for He existed before me.'"

16 For of His fullness we have all received, and grace upon grace.

17 For the Law was given through Moses; grace and truth came through Jesus Christ.

18 No one has seen God at any time; the only begotten God who is in the bosom of the Father, He has explained *Him*.

A Voice in the Wilderness

19 And this is the witness of John, when the Jews sent to him priests and Levites from Jerusalem to ask him, "Who are you?"

20 And he confessed and did not deny, but confessed, "I am not the Christ."

21 And they asked him, "What then? Are you Elijah?" And he *said, "I am not." "Are you the Prophet?" And he answered, "No."

22 Therefore, they said to him, "Who are you, so that we may give an answer to those who sent us? What do you say about yourself?"

23 He said, "I am A VOICE OF ONE CRYING IN THE WILDERNESS, 'MAKE STRAIGHT THE WAY OF THE LORD,' as Isaiah the prophet said."

24 Now they had been sent from the Pharisees.

25 And they asked him, and said to him, "Why then are you baptizing, if you are not the Christ, nor Elijah, nor the Prophet?"

26 John answered them, saying, "I baptize with water, *but* among you stands One whom you do not know.

27 *This One is* He who comes after me, of whom I am not worthy to untie the strap of His sandal."

28 These things took place in Bethany beyond the Jordan, where John was baptizing.

29 On the next day, he *saw Jesus coming to him and *said, "Behold, the Lamb of God who takes away the sin of the world!

30 "This is He of whom I said, 'After me comes a man who has been ahead of me, for He existed before me.'

31 "I did not know Him, but so that He might be manifested to Israel, I came baptizing with water."

32 And John bore witness saying, "I have beheld the Spirit descending as a dove out of heaven, and He abided on Him.

33 "And I did not know Him, but He who sent me to baptize with water said to me, 'The One upon whom you see the Spirit descending and abiding on Him, this is the One who baptizes with the Holy Spirit.'

34 "And I myself have seen, and have borne witness that this is the Son of God."

Behold, the Lamb of God

35 On the next day, John again was standing with two of his disciples,

36 and he looked at Jesus as He walked, and *said, "Behold, the Lamb of God!"

37 And the two disciples heard him speak and followed Jesus.

38 And when Jesus turned and noticed them following, He *said to them, "What do you seek?" They said to Him, "Rabbi (which translated means Teacher), where are You staying?"

39 He *said to them, "Come, and you will see." So they came and saw where He was staying; and they stayed with Him that day. It was about the tenth hour.

40 One of the two who heard John *speak* and followed Him, was Andrew, Simon Peter's brother.

41 He first *found his own brother Simon and *said to him, "We have found the Messiah" (which translated means Christ).

42 He brought him to Jesus. When Jesus looked at him, He said, "You are

Simon the son of John; you shall be called Cephas" (which is translated Peter).

43 On the next day, He desired to go into Galilee, and He *found Philip. And Jesus *said to him, "Follow Me."

44 Now Philip was from Bethsaida, the city of Andrew and Peter.

45 Philip *found Nathanael and *said to him, "We have found Him of whom Moses in the Law and *also* the Prophets wrote—Jesus of Nazareth, the son of Joseph."

46 And Nathanael said to him, "Can any good thing come out of Nazareth?" Philip *said to him, "Come and see."

47 Jesus saw Nathanael coming to Him, and *said about him, "Behold, truly an Israelite in whom there is no deceit!"

48 Nathanael *said to Him, "From where do You know me?" Jesus answered and said to him, "Before Philip called you, when you were under the fig tree, I saw you."

49 Nathanael answered Him, "Rabbi, You are the Son of God; You are the King of Israel."

50 Jesus answered and said to him, "Because I said to you that I saw you under the fig tree, do you believe? You will see greater things than these."

51 And He *said to him, "Truly, truly, I say to you, you will see THE HEAVENS OPENED AND THE ANGELS OF GOD ASCENDING AND DESCENDING on the Son of Man."

CHAPTER 2

The Wedding at Cana

AND on the third day there was a wedding in Cana of Galilee, and the mother of Jesus was there;

2 and both Jesus and His disciples were invited to the wedding.

3 And when the wine ran out, the mother of Jesus *said to Him, "They have no wine."

4 And Jesus *said to her, "Woman, what do I have to do with you? My hour has not yet come."

5 His mother *said to the servants, "Whatever He says to you, do *it.*"

6 Now there were six stone water jars set there for the Jewish custom of purification, containing [1]two or three measures each.

7 Jesus *said to them, "Fill the water jars with water." So they filled them up to the brim.

8 And He *said to them, "Draw *some* out now and take it to the headwaiter." So they took it *to him.*

9 Now when the headwaiter tasted the water which had become wine, and did not know where it came from (but the servants who had drawn the water knew), the headwaiter *called the bridegroom,

10 and *said to him, "Every man serves the good wine first, and when *the people* have drunk freely, *then* the inferior *wine*; *but* you have kept the good wine until now."

11 Jesus did this in Cana of Galilee

---

[1] Approx. 20–30 gal. or 75–115 l, a measure was approx. 10 gal. or 38 l

as the beginning of *His* signs, and manifested His glory, and His disciples believed in Him.

12 After this He went down to Capernaum, He and His mother and *His* brothers and His disciples; and they stayed there a few days.

Jesus Cleanses the Temple

13 And the Passover of the Jews was near, and Jesus went up to Jerusalem.

14 And He found in the temple those who were selling oxen and sheep and doves, and the money changers seated *at their tables.*

15 And He made a scourge of cords, and drove *them* all out of the temple, with the sheep and the oxen; and He poured out the coins of the money changers and overturned their tables;

16 and to those who were selling the doves He said, "Take these things away; stop making My Father's house a place of business."

17 His disciples remembered that it was written, "ZEAL FOR YOUR HOUSE WILL CONSUME ME."

18 The Jews then said to Him, "What sign do You show us as your authority for doing these things?"

19 Jesus answered them, "Destroy this sanctuary, and in three days I will raise it up."

20 The Jews then said, "It took forty-six years to build this sanctuary, and will You raise it up in three days?"

21 But He was speaking about the sanctuary of His body.

22 So when He was raised from the dead, His disciples remembered that He said this; and they believed the Scripture and the word which Jesus had spoken.

23 Now when He was in Jerusalem at the Passover, during the feast, many believed in His name, when they saw His signs which He was doing.

24 But Jesus, on His part, was not entrusting Himself to them, for He knew all men,

25 and because He had no need that anyone bear witness concerning man, for He Himself knew what was in man.

CHAPTER 3

You Must Be Born Again

NOW there was a man of the Pharisees, named Nicodemus, a ruler of the Jews;

2 this man came to Jesus by night and said to Him, "Rabbi, we know that You have come from God *as* a teacher; for no one can do these signs that You do unless God is with him."

3 Jesus answered and said to him, "Truly, truly, I say to you, unless one is born again he cannot see the kingdom of God."

4 Nicodemus *said to Him, "How can a man be born when he is old? Can he enter a second time into his mother's womb and be born?"

5 Jesus answered, "Truly, truly, I say to you, unless one is born of water and the Spirit he cannot enter into the kingdom of God.

6 "That which has been born of the flesh is flesh, and that which has been born of the Spirit is spirit.

7 "Do not marvel that I said to you, 'You must be born again.'

8 "The wind blows where it wishes and you hear its sound, but do not know where it comes from and where it is going; so is everyone who has been born of the Spirit."

9 Nicodemus answered and said to Him, "How can these things be?"

10 Jesus answered and said to him, "Are you the teacher of Israel and do not understand these things?

11 "Truly, truly, I say to you, we speak of what we know and bear witness of what we have seen, and you do not accept our witness.

12 "If I told you earthly things and you do not believe, how will you believe if I tell you heavenly things?

13 "And no one has ascended into heaven, but He who descended from heaven, the Son of Man.

14 "And as Moses lifted up the serpent in the wilderness, even so must the Son of Man be lifted up;

15 so that whoever believes will in Him have eternal life.

16 "For God so loved the world, that He gave His only begotten Son, that whoever believes in Him shall not perish, but have eternal life.

17 "For God did not send the Son into the world to judge the world, but that the world might be saved through Him.

18 "He who believes in Him is not judged; he who does not believe has been judged already, because he has not believed in the name of the only begotten Son of God.

19 "And this is the judgment, that the Light has come into the world, and men loved the darkness rather than the Light, for their deeds were evil.

20 "For everyone who does evil hates the Light, and does not come to the Light lest his deeds be exposed.

21 "But he who practices the truth comes to the Light, so that his deeds may be manifested as having been done by God."

John the Baptist's Last Witness

22 After these things Jesus and His disciples came into the land of Judea, and there He was spending time with them and baptizing.

23 And John also was baptizing in Aenon near Salim, because there was much water there; and *people* were coming and were being baptized—

24 for John had not yet been thrown into prison.

25 Therefore there arose a debate between John's disciples and a Jew about purification.

26 And they came to John and said to him, "Rabbi, He who was with you beyond the Jordan, to whom you have borne witness, behold, He is baptizing and all are coming to Him."

27 John answered and said, "A man can receive nothing unless it has been given him from heaven.

28 "You yourselves are my witnesses that I said, 'I am not the Christ,' but, 'I have been sent ahead of Him.'

29 "He who has the bride is the bridegroom; but the friend of the bridegroom, who stands and hears him, rejoices greatly because of the bridegroom's voice. So this joy of mine has been made full.

30 "He must increase, but I must decrease.

31 "He who comes from above is above all, he who is of the earth is from the earth and speaks of the earth. He who comes from heaven is above all.

32 "What He has seen and heard, of that He bears witness; and no one receives His witness.

33 "He who has received His witness has set his seal to *this*, that God is true.

34 "For He whom God has sent speaks the words of God; for He gives the Spirit without measure.

35 "The Father loves the Son and has given all things into His hand.

36 "He who believes in the Son has eternal life; but he who does not obey the Son will not see life, but the wrath of God abides on him."

CHAPTER 4

Jesus Goes to Galilee

THEREFORE when Jesus knew that the Pharisees had heard that Jesus was making and baptizing more disciples than John

2 (although Jesus Himself was not baptizing, but His disciples *were*),

3 He left Judea and went away again into Galilee.

4 And He had to pass through Samaria.

5 So He *came to a city of Samaria called Sychar, near the field that Jacob gave to his son Joseph;

6 and Jacob's well was there. So Jesus, being wearied from His journey, was sitting thus by the well. It was about the sixth hour.

Jesus and the Samaritan Woman

7 A woman of Samaria *came to draw water. Jesus *said to her, "Give Me a drink."

8 For His disciples had gone away into the city to buy food.

9 Therefore the Samaritan woman *said to Him, "How do You, being a Jew, ask for a drink from me, being a Samaritan woman?" (For Jews have no dealings with Samaritans.)

10 Jesus answered and said to her, "If you knew the gift of God, and who it is who says to you, 'Give Me a drink,' you would have asked Him, and He would have given you living water."

11 She *said to Him, "Sir, You have nothing to draw with and the well is deep. Where then do You get that living water?

12 "Are You greater than our father Jacob, who gave us this well, and drank of it himself and his sons and his cattle?"

13 Jesus answered and said to her, "Everyone who drinks of this water will thirst again;

14 but whoever drinks of the water that I will give him will never

thirst—ever; but the water that I will give him will become in him a well of water springing up to eternal life."

15 The woman *said to Him, "Sir, give me this water, so I will not be thirsty nor come *back* here to draw."

16 He *said to her, "Go, call your husband and come *back* here."

17 The woman answered and said, "I have no husband." Jesus *said to her, "You have correctly said, 'I have no husband';

18 for you had five husbands, and the one you now have is not your husband; this you have said truly."

19 The woman *said to Him, "Sir, I see that You are a prophet.

20 "Our fathers worshiped on this mountain, and you *people* say that in Jerusalem is the place where men ought to worship."

21 Jesus *said to her, "Woman, believe Me, an hour is coming when neither in this mountain nor in Jerusalem will you worship the Father.

22 "You worship what you do not know; we worship what we know, for salvation is from the Jews.

23 "But an hour is coming, and now is, when the true worshipers will worship the Father in spirit and truth; for such people the Father seeks to be His worshipers.

24 "God is spirit, and those who worship Him must worship in spirit and truth."

25 The woman *said to Him, "I know that Messiah is coming (He who is called Christ); when He comes, He will declare all things to us."

26 Jesus *said to her, "I who speak to you am *He*."

27 And at this point His disciples came, and they were marveling that He was speaking with a woman, yet no one said, "What do You seek?" or, "Why are You speaking with her?"

28 So the woman left her water jar, and went into the city and *said to the men,

29 "Come, see a man who told me all the things that I *have* done; is this not the Christ?"

30 They went out of the city, and were coming to Him.

31 Meanwhile the disciples were urging Him, saying, "Rabbi, eat."

32 But He said to them, "I have food to eat that you do not know about."

33 So the disciples were saying to one another, "Has anyone brought Him *anything* to eat?"

34 Jesus *said to them, "My food is to do the will of Him who sent Me and to finish His work.

35 "Do you not say, 'There are yet four months, and *then* comes the harvest'? Behold, I say to you, lift up your eyes and look on the fields, that they are white for harvest.

36 "Even now he who reaps is receiving wages and is gathering fruit for life eternal; so that he who sows and he who reaps may rejoice together.

37 "For in this *case* the saying is true, 'One sows and another reaps.'

38 "I sent you to reap that for which you have not labored; others have

labored and you have entered into their labor."

Many Samaritans Believe

39 From that city many of the Samaritans believed in Him because of the word of the woman who bore witness, "He told me all the things that I *have* done."

40 So when the Samaritans came to Jesus, they were asking Him to stay with them; and He stayed there two days.

41 And many more believed because of His word;

42 and they were saying to the woman, "It is no longer because of what you said that we believe, for we have heard for ourselves and know that this One is truly the Savior of the world."

43 And after the two days He went from there into Galilee.

44 For Jesus Himself bore witness that a prophet has no honor in his own country.

45 So when He came to Galilee, the Galileans received Him, having seen all the things that He did in Jerusalem at the feast; for they themselves also went to the feast.

Jesus Heals a Royal Official's Son

46 Then He came again to Cana of Galilee where He had made the water wine. And there was a royal official whose son was sick at Capernaum.

47 When he heard that Jesus had come out of Judea into Galilee, he went to Him and was asking *Him* to come down and heal his son; for he was about to die.

48 So Jesus said to him, "Unless you *people* see signs and wonders, you will never believe."

49 The royal official *said to Him, "Sir, come down before my child dies."

50 Jesus *said to him, "Go; your son lives." The man believed the word that Jesus spoke to him and started on his way.

51 And while he was still going down, his slaves met him, saying that his son was alive.

52 So he inquired of them the hour when he began to get better. Then they said to him, "Yesterday at the seventh hour the fever left him."

53 So the father knew that *it was* at that hour in which Jesus said to him, "Your son lives"; and he himself believed and his whole household.

54 This is again a second sign that Jesus did when He had come out of Judea into Galilee.

CHAPTER 5

The Healing at Bethesda

AFTER these things there was a feast of the Jews, and Jesus went up to Jerusalem.

2 Now there is in Jerusalem by the sheep *gate* a pool, which is called in Hebrew Bethesda, having five porticoes.

3 In these lay a multitude of those who were sick, blind, lame, and withered, [waiting for the moving of the waters;

4 for an angel of the Lord went down at certain seasons into the pool and stirred up the water; whoever then first, after the stirring up of the water, stepped in was made well from whatever sickness with which he was afflicted.]

5 And a man was there who had been sick for thirty-eight years.

6 When Jesus saw him lying *there* and knew that he had already been *sick* a long time, He *said to him, "Do you wish to get well?"

7 The sick man answered Him, "Sir, I have no man to put me into the pool when the water is stirred up, but while I am coming, another steps down before me."

8 Jesus *said to him, "Get up, pick up your mat and walk."

9 And immediately the man became well, and picked up his mat and *began to* walk.

Now it was the Sabbath on that day.

10 So the Jews were saying to the man who had been healed, "It is the Sabbath, and it is not lawful for you to carry your mat."

11 But he answered them, "He who made me well was the one who said to me, 'Pick up your mat and walk.'"

12 They asked him, "Who is the man who said to you, 'Pick up *your mat* and walk'?"

13 But the man who was healed did not know who it was, for Jesus had slipped away while there was a crowd in *that* place.

14 Afterward Jesus *found him in the temple and said to him, "Behold, you have become well; do not sin anymore, so that nothing worse happens to you."

15 The man went away, and disclosed to the Jews that it was Jesus who had made him well.

16 And for this reason the Jews were persecuting Jesus, because He was doing these things on the Sabbath.

17 But He answered them, "My Father is working until now, and I Myself am working."

Jesus' Equality with the Father

18 For this reason therefore the Jews were seeking all the more to kill Him, because He not only was breaking the Sabbath, but also was calling God His own Father, making Himself equal with God.

19 Therefore Jesus answered and was saying to them, "Truly, truly, I say to you, the Son can do nothing from Himself, unless *it is* something He sees the Father doing; for whatever the Father does, these things the Son also does in the same manner.

20 "For the Father loves the Son, and shows Him all things that He Himself is doing; and *the Father* will show Him greater works than these, so that you will marvel.

21 "For just as the Father raises the dead and gives *them* life, even so the Son also gives life to whom He wishes.

22 "For not even the Father judges

anyone, but He has given all judgment to the Son,

23 so that all will honor the Son even as they honor the Father. He who does not honor the Son does not honor the Father who sent Him.

24 "Truly, truly, I say to you, he who hears My word, and believes Him who sent Me, has eternal life, and does not come into judgment, but has passed out of death into life.

Two Resurrections

25 "Truly, truly, I say to you, an hour is coming and now is, when the dead will hear the voice of the Son of God, and those who hear will live.

26 "For just as the Father has life in Himself, even so He gave to the Son also to have life in Himself;

27 and He gave Him authority to execute judgment, because He is the Son of Man.

28 "Do not marvel at this; for an hour is coming, in which all who are in the tombs will hear His voice,

29 and will come forth; those who did the good deeds to a resurrection of life, those who committed the evil deeds to a resurrection of judgment.

30 "I can do nothing from Myself. As I hear, I judge; and My judgment is righteous, because I do not seek My own will, but the will of Him who sent Me.

31 "If I *alone* bear witness about Myself, My witness is not true.

32 "There is another who bears witness about Me, and I know that the witness which He gives about Me is true.

Witness to Jesus: the Father and the Scriptures

33 "You have sent to John, and he has borne witness to the truth.

34 "But the witness I receive is not from man, but I say these things so that you may be saved.

35 "He was the lamp that was burning and shining and you were willing to rejoice for a while in his light.

36 "But the witness I have is greater than *the witness of* John; for the works which the Father has given Me to finish—the very works that I do—bear witness about Me, that the Father has sent Me.

37 "And the Father who sent Me, He has borne witness about Me. You have neither heard His voice at any time nor seen His form.

38 "And you do not have His word abiding in you, for you do not believe Him whom He sent.

39 "You search the Scriptures because you think that in them you have eternal life; it is these that bear witness about Me;

40 and you are unwilling to come to Me so that you may have life.

41 "I do not receive glory from men;

42 but I know you, that you do not have the love of God in yourselves.

43 "I have come in My Father's name, and you do not receive Me; if another comes in his own name, you will receive him.

44 "How can you believe, when you

receive glory from one another and you do not seek the glory that is from the only God?

45 "Do not think that I will accuse you to the Father; the one who accuses you is Moses, in whom you have set your hope.

46 "For if you believed Moses, you would believe Me, for he wrote about Me.

47 "But if you do not believe his writings, how will you believe My words?"

CHAPTER 6

Jesus Feeds Five Thousand

AFTER these things Jesus went away to the other side of the Sea of Galilee (or Tiberias).

2 Now a large crowd was following Him, because they were seeing the signs which He was doing on those who were sick.

3 Then Jesus went up on the mountain, and there He was sitting down with His disciples.

4 Now the Passover, the feast of the Jews, was near.

5 Therefore Jesus, lifting up His eyes and seeing that a large crowd was coming to Him, *said to Philip, "Where should we buy bread, so that these people may eat?"

6 And this He was saying to test him, for He Himself knew what He was going to do.

7 Philip answered Him, "Two

hundred ¹denarii worth of bread is not sufficient for them, for everyone to receive a little."

8 One of His disciples, Andrew, Simon Peter's brother, *said to Him,

9 "There is a boy here who has five barley loaves and two fish, but what are these for so many people?"

10 Jesus said, "Have the people sit down." Now there was much grass in the place. So the men sat down, in number about five thousand.

11 Jesus then took the loaves, and having given thanks, He distributed *them* to those who were seated; likewise also of the fish, as much as they wanted.

12 And when they were filled, He *said to His disciples, "Gather up the leftover pieces so that nothing will be lost."

13 So they gathered them up, and filled twelve baskets with pieces of the five barley loaves left over by those who had eaten.

14 Therefore when the people saw the sign which He had done, they were saying, "This is truly the Prophet who is to come into the world."

Jesus Walks on the Sea

15 So Jesus, knowing that they were going to come and take Him by force to make Him king, withdrew again to the mountain by Himself alone.

16 Now when evening came, His disciples went down to the sea,

17 and after getting into a boat, they *began to* cross the sea to Capernaum.

---

¹ A Roman silver coin, approx. a laborer's daily wage

It had already become dark, and Jesus had not yet come to them.

18 And the sea *was stirred up because a strong wind was blowing.

19 Then, when they had rowed about [1]twenty-five or thirty stadia, they *saw Jesus walking on the sea and drawing near to the boat; and they were frightened.

20 But He *said to them, "It is I; do not be afraid."

21 So they were willing to receive Him into the boat, and immediately the boat was at the land to which they were going.

22 On the next day, the crowd which stood on the other side of the sea saw that there was no other small boat there, except one, and that Jesus had not entered with His disciples into the boat, but *that* His disciples had gone away alone.

23 Other small boats came from Tiberias near to the place where they ate the bread after the Lord had given thanks.

24 So when the crowd saw that Jesus was not there, nor His disciples, they themselves got into the small boats, and came to Capernaum seeking Jesus.

25 And when they found Him on the other side of the sea, they said to Him, "Rabbi, when did You come here?"

I Am the Bread of Life

26 Jesus answered them and said, "Truly, truly, I say to you, you seek Me, not because you saw signs, but because you ate of the loaves and were filled.

27 "Do not work for the food which perishes, but for the food which endures to eternal life, which the Son of Man will give to you, for on Him the Father, God, set His seal."

28 Therefore they said to Him, "What should we do, so that we may work the works of God?"

29 Jesus answered and said to them, "This is the work of God, that you believe in Him whom He has sent."

30 So they said to Him, "What then do You do for a sign so that we may see, and believe You? What work do You perform?

31 "Our fathers ate the manna in the wilderness; as it is written, 'HE GAVE THEM BREAD FROM HEAVEN TO EAT.'"

32 Jesus then said to them, "Truly, truly, I say to you, Moses has not given you the bread from heaven, but My Father gives you the true bread from heaven.

33 "For the bread of God is that which comes down from heaven and gives life to the world."

34 Then they said to Him, "Lord, always give us this bread."

35 Jesus said to them, "I am the bread of life. He who comes to Me will never hunger, and he who believes in Me will never thirst.

36 "But I said to you that you have seen Me, and yet do not believe.

37 "All that the Father gives Me will

[1] Approx. 2.8–3.5 mi. or 4.6–5.5 km, a stadion was about 607 ft. or 185 m

come to Me, and the one who comes to Me I will never cast out.

38 "For I have come down from heaven, not to do My own will, but the will of Him who sent Me.

39 "Now this is the will of Him who sent Me, that of all that He has given Me I lose nothing, but raise it up on the last day.

40 "For this is the will of My Father, that everyone who sees the Son and believes in Him will have eternal life, and I Myself will raise him up on the last day."

Words to the Jews

41 Therefore the Jews were grumbling about Him, because He said, "I am the bread that came down from heaven."

42 They were saying, "Is not this Jesus, the son of Joseph, whose father and mother we know? How does He now say, 'I have come down from heaven'?"

43 Jesus answered and said to them, "Stop grumbling among yourselves.

44 "No one can come to Me unless the Father who sent Me draws him; and I will raise him up on the last day.

45 "It is written in the prophets, 'AND THEY SHALL ALL BE TAUGHT BY GOD.' Everyone who has heard and learned from the Father comes to Me.

46 "Not that anyone has seen the Father, except the One who is from God; He has seen the Father.

47 "Truly, truly, I say to you, he who believes has eternal life.

48 "I am the bread of life.

49 "Your fathers ate the manna in the wilderness, and they died.

50 "This is the bread which comes down from heaven, so that one may eat of it and not die.

51 "I am the living bread that came down from heaven; if anyone eats of this bread, he will live forever; and also the bread which I will give for the life of the world is My flesh."

52 Then the Jews *began to* argue with one another, saying, "How can this man give us *His* flesh to eat?"

53 So Jesus said to them, "Truly, truly, I say to you, unless you eat the flesh of the Son of Man and drink His blood, you have no life in yourselves.

54 "He who eats My flesh and drinks My blood has eternal life, and I will raise him up on the last day.

55 "For My flesh is true food, and My blood is true drink.

56 "He who eats My flesh and drinks My blood abides in Me, and I in him.

57 "As the living Father sent Me, and I live because of the Father, so he who eats Me, he also will live because of Me.

58 "This is the bread which came down out of heaven, not as the fathers ate and died. He who eats this bread will live forever."

Words to the Disciples

59 These things He said in the synagogue as He taught in Capernaum.

60 Therefore many of His disciples, when they heard *this* said, "This is a difficult statement; who can listen to it?"

61 But Jesus, knowing in Himself that His disciples were grumbling at this, said to them, "Does this cause you to stumble?

62 "*What* then if you see the Son of

Man ascending to where He was before?

63 "The Spirit is the One who gives life; the flesh profits nothing; the words that I have spoken to you are spirit and are life.

64 "But there are some of you who do not believe." For Jesus knew from the beginning who they were who did not believe, and who it was that would betray Him.

65 And He was saying, "For this reason I have said to you, that no one can come to Me unless it has been granted him from the Father."

Peter Confesses Jesus Is the Christ

66 As a result of this many of His disciples went away and were not walking with Him anymore.

67 So Jesus said to the twelve, "Do you also want to go?"

68 Simon Peter answered Him, "Lord, to whom shall we go? You have words of eternal life.

69 "And we have believed and have come to know that You are the Holy One of God."

70 Jesus answered them, "Did I Myself not choose you, the twelve, and *yet* one of you is a devil?"

71 Now He was speaking of Judas *the son* of Simon Iscariot, for he, one of the twelve, was going to betray Him.

CHAPTER 7

Jesus Teaches at the Feast of Booths

AND after these things Jesus was walking in Galilee, for He was unwilling to walk in Judea because the Jews were seeking to kill Him.

2 Now the feast of the Jews, the Feast of Booths, was near.

3 Therefore His brothers said to Him, "Leave here and go into Judea, so that Your disciples also may see Your works which You are doing.

4 "For no one does anything in secret when he himself seeks to be *known* openly. If You do these things, show Yourself publicly to the world."

5 For not even His brothers were believing in Him.

6 So Jesus *said to them, "My time is not yet here, but your time is always here.

7 "The world cannot hate you, but it hates Me because I bear witness about it, that its deeds are evil.

8 "Go up to the feast yourselves; I am not yet going up to this feast because My time has not yet been fulfilled."

9 Having said these things to them, He stayed in Galilee.

10 But when His brothers had gone up to the feast, then He Himself also went up, not publicly, but as in secret.

11 So the Jews were seeking Him at the feast and saying, "Where is He?"

12 And there was much grumbling among the crowds concerning Him; some were saying, "He is a good man"; others were saying, "No, on the contrary, He leads the crowd astray."

13 Yet no one was speaking openly about Him for fear of the Jews.

14 But when it was now the middle of the feast Jesus went up into the temple, and *began to* teach.

15 The Jews then were marveling, saying, "How has this man become learned, not having been educated?"

16 So Jesus answered them and said, "My teaching is not Mine, but from Him who sent Me.

17 "If anyone is willing to do His will, he will know about the teaching, whether it is of God or I speak from Myself.

18 "He who speaks from himself seeks his own glory; but He who is seeking the glory of the One who sent Him, He is true, and there is no unrighteousness in Him.

19 "Did not Moses give you the Law? And *yet* none of you does the Law. Why do you seek to kill Me?"

20 The crowd answered, "You have a demon! Who seeks to kill You?"

21 Jesus answered them, "I did one work, and you all marvel.

22 "For this reason Moses has given you circumcision (not because it is from Moses, but from the fathers), and on *the* Sabbath you circumcise a man.

23 "If a man receives circumcision on the Sabbath so that the Law of Moses will not be broken, are you angry with Me because I made an entire man well on *the* Sabbath?

24 "Do not judge according to appearance, but judge with righteous judgment."

25 So some of the people of Jerusalem were saying, "Is this not the man whom they are seeking to kill?

26 "And look, He is speaking openly, and they are saying nothing to Him. Do the rulers truly know that this is the Christ?

27 "However, we know where this man is from; but whenever the Christ comes, no one knows where He is from."

28 Then Jesus cried out in the temple, teaching and saying, "You both know Me and know where I am from; and I have not come of Myself, but He who sent Me is true, whom you do not know.

29 "I know Him, because I am from Him, and He sent Me."

30 So they were seeking to seize Him; yet no man laid his hand on Him, because His hour had not yet come.

31 But many of the crowd believed in Him; and they were saying, "When the Christ comes, will He do more signs than this man did?"

32 The Pharisees heard the crowd whispering these things about Him, and the chief priests and the Pharisees sent officers to seize Him.

33 Therefore Jesus said, "For a little while longer I am with you, then I go to Him who sent Me.

34 "You will seek Me, and will not find Me; and where I am, you cannot come."

35 The Jews then said to one another, "Where does this man intend to go that we will not find Him? Is He intending to go to the Dispersion among the Greeks and teach the Greeks?

36 "What is this statement that He

said, 'You will seek Me, and will not find Me; and where I am, you cannot come'?"

37 Now on the last day, the great *day* of the feast, Jesus stood and cried out, saying, "If anyone is thirsty, let him come to Me and drink.

38 "He who believes in Me, as the Scripture said, 'From his innermost being will flow rivers of living water.' "

39 But this He spoke of the Spirit, whom those who believed in Him were going to receive; for the Spirit was not yet *given*, because Jesus was not yet glorified.

Division of People over Jesus

40 *Some* of the crowd therefore, when they heard these words, were saying, "This truly is the Prophet."

41 Others were saying, "This is the Christ." Still others were saying, "*No*, for is the Christ going to come from Galilee?

42 "Has not the Scripture said that the Christ comes from the seed of David and from Bethlehem, the village where David was?"

43 So a division occurred in the crowd because of Him.

44 Some of them were wanting to seize Him, but no one laid hands on Him.

45 The officers then came to the chief priests and Pharisees, and they said to them, "Why did you not bring Him?"

46 The officers answered, "Never has a man spoken like this!"

47 The Pharisees then answered them, "Have you also been led astray?

48 "Have any of the rulers or Pharisees believed in Him?

49 "But this crowd which does not know the Law is accursed."

50 Nicodemus (he who came to Him before), being one of them, *said to them,

51 "Does our Law judge a man unless it first hears from him and knows what he is doing?"

52 They answered him, "Are you also from Galilee? Search and see that no prophet arises out of Galilee."

53 [Everyone went to his home.

CHAPTER 8

An Adulteress Forgiven

BUT Jesus went to the Mount of Olives.

2 Early in the morning He came again into the temple, and all the people were coming to Him; and He sat down and *began to* teach them.

3 The scribes and the Pharisees *brought a woman caught in adultery, and having set her in the center *of the court*,

4 they *said to Him, "Teacher, this woman has been caught in adultery, in the very act.

5 "Now in the Law Moses commanded us to stone such women; what then do You say?"

6 They were saying this, testing Him, so that they might have *evidence* to accuse Him. But Jesus

stooped down and with His finger wrote on the ground.

7 But when they persisted in asking Him, He straightened up and said to them, "Let him who is without sin among you *be the* first to throw a stone at her."

8 Again He stooped down and wrote on the ground.

9 When they heard it, they *began* to go out one by one, beginning with the older ones, and He was left alone, and the woman, where she was, in the center *of the court.*

10 Straightening up, Jesus said to her, "Woman, where are they? Did no one condemn you?"

11 She said, "No one, Lord." And Jesus said, "I do not condemn you, either. Go, and from now on sin no more."]

I Am the Light of the World

12 Then Jesus again spoke to them, saying, "I am the Light of the world; he who follows Me will never walk in the darkness, but will have the Light of life."

13 So the Pharisees said to Him, "You are bearing witness about Yourself; Your witness is not true."

14 Jesus answered and said to them, "Even if I bear witness about Myself, My witness is true, for I know where I came from and where I am going; but you do not know where I come from or where I am going.

15 "You judge according to the flesh; I am not judging anyone.

16 "But even if I do judge, My judgment is true; for I am not alone in *it*, but I and the Father who sent Me.

17 "Even in your law it has been written that the witness of two men is true.

18 "I am He who bears witness about Myself, and the Father who sent Me bears witness about Me."

19 So they were saying to Him, "Where is Your Father?" Jesus answered, "You know neither Me nor My Father; if you knew Me, you would know My Father also."

20 These words He spoke in the treasury, as He was teaching in the temple; and no one seized Him, because His hour had not yet come.

21 Then He said again to them, "I am going away, and you will seek Me, and will die in your sin. Where I am going, you cannot come."

22 So the Jews were saying, "Surely He will not kill Himself, since He says, 'Where I am going, you cannot come'?"

23 And He was saying to them, "You are from below, I am from above. You are of this world, I am not of this world.

24 "Therefore I said to you that you will die in your sins. For unless you believe that I am *He*, you will die in your sins."

25 So they were saying to Him, "Who are You?" Jesus said to them, "What have I been saying to you *from* the beginning?

26 "I have many things to say and to judge concerning you, but He who sent Me is true; and the things which

I heard from Him, these I am saying to the world."

27 They did not know that He had been speaking to them about the Father.

28 So Jesus said, "When you lift up the Son of Man, then you will know that I am *He*, and I do nothing from Myself, but I speak these things as the Father taught Me.

29 "And He who sent Me is with Me; He has not left Me alone, for I always do the things that are pleasing to Him."

30 As He was speaking these things, many believed in Him.

The Son Will Make You Free

31 So Jesus was saying to those Jews who had believed Him, "If you abide in My word, *then* you are truly My disciples;

32 and you will know the truth, and the truth will make you free."

33 They answered Him, "We are Abraham's seed and have never yet been enslaved to anyone. How is it that You say, 'You will become free'?"

34 Jesus answered them, "Truly, truly, I say to you, everyone who commits sin is the slave of sin.

35 "And the slave does not remain in the house forever; the son does remain forever.

36 "So if the Son makes you free, you will be free indeed.

37 "I know that you are Abraham's seed; yet you are seeking to kill Me, because My word has no place in you.

38 "I speak the things which I have seen with *My* Father; therefore you also do the things which you heard from *your* father."

39 They answered and said to Him, "Abraham is our father." Jesus *said to them, "If you are Abraham's children, you would do the deeds of Abraham.

40 "But now you are seeking to kill Me, a man who has told you the truth, which I heard from God. This Abraham did not do.

41 "You are doing the deeds of your father." They said to Him, "We were not born of sexual immorality; we have one Father: God."

42 Jesus said to them, "If God were your Father, you would love Me, for I proceeded forth and have come from God, for I have not even come of Myself, but He sent Me.

43 "Why do you not understand what I am saying? *It is* because you cannot hear My word.

44 "You are of *your* father the devil, and you want to do the desires of your father. He was a murderer from the beginning, and does not stand in the truth because there is no truth in him. Whenever he speaks a lie, he speaks from his own *nature*, for he is a liar and the father of lies.

45 "But because I speak the truth, you do not believe Me.

46 "Which one of you convicts Me of sin? If I speak truth, why do you not believe Me?

47 "He who is of God hears the words of God; for this reason you do

not hear *them*, because you are not of God."

48 The Jews answered and said to Him, "Do we not say rightly that You are a Samaritan and have a demon?"

49 Jesus answered, "I do not have a demon, but I honor My Father, and you dishonor Me.

50 "But I do not seek My glory; there is One who seeks and judges.

51 "Truly, truly, I say to you, if anyone keeps My word he will never see death—ever."

52 The Jews said to Him, "Now we know that You have a demon. Abraham died, and the prophets *also*; and You say, 'If anyone keeps My word, he will never taste of death—ever.'

53 "Surely You are not greater than our father Abraham who died? The prophets died too; whom do You make Yourself out *to be*?"

54 Jesus answered, "If I glorify Myself, My glory is nothing; it is My Father who glorifies Me, of whom you say, 'He is our God';

55 and you have not known Him, but I know Him; and if I say that I do not know Him, I will be a liar like you, but I do know Him and keep His word.

56 "Your father Abraham rejoiced to see My day, and he saw *it* and was glad."

57 So the Jews said to Him, "You are not yet fifty years old, and have You seen Abraham?"

58 Jesus said to them, "Truly, truly, I say to you, before Abraham was, I am."

59 Therefore they picked up stones to throw at Him, but Jesus hid Himself and went out of the temple.

CHAPTER 9

Jesus Heals a Man Born Blind

AS He passed by, He saw a man blind from birth.

2 And His disciples asked Him, saying, "Rabbi, who sinned, this man or his parents, that he would be born blind?"

3 Jesus answered, "Neither this man nor his parents sinned, but *this was* so that the works of God might be manifested in him.

4 "We must work the works of Him who sent Me as long as it is day; night is coming when no one can work.

5 "While I am in the world, I am the light of the world."

6 When He had said this, He spat on the ground, made clay of the saliva, and rubbed the clay on his eyes,

7 and said to him, "Go, wash in the pool of Siloam" (which is translated, Sent). So he went away and washed, and came *back* seeing.

8 Therefore the neighbors, and those who previously saw him as a beggar, were saying, "Is not this the one who used to sit and beg?"

9 Others were saying, "This is he," *still* others were saying, "No, but he is like him." He kept saying, "I am the one."

10 So they were saying to him, "How then were your eyes opened?"

11 He answered, "The man who is called Jesus made clay, and rubbed my eyes, and said to me, 'Go to Siloam and wash'; so when I went away and washed, I received sight."

12 And they said to him, "Where is He?" He *said, "I do not know."

Controversy over the Man Born Blind

13 They *brought to the Pharisees the man who was formerly blind.

14 Now it was a Sabbath on the day when Jesus made the clay and opened his eyes.

15 So the Pharisees also were asking him again how he received his sight. And he said to them, "He applied clay to my eyes, and I washed, and I see."

16 So then some of the Pharisees were saying, "This man is not from God, because He does not keep the Sabbath." But others were saying, "How can a sinful man do such signs?" And there was a division among them.

17 Therefore, they *said to the blind man again, "What do you say about Him, since He opened your eyes?" And he said, "He is a prophet."

18 Then, the Jews did not believe *it* of him that he was blind and had received sight, until they called the parents of the very one who had received his sight,

19 and questioned them, saying, "Is this your son, who you say was born blind? Then how does he now see?"

20 So his parents answered and said, "We know that this is our son, and that he was born blind;

21 but how he now sees, we do not know; or who opened his eyes, we do not know. Ask him; he is of age, he will speak for himself."

22 His parents said this because they were afraid of the Jews; for the Jews had already agreed that if anyone confessed Him to be Christ, he was to be put out of the synagogue.

23 For this reason his parents said, "He is of age; ask him."

24 Therefore, a second time they called the man who had been blind, and said to him, "Give glory to God; we know that this man is a sinner."

25 He then answered, "Whether He is a sinner, I do not know; one thing I do know, that though I was blind, now I see."

26 So they said to him, "What did He do to you? How did He open your eyes?"

27 He answered them, "I told you already and you did not listen. Why do you want to listen again? Do you want to become His disciples too?"

28 And they reviled him and said, "You are His disciple, but we are disciples of Moses.

29 "We know that God has spoken to Moses, but as for this man, we do not know where He is from."

30 The man answered and said to them, "Well, here is a marvelous thing, that you do not know where He is from, and He opened my eyes.

31 "We know that God does not listen to sinners; but if anyone is God-fearing and does His will, He listens to him.

32 "Since the beginning of time it has never been heard that anyone opened the eyes of a person born blind.

33 "If this man were not from God, He could do nothing."

34 They answered and said to him, "You were born entirely in sins, and are you teaching us?" So they put him out.

Jesus Affirms His Deity

35 Jesus heard that they had put him out, and after finding him, He said, "Do you believe in the Son of Man?"

36 He answered and said, "Who is He, Lord, that I may believe in Him?"

37 Jesus said to him, "You have both seen Him, and He is the one who is talking with you."

38 And he said, "Lord, I believe." And he worshiped Him.

39 And Jesus said, "For judgment I came into this world, so that those who do not see may see, and that those who see may become blind."

40 Some of the Pharisees who were with Him heard these things and said to Him, "Are we blind too?"

41 Jesus said to them, "If you were blind, you would have no sin; but now *that* you say, 'We see,' your sin remains.

CHAPTER 10

I Am the Good Shepherd

"TRULY, truly, I say to you, he who does not enter by the door into the fold of the sheep, but climbs up some other way, he is a thief and a robber.

2 "But he who enters by the door is a shepherd of the sheep.

3 "To him the doorkeeper opens, and the sheep hear his voice, and he calls his own sheep by name and leads them out.

4 "When he brings all his own out, he goes ahead of them, and the sheep follow him because they know his voice.

5 "A stranger they will never follow, but will flee from him, because they do not know the voice of strangers."

6 This figure of speech Jesus spoke to them, but they did not understand what those things were which He had been saying to them.

7 So Jesus said to them again, "Truly, truly, I say to you, I am the door of the sheep.

8 "All who came before Me are thieves and robbers, but the sheep did not hear them.

9 "I am the door; if anyone enters through Me, he will be saved, and will go in and out and find pasture.

10 "The thief comes only to steal and kill and destroy; I came that they may have life, and have *it* abundantly.

11 "I am the good shepherd; the good shepherd lays down His life for the sheep.

12 "He who is a hired hand, and not a shepherd, who is not the owner of the sheep, sees the wolf coming, and leaves the sheep and flees—and the wolf snatches and scatters them—

13 "because he is a hired hand and is not concerned about the sheep.

14 "I am the good shepherd, and I know My own and My own know Me,

15 even as the Father knows Me and I know the Father; and I lay down My life for the sheep.

16 "And I have other sheep, which are not from this fold; I must bring them also, and they will hear My voice; and they will become one flock *with* one shepherd.

17 "For this reason the Father loves Me, because I lay down My life so that I may take it again.

18 "No one takes it away from Me, but from Myself, I lay it down. I have authority to lay it down, and I have authority to take it up again. This commandment I received from My Father."

19 A division occurred again among the Jews because of these words.

20 And many of them were saying, "He has a demon and is insane. Why do you listen to Him?"

21 Others were saying, "These are not the words of someone demon-possessed. Can a demon open the eyes of the blind?"

I and the Father Are One

22 At that time the Feast of the Dedication took place at Jerusalem;

23 it was winter, and Jesus was walking in the temple in the Portico of Solomon.

24 The Jews then gathered around Him, and were saying to Him, "How long will You keep us in suspense? If You are the Christ, tell us openly."

25 Jesus answered them, "I told you, and you do not believe; the works that I do in My Father's name, these bear witness of Me.

26 "But you do not believe because you are not of My sheep.

27 "My sheep hear My voice, and I know them, and they follow Me;

28 and I give eternal life to them, and they will never perish—ever; and no one will snatch them out of My hand.

29 "My Father, who has given *them* to Me, is greater than all; and no one is able to snatch *them* out of the Father's hand.

30 "I and the Father are one."

31 The Jews picked up stones again to stone Him.

32 Jesus answered them, "I showed you many good works from the Father; for which of them are you stoning Me?"

33 The Jews answered Him, "For a good work we do not stone You, but for blasphemy; and because You, being a man, make Yourself God."

34 Jesus answered them, "Has it not been written in your Law, 'I SAID, YOU ARE GODS'?

35 "If he called them gods, to whom the word of God came (and the Scripture cannot be broken),

36 do you say of Him, whom the Father sanctified and sent into the world, 'You are blaspheming,' because I said, 'I am the Son of God'?

37 "If I do not do the works of My Father, do not believe Me;

38 but if I do them, though you do not believe Me, believe the works,

so that you may know and continue knowing that the Father is in Me, and I in the Father."

39 Therefore they were seeking again to seize Him, and He eluded their grasp.

40 And He went away again beyond the Jordan to the place where John was first baptizing, and He was staying there.

41 And many came to Him and were saying, "While John did no sign, yet everything John said about this man was true."

42 And many believed in Him there.

CHAPTER 11

The Death and Resurrection of Lazarus

NOW a certain man was sick, Lazarus from Bethany, the village of Mary and her sister Martha.

2 And it was *the* Mary who anointed the Lord with perfume, and wiped His feet with her hair, whose brother Lazarus was sick.

3 So the sisters sent to Him, saying, "Lord, behold, he whom You love is sick."

4 But when Jesus heard *this*, He said, "This sickness is not to end in death, but is for the glory of God, so that the Son of God may be glorified by it."

5 Now Jesus loved Martha and her sister and Lazarus.

6 So when He heard that he was sick, He then stayed two days in the place where He was.

7 Then after this He *said to the disciples, "Let us go to Judea again."

8 The disciples *said to Him, "Rabbi, the Jews were just now seeking to stone You, and are You going there again?"

9 Jesus answered, "Are there not twelve hours in the day? If anyone walks in the day, he does not stumble, because he sees the light of this world.

10 "But if anyone walks in the night, he stumbles, because the light is not in him."

11 He said these things, and after that He *said to them, "Our friend Lazarus has fallen asleep; but I go, so that I may awaken him."

12 The disciples then said to Him, "Lord, if he has fallen asleep, he will be saved *from his sickness.*"

13 Now Jesus had spoken of his death, but they thought that He was speaking of actual sleep.

14 So Jesus then said to them plainly, "Lazarus is dead,

15 and I am glad for your sakes that I was not there, so that you may believe; but let us go to him."

16 Therefore Thomas, who is called Didymus, said to *his* fellow disciples, "Let us also go, so that we may die with Him."

17 So when Jesus came, He found that he had already been in the tomb four days.

18 Now Bethany was near Jerusalem, about [1]fifteen stadia away;

19 and many of the Jews had come

---

[1] Approx. 1.7 mi. or 2.7 km, a stadion was approx. 607 ft. or 185 m

to Martha and Mary, to console them about their brother.

20 Martha therefore, when she heard that Jesus was coming, went to meet Him, but Mary was sitting in the house.

21 Martha then said to Jesus, "Lord, if You had been here, my brother would not have died.

22 "But even now I know that whatever You ask from God, God will give You."

23 Jesus *said to her, "Your brother will rise again."

24 Martha *said to Him, "I know that he will rise again in the resurrection on the last day."

25 Jesus said to her, "I am the resurrection and the life; he who believes in Me will live even if he dies,

26 and everyone who lives and believes in Me will never die—ever. Do you believe this?"

27 She *said to Him, "Yes, Lord; I have believed that You are the Christ, the Son of God, the One who comes into the world."

28 And when she had said this, she went away and called Mary her sister, saying secretly, "The Teacher is here and is calling for you."

29 And when she heard it, she *got up quickly and was coming to Him.

30 Now Jesus had not yet come into the village, but was still in the place where Martha met Him.

31 Then the Jews—who were with her in the house and consoling her—when they saw that Mary rose up quickly and went out, they followed her, thinking that she was going to the tomb to cry there.

32 Therefore, when Mary came where Jesus was, she saw Him, and fell at His feet, saying to Him, "Lord, if You had been here, my brother would not have died."

33 When Jesus therefore saw her crying, and the Jews who came with her *also* crying, He was deeply moved in spirit and was troubled,

34 and said, "Where have you laid him?" They *said to Him, "Lord, come and see."

35 Jesus wept.

36 So the Jews were saying, "See how He loved him!"

37 But some of them said, "Could not this man, who opened the eyes of the blind man, have kept this man also from dying?"

38 So Jesus, again being deeply moved within, *came to the tomb. Now it was a cave, and a stone was lying against it.

39 Jesus *said, "Remove the stone." Martha, the sister of the deceased, *said to Him, "Lord, by this time he smells, for he has been *dead* four days."

40 Jesus *said to her, "Did I not say to you that if you believe, you will see the glory of God?"

41 So they removed the stone. Then Jesus raised His eyes, and said, "Father, I thank You that You have heard Me.

42 "And I knew that You always hear Me; but because of the crowd standing around I said this, so that they may believe that You sent Me."

43 And when He had said these things, He cried out with a loud voice, "Lazarus, come forth."

44 The man who had died came forth, bound hand and foot with wrappings, and his face was wrapped around with a cloth. Jesus *said to them, "Unbind him, and let him go."

45 Therefore many of the Jews who came to Mary, and saw what He had done, believed in Him.

46 But some of them went to the Pharisees and told them the things which Jesus had done.

The Leaders Plot to Kill Jesus

47 Therefore the chief priests and the Pharisees gathered the Sanhedrin together, and were saying, "What are we doing? For this man is doing many signs.

48 "If we let Him *go on* like this, all will believe in Him, and the Romans will come and take away both our place and our nation."

49 But one of them, Caiaphas, who was high priest that year, said to them, "You know nothing at all,

50 nor do you take into account that it is better for you that one man should die for the people, and that the whole nation not perish."

51 Now he did not say this from himself, but being high priest that year, he prophesied that Jesus was going to die for the nation,

52 and not for the nation only, but in order that He might also gather together into one the children of God who are scattered abroad.

53 So from that day on they planned together to kill Him.

54 Therefore Jesus no longer continued to walk openly among the Jews, but went away from there to the region near the wilderness, into a city called Ephraim; and there He stayed with the disciples.

55 Now the Passover of the Jews was near, and many went up to Jerusalem from the region before the Passover to purify themselves.

56 So they were seeking Jesus, and were saying to one another as they stood in the temple, "What do you think? That He will not come to the feast at all?"

57 Now the chief priests and the Pharisees had given orders that if anyone knew where He was, he was to report it, so that they might seize Him.

CHAPTER 12

Mary Anoints Jesus with Costly Perfume

JESUS, therefore, six days before the Passover, came to Bethany where Lazarus was, whom Jesus had raised from the dead.

2 So they made Him a supper there, and Martha was serving; and Lazarus was one of those reclining *at the table* with Him.

3 Mary then took a [1]litra of perfume

---

[1] A Roman pound, approx. 12 oz. or 340 gm

of very costly pure nard, and anointed the feet of Jesus and wiped His feet with her hair; and the house was filled with the fragrance of the perfume.

4 But Judas Iscariot, one of His disciples, who was going to betray Him, *said,

5 "Why was this perfume not sold for three hundred denarii and given to the poor?"

6 Now he said this, not because he was concerned about the poor, but because he was a thief, and as he had the money box, he used to take from what was put into it.

7 Therefore Jesus said, "Let her alone, so that she may keep it for the day of My burial.

8 "For you always have the poor with you, but you do not always have Me."

9 Then the large crowd from the Jews learned that He was there. And they came, not because of Jesus only, but that they might also see Lazarus, whom He raised from the dead.

10 But the chief priests planned to put Lazarus to death also;

11 because on account of him many of the Jews were going away and were believing in Jesus.

The Triumphal Entry

12 On the next day the large crowd who had come to the feast, when they heard that Jesus was coming to Jerusalem,

13 took the branches of the palm trees and went out to meet Him, and *began to* shout, "Hosanna! BLESSED IS HE WHO COMES IN THE NAME OF THE LORD, even the King of Israel."

14 And Jesus, finding a young donkey, sat on it; as it is written,

15 "FEAR NOT, DAUGHTER OF ZION; BEHOLD, YOUR KING IS COMING, SEATED ON A DONKEY'S COLT."

16 These things His disciples did not understand at the first; but when Jesus was glorified, then they remembered that these things were written about Him, and that they had done these things to Him.

17 So the crowd, who was with Him when He called Lazarus out of the tomb and raised him from the dead, continued to bear witness *about Him.*

18 For this reason also the crowd went and met Him, because they heard that He had done this sign.

19 So the Pharisees said to one another, "You see that you are gaining nothing; look, the world has gone after Him."

Some Greeks Seek Jesus

20 Now there were some Greeks among those who were going up to worship at the feast;

21 these then came to Philip, who was from Bethsaida of Galilee, and *began to* ask him, saying, "Sir, we wish to see Jesus."

22 Philip *came and *told Andrew; Andrew and Philip *came and *told Jesus.

23 And Jesus *answered them, saying, "The hour has come for the Son of Man to be glorified.

24 "Truly, truly, I say to you, unless

a grain of wheat falls into the earth and dies, it remains alone; but if it dies, it bears much fruit.

25 "He who loves his life loses it, and he who hates his life in this world will keep it to life eternal.

26 "If anyone serves Me, he must follow Me; and where I am, there My servant will be also; if anyone serves Me, the Father will honor him.

The Son of Man Must Be Lifted Up

27 "Now MY SOUL HAS BECOME DISMAYED; and what shall I say, 'Father, SAVE ME from this hour'? But for this purpose I came to this hour.

28 "Father, glorify Your name." Then a voice came from heaven: "I have both glorified it, and will glorify it again."

29 So the crowd *of people* who stood by and heard it were saying that it had thundered; others were saying, "An angel has spoken to Him."

30 Jesus answered and said, "This voice has not come for My sake, but for your sake.

31 "Now judgment is upon this world; now the ruler of this world will be cast out.

32 "And I, if I am lifted up from the earth, will draw all men to Myself."

33 But He was saying this to indicate the kind of death by which He was about to die.

34 The crowd then answered Him, "We have heard from the Law that the Christ is to remain forever; and how do You say, 'The Son of Man must be lifted up'? Who is this Son of Man?"

35 So Jesus said to them, "For a little while longer the Light is among you. Walk while you have the Light, so that darkness will not overtake you; he who walks in the darkness does not know where he goes.

36 "While you have the Light, believe in the Light, so that you may become sons of Light."

These things Jesus spoke, and He went away and hid Himself from them.

37 But though He had done so many signs before them, they *still* were not believing in Him,

38 so that the word of Isaiah the prophet would be fulfilled, which he spoke: "LORD, WHO HAS BELIEVED OUR REPORT? AND TO WHOM HAS THE ARM OF THE LORD BEEN REVEALED?"

39 For this reason they could not believe, for Isaiah said again,

40 "HE HAS BLINDED THEIR EYES AND HE HARDENED THEIR HEART, LEST THEY SEE WITH THEIR EYES AND UNDERSTAND WITH THEIR HEART, AND RETURN AND I HEAL THEM."

41 These things Isaiah said because he saw His glory, and he spoke about Him.

42 Nevertheless many even of the rulers believed in Him, but because of the Pharisees they were not confessing *Him*, for fear that they would be put out of the synagogue;

43 for they loved the glory of men rather than the glory of God.

44 And Jesus cried out and said, "He who believes in Me, does not believe in Me but in Him who sent Me.

45 "And he who sees Me sees the One who sent Me.

46 "I have come *as* Light into the world, so that everyone who believes in Me will not remain in darkness.

47 "And if anyone hears My words and does not keep them, I do not judge him; for I did not come to judge the world, but to save the world.

48 "He who rejects Me and does not receive My words, has one who judges him; the word I spoke is what will judge him on the last day.

49 "For I did not speak from Myself, but the Father Himself who sent Me has given Me a commandment— what to say and what to speak.

50 "And I know that His commandment is eternal life; therefore the things I speak, I speak just as the Father has told Me."

CHAPTER 13

The Lord's Supper

NOW before the Feast of the Passover, Jesus knowing that His hour had come that He would depart out of this world to the Father, having loved His own who were in the world, He loved them to the end.

2 And during supper, the devil having already put into the heart of Judas Iscariot, *the son* of Simon, to betray Him,

3 Jesus, knowing that the Father had given all things into His hands, and that He had come forth from God and was going back to God,

4 *got up from supper, and *laid aside His garments; and taking a towel, He tied it around Himself.

Jesus Washes the Disciples' Feet

5 Then He *poured water into the washbasin, and began to wash the disciples' feet and to wipe them with the towel which He had tied around *Himself.

6 So He *came to Simon Peter. He *said to Him, "Lord, are You going to wash my feet?"

7 Jesus answered and said to him, "What I am doing you do not realize now, but you will understand afterwards."

8 Peter *said to Him, "You will never wash my feet—ever!" Jesus answered him, "If I do not wash you, you have no part with Me."

9 Simon Peter *said to Him, "Lord, not only my feet, but also my hands and my head."

10 Jesus *said to him, "He who has bathed needs only to wash his feet, but is completely clean; and you are clean, but not all *of you.*"

11 For He knew the one who was betraying Him; for this reason He said, "Not all of you are clean."

12 So when He had washed their feet, and taken His garments and reclined *at the table* again, He said to them, "Do you know what I have done to you?

13 "You call Me Teacher and Lord; and you are right, for *so* I am.

14 "If I then, the Lord and the Teacher, washed your feet, you also ought to wash one another's feet.

15 "For I gave you an example that you also should do as I did to you.

16 "Truly, truly, I say to you, a slave is not greater than his master, nor *is* one who is sent greater than the one who sent him.

17 "If you know these things, you are blessed if you do them.

18 "I do not speak about all of you. I know the ones I have chosen; but that the Scripture would be fulfilled, 'HE WHO EATS MY BREAD HAS LIFTED UP HIS HEEL AGAINST ME.'

19 "From now on I am telling you before *it* occurs, so that when it does occur, you may believe that I am *He*.

20 "Truly, truly, I say to you, he who receives anyone I send receives Me; and he who receives Me receives Him who sent Me."

Jesus Predicts His Betrayal

21 When Jesus had said these things, He became troubled in spirit, and bore witness and said, "Truly, truly, I say to you, that one of you will betray Me."

22 The disciples *began* looking at one another, perplexed about whom He *spoke.

23 There was reclining on Jesus' bosom one of His disciples, whom Jesus loved.

24 So Simon Peter *gestured to him to inquire, "Who is the one of whom He is speaking?"

25 He, leaning back thus on Jesus' bosom, *said to Him, "Lord, who is it?"

26 Jesus *answered, "He is the one for whom I shall dip the piece of bread and give it to him." So when He had dipped the piece of bread, He *took and *gave it to Judas, *the son* of Simon Iscariot.

27 And after the piece of bread, Satan then entered into him. Therefore Jesus *said to him, "What you do, do quickly."

28 Now no one of those reclining *at the table* knew for what purpose He had said this to him.

29 For some were thinking, because Judas had the money box, that Jesus was saying to him, "Buy the things we have need of for the feast"; or else, that he should give something to the poor.

30 So after receiving the piece of bread, he went out immediately. And it was night.

31 Therefore when he had gone out, Jesus *said, "Now is the Son of Man glorified, and God is glorified in Him;

32 if God is glorified in Him, God will also glorify Him in Himself, and will glorify Him immediately.

33 "Little children, I am with you a little while longer. You will seek Me; and as I said to the Jews, now I also say to you, 'Where I am going, you cannot come.'

34 "A new commandment I give to you, that you love one another, even as I have loved you, that you also love one another.

35 "By this all will know that you are My disciples, if you have love for one another."

36 Simon Peter *said to Him, "Lord, where are You going?" Jesus answered,

"Where I go, you cannot follow Me now; but you will follow later."

37 Peter *said to Him, "Lord, why can I not follow You right now? I will lay down my life for You."

38 Jesus *answered, "Will you lay down your life for Me? Truly, truly, I say to you, a rooster will not crow until you deny Me three times.

CHAPTER 14

I Am the Way, the Truth, and the Life

"DO not let your heart be troubled; believe in God, believe also in Me.

2 "In My Father's house are many dwelling places; if it were not so, I would have told you; for I go to prepare a place for you.

3 "And if I go and prepare a place for you, I will come again and receive you to Myself, that where I am, *there* you may be also.

4 "And you know the way where I am going."

5 Thomas *said to Him, "Lord, we do not know where You are going. How do we know the way?"

6 Jesus *said to him, "I am the way, and the truth, and the life. No one comes to the Father but through Me.

Oneness with the Father

7 "If you have come to know Me, you will know My Father also; from now on you know Him, and have seen Him."

8 Philip *said to Him, "Lord, show us the Father, and it is enough for us."

9 Jesus *said to him, "Have I been with you all so long and have you not come to know Me, Philip? He who has seen Me has seen the Father; how *can* you say, 'Show us the Father'?

10 "Do you not believe that I am in the Father, and the Father is in Me? The words that I say to you I do not speak from Myself, but the Father abiding in Me does His works.

11 "Believe Me that I am in the Father and the Father is in Me; otherwise believe because of the works themselves.

12 "Truly, truly, I say to you, he who believes in Me, the works that I do, he will do also; and greater *works* than these he will do because I go to the Father.

13 "Whatever you ask in My name, this will I do, so that the Father may be glorified in the Son.

14 "If you ask Me anything in My name, I will do *it*.

15 "If you love Me, you will keep My commandments.

Jesus Promises the Holy Spirit

16 "And I will ask the Father, and He will give you another Advocate, that He may be with you forever;

17 the Spirit of truth, whom the world cannot receive, because it does not see Him or know Him. You know Him because He abides with you and will be in you.

18 "I will not leave you as orphans; I will come to you.

19 "After a little while the world will

no longer see Me, but you *will* see Me; because I live, you will live also.

20 "On that day you will know that I am in My Father, and you in Me, and I in you.

21 "He who has My commandments and keeps them is the one who loves Me; and he who loves Me will be loved by My Father, and I will love him and will disclose Myself to him."

22 Judas (not Iscariot) *said to Him, "Lord, what then has happened that You are going to disclose Yourself to us and not to the world?"

23 Jesus answered and said to him, "If anyone loves Me, he will keep My word; and My Father will love him, and We will come to him and make Our dwelling with him.

24 "He who does not love Me does not keep My words; and the word which you hear is not Mine, but the Father's who sent Me.

25 "These things I have spoken to you while abiding with you.

26 "But the Advocate, the Holy Spirit, whom the Father will send in My name, He will teach you all things, and bring to your remembrance all that I said to you.

27 "Peace I leave with you; My peace I give to you; not as the world gives do I give to you. Do not let your heart be troubled, nor let it be fearful.

28 "You heard that I said to you, 'I go away, and I will come to you.' If you loved Me, you would have rejoiced because I go to the Father, for the Father is greater than I.

29 "And now I have told you before it happens, so that when it happens, you may believe.

30 "I will not speak much more with you, for the ruler of the world is coming, and he has nothing in Me;

31 but so that the world may know that I love the Father, I do exactly as the Father commanded Me. Get up, let us go from here.

CHAPTER 15

I Am the True Vine

"I am the true vine, and My Father is the vine-grower.

2 "Every branch in Me that does not bear fruit, He takes away; and every *branch* that bears fruit, He cleans it so that it may bear more fruit.

3 "You are already clean because of the word which I have spoken to you.

4 "Abide in Me, and I in you. As the branch cannot bear fruit from itself unless it abides in the vine, so neither *can* you unless you abide in Me.

5 "I am the vine, you are the branches; he who abides in Me and I in him, he bears much fruit, for apart from Me you can do nothing.

6 "If anyone does not abide in Me, he is thrown away as a branch and dries up; and they gather them, and cast them into the fire and they are burned.

7 "If you abide in Me, and My words abide in you, ask whatever you wish, and it will be done for you.

8 "My Father is glorified by this, that you bear much fruit, and *so* prove to be My disciples.

9 "Just as the Father has loved Me, I have also loved you; abide in My love.

10 "If you keep My commandments, you will abide in My love; just as I have kept My Father's commandments and abide in His love.

11 "These things I have spoken to you so that My joy may be in you, and *that* your joy may be complete.

Jesus' Commandment Is Love

12 "This is My commandment, that you love one another, just as I have loved you.

13 "Greater love has no one than this, that one lay down his life for his friends.

14 "You are My friends if you do what I command you.

15 "No longer do I call you slaves, for the slave does not know what his master is doing; but I have called you friends, for all things that I have heard from My Father I have made known to you.

16 "You did not choose Me but I chose you, and appointed you that you would go and bear fruit, and *that* your fruit would abide, so that whatever you ask of the Father in My name He may give to you.

17 "This I command you, that you love one another.

If the World Hates You

18 "If the world hates you, know that it has hated Me before *it hated* you.

19 "If you were of the world, the world would love its own; but because you are not of the world, but I chose you out of the world, because of this the world hates you.

20 "Remember the word that I said to you, 'A slave is not greater than his master.' If they persecuted Me, they will also persecute you; if they kept My word, they will keep yours also.

21 "But all these things they will do to you for My name's sake, because they do not know the One who sent Me.

22 "If I had not come and spoken to them, they would not have sin, but now they have no excuse for their sin.

23 "He who hates Me hates My Father also.

24 "If I had not done among them the works which no one else did, they would not have sin; but now they have both seen and hated Me and My Father as well.

25 "But *this happened* to fulfill the word that is written in their Law, 'THEY HATED ME WITHOUT CAUSE.'

26 "When the Advocate comes, whom I will send to you from the Father, the Spirit of truth who proceeds from the Father, He will bear witness about Me,

27 and you *will* bear witness also, because you have been with Me from the beginning.

CHAPTER 16

Jesus' Warning

"THESE things I have spoken to you so that you may be kept from stumbling.

2 "They will put you out of the synagogue, but an hour is coming for everyone who kills you to think that he is offering service to God.

3 "These things they will do because they did not know the Father or Me.

4 "But these things I have spoken to you, so that when their hour comes, you may remember that I told you of them. These things I did not say to you at the beginning, because I was with you.

The Spirit Is Promised Again

5 "But now I am going to Him who sent Me; and none of you asks Me, 'Where are You going?'

6 "But because I have said these things to you, sorrow has filled your heart.

7 "But I tell you the truth, it is to your advantage that I go away; for if I do not go away, the Advocate will not come to you; but if I go, I will send Him to you.

8 "And He, when He comes, will convict the world concerning sin and righteousness and judgment;

9 concerning sin, because they do not believe in Me;

10 and concerning righteousness, because I go to the Father and you no longer see Me;

11 and concerning judgment, because the ruler of this world has been judged.

12 "I still have many more things to say to you, but you cannot bear *them* now.

13 "But when He, the Spirit of truth, comes, He will guide you into all the truth; for He will not speak from Himself, but whatever He hears, He will speak; and He will disclose to you what is to come.

14 "He will glorify Me, for He will take of Mine and will disclose *it* to you.

15 "All things that the Father has are Mine; therefore I said that He takes of Mine and will disclose *it* to you.

Sorrow Turned to Joy

16 "A little while, and you will no longer see Me; and again a little while, and you will see Me."

17 *Some* of His disciples then said to one another, "What is this He is telling us, 'A little while, and you will not see Me; and again a little while, and you will see Me'; and, 'because I go to the Father'?"

18 So they were saying, "What is this that He says, 'A little while'? We do not know what He is talking about."

19 Jesus knew that they were wishing to question Him, and He said to them, "Are you deliberating together about this, that I said, 'A little while, and you will not see Me, and again a little while, and you will see Me'?

20 "Truly, truly, I say to you, that you will cry and lament, but the world will rejoice; you will be sorrowful, but your sorrow will be turned into joy.

21 "Whenever a woman is in labor she has sorrow, because her hour has come; but when she gives birth to the

child, she no longer remembers the suffering because of the joy that a child has been born into the world.

22 "Therefore you too have sorrow now; but I will see you again, and your heart will rejoice, and no one *will* take your joy away from you.

I Have Overcome the World

23 "And on that day you will not question Me about anything. Truly, truly, I say to you, if you ask the Father for anything in My name, He will give it to you.

24 "Until now you have asked for nothing in My name; ask and you will receive, so that your joy may be made complete.

25 "These things I have spoken to you in figures of speech; an hour is coming when I will no longer speak to you in figures of speech, but will tell you openly of the Father.

26 "On that day you will ask in My name, and I do not say to you that I will request of the Father on your behalf;

27 for the Father Himself loves you, because you have loved Me and have believed that I came forth from the Father.

28 "I came forth from the Father and have come into the world; I am leaving the world again and going to the Father."

29 His disciples *said, "Behold, now You are speaking openly and are not using a figure of speech.

30 "Now we know that You know all things, and have no need for anyone

to question You; by this we believe that You came from God."

31 Jesus answered them, "Do you now believe?

32 "Behold, an hour is coming, and has *already* come, for you to be scattered, each to his own *home*, and to leave Me alone; and *yet* I am not alone, because the Father is with Me.

33 "These things I have spoken to you, so that in Me you may have peace. In the world you have tribulation, but take courage; I have overcome the world."

CHAPTER 17

The High Priestly Prayer

JESUS spoke these things; and lifting up His eyes to heaven, He said, "Father, the hour has come; glorify Your Son, that the Son may glorify You,

2 even as You gave Him authority over all flesh, that to all whom You have given Him, He may give eternal life.

3 "And this is eternal life, that they may know You, the only true God, and Jesus Christ whom You have sent.

4 "I glorified You on the earth, having finished the work which You have given Me to do.

5 "Now, Father, glorify Me together with Yourself, with the glory which I had with You before the world was.

Jesus Prays for His Disciples

6 "I have manifested Your name to the men whom You gave Me out of the world; they were Yours and You

gave them to Me, and they have kept Your word.

7 "Now they have come to know that everything You have given Me is from You;

8 for the words which You gave Me I have given to them; and they received *them* and truly understood that I came forth from You, and they believed that You sent Me.

9 "I ask on their behalf; I do not ask on behalf of the world but of those whom You have given Me; for they are Yours;

10 and all things that are Mine are Yours, and Yours are Mine; and I have been glorified in them.

11 "And I am no longer in the world; and *yet* they themselves are in the world, and I come to You. Holy Father, keep them in Your name, *the name* which You have given Me, that they may be one even as We *are*.

12 "While I was with them, I was keeping them in Your name which You have given Me; and I guarded them and not one of them perished but the son of perdition, so that the Scripture would be fulfilled.

13 "But now I come to You; and these things I speak in the world so that they may have My joy made full in themselves.

14 "I have given them Your word; and the world has hated them, because they are not of the world, even as I am not of the world.

15 "I do not ask You to take them out of the world, but to keep them from the evil one.

16 "They are not of the world, even as I am not of the world.

17 "Sanctify them by the truth; Your word is truth.

18 "As You sent Me into the world, I also sent them into the world.

19 "For their sake I sanctify Myself, that they themselves also may be sanctified in truth.

20 "I do not ask on behalf of these alone, but for those also who believe in Me through their word;

21 that they may all be one; even as You, Father, *are* in Me and I in You, that they also may be in Us, so that the world may believe that You sent Me.

22 "The glory which You have given Me I have given to them, that they may be one, just as We are one;

23 I in them and You in Me, that they may be perfected in unity, so that the world may know that You sent Me, and loved them, even as You have loved Me.

24 "Father, I desire that they also, whom You have given Me, be with Me where I am, so that they may see My glory which You have given Me, for You loved Me before the foundation of the world.

25 "O righteous Father, although the world has not known You, yet I have known You; and these have known that You sent Me;

26 and I have made Your name known to them, and will make it known, so that the love with which You loved Me may be in them, and I in them."

CHAPTER 18

Jesus Betrayed and Arrested

WHEN Jesus had spoken these words, He went forth with His disciples to the other side of the Kidron Valley, where there was a garden, into which He entered with His disciples.

2 Now Judas also, who was betraying Him, knew the place, for Jesus had often gathered there with His disciples.

3 Judas then, having received the *Roman* cohort and officers from the chief priests and the Pharisees, *came there with lanterns and torches and weapons.

4 So Jesus, knowing all the things that were coming upon Him, went forth and *said to them, "Whom do you seek?"

5 They answered Him, "Jesus the Nazarene." He *said to them, "I am *He*." And Judas also, who was betraying Him, was standing with them.

6 So when He said to them, "I am *He*," they drew back and fell to the ground.

7 Therefore He again asked them, "Whom do you seek?" And they said, "Jesus the Nazarene."

8 Jesus answered, "I told you that I am *He*; so if you seek Me, let these go their way,"

9 in order that the word which He spoke would be fulfilled, "Of those whom You have given Me, I lost not one."

10 Simon Peter then, having a sword, drew it and struck the high priest's slave, and cut off his right ear; and the slave's name was Malchus.

11 So Jesus said to Peter, "Put the sword into the sheath; the cup which the Father has given Me, shall I not drink it?"

Jesus Before the Priests;
Peter Denies Jesus

12 So the *Roman* cohort and the commander and the officers of the Jews, arrested Jesus and bound Him,

13 and led Him to Annas first; for he was father-in-law of Caiaphas, who was high priest that year.

14 Now Caiaphas was the one who had advised the Jews that it was better for one man to die on behalf of the people.

15 And Simon Peter was following Jesus, and *so was* another disciple. Now that disciple was known to the high priest, and entered with Jesus into the court of the high priest,

16 but Peter was standing at the door outside. So the other disciple, who was known to the high priest, went out and spoke to the doorkeeper, and brought Peter in.

17 Then the servant-girl who kept the door *said to Peter, "Are you not also *one* of this man's disciples?" He *said, "I am not."

18 Now the slaves and the officers were standing *there*, having made a charcoal fire, for it was cold and they were warming themselves; and Peter was also with them, standing and warming himself.

19 The high priest then questioned Jesus about His disciples, and about His teaching.

20 Jesus answered him, "I have spoken openly to the world; I always taught in synagogues and in the temple, where all the Jews come together; and I spoke nothing in secret.

21 "Why do you question Me? Question those who have heard what I spoke to them; behold, they know what I said."

22 And when He had said this, one of the officers standing nearby gave Jesus a slap, saying, "Is that the way You answer the high priest?"

23 Jesus answered him, "If I have spoken wrongly, bear witness of the wrong; but if rightly, why do you strike Me?"

24 So Annas sent Him bound to Caiaphas the high priest.

25 Now Simon Peter was standing and warming himself. So they said to him, "You are not also one of His disciples, are you?" He denied it, and said, "I am not."

26 One of the slaves of the high priest, being a relative of the one whose ear Peter cut off, *said, "Did I not see you in the garden with Him?"

27 Peter then denied it again, and immediately a rooster crowed.

Jesus Before Pilate

28 Then they *led Jesus from Caiaphas into the Praetorium, and it was early; and they themselves did not enter into the Praetorium so that they would not be defiled, but might eat the Passover.

29 Therefore Pilate went out to them and *said, "What accusation do you bring against this man?"

30 They answered and said to him, "If this man were not an evildoer, we would not have delivered Him to you."

31 So Pilate said to them, "Take Him yourselves, and judge Him according to your law." The Jews said to him, "It is not lawful for us to put anyone to death,"

32 in order that the word of Jesus which He spoke would be fulfilled, signifying by what kind of death He was about to die.

33 Therefore Pilate entered again into the Praetorium, and summoned Jesus and said to Him, "Are You the King of the Jews?"

34 Jesus answered, "Are you saying this from yourself, or did others tell you about Me?"

35 Pilate answered, "Am I a Jew? Your own nation and the chief priests delivered You to me; what did You do?"

36 Jesus answered, "My kingdom is not of this world. If My kingdom were of this world, then My servants would be fighting so that I would not be delivered over to the Jews; but as it is, My kingdom is not from here."

37 Therefore Pilate said to Him, "So You are a king?" Jesus answered, "You yourself said I am a king. For this I have been born, and for this I have come into the world, to bear witness to the truth. Everyone who is of the truth hears My voice."

38 Pilate *said to Him, "What is truth?"

And when he had said this, he went out again to the Jews and *said to them, "I find no guilt in Him.

39 "But you have a custom that I release someone for you at the Passover; do you wish then that I release for you the King of the Jews?"

40 So they cried out again, saying, "Not this man, but Barabbas." Now Barabbas was a robber.

CHAPTER 19

Jesus Flogged and Rejected as King

PILATE then took Jesus and flogged Him.

2 And when the soldiers twisted together a crown of thorns, they put it on His head, and put a purple robe on Him;

3 and they were coming to Him and saying, "Hail, King of the Jews!" and were giving Him slaps *in the face.*

4 And Pilate came out again and *said to them, "Behold, I am bringing Him out to you so that you may know that I find no guilt in Him."

5 Jesus then came out, wearing the crown of thorns and the purple robe. *Pilate* *said to them, "Behold, the man!"

6 So when the chief priests and the officers saw Him, they cried out saying, "Crucify, crucify!" Pilate *said to them, "Take Him yourselves and crucify Him, for I find no guilt in Him."

7 The Jews answered him, "We have a law, and by that law He ought to die because He made Himself out *to be* the Son of God."

8 Therefore when Pilate heard this statement, he became more afraid;

9 and he entered into the Praetorium again and *said to Jesus, "Where are You from?" But Jesus gave him no answer.

10 So Pilate *said to Him, "You do not speak to me? Do You not know that I have authority to release You, and I have authority to crucify You?"

11 Jesus answered, "You would have no authority over Me, unless it had been given you from above; for this reason he who delivered Me to you has *the* greater sin."

12 As a result of this Pilate kept seeking to release Him, but the Jews cried out saying, "If you release this man, you are no friend of Caesar; everyone who makes himself *to be* a king opposes Caesar."

13 Therefore when Pilate heard these words, he brought Jesus out, and sat down on the judgment seat at a place called The Stone Pavement, but in Hebrew, Gabbatha.

14 Now it was the day of Preparation for the Passover; it was about the sixth hour. And he *said to the Jews, "Behold, your King!"

15 So they cried out, "Away with *Him*! Away with *Him*! Crucify Him!" Pilate *said to them, "Shall I crucify your King?" The chief priests answered, "We have no king but Caesar."

The Crucifixion

16 So he then delivered Him over to them to be crucified.

17 They took Jesus, therefore, and He went out, bearing His own cross, to the place called the Place of a Skull, which is called in Hebrew, Golgotha.

18 There they crucified Him, and

with Him two other men, one on either side, and Jesus in between.

19 And Pilate also wrote an inscription and put it on the cross. It was written, "JESUS THE NAZARENE, THE KING OF THE JEWS."

20 Therefore many of the Jews read this inscription, for the place where Jesus was crucified was near the city; and it was written in Hebrew, Latin, *and* in Greek.

21 So the chief priests of the Jews were saying to Pilate, "Do not write, 'The King of the Jews;' but that He said, 'I am King of the Jews.'"

22 Pilate answered, "What I have written I have written."

23 Then the soldiers, when they had crucified Jesus, took His garments and made four parts, a part to each soldier and *also* His tunic; now that tunic was seamless, woven in one piece from the top.

24 So they said to one another, "Let us not tear it, but cast lots for it, *to decide* whose it shall be;" *this was* in order that the Scripture would be fulfilled: "They divided My garments among them, and for My clothing they cast lots."

25 Therefore the soldiers did these things.

But standing by the cross of Jesus were His mother, and His mother's sister, Mary the *wife* of Clopas, and Mary Magdalene.

26 When Jesus then saw His mother, and the disciple whom He loved standing nearby, He *said to His mother, "Woman, behold, your son!"

27 Then He *said to the disciple, "Behold, your mother!" From that hour the disciple took her into his *home*.

Scripture Fulfilled—It Is Finished

28 After this, Jesus, knowing that all things had already been finished, in order to finish the Scripture, *said, "I am thirsty."

29 A jar full of sour wine was standing there; so they put a sponge full of the sour wine upon *a branch of* hyssop and brought it up to His mouth.

30 Therefore when Jesus had received the sour wine, He said, "It is finished!" And bowing His head, He gave up His spirit.

31 Then the Jews, because it was the day of Preparation, so that the bodies would not remain on the cross on the Sabbath (for that Sabbath was a high day), asked Pilate that their legs might be broken, and *that* they might be taken away.

32 So the soldiers came, and broke the legs of the first man and of the other who was crucified with Him;

33 but coming to Jesus, when they saw that He was already dead, they did not break His legs.

34 But one of the soldiers pierced His side with a spear, and immediately blood and water came out.

35 And he who has seen has borne witness, and his witness is true; and he knows that he is telling the truth, so that you also may believe.

36 For these things came to pass in order that the Scripture would be fulfilled, "Not a bone of Him shall be broken."

37 And again another Scripture says, "THEY SHALL LOOK ON HIM WHOM THEY PIERCED."

Jesus Is Buried

38 Now after these things Joseph of Arimathea, being a disciple of Jesus, but secretly because of his fear of the Jews, asked Pilate that he might take away the body of Jesus; and Pilate granted permission. So he came and took away His body.

39 And Nicodemus, who had first come to Him by night, also came, bringing a mixture of myrrh and aloes, *weighing* about one hundred litras.

40 So they took the body of Jesus and bound it in linen wrappings with the spices, as is the burial custom of the Jews.

41 Now in the place where He was crucified there was a garden, and in the garden a new tomb in which no one had yet been laid.

42 Therefore because of the Jewish day of Preparation, since the tomb was nearby, they laid Jesus there.

CHAPTER 20

The Empty Tomb

NOW on the first *day* of the week, Mary Magdalene *came early to the tomb, while it *was still dark, and *saw the stone *already* taken away from the tomb.

2 So she *ran and *came to Simon Peter and to the other disciple whom Jesus loved, and *said to them, "They have taken away the Lord out of the tomb, and we do not know where they have laid Him."

3 So Peter and the other disciple went forth, and they were going to the tomb.

4 And the two were running together; and the other disciple ran ahead faster than Peter and came to the tomb first;

5 and stooping and looking in, he *saw the linen wrappings lying *there*; but he did not go in.

6 And so Simon Peter also *came, following him, and entered the tomb; and he *saw the linen wrappings lying there,

7 and the face-cloth which had been on His head, not lying with the linen wrappings, but folded up in a place by itself.

8 So the other disciple who had first come to the tomb then also entered, and he saw and believed.

9 For as yet they did not understand the Scripture, that He must rise again from the dead.

10 So the disciples went away again to where they were staying.

Jesus Appears to Mary Magdalene

11 But Mary was standing outside the tomb crying; and so, as she was crying, she stooped to look into the tomb;

12 and she *saw two angels in white sitting, one at the head and one at the feet, where the body of Jesus had been lying.

13 And they *said to her, "Woman, why are you crying?" She *said to them, "Because they have taken away my Lord, and I do not know where they have laid Him."

14 When she had said this, she turned around and *saw Jesus standing *there*, and did not know that it was Jesus.

15 Jesus *said to her, "Woman, why are you crying? Whom are you seeking?" Thinking Him to be the gardener, she *said to Him, "Sir, if you have carried Him away, tell me where you have laid Him, and I will take Him away."

16 Jesus *said to her, "Mary!" She turned and *said to Him in Hebrew, "Rabboni!" (which means, Teacher).

17 Jesus *said to her, "Stop clinging to Me, for I have not yet ascended to the Father; but go to My brothers and say to them, 'I ascend to My Father and your Father, and My God and your God.'"

18 Mary Magdalene *came, announcing to the disciples, "I have seen the Lord," and *that* He had said these things to her.

Jesus Appears to His Disciples

19 So while it was evening on that day, the first *day* of the week, and while the doors were shut where the disciples were, for fear of the Jews, Jesus came and stood in their midst and *said to them, "Peace *be* with you."

20 And when He had said this, He showed them both His hands and His side. The disciples then rejoiced when they saw the Lord.

21 So Jesus said to them again, "Peace *be* with you; as the Father has sent Me, I also send you."

22 And when He had said this, He breathed on *them* and *said to them, "Receive the Holy Spirit.

23 "If you forgive the sins of any, *their sins* have been forgiven them; if you retain the *sins* of any, they have been retained."

24 But Thomas, one of the twelve, called Didymus, was not with them when Jesus came.

25 So the other disciples were saying to him, "We have seen the Lord!" But he said to them, "Unless I see in His hands the imprint of the nails, and put my finger into the place of the nails, and put my hand into His side, I will not believe."

26 And after eight days His disciples were again inside, and Thomas with them. Jesus *came, the doors having been shut, and stood in their midst and said, "Peace *be* with you."

27 Then He *said to Thomas, "Bring your finger here, and see My hands; and bring your hand *here* and put it into My side; and do not be unbelieving, but believing."

28 Thomas answered and said to Him, "My Lord and my God!"

29 Jesus *said to him, "Because you have seen Me, have you believed? Blessed *are* those who did not see, and *yet* believed."

Why This Gospel Was Written

30 Therefore many other signs Jesus also did in the presence of the disciples, which are not written in this book;

31 but these have been written so that you may believe that Jesus is the Christ, the Son of God; and that believing you may have life in His name.

CHAPTER 21

Jesus Appears at the Sea of Galilee

1 AFTER these things Jesus manifested Himself again to the disciples at the Sea of Tiberias, and He manifested Himself in this way:

2 Simon Peter, and Thomas called Didymus, and Nathanael of Cana in Galilee, and the sons of Zebedee, and two others of His disciples were together.

3 Simon Peter *said to them, "I am going fishing." They *said to him, "We will also come with you." They went out and got into the boat; and that night they caught nothing.

4 But when the day was now breaking, Jesus stood on the beach; yet the disciples did not know that it was Jesus.

5 So Jesus *said to them, "Children, do you have any fish?" They answered Him, "No."

6 And He said to them, "Cast the net on the right side of the boat and you will find some." So they cast, and then they were not able to haul it in because of the great number of fish.

7 Therefore that disciple whom Jesus loved *said to Peter, "It is the Lord." So when Simon Peter heard

that it was the Lord, he put his outer garment on (for he was stripped for *work*), and cast himself into the sea.

8 But the other disciples came in the little boat, for they were not far from the land, but about two hundred cubits away, dragging the net *full of fish*.

9 So when they got out on the land, they *saw a charcoal fire in place and fish placed on it, and bread.

10 Jesus *said to them, "Bring some of the fish which you have now caught."

11 Simon Peter went up and drew the net to land, full of large fish, 153; and although there were so many, the net was not torn.

Jesus Provides Breakfast

12 Jesus *said to them, "Come, have breakfast." None of the disciples dared to question Him, "Who are You?" knowing that it was the Lord.

13 Jesus *came and *took the bread and *gave *it* to them, and the fish likewise.

14 This is now the third time that Jesus was manifested to the disciples, after He was raised from the dead.

Peter's Restoration and Commission

15 So when they had finished breakfast, Jesus *said to Simon Peter, "Simon, son of John, do you love Me more than these?" He *said to Him, "Yes, Lord; You know that I love You." He *said to him, "Tend My lambs."

16 He *said to him again a second time, "Simon, son of John, do you

---

1 Approx. 100 yd. or 91 m, a cubit was approx. 18 in. or 45 cm

love Me?" He *said to Him, "Yes, Lord; You know that I love You." He *said to him, "Shepherd My sheep."

17 He *said to him the third time, "Simon, son of John, do you love Me?" Peter was grieved because He said to him the third time, "Do you love Me?" And he said to Him, "Lord, You know all things; You know that I love You." Jesus *said to him, "Tend My sheep.

18 "Truly, truly, I say to you, when you were younger, you used to gird yourself and walk wherever you wished; but when you grow old, you will stretch out your hands and someone else will gird you, and bring you where you do not wish to go."

19 Now this He said, signifying by what kind of death he would glorify God. And when He had spoken this, He *said to him, "Follow Me!"

Jesus' Command to Follow Him

20 Peter, turning around, *saw the disciple whom Jesus loved following

them; the one who also had leaned back on His bosom at the supper and said, "Lord, who is the one who betrays You?"

21 So Peter seeing him *said to Jesus, "Lord, and what about this man?"

22 Jesus *said to him, "If I want him to remain until I come, what is that to you? You follow Me!"

23 Therefore this saying went out among the brothers that this disciple would not die; yet Jesus did not say to him that he would not die, but only, "If I want him to remain until I come, what is that to you?"

24 This is the disciple who is bearing witness to these things and wrote these things, and we know that his witness is true.

25 And there are also many other things which Jesus did, which if they *were written one after the other, I suppose that even the world itself *could not contain the books that *would be written.

THE ACTS
OF THE APOSTLES

CHAPTER 1

The Promise of the Holy Spirit

THE first account, O Theophilus, I composed, about all that Jesus began to do and teach,

2 until the day when He was taken up *to heaven*, after He had by the Holy Spirit given orders to the apostles whom He had chosen,

3 to whom He also presented Himself alive after His suffering by many convincing proofs, appearing to them over forty days and speaking about the things concerning the kingdom of God.

4 And gathering them together, He commanded them not to leave Jerusalem, but to wait for the promise of the Father, "Which," He said, "you heard of from Me;

5 for John baptized with water, but you will be baptized with the Holy Spirit not many days from now."

6 So when they had come together, they were asking Him, saying, "Lord, is it at this time You are restoring the kingdom to Israel?"

7 But He said to them, "It is not for you to know times or seasons which the Father has set by His own authority;

8 but you will receive power when the Holy Spirit has come upon you, and

The Ascension

9 And after He had said these things, He was lifted up while they were looking on, and a cloud received Him out of their sight.

10 And as they were gazing intently into the sky while He was going, behold, two men in white clothing stood beside them.

11 They also said, "Men of Galilee, why do you stand looking toward heaven? This Jesus, who has been taken up from you into heaven, will come in just the same way as you have watched Him go into heaven."

Matthias Chosen to Replace Judas

12 Then they returned to Jerusalem from the mount called Olivet, which is near Jerusalem, a Sabbath day's journey away.[1]

13 And when they had entered the *city*, they went up to the upper room where they were staying; that is, Peter and John and James and Andrew, Philip and Thomas, Bartholomew and Matthew, James *the son of Alphaeus*, and Simon the Zealot, and Judas *the son of James*.

you shall be My witnesses both in Jerusalem, and in all Judea and Samaria, and even to the END OF THE EARTH."

14 These all with one accord were continually devoting themselves to prayer, along with the women, and Mary the mother of Jesus, and His brothers.

15 And in those days, Peter stood up in the midst of the brothers (a crowd of about 120 persons was there together), and said,

16 "Men, brothers, the Scripture had to be fulfilled, which the Holy Spirit foretold by the mouth of David concerning Judas, who became a guide to those who arrested Jesus.

17 "For he was counted among us and received his share in this ministry."

18 (Now this man acquired a field with the price of his unrighteousness, and falling headlong, he burst open in the middle and all his intestines gushed out.

19 And it became known to all who were living in Jerusalem; so that in their own language that field was called Hakeldama, that is, Field of Blood.)

20 "For it is written in the book of Psalms,

'LET HIS RESIDENCE BE MADE DESOLATE,
AND LET NO ONE DWELL IN IT';
and,
'LET ANOTHER MAN TAKE HIS OFFICE.'

21 "Therefore it is necessary that of the men who have accompanied us all the time that the Lord Jesus went in and out among us—

22 beginning with the baptism of John until the day that He was taken up from us—one of these must become a witness with us of His resurrection."

23 And they put forward two men, Joseph called Barsabbas (who was also called Justus), and Matthias.

24 And they prayed and said, "You, Lord, who know the hearts of all men, show which one of these two You have chosen

25 to take the place of this ministry and apostleship from which Judas turned aside to go to his own place."

26 And they cast lots for them, and the lot fell to Matthias; and he was added to the eleven apostles.

CHAPTER 2

The Holy Spirit Comes at Pentecost

AND when the day of Pentecost had fully come, they were all together in one place.

2 And suddenly there came from heaven a noise like a violent rushing wind, and it filled the whole house where they were sitting.

3 And there appeared to them tongues like fire distributing themselves, and they rested on each one of them.

4 And they were all filled with the Holy Spirit and began to speak with other tongues, as the Spirit was giving them utterance.

5 Now there were Jews living in Jerusalem, devout men from every nation under heaven.

6 And when this sound occurred,

the multitude came together, and were bewildered because each one of them was hearing them speak in his own language.

7 So they were astounded and marveling, saying, "Behold, are not all these who are speaking Galileans?

8 "And how is it that we each hear *them* in our own language in which we were born?

9 "Parthians and Medes and Elamites, and residents of Mesopotamia, Judea and Cappadocia, Pontus and Asia,

10 Phrygia and Pamphylia, Egypt and the district of Libya around Cyrene, and visitors from Rome, both Jews and proselytes,

11 Cretans and Arabs—we hear them in our *own* tongues speaking of the mighty deeds of God."

12 And they all continued in astonishment and great perplexity, saying to one another, "What does this mean?"

13 But others, mocking, were saying, "They are full of new wine."

Peter's Sermon at Pentecost

14 But Peter, taking his stand with the eleven, raised his voice and declared to them: "Men of Judea and all you who live in Jerusalem, let this be known to you and give heed to my words.

15 "For these men are not drunk, as you suppose, for it is the third hour of the day;

16 but this is what was spoken through the prophet Joel:

17 'AND IT SHALL BE IN THE LAST
        DAYS,' God says,
    'THAT I WILL POUR OUT MY SPIRIT
        ON ALL MANKIND;
    AND YOUR SONS AND YOUR
        DAUGHTERS SHALL PROPHESY,
    AND YOUR YOUNG MEN SHALL SEE
        VISIONS,
    AND YOUR OLD MEN SHALL DREAM
        DREAMS;
18 EVEN ON MY MALE SLAVES AND
        FEMALE SLAVES,
    I WILL IN THOSE DAYS POUR OUT
        MY SPIRIT
    And they shall prophesy.
19 'AND I WILL PUT WONDERS IN THE
        SKY ABOVE
    AND SIGNS ON THE EARTH BELOW,
    BLOOD, AND FIRE, AND VAPOR OF
        SMOKE.
20 'THE SUN WILL BE TURNED INTO
        DARKNESS
    AND THE MOON INTO BLOOD,
    BEFORE THE GREAT AND AWESOME
        DAY OF THE LORD COMES.
21 'AND IT WILL BE THAT EVERYONE
        WHO CALLS ON THE NAME OF
        THE LORD WILL BE SAVED.'

22 "Men of Israel, listen to these words: Jesus the Nazarene, a man attested to you by God with miracles and wonders and signs which God did through Him in your midst, just as you yourselves know—

23 this *Man*, delivered over by the predetermined plan and foreknowledge of God, you nailed to a cross by the hands of lawless men and put *Him* to death.

24 "But God raised Him up again,

putting an end to the agony of death, since it was impossible for Him to be held in its power.

25 "For David says of Him,
'I SAW THE LORD CONTINUALLY
    BEFORE ME;
BECAUSE HE IS AT MY RIGHT HAND,
    SO THAT I WILL NOT BE SHAKEN.

26 'THEREFORE MY HEART WAS GLAD
    AND MY TONGUE EXULTED;
MOREOVER MY FLESH ALSO WILL
    LIVE IN HOPE;

27 BECAUSE YOU WILL NOT FORSAKE
    MY SOUL TO HADES,
NOR GIVE YOUR HOLY ONE OVER
    TO SEE CORRUPTION.

28 'YOU HAVE MADE KNOWN TO ME
    THE WAYS OF LIFE;
YOU WILL MAKE ME FULL OF
    GLADNESS WITH YOUR
    PRESENCE.'

29 "Men, brothers, I may confidently say to you regarding the patriarch David that he both died and was buried, and his tomb is with us to this day.

30 "And so, because he was a prophet and knew that GOD HAD SWORN TO HIM WITH AN OATH TO SET *one* OF THE FRUIT OF HIS BODY ON HIS THRONE,

31 he looked ahead and spoke of the resurrection of the Christ, that HE WAS NEITHER FORSAKEN TO HADES, NOR DID His flesh SEE CORRUPTION.

32 "This Jesus God raised up again, to which we are *all* witnesses.

33 "Therefore having been exalted to the right hand of God, and having received from the Father the promise of the Holy Spirit, He has poured out this which you both see and hear.

34 "For David did not ascend into the heavens, but he himself says:
'THE LORD SAID TO MY LORD,
"SIT AT MY RIGHT HAND,

35 UNTIL I PUT YOUR ENEMIES AS A
    FOOTSTOOL FOR YOUR FEET."'

36 "Therefore let all the house of Israel know for certain that God has made Him both Lord and Christ— this Jesus whom you crucified."

About Three Thousand Souls Saved

37 Now when they heard *this*, they were pierced to the heart, and said to Peter and the rest of the apostles, "Men, brothers, what should we do?"

38 And Peter *said* to them, "Repent, and each of you be baptized in the name of Jesus Christ for the forgiveness of your sins; and you will receive the gift of the Holy Spirit.

39 "For the promise is for you and your children and for all who are far off, as many as the Lord our God will call to Himself."

40 And with many other words he solemnly bore witness and kept on exhorting them, saying, "Be saved from this crooked generation!"

41 So then, those who had received his word were baptized; and that day there were added about three thousand souls.

42 And they were continually devoting themselves to the apostles' teaching and to the fellowship, to the breaking of bread and to the prayers.

43 And fear came upon every soul; and many wonders and signs were taking place through the apostles.

44 And all those who had believed were together and had all things in common;

45 and they *began* selling their property and possessions and were dividing them up with all, as anyone might have need.

46 And daily devoting themselves with one accord in the temple and breaking bread from house to house, they were taking their meals together with gladness and sincerity of heart,

47 praising God and having favor with all the people. And the Lord was adding to their number daily those who were being saved.

CHAPTER 3

The Lame Beggar Healed

NOW Peter and John were going up to the temple at the ninth *hour*, the hour of prayer.

2 And a man who had been lame from his mother's womb was being carried, whom they used to set down daily at the gate of the temple which is called Beautiful, in order to beg alms of those who were entering the temple.

3 When he saw Peter and John about to go into the temple, he *began* asking to receive alms.

4 But when Peter, along with John, fixed his gaze on him, he said, "Look at us!"

5 And he *began to* give them his attention, expecting to receive something from them.

6 But Peter said, "I do not possess silver and gold, but what I do have I give to you: In the name of Jesus Christ the Nazarene—walk!"

7 And seizing him by the right hand, he raised him up; and immediately his feet and his ankles were strengthened.

8 And leaping up, he stood upright and *began to* walk; and he entered the temple with them, walking and leaping and praising God.

9 And all the people saw him walking and praising God;

10 and they were recognizing him, that he was the one who used to sit at the Beautiful Gate of the temple to *beg* alms, and they were filled with wonder and amazement at what had happened to him.

Peter's Sermon in Solomon's Portico

11 And while he was clinging to Peter and John, all the people ran together to them at the portico called Solomon's, full of wonder.

12 But when Peter saw *this*, he replied to the people, "Men of Israel, why do you marvel at this, or why do you gaze at us, as if by our own power or piety we had made him walk?

13 "The God of Abraham, Isaac, and Jacob, the God of our fathers, has glorified His Servant Jesus, whom you delivered and denied in the presence of Pilate, when he had decided to release Him.

14 "But you denied the Holy and Righteous One and asked for a murderer to be granted to you,

15 but put to death the Author of life, whom God raised from the dead, *a fact* to which we are witnesses.

16 "And on the basis of faith in His name, *it is* the name of Jesus which has strengthened this man whom you see and know; and the faith which *is* through Him has given him this perfect health in the presence of you all.

17 "And now, brothers, I know that you acted in ignorance, just as your rulers did also.

18 "But the things which God announced beforehand by the mouth of all the prophets, that His Christ would suffer, He has thus fulfilled.

19 "Therefore repent and return, so that your sins may be wiped away, in order that times of refreshing may come from the presence of the Lord;

20 and that He may send Jesus, the Christ appointed for you,

21 whom heaven must receive until *the* period of restoration of all things about which God spoke by the mouth of His holy prophets from ancient time.

22 "Moses said, 'THE LORD GOD WILL RAISE UP FOR YOU A PROPHET LIKE ME FROM YOUR BROTHERS; TO HIM YOU SHALL LISTEN to everything He says to you.

23 'AND IT WILL BE THAT EVERY SOUL THAT DOES NOT HEED THAT PROPHET SHALL BE UTTERLY DESTROYED FROM AMONG THE PEOPLE.'

24 "And likewise, all the prophets who have spoken, from Samuel and *his* successors onward, also proclaimed these days.

25 "It is you who are the sons of the prophets and of the covenant which God made with your fathers, saying to Abraham, 'AND IN YOUR SEED ALL THE FAMILIES OF THE EARTH SHALL BE BLESSED.'

26 "For you first, God raised up His Servant and sent Him to bless you by turning every one *of you* from your wicked ways."

CHAPTER 4

Peter and John Arrested

NOW as they were speaking to the people, the priests and the captain of the temple *guard* and the Sadducees came up to them,

2 being greatly agitated because they were teaching the people and proclaiming in Jesus the resurrection from the dead.

3 And they laid hands on them and put them in jail until the next day, for it was already evening.

4 But many of those who had heard the message believed, and the number of the men came to be about five thousand.

5 Now it happened that on the next day, their rulers and elders and scribes were gathered together in Jerusalem;

6 and Annas the high priest *was there*, and Caiaphas and John and Alexander, and all who were of high-priestly descent.

7 And when they had placed them in their midst, they *began to* inquire,

"By what power, or in what name, have you done this?"

8 Then Peter, filled with the Holy Spirit, said to them, "Rulers and elders of the people,

9 if we are being examined today for a good deed *done* to a sick man, as to how this man has been saved *from his sickness,*

10 let it be known to all of you and to all the people of Israel, that by the name of Jesus Christ the Nazarene, whom you crucified, whom God raised from the dead—by this *name* this man stands here before you in good health.

11 "He is the STONE WHICH WAS REJECTED by you, THE BUILDERS, *but* WHICH BECAME THE CHIEF CORNER *stone.*

12 "And there is salvation in no one else, for there is no other name under heaven that has been given among men by which we must be saved."

Peter and John Threatened and Released

13 Now as they observed the confidence of Peter and John and comprehended that they were uneducated and ordinary men, they were marveling, and *began to* recognize them as having been with Jesus.

14 And seeing the man who had been healed standing with them, they had nothing to say in reply.

15 But when they had ordered them to leave the Sanhedrin, they *began to* confer with one another,

16 saying, "What should we do with these men? For the fact that a noteworthy sign has happened through them is apparent to all who live in Jerusalem, and we cannot deny it.

17 "But lest it spread any further among the people, let us warn them to speak no longer to any man in this name."

18 And when they had summoned them, they commanded them not to speak or teach at all in the name of Jesus.

19 But Peter and John answered and said to them, "Whether it is right in the sight of God to hear you rather than God, you be the judge;

20 for we cannot stop speaking about what we have seen and heard."

21 And when they had threatened them further, they let them go (finding no basis on which to punish them) on account of the people, because they were all glorifying God for what had happened;

22 for the man was more than forty years old on whom this sign of healing had occurred.

23 So when they were released, they went to their own *companions* and reported all that the chief priests and the elders had said to them.

24 And when they heard *this,* they lifted their voices to God with one accord and said, "O Master, it is You who MADE THE HEAVEN AND THE EARTH AND THE SEA, AND ALL THAT IS IN THEM,

25 who by the Holy Spirit, *through* the mouth of our father David Your servant, said,

'WHY DID THE GENTILES RAGE,
AND THE PEOPLES DEVISE VAIN
THINGS?
26 'THE KINGS OF THE EARTH TOOK
THEIR STAND,
AND THE RULERS WERE GATHERED
TOGETHER
AGAINST THE LORD AND AGAINST
HIS CHRIST.'

27 "For truly in this city there were gathered together against Your holy Servant Jesus, whom You anointed, both Herod and Pontius Pilate, along with the Gentiles and the peoples of Israel,

28 to do whatever Your hand and Your purpose predestined to occur.

29 "And now, Lord, take note of their threats, and grant that Your slaves may speak Your word with all confidence,

30 while You extend Your hand to heal, and signs and wonders happen through the name of Your holy Servant Jesus."

31 And when they had prayed earnestly, the place where they had gathered together was shaken, and they were all filled with the Holy Spirit and *began to* speak the word of God with confidence.

Distribution Among Needy Believers

32 And the congregation of those who believed were of one heart and soul, and not one was saying that any of his possessions was his own, but, for them, everything was common.

33 And with great power the apostles were bearing witness to the resurrection of the Lord Jesus, and great grace was upon them all.

34 For there was not a needy person among them, for all who were owners of land or houses would sell them and bring the proceeds of the sales

35 and lay them at the apostles' feet, and they would be distributed to each as any had need.

36 Now Joseph, a Levite of Cyprian birth, who was also called Barnabas by the apostles (which translated means Son of Encouragement),

37 and who owned a field, sold it and brought the money and laid it at the apostles' feet.

CHAPTER 5

Ananias and Sapphira

BUT a man named Ananias, with his wife Sapphira, sold a piece of property,

2 and kept back *some* of the price for himself, with his wife's full knowledge. And bringing a portion of it, he laid it at the apostles' feet.

3 But Peter said, "Ananias, why has Satan filled your heart to lie to the Holy Spirit and to keep back *some* of the price of the land?

4 "While it remained *unsold*, did it not remain your own? And after it was sold, was it not under your authority? Why is it that you laid this deed in your heart? You have not lied to men but to God."

5 And as he heard these words, Ananias fell down and breathed his

last; and great fear came over all who heard.

6 And the young men rose up and wrapped him up, and after carrying him out, they buried him.

7 Now there was an interval of about three hours, and his wife came in, not knowing what had happened.

8 And Peter responded to her, "Tell me whether you were paid this much for the land?" And she said, "Yes, that much."

9 Then Peter *said* to her, "Why is it that you have agreed together to put the Spirit of the Lord to the test? Behold, the feet of those who buried your husband are at the door, and they will carry you out *as well.*"

10 And immediately she fell at his feet and breathed her last, and the young men came in and found her dead, and they carried her out and buried her beside her husband.

11 And great fear came over the whole church, and over all who heard these things.

12 Now at the hands of the apostles many signs and wonders were happening among the people, and they were all with one accord in Solomon's Portico.

13 But none of the rest dared to associate with them; however, the people were holding them in high esteem.

14 And more than ever believers in the Lord were added to *their number*, multitudes of men and women,

15 to such an extent that they even carried the sick out into the streets and laid them on cots and mats, so that when Peter came by at least his shadow might fall on any one of them.

16 Also the multitude from the cities in the vicinity of Jerusalem were coming together, bringing people who were sick or afflicted with unclean spirits, and they were all being healed.

The Apostles Jailed and Freed

17 But the high priest rose up and those with him (that is the sect of the Sadducees), and they were filled with jealousy.

18 And they laid hands on the apostles and put them in a public jail.

19 But during the night an angel of the Lord opened the doors of the prison, and taking them out, he said,

20 "Go, stand and speak to the people in the temple the whole message of this Life."

21 Upon hearing *this*, they entered into the temple about daybreak and *began to* teach.

Now when the high priest and those with him came, they called the Sanhedrin together, even all the Council of the sons of Israel, and sent *orders* to the jailhouse for them to be brought.

22 But the officers who came did not find them in the prison, and they returned and reported back,

23 saying, "We found the jailhouse locked quite securely and the guards standing at the doors, but we opened it and found no one inside."

24 Now when the captain of the

temple *guard* and the chief priests heard these words, they were greatly perplexed about them as to what would come of this.

25 But someone came and reported to them, "The men whom you put in prison are standing in the temple and teaching the people!"

26 Then the captain went along with the officers and *proceeded* to bring them *back* without violence (for they were afraid of the people, that they might be stoned).

27 And when they had brought them, they stood them before the Sanhedrin. And the high priest questioned them,

28 saying, "We strictly commanded you not to continue teaching in this name, and yet, you have filled Jerusalem with your teaching and intend to bring this man's blood upon us."

29 But Peter and the apostles answered and said, "We must obey God rather than men.

30 "The God of our fathers raised up Jesus, whom you put to death by hanging Him on a tree.

31 "This One God exalted to His right hand as a Leader and a Savior, to grant repentance to Israel, and forgiveness of sins.

32 "And we are witnesses of these things, and *so is* the Holy Spirit, whom God gave to those who obey Him."

Gamaliel's Counsel

33 But when they heard this, they became furious and intended to kill them.

34 But a Pharisee named Gamaliel, a teacher of the Law, respected by all the people, stood up in the Sanhedrin and gave orders to put the men outside for a short time.

35 And he said to them, "Men of Israel, take care what you propose to do with these men.

36 "For some time ago Theudas rose up, claiming to be somebody, and a group of about four hundred men joined up with him. But he was killed, and all who were following him were dispersed and came to nothing.

37 "After this man, Judas the Galilean rose up in the days of the census and drew away people after him. He too perished, and all those who were following him were scattered.

38 "So in the present case, I also say to you, stay away from these men and let them alone, for if this plan or action is of men, it will be overthrown;

39 but if it is of God, you will not be able to overthrow them; or you may even be found fighting against God."

40 So they followed his advice. And after calling the apostles in *and* beating them, they commanded them not to speak in the name of Jesus, and *then* released them.

41 So they went on their way from the presence of the Sanhedrin, rejoicing that they had been considered worthy to suffer shame for the Name.

42 And every day, in the temple and from house to house, they did not cease teaching and proclaiming the good news that Jesus *is* the Christ.

CHAPTER 6

Selection of the Seven

NOW in those days, while the disciples were multiplying *in number*, there was grumbling from the Hellenists against the Hebrews, because their widows were being overlooked in the daily serving *of food*.

2 So the twelve summoned the congregation of the disciples and said, "It is not pleasing *to God* for us to neglect the word of God in order to serve tables.

3 "Therefore, brothers, select from among you seven men of good reputation, full of the Spirit and of wisdom, whom we may put in charge of this need.

4 "But we will devote ourselves to prayer and to the service of the word."

5 And this word pleased the whole congregation, and they chose Stephen, a man full of faith and of the Holy Spirit, and Philip, Prochorus, Nicanor, Timon, Parmenas, and Nicolas, a proselyte from Antioch.

6 And these they stood before the apostles, and after praying, they laid their hands on them.

7 And the word of God kept on spreading, and the number of the disciples continued to multiply greatly in Jerusalem, and a great many of the priests were becoming obedient to the faith.

Stephen Accused of Blasphemy

8 And Stephen, full of grace and power, was doing great wonders and signs among the people.

9 But some men from what was called the Synagogue of the Freedmen, *including* both Cyrenians and Alexandrians, and some from Cilicia and Asia, rose up and were arguing with Stephen.

10 But they were unable to oppose the wisdom and the Spirit by whom he was speaking.

11 Then they secretly induced men to say, "We have heard him speak blasphemous words against Moses and God."

12 And they stirred up the people, the elders, and the scribes, and they came up to him, dragged him away, and brought him to the Sanhedrin.

13 And they put forward false witnesses who said, "This man never ceases speaking words against this holy place and the Law;

14 for we have heard him say that this Jesus the Nazarene will destroy this place and alter the customs which Moses handed down to us."

15 And fixing their gaze on him, all who were sitting in the Sanhedrin saw his face like the face of an angel.

CHAPTER 7

Stephen's Defense

AND the high priest said, "Are these things so?"

2 And he said, "Hear me, brothers and fathers! The God of glory appeared to our father Abraham when he was in Mesopotamia, before he lived in Haran,

3 and said to him, 'LEAVE YOUR COUNTRY AND YOUR RELATIVES, AND COME INTO THE LAND THAT I WILL SHOW YOU.'

4 "Then he left the land of the Chaldeans and settled in Haran. From there, after his father died, *God* had him move to this country in which you are now living.

5 "But He gave him no inheritance in it, not even a foot of ground, and He promised that HE WOULD GIVE IT TO HIM AS A POSSESSION, AND TO HIS SEED AFTER HIM, even when he had no child.

6 "But God spoke in this way, that his SEED WOULD BE SOJOURNERS IN A FOREIGN LAND, AND THAT THEY WOULD BE ENSLAVED AND MISTREATED FOR FOUR HUNDRED YEARS.

7 " 'AND I MYSELF WILL JUDGE THE NATION TO WHICH THEY WILL BE ENSLAVED,' said God, 'AND AFTER THAT THEY WILL COME OUT AND SERVE ME IN THIS PLACE.'

8 "And He gave him the covenant of circumcision; and so *Abraham* was the father of Isaac, and circumcised him on the eighth day; and Isaac *was the father of* Jacob, and Jacob *of* the twelve patriarchs.

9 "And the patriarchs, becoming jealous of Joseph, sold him into Egypt. *Yet* God was with him,

10 and rescued him from all his afflictions, and granted him favor and wisdom in the sight of Pharaoh, king of Egypt, and he appointed him governor over Egypt and all his household.

11 "Now a famine came over all Egypt and Canaan, and great affliction *with it*, and our fathers could find no food.

12 "But when Jacob heard that there was grain in Egypt, he sent our fathers *there* the first time.

13 "And on the second *visit* Joseph made himself known to his brothers, and Joseph's family was disclosed to Pharaoh.

14 "Then Joseph sent *word* and invited Jacob his father and all his relatives to come to him, seventy-five persons *in all*.

15 "And Jacob went down to Egypt and *there* he and our fathers died.

16 "*And from there* they were removed to Shechem and placed in the tomb which Abraham had purchased for a sum of money from the sons of Hamor in Shechem.

17 "But as the time of the promise was drawing near which God had assured to Abraham, the people increased and multiplied in Egypt,

18 until ANOTHER KING AROSE OVER EGYPT WHO DID NOT KNOW ABOUT JOSEPH.

19 "It was he who deceitfully took advantage of our family and mistreated our fathers to set their infants outside so that they would not survive.

20 "It was at this time that Moses was born, and he was lovely in the sight of God, and he was nurtured three months in his father's home.

21 "And after he had been set outside, Pharaoh's daughter took him

away and nurtured him as her own son.

22 "And Moses was educated in all the wisdom of the Egyptians, and he was powerful in words and deeds.

23 "But when he was approaching the age of forty, it entered his heart to visit his brothers, the sons of Israel.

24 "And when he saw one *of them* being treated unjustly, he defended him and took justice for the oppressed by striking down the Egyptian.

25 "And he supposed that his brothers understood that God was granting them salvation through him, but they did not understand.

26 "On the following day he appeared to them as they were fighting together, and he tried to reconcile them in peace, saying, 'Men, you are brothers, why are you treating one another unjustly?'

27 "But the one who was treating his neighbor unjustly pushed him away, saying, 'WHO MADE YOU A RULER AND JUDGE OVER US?

28 'DO YOU INTEND TO KILL ME AS YOU KILLED THE EGYPTIAN YESTERDAY?'

29 "At this remark, MOSES FLED AND BECAME A SOJOURNER IN THE LAND OF MIDIAN, where he was the father of two sons.

30 "And after forty years had passed, AN ANGEL APPEARED TO HIM IN THE WILDERNESS OF MOUNT SINAI, IN THE FLAME OF A BURNING BUSH.

31 "When Moses saw it, he was marveling at the sight; and as he approached to look *more* closely, there came the voice of the Lord:

32 'I AM THE GOD OF YOUR FATHERS, THE GOD OF ABRAHAM AND ISAAC AND JACOB.' Moses trembled with fear and would not dare to look.

33 "BUT THE LORD SAID TO HIM, 'REMOVE THE SANDALS FROM YOUR FEET, FOR THE PLACE ON WHICH YOU ARE STANDING IS HOLY GROUND.

34 'I HAVE SURELY SEEN THE OPPRESSION OF MY PEOPLE IN EGYPT AND HAVE HEARD THEIR GROANS, AND I HAVE COME DOWN TO DELIVER THEM; COME NOW, AND I WILL SEND YOU TO EGYPT.'

35 "This Moses whom they disowned, saying, 'WHO MADE YOU A RULER AND A JUDGE?' is the one whom God sent *to be* both a ruler and a deliverer with the help of the angel who appeared to him in the bush.

36 "This man led them out, doing wonders and signs in the land of Egypt and in the Red Sea and in the wilderness for forty years.

37 "This is the Moses who said to the sons of Israel, 'GOD WILL RAISE UP FOR YOU A PROPHET LIKE ME FROM YOUR BROTHERS.'

38 "This is the one who, in the congregation in the wilderness, was with the angel who was speaking to him on Mount Sinai and with our fathers; the one who received living oracles to pass on to you.

39 "Our fathers were unwilling to be obedient to him, but rejected him and in their hearts turned back to Egypt,

40 SAYING TO AARON, 'MAKE FOR US GODS WHO WILL GO BEFORE US; FOR

THIS MOSES WHO LED US OUT OF THE LAND OF EGYPT—WE DO NOT KNOW WHAT HAS BECOME OF HIM.'

41 "At that time they made a calf and brought a sacrifice to the idol, and were rejoicing in the works of their hands.

42 "But God turned away and delivered them up to serve the host of heaven; as it is written in the book of the prophets, 'DID YOU PRESENT ME WITH SLAIN BEASTS AND SACRIFICES FORTY YEARS IN THE WILDERNESS, O HOUSE OF ISRAEL?

43 'YOU ALSO TOOK ALONG THE TABERNACLE OF MOLOCH AND THE STAR OF THE GOD ROMPHA, THE IMAGES WHICH YOU MADE TO WORSHIP. I ALSO WILL REMOVE YOU BEYOND BABYLON.'

44 "Our fathers had the tabernacle of testimony in the wilderness, just as He, who spoke to Moses, directed *him* to make it according to the pattern which he had seen.

45 "And having received it in their turn, our fathers brought it in with Joshua when they dispossessed the nations whom God drove out before our fathers, until the time of David.

46 "*David* found favor in the sight of God, and asked that he might find a dwelling place for the God of Jacob.

47 "But Solomon built a house for Him.

48 "However, the Most High does not dwell in *houses* made by *human* hands, as the prophet says:

49 'HEAVEN IS MY THRONE,
AND EARTH IS THE FOOTSTOOL OF MY FEET.

WHAT KIND OF HOUSE WILL YOU BUILD FOR ME?' says the Lord,
'OR WHAT PLACE IS THERE FOR MY REST?

50 'WAS IT NOT MY HAND WHICH MADE ALL THESE THINGS?'

51 "You men—stiff-necked and uncircumcised in heart and ears—are always resisting the Holy Spirit. As your fathers did, so do you.

52 "And which one of the prophets did your fathers not persecute? They killed those who had previously announced the coming of the Righteous One, whose betrayers and murderers you have now become;

53 you who received the Law as ordained by angels, and *yet* did not observe it."

Stephen Is Stoned to Death

54 Now when they heard this, they became furious in their hearts, and they *began* gnashing their teeth at him.

55 But being full of the Holy Spirit, he gazed intently into heaven and saw the glory of God, and Jesus standing at the right hand of God;

56 and he said, "Behold, I see the heavens opened up and the Son of Man standing at the right hand of God."

57 But crying out with a loud voice, they covered their ears and rushed at him with one accord.

58 And when they had driven him out of the city, they *began* stoning *him*; and the witnesses laid aside their garments at the feet of a young man named Saul.

59 They went on stoning Stephen as he was calling out and saying, "Lord Jesus, receive my spirit!"

60 Then falling on his knees, he cried out with a loud voice, "Lord, do not hold this sin against them!" And having said this, he fell asleep.

CHAPTER 8

Saul Persecutes the Church

NOW Saul was in hearty agreement with putting him to death.

And on that day a great persecution began against the church in Jerusalem, and they were all scattered throughout the regions of Judea and Samaria, except the apostles.

2 And *some* devout men buried Stephen and made loud lamentation over him.

3 But Saul *began* ravaging the church, entering house after house, and dragging off men and women, he was delivering them into prison.

Philip Preaches in Samaria

4 Therefore, those who had been scattered went about, proclaiming the good news of the word.

5 Now Philip went down to the city of Samaria and *began* preaching Christ to them.

6 And the crowds with one accord were giving attention to what was being said by Philip, as they heard and saw the signs which he was doing.

7 For *in the case of* many who had unclean spirits, they were coming out *of them* shouting with a loud voice; and many who had been paralyzed and lame were healed.

8 So there was great joy in that city.

9 Now there was a man named Simon, who formerly was practicing magic in the city and astounding the people of Samaria, claiming to be someone great;

10 and they all, from smallest to greatest, were giving attention to him, saying, "This man is what is called the Great Power of God."

11 And they were giving him attention because he had for a long time astounded them with his magic arts.

12 But when they believed Philip proclaiming the good news about the kingdom of God and the name of Jesus Christ, they were being baptized, both men and women.

13 Even Simon himself believed; and after being baptized, he continued on with Philip, and as he observed signs and great miracles taking place, he was constantly astounded.

14 Now when the apostles in Jerusalem heard that Samaria had received the word of God, they sent them Peter and John,

15 who came down and prayed for them that they might receive the Holy Spirit.

16 For He had not yet fallen upon any of them; they had simply been baptized in the name of the Lord Jesus.

17 Then they *began* laying their hands on them, and they were receiving the Holy Spirit.

18 Now when Simon saw that the Spirit had been bestowed through the laying on of the apostles' hands, he offered them money,

19 saying, "Give this authority to me as well, so that everyone on whom I lay my hands may receive the Holy Spirit."

20 But Peter said to him, "May your silver perish with you, because you supposed you could obtain the gift of God with money!

21 "You have no part or portion in this matter, for your heart is not right before God.

22 "Therefore repent of this wickedness of yours, and pray earnestly to the Lord that, if possible, the intention of your heart may be forgiven you.

23 "For I see that you are in the gall of bitterness and in the bondage of unrighteousness."

24 But Simon answered and said, "Pray earnestly to the Lord for me yourselves, so that nothing of what you have said may come upon me."

An Ethiopian Receives Christ

25 So, when they had solemnly borne witness and spoken the word of the Lord, they started back to Jerusalem, and were proclaiming the gospel to many villages of the Samaritans.

26 But an angel of the Lord spoke to Philip saying, "Rise up and go south to the road that descends from Jerusalem to Gaza." (This is a desert *road*.)

27 So he rose up and went; and behold, there was an Ethiopian eunuch, a court official of Candace, queen of the Ethiopians, who was in charge of all her treasure; and he had come to Jerusalem to worship,

28 and he was returning and sitting in his chariot, and was reading the prophet Isaiah.

29 Then the Spirit said to Philip, "Go over and join this chariot."

30 And Philip ran up and heard him reading Isaiah the prophet, and said, "Do you understand what you are reading?"

31 And he said, "Well, how could I, unless someone guides me?" And he invited Philip to come up and sit with him.

32 Now the passage of Scripture which he was reading was this:

"AS A SHEEP IS LED TO SLAUGHTER;
AND AS A LAMB BEFORE ITS
    SHEARER IS SILENT,
SO HE DOES NOT OPEN HIS MOUTH.

33 "IN HUMILIATION HIS JUDGMENT
    WAS TAKEN AWAY;
WHO WILL RECOUNT HIS
    GENERATION?
FOR HIS LIFE IS REMOVED FROM
    THE EARTH."

34 And the eunuch answered Philip and said, "I ask you earnestly, of whom does the prophet say this? Of himself or of someone else?"

35 Then Philip opened his mouth, and beginning from this Scripture he proclaimed the good news about Jesus to him.

36 And as they went along the road they came to some water; and the eunuch *said, "Look! Water! What prevents me from being baptized?"

37 [And Philip said, "If you believe with all your heart, you may." And he answered and said, "I believe that Jesus Christ is the Son of God."]

38 And he ordered the chariot to stop, and they both went down into the water, Philip as well as the eunuch, and he baptized him.

39 When they came up out of the water, the Spirit of the Lord snatched Philip away, and the eunuch no longer saw him, but went on his way rejoicing.

40 But Philip found himself at Azotus, and as he passed through he kept proclaiming the gospel to all the cities until he came to Caesarea.

CHAPTER 9

The Conversion of Saul

NOW Saul, still breathing threats and murder against the disciples of the Lord, went to the high priest,

2 and asked for letters from him to the synagogues at Damascus, so that if he found any belonging to the Way, both men and women, he might bring them bound to Jerusalem.

3 And as he was traveling, it happened that when he was approaching Damascus, suddenly a light from heaven flashed around him;

4 and falling to the ground, he heard a voice saying to him, "Saul, Saul, why are you persecuting Me?"

5 And he said, "Who are You, Lord?" And He *said*, "I am Jesus whom you are persecuting,

6 but rise up and enter the city, and it will be told you what you must do."

7 And the men who traveled with him stood speechless, hearing the voice but seeing no one.

8 And Saul got up from the ground, and though his eyes were open, he could see nothing. Leading him by the hand, they brought him into Damascus.

9 And he was three days without sight, and neither ate nor drank.

10 Now there was a disciple at Damascus named Ananias, and the Lord said to him in a vision, "Ananias." And he said, "Here I am, Lord."

11 And the Lord *said* to him, "Rise up and go to the street called Straight, and inquire at the house of Judas for a man from Tarsus named Saul, for behold, he is praying,

12 and he has seen in a vision a man named Ananias come in and lay his hands on him, so that he might regain his sight."

13 But Ananias answered, "Lord, I have heard from many about this man, how much harm he did to Your saints at Jerusalem.

14 And here he has authority from the chief priests to bind all who call on Your name."

15 But the Lord said to him, "Go, for he is a chosen instrument of Mine, to bear My name before the Gentiles and kings and the sons of Israel;

16 for I will show him how much he must suffer for My name."

17 So Ananias departed and entered the house. And he laid his hands on

him and said, "Brother Saul, the Lord sent me—*that is* Jesus who appeared to you on the road by which you were coming—so that you may regain your sight and be filled with the Holy Spirit."

18 And immediately there fell from his eyes something like scales, and he regained his sight, and he rose up and was baptized;

19 and he took food and was strengthened.

Saul Begins to Preach Christ

Now for several days he was with the disciples who were at Damascus,

20 and immediately he *began to* proclaim Jesus in the synagogues, saying, "He is the Son of God."

21 And all those hearing him continued to be astounded, and were saying, "Is this not the one who in Jerusalem destroyed those that called on this name, and *who* had come here for the purpose of bringing them bound before the chief priests?"

22 But Saul kept increasing in strength and confounding the Jews who lived at Damascus by proving that this One is the Christ.

23 And when many days had elapsed, the Jews plotted together to put him to death,

24 but their plot became known to Saul. They were also watching the gates day and night so that they might put him to death;

25 but his disciples took him by night and let him down through the wall, lowering him in a *large* basket.

26 And when he came to Jerusalem, he was trying to associate with the disciples, but they were all afraid of him, not believing that he was a disciple.

27 But Barnabas took him and brought him to the apostles and recounted to them how he had seen the Lord on the road, and that He had talked to him, and how at Damascus he had spoken out boldly in the name of Jesus.

28 So he was with them, moving about freely in Jerusalem, speaking out boldly in the name of the Lord.

29 And he was talking and arguing with the Hellenistic *Jews*, but they were attempting to put him to death.

30 But when the brothers learned *of it*, they brought him down to Caesarea and sent him away to Tarsus.

31 So the church throughout all Judea and Galilee and Samaria having peace, being built up. And going on in the fear of the Lord and in the encouragement of the Holy Spirit, it continued to multiply.

Peter Heals Aeneas

32 Now it happened that as Peter was traveling through all *those regions*, he came down also to the saints who lived at Lydda.

33 And there he found a man named Aeneas, who had been bedridden eight years, for he was paralyzed.

34 And Peter said to him, "Aeneas, Jesus Christ heals you. Rise up and make your bed." Immediately he rose up.

35 And all who lived at Lydda and Sharon saw him, and they turned to the Lord.

Peter Raises Tabitha to Life

36 Now in Joppa there was a disciple named Tabitha (which translated is called Dorcas). This woman was full of good works and charity which she continually did.

37 And it happened at that time that she fell sick and died; and when they had washed her body, they laid it in an upper room.

38 Now since Lydda was near Joppa, the disciples, having heard that Peter was there, sent two men to him, pleading with him, "Do not delay in coming to us."

39 So Peter arose and went with them. When he arrived, they brought him into the upper room; and all the widows stood beside him, crying and showing all the tunics and garments that Dorcas used to make while she was with them.

40 But Peter sent them all out and knelt down and prayed, and turning to the body, he said, "Tabitha, arise." And she opened her eyes, and when she saw Peter, she sat up.

41 And he gave her his hand and raised her up. And calling the saints and widows, he presented her alive.

42 And it became known all over Joppa, and many believed in the Lord.

43 And it happened that he stayed many days in Joppa with a tanner *named* Simon.

CHAPTER 10

Cornelius' and Peter's Visions

NOW *there was* a man at Caesarea named Cornelius, a centurion of what was called the Italian cohort,

2 a devout man and one who feared God with all his household, and gave many alms to the people and prayed to God continually.

3 About the ninth hour of the day he clearly saw in a vision an angel of God who had come in and said to him, "Cornelius!"

4 And looking intently on him and becoming afraid, he said, "What is it, Lord?" And he said to him, "Your prayers and alms have ascended as a memorial before God.

5 "Now send *some* men to Joppa and summon a man *named* Simon, who is also called Peter;

6 he is lodging with a tanner *named* Simon, whose house is by the sea."

7 And when the angel who was speaking to him had left, he called two of his servants and a devout soldier of those who were his personal attendants,

8 and after he explained everything to them, he sent them to Joppa.

9 And on the next day, as they were on their way and approaching the city, Peter went up on the housetop about the sixth hour to pray.

10 But he became hungry and was desiring to eat. And while they were making preparations, he fell into a trance

11 and *saw heaven opened up, and

an object like a great sheet coming down, lowered by four corners to the ground,

12 and there were in it all *kinds of* four-footed animals and crawling creatures of the earth and birds of the sky.

13 And a voice came to him, "Rise up, Peter, slaughter and eat!"

14 But Peter said, "By no means, Lord, for I have never eaten anything defiled and unclean."

15 Again a voice *came* to him a second time, "What God has cleansed, no *longer* consider defiled."

16 And this happened three times and immediately the object was taken up into heaven.

17 Now while Peter was greatly perplexed in mind as to what the vision which he had seen might be, behold, the men who had been sent by Cornelius, having asked directions for Simon's house, appeared at the gate;

18 and calling out, they were asking whether Simon, who was also called Peter, was lodging there.

19 And while Peter was reflecting on the vision, the Spirit said to him, "Behold, three men are looking for you.

20 "But rise up, go down and accompany them without taking issue at all, for I have sent them Myself."

21 And Peter went down to the men and said, "Behold, I am the one you are looking for; what is the reason for which you have come?"

22 And they said, "Cornelius, a centurion, a righteous and God-fearing man well spoken of by the entire nation of the Jews, was directed by a holy angel to summon you to his house and hear a message from you."

23 So he invited them in and gave them lodging.

Peter at Caesarea

And on the next day he rose up and went away with them, and some of the brothers from Joppa went with him.

24 And on the following day he entered Caesarea. Now Cornelius was waiting for them and had called together his relatives and close friends.

25 And when Peter entered, Cornelius met him, and fell at his feet and worshiped *him*.

26 But Peter raised him up, saying, "Stand up; I too am *just* a man."

27 As he talked with him, he entered and *found many people assembled.

28 And he said to them, "You yourselves know how unlawful it is for a man who is a Jew to associate with a foreigner or to visit him; and *yet* God has shown me that I should not call any man defiled or unclean.

29 "That is why I came without even raising any objection when I was summoned. So I ask for what reason you have summoned me."

30 And Cornelius said, "Four days ago to this hour, I was praying in my house during the ninth hour; and behold, a man stood before me in shining garments,

31 and he *said, 'Cornelius, your prayer has been heard and your alms have been remembered before God.

32 'Therefore send to Joppa and

invite Simon, who is also called Peter, to come to you; he is lodging at the house of Simon *the* tanner by the sea.'

33 "So I sent for you immediately, and you have been kind enough to come. Now then, we are all here present before God to hear all that you have been ordered by the Lord."

The Holy Spirit Poured Out on the Gentiles

34 And opening his mouth, Peter said:

"I most truly comprehend *now* that God is not one to show partiality,

35 but in every nation the one who fears Him and does righteousness is welcome to Him.

36 "As for the word which He sent to the sons of Israel, proclaiming the good news of peace through Jesus Christ—He is Lord of all—

37 you yourselves know the thing which happened throughout all Judea, starting from Galilee, after the baptism which John proclaimed.

38 "*You know of* Jesus of Nazareth, how God anointed Him with the Holy Spirit and with power, and *how* He went about doing good and healing all who were oppressed by the devil, for God was with Him.

39 "And we are witnesses of all the things He did both in the land of the Jews and in Jerusalem. They also put Him to death by hanging Him on a tree.

40 "God raised Him up on the third day and granted that He appear,

41 not to all the people, but to witnesses who were chosen beforehand by God, *that is*, to us who ate and drank with Him after He arose from the dead.

42 "And He commanded us to preach to the people, and solemnly to bear witness that this is the One who has been designated by God as Judge of the living and the dead.

43 "Of Him all the prophets bear witness that through His name everyone who believes in Him receives forgiveness of sins."

44 While Peter was still speaking these things, the Holy Spirit fell upon all those who were listening to the word.

45 And all the circumcised believers who came with Peter were astounded that the gift of the Holy Spirit had been poured out on the Gentiles also.

46 For they were hearing them speaking with tongues and magnifying God. Then Peter answered,

47 "Can anyone refuse water for these to be baptized who have received the Holy Spirit just as we *did*?"

48 And he ordered them to be baptized in the name of Jesus Christ. Then they asked him to remain for a few days.

CHAPTER 11

Peter's Report in Jerusalem

NOW the apostles and the brothers who were throughout Judea heard that the Gentiles also had received the word of God.

2 And when Peter came up to Jerusalem, those who were circumcised took issue with him,

3 saying, "You went to uncircumcised men and ate with them."

4 But Peter began *speaking* and *proceeded* to explain to them in orderly sequence, saying,

5 "I was in the city of Joppa praying; and in a trance I saw a vision, an object coming down like a great sheet lowered by four corners from heaven, and it came right down to me,

6 and when looking closely at it, I was observing it and saw the four-footed animals of the earth and the wild beasts and the crawling creatures and the birds of the sky.

7 "And I also heard a voice saying to me, 'Rise up, Peter; slaughter and eat.'

8 "But I said, 'By no means, Lord, for nothing defiled or unclean has ever entered my mouth.'

9 "But a voice from heaven answered a second time, 'What God has cleansed, no longer consider defiled.'

10 "And this happened three times, and everything was drawn back up into heaven.

11 "And behold, immediately three men appeared at the house in which we were, having been sent to me from Caesarea.

12 "And the Spirit told me to go with them without taking issue at all. These six brothers also went with me and we entered the man's house.

13 "And he reported to us how he had seen the angel standing in his house, and saying, 'Send to Joppa and summon Simon, who is also called Peter;

14 and he will speak words to you by which you will be saved, you and all your household.'

15 "And as I began to speak, the Holy Spirit fell upon them just as *He did* upon us at the beginning.

16 "And I remembered the word of the Lord, how He used to say, 'John baptized with water, but you will be baptized with the Holy Spirit.'

17 "Therefore if God gave to them the same gift as *He gave* to us also after believing in the Lord Jesus Christ, who was I that I could prevent God's way?"

18 And when they heard this, they quieted down and glorified God, saying, "Well then, God has granted to the Gentiles also the repentance *that leads* to life."

The Church in Antioch

19 So then those who were scattered because of the persecution that occurred in connection with Stephen made their way to Phoenicia and Cyprus and Antioch, speaking the word to no one except to Jews alone.

20 But there were some of them, men of Cyprus and Cyrene, who came to Antioch and *began* speaking to the Greeks also, proclaiming the good news of the Lord Jesus.

21 And the hand of the Lord was with them, and a large number who believed turned to the Lord.

22 Now the news about them reached

the ears of the church at Jerusalem, and they sent Barnabas off to Antioch,

23 who, when he arrived and saw the grace of God, rejoiced and *began to* encourage them all with a purposeful heart to remain *true* to the Lord;

24 for he was a good man, and full of the Holy Spirit and of faith. And a considerable crowd was brought to the Lord.

25 And he left for Tarsus to search for Saul;

26 and when he found him, he brought him to Antioch. And it happened that for an entire year they met with the church and taught a considerable crowd. And the disciples were first called Christians in Antioch.

27 Now in those days, some prophets came down from Jerusalem to Antioch.

28 And one of them named Agabus stood up and indicated by the Spirit that there was going to be a great famine all over the world. And this took place in the *reign* of Claudius.

29 And as any of the disciples had means, each of them determined to send *a contribution* for the service of the brothers living in Judea.

30 And this they did, sending it in charge of Barnabas and Saul to the elders.

CHAPTER 12

An Angel Frees Peter from Prison

NOW about that time Herod the king laid hands on some who belonged to the church in order to harm them.

2 And he had James the brother of John put to death with a sword.

3 And when he saw that it pleased the Jews, he proceeded to arrest Peter also. Now it was during the days of Unleavened Bread.

4 When he had seized him, he put him in prison, delivering him to four squads of soldiers to guard him, intending after the Passover to bring him out before the people.

5 So Peter was kept in the prison, but prayer for him was being made fervently by the church to God.

6 Now on the very night when Herod was about to bring him forward, Peter was sleeping between two soldiers, bound with two chains, and guards in front of the door were watching over the prison.

7 And behold, an angel of the Lord suddenly appeared and a light shone in the cell; and he struck Peter's side and woke him up, saying, "Rise up quickly." And his chains fell off his hands.

8 And the angel said to him, "Gird yourself and put on your sandals." And he did so. And he *said to him, "Wrap your garment around yourself and follow me."

9 And he went out and continued to follow, and he did not know that what was being done by the angel was real, but was thinking he was seeing a vision.

10 And when they had passed the first and second guard posts, they came to the iron gate that leads into the city, which opened for them by

itself; and they went out and went along one street, and immediately the angel departed from him.

11 When Peter came to himself, he said, "Now truly I know that the Lord has sent His angel and rescued me from the hand of Herod and from all that the Jewish people were expecting."

12 And when he realized *this*, he went to the house of Mary, the mother of John who was also called Mark, where many were gathered together and were praying.

13 And when he knocked at the door of the gate, a servant-girl named Rhoda came to answer.

14 And when she recognized Peter's voice, because of her joy she did not open the gate. But she ran in and reported that Peter was standing in front of the gate.

15 And they said to her, "You are out of your mind!" But she kept insisting that it was so. They kept saying, "It is his angel."

16 But Peter continued knocking, and when they opened *the door*, they saw him and were astounded.

17 But motioning to them with his hand to be silent, he recounted to them how the Lord had led him out of the prison. And he said, "Report these things to James and the brothers." Then he left and went to another place.

18 Now when day came, there was no small disturbance among the soldiers *as to* what had become of Peter.

19 And when Herod had searched for him and had not found him, he examined the guards and ordered that they be led away *to execution*. Then he went down from Judea to Caesarea and was spending time there.

The Death of Herod

20 Now he was very angry with the people of Tyre and Sidon; and with one accord they came to him, and having won over Blastus the king's chamberlain, they were asking for peace, because their country was fed by the king's country.

21 And on an appointed day Herod, having put on his royal apparel and sitting on the judgment seat, *began* delivering an address to them.

22 And the assembly kept crying out, "The voice of a god and not of a man!"

23 And immediately an angel of the Lord struck him because he did not give God the glory, and he was eaten by worms and breathed his last.

24 But the word of the Lord continued to grow and to be multiplied.

25 And Barnabas and Saul returned to Jerusalem, fulfilling their ministry, taking along with *them* John, who was also called Mark.

CHAPTER 13

Barnabas and Saul Sent from Antioch by the Holy Spirit

NOW there were at Antioch, in the church that was *there*, prophets and teachers: Barnabas, and Simeon who was called Niger, and Lucius of Cyrene, and Manaen who had been brought up with Herod the tetrarch, and Saul.

2 And while they were ministering to the Lord and fasting, the Holy Spirit said, "Set apart for Me Barnabas and Saul for the work to which I have called them."

3 Then, when they had fasted and prayed and laid their hands on them, they sent them away.

On Cyprus

4 So, being sent out by the Holy Spirit, they went down to Seleucia and from there they sailed to Cyprus.

5 And when they reached Salamis, they *began to* proclaim the word of God in the synagogues of the Jews, and they also had John as their helper.

6 And when they had gone through the whole island as far as Paphos, they found a magician, a Jewish false prophet whose name was Bar-Jesus,

7 who was with the proconsul, Sergius Paulus, a man of intelligence. This man summoned Barnabas and Saul and sought to hear the word of God.

8 But Elymas the magician (for so his name is translated) was opposing them, seeking to turn the proconsul away from the faith.

9 But Saul, who was also *known as* Paul, filled with the Holy Spirit, fixed his gaze on him,

10 and said, "You who are full of all deceit and fraud, you son of the devil, you enemy of all righteousness,

will you not cease to make crooked the straight ways of the Lord?

11 "Now, behold, the hand of the Lord is upon you, and you will be blind and not see the sun for a time." And immediately a mist and a darkness fell upon him, and he went about seeking those who would lead him by the hand.

12 Then the proconsul believed when he saw what had happened, being astonished at the teaching of the Lord.

In Pisidian Antioch

13 Now after Paul and his companions set sail from Paphos, they came to Perga in Pamphylia, but John left them and returned to Jerusalem.

14 But going on from Perga, they arrived at Pisidian Antioch. And on the Sabbath day, they went into the synagogue and sat down.

15 And after the reading of the Law and the Prophets the synagogue officials sent to them, saying, "Brothers, if you have any word of exhortation for the people, say it."

16 So Paul stood up, and motioning with his hand said,

"Men of Israel, and you who fear God, listen:

17 "The God of this people Israel chose our fathers and lifted up the people during their stay in the land of Egypt, and with an uplifted arm He led them out from it.

18 "And for a period of about forty years He put up with them in the wilderness.

19 "And when He destroyed seven nations in the land of Canaan, He distributed their land as an inheritance— *all of which took* about 450 years.

20 "After these things He gave *them* judges until Samuel the prophet.

21 "Then they asked for a king, and God gave them Saul the son of Kish, a man of the tribe of Benjamin, for forty years.

22 "And after He had removed him, He raised up David to be their king, about whom He also said, bearing witness, 'I HAVE FOUND DAVID the son of Jesse, A MAN AFTER MY HEART, who will do all My will.'

23 "From the seed of this man, according to promise, God has brought to Israel a Savior, Jesus,

24 after John had preached before His coming a baptism of repentance to all the people of Israel.

25 "And as John was fulfilling his course, he kept saying, 'What do you suppose that I am? I am not *He.* But behold, one is coming after me of whom I am not worthy to untie the sandals of His feet.'

26 "Brothers, sons of Abraham's family, and those among you who fear God, to us the word of this salvation was sent.

27 "For those who live in Jerusalem, and their rulers, recognizing neither *Him nor the utterances* of the prophets which are read every Sabbath, fulfilled *them* by condemning *Him.*

28 "And though they found no ground for death, they asked Pilate that He be executed.

29 "And when they had finished all that was written concerning Him, they took Him down from the tree and laid Him in a tomb.

30 "But God raised Him from the dead;

31 and for many days He appeared to those who came up with Him from Galilee to Jerusalem, the very ones who are now His witnesses to the people.

32 "And we proclaim to you the good news of the promise made to the fathers,

33 that God has fulfilled this *promise* to our children in that He raised up Jesus, as it is also written in the second Psalm, 'YOU ARE MY SON; TODAY I HAVE BEGOTTEN YOU.'

34 "*But* that He raised Him up from the dead, no longer to return to corruption, He has spoken in this way: 'I WILL GIVE YOU THE HOLY *and* FAITHFUL *lovingkindnesses* OF DAVID.'

35 "Therefore He also says in another *Psalm,* 'YOU WILL NOT GIVE YOUR HOLY ONE OVER TO SEE CORRUPTION.'

36 "For David, after he had served the purpose of God in his own generation, fell asleep and was laid among his fathers and saw corruption;

37 but He whom God raised did not see corruption.

38 "Therefore let it be known to you, brothers, that through Him forgiveness of sins is proclaimed to you,

39 and *that* in Him, everyone who believes is justified from all things which you could not be justified from through the Law of Moses.

40 "Therefore watch out, so that the thing spoken of in the Prophets may not come upon *you*:

41 'LOOK, YOU SCOFFERS, AND MAR-
    VEL, AND PERISH;
   FOR I AM ACCOMPLISHING A WORK
    IN YOUR DAYS,
   A WORK WHICH YOU WILL NEVER
    BELIEVE, THOUGH SOMEONE
    SHOULD RECOUNT IT TO
    YOU.' "

42 And as Paul and Barnabas were leaving, the people kept pleading that these words might be spoken to them the next Sabbath.

43 Now when *the meeting of* the synagogue had broken up, many of the Jews and of the God-fearing proselytes followed Paul and Barnabas, who, speaking to them, were urging them to continue in the grace of God.

Many Gentiles Believe

44 And the next Sabbath, nearly the whole city assembled to hear the word of the Lord.

45 But when the Jews saw the crowds, they were filled with jealousy and *began* contradicting the things spoken by Paul, blaspheming.

46 Paul and Barnabas spoke out boldly and said, "It was necessary that the word of God be spoken to you first. Since you reject it and judge yourselves unworthy of eternal life, behold, we are turning to the Gentiles.

47 "For so the Lord has commanded us,

   'I HAVE PLACED YOU AS A LIGHT
    FOR THE GENTILES,
   THAT YOU MAY BRING SALVATION
    TO THE END OF THE EARTH.' "

48 And when the Gentiles heard this, they *began* rejoicing and glorifying the word of the Lord, and as many as had been appointed to eternal life believed.

49 And the word of the Lord was being spread through the whole region.

50 But the Jews incited the God-fearing women of prominence and the leading men of the city, and instigated a persecution against Paul and Barnabas, and drove them out of their district.

51 But having shaken off the dust of their feet against them, they went to Iconium.

52 And the disciples were continually filled with joy and with the Holy Spirit.

CHAPTER 14

In Iconium

NOW it happened that in Iconium they entered the synagogue of the Jews together and spoke in such a manner that a large number of people believed, both of Jews and of Greeks.

2 But the unbelieving Jews instigated and embittered the minds of the Gentiles against the brothers.

3 Therefore they spent a long time *there* speaking boldly *with reliance* upon the Lord, who was testifying to the word of His grace, granting that signs and wonders be done through their hands.

4 But the multitude of the city was divided; and some sided with the Jews, and some with the apostles.

5 And when an attempt was made by both the Gentiles and the Jews with their rulers to mistreat and to stone them,

6 they became aware of it and fled to the cities of Lycaonia, Lystra and Derbe, and the surrounding region;

7 and there they continued to proclaim the gospel.

In Lystra and Derbe

8 And at Lystra a man was sitting who had no strength in his feet, lame from his mother's womb, who had never walked.

9 This man listened to Paul as he spoke, who, when he fixed his gaze on him and saw that he had faith to be saved *from being lame*,

10 said with a loud voice, "Stand upright on your feet." And he leaped up and *began to* walk.

11 And when the crowds saw what Paul had done, they raised their voice, saying in the Lycaonian language, "The gods have become like men and have come down to us."

12 And they *began* calling Barnabas, Zeus, and Paul, Hermes, because he was the chief speaker.

13 And the priest of Zeus, whose *temple* was just outside the city, brought oxen and garlands to the gates, and was wanting to offer sacrifice with the crowds.

14 But when the apostles Barnabas and Paul heard of it, they tore their garments and rushed out into the crowd, crying out

15 and saying, "Men, why are you doing these things? We are also men of the same nature as you, proclaiming the gospel to you that you should turn from these vain things to a living God, WHO MADE THE HEAVEN AND THE EARTH AND THE SEA AND ALL THAT IS IN THEM.

16 "In the generations gone by He permitted all the nations to go their own ways;

17 and yet He did not leave Himself without witness, in that He did good and gave you rains from heaven and fruitful seasons, filling your hearts with food and gladness."

18 And saying these things, with difficulty they restrained the crowds from offering sacrifice to them.

19 But Jews came from Antioch and Iconium, and after winning over the crowds and stoning Paul, they were dragging him out of the city, supposing him to be dead.

20 But while the disciples stood around him, he rose up and entered the city. The next day he went away with Barnabas to Derbe.

21 And after they had proclaimed the gospel to that city and had made many disciples, they returned to Lystra and to Iconium and to Antioch,

22 strengthening the souls of the disciples, encouraging them to continue in the faith, and *saying*, "Through many afflictions we must enter the kingdom of God."

23 And when they had appointed elders for them in every church,

having prayed with fasting, they commended them to the Lord in whom they had believed.

The Return to Antioch

24 And when they passed through Pisidia, they came into Pamphylia.

25 And when they had spoken the word in Perga, they went down to Attalia.

26 And from there they sailed to Antioch, from where they had been committed to the grace of God for the work that they had fulfilled.

27 And when they had arrived and gathered the church together, they *began to* report all things that God had done with them and how He had opened a door of faith to the Gentiles.

28 And they spent not a little time with the disciples.

CHAPTER 15

The Jerusalem Council

SOME men came down from Judea and *began* teaching the brothers, "Unless you are circumcised according to the custom of Moses, you cannot be saved."

2 And when Paul and Barnabas had not a little dissension and debate with them, *the brothers* determined that Paul and Barnabas and some others of them should go up to Jerusalem to the apostles and elders concerning this issue.

3 Therefore, being sent on their way by the church, they were passing through both Phoenicia and Samaria, recounting in detail the conversion of the Gentiles, and were bringing great joy to all the brothers.

4 When they arrived at Jerusalem, they were received by the church and the apostles and the elders, and they reported all that God had done with them.

5 But some of the sect of the Pharisees who had believed stood up, saying, "It is necessary to circumcise them and to command them to keep the Law of Moses."

6 Both the apostles and the elders came together to look into this matter.

7 And after there had been much debate, Peter stood up and said to them, "Brothers, you know that in the early days God made a choice among you, that by my mouth the Gentiles would hear the word of the gospel and believe.

8 "And God, who knows the heart, testified to them giving them the Holy Spirit, just as He also did to us;

9 and He made no distinction between us and them, cleansing their hearts by faith.

10 "Now therefore why do you put God to the test by placing upon the neck of the disciples a yoke which neither our fathers nor we have been able to bear?

11 "But we believe that we are saved through the grace of the Lord Jesus, in the same way as they also are."

12 And all the multitude kept silent, and they were listening to Barnabas and Paul as they were relating what signs and wonders God had done through them among the Gentiles.

James Issues a Judgment

13 Now after they had stopped speaking, James answered, saying, "Brothers, listen to me.

14 "Simeon has related how God first concerned Himself about taking from among the Gentiles a people for His name.

15 "And with this the words of the Prophets agree, just as it is written,

16 'AFTER THESE THINGS I will return,
AND I WILL REBUILD THE FALLEN BOOTH OF DAVID,
AND I WILL REBUILD ITS RUINS,
AND I WILL RESTORE IT,

17 SO THAT THE REST OF MANKIND MAY SEEK THE LORD,
AND ALL THE GENTILES WHO ARE CALLED BY MY NAME,'

18 SAYS THE LORD, WHO MAKES THESE THINGS KNOWN FROM LONG AGO.

19 "Therefore I judge that we do not trouble those who are turning to God from among the Gentiles,

20 but that we write to them that they abstain from things contaminated by idols and from sexual immorality and from what is strangled and from blood.

21 "For from ancient generations, Moses has those who preach him in every city, since he is read in the synagogues every Sabbath."

22 Then it seemed good to the apostles and the elders, with the whole church, to choose men from among them—Judas called Barsabbas, and Silas, leading men among the brothers—to send to Antioch with Paul and Barnabas,

23 and they sent this letter by them, "The apostles and the brothers who are elders, to the brothers in Antioch and Syria and Cilicia who are from the Gentiles, greetings.

24 "Since we have heard that some of us, to whom we gave no instruction, have gone out and disturbed you with *their* words, unsettling your souls,

25 it seemed good to us, having come to one accord, to select men to send to you with our beloved Barnabas and Paul,

26 men who have risked their lives for the name of our Lord Jesus Christ.

27 "Therefore we have sent Judas and Silas, and they themselves will report the same things by word *of mouth*.

28 "For it seemed good to the Holy Spirit and to us to lay upon you no greater burden than these essentials:

29 that you abstain from things sacrificed to idols and from blood and from things strangled and from sexual immorality, from which if you keep yourselves, you will do well. Farewell."

30 So when they were sent away, they went down to Antioch; and

having gathered the congregation together, they delivered the letter.

31 And when they had read it, they rejoiced because of its encouragement.

32 And both Judas and Silas, also being prophets themselves, encouraged and strengthened the brothers with a lengthy message.

33 And after they had spent time *there*, they were sent away from the brothers in peace to those who had sent them.

34 [But it seemed good to Silas to remain there.]

35 But Paul and Barnabas spent a long time in Antioch, teaching and preaching with many others also, the word of the Lord.

Disagreement Between Paul and Barnabas

36 Now after some days Paul said to Barnabas, "Let us return and visit the brothers in every city in which we proclaimed the word of the Lord, *and see* how they are."

37 And Barnabas wanted to take John, called Mark, along with them also.

38 But Paul kept insisting that they should not take him along who had deserted them in Pamphylia and had not gone with them to the work.

39 And there was such a sharp disagreement that they separated from one another, and Barnabas took Mark with him and sailed away to Cyprus.

40 But Paul chose Silas and left, being committed by the brothers to the grace of the Lord.

41 And he was traveling through Syria and Cilicia, strengthening the churches.

CHAPTER 16

Timothy Joins Paul and Silas

NOW Paul also arrived at Derbe and at Lystra. And behold, a disciple was there, named Timothy, the son of a Jewish woman who was a believer, but his father was a Greek,

2 and he was well spoken of by the brothers who were in Lystra and Iconium.

3 Paul wanted this man to go with him, and he took him and circumcised him because of the Jews who were in those parts, for they all knew that his father was a Greek.

4 Now while they were passing through the cities, they were delivering the decrees which had been decided upon by the apostles and elders who were in Jerusalem, for them to keep.

5 So the churches were being strengthened in the faith, and were abounding in number daily.

The Macedonian Vision

6 And they passed through the Phrygian and Galatian region, having been forbidden by the Holy Spirit to speak the word in Asia;

7 and after they came to Mysia, they were trying to go into Bithynia,

and the Spirit of Jesus did not permit them;

8 and passing by Mysia, they came down to Troas.

9 And a vision appeared to Paul in the night: a man of Macedonia was standing and appealing to him, and saying, "Come over to Macedonia and help us."

10 And when he had seen the vision, immediately we sought to go into Macedonia, concluding that God had called us to proclaim the gospel to them.

Lydia's Conversion in Philippi

11 So setting sail from Troas, we ran a straight course to Samothrace, and on the day following to Neapolis;

12 and from there to Philippi, which is a leading city of the district of Macedonia, a Roman colony; and we were staying in this city for some days.

13 And on the Sabbath day we went outside the gate to a riverside, where we were supposing that there would be a place of prayer; and sitting down, we *began* speaking to the women who had assembled.

14 And a woman named Lydia, from the city of Thyatira, a seller of purple fabrics, a worshiper of God, was listening, whose heart the Lord opened to pay attention to the things spoken by Paul.

15 And when she and her household had been baptized, she urged us, saying, "If you have judged me to be faithful to the Lord, come into my house and stay." And she prevailed upon us.

Paul and Silas in Prison

16 Now it happened that as we were going to the place of prayer, a servant-girl having a spirit of divination met us, who was bringing her masters much profit by fortune-telling.

17 Following after Paul and us, she kept crying out, saying, "These men are slaves of the Most High God, who are proclaiming to you the way of salvation."

18 And she continued doing this for many days. But being greatly annoyed, Paul turned and said to the spirit, "I command you in the name of Jesus Christ to leave her!" And it left at that very moment.

19 But when her masters saw that their hope of profit had left, they seized Paul and Silas and dragged them into the marketplace before the authorities,

20 and when they had brought them to the chief magistrates, they said, "These men are throwing our city into confusion, being Jews,

21 and are proclaiming customs that are not lawful for us to accept or to observe, being Romans."

22 And the crowd joined together to attack them, and the chief magistrates, tearing their garments off of them, proceeded to order *them* to be beaten with rods.

23 And when they had inflicted them with many wounds, they threw them into prison, commanding the jailer to guard them securely,

24 who, having received such a command, threw them into the inner prison and fastened their feet in the stocks.

The Philippian Jailer Converted

25 But about midnight Paul and Silas were praying and singing hymns of praise to God, and the prisoners were listening to them.

26 And suddenly there came a great earthquake, so that the foundations of the jailhouse were shaken; and immediately all the doors were opened and everyone's chains were unfastened.

27 And when the jailer awoke and saw the prison doors opened, he drew his sword and was about to kill himself, supposing that the prisoners had escaped.

28 But Paul cried out with a loud voice, saying, "Do not harm yourself, for we are all here!"

29 And he called for lights and rushed in, and trembling with fear he fell down before Paul and Silas,

30 and after he brought them out, he said, "Sirs, what must I do to be saved?"

31 And they said, "Believe in the Lord Jesus, and you will be saved, you and your house."

32 And they spoke the word of the Lord to him together with all who were in his household.

33 And he took them that *very* hour of the night and washed their wounds, and immediately he was baptized, he and all his *household*.

34 And he brought them into his house and set food before them, and rejoiced greatly with his whole household, because he had believed in God.

35 Now when day came, the chief magistrates sent their policemen, saying, "Release those men."

36 And the jailer reported these words to Paul, *saying*, "The chief magistrates have sent to release you. Therefore come out now and go in peace."

37 But Paul said to them, "Having beaten us in public without trial, men who are Romans, they have thrown us into prison. And now are they sending us away secretly? No indeed! But let them come themselves and bring us out."

38 And the policemen reported these words to the chief magistrates. They were afraid when they heard that they were Romans,

39 and they came and appealed to them, and when they had brought them out, they kept requesting them to leave the city.

40 And they went out of the prison and entered *the house of* Lydia, and when they saw the brothers, they encouraged them and left.

CHAPTER 17

Paul and Silas in Thessalonica

NOW when they had traveled through Amphipolis and Apollonia, they came to Thessalonica, where there was a synagogue of the Jews.

2 And according to Paul's custom, he went to them, and for three Sabbaths reasoned with them from the Scriptures,

3 explaining and setting before them that the Christ had to suffer and rise again from the dead, and *saying*, "This Jesus whom I am proclaiming to you is that Christ."

4 And some of them were persuaded and joined Paul and Silas, along with a great multitude of the God-fearing Greeks and not a few of the leading women.

5 But the Jews, becoming jealous, taking along some wicked men from the marketplace, and forming a mob, set the city in an uproar. And attacking the house of Jason, they were seeking to bring them out to the assembly.

6 And when they did not find them, they *began* dragging Jason and some brothers before the city authorities, shouting, "These men who have upset the world have come here also;

7 and Jason has welcomed them, and they all act contrary to the decrees of Caesar, saying that there is another king, Jesus."

8 And they disturbed the crowd and the city authorities who heard these things.

9 And when they had received the bond from Jason and the others, they released them.

In Berea

10 And the brothers immediately sent Paul and Silas away by night to Berea, and when they arrived, they went into the synagogue of the Jews.

11 Now these were more noble-minded than those in Thessalonica, for they received the word with great eagerness, examining the Scriptures daily *to see* whether these things were so.

12 Therefore many of them believed, along with not a few prominent Greek women and men.

13 But when the Jews of Thessalonica found out that the word of God had been proclaimed by Paul in Berea also, they came there as well, shaking up and disturbing the crowds.

14 Then immediately the brothers sent Paul out to go as far as the sea; and Silas and Timothy remained there.

15 Now those who escorted Paul brought him as far as Athens; and after receiving a command for Silas and Timothy to come to him as soon as possible, they left.

In Athens

16 Now while Paul was waiting for them at Athens, his spirit was being provoked within him as he was observing the city full of idols.

17 So he was reasoning in the synagogue with the Jews and the God-fearing *Gentiles*, and in the marketplace every day with those who happened to be present.

18 And also some of the Epicurean and Stoic philosophers were conversing with him. Some were saying, "What would this idle babbler wish

to say?" Others, "He seems to be a proclaimer of strange deities,"—because he was proclaiming the good news of Jesus and the resurrection.

19 And they took him and brought him to the Areopagus, saying, "May we know what this new teaching is which you are speaking?

20 "For you are bringing some strange things to our ears. So we want to know what these things mean."

21 (Now all the Athenians and the strangers visiting there used to spend their time in nothing other than telling or hearing something newer.)

22 So Paul stood in the midst of the Areopagus and said, "Men of Athens, I observe that you are very religious in all respects.

23 "For while I was passing through and examining the objects of your worship, I also found an altar with this inscription, 'TO AN UNKNOWN GOD.' Therefore what you worship in ignorance, this I proclaim to you.

24 "The God who made the world and all things in it, since He is Lord of heaven and earth, does not dwell in temples made with hands;

25 nor is He served by human hands, as though He needed anything, since He Himself gives to all *people* life and breath and all things;

26 and He made from one *man* every nation of mankind to inhabit all the face of the earth, having determined *their* appointed times and the boundaries of their habitation,

27 that they would seek God, if perhaps they might grope for Him and find Him, though He is not far from each one of us;

28 for in Him we live and move and exist, as even some of your own poets have said, 'For we also are His offspring.'

29 "Being then the offspring of God, we ought not to suppose that the Divine Nature is like gold or silver or stone, an image formed by the craft and thought of man.

30 "Therefore having overlooked the times of ignorance, God is now commanding men that everyone everywhere should repent,

31 because He has fixed a day in which He will judge the world in righteousness through a Man whom He determined, having furnished proof to all by raising Him from the dead."

32 Now when they heard about the resurrection of the dead, some *began to* sneer, but others said, "We shall hear you again concerning this."

33 In this way, Paul went out of their midst.

34 But some men joined him and believed, among whom also were Dionysius the Areopagite and a woman named Damaris and others with them.

CHAPTER 18

In Corinth

AFTER these things he departed Athens and went to Corinth.

2 And he found a Jew named Aquila, a native of Pontus, and his wife Priscilla, who recently came from Italy

because Claudius had commanded all the Jews to depart from Rome. He came to them,

3 and because he was of the same trade, he was staying with them and they were working, for by trade they were tent-makers.

4 And he was reasoning in the synagogue every Sabbath and trying to persuade both Jews and Greeks.

5 But when Silas and Timothy came down from Macedonia, Paul *began* devoting himself completely to the word, solemnly bearing witness to the Jews that Jesus is the Christ.

6 But when they resisted and blasphemed, he shook out his garments and said to them, "Your blood *be* on your own heads! I am clean. From now on I will go to the Gentiles."

7 Then he left there and went to the house of a man named Titius Justus, a God-fearer, whose house was next to the synagogue.

8 And Crispus, the leader of the synagogue, believed in the Lord with all his household, and many of the Corinthians when they heard were believing and being baptized.

9 And the Lord said to Paul in the night by a vision, "Do not be afraid, but go on speaking and do not be silent;

10 for I am with you, and no man will lay *a hand* on you in order to harm you, for I have many people in this city."

11 And he stayed *there* a year and six months, teaching the word of God among them.

12 But while Gallio was proconsul of Achaia, the Jews with one accord rose up against Paul and brought him before the judgment seat,

13 saying, "This man persuades men to worship God contrary to the law."

14 But when Paul was about to open his mouth, Gallio said to the Jews, "If it were a wrongdoing or vicious crime, O Jews, it would be reasonable for me to put up with you;

15 but if there are questions about words and names and your own law, see to it yourselves; I am not willing to be a judge of these matters."

16 And he drove them away from the judgment seat.

17 And they all took hold of Sosthenes, the leader of the synagogue, and *began* beating him in front of the judgment seat. But Gallio was not concerned about any of these things.

Priscilla, Aquila, and Apollos

18 And Paul, having remained many days longer, took leave of the brothers and put out to sea for Syria, and with him were Priscilla and Aquila. In Cenchreae he had his hair cut, for he was keeping a vow.

19 And they arrived at Ephesus, and he left them there. Now he himself entered the synagogue and reasoned with the Jews.

20 When they asked him to stay for a longer time, he did not consent,

21 but taking leave of them and saying, "I will return to you again if God wills," he set sail from Ephesus.

22 And when he had landed at Caesarea, he went up and greeted the church, and went down to Antioch.

23 And having spent some time *there*, he left and passed successively through the Galatian region and Phrygia, strengthening all the disciples.

24 Now a Jew named Apollos, an Alexandrian by birth, an eloquent man, arrived at Ephesus; and he was mighty in the Scriptures.

25 This man had been instructed in the way of the Lord; and being fervent in spirit, he was speaking and teaching accurately the things concerning Jesus, being acquainted only with the baptism of John;

26 and he began to speak out boldly in the synagogue. But when Priscilla and Aquila heard him, they took him aside and explained to him the way of God more accurately.

27 And when he wanted to go across to Achaia, the brothers encouraged him and wrote to the disciples to welcome him; and when he had arrived, he greatly helped those who had believed through grace,

28 for he powerfully refuted the Jews in public, demonstrating by the Scriptures that Jesus is the Christ.

CHAPTER 19

Paul in Ephesus

NOW it happened that while Apollos was at Corinth, Paul passed through the upper regions and came to Ephesus and found some disciples.

2 And he said to them, "Did you receive the Holy Spirit when you believed?" And they *said* to him, "No, we have not even heard if the Holy Spirit is *being received*."

3 And he said, "Into what then were you baptized?" And they said, "Into John's baptism."

4 Then Paul said, "John baptized with the baptism of repentance, telling the people to believe in Him who was coming after him, that is, in Jesus."

5 And when they heard this, they were baptized in the name of the Lord Jesus.

6 And when Paul had laid his hands upon them, the Holy Spirit came on them, and they *began* speaking with tongues and prophesying.

7 Now there were in all about twelve men.

8 And after he entered the synagogue, he continued speaking out boldly for three months, reasoning and persuading *them* about the kingdom of God.

9 But when some were becoming hardened and were not believing, speaking evil of the Way before the multitude, he left them and took away the disciples, reasoning daily in the school of Tyrannus.

10 This took place for two years, so that all who lived in Asia heard the word of the Lord, both Jews and Greeks.

Miracles in Ephesus

11 And God was doing extraordinary miracles by the hands of Paul,

12 so that cloths or aprons were even carried from his body to the sick, and the diseases left them and the evil spirits went out.

13 But also some of the Jewish exorcists, who went from place to place, attempted to invoke over those who had the evil spirits the name of the Lord Jesus, saying, "I implore you by Jesus whom Paul preaches."

14 Now seven sons of one *named* Sceva, a Jewish chief priest, were doing this.

15 And the evil spirit answered and said to them, "I recognize Jesus, and I know about Paul, but who are you?"

16 And the man, in whom was the evil spirit, leaped on them, subdued all of them, and utterly prevailed against them, so that they fled out of that house naked and wounded.

17 And this became known to all, both Jews and Greeks, who lived in Ephesus; and fear fell upon them all and the name of the Lord Jesus was being magnified.

18 Also, many of those who had believed kept coming, confessing and disclosing their practices.

19 And many of those who practiced magic brought their books together and were burning them in the sight of everyone; and they counted up the price of them and found it fifty thousand ¹pieces of silver.

20 So the word of the Lord was growing mightily and prevailing.

Riots in Ephesus

21 Now after these things were finished, Paul purposed in the Spirit to go to Jerusalem after he had passed through Macedonia and Achaia, saying, "After I have been there, I must also see Rome."

22 And having sent into Macedonia two of those who ministered to him, Timothy and Erastus, he himself stayed in Asia for a while.

23 Now about that time there occurred no small disturbance concerning the Way.

24 For a man named Demetrius, a silversmith, who made silver shrines of Artemis, was bringing no little business to the craftsmen;

25 these he gathered together with the workers of similar *trades*, and said, "Men, you know that our prosperity is from this business.

26 "And you see and hear that not only in Ephesus, but in almost all of Asia, this Paul has persuaded and turned away a considerable crowd, saying that things made with hands are not gods.

27 "And not only is there danger that this trade of ours fall into disrepute, but also that the temple of the great goddess Artemis be considered as worthless and that she, whom all of Asia and the world worship, is even about to be brought down from her majesty."

28 When they heard *this* and were filled with rage, they *began* crying out, saying, "Great is Artemis of the Ephesians!"

29 And the city was filled with the confusion, and they rushed with

¹ A silver piece was approx. a laborer's daily wage

one accord into the theater, dragging along Gaius and Aristarchus, Paul's traveling companions from Macedonia.

30 And when Paul wanted to go into the assembly, the disciples would not let him.

31 Also some of the Asiarchs who were friends of his sent to him and repeatedly urged him not to venture into the theater.

32 So then, some were shouting one thing and some another, for the meeting was in confusion and the majority did not know for what reason they had come together.

33 And some of the crowd concluded *it was* Alexander, since the Jews had put him forward; and having motioned with his hand, Alexander was intending to make a defense to the assembly.

34 But when they recognized that he was a Jew, a single cry arose from them all as they shouted for about two hours, "Great is Artemis of the Ephesians!"

35 Now after calming the crowd, the city clerk *said, "Men of Ephesus, what man is there after all who does not know that the city of the Ephesians is guardian of the temple of the great Artemis and of the *image* which fell down from heaven?

36 "So, since these are undeniable facts, you ought to keep calm and to do nothing rash.

37 "For you have brought these men *here* who are neither robbers of temples nor blasphemers of our goddess.

38 "So then, if Demetrius and the craftsmen who are with him have a complaint against anyone, the courts are in session and proconsuls are *available*; let them bring charges against one another.

39 "But if you want anything beyond this, it shall be settled in the lawful meeting.

40 "For indeed we are in danger of being accused of a riot in connection with today's events, since there is no cause for which we can give as an account for this disorderly gathering."

41 After saying this he dismissed the meeting.

CHAPTER 20

Through Macedonia and Greece

NOW after the uproar had ceased, Paul having summoned and exhorted the disciples, said farewell and left to go to Macedonia.

2 And when he had gone through those districts and had given them much exhortation, he came to Greece.

3 And *there* he spent three months, and when a plot was formed against him by the Jews as he was about to set sail for Syria, he decided to return through Macedonia.

4 And he was accompanied by Sopater of Berea, *the son* of Pyrrhus, and by Aristarchus and Secundus of the Thessalonians, and Gaius of Derbe, and Timothy, and Tychicus and Trophimus of Asia.

5 But these had gone on ahead and were waiting for us at Troas.

6 And we sailed from Philippi after the days of Unleavened Bread, and came to them at Troas within five days; and there we stayed seven days.

Eutychus Raised from the Dead in Troas

7 And on the first day of the week, when we were gathered together to break bread, Paul *began* speaking to them, intending to leave the next day, and he prolonged his message until midnight.

8 Now there were many lamps in the upper room where we were gathered together.

9 And there was a young man named Eutychus sitting on the windowsill, sinking into a deep sleep. And as Paul kept on talking, he sunk into that sleep and fell down from the third floor and was picked up dead.

10 But Paul went down and fell upon him, and after embracing him, he said, "Do not be troubled, for his life is in him."

11 And when he had gone *back* up and had broken the bread and eaten, he talked with them a long while until daybreak, and then left.

12 And they took away the boy alive, and were not a little comforted.

Paul's Farewell to the Ephesian Elders

13 But we, going ahead to the ship, set sail for Assos, intending from there to take Paul on board; for so he had arranged it, intending himself to go by land.

14 And when he met us at Assos, we took him on board and came to Mitylene.

15 And sailing from there, we arrived the following day opposite Chios; and the next day we crossed over to Samos; and the day following we came to Miletus.

16 For Paul had decided to sail past Ephesus so that he would not have to spend time in Asia; for he was hurrying to be in Jerusalem, if possible, on the day of Pentecost.

17 Now from Miletus he sent to Ephesus and called to him the elders of the church.

18 And when they had come to him, he said to them,

"You yourselves know, from the first day that I set foot in Asia, how I was with you the whole time,

19 serving the Lord with all humility and with tears and with trials which came upon me through the plots of the Jews;

20 how I did not shrink from declaring to you anything that was profitable, and teaching you publicly and from house to house,

21 solemnly testifying to both Jews and Greeks about repentance toward God and faith in our Lord Jesus Christ.

22 "And now, behold, bound by the Spirit, I am on my way to Jerusalem, not knowing what will happen to me there,

23 except that the Holy Spirit solemnly testifies to me in every city,

saying that chains and afflictions await me.

24 "But I do not make my life of any account nor dear to myself, so that I may finish my course and the ministry which I received from the Lord Jesus, to testify solemnly of the gospel of the grace of God.

25 "And now, behold, I know that all of you, among whom I went about preaching the kingdom, will no longer see my face.

26 "Therefore, I testify to you this day that I am innocent of the blood of all.

27 "For I did not shrink from declaring to you the whole purpose of God.

28 "Be on guard for yourselves and for all the flock, among which the Holy Spirit has made you overseers, to shepherd the church of God which He purchased with His own blood.

29 "I know that after my departure savage wolves will come in among you, not sparing the flock;

30 and from among your own selves men will arise, speaking perverse things, to draw away the disciples after them.

31 "Therefore be watchful, remembering that night and day for a period of three years I did not cease to admonish each one with tears.

32 "And now I commend you to God and to the word of His grace, which is able to build *you* up and to give *you* the inheritance among all those who have been sanctified.

33 "I have coveted no one's silver or gold or clothes.

34 "You yourselves know that these hands ministered to my *own* needs and to those who were with me.

35 "In everything I showed you that by laboring in this manner you must help the weak and remember the words of the Lord Jesus, that He Himself said, 'It is more blessed to give than to receive.'"

36 And when he had said these things, he knelt down and prayed with them all.

37 And they *began* to weep aloud and falling on Paul's neck, they were kissing him,

38 being in agony especially over the word which he had spoken, that they would not see his face again. And they were accompanying him to the ship.

CHAPTER 21

Paul Sets Out for Jerusalem

NOW when we had parted from them and had set sail, we came by a straight course to Cos and the next day to Rhodes and from there to Patara;

2 and having found a ship crossing over to Phoenicia, we went aboard and set sail.

3 And when we came in sight of Cyprus, leaving it on the left, we kept sailing to Syria and landed at Tyre; for there the ship was to unload its cargo.

4 And after looking up the disciples, we stayed there seven days; and

they kept telling Paul through the Spirit not to set foot in Jerusalem.

5 And when our days there were ended, we left and started on our journey, while they all, with wives and children, escorted us until *we were* out of the city. After kneeling down on the beach and praying, we said farewell to one another.

6 Then we went on board the ship, and they returned home again.

7 And when we had finished the voyage from Tyre, we arrived at Ptolemais, and after greeting the brothers, we stayed with them for a day.

8 And on the next day we left and came to Caesarea, and entering the house of Philip the evangelist, who was one of the seven, we stayed with him.

9 Now this man had four virgin daughters who prophesied.

10 And as we were staying there for some days, a prophet named Agabus came down from Judea.

11 And coming to us, he took Paul's belt and bound his own feet and hands, and said, "This is what the Holy Spirit says: 'In this way the Jews at Jerusalem will bind the man who owns this belt and deliver him into the hands of the Gentiles.'"

12 And when we had heard this, we as well as the local residents *began* begging him not to go up to Jerusalem.

13 Then Paul answered, "What are you doing, crying and breaking my heart? For I am ready not only to be bound, but even to die at Jerusalem for the name of the Lord Jesus."

14 And since he would not be persuaded, we fell silent, saying, "The will of the Lord be done!"

15 Now after these days we got ready and started on our way up to Jerusalem.

16 And *some* of the disciples from Caesarea also came with us, taking us to Mnason of Cyprus, an early disciple with whom we were to lodge.

In Jerusalem

17 And after we arrived in Jerusalem, the brothers welcomed us gladly.

18 And the following day Paul went in with us to James, and all the elders were present.

19 And after he had greeted them, he *began to* relate one by one the things which God did among the Gentiles through his ministry.

20 And when they heard it they *began* glorifying God; and they said to him, "You see, brother, how many thousands there are among the Jews of those who have believed, and they are all zealous for the Law;

21 and they have been told about you, that you are teaching all the Jews who are among the Gentiles to forsake Moses, telling them not to circumcise their children nor to walk according to the customs.

22 "What, then, is *to be done*? They will certainly hear that you have come.

23 "Therefore do this that we tell you. We have four men who are under a vow;

24 take them and purify yourself along with them, and pay their

expenses so that they may shave their heads. Then all will know that there is nothing to the things which they have been told about you, but that you yourself also walk orderly, keeping the Law.

25 "But concerning the Gentiles who have believed, we wrote, having decided that they should keep from meat sacrificed to idols and from blood and from what is strangled and from sexual immorality."

26 Then Paul took the men, and the next day, purifying himself along with them, went into the temple giving notice of the completion of the days of purification, until the sacrifice was offered for each one of them.

Paul Is Arrested

27 Now when the seven days were almost over, the Jews from Asia, upon noticing him in the temple, *began to* throw all the crowd into confusion and laid hands on him,

28 crying out, "Men of Israel, help! This is the man who teaches to everyone everywhere against our people and the Law and this place; and besides, he has even brought Greeks into the temple and has defiled this holy place."

29 For they had previously seen Trophimus the Ephesian in the city with him, and they supposed that Paul had brought him into the temple.

30 Then all the city was stirred, and the people rushed together, and taking hold of Paul they dragged him out of the temple, and immediately the doors were shut.

31 While they were seeking to kill him, a report came up to the commander of the *Roman* cohort that all Jerusalem was in confusion.

32 At once he took along soldiers and centurions and ran down to them; and when they saw the commander and the soldiers, they stopped beating Paul.

33 Then the commander came up and took hold of him, and ordered him to be bound with two chains; and he *began* asking who he was and what he had done.

34 But among the crowd some were shouting one thing *and* some another, and when he could not find out the facts because of the uproar, he ordered him to be brought into the barracks.

35 And when he got to the stairs, he actually was carried by the soldiers because of the violence of the crowd;

36 for the multitude of the people kept following them, shouting, "Away with him!"

Paul's Defense Before the Jews

37 As Paul was about to be brought into the barracks, he said to the commander, "May I say something to you?" And he *said, "Do you know Greek?

38 "Then you are not the Egyptian who some time ago raised a revolt and led the four thousand men of the Assassins out into the wilderness?"

39 But Paul said, "I am a Jew of Tarsus in Cilicia, a citizen of no insignificant city; and I beg you, allow me to speak to the people."

40 And when he had given him permission, Paul, standing on the stairs, motioned to the people with his hand; and when there was a great hush, he spoke to them in the Hebrew language, saying,

CHAPTER 22

"MEN, brothers, and fathers, hear my defense which I now *offer* to you."

2 And when they heard that he was addressing them in the Hebrew language, they became even quieter; and he *said,

3 "I am a Jew, born in Tarsus of Cilicia, but having been brought up in this city, having been instructed at the feet of Gamaliel according to the strictness of the law of our fathers, being zealous for God just as you all are today,

4 I persecuted this Way to the death, binding and delivering both men and women into prisons,

5 as also the high priest and all the Council of the elders can testify. From them I also received letters to the brothers, and started off for Damascus in order to bring even those who were there to Jerusalem as prisoners to be punished.

6 "But it happened that as I was on my way, approaching Damascus about noontime, a very bright light suddenly flashed from heaven all around me,

7 and I fell to the ground and heard a voice saying to me, 'Saul, Saul, why are you persecuting Me?'

8 "And I answered, 'Who are You, Lord?' And He said to me, 'I am Jesus the Nazarene, whom you are persecuting.'

9 "And those who were with me beheld the light, to be sure, but did not understand the voice of the One who was speaking to me.

10 "And I said, 'What should I do, Lord?' And the Lord said to me, 'Rise up and go on into Damascus, and there you will be told of all that has been determined for you to do.'

11 "But since I could not see because of the glory of that light, being led by the hand by those who were with me, I came into Damascus.

12 "Now a certain Ananias, a man who was devout by the standard of the Law, *and* well spoken of by all the Jews who lived there,

13 came to me, and standing near, said to me, 'Brother Saul, regain your sight!' And at that very hour I regained my sight and *saw* him.

14 "And he said, 'The God of our fathers has appointed you to know His will and to see the Righteous One and to hear a voice from His mouth.

15 'For you will be a witness for Him to all men of what you have seen and heard.

16 'Now why do you delay? Rise up and be baptized, and wash away your sins, calling on His name.'

17 "Now it happened when I returned to Jerusalem and was praying in the temple, that I fell into a trance,

18 and I saw Him saying to me, 'Hurry and get out of Jerusalem quickly, because they will not accept your witness about Me.'

19 "And I said, 'Lord, they themselves understand that in one synagogue after another I used to imprison and beat those who believed in You.

20 'And when the blood of Your witness Stephen was being shed, I also was standing by approving, and guarding the garments of those who were slaying him.'

21 "And He said to me, 'Go! For I will send you far away to the Gentiles.' "

Paul, a Citizen of Rome

22 And they were listening to him up to this statement, and *then* they raised their voices and said, "Away with such a fellow from the earth, for he should not be allowed to live!"

23 And as they were crying out and throwing off their garments and tossing dust into the air,

24 the commander ordered him to be brought into the barracks, stating that he should be examined by flogging so that he might find out the reason why they were shouting against him that way.

25 But when they stretched him out with leather straps, Paul said to the centurion who was standing by, "Is it lawful for you to flog a man who is a Roman and uncondemned?"

26 And when the centurion heard *this*, he went to the commander and reported to him, saying, "What are

you about to do? For this man is a Roman."

27 And the commander came and said to him, "Tell me, are you a Roman?" And he said, "Yes."

28 And the commander answered, "I acquired this citizenship with a large sum of money." And Paul said, "But I have been born *a citizen.*"

29 Therefore those who were about to examine him immediately withdrew from him; and the commander also was afraid when he learned that he was a Roman, and because he had bound him.

Paul Before the Sanhedrin

30 But on the next day, wishing to know for certain why he had been accused by the Jews, he released him and ordered the chief priests and all the Sanhedrin to come together, and brought Paul down and set him before them.

CHAPTER 23

NOW Paul, looking intently at the Sanhedrin, said, "Brothers, I have lived my life in all good conscience before God up to this day."

2 And the high priest Ananias commanded those standing beside him to strike him on the mouth.

3 Then Paul said to him, "God is going to strike you, you whitewashed wall! Do you sit to try me according to the Law, and in violation of the Law order me to be struck?"

4 But those standing nearby said, "Do you revile the high priest of God?"

5 And Paul said, "I was not aware, brothers, that he was high priest; for it is written, 'YOU SHALL NOT SPEAK EVIL OF A RULER OF YOUR PEOPLE.'"

6 But knowing that one group were Sadducees and the other Pharisees, Paul *began* crying out in the Sanhedrin, "Brothers, I am a Pharisee, a son of Pharisees; I am on trial for the hope and resurrection of the dead!"

7 As he said this, there was dissension between the Pharisees and Sadducees, and the assembly was divided.

8 For the Sadducees say that there is no resurrection, nor an angel, nor a spirit, but the Pharisees acknowledge them all.

9 And there occurred a great outcry; and some of the scribes of the Pharisaic party stood up and *began to* argue heatedly, saying, "We find nothing wrong with this man. Suppose a spirit or an angel has spoken to him?"

10 And as a great dissension was developing, because the commander was afraid Paul would be torn to pieces by them, he ordered the troops to go down and take him away from them by force, and bring him into the barracks.

11 But on that very night, the Lord stood at his side and said, "Take courage; for as you have solemnly borne witness to My cause at Jerusalem, so you must bear witness at Rome also."

A Plot to Kill Paul

12 Now when it was day, the Jews formed a conspiracy and bound themselves under a curse, saying that they would neither eat nor drink until they had killed Paul.

13 And there were more than forty who formed this scheme.

14 They came to the chief priests and the elders and said, "We have bound ourselves under a curse to taste nothing until we have killed Paul.

15 "So now you, along with the Sanhedrin, notify the commander to bring him down to you, as though you were going to determine his case more carefully; and we for our part are ready to slay him before he comes near."

16 But when the son of Paul's sister heard of their ambush, he came and entered the barracks and reported *it* to Paul.

17 And Paul called one of the centurions to him and said, "Lead this young man to the commander, for he has something to report to him."

18 So he took him and led him to the commander and *said, "Paul the prisoner called me to him and asked me to lead this young man to you since he has something to tell you."

19 And the commander took him by the hand and stepping aside, *began to* inquire of him privately, "What is it that you have to report to me?"

20 And he said, "The Jews have agreed to ask you to bring Paul down tomorrow to the Sanhedrin, as though they were going to inquire somewhat more carefully about him.

21 "So do not be persuaded by them, for more than forty of them—who have bound themselves under a curse not to eat or drink until they slay him—are lying in wait for him and now they are ready and waiting for the promise from you."

22 So the commander let the young man go, instructing him, "Tell no one that you have notified me of these things."

Paul Is Brought to Caesarea

23 And when he called to him two of the centurions, he said, "Make ready two hundred soldiers, seventy horsemen, and two hundred spearmen to proceed to Caesarea by the third hour of the night,

24 and provide mounts to put Paul on and bring him safely to Felix the governor."

25 And he wrote a letter having this form:

26 "Claudius Lysias, to the most excellent governor Felix, greetings.

27 "When this man was arrested by the Jews and was about to be slain by them, I came up to them with the troops and rescued him, having learned that he was a Roman.

28 "And wanting to ascertain the charge for which they were accusing him, I brought him down to their Sanhedrin;

29 and I found him to be accused over questions about their Law, but under no accusation deserving death or imprisonment.

30 "And when I was informed that there would be a plot against the man, I sent him to you at once, also instructing his accusers to speak against him before you."

31 So the soldiers, according to their orders, took Paul and brought him by night to Antipatris.

32 But the next day, leaving the horsemen to go on with him, they returned to the barracks.

33 When these had come to Caesarea and delivered the letter to the governor, they also presented Paul to him.

34 And when he had read it, he asked from what province he was, and when he learned that he was from Cilicia,

35 he said, "I will give you a hearing after your accusers arrive also," giving orders for him to be kept in Herod's Praetorium.

CHAPTER 24

Paul's Trial Before Felix the Governor

NOW after five days the high priest Ananias came down with some elders, with an attorney *named* Tertullus, and they brought charges to the governor against Paul.

2 And after *Paul* had been summoned, Tertullus began to accuse him, saying,

"As we have attained much peace through you—and because by your provision reforms are being carried out for this nation—

3 we welcome *this* in every way and everywhere, most excellent Felix, with all thankfulness.

4 "But, that I may not weary you any further, I plead with you by your forbearance to hear us briefly.

5 "For we have found this man a real pest and a fellow who stirs up dissension among all the Jews throughout the world, and a ringleader of the sect of the Nazarenes.

6 "And he even tried to desecrate the temple; and then we arrested him. [We wanted to judge him according to our own Law.

7 "But Lysias the commander came along, and with much violence took him out of our hands,

8 ordering his accusers to come before you.] By examining him yourself concerning all these matters you will be able to ascertain the things of which we accuse him."

9 And the Jews also joined in the attack, asserting that these things were so.

10 And when the governor had nodded for him to speak, Paul answered:

"Knowing that for many years you have been a judge to this nation, I cheerfully make my defense,

11 since you are able to ascertain the fact that no more than twelve days ago I went up to Jerusalem to worship.

12 "And neither in the temple, nor in the synagogues, nor across the city did they find me carrying on a discussion with anyone or causing a riot.

13 "Nor are they able to prove to you of what they are now accusing me.

14 "But this I confess to you, that according to the Way, which they call a sect, I do serve the God of our fathers, believing everything that is in accordance with the Law and that is written in the Prophets;

15 having a hope in God, for which these men are waiting, that there shall certainly be a resurrection of both the righteous and the unrighteous.

16 "In view of this, I also do my best to maintain always a conscience without fault *both* before God and before men.

17 "Now after several years I came to bring alms to my nation and offerings;

18 in which they found me, having been purified in the temple, without *any* crowd or uproar. But *there were* some Jews from Asia—

19 who ought to have been present before you and to make accusation, if they should have anything against me.

20 "Or else let these men themselves tell what wrongdoing they found when I stood before the Sanhedrin,

21 other than for this one statement which I shouted out while standing among them, 'For the resurrection

of the dead I am on trial before you today.'"

22 But Felix, having a more accurate knowledge about the Way, put them off, saying, "When Lysias the commander comes down, I will decide your case."

23 Then he gave orders to the centurion for him to be kept in custody and *yet* have *some* rest, and not to prevent any of his friends from ministering to him.

24 But some days later Felix arrived with Drusilla, his wife who was a Jewess, and summoned Paul and heard him *speak* about faith in Christ Jesus.

25 But as he was discussing righteousness, self-control, and the judgment to come, Felix became frightened and answered, "Go away for the present, and when I find time I will call for you."

26 At the same time, he was also hoping that money would be given him by Paul; therefore he also used to summon for him quite often and converse with him.

27 But after two years had passed, Felix was succeeded by Porcius Festus, and wishing to do the Jews a favor, Felix left Paul imprisoned.

CHAPTER 25

Paul Before Festus

FESTUS then, having arrived in the province, after three days went up to Jerusalem from Caesarea.

2 And the chief priests and the leading men of the Jews brought charges against Paul, and they were pleading with him,

3 requesting a favor against Paul, that he might have him brought to Jerusalem (while they set an ambush to kill him on the way).

4 Festus then answered that Paul was being kept in custody at Caesarea and that he himself was about to leave shortly.

5 "Therefore," he *said, "let the influential men among you go down there with me, and if there is anything wrong about the man, let them accuse him."

6 And after he had spent not more than eight or ten days among them, he went down to Caesarea, and on the next day he took his seat on the judgment seat and ordered Paul to be brought.

7 And after Paul arrived, the Jews who had come down from Jerusalem stood around him, bringing many and serious charges against him which they could not prove,

8 while Paul said in his own defense, "I have committed no sin either against the Law of the Jews or against the temple or against Caesar."

9 But Festus, wishing to do the Jews a favor, answered Paul and said, "Are you willing to go up to Jerusalem and to be tried before me on these *matters*?"

10 But Paul said, "I am standing before Caesar's judgment seat, where I ought to be tried. I have done no wrong to *the* Jews, as you also very well know.

11 "If, then, I am a wrongdoer and have committed anything worthy of death, I do not refuse to die; but if none of those things is *true* of which these men accuse me, no one can hand me over to them. I appeal to Caesar."

12 Then when Festus had conferred with his council, he answered, "You have appealed to Caesar, to Caesar you shall go."

Festus and Agrippa Discuss Paul's Trial

13 Now when several days had passed, King Agrippa and Bernice arrived at Caesarea and greeted Festus.

14 And while they were spending many days there, Festus laid Paul's case before the king, saying, "There is a man who was left as a prisoner by Felix;

15 and when I was at Jerusalem, the chief priests and the elders of the Jews brought charges against him, asking for a sentence of condemnation against him.

16 "I answered them that it is not the custom of the Romans to hand over any man before the accused meets his accusers face to face and has an opportunity to make his defense against the charges.

17 "So after they had assembled here, I did not delay, but on the next day took my seat on the judgment seat and ordered the man to be brought before me.

18 "When the accusers stood up, they were not bringing any charges against him for the evil deeds I was expecting,

19 but they had some points of disagreement with him about their own religion and about a certain Jesus, a dead man whom Paul asserted to be alive.

20 "And being perplexed about how to investigate such matters, I was asking whether he was willing to go to Jerusalem and there to be tried on these matters.

21 "But when Paul appealed to be held in custody for the Emperor's decision, I ordered him to be kept in custody until I send him to Caesar."

22 Then Agrippa *said* to Festus, "I also would like to hear the man myself." "Tomorrow," he *said*, "you shall hear him."

Paul Before Agrippa and Bernice

23 So, on the next day when Agrippa came together with Bernice amid great pomp, and entered the hall accompanied by the commanders and the prominent men of the city, at the order of Festus, Paul was brought in.

24 And Festus *said*, "King Agrippa, and all you gentlemen here present with us, you see this man about whom all the people of the Jews appealed to me, both at Jerusalem and here, loudly declaring that he ought not to live any longer.

25 "But I found that he had committed nothing worthy of death, and since he himself appealed to the Emperor, I decided to send him.

26 "Yet I have nothing definite about him to write to my lord. Therefore I have brought him before you *all* and especially before you, King Agrippa, so that after the investigation has taken place, I may have something to write.

27 "For it seems absurd to me in sending a prisoner, not to indicate also the charges against him."

CHAPTER 26

NOW Agrippa said to Paul, "You are permitted to speak for yourself." Then Paul, stretching out his hand, *began to* make his defense:

2 "Concerning all the things of which I am accused by the Jews, I regard myself blessed, King Agrippa, that I am about to make my defense before you today;

3 especially because you are an expert in all customs and questions among *the* Jews; therefore I beg you to listen to me patiently.

4 "So then, all Jews know my manner of life from my youth, which from the beginning was spent among my *own* nation and at Jerusalem;

5 since they have known about me for a long time, if they are willing to testify, that I lived *as* a Pharisee according to the strictest sect of our religion.

6 "And now I am standing here being tried for the hope of the promise made by God to our fathers;

7 *the promise* to which our twelve tribes hope to attain, as they earnestly serve *God* night and day. And for this hope, O King, I am being accused by Jews.

8 "Why is it considered unbelievable among all of you if God does raise the dead?

9 "So then, I thought to myself that I had to do many things hostile to the name of Jesus the Nazarene.

10 "And this is just what I did in Jerusalem; not only did I lock up many of the saints in prisons, having received authority from the chief priests, but also when they were being put to death I cast my vote against them.

11 "And as I punished them often in all the synagogues, I tried to force them to blaspheme; and being furiously enraged at them, I kept pursuing them even to foreign cities.

Paul Tells of His Conversion

12 "While so engaged as I was journeying to Damascus with the authority and commission of the chief priests,

13 at midday, O King, I saw on the way a light from heaven, brighter than the sun, shining all around me and those who were journeying with me.

14 "And when we had all fallen to the ground, I heard a voice saying to me in the Hebrew language, 'Saul, Saul, why are you persecuting Me? It is hard for you to kick against the goads.'

15 "And I said, 'Who are You, Lord?' And the Lord said, 'I am Jesus whom you are persecuting.

16 'But rise up and stand on your feet; for this purpose I have appeared to you, to appoint you a servant and a witness not only to the things which you have seen, but also to the things in which I will appear to you;

17 rescuing you from the *Jewish* people and from the Gentiles, to whom I am sending you,

18 to open their eyes so that they may turn from darkness to light and from the authority of Satan to God, that they may receive forgiveness of sins and an inheritance among those who have been sanctified by faith in Me.'

19 "So, King Agrippa, I did not prove disobedient to the heavenly vision,

20 but *kept* declaring both to those of Damascus first, and *also* at Jerusalem and *then* throughout all the region of Judea, and *even* to the Gentiles, that they should repent and turn to God, practicing deeds appropriate to repentance.

21 "For this reason *some* Jews seized me in the temple and were trying to put me to death.

22 "Therefore, having obtained help from God to this day, I stand here bearing witness both to small and great, stating nothing but what the Prophets and Moses said was going to take place;

23 that the Christ was to suffer, *and* that as first of the resurrection from the dead, He was going to proclaim light both to the *Jewish* people and to the Gentiles."

24 Now while Paul was saying this in his defense, Festus *said in a loud voice, "Paul, you are out of your mind! Great learning is driving you out of your mind."

25 But Paul *said, "I am not out of my mind, most excellent Festus, but I utter words of sober truth.

26 "For the king knows about these matters, and I speak to him also with confidence, since I am persuaded that none of these things escape his notice; for this has not been done in a corner.

27 "King Agrippa, do you believe the Prophets? I know you believe."

28 But Agrippa *replied* to Paul, "In *such* short time are you persuading me to become a Christian?"

29 And Paul *said*, "I would pray to God, that whether in a short or long time, not only you, but also all who hear me this day, might become such as I am, except for these chains."

30 And the king stood up and the governor and Bernice, and those who were sitting with them,

31 and when they had gone aside, they *began* talking to one another, saying, "This man is not doing anything worthy of death or imprisonment."

32 And Agrippa said to Festus, "This man could have been set free if he had not appealed to Caesar."

CHAPTER 27

Paul Is Sent to Rome

NOW when it was decided that we would sail for Italy, they proceeded to deliver Paul and some other prisoners to a centurion of the Augustan cohort named Julius.

2 And getting aboard an Adramyttian ship, which was about to sail to the regions along the coast of Asia, we set sail accompanied by Aristarchus, a Macedonian of Thessalonica.

3 The next day we put in at Sidon, and Julius treated Paul with consideration and allowed him to go to his friends and receive care.

4 And from there we set sail and sailed under the shelter of Cyprus because the winds were against *us*.

5 And when we had sailed through the sea along the coast of Cilicia and Pamphylia, we landed at Myra in Lycia.

6 There the centurion found an Alexandrian ship sailing for Italy, and he put us aboard it.

7 And when we had sailed slowly for a good many days, and with difficulty had arrived off Cnidus, since the wind did not permit us to go farther, we sailed under the shelter of Crete, off Salmone;

8 and with difficulty, we sailed past it and came to a place called Fair Havens, near which was the city of Lasea.

9 And when considerable time had passed and the voyage was now dangerous, since even the Fast was already over, Paul *began to* advise them,

10 and said to them, "Men, I perceive that the voyage will certainly be with damage and great loss, not only of the cargo and the ship, but also of our lives."

11 But the centurion was being more persuaded by the pilot and the captain of the ship than by what was being said by Paul.

12 And because the harbor was not suitable for wintering, the majority reached a decision to set sail from there, if somehow they could arrive at Phoenix, a harbor of Crete facing southwest and northwest, to spend the winter *there*.

13 And when a moderate south wind came up, thinking that they had attained their purpose, they weighed anchor and *began* sailing along the shore of Crete.

The Storm at Sea

14 But before very long there rushed down from the land a violent wind, called Euraquilo;

15 and when the ship was caught in *it* and could not face the wind, we gave way *to it* and let ourselves be carried along.

16 And running under the shelter of a small island called Clauda, we were scarcely able to get the *ship's* boat under control.

17 After they had hoisted it up, they used supporting cables in undergirding the ship. Fearing that they might run aground on *the shallows* of Syrtis, they let down the sea anchor and in this way let themselves be carried along.

18 And the next day as we were being violently storm-tossed, they *began to* jettison the cargo;

19 and on the third day they cast

the ship's tackle overboard with their own hands.

20 And since neither sun nor stars appeared for many days, and no small storm was assailing *us*, from then on all hope of our being saved was gradually abandoned.

21 And when they had gone a long time without food, then Paul stood up in their midst and said, "Men, you ought to have followed my advice to not set sail from Crete and to avoid this damage and loss.

22 "And now I advise you to be cheerful, for there will be no loss of life among you, but *only* of the ship.

23 "For this very night an angel of the God to whom I belong and whom I serve stood before me,

24 saying, 'Do not be afraid, Paul; you must stand before Caesar; and behold, God has granted you all those who are sailing with you.'

25 "Therefore, be cheerful, men, for I believe God that it will turn out exactly as I have been told.

26 "But we must run aground on some island."

27 But when the fourteenth night came, as we were being carried about in the Adriatic Sea, about midnight the sailors *began to* suspect that some land was approaching them.

28 And when they *took soundings*, *they found it to be* [1]twenty fathoms; and a little farther on they took another sounding and found *it to be* [2]fifteen fathoms.

29 And fearing that we might run aground somewhere on the rocks, they cast four anchors from the stern and were praying for daybreak.

30 But as the sailors were trying to escape from the ship and had let down the *ship's* boat into the sea, on the pretense of intending to lay out anchors from the bow,

31 Paul said to the centurion and to the soldiers, "Unless these men remain in the ship, you yourselves cannot be saved."

32 Then the soldiers cut away the ropes of the *ship's* boat and let it fall away.

33 Until the day was about to dawn, Paul was encouraging them all to take some food, saying, "Today is the fourteenth day that you have been constantly watching and going without eating, having taken nothing.

34 "Therefore I encourage you to take some food, for this is for your salvation, for not a hair from the head of any of you will perish."

35 And having said these things, he took bread and gave thanks to God in the presence of all. And he broke it and began to eat.

36 And all of them became cheerful and they themselves also took food.

37 And all of us in the ship were 276 persons.

38 And when they had eaten enough,

---

[1] Approx. 120 ft. or 36 m, a fathom was approx. 6 ft. or 1.8 m
[2] Approx. 90 ft. or 27 m

they *began to* lighten the ship by throwing out the wheat into the sea.

The Shipwreck

39 Now when day came, they could not recognize the land; but they were noticing a bay with a beach, and they were resolving to drive the ship onto it if they could.

40 And casting off the anchors, they left them in the sea while at the same time they were loosening the ropes of the rudders. And hoisting the foresail to the wind, they were heading for the beach.

41 But striking a reef where two seas met, they ran the vessel aground; and the bow stuck fast and remained immovable, but the stern *began to* be broken up by the force *of the waves.*

42 Now the soldiers' plan was to kill the prisoners, so that none *of them* would swim away and escape;

43 but the centurion, wanting to bring Paul safely through, kept them from their intention, and ordered that those who could swim should jump overboard first and get to land,

44 and the rest *should follow,* some on planks, and others on various things from the ship. And so it happened that they all were brought safely to land.

CHAPTER 28

On the Island of Malta

AND when they had been brought safely through *to shore,* then we learned that the island was called Malta.

2 And the natives showed us extraordinary affection; for because of the rain that had set in and because of the cold, they kindled a fire and received us all.

3 But when Paul had gathered a bundle of sticks and laid them on the fire, a viper came out because of the heat and fastened itself on his hand.

4 And when the natives saw the creature hanging from his hand, they *began* saying to one another, "Undoubtedly this man is a murderer, and though he has been saved from the sea, Justice has not allowed him to live."

5 However he shook the creature off into the fire and suffered no harm.

6 But they were waiting for him to soon swell up or suddenly fall down dead. But after they had waited a long time and had seen nothing unusual happen to him, changing their minds, they *began to* say that he was a god.

7 Now in the areas around that place were lands belonging to the leading man of the island, named Publius, who welcomed us and entertained us courteously three days.

8 And it happened that the father of Publius was lying afflicted with fever and dysentery; and Paul, going *to see* him and having prayed, laid his hands on him and healed him.

9 And after this had happened, the rest of the people on the island who

had diseases were coming to him and being healed.

10 They also bestowed on us many honors of respect; and when we were setting sail, they supplied *us* with all we needed.

Paul Arrives in Rome

11 Now at the end of three months we set sail on an Alexandrian ship which had wintered at the island, and which had the Twin Brothers for its figurehead.

12 After we put into Syracuse, we stayed there for three days.

13 From there we sailed around and arrived at Rhegium, and after a day when a south wind sprang up, on the second day we came to Puteoli.

14 There we found *some* brothers, and were invited to stay with them for seven days; and thus we came to Rome.

15 And the brothers, when they heard about us, came from there as far as the Market of Appius and Three Inns to meet us. When Paul saw them, he thanked God and took courage.

16 And when we entered Rome, Paul was allowed to stay by himself, with the soldier who was guarding him.

Paul's Ministry in Rome

17 And it happened that after three days Paul called together those who were the leading men of the Jews, and when they came together, he *began* saying to them, "Brothers, though I had done nothing against our people or the customs of our fathers, yet I was delivered as a prisoner from Jerusalem into the hands of the Romans.

18 "And when they had examined me, they were willing to release me because there was no ground for putting me to death.

19 "But when the Jews objected, I was forced to appeal to Caesar, not that I had any accusation against my nation.

20 "For this reason, therefore, I requested to see you and to speak with you, for I am wearing this chain for the sake of the hope of Israel."

21 And they said to him, "We have neither received letters from Judea concerning you, nor have any of the brothers come here and reported or spoken anything bad about you.

22 "But we desire to hear from you what you think; for concerning this sect, it is known to us that it is spoken against everywhere."

23 And when they had set a day for Paul, they came to him at his lodging in large numbers; and he was explaining to them by solemnly bearing witness about the kingdom of God and trying to persuade them concerning Jesus, from both the Law of Moses and from the Prophets, from morning until evening.

24 And some were being persuaded by the things spoken, but others were not believing.

25 And when they disagreed with one another, they *began* leaving after Paul had spoken one word, "The

Holy Spirit rightly spoke through Isaiah the prophet to your fathers,
26 saying,

'GO TO THIS PEOPLE AND SAY,
  "YOU WILL KEEP ON HEARING, BUT
      WILL NOT UNDERSTAND;
  AND YOU WILL KEEP ON SEEING,
      BUT WILL NOT PERCEIVE;
27 FOR THE HEART OF THIS PEOPLE
      HAS BECOME DULL,
  AND WITH THEIR EARS THEY
      SCARCELY HEAR,
  AND THEY HAVE CLOSED THEIR
      EYES;
  LEST THEY MIGHT SEE WITH
      THEIR EYES,
  AND HEAR WITH THEIR EARS,

  AND UNDERSTAND WITH THEIR
      HEART AND RETURN,
  AND I HEAL THEM." '

28 "Therefore let it be known to you that this salvation of God was sent to the Gentiles—they will also hear."

29 [When he had spoken these words, the Jews departed, having a great dispute among themselves.]

30 And he stayed two full years in his own rented quarters and was welcoming all who came to him,

31 preaching the kingdom of God and teaching concerning the Lord Jesus Christ with all confidence, unhindered.

THE LETTER OF PAUL TO THE

ROMANS

CHAPTER 1

The Gospel Exalted

PAUL, a slave of Christ Jesus, called *as* an apostle, having been set apart for the gospel of God,

2 which He promised beforehand through His prophets in the holy Scriptures,

3 concerning His Son, who was born of the seed of David according to the flesh,

4 who was designated as the Son of God in power, according to the Spirit of holiness, by the resurrection from the dead, Jesus Christ our Lord,

5 through whom we received grace and apostleship for *the* obedience of faith among all the Gentiles for the sake of His name,

6 among whom you also are the called of Jesus Christ;

7 to all who are beloved of God in Rome, called *as* saints: Grace to you and peace from God our Father and the Lord Jesus Christ.

8 First, I thank my God through Jesus Christ for you all, because your

faith is being proclaimed throughout the whole world.

9 For God, whom I serve in my spirit in the gospel of His Son, is my witness *as to* how without ceasing I make mention of you,

10 always in my prayers earnestly asking, if perhaps now at last by the will of God I may succeed in coming to you.

11 For I long to see you so that I may impart some spiritual gift to you, that you may be strengthened;

12 that is, to be mutually encouraged, *while* among you, by each other's faith, both yours and mine.

13 I do not want you to be unaware, brothers, that often I have planned to come to you (and have been prevented so far) so that I may have some fruit among you also, even as among the rest of the Gentiles.

14 I am under obligation both to Greeks and to barbarians, both to the wise and to the foolish.

15 In this way, for my part, I am eager to proclaim the gospel to you also who are in Rome.

16 For I am not ashamed of the gospel, for it is the power of God for salvation to everyone who believes, to the Jew first and also to the Greek.

17 For in it *the* righteousness of God is revealed from faith to faith; as it is written, "BUT THE RIGHTEOUS WILL LIVE BY FAITH."

God's Wrath on Unrighteousness

18 For the wrath of God is revealed from heaven against all ungodliness and unrighteousness of men who suppress the truth in unrighteousness,

19 because that which is known about God is evident within them; for God made it evident to them.

20 For since the creation of the world His invisible attributes, both His eternal power and divine nature, have been clearly seen, being understood through what has been made, so that they are without excuse.

21 For even though they knew God, they did not glorify Him as God or give thanks, but they became futile in their thoughts, and their foolish heart was darkened.

22 Professing to be wise, they became fools,

23 and exchanged the glory of the incorruptible God for an image in the likeness of corruptible man and of birds and four-footed animals and crawling creatures.

24 Therefore God gave them over in the lusts of their hearts to impurity, so that their bodies would be dishonored among them.

25 For they exchanged the truth of God for a lie, and worshiped and served the creature rather than the Creator, who is blessed forever. Amen.

26 For this reason God gave them over to dishonorable passions; for their females exchanged the natural function for that which is unnatural,

27 and in the same way also the males abandoned the natural function of the female and burned in

their desire toward one another, males with males committing indecent acts and receiving in their own persons the due penalty of their error.

28 And just as they did not see fit to acknowledge God, God gave them over to an unfit mind, to do those things which are not proper,

29 having been filled with all unrighteousness, wickedness, greed, evil; full of envy, murder, strife, deceit, malice; *they are* gossips,

30 slanderers, haters of God, violent, arrogant, boastful, inventors of evil, disobedient to parents,

31 without understanding, untrustworthy, unloving, unmerciful;

32 and although they know the righteous requirement of God, that those who practice such things are worthy of death, they not only do the same, but also give hearty approval to those who practice *them.*

CHAPTER 2

God's Righteous Judgment

THEREFORE you are without excuse, O man, everyone who passes judgment, for in that which you judge another, you condemn yourself; for you who judge practice the same things.

2 And we know that the judgment of God rightly falls upon those who practice such things.

3 But do you presume this, O man—who passes judgment on those who practice such things and does the same—that you will escape the judgment of God?

4 Or do you think lightly of the riches of His kindness and forbearance and patience, not knowing that the kindness of God leads you to repentance?

5 But because of your stubbornness and unrepentant heart you are storing up wrath for yourself in the day of wrath and revelation of the righteous judgment of God,

6 who WILL REPAY TO EACH ACCORDING TO HIS WORKS:

7 to those who by perseverance in doing good seek for glory and honor and immortality, eternal life;

8 but to those who are selfishly ambitious and do not obey the truth, but obey unrighteousness, wrath and anger.

9 *There will be* affliction and turmoil for every soul of man who works out evil, of the Jew first and also of the Greek,

10 but glory and honor and peace to everyone who works good, to the Jew first and also to the Greek.

11 For there is no partiality with God.

12 For all who have sinned without the Law will also perish without the Law, and all who have sinned under the Law will be judged by the Law.

13 For *it is* not the hearers of the Law *who* are just before God, but the doers of the Law will be justified.

14 For when Gentiles who do not have the Law naturally do the things

of the Law, these, not having the Law, are a law to themselves,

15 in that they demonstrate the work of the Law written in their hearts, their conscience bearing witness and their thoughts alternately accusing or else defending them,

16 on the day when, according to my gospel, God will judge the secrets of men through Christ Jesus.

The Jew Is Judged by the Law

17 But if you bear the name "Jew" and rely upon the Law and boast in God,

18 and know *His* will and approve the things that are essential, being instructed out of the Law,

19 and are confident that you yourself are a guide to the blind, a light to those who are in darkness,

20 a corrector of the foolish, a teacher of the immature, having in the Law the embodiment of knowledge and of the truth,

21 you, therefore, who teach another, do you not teach yourself? You who preach that one shall not steal, do you steal?

22 You who say that one should not commit adultery, do you commit adultery? You who abhor idols, do you rob temples?

23 You who boast in the Law, through your transgression of the Law, do you dishonor God?

24 For "THE NAME OF GOD IS BLAS-PHEMED AMONG THE GENTILES BE-CAUSE OF YOU," just as it is written.

25 For indeed circumcision is of value if you practice the Law, but if you are a transgressor of the Law, your circumcision has become uncircumcision.

26 So if the uncircumcised man observes the righteous requirements of the Law, will not his uncircumcision be counted as circumcision?

27 And he who is physically uncircumcised, if he fulfills the Law, will he not judge you who, through the letter *of the Law* and circumcision, are a transgressor of the Law?

28 For he is not a Jew who is one outwardly, nor is circumcision that which is outward in the flesh.

29 But he is a Jew who is one inwardly; and circumcision is that which is of the heart, by the Spirit, not by the letter; and his praise is not from men, but from God.

CHAPTER 3

There Is None Righteous

THEN what advantage has the Jew? Or what is the value of circumcision?

2 Great in every respect. First of all, that they were entrusted with the oracles of God.

3 What then? If some did not believe, does their unbelief abolish the faithfulness of God?

4 May it never be! Rather, let God be true and every man a liar, as it is written,

> "THAT YOU MAY BE JUSTIFIED IN
>   YOUR WORDS,
> AND OVERCOME WHEN YOU ARE
>   JUDGED."

5 But if our unrighteousness demonstrates the righteousness of God, what shall we say? Is the God who inflicts wrath unrighteous? (I am speaking in human terms.)

6 May it never be! For otherwise, how will God judge the world?

7 But if through my lie the truth of God abounded to His glory, why am I also still being judged as a sinner?

8 And why not *say* (as we are slanderously reported and as some claim that we say), "Let us do evil that good may come"? Their condemnation is just.

9 What then? Are we better? Not at all; for we have already charged that both Jews and Greeks are all under sin;

10 as it is written,
"THERE IS NONE RIGHTEOUS, NOT
    EVEN ONE;
11 THERE IS NONE WHO UNDERSTANDS,
    THERE IS NONE WHO SEEKS FOR
        GOD;
12 ALL HAVE TURNED ASIDE, TOGETHER
        THEY HAVE BECOME WORTHLESS;
    THERE IS NONE WHO DOES GOOD,
    THERE IS NOT EVEN ONE."
13 "THEIR THROAT IS AN OPEN TOMB,
    WITH THEIR TONGUES THEY KEEP
        DECEIVING,"
    "THE POISON OF ASPS IS UNDER
        THEIR LIPS";
14 "WHOSE MOUTH IS FULL OF
        CURSING AND BITTERNESS";
15 "THEIR FEET ARE SWIFT TO SHED
        BLOOD,
16 DESTRUCTION AND MISERY ARE IN
        THEIR PATHS,
17 AND THE PATH OF PEACE THEY
        HAVE NOT KNOWN."
18 "THERE IS NO FEAR OF GOD
        BEFORE THEIR EYES."

19 Now we know that whatever the Law says, it speaks to those who are in the Law, so that every mouth may be shut and all the world may become accountable to God;

20 because by the works of the Law NO FLESH WILL BE JUSTIFIED IN HIS SIGHT, for through the Law *comes* the knowledge of sin.

The Righteousness of God
Through Faith

21 But now apart from the Law *the* righteousness of God has been manifested, being witnessed by the Law and the Prophets,

22 even *the* righteousness of God through faith in Jesus Christ for all those who believe; for there is no distinction;

23 for all have sinned and fall short of the glory of God,

24 being justified as a gift by His grace through the redemption which is in Christ Jesus;

25 whom God displayed publicly as a propitiation in His blood through faith, for a demonstration of His righteousness, because in the forbearance of God He passed over the sins previously committed;

26 for the demonstration of His righteousness at the present time, so that He would be just and the justifier of the one who has faith in Jesus.

27 Where then is boasting? It is

excluded. By what kind of law? Of works? No, but by a law of faith.

28 For we maintain that a man is justified by faith apart from works of the Law.

29 Or is God *the God* of Jews only? Is He not *the God* of Gentiles also? Yes, of Gentiles also,

30 since indeed God, who will justify the circumcised by faith and the uncircumcised through that faith, is one.

31 Do we then abolish the Law through faith? May it never be! On the contrary, we establish the Law.

CHAPTER 4

Abraham and David's Faith
Counted as Righteousness

WHAT then shall we say that Abraham, our forefather according to the flesh, has found?

2 For if Abraham was justified by works, he has something to boast about—but not before God!

3 For what does the Scripture say? "ABRAHAM BELIEVED GOD, AND IT WAS COUNTED TO HIM AS RIGHTEOUSNESS."

4 Now to the one who works, his wage is not counted according to grace, but according to what is due.

5 But to the one who does not work, but believes upon Him who justifies the *ungodly, his faith is* counted as righteousness,

6 just as David also speaks of the blessing on the man to whom God counts righteousness apart from works:

7 "BLESSED ARE THOSE WHOSE
    LAWLESS DEEDS HAVE BEEN
    FORGIVEN,
  AND WHOSE SINS HAVE BEEN
    COVERED.

8 "BLESSED IS THE MAN WHOSE SIN
    THE LORD WILL NOT TAKE
    INTO ACCOUNT."

9 Therefore, is this blessing on the circumcised, or on the uncircumcised also? For we say, "FAITH WAS COUNTED TO ABRAHAM AS RIGHTEOUSNESS."

10 How then was it counted? While he was circumcised, or uncircumcised? Not while circumcised, but while uncircumcised;

11 and he received the sign of circumcision, a seal of the righteousness of the faith which he had while uncircumcised, so that he might be the father of all who believe without being circumcised, that righteousness might be counted to them,

12 and the father of circumcision to those who not only are of the circumcision, but who also follow in the steps of the faith of our father Abraham which he had while uncircumcised.

13 For the promise to Abraham or to his seed that he would be heir of the world was not through the Law, but through the righteousness of faith.

14 For if those who are of the Law are heirs, faith has been made empty and the promise has been abolished;

15 for the Law brings about wrath, but where there is no law, there also is no trespass.

16 For this reason *it is* by faith, in

order that *it may be* according to grace, so that the promise will be guaranteed to all the seed, not only to those who are of the Law, but also to those who are of the faith of Abraham, who is the father of us all—

17 as it is written, "A FATHER OF MANY NATIONS HAVE I MADE YOU"—in the presence of Him whom he believed, *even* God, who gives life to the dead and calls into being that which does not exist.

18 In hope against hope he believed, so that he might become a father of many nations according to that which had been spoken, "So SHALL YOUR SEED BE."

19 And without becoming weak in faith he contemplated his own body, now as good as dead since he was about a hundred years old, and the deadness of Sarah's womb;

20 yet, with respect to the promise of God, he did not waver in unbelief but grew strong in faith, giving glory to God,

21 and being fully assured that what God had promised, He was able also to do.

22 Therefore IT WAS ALSO COUNTED TO HIM AS RIGHTEOUSNESS.

23 Now not for his sake only was it written THAT IT WAS COUNTED TO HIM,

24 but for our sake also, to whom it will be counted, as those who believe upon Him who raised Jesus our Lord from the dead,

25 *He* who was delivered over on account of our transgressions, and was raised on account of our justification.

CHAPTER 5

Results of Justification by Faith

THEREFORE, having been justified by faith, we have peace with God through our Lord Jesus Christ,

2 through whom also we have obtained our introduction by faith into this grace in which we stand; and we boast in hope of the glory of God.

3 And not only this, but we also boast in our afflictions, knowing that affliction brings about perseverance;

4 and perseverance, proven character; and proven character, hope;

5 and hope does not put to shame, because the love of God has been poured out within our hearts through the Holy Spirit who was given to us.

6 For while we were still weak, at the right time Christ died for the ungodly.

7 For one will hardly die for a righteous man, though perhaps for the good man someone would dare even to die.

8 But God demonstrates His own love toward us, in that while we were yet sinners, Christ died for us.

9 Much more then, having now been justified by His blood, we shall be saved from the wrath *of God* through Him.

10 For if while we were enemies we were reconciled to God through the death of His Son, much more, having been reconciled, we shall be saved by His life.

11 And not only this, but we also

boast in God through our Lord Jesus Christ, through whom we have now received the reconciliation.

The Gift of Righteousness in Christ

12 Therefore, just as through one man sin entered into the world, and death through sin, and so death spread to all men, because all sinned—

13 for until the Law sin was in the world, but sin is not imputed when there is no law.

14 Nevertheless death reigned from Adam until Moses, even over those who had not sinned in the likeness of the trespass of Adam, who is a type of Him who was to come.

15 But the gracious gift is not like the transgression. For if by the transgression of the one the many died, much more did the grace of God and the gift by the grace of the one Man, Jesus Christ, abound to the many.

16 And the gift is not like *that which came* through the one who sinned; for on the one hand the judgment *arose* from one *transgression* resulting in condemnation, but on the other hand the gracious gift *arose* from many transgressions resulting in justification.

17 For if by the transgression of the one, death reigned through the one, much more those who receive the abundance of grace and of the gift of righteousness will reign in life through the One, Jesus Christ.

18 So then as through one transgression there resulted condemnation to all men, even so through one act of righteousness there resulted justification of life to all men.

19 For as through the one man's disobedience the many were appointed sinners, even so through the obedience of the One the many will be appointed righteous.

20 Now the Law came in so that the transgression would increase, but where sin increased, grace abounded all the more,

21 so that, as sin reigned in death, even so grace would reign through righteousness to eternal life through Jesus Christ our Lord.

CHAPTER 6

Dead to Sin, Alive to God

WHAT shall we say then? Are we to continue in sin so that grace may increase?

2 May it never be! How shall we who died to sin still live in it?

3 Or do you not know that all of us who were baptized into Christ Jesus were baptized into His death?

4 Therefore we were buried with Him through baptism into death, so that as Christ was raised from the dead through the glory of the Father, so we too might walk in newness of life.

5 For if we have become united with *Him* in the likeness of His death, certainly we shall also be *in the likeness* of His resurrection,

6 knowing this, that our old man was crucified with *Him*, in order that

our body of sin might be done away with, so that we would no longer be slaves to sin;

7 for he who has died has been justified from sin.

8 Now if we died with Christ, we believe that we shall also live with Him,

9 knowing that Christ, having been raised from the dead, is never to die again; death no longer is master over Him.

10 For the death that He died, He died to sin once for all, but the life that He lives, He lives to God.

11 Even so consider yourselves to be dead to sin, but alive to God in Christ Jesus.

12 Therefore do not let sin reign in your mortal body so that you obey its lusts,

13 and do not go on presenting your members to sin *as* instruments of unrighteousness, but present yourselves to God as those alive from the dead, and your members *as* instruments of righteousness to God.

14 For sin shall not be master over you, for you are not under law but under grace.

Slaves of Righteousness

15 What then? Shall we sin because we are not under law but under grace? May it never be!

16 Do you not know that when you go on presenting yourselves to someone *as* slaves for obedience, you are slaves of the one whom you obey, either of sin leading to death, or of obedience leading to righteousness?

17 But thanks be to God that *though* you were slaves of sin, you obeyed from the heart that pattern of teaching to which you were given over,

18 and having been freed from sin, you became slaves of righteousness.

19 I am speaking in human terms because of the weakness of your flesh. For just as you presented your members as slaves to impurity and to lawlessness, leading to *further* lawlessness, so now present your members as slaves to righteousness, leading to sanctification.

20 For when you were slaves of sin, you were free in regard to righteousness.

21 Therefore what benefit were you then having from the things of which you are now ashamed? For the end of those things is death.

22 But now having been freed from sin and enslaved to God, you have your benefit, leading to sanctification, and the end, eternal life.

23 For the wages of sin is death, but the gracious gift of God is eternal life in Christ Jesus our Lord.

CHAPTER 7

Released from the Law

OR do you not know, brothers—for I am speaking to those who know the law—that the law is master over a person as long as he lives?

2 For the married woman has been bound by law to her husband while he is living, but if her husband dies,

she is released from the law concerning the husband.

3 So then, if while her husband is living she is joined to another man, she shall be called an adulteress. But if her husband dies, she is free from the law, so that she is not an adulteress though she is joined to another man.

4 So, my brothers, you also were made to die to the Law through the body of Christ, so that you might be joined to another, to Him who was raised from the dead, in order that we might bear fruit for God.

5 For while we were in the flesh, the sinful passions, which were *aroused* by the Law, were at work in our members to bear fruit for death.

6 But now we have been released from the Law, having died to that by which we were constrained, so that we serve in newness of the Spirit and not in oldness of the letter.

7 What shall we say then? Is the Law sin? May it never be! Rather, I would not have come to know sin except through the Law. For I would not have known about coveting if the Law had not said, "YOU SHALL NOT COVET."

8 But sin, taking opportunity through the commandment, worked out in me coveting of every kind. For apart from the Law sin *is* dead.

9 *Now I was once alive apart from* the Law, but when the commandment came, sin revived and I died;

10 and this commandment, which was to lead to life, was found to lead to death for me.

11 For sin, taking an opportunity through the commandment, deceived me and through it killed me.

12 So, the Law is holy, and the commandment is holy and righteous and good.

The Conflict of Two Natures

13 Therefore did that which is good become *a cause of* death for me? May it never be! Rather it was sin, in order that it might be shown to be sin by working out my death through that which is good, so that through the commandment sin would become utterly sinful.

14 For we know that the Law is spiritual, but I am fleshly, having been sold into bondage under sin.

15 For what I am working out, I do not understand; for I am not practicing what I *would* like to *do*, but I am doing the very thing I hate.

16 But if I do the very thing I do not want, I agree with the Law, that it is good.

17 So now, no longer am I the one working it out, but sin which dwells in me.

18 For I know that nothing good dwells in me, that is, in my flesh; for the willing is present in me, but the working out of the good *is* not.

19 For the good that I want, I do not do, but I practice the very evil that I do not want.

20 But if I am doing the very thing I do not want, I am no longer the one working it out, but sin which dwells in me.

21 I find then the principle that in me evil is present—in me who wants to do good.

22 For I joyfully concur with the law of God in the inner man,

23 but I see a different law in my members, waging war against the law of my mind and making me a captive to the law of sin which is in my members.

24 Wretched man that I am! Who will deliver me from the body of this death?

25 Thanks be to God through Jesus Christ our Lord! So then, on the one hand I myself with my mind am serving the law of God, but on the other, with my flesh the law of sin.

CHAPTER 8

The Spirit of God Dwells in You

THEREFORE there is now no condemnation for those who are in Christ Jesus.

2 For the law of the Spirit of life in Christ Jesus has set you free from the law of sin and of death.

3 For what the Law could not do, weak as it was through the flesh, God *did*: sending His own Son in the likeness of sinful flesh and *as an offering* for sin, He condemned sin in the flesh,

4 so that the righteous requirement of the Law might be fulfilled in us, who do not walk according to the flesh but according to the Spirit.

5 For those who are according to the flesh set their minds on the things of the flesh, but those who are according to the Spirit, the things of the Spirit.

6 For the mind set on the flesh is death, but the mind set on the Spirit is life and peace,

7 because the mind set on the flesh is *at* enmity toward God, for it does not subject itself to the law of God, for it is not even able *to do so*,

8 and those who are in the flesh are not able to please God.

9 However, you are not in the flesh but in the Spirit, if indeed the Spirit of God dwells in you. But if anyone does not have the Spirit of Christ, he does not belong to Him.

10 But if Christ is in you, though the body is dead because of sin, yet the spirit is alive because of righteousness.

11 But if the Spirit of Him who raised Jesus from the dead dwells in you, He who raised Christ Jesus from the dead will also give life to your mortal bodies through His Spirit who dwells in you.

12 So then, brothers, we are under obligation, not to the flesh, to live according to the flesh—

13 for if you are living according to the flesh, you must die, but if by the Spirit you are putting to death the practices of the body, you will live.

14 For as many as are being led by the Spirit of God, these are sons of God.

15 For you have not received a spirit of slavery leading to fear again, but you have received *the* Spirit of adoption as sons by whom we cry out, "Abba! Father!"

16 The Spirit Himself testifies with our spirit that we are children of God,

17 and if children, also heirs, heirs of God and fellow heirs with Christ, if indeed we suffer with *Him* so that we may also be glorified with *Him*.

Present Suffering and Future Glory

18 For I consider that the sufferings of this present time are not worthy to be compared with the glory that is to be revealed to us.

19 For the anxious longing of the creation eagerly waits for the revealing of the sons of God.

20 For the creation was subjected to futility, not willingly, but because of Him who subjected it, in hope

21 that the creation itself also will be set free from its slavery to corruption into the freedom of the glory of the children of God.

22 For we know that the whole creation groans and suffers the pains of childbirth together until now.

23 And not only this, but also we ourselves, having the first fruits of the Spirit, even we ourselves groan within ourselves, eagerly waiting for *our* adoption as sons, the redemption of our body.

24 For in hope we were saved, but hope that is seen is not hope, for who hopes for what he *already* sees?

25 But if we hope for what we do not see, with perseverance we eagerly wait for it.

26 And in the same way the Spirit also helps our weakness, for we do not know how to pray as we should, but the Spirit Himself intercedes for *us* with groanings too deep for words;

27 and He who searches the hearts knows what the mind of the Spirit is, because He intercedes for the saints according to *the will of* God.

28 And we know that for those who love God all things work together for good, for those who are called according to *His* purpose.

29 Because those whom He foreknew, He also predestined *to become* conformed to the image of His Son, so that He would be the firstborn among many brothers;

30 and those whom He predestined, He also called; and those whom He called, He also justified; and those whom He justified, He also glorified.

God Is for Us

31 What then shall we say to these things? If God *is* for us, who *is* against us?

32 He who indeed did not spare His own Son, but delivered Him over for us all, how will He not also with Him graciously give us all things?

33 Who will bring a charge against God's elect? God is the one who justifies;

34 who is the one who condemns? Christ Jesus is He who died, yes, rather who was raised, who is at the right hand of God, who also intercedes for us.

35 Who will separate us from the love of Christ? Will affliction, or turmoil, or persecution, or famine, or nakedness, or peril, or sword?

36 Just as it is written,

"FOR YOUR SAKE WE ARE BEING
   PUT TO DEATH ALL DAY LONG;
WE WERE COUNTED AS SHEEP FOR
   the SLAUGHTER."

37 But in all these things we overwhelmingly conquer through Him who loved us.

38 For I am convinced that neither death, nor life, nor angels, nor rulers, nor things present, nor things to come, nor powers,

39 nor height, nor depth, nor any other created thing, will be able to separate us from the love of God, which is in Christ Jesus our Lord.

CHAPTER 9

God's Chosen People, Israel

I am telling the truth in Christ, I am not lying, my conscience testifies with me in the Holy Spirit,

2 that I have great sorrow and unceasing grief in my heart.

3 For I could wish that I myself were accursed, *separated* from Christ for the sake of my brothers, my kinsmen according to the flesh,

4 who are Israelites, to whom belongs the adoption as sons, and the glory and the covenants and the giving of the Law and the *temple* service and the promises,

5 whose are the fathers, and from whom is the Christ according to the flesh, who is God over all, blessed forever. Amen.

6 But *it is* not as though the word of God has failed. For they are not all Israel who are *descended* from Israel;

7 nor are they all children because they are Abraham's seed, but: "THROUGH ISAAC YOUR SEED WILL BE NAMED."

8 That is, the children of the flesh are not the children of God, but the children of the promise are considered as seed.

9 For this is the word of promise: "AT THIS TIME I WILL COME, AND SARAH SHALL HAVE A SON."

10 And not only this, but there was Rebekah also, when she had conceived *twins* by one man, our father Isaac;

11 for though *the twins* were not yet born and had not done anything good or bad, so that the purpose of God according to *His* choice would stand, not because of works but because of Him who calls,

12 it was said to her, "THE OLDER SHALL SERVE THE YOUNGER."

13 Just as it is written, "JACOB I LOVED, BUT ESAU I HATED."

14 What shall we say then? Is there any unrighteousness with God? May it never be!

15 For He says to Moses, "I WILL HAVE MERCY ON WHOM I HAVE MERCY, AND I WILL HAVE COMPASSION ON WHOM I HAVE COMPASSION."

16 So then it *does* not *depend* on the one who wills or the one who runs, but on God who has mercy.

17 For the Scripture says to Pharaoh, "FOR THIS VERY PURPOSE I RAISED YOU UP, IN ORDER TO DEMONSTRATE

MY POWER IN YOU, AND IN ORDER THAT MY NAME MIGHT BE PROCLAIMED THROUGHOUT THE WHOLE EARTH."

18 So then He has mercy on whom He desires, and He hardens whom He desires.

19 You will say to me then, "Why does He still find fault? For who resists His will?"

20 On the contrary, who are you, O man, who answers back to God? WILL THE THING MOLDED SAY TO THE MOLDER, "WHY DID YOU MAKE ME LIKE THIS"?

21 Or does not the potter have authority over the clay, to make from the same lump one vessel for honorable use and another for dishonorable use?

22 And what if God, wanting to demonstrate His wrath and to make His power known, endured with much patience vessels of wrath having been prepared for destruction,

23 and in order that He might make known the riches of His glory upon vessels of mercy, which He prepared beforehand for glory—

24 *even* us, whom He also called, not from among Jews only, but also from among Gentiles?

25 As He says also in Hosea,
"I WILL CALL THOSE WHO WERE
    NOT MY PEOPLE, 'MY PEOPLE,'
AND HER WHO WAS NOT BELOVED,
    'BELOVED.'"

26 "AND IT SHALL BE THAT IN THE
    PLACE WHERE IT WAS SAID
    TO THEM, 'YOU ARE NOT MY
    PEOPLE,'

THERE THEY SHALL BE CALLED
    SONS OF THE LIVING GOD."

27 And Isaiah cries out concerning Israel, "THOUGH THE NUMBER OF THE SONS OF ISRAEL BE LIKE THE SAND OF THE SEA, IT IS THE REMNANT THAT WILL BE SAVED;

28 FOR THE LORD WILL EXECUTE HIS WORD ON THE LAND, THOROUGHLY AND QUICKLY."

29 And just as Isaiah foretold,
"UNLESS THE LORD OF SABAOTH
    HAD LEFT TO US A SEED,
WE WOULD HAVE BECOME LIKE
    SODOM, AND WOULD HAVE
    RESEMBLED GOMORRAH."

30 What shall we say then? That Gentiles, who did not pursue righteousness, laid hold of righteousness, even the righteousness which is by faith;

31 but Israel, pursuing a law of righteousness, did not attain *that* law.

32 Why? Because *they did* not *pursue it* by faith, but as though *it were* by works. They stumbled over the stumbling stone,

33 just as it is written,
"BEHOLD, I AM LAYING IN ZION A
    STONE OF STUMBLING AND A
    ROCK OF OFFENSE,
AND THE ONE WHO BELIEVES
    UPON HIM WILL NOT BE PUT
    TO SHAME."

CHAPTER 10

BROTHERS, my heart's desire and my prayer to God for them is for *their* salvation.

2 For I testify about them that they

have a zeal for God, but not according to knowledge.

3 For not knowing about the righteousness of God and seeking to establish their own, they did not subject themselves to the righteousness of God.

4 For Christ is the end of the law for righteousness to everyone who believes.

Faith Comes by Hearing

5 For Moses writes about the righteousness which is of law: "THE MAN WHO DOES THESE THINGS SHALL LIVE BY THEM."

6 But the righteousness of faith speaks in this way: "DO NOT SAY IN YOUR HEART, 'WHO WILL GO UP INTO HEAVEN?' (that is, to bring Christ down),

7 or 'WHO WILL GO DOWN INTO THE ABYSS?' (that is, to bring Christ up from the dead)."

8 But what does it say? "THE WORD IS NEAR YOU, IN YOUR MOUTH AND IN YOUR HEART"—that is, the word of faith which we are preaching,

9 that if you confess with your mouth Jesus *as* Lord, and believe in your heart that God raised Him from the dead, you will be saved;

10 for with the heart a person believes, leading to righteousness, and with the mouth he confesses, leading to salvation.

11 For the Scripture says, "WHOEVER BELIEVES UPON HIM WILL NOT BE PUT TO SHAME."

12 For there is no distinction between Jew and Greek, for the same *Lord* is Lord of all, abounding in riches for all who call on Him,

13 for "WHOEVER CALLS ON THE NAME OF THE LORD WILL BE SAVED."

14 How then will they call on Him in whom they have not believed? How will they believe in Him whom they have not heard? And how will they hear without a preacher?

15 And how will they preach unless they are sent? Just as it is written, "How BEAUTIFUL ARE THE FEET OF THOSE WHO PROCLAIM GOOD NEWS OF GOOD THINGS!"

16 However, they did not all heed the good news, for Isaiah says, "LORD, WHO HAS BELIEVED OUR REPORT?"

17 So faith *comes* from hearing, and hearing by the word of Christ.

18 But I say, have they never heard? On the contrary, they have;

"THEIR VOICE HAS GONE OUT INTO
    ALL THE EARTH,
AND THEIR WORDS TO THE ENDS
    OF THE WORLD."

19 But I say, did Israel not know? First Moses says,

"I WILL MAKE YOU JEALOUS BY
    THAT WHICH IS NOT A NATION,
BY A NATION WITHOUT
    UNDERSTANDING WILL I
    ANGER YOU."

20 And Isaiah is very bold and says,

"I WAS FOUND BY THOSE WHO DID
    NOT SEEK ME,
I BECAME MANIFEST TO THOSE
    WHO DID NOT ASK FOR ME."

21 But as for Israel He says, "ALL DAY LONG I HAVE STRETCHED OUT MY HANDS TO A DISOBEDIENT AND OBSTINATE PEOPLE."

CHAPTER 11

God Has Not Rejected Israel

I say then, has God rejected His people? May it never be! For I too am an Israelite, a seed of Abraham, of the tribe of Benjamin.

2 GOD HAS NOT REJECTED HIS PEOPLE whom He foreknew. Or do you not know what the Scripture says in *the passage about* Elijah, how he appeals to God against Israel?

3 "Lord, THEY HAVE KILLED YOUR PROPHETS, THEY HAVE TORN DOWN YOUR ALTARS, AND I ALONE AM LEFT, AND THEY ARE SEEKING MY LIFE."

4 But what does the divine response say to him? "I HAVE LEFT for Myself SEVEN THOUSAND MEN WHO HAVE NOT BOWED THE KNEE TO BAAL."

5 In this way then, at the present time, a remnant according to *God's* gracious choice has also come to be.

6 But if it is by grace, it is no longer of works, otherwise grace is no longer grace.

7 What then? What Israel is seeking, it has not obtained, but the chosen obtained it, and the rest were hardened;

8 just as it is written,

"GOD GAVE THEM A SPIRIT OF
    STUPOR,
EYES TO SEE NOT AND EARS TO
    HEAR NOT,
DOWN TO THIS VERY DAY."

9 And David says,

"LET THEIR TABLE BECOME A
    SNARE AND A TRAP,
AND A STUMBLING BLOCK AND A
    RETRIBUTION TO THEM.

10 "LET THEIR EYES BE DARKENED TO
    SEE NOT,
AND BEND THEIR BACKS FOREVER."

Gentiles Grafted In

11 I say then, did they stumble so as to fall? May it never be! But by their transgression salvation *has come* to the Gentiles, to make them jealous.

12 Now if their transgression is riches for the world and their failure is riches for the Gentiles, how much more will their fullness be!

13 But I am speaking to you who are Gentiles. Inasmuch then as I am an apostle of Gentiles, I magnify my ministry,

14 if somehow I might move to jealousy my fellow countrymen and save some of them.

15 For if their rejection is the reconciliation of the world, what will *their* acceptance be but life from the dead?

16 And if the first piece *of dough* is holy, the lump is also; and if the root is holy, the branches are too.

17 But if some of the branches were broken off, and you, being a wild olive, were grafted in among them and became a partaker with them of the rich root of the olive tree,

18 do not boast against the branches. But if you do boast against *them*, *remember that* it is not you who supports the root, but the root *supports* you.

19 You will say then, "Branches were broken off so that I might be grafted in."

20 Quite right! They were broken

off for their unbelief, but you stand by your faith. Do not be haughty, but fear,

21 for if God did not spare the natural branches, He will not spare you, either.

22 Behold then the kindness and severity of God; to those who fell, severity, but to you, God's kindness, if you continue in His kindness; otherwise you also will be cut off.

23 And they also, if they do not continue in their unbelief, will be grafted in, for God is able to graft them in again.

24 For if you were cut off from what is by nature a wild olive tree, and were grafted contrary to nature into a cultivated olive tree, how much more will these who are the natural *branches* be grafted into their own olive tree?

All Israel Will Be Saved

25 For I do not want you, brothers, to be uninformed of this mystery—so that you will not be wise in your own estimation—that a partial hardening has happened to Israel until the fullness of the Gentiles has come in;

26 and so all Israel will be saved; just as it is written,

"The Deliverer will come from Zion,

He will remove ungodliness from Jacob."

27 "And this is My covenant with them,

When I take away their sins."

28 From the standpoint of the gospel they are enemies for your sake, but from the standpoint of *God's* choice they are beloved for the sake of the fathers;

29 for the gifts and the calling of God are irrevocable.

30 For just as you once were disobedient to God, but now have been shown mercy because of their disobedience,

31 so these also now have been disobedient, that because of the mercy shown to you they also may now be shown mercy.

32 For God has shut up all in disobedience so that He may show mercy to all.

33 Oh, the depth of the riches and wisdom and knowledge of God! How unsearchable are His judgments and unfathomable His ways!

34 For who has known the mind of the Lord, or who became His counselor?

35 Or who has first given to Him that it might be repaid to him?

36 For from Him and through Him and to Him are all things. To Him *be* the glory forever. Amen.

CHAPTER 12

A Living and Holy Sacrifice

THEREFORE I exhort you, brothers, by the mercies of God, to present your bodies as a sacrifice—living, holy, *and* pleasing to God, *which is* your spiritual service of worship.

2 And do not be conformed to this world, but be transformed by the

renewing of your mind, so that you may approve what the will of God is, that which is good and pleasing and perfect.

3 For through the grace given to me I say to each one among you not to think more highly of himself than he ought to think; but to think so as to have sound thinking, as God has allotted to each a measure of faith.

4 For just as we have many members in one body and all the members do not have the same function,

5 so we, who are many, are one body in Christ, and individually members one of another,

6 but having gifts that differ according to the grace given to us: whether prophecy, in agreement with the faith;

7 or service, in his serving; or he who teaches, in his teaching;

8 or he who exhorts, in his exhortation; he who gives, with generosity; he who leads, with diligence; he who shows mercy, with cheerfulness.

9 *Let* love *be* without hypocrisy— by abhorring what is evil, clinging to what is good,

10 *being* devoted to one another in brotherly love, giving preference to one another in honor,

11 not lagging behind in diligence, being fervent in spirit, serving the Lord,

12 *rejoicing in hope, persevering in* affliction, being devoted to prayer,

13 contributing to the needs of the saints, pursuing hospitality.

14 Bless those who persecute you; bless, and do not curse.

15 Rejoice with those who rejoice; weep with those who weep,

16 by being of the same mind toward one another, not being haughty in mind, but associating with the humble. Do not be wise in your own mind.

17 Never paying back evil for evil to anyone, respecting what is good in the sight of all men,

18 if possible, so far as it depends on you, being at peace with all men,

19 never taking your own revenge, beloved—instead leave room for the wrath *of God.* For it is written, "VEN-GEANCE IS MINE, I WILL REPAY," says the Lord.

20 "BUT IF YOUR ENEMY IS HUNGRY, FEED HIM, AND IF HE IS THIRSTY, GIVE HIM A DRINK; FOR IN SO DOING YOU WILL HEAP BURNING COALS ON HIS HEAD."

21 Do not be overcome by evil, but overcome evil with good.

CHAPTER 13

Be Subject to Government

EVERY person is to be in subjection to the governing authorities. For there is no authority except from God, and those which exist have been appointed by God.

2 Therefore whoever resists that authority has opposed the ordinance of God; and they who have opposed will receive condemnation upon themselves.

3 For rulers are not *a cause of* fear

for good behavior, but for evil. Do you want to have no fear of that authority? Do what is good, and you will have praise from the same;

4 for it is a minister of God to you for good. But if you do what is evil, be afraid; for it does not bear the sword in vain, for it is a minister of God, an avenger who brings wrath on the one who practices evil.

5 Therefore it is necessary to be in subjection, not only because of that wrath, but also because of conscience.

6 For because of this you also pay taxes, for *rulers* are servants of God, devoting themselves to this very thing.

7 Render to all what is due them: tax to whom tax *is due*; custom to whom custom; fear to whom fear; honor to whom honor.

8 Owe nothing to anyone except to love one another; for he who loves his neighbor has fulfilled *the* law.

9 For this, "YOU SHALL NOT COMMIT ADULTERY, YOU SHALL NOT MURDER, YOU SHALL NOT STEAL, YOU SHALL NOT COVET," and if there is any other commandment, it is summed up in this word, "YOU SHALL LOVE YOUR NEIGHBOR AS YOURSELF."

10 Love does not work evil against a neighbor; therefore love is the fulfillment of *the* Law.

11 And *do* this, knowing the time, that it is already the hour for you to awaken from sleep; for now salvation is nearer to us than when we believed.

12 The night is almost gone, and the day is at hand. Therefore let us lay aside the deeds of darkness and put on the armor of light.

13 Let us walk properly as in the day, not in carousing and drunkenness, not in sexual promiscuity and sensuality, not in strife and jealousy.

14 But put on the Lord Jesus Christ, and make no provision for the flesh in regard to *its* lusts.

CHAPTER 14

Do Not Pass Judgment on One Another

NOW accept the one who is weak in faith, *but* not for *the purpose of* passing judgment on opinions.

2 One person has faith that he may eat all things, but he who is weak eats vegetables *only*.

3 The one who eats must not view the one who does not eat with contempt, and the one who does not eat must not judge the one who eats, for God accepted him.

4 Who are you to judge the servant of another? To his own master he stands or falls; and he will stand, for the Lord is able to make him stand.

5 One person judges one day above another, another judges every day *alike*. Each person must be fully convinced in his own mind.

6 He who regards the day, regards it for the Lord, and he who eats, eats for the Lord, for he gives thanks to God; and he who does not eat, for the Lord he does not eat and gives thanks to God.

7 For not one of us lives for himself, and not one dies for himself;

8 for if we live, we live for the Lord, or if we die, we die for the Lord; therefore whether we live or die, we are the Lord's.

9 For to this end Christ died and lived again, that He might be Lord both of the dead and of the living.

10 But you, why do you judge your brother? Or you again, why do you view your brother with contempt? For we will all stand before the judgment seat of God.

11 For it is written,

"As I LIVE, SAYS THE LORD, TO ME
  EVERY KNEE SHALL BOW,
AND EVERY TONGUE SHALL
  CONFESS TO GOD."

12 So then each one of us will give an account of himself to God.

13 Therefore let us not judge one another anymore, but rather judge this—not to put a stumbling block or offense before a brother.

14 I know and am convinced in the Lord Jesus that nothing is defiled in itself; but to him who considers anything to be defiled, to him it is defiled.

15 For if because of food your brother is grieved, you are no longer walking according to love. Do not destroy with your food him for whom Christ died.

16 Therefore do not let what is for you a good thing be slandered;

17 for the kingdom of God is not eating and drinking, but righteousness and peace and joy in the Holy Spirit.

18 For he who in this *way* serves Christ is pleasing to God and approved by men.

19 So then let us pursue the things which make for peace and the building up of one another.

20 Do not tear down the work of God for the sake of food. All things indeed are clean, but they are evil for the man who eats and gives offense.

21 It is good not to eat meat or to drink wine, or *to do anything* by which your brother stumbles.

22 The faith which you have, have as your own conviction before God. Blessed is he who does not judge himself in what he approves.

23 But he who doubts is condemned if he eats, because *his eating is* not from faith; and whatever is not from faith is sin.

CHAPTER 15

Bearing the Weaknesses of Others

NOW we who are strong ought to bear the weaknesses of those without strength and not *just* please ourselves.

2 Each of us is to please his neighbor for his good, to his building up.

3 For even Christ did not please Himself; but as it is written, "THE REPROACHES OF THOSE WHO REPROACHED YOU FELL ON ME."

4 For whatever was written in earlier times was written for our instruction, so that through the perseverance and the encouragement of the Scriptures we might have hope.

5 Now may the God of perseverance and encouragement grant you to be of the same mind with one another according to Christ Jesus,

6 so that with one accord you may with one voice glorify the God and Father of our Lord Jesus Christ.

Christ, the Hope of Jews and Gentiles

7 Therefore, accept one another, just as Christ also accepted us to the glory of God.

8 For I say that Christ has become a servant to the circumcision on behalf of the truth of God to confirm the promises *given* to the fathers,

9 and for the Gentiles to glorify God for His mercy; as it is written,

"THEREFORE I WILL GIVE PRAISE TO
    YOU AMONG THE GENTILES,
AND I WILL SING TO YOUR NAME."

10 And again he says,

"REJOICE, O GENTILES, WITH HIS
    PEOPLE."

11 And again,

"PRAISE THE LORD ALL YOU
    GENTILES,
AND LET ALL THE PEOPLES PRAISE
    HIM."

12 And again Isaiah says,

"THERE SHALL COME THE ROOT
    OF JESSE,
AND HE WHO ARISES TO RULE
    OVER THE GENTILES,
IN HIM SHALL THE GENTILES
    HOPE."

13 Now may the God of hope fill you with all joy and peace in believing, so that you will abound in hope by the power of the Holy Spirit.

Paul's Ministry Plans

14 But I myself am also convinced about you, my brothers, that you yourselves are full of goodness, having been filled with all knowledge and being able also to admonish one another.

15 But I have written very boldly to you on some points so as to remind you again, because of the grace that was given me by God

16 for me to be a minister of Christ Jesus to the Gentiles, ministering as a priest the gospel of God, so that *my* offering of the Gentiles may become acceptable, having been sanctified by the Holy Spirit.

17 Therefore in Christ Jesus I have reason for boasting in things pertaining to God.

18 For I will not be bold to speak of anything except what Christ has brought about through me, leading to the obedience of the Gentiles by word and deed,

19 in the power of signs and wonders, in the power of the Spirit; so that from Jerusalem and all around as far as Illyricum I have fully preached the gospel of Christ.

20 And in this way I make it my ambition to proclaim the gospel, not where Christ was *already* named, so that I would not build on another man's foundation;

21 but as it is written,

"THEY WHO HAD NO DECLARATION
    OF HIM SHALL SEE,
AND THEY WHO HAVE NOT HEARD
    SHALL UNDERSTAND."

22 For this reason I have often been prevented from coming to you;

23 but now, with no further place for me in these regions, and since I have had for many years a longing to come to you

24 whenever I go to Spain—for I hope, passing through, to see you, and to be helped on my way there by you, when I have first enjoyed your company for a while.

25 But now I am going to Jerusalem to serve the saints.

26 For Macedonia and Achaia were pleased to share with the poor among the saints in Jerusalem.

27 Yes, they were pleased *to do so*, and they are indebted to them. For if the Gentiles have shared in their spiritual things, they are indebted to minister to them also in material things.

28 Therefore, when I have completed this and have put my seal on this fruit of theirs, I will go on by way of you to Spain.

29 And I know that when I come to you, I will come in the fullness of the blessing of Christ.

30 Now I urge you, brothers, by our Lord Jesus Christ and by the love of the Spirit, to strive together with me in your prayers to God for me,

31 that I may be rescued from those *who are disobedient in* Judea, and *that* my service for Jerusalem may prove acceptable to the saints;

32 so that I may come to you in joy by the will of God and find rest in your company.

33 Now may the God of peace be with you all. Amen.

CHAPTER 16

Final Instructions and Greetings

NOW I commend to you our sister Phoebe, who is a servant of the church which is at Cenchrea;

2 that you receive her in the Lord in a manner worthy of the saints, and that you help her in whatever matter she may have need of you; for she herself has also been a benefactor of many, and of myself as well.

3 Greet Prisca and Aquila, my fellow workers in Christ Jesus,

4 who for my life risked their own necks, to whom not only do I give thanks, but also all the churches of the Gentiles;

5 also *greet* the church that is in their house. Greet Epaenetus, my beloved, who is the first convert to Christ from Asia.

6 Greet Mary, who has labored much for you.

7 Greet Andronicus and Junia, my kinsmen and my fellow prisoners, who are outstanding to the apostles, who also were in Christ before me.

8 Greet Ampliatus, my beloved in the Lord.

9 Greet Urbanus, our fellow worker in Christ, and Stachys my beloved.

10 Greet Apelles, the approved in Christ. Greet those who are of the *household* of Aristobulus.

11 Greet Herodion, my kinsman.

Greet those of the *household* of Narcissus, who are in the Lord.

12 Greet Tryphaena and Tryphosa, laborers in the Lord. Greet Persis the beloved, who labored much in the Lord.

13 Greet Rufus, a choice man in the Lord, also his mother and mine.

14 Greet Asyncritus, Phlegon, Hermes, Patrobas, Hermas and the brothers with them.

15 Greet Philologus and Julia, Nereus and his sister, and Olympas, and all the saints who are with them.

16 Greet one another with a holy kiss. All the churches of Christ greet you.

17 Now I urge you, brothers, to keep your eye on those who cause dissensions and stumblings contrary to the teaching which you learned, and turn away from them.

18 For such men are slaves, not of our Lord Christ but of their own appetites, and by their smooth and flattering speech they deceive the hearts of the unsuspecting.

19 For the report of your obedience has reached to all. Therefore I am rejoicing over you, but I want you to be wise in what is good and innocent in what is evil.

20 And the God of peace will soon crush Satan under your feet.

The grace of our Lord Jesus be with you.

21 Timothy my fellow worker greets you, and *so do* Lucius and Jason and Sosipater, my kinsmen.

22 I, Tertius, who wrote this letter, greet you in the Lord.

23 Gaius, host to me and to the whole church, greets you. Erastus, the city treasurer greets you, and Quartus, the brother.

24 [The grace of our Lord Jesus Christ be with you all. Amen.]

25 Now to Him who is able to strengthen you according to my gospel and the preaching of Jesus Christ, according to the revelation of the mystery which has been kept secret for long ages past,

26 but now is manifested, and by the Scriptures of the prophets, according to the commandment of the eternal God, has been made known to all the Gentiles, *leading* to obedience of faith;

27 to the only wise God, through Jesus Christ, be the glory forever. Amen.

THE FIRST LETTER OF PAUL TO THE

CORINTHIANS

CHAPTER 1

Christ Is Undivided

PAUL, called *as* an apostle of Jesus Christ by the will of God, and Sosthenes our brother,

2 To the church of God which is at Corinth, to those who have been sanctified in Christ Jesus, called as saints, with all who in every place call on the name of our Lord Jesus Christ, their *Lord* and ours:

3 Grace to you and peace from God our Father and the Lord Jesus Christ.

4 I thank my God always concerning you for the grace of God which was given you in Christ Jesus,

5 that in everything you were enriched in Him, in all word and all knowledge,

6 even as the witness about Christ was confirmed in you,

7 so that you are not lacking in any gift, eagerly awaiting the revelation of our Lord Jesus Christ,

8 who will also confirm you to the end, beyond reproach in the day of our Lord Jesus Christ.

9 God is faithful, through whom you were called into fellowship with His Son, Jesus Christ our Lord.

10 Now I exhort you, brothers, by the name of our Lord Jesus Christ, that you all agree and that there be no divisions among you, but that you be made complete in the same mind and in the same judgment.

11 For I have been informed concerning you, my brothers, by Chloe's *people,* that there are quarrels among you.

12 Now I mean this, that each one of you is saying, "I am of Paul," and "I of Apollos," and "I of Cephas," and "I of Christ."

13 Has Christ been divided? Was Paul crucified for you? Or were you baptized in the name of Paul?

14 I thank God that I baptized none of you except Crispus and Gaius,

15 so that no one would say you were baptized in my name.

16 Now I did baptize also the household of Stephanas; beyond that, I do not know whether I baptized any other.

17 For Christ did not send me to baptize, but to proclaim the gospel, not in wisdom of word, so that the cross of Christ will not be made empty.

Christ the Power and Wisdom of God

18 For the word of the cross is foolishness to those who are perishing, but to us who are being saved, it is the power of God.

19 For it is written,

"I WILL DESTROY THE WISDOM OF THE WISE,

AND THE CLEVERNESS OF THE
    CLEVER I WILL SET ASIDE."

20 Where is the wise man? Where is the scribe? Where is the debater of this age? Has not God made foolish the wisdom of the world?

21 For since, in the wisdom of God, the world through its wisdom did not *come to* know God, God was well-pleased, through the foolishness of the message preached, to save those who believe.

22 For indeed Jews ask for signs and Greeks search for wisdom,

23 but we preach Christ crucified, to Jews a stumbling block and to Gentiles foolishness,

24 but to those who are the called, both Jews and Greeks, Christ the power of God and the wisdom of God.

25 Because the foolishness of God is wiser than men, and the weakness of God is stronger than men.

26 For consider your calling, brothers, that there were not many wise according to the flesh, not many mighty, not many noble.

27 But God has chosen the foolish things of the world to shame the wise, and God has chosen the weak things of the world to shame the things which are strong,

28 and the base things of the world and the despised God has chosen, the things that are not, so that He may abolish the things that are,

29 so that no flesh may boast before God.

30 But by His doing you are in Christ Jesus, who became to us wisdom from God, and righteousness and sanctification, and redemption,

31 so that, just as it is written, "LET HIM WHO BOASTS, BOAST IN THE LORD."

CHAPTER 2

Paul's Reliance upon the Spirit

AND when I came to you, brothers, I did not come with superiority of word or of wisdom, proclaiming to you the witness of God.

2 For I determined to know nothing among you except Jesus Christ, and Him crucified.

3 And I was with you in weakness and in fear and in much trembling,

4 and my word and my preaching were not in persuasive words of wisdom, but in demonstration of the Spirit and of power,

5 so that your faith would not be in the wisdom of men, but in the power of God.

6 Yet we do speak wisdom among those who are mature, a wisdom, however, not of this age nor of the rulers of this age, who are being abolished.

7 But we speak God's wisdom in a mystery, the *wisdom* which has been hidden, which God predestined before the ages to our glory,

8 which none of the rulers of this age has understood; for if they had understood it, they would not have crucified the Lord of glory.

9 But just as it is written,

"THINGS WHICH EYE HAS NOT SEEN
    AND EAR HAS NOT HEARD,

And *which* have not entered
the heart of man,
All that God has prepared for
those who love Him."

10 But to us God revealed *them* through the Spirit, for the Spirit searches all things, even the depths of God.

11 For who among men knows the *depths* of a man except the spirit of the man which is in him? Even so the *depths* of God no one knows except the Spirit of God.

12 Now we have received, not the spirit of the world, but the Spirit who is from God, so that we may know the *depths* graciously given to us by God,

13 of which *depths* we also speak, not in words taught by human wisdom, but in those taught by the Spirit, combining spiritual *depths* with spiritual *words*.

14 But a natural man does not accept the *depths* of the Spirit of God, for they are foolishness to him, and he cannot understand them, because they are spiritually examined.

15 But he who is spiritual examines all things, yet he himself is examined by no one.

16 For who has known the mind of the Lord, that he will direct Him? But we have the mind of Christ.

CHAPTER 3

Jesus Christ, Our Foundation

AND I, brothers, was not able to speak to you as to spiritual men, but as to fleshly men, as to infants in Christ.

2 I gave you milk to drink, not solid food, for you were not yet able *to receive it*. Indeed, even now you are still not able,

3 for you are still fleshly. For since there is jealousy and strife among you, are you not fleshly, and are you not walking like mere men?

4 For when one says, "I am of Paul," and another, "I am of Apollos," are you not *mere* men?

5 What then is Apollos? And what is Paul? Servants through whom you believed, even as the Lord gave to each one.

6 I planted, Apollos watered, but God was causing the growth.

7 So then neither the one who plants nor the one who waters is anything, but God who causes the growth.

8 Now he who plants and he who waters are one, but each will receive his own reward according to his own labor.

9 For we are God's fellow workers; you are God's field, God's building.

10 According to the grace of God which was given to me, like a wise master builder I laid a foundation, and another is building on it. But each man must be careful how he builds on it.

11 For no one can lay a foundation other than the one which is laid, which is Jesus Christ.

12 Now if anyone builds on the

foundation with gold, silver, precious stones, wood, hay, straw,

13 each man's work will become evident, for the day will indicate it because it is revealed with fire, and the fire itself will test the quality of each man's work.

14 If any man's work which he has built on it remains, he will receive a reward.

15 If any man's work is burned up, he will suffer loss, but he himself will be saved, yet so as through fire.

16 Do you not know that you are a sanctuary of God and *that* the Spirit of God dwells in you?

17 If any man destroys the sanctuary of God, God will destroy him, for the sanctuary of God is holy, and that is what you are.

18 Let no man deceive himself. If any man among you thinks that he is wise in this age, he must become foolish, so that he may become wise.

19 For the wisdom of this world is foolishness before God. For it is written, "*He is* THE ONE WHO CATCHES THE WISE IN THEIR CRAFTINESS";

20 and again, "THE LORD KNOWS THE REASONINGS of the wise, THAT THEY ARE USELESS."

21 So then let no one boast in men. For all things belong to you,

22 whether Paul or Apollos or Cephas or the world or life or death or things present or things to come; all things belong to you,

23 and you belong to Christ, and Christ belongs to God.

CHAPTER 4

Servants of Christ

LET a man consider us in this manner, as servants of Christ and stewards of the mysteries of God.

2 In this case, moreover, it is required of stewards that one be found faithful.

3 But to me it is a very small thing that I may be examined by you, or by *any* human court. In fact, I do not even examine myself.

4 For I am conscious of nothing against myself, yet I am not by this acquitted. But the one who examines me is the Lord.

5 Therefore do not go on passing judgment before the time, *but wait* until the Lord comes who will both bring to light the things hidden in the darkness and make manifest the motives of hearts. And then each one's praise will come to him from God.

6 Now these things, brothers, I have applied to myself and Apollos for your sakes, so that in us you may learn not to go beyond what is written, so that no one of you will become puffed up on behalf of one against the other.

7 For who regards you as superior? What do you have that you did not receive? And if you did receive it, why do you boast as if you had not received it?

8 You are already filled, you have already become rich, you have ruled without us—and *how* I wish that you had ruled indeed so that we also might rule with you.

9 For, I think that God has exhibited us apostles last of all, as men condemned to death, because we have become a spectacle to the world, and to angels, and to men.

10 We are fools for the sake of Christ, but you are prudent in Christ! We are weak, but you are strong! You are glorious, but we are without honor!

11 To this present hour we hunger and thirst, and are poorly clothed, and roughly treated, and homeless;

12 and we labor, working with our own hands; when we are reviled, we bless; when we are persecuted, we endure;

13 when we are slandered, we try to plead; we have become as the scum of the world, the grime of all things, *even* until now.

14 I do not write these things to shame you, but to admonish you as my beloved children.

15 For if you were to have countless tutors in Christ, yet *you would* not *have* many fathers, for in Christ Jesus I became your father through the gospel.

16 Therefore I exhort you, be imitators of me.

17 For this reason I have sent to you Timothy, who is my beloved and faithful child in the Lord, and who will remind you of my ways which are in Christ, just as I teach everywhere in every church.

18 Now some have become puffed up, as though I were not coming to you.

19 But I will come to you soon, if the Lord wills, and I shall know, not the words of those who are puffed up but their power.

20 For the kingdom of God does not consist in words but in power.

21 What do you desire? Shall I come to you with a rod, or with love and a spirit of gentleness?

CHAPTER 5

Sexual Immorality in the Church

IT is actually reported that there is sexual immorality among you, and sexual immorality of such a kind as does not exist even among the Gentiles, that someone has his father's wife.

2 And you have become puffed up and have not mourned instead, so that the one who had done this deed would be removed from your midst.

3 For I, on my part, though absent in body but present in spirit, have already judged him who has so committed this, as though I were present:

4 in the name of our Lord Jesus, when you are assembled, and I with you in spirit, with the power of our Lord Jesus,

5 deliver such a one to Satan for the destruction of his flesh, so that his spirit may be saved in the day of the Lord.

6 Your boasting is not good. Do you not know that a little leaven leavens the whole lump?

7 Clean out the old leaven so that

you may be a new lump, just as you are *in fact* unleavened. For Christ, our Passover lamb, also was sacrificed.

8 Therefore let us celebrate the feast, not with old leaven, nor with the leaven of malice and wickedness, but with the unleavened bread of sincerity and truth.

9 I wrote you in my letter not to associate with sexually immoral people;

10 I *did* not at all *mean* with the sexually immoral people of this world, or with the greedy and swindlers, or with idolaters, for then you would have to go out of the world.

11 But now I am writing to you not to associate with any so-called brother if he is a sexually immoral person, or greedy, or an idolater, or a reviler, or a drunkard, or a swindler—not even to eat with such a one.

12 For what have I to do with judging outsiders? Are you not to judge those who are within *the church*?

13 But those who are outside, God will judge. REMOVE THE WICKED MAN FROM AMONG YOURSELVES.

CHAPTER 6

Lawsuits Among Believers

DOES any one of you, when he has a case against another, dare to be tried before the unrighteous and not before the saints?

2 Or do you not know that the saints will judge the world? If the world is judged by you, are you not worthy *to constitute* the smallest law courts?

3 Do you not know that we will judge angels? How much more matters of this life?

4 So if you have law courts dealing with matters of this life, do you appoint those who are of no account in the church as judges?

5 I say *this* to your shame. *Is it really* this way: there is not one wise man among you who will be able to pass judgment between his brothers?

6 On the contrary, brother is tried with brother, and that before unbelievers!

7 Actually, then, it is already a failure for you, that you have lawsuits with one another. Why not rather be wronged? Why not rather be defrauded?

8 On the contrary, you yourselves wrong and defraud. *You do* this even to *your* brothers.

9 Or do you not know that the unrighteous will not inherit the kingdom of God? Do not be deceived; neither *the* sexually immoral, nor idolaters, nor adulterers, nor effeminate, nor homosexuals,

10 nor thieves, nor *the* greedy, nor drunkards, nor revilers, nor swindlers, will inherit the kingdom of God.

11 And such were some of you; but you were washed, but you were sanctified, but you were justified in the name of the Lord Jesus Christ and in the Spirit of our God.

Flee Sexual Immorality

12 All things are lawful for me, but not all things are profitable. All things are lawful for me, but I will not be mastered by anything.

13 Food is for the stomach and the stomach is for food, but God will do away with both of them. Yet the body is not for sexual immorality, but for the Lord, and the Lord is for the body.

14 Now God has not only raised the Lord, but will also raise us up through His power.

15 Do you not know that your bodies are members of Christ? Shall I then take away the members of Christ and make them members of a prostitute? May it never be!

16 Or do you not know that the one who joins himself to a prostitute is one body *with her*? For He says, "THE TWO SHALL BECOME ONE FLESH."

17 But the one who joins himself to the Lord is one spirit *with Him.*

18 Flee sexual immorality. Every *other* sin that a man commits is outside the body, but the sexually immoral man sins against his own body.

19 Or do you not know that your body is a sanctuary of the Holy Spirit who is in you, whom you have from God, and that you are not your own?

20 For you were bought with a price: therefore glorify God in your body.

CHAPTER 7

Concerning Marriage and Singleness

NOW concerning the things about which you wrote, it is good for a man not to touch a woman.

2 But because of sexual immoralities, each man is to have his own wife, and each woman is to have her own husband.

3 The husband must fulfill his duty to his wife, and likewise also the wife to her husband.

4 The wife does not have authority over her own body, but the husband *does*; and likewise also the husband does not have authority over his own body, but the wife *does.*

5 Stop depriving one another, except by agreement for a time, so that you may devote yourselves to prayer, and come together again so that Satan will not tempt you because of your lack of self-control.

6 But this I say as a concession, not as a command.

7 Yet I wish that all men were even as I myself am. However, each man has his own gift from God, one this way, and another that.

8 But I say to the unmarried and to widows that it is good for them if they remain even as I.

9 But if they do not have self-control, let them marry, for it is better to marry than to burn *with passion.*

10 But to the married I give instructions, not I, but the Lord, that the wife should not leave her husband

11 (but if she does leave, she must remain unmarried, or else be reconciled to her husband), and that the husband should not divorce his wife.

12 But to the rest I say, not the Lord, that if any brother has a wife who

is an unbeliever, and she consents to live with him, he must not divorce her.

13 And a woman who has an unbelieving husband, and he consents to live with her, she must not divorce her husband.

14 For the unbelieving husband is sanctified through his wife, and the unbelieving wife is sanctified through her believing husband. For otherwise your children are unclean, but now they are holy.

15 Yet if the unbelieving one leaves, let him leave. The brother or the sister is not enslaved in such *cases*, but God has called us to peace.

16 For how do you know, O wife, whether you will save your husband? Or how do you know, O husband, whether you will save your wife?

17 Only, as the Lord has assigned to each one, as God has called each, in this manner let him walk. And so I direct in all the churches.

18 Was any man called *when he was already* circumcised? He is not to become uncircumcised. Has anyone been called in uncircumcision? He is not to be circumcised.

19 Circumcision is nothing, and uncircumcision is nothing, but *what matters is* the keeping of the commandments of God.

20 Each man must remain in that condition in which he was called.

21 Were you called while a slave? Do not worry about it. But if you are able also to become free, rather do that.

22 For he who was called in the Lord while a slave, is the Lord's freedman. Likewise he who was called while free, is Christ's slave.

23 You were bought with a price; do not become slaves of men.

24 Brothers, each one is to remain with God in that *condition* in which he was called.

25 Now concerning virgins I have no command of the Lord, but I give an opinion as one who by the mercy of the Lord is trustworthy.

26 I think then that this is good because of the present distress, that it is good for a man to remain as he is.

27 Are you bound to a wife? Do not seek to be released. Are you released from a wife? Do not seek a wife.

28 But if you marry, you have not sinned. And if a virgin marries, she has not sinned. Yet such will have trouble in this life, and I am trying to spare you.

29 But this I say, brothers, the time has been shortened, so that from now on those who have wives should be as though they had none;

30 and those who cry, as though they did not cry; and those who rejoice, as though they did not rejoice; and those who buy, as though they did not possess;

31 and those who use the world, as though they did not make full use of it. For the form of this world is passing away.

32 But I want you to be free from concern. One who is unmarried is concerned about the things of the Lord, how he may please the Lord.

33 But one who is married is concerned about the things of the world, how he may please his wife,

34 and *his interests* have been divided. The woman who is unmarried, and the virgin, is concerned about the things of the Lord, that she may be holy both in body and spirit. But one who is married is concerned about the things of the world, how she may please her husband.

35 Now this I say for your own benefit, not to put a restraint upon you, but to promote propriety and undistracted devotion to the Lord.

36 But if any man thinks that he is acting unbecomingly toward his virgin *daughter*, if she is past her youth, and if it must be so, let him do what he wishes, he does not sin; let her marry.

37 But he who stands firm in his heart, being under no compulsion, but has authority over his own will, and has decided this in his own heart, to keep his own virgin *daughter*, he will do well.

38 So then both he who gives his own virgin *daughter* in marriage does well, and he who does not give her in marriage will do better.

39 A wife is bound as long as her husband lives; but if her husband has fallen asleep, she is free to be married to whom she wishes, only in the Lord.

40 But in my opinion she is happier if she remains as she is. And I think that I also have the Spirit of God.

CHAPTER 8

Take Care with Your Liberty

NOW concerning things sacrificed to idols, we know that we all have knowledge. Knowledge puffs up, but love builds up.

2 If anyone thinks that he has known anything, he has not yet known as he ought to know;

3 but if anyone loves God, he has been known by Him.

4 Therefore, concerning the eating of things sacrificed to idols, we know that an idol is nothing in the world, and that there is no God but one.

5 For even if there are so-called gods whether in heaven or on earth, as indeed there are many gods and many lords,

6 yet for us there is one God, the Father, from whom are all things and we *exist* for Him, and one Lord, Jesus Christ, by whom are all things, and we *exist* through Him.

7 However, not all men have this knowledge; but some, being accustomed to the idol until now, eat *food* as if it were sacrificed to an idol; and their conscience, being weak, is defiled.

8 But food will not commend us to God. We neither lack if we do not eat, nor abound if we do eat.

9 But see *to it* that this authority of yours does not somehow become a stumbling block to the weak.

10 For if someone sees you, who have knowledge, dining in an idol's temple, will not his conscience, if he

is weak, be built up to eat things sacrificed to idols?

11 For through your knowledge he who is weak is ruined, the brother for whose sake Christ died.

12 And in that way, by sinning against the brothers and wounding their conscience when it is weak, you sin against Christ.

13 Therefore, if food causes my brother to stumble, I will never eat meat again—ever, so that I will not cause my brother to stumble.

CHAPTER 9

Paul Gives Up His Rights

AM I not free? Am I not an apostle? Have I not seen Jesus our Lord? Are you not my work in the Lord?

2 If to others I am not an apostle, at least I am to you, for you are the seal of my apostleship in the Lord.

3 My defense to those who examine me is this:

4 Do we not have authority to eat and drink?

5 Do we not have authority to take along a believing wife, even as the rest of the apostles and the brothers of the Lord and Cephas?

6 Or do only Barnabas and I not have authority to refrain from working?

7 Who at any time serves as a soldier at his own expense? Who plants a vineyard and does not consume the fruit of it? Or who shepherds a flock and does not consume the milk of the flock?

8 Am I speaking these things according to human judgment? Or does not the Law also say these things?

9 For it is written in the Law of Moses, "YOU SHALL NOT MUZZLE THE OX WHILE IT IS THRESHING." Is God *merely* concerned about oxen?

10 Or is He speaking altogether for our sake? Yes, for our sake it was written, because the plowman ought to plow in hope, and the thresher *to thresh* in hope of sharing *the crops.*

11 If we sowed spiritual things in you, is it too much if we reap material things from you?

12 If others share this authority over you, do we not more? Nevertheless, we did not use this authority, but we endure all things so that we will cause no hindrance to the gospel of Christ.

13 Do you not know that those who perform sacred services eat the *food* of the temple, *and* those who attend regularly to the altar have their share from the altar?

14 So also the Lord directed those who proclaim the gospel to get their living from the gospel.

15 But I have used none of these things. And I am not writing these things so that it will be done so in my case, for it would be better for me to die than have anyone make my boast an empty one.

16 For if I proclaim the gospel, I have nothing to boast, for I am under compulsion. For woe is me if I do not proclaim the gospel.

17 For if I do this voluntarily, I have

a reward; but if against my will, I have a stewardship entrusted to me.

18 What then is my reward? That, when I proclaim the gospel, I may offer the gospel without charge, so as not to make full use of my authority in the gospel.

19 For though I am free from all, I have made myself a slave to all, so that I may win more.

20 And to the Jews I became as a Jew, so that I might win Jews. To those who are under the Law, as under the Law though not being myself under the Law, so that I might win those who are under the Law.

21 To those who are without law, as without law, though not being without the law of God but under the law of Christ, so that I might win those who are without law.

22 To the weak I became weak, that I might win the weak. I have become all things to all men, so that I may by all means save some.

23 So I do all things for the sake of the gospel, so that I may become a fellow partaker of it.

24 Do you not know that those who run in a race all run, but *only* one receives the prize? Run in such a way that you may win.

25 Now everyone who competes in the games exercises self-control in all things. They then *do it* to receive a corruptible crown, but we an incorruptible.

26 Therefore I run in such a way, as not without aim; I box in such a way, as not beating the air;

27 but I discipline my body and make it my slave, so that, after I have preached to others, I myself will not be disqualified.

CHAPTER 10

Temptation and God's Faithfulness

FOR I do not want you to be unaware, brothers, that our fathers were all under the cloud and all passed through the sea;

2 and all were baptized into Moses in the cloud and in the sea;

3 and all ate the same spiritual food;

4 and all drank the same spiritual drink, for they were drinking from a spiritual rock which followed them, and the rock was Christ.

5 Nevertheless, with most of them God was not well-pleased. For THEY WERE STRUCK DOWN IN THE WILDERNESS.

6 Now these things happened as examples for us, so that we would not crave evil things as they also craved.

7 Do not be idolaters, as some of them were. As it is written, "THE PEOPLE SAT DOWN TO EAT AND DRINK, AND STOOD UP TO PLAY."

8 Nor let us act in sexual immorality, as some of them did, and twenty-three thousand fell in one day.

9 Nor let us put Christ to the test, as some of them did, and were destroyed by the serpents.

10 Nor grumble, as some of them did, and were destroyed by the destroyer.

11 Now these things happened to them as an example, and they were

written for our instruction, upon whom the ends of the ages have arrived.

12 Therefore let him who thinks he stands take heed that he does not fall.

13 No temptation has overtaken you but such as is common to man, but God is faithful, who will not allow you to be tempted beyond what you are able, but with the temptation will provide the way of escape also, so that you will be able to endure it.

14 Therefore, my beloved, flee from idolatry.

15 I speak as to prudent people. You judge what I say.

16 Is not the cup of blessing which we bless a sharing in the blood of Christ? Is not the bread which we break a sharing in the body of Christ?

17 Since there is one bread, we who are many are one body, for we all partake of the one bread.

18 Look at the nation Israel. Are not those who eat the sacrifices sharers in the altar?

19 What do I mean then? That a thing sacrificed to idols is anything, or that an idol is anything?

20 *No*, but *I say* that the things which the Gentiles sacrifice, they SACRIFICE TO DEMONS AND NOT TO GOD. And I do not want you to become sharers in demons.

21 You cannot drink the cup of the Lord and the cup of demons. You cannot partake of the table of the Lord and the table of demons.

22 Or do we PROVOKE THE LORD TO JEALOUSY? Are we stronger than He?

23 All things are lawful, but not all things are profitable. All things are lawful, but not all things build up.

24 Let no one seek his own *good*, but that of the other person.

25 Eat anything that is sold in the meat market without asking questions for conscience' sake.

26 FOR THE EARTH IS THE LORD'S, AS WELL AS ITS FULLNESS.

27 If one of the unbelievers invites you and you want to go, eat anything that is set before you without asking questions for conscience' sake.

28 But if anyone says to you, "This is meat consecrated to idols," do not eat *it*, for the sake of the one who informed *you*, and for conscience' sake.

29 I do not mean your own conscience, but the other *person's*. For why is my freedom judged by another's conscience?

30 If I partake with gratefulness, why am I slandered concerning that for which I give thanks?

31 Whether, then, you eat or drink or whatever you do, do all to the glory of God.

32 Give no offense either to Jews or to Greeks or to the church of God;

33 just as I also please all men in all things, not seeking my own profit but the *profit* of the many, so that they may be saved.

CHAPTER 11

BE imitators of me, just as I also am of Christ.

Head Coverings

2 Now I praise you because you remember me in everything and hold firmly to the traditions, just as I delivered them to you.

3 But I want you to understand that Christ is the head of every man, and the man is the head of a woman, and God is the head of Christ.

4 Every man who has *something* on his head while praying or prophesying, shames his head.

5 But every woman who has her head uncovered while praying or prophesying, shames her head, for she is one and the same as the woman whose head is shaved.

6 For if a woman does not cover her head, let her also have her hair cut short. But if it is disgraceful for a woman to have her hair cut short or her head shaved, let her cover her head.

7 For a man ought not to have his head covered, since he is the image and glory of God, but the woman is the glory of man.

8 For man does not originate from woman, but woman from man.

9 For indeed man was not created for the woman's sake, but woman for the man's sake.

10 Therefore the woman ought to have *a symbol of* authority on her head, because of the angels.

11 Nevertheless, in the Lord, neither is woman independent of man, nor is man independent of woman.

12 For as the woman originates from the man, so also the man *has* his *birth* through the woman, but all things originate from God.

13 Judge for yourselves: is it proper for a woman to pray to God *with her head* uncovered?

14 Does not even nature itself teach you that if a man has long hair, it is a dishonor to him,

15 but if a woman has long hair, it is a glory to her? For her hair is given to her for a covering.

16 But if one is inclined to be contentious, we have no other practice, nor have the churches of God.

The Lord's Supper

17 But in giving this instruction, I do not praise you, because you come together not for the better but for the worse.

18 For, in the first place, when you come together as a church, I hear that divisions exist among you, and in part I believe it.

19 For there must also be factions among you, so that those who are approved may become evident among you.

20 Therefore when you meet together in the same *place*, it is not to eat the Lord's Supper,

21 for in your eating each one takes his own supper first, and one is hungry and another is drunk.

22 For do you not have houses in which to eat and drink? Or do you despise the church of God and shame those who have nothing? What shall I say to you? Shall I praise you? In this I will not praise you.

23 For I received from the Lord that which I also delivered to you, that the Lord Jesus in the night in which He was being betrayed took bread,

24 and when He had given thanks, He broke it and said, "This is My body, which is for you. Do this in remembrance of Me."

25 In the same way *He took* the cup also after supper, saying, "This cup is the new covenant in My blood; do this, as often as you drink *it*, in remembrance of Me."

26 For as often as you eat this bread and drink the cup, you proclaim the death of the Lord until He comes.

27 Therefore whoever eats the bread or drinks the cup of the Lord in an unworthy manner, shall be guilty of the body and the blood of the Lord.

28 But a man must test himself, and in so doing he is to eat of the bread and drink of the cup.

29 For he who eats and drinks, eats and drinks judgment to himself if he does not judge the body rightly.

30 For this reason many among you are weak and sick, and a number sleep.

31 But if we judged ourselves rightly, we would not be judged.

32 But when we are judged, we are disciplined by the Lord so that we will not be condemned along with the world.

33 So then, my brothers, when you come together to eat, wait for one another.

34 If anyone is hungry, let him eat at home, so that you will not come together for judgment. The remaining matters I will direct when I come.

CHAPTER 12

Concerning Spiritual Gifts

NOW concerning spiritual *gifts*, brothers, I do not want you to be ignorant.

2 You know that when you were pagans, *you were* being led astray to the mute idols, however you were led.

3 Therefore I make known to you that no one speaking by the Spirit of God says, "Jesus is accursed," and no one can say, "Jesus is Lord," except by the Holy Spirit.

4 Now there are varieties of gifts, but the same Spirit.

5 And there are varieties of ministries, and the same Lord.

6 And there are varieties of workings, but the same God who works everything in everyone.

7 But to each one is given the manifestation of the Spirit for what is profitable.

8 For to one is given the word of wisdom through the Spirit, and to another the word of knowledge according to the same Spirit;

9 to someone else faith by the same Spirit, and to another gifts of healing by the one Spirit,

10 and to another the workings of miracles, and to another prophecy, and to another the distinguishing of spirits, to someone else *various* kinds of tongues, and to another the translation of tongues.

11 But one and the same Spirit works all these things, distributing to each one individually just as He wills.

12 For even as the body is one and *yet* has many members, and all the members of the body, though they are many, are one body, so also is Christ.

13 For also by one Spirit we were all baptized into one body, whether Jews or Greeks, whether slaves or free, and we were all made to drink of one Spirit.

14 For also the body is not one member, but many.

15 If the foot says, "Because I am not a hand, I am not *a part* of the body," it is not for this reason any the less *a part* of the body.

16 And if the ear says, "Because I am not an eye, I am not *a part* of the body," it is not for this reason any the less *a part* of the body.

17 If the whole body were an eye, where would the hearing be? If the whole were hearing, where would the sense of smell be?

18 But now God has appointed the members, each one of them, in the body, just as He desired.

19 And if they were all one member, where would the body be?

20 But now there are many members, but one body.

21 And the eye cannot say to the hand, "I have no need of you"; or again the head to the feet, "I have no need of you."

22 On the contrary, *how* much more is it that the members of the body which seem to be weaker are necessary,

23 and those *members* of the body which we think as less honorable, on these we bestow more abundant honor, and our less presentable members become much more presentable,

24 whereas our more presentable members have no *such* need. But God has *so* composed the body, giving more abundant honor to that *member* which lacked,

25 so that there may be no division in the body, but *that* the members may have the same care for one another.

26 And if one member suffers, all the members suffer with it; if *one* member is honored, all the members rejoice with it.

27 Now you are Christ's body, and individually members of it.

28 And God has appointed in the church, first apostles, second prophets, third teachers, then miracles, then gifts of healings, helps, administrations, *various* kinds of tongues.

29 Are all apostles? Are all prophets? Are all teachers? Are all *workers of* miracles?

30 Do all have gifts of healings? Do all speak with tongues? Do all translate?

31 But you earnestly desire the greater gifts.

And I will yet show you a more excellent way.

CHAPTER 13

The Excellence of Love

IF I speak with the tongues of men and of angels, but do not have love, I have become a noisy gong or a clanging cymbal.

2 And if I have *the gift of* prophecy, and know all mysteries and all knowledge; and if I have all faith, so as to remove mountains, but do not have love, I am nothing.

3 And if I give all my possessions to feed *the poor*, and if I surrender my body to be burned, but do not have love, it profits me nothing.

4 Love is patient, love is kind, is not jealous, does not brag, is not puffed up;

5 it does not act unbecomingly, does not seek its own, is not provoked, does not take into account a wrong *suffered*;

6 it does not rejoice in unrighteousness, but rejoices with the truth;

7 it bears all things, believes all things, hopes all things, endures all things.

8 Love never fails, but if *there are gifts of* prophecy, they will be done away; if *there are* tongues, they will cease; if *there is* knowledge, it will be done away.

9 For we know in part and we prophesy in part,

10 but when the perfect comes, the partial will be done away.

11 When I was a child, I used to speak like a child, think like a child, reason like a child. When I became a man, I did away with childish things.

12 For now we see in a mirror dimly, but then face to face. Now I know in part, but then I will know fully just as I also have been fully known.

13 But now abide faith, hope, love— these three; but the greatest of these is love.

CHAPTER 14

Prophecy and Tongues

PURSUE love, yet earnestly desire spiritual *gifts*, but especially that you may prophesy.

2 For one who speaks in a tongue does not speak to men but to God, for no one understands, but in *his* spirit he speaks mysteries.

3 But one who prophesies speaks to men for edification and exhortation and encouragement.

4 One who speaks in a tongue edifies himself; but one who prophesies edifies the church.

5 But I wish that you all spoke in tongues, but *even* more that you would prophesy. And greater is one who prophesies than one who speaks in tongues, unless he translates, so that the church may receive edification.

6 But now, brothers, if I come to you speaking in tongues, what will I profit you unless I speak to you either by way of revelation or of knowledge or of prophecy or of teaching?

7 Yet *even* lifeless things, either flute or harp, in producing a sound, if they do not produce a distinction in the tones, how will it be known what is played on the flute or on the harp?

8 For if the trumpet produces an indistinct sound, who will prepare himself for battle?

9 So also you, unless you utter by the tongue a word that is clear, how will it be known what is spoken? For you will be speaking into the air.

10 There are, perhaps, a great many kinds of sounds in the world, and none is without meaning.

11 If then I do not know the meaning of the sound, I will be to the one who speaks a barbarian, and the one who speaks will be a barbarian to me.

12 So also you, since you are zealous for spiritual *gifts*, seek to abound for the edification of the church.

13 Therefore let one who speaks in a tongue pray that he may translate.

14 For if I pray in a tongue, my spirit prays, but my mind is unfruitful.

15 What is *the outcome* then? I will pray with the spirit and I will pray with the mind also; I will sing with the spirit and I will sing with the mind also.

16 Otherwise if you bless in the spirit *only*, how will the one who fills the place of the uninformed say the "Amen" at your giving of thanks, since he does not know what you are saying?

17 For you are giving thanks well enough, but the other person is not edified.

18 I thank God that I speak in tongues more than you all;

19 however, in the church I desire to speak five words with my mind so that I may instruct others also, rather than ten thousand words in a tongue.

20 Brothers, do not be children in your thinking; rather in evil be infants, but in your thinking be mature.

21 In the Law it is written, "By men of strange tongues and by the lips of strangers I will speak to this people, and even so they will not listen to Me," says the Lord.

22 So then tongues are for a sign, not to those who believe but to unbelievers; but prophecy *is for a sign* not to unbelievers but to those who believe.

23 Therefore if the whole church assembles together and all speak in tongues, and uninformed men or unbelievers enter, will they not say that you are out of your mind?

24 But if all prophesy, and an unbeliever or an uninformed man enters, he is convicted by all, he is called to account by all;

25 the secrets of his heart are disclosed; and so he will fall on his face and worship God, declaring that surely God is among you.

Orderly Worship

26 What is *the outcome* then, brothers? When you assemble, each one has a psalm, has a teaching, has a revelation, has a tongue, has a translation. Let all things be done for edification.

27 If anyone speaks in a tongue, *it should be* by two or at the most three, and *each* in turn, and one must translate;

28 but if there is no translator, he must keep silent in the church, and let him speak to himself and to God.

29 And let two or three prophets speak, and let the others pass judgment.

30 But if a revelation is made to

another who is seated, the first one must keep silent.

31 For you can all prophesy one by one, so that all may learn and all may be exhorted.

32 And the spirits of prophets are subject to prophets;

33 for God is not *a God* of confusion but of peace, as in all the churches of the saints.

34 The women are to keep silent in the churches, for they are not permitted to speak, but are to subject themselves, just as the Law also says.

35 But if they desire to learn anything, let them ask their own husbands at home, for it is disgraceful for a woman to speak in church.

36 Was it from you that the word of God *first* went forth? Or has it arrived to you only?

37 If anyone thinks he is a prophet or spiritual, let him recognize that the things which I write to you are the Lord's commandment.

38 But if anyone remains ignorant about *this*, he is ignored *by God*.

39 Therefore, my brothers, earnestly *desire to* prophesy, and do not forbid to speak in tongues.

40 But all things must be done properly and in an orderly manner.

CHAPTER 15

The Resurrection of Christ

NOW I make known to you, brothers, the gospel which I proclaimed as good news to you, which also you received, in which also you stand,

2 by which also you are saved, if you hold fast the word which I proclaimed to you as good news, unless you believed for nothing.

3 For I delivered to you as of first importance what I also received, that Christ died for our sins according to the Scriptures,

4 and that He was buried, and that He was raised on the third day according to the Scriptures,

5 and that He appeared to Cephas, then to the twelve.

6 After that He appeared to more than five hundred brothers at one time, most of whom remain until now, but some have fallen asleep.

7 After that, He appeared to James, then to all the apostles,

8 and last of all, as to one untimely born, He appeared to me also.

9 For I am the least of the apostles, and not worthy to be called an apostle, because I persecuted the church of God.

10 But by the grace of God I am what I am, and His grace toward me did not prove vain; but I labored even more than all of them, yet not I, but the grace of God with me.

11 Whether then *it was* I or they, so we preach and so you believed.

The Resurrection of the Dead

12 Now if Christ is preached, that He has been raised from the dead, how do some among you say that there is no resurrection of the dead?

13 But if there is no resurrection of the dead, not even Christ has been raised.

14 And if Christ has not been raised, then our preaching is vain, your faith also is vain.

15 Moreover we are even found *to be* false witnesses of God, because we bore witness against God that He raised Christ, whom He did not raise, if in fact the dead are not raised.

16 For if the dead are not raised, not even Christ has been raised.

17 And if Christ has not been raised, your faith is worthless; you are still in your sins.

18 Then those also who have fallen asleep in Christ have perished.

19 If we have hoped in Christ in this life only, we are of all men most to be pitied.

20 But now Christ has been raised from the dead, the first fruits of those who have fallen asleep.

21 For since by a man *came* death, by a man also *came* the resurrection of the dead.

22 For as in Adam all die, so also in Christ all will be made alive.

23 But each in his own order: Christ the first fruits, after that those who are Christ's at His coming.

24 Then *comes* the end, when He hands over the kingdom to the God *and* Father, when He has abolished all rule and all authority and power.

25 For He must reign UNTIL HE HAS PUT ALL HIS ENEMIES UNDER HIS FEET.

26 The last enemy to be abolished is death.

27 For He HAS PUT ALL THINGS IN SUBJECTION UNDER HIS FEET. But when He says, "All things are put in subjection," it is evident that He is excepted who put all things in subjection to Him.

28 And when all things are subjected to Him, then the Son Himself also will be subjected to the One who subjected all things to Him, so that God may be all in all.

29 Otherwise, what will those do who are baptized for the dead? If the dead are not raised at all, why then are they baptized for them?

30 Why are we also in danger every hour?

31 I affirm, brothers, by the boasting in you which I have in Christ Jesus our Lord, I die daily.

32 If from human motives I fought with wild beasts at Ephesus, what does it profit me? If the dead are not raised, LET US EAT AND DRINK, FOR TOMORROW WE DIE.

33 Do not be deceived: "Bad company corrupts good morals."

34 Become righteously sober-minded, and stop sinning; for some have no knowledge of God. I speak *this* to your shame.

The Resurrection Body

35 But someone will say, "How are the dead raised? And with what kind of body do they come?"

36 You fool! That which you sow does not come to life unless it dies;

37 and that which you sow, you do not sow the body which is to be, but

a bare grain, perhaps of wheat or of something else.

38 But God gives it a body just as He wished, and to each of the seeds a body of its own.

39 All flesh is not the same flesh, but there is one *flesh* of men, and another flesh of beasts, and another flesh of birds, and another of fish.

40 There are also heavenly bodies and earthly bodies, but the glory of the heavenly is one, and the *glory* of the earthly is another.

41 There is one glory of the sun, and another glory of the moon, and another glory of the stars; for star differs from star in glory.

42 So also is the resurrection of the dead. It is sown a corruptible *body*, it is raised an incorruptible *body*;

43 it is sown in dishonor, it is raised in glory; it is sown in weakness, it is raised in power;

44 it is sown a natural body, it is raised a spiritual body. If there is a natural body, there is also a spiritual *body*.

45 So also it is written, "The first MAN, Adam, BECAME A LIVING SOUL." The last Adam *became* a life-giving spirit.

46 However, the spiritual is not first, but the natural; then the spiritual.

47 The first man is from the earth, earthy; the second man is from heaven.

48 As is the earthy, so also are those who are earthy; and as is the heavenly, so also are those who are heavenly.

49 And just as we have borne the image of the earthy, we will also bear the image of the heavenly.

50 Now I say this, brothers, that flesh and blood cannot inherit the kingdom of God, nor does the corruptible inherit the incorruptible.

51 Behold, I tell you a mystery: we will not all sleep, but we will all be changed,

52 in a moment, in the twinkling of an eye, at the last trumpet. For the trumpet will sound, and the dead will be raised incorruptible, and we will be changed.

53 For this corruptible must put on the incorruptible, and this mortal must put on immortality.

54 But when this corruptible puts on the incorruptible, and this mortal puts on immortality, then will come about the word that is written, "DEATH IS SWALLOWED UP in victory.

55 "O DEATH, WHERE IS YOUR VICTORY? O DEATH, WHERE IS YOUR STING?"

56 Now the sting of death is sin, and the power of sin is the law;

57 but thanks be to God, who gives us the victory through our Lord Jesus Christ!

58 Therefore, my beloved brothers, be steadfast, immovable, always abounding in the work of the Lord, knowing that your labor is not *in* vain in the Lord.

CHAPTER 16

The Collection of Gifts

NOW concerning the collection for the saints, as I directed the churches of Galatia, so do you also.

2 On the first day of every week each one of you is to set *something* aside, saving whatever he has prospered, so that no collections be made when I come.

3 And when I arrive, whomever you may approve, I will send them with letters to carry your gracious gift to Jerusalem,

4 and if it is fitting for me to go also, they will go with me.

5 But I will come to you after I go through Macedonia, for I am going through Macedonia;

6 and perhaps I will stay with you, or even spend the winter, so that you may send me on my way wherever I may go.

7 For I do not wish to see you now *just* in passing, for I hope to remain with you for some time, if the Lord permits.

8 But I will remain in Ephesus until Pentecost,

9 for a wide and effective door has opened to me, and there are many adversaries.

10 Now if Timothy comes, take care that he is with you without fear, for he is doing the Lord's work, as I also am.

11 So let no one despise him. But send him on his way in peace, so that he may come to me, for I expect him with the brothers.

12 Now concerning Apollos our brother, I encouraged him greatly to come to you with the brothers, and it was not at all *his* desire to come now, but he will come when he has opportunity.

Final Instructions and Greetings

13 Be watchful, stand firm in the faith, act like men, be strong.

14 Let all that you do be done in love.

15 Now I exhort you, brothers (you know the household of Stephanas, that they were the first fruits of Achaia, and that they have devoted themselves for service to the saints),

16 that you also be in subjection to such men and to everyone who helps in the work and labors.

17 And I rejoice over the coming of Stephanas and Fortunatus and Achaicus, because they have supplied what was lacking on your part.

18 For they have refreshed my spirit and yours. Therefore recognize such men.

19 The churches of Asia greet you. Aquila and Prisca greet you heartily in the Lord, with the church that is in their house.

20 All the brothers greet you. Greet one another with a holy kiss.

21 The greeting is in my own hand—Paul.

22 If anyone does not love the Lord, he is to be accursed. Maranatha.

23 The grace of the Lord Jesus be with you.

24 My love be with you all in Christ Jesus. Amen.

THE SECOND LETTER OF PAUL TO THE
CORINTHIANS

CHAPTER 1

God of All Comfort

PAUL, an apostle of Christ Jesus by the will of God, and Timothy *our* brother,

To the church of God which is at Corinth with all the saints who are throughout Achaia:

2 Grace to you and peace from God our Father and the Lord Jesus Christ.

3 Blessed *be* the God and Father of our Lord Jesus Christ, the Father of mercies and God of all comfort,

4 who comforts us in all our affliction so that we will be able to comfort those who are in any affliction with the comfort with which we ourselves are comforted by God.

5 For just as the sufferings of Christ abound to us, so also our comfort abounds through Christ.

6 But whether we are afflicted, it is for your comfort and salvation; or whether we are comforted, it is for your comfort, which is working in *your* perseverance in the same sufferings which we also suffer.

7 And our hope for you is firmly grounded, knowing that as you are *sharers* of our sufferings, so also you are *sharers* of our comfort.

8 For we do not want you to be unaware, brothers, of our affliction which came *to us* in Asia, that we were burdened excessively, beyond our strength, so that we despaired even to live.

9 Indeed, we had the sentence of death within ourselves so that we would not have confidence in ourselves, but in God who raises the dead;

10 who rescued us from so great a *peril of* death, and will rescue *us*, He on whom we have set our hope. And He will yet rescue us,

11 you also joining in helping *us* through your prayers on our behalf, so that thanks may be given on our behalf by many persons for the gracious gift bestowed on us through *the prayers of* many.

Paul's Change of Plans

12 For our boasting is this: the testimony of our conscience, that in holiness and godly sincerity, not in fleshly wisdom but in the grace of God, we have conducted ourselves in the world, and especially toward you.

13 For we write nothing else to you than what you read and understand, and I hope you will understand until the end,

14 just as you also partially did understand us, that we are your reason for boasting as you also are ours, in the day of our Lord Jesus.

15 And in this confidence I intended

at first to come to you, so that you might receive grace twice;

16 that is, to pass your way into Macedonia, and again from Macedonia to come to you, and by you to be helped on my journey to Judea.

17 Therefore, was I vacillating when I intended to do this? Or what I purpose, do I purpose according to the flesh, so that with me there will be yes, yes and no, no *at the same time*?

18 But as God is faithful, our word to you is not yes and no.

19 For the Son of God, Jesus Christ, who was preached among you by us— by me and Silvanus and Timothy— was not yes and no, but has become yes in Him.

20 For as many as are the promises of God, in Him they are yes. Therefore also through Him is our Amen to the glory of God through us.

21 Now He who establishes us with you in Christ and anointed us is God,

22 who also sealed us and gave the pledge of the Spirit in our hearts.

23 But I call God as witness to my soul, that to spare you I did not come again to Corinth.

24 Not that we lord it over your faith, but are workers with you for your joy; for in your faith you are standing firm.

CHAPTER 2

BUT I determined this for my own sake, that I would not come to you again in sorrow.

2 For if I cause you sorrow, who then makes me glad but the one whom I made sorrowful?

3 And this is the very thing I wrote you, so that when I came, I would not have sorrow from those who ought to make me rejoice; having confidence in you all that my joy would be *the joy* of you all.

4 For out of much affliction and anguish of heart I wrote to you with many tears; not so that you would be made sorrowful, but that you might know the love which I have abundantly for you.

Forgive and Love the Sinner

5 But if any has caused sorrow, he has caused sorrow not to me, but in some degree—in order not to say too much—to all of you.

6 Sufficient for such a one is this punishment which *was inflicted* by the majority,

7 so that on the contrary you should rather graciously forgive and comfort *him*, lest such a one be swallowed up by excessive sorrow.

8 Therefore I encourage you to reaffirm *your* love for him.

9 For to this end also I wrote, so that I might know your proven character, whether you are obedient in all things.

10 But one whom you graciously forgive anything, I *graciously forgive* also. For indeed what I have graciously forgiven, if I have graciously forgiven anything, *I did it* for your sakes in the presence of Christ,

11 so that no advantage would be taken of us by Satan, for we are not ignorant of his schemes.

12 Now when I came to Troas for the gospel of Christ and when a door was opened for me in the Lord,

13 I had no rest for my spirit, not finding Titus my brother. But saying farewell to them, I went on to Macedonia.

14 But thanks be to God, who always leads us in triumphal procession in Christ, and manifests through us the aroma of the knowledge of Him in every place.

15 For we are a fragrance of Christ to God among those who are being saved and among those who are perishing;

16 to the one an aroma from death to death, to the other an aroma from life to life. And who is sufficient for these things?

17 For we are not like many, peddling the word of God, but as from sincerity, but as from God, in the sight of God, we speak in Christ.

CHAPTER 3

Ministers of a New Covenant

ARE we beginning to commend ourselves again? Or do we need, as some, letters of commendation to you or from you?

2 You are our letter, having been written in our hearts, known and read by all men,

3 being manifested that you are a letter of Christ, ministered to by us, having been written not with ink but with the Spirit of the living God, not on tablets of stone but on tablets of hearts of flesh.

4 And such confidence we have through Christ toward God.

5 Not that we are sufficient in ourselves to consider anything as *coming* from ourselves, but our sufficiency is from God,

6 who also made us sufficient *as* ministers of a new covenant, not of the letter but of the Spirit; for the letter kills, but the Spirit gives life.

7 But if the ministry of death, in letters having been engraved on stones, came with glory, so that the sons of Israel could not look intently at the face of Moses because of the glory of his face, which was being brought to an end,

8 how will the ministry of the Spirit not be even more in glory?

9 For if the ministry of condemnation has glory, much more does the ministry of righteousness abound in glory.

10 For indeed what had been glorious, in this case has no glory because of the glory that surpasses *it*.

11 For if that which was being brought to an end *was* with glory, much more that which remains *is* in glory.

12 Therefore having such a hope, we use great boldness,

13 and *are* not like Moses, *who* used to put a veil over his face so that the sons of Israel would not look intently

at the consequence of what was being brought to an end.

14 But their minds were hardened; for until this very day at the reading of the old covenant the same veil remains unlifted, because it is brought to an end in Christ.

15 But to this day whenever Moses is read, a veil lies over their heart,

16 but whenever a person TURNS TO THE LORD, THE VEIL IS TAKEN AWAY.

17 Now the Lord is the Spirit, and where the Spirit of the Lord is, *there* is freedom.

18 But we all, with unveiled face, beholding as in a mirror the glory of the Lord, are being transformed into the same image from glory to glory, just as from the Lord, the Spirit.

CHAPTER 4

The Gospel of the Glory of Christ

THEREFORE, since we have this ministry, as we received mercy, we do not lose heart,

2 but we have renounced the hidden things of shame, not walking in craftiness or adulterating the word of God, but by the manifestation of truth commending ourselves to every man's conscience in the sight of God.

3 And even if our gospel is veiled, it is veiled to those who are perishing,

4 in whose case the god of this age has blinded the minds of the unbelieving so that they might not see the light of the gospel of the glory of Christ, who is the image of God.

5 For we do not preach ourselves but Jesus Christ as Lord, and ourselves as your slaves for the sake of Jesus.

6 For God, who said, "Light shall shine out of darkness," is the One who has shone in our hearts to give the Light of the knowledge of the glory of God in the face of Christ.

7 But we have this treasure in earthen vessels, so that the surpassing greatness of the power will be of God and not from ourselves;

8 in every way afflicted, but not crushed; perplexed, but not despairing;

9 persecuted, but not forsaken; struck down, but not destroyed;

10 always carrying about in the body the dying of Jesus, so that the life of Jesus also may be manifested in our body.

11 For we who live are constantly being delivered over to death for Jesus' sake, so that the life of Jesus also may be manifested in our mortal flesh.

12 So death works in us, but life in you.

13 But having the same spirit of faith, according to what is written, "I BELIEVED, THEREFORE I SPOKE," we also believe, therefore we also speak,

14 knowing that He who raised the Lord Jesus will raise us also with Jesus and will present us with you.

15 For all things *are* for your sakes, so that the grace which is spreading to more and more people may cause the giving of thanks to abound to the glory of God.

16 Therefore we do not lose heart, but though our outer man is decaying,

yet our inner man is being renewed day by day.

17 For our momentary, light affliction is working out for us an eternal weight of glory far beyond all comparison.

18 while we look not at the things which are seen, but at the things which are not seen; for the things which are seen are temporal, but the things which are not seen are eternal.

CHAPTER 5

The Temporal and Eternal

FOR we know that if the earthly tent which is our house is torn down, we have a building from God, a house not made with hands, eternal in the heavens.

2 For indeed in this we groan, longing to be clothed with our dwelling from heaven,

3 inasmuch as we, having put it on, will not be found naked.

4 For indeed while we are in this tent, we groan, being burdened, because we do not want to be unclothed but to be clothed, so that what is mortal will be swallowed up by life.

5 Now He who prepared us for this very purpose is God, who gave to us the Spirit as a pledge.

6 Therefore, being always of good courage, and knowing that while we are at home in the body we are absent from the Lord—

7 for we walk by faith, not by sight—

8 we are of good courage and prefer rather to be absent from the body and to be at home with the Lord.

9 Therefore we also have as our ambition, whether at home or absent, to be pleasing to Him.

10 For we must all appear before the judgment seat of Christ, so that each one may be recompensed for his deeds in the body, according to what he has done, whether good or bad.

11 So then, knowing the fear of the Lord, we persuade men, but we have been made manifest to God; and I hope that we have been made manifest also in your consciences.

12 We are not again commending ourselves to you but *are* giving you an opportunity to boast of us, so that you will have *an answer* for those who boast in appearance and not in heart.

13 For if we are out of our mind, it is for God, or if we are of right mind, it is for you.

14 For the love of Christ controls us, having concluded this, that one died for all, therefore all died.

15 And He died for all, so that they who live would no longer live for themselves, but for Him who died and rose again on their behalf.

16 Therefore from now on we recognize no one according to the flesh; even though we have known Christ according to the flesh, yet now we know *Him in this way* no longer.

17 Therefore if anyone is in Christ, *he is* a new creation; the old things passed away; behold, new things have come.

18 Now all *these* things are from God, who reconciled us to Himself through Christ and gave us the ministry of reconciliation,

19 namely, that God was in Christ reconciling the world to Himself, not counting their transgressions against them, and He has committed to us the word of reconciliation.

20 So then, we are ambassadors for Christ, as God is pleading through us. We beg you on behalf of Christ, be reconciled to God.

21 He made Him who knew no sin *to be* sin on our behalf, so that we might become the righteousness of God in Him.

CHAPTER 6

Commendable Ministers of God

AND working together *with Him*, we also plead with you not to receive the grace of God in vain—

2 for He says,

"AT THE ACCEPTABLE TIME I LIS-
    TENED TO YOU,
AND ON THE DAY OF SALVATION I
    HELPED YOU."

Behold, now is "THE ACCEPTABLE TIME," behold, now is "THE DAY OF SALVATION"—

3 giving no cause for offense in anything, so that the ministry will not be discredited,

4 but in everything commending ourselves as ministers of God, in much perseverance, in afflictions, in distresses, in hardships,

5 in beatings, in imprisonments, in disturbances, in labors, in sleeplessness, in hunger,

6 in purity, in knowledge, in patience, in kindness, in the Holy Spirit, in unhypocritical love,

7 in the word of truth, in the power of God; by the weapons of righteousness for the right hand and the left,

8 by glory and dishonor, by evil report and good report; *regarded* as deceivers and *yet* true;

9 as unknown and *yet* well-known, as dying and *yet* behold, we live; as punished and *yet* not put to death,

10 as sorrowful but always rejoicing, as poor but making many rich, as having nothing and *yet* possessing all things.

11 Our mouth has spoken freely to you, O Corinthians, our heart is opened wide.

12 You are not restrained by us, but you are restrained in your own affections.

13 Now in a like exchange—I speak as to children—open wide *to us* also.

14 Do not be unequally yoked with unbelievers; for what partnership have righteousness and lawlessness, or what fellowship has light with darkness?

15 Or what harmony has Christ with Belial, or what has a believer in common with an unbeliever?

16 Or what agreement has a sanctuary of God with idols? For we are a sanctuary of the living God; just as God said,

"I WILL DWELL IN THEM AND WALK
    AMONG THEM;
AND I WILL BE THEIR GOD, AND
    THEY SHALL BE MY PEOPLE.
17 "Therefore, COME OUT FROM
    THEIR MIDST AND BE
    SEPARATE," says the Lord.
"AND DO NOT TOUCH WHAT IS
    UNCLEAN,
And I will welcome you.
18 "AND I WILL BE A FATHER TO YOU,
And you shall be sons and
    daughters to Me,"
SAYS THE LORD ALMIGHTY.

CHAPTER 7

THEREFORE, having these promises, beloved, let us cleanse ourselves
from all defilement of flesh and
spirit, perfecting holiness in the fear
of God.

Godly Sorrow Produces Repentance

2 Make room for us *in your
hearts.* We wronged no one, we corrupted no one, we took advantage of
no one.

3 I do not speak to condemn you,
for I have said before that you are in
our hearts to die together and to live
together.

4 Great is my boldness toward you;
great is my boasting on your behalf.
I have been filled with comfort; I
am overflowing with joy in all our
affliction.

5 For even when we came into
Macedonia our flesh had no rest, but
we were afflicted on every side—
conflicts without, fears within.

6 But God, who comforts the humbled, comforted us by the coming of
Titus;

7 and not only by his coming, but
also by the comfort with which he
was comforted in you, as he reported
to us your longing, your mourning,
your zeal for me, so that I rejoiced
even more.

8 For though I caused you sorrow
by my letter, I do not regret it, though
I did regret it—*for* I see that that letter caused you sorrow, though only
for a while—

9 I now rejoice, not that you were
made sorrowful, but that you were
made sorrowful to repentance. For
you were made to have godly sorrow,
so that you might not suffer loss in
anything through us.

10 For godly sorrow produces a
repentance without regret, *leading*
to salvation, but the sorrow of the
world brings about death.

11 For behold what earnestness this
very thing—this godly sorrow—has
brought about in you: what vindication of yourselves, what indignation,
what fear, what longing, what zeal,
what avenging of wrong! In everything you demonstrated yourselves
to be innocent in the matter.

12 So although I wrote to you, *it
was* not for the sake of the offender
nor for the sake of the one offended,
but that your earnestness on our behalf might be manifested to you in
the sight of God.

13 For this reason we have been comforted.

And besides our comfort, we rejoiced even much more for the joy of Titus, because his spirit has been refreshed by you all.

14 For if in anything I have boasted to him about you, I was not put to shame, but as we spoke all things to you in truth, so also our boasting before Titus proved to be *the* truth.

15 And his affection abounds all the more toward you, as he remembers the obedience of you all, how you received him with fear and trembling.

16 I rejoice that in everything I am encouraged about you.

CHAPTER 8

Generosity and Grace

NOW brothers, we make known to you the grace of God which has been given in the churches of Macedonia,

2 that in a great testing by affliction their abundance of joy and their deep poverty abounded unto the richness of their generosity.

3 For I testify that according to their ability, and beyond their ability, *they gave* of their own accord,

4 begging us with much urging for the grace of sharing in the ministry to the saints,

5 and *this*, not as we had expected, but they first gave themselves to the Lord and to us by the will of God.

6 So we encouraged Titus that as he had previously made a beginning, so he would also complete in you this gracious work as well.

7 But just as you abound in everything, in faith and word and knowledge and in all earnestness and in the love we inspired in you, *see* that you abound in this gracious work also.

8 I am not speaking *this* as a command, but as proving through the earnestness of others the sincerity of your love also.

9 For you know the grace of our Lord Jesus Christ, that though being rich, yet for your sake He became poor, so that you through His poverty might become rich.

10 And I give *my* opinion in this matter, for this is profitable for you, who were the first to begin a year ago not only to do *this*, but also to desire *to do it.*

11 But now complete doing it also, so that just as *there was* the readiness to desire it, so *there may be* also the completion of it from what you have.

12 For if the readiness is present, it is acceptable according to what *a person* has, not according to what he does not have.

13 For *this* is not for the relief of others *and* for your affliction, but by way of equality—

14 at this present time your abundance *being a supply* for their need, so that their abundance also may become *a supply* for your need, that there may be equality.

15 As it is written, "HE WHO *gathered* MUCH DID NOT HAVE TOO MUCH, AND HE WHO *gathered* LITTLE HAD NO LACK."

16 But thanks be to God who puts the same earnestness on your behalf in the heart of Titus.

17 For he not only accepted our plea, but being himself very earnest, he has gone out to you of his own accord.

18 And we have sent along with him the brother whose praise in *the things of* the gospel is throughout all the churches.

19 And not only *this*, but he has also been appointed by the churches to travel with us in this gracious work that is being ministered by us for the glory of the Lord Himself, and *to show* our readiness,

20 taking precaution lest anyone discredits us in our ministering of this generous gift,

21 for we respect what is good, not only in the sight of the Lord, but also in the sight of men.

22 And we have sent with them our brother, whom we have often tested and found earnest in many things, but now even more earnest because of *his* great confidence in you.

23 As for Titus, *he is* my partner and fellow worker among you; as for our brothers, *they are* messengers of the churches, a glory to Christ.

24 Therefore openly before the churches, show them the proof of your love and of our reason for boasting about you.

CHAPTER 9

God Loves a Cheerful Giver

FOR it is superfluous for me to write to you about this ministry to the saints;

2 for I know your readiness, of which I boast about you to the Macedonians, that Achaia has been prepared since last year, and your zeal stirred up most of them.

3 But I have sent the brothers, in order that our boasting about you may not be made empty in this case, so that, as I was saying, you may be prepared;

4 lest if any Macedonians come with me and find you unprepared, we—not to speak of you—be put to shame in this certainty *of ours*.

5 So I regarded it necessary to encourage the brothers that they would go on ahead to you and arrange beforehand your previously promised blessing, so that the same would be ready as a blessing and not as a begrudging obligation.

6 Now this *I say*, he who sows sparingly will also reap sparingly, and he who sows with blessing will also reap with blessing.

7 Each one *must do* just as he has purposed in his heart, not grudgingly or under compulsion, for God loves a cheerful giver.

8 And God is able to make every grace abound to you, so that in everything at every time having every sufficiency, you may have an abundance for every good deed;

9 as it is written,

> "HE SCATTERED ABROAD, HE GAVE
> TO THE NEEDY,
> HIS RIGHTEOUSNESS STANDS
> FOREVER."

10 Now He who supplies SEED TO THE SOWER AND BREAD FOR FOOD will supply and multiply your seed and increase the harvest of your righteousness;

11 you will be enriched in everything for all generosity, which through us is bringing about thanksgiving to God.

12 For the ministry of this service is not only fully supplying the needs of the saints, but is also abounding through many thanksgivings to God.

13 Because of the proven character given by this ministry, they will glorify God for *your* obedience to your confession of the gospel of Christ and for the generosity of your fellowship toward them and toward all,

14 while they also, by prayer on your behalf, long for you because of the surpassing grace of God on you.

15 Thanks be to God for His indescribable gift!

CHAPTER 10

Paul Defends His Authority

NOW I, Paul, myself plead with you by the gentleness and forbearance of Christ—I who am humble when face-to-face with you, but courageous toward you when absent!

2 But I beg that when I am present I *need* not act *so* courageously with the confidence that I consider to daringly *use* against some, who consider us as if we walked according to the flesh.

3 For though we walk in the flesh, we do not war according to the flesh,

4 for the weapons of our warfare are not of the flesh, but divinely powerful for the tearing down of strongholds,

5 as we tear down speculations and every lofty thing raised up against the knowledge of God, and take every thought captive to the obedience of Christ,

6 and are ready to punish all disobedience, whenever your obedience is fulfilled.

7 You are looking at things as they are outwardly. If anyone is confident in himself that he is Christ's, let him consider this again within himself, that just as he is Christ's, so also are we.

8 For even if I boast somewhat further about our authority, which the Lord gave for building you up and not for tearing you down, I will not be put to shame;

9 for I do not wish to seem as if I would terrify you by my letters.

10 For they say, "His letters are weighty and strong, but his personal presence is weak and his words contemptible."

11 Let such a person consider this, that what we are in word by letters when absent, such persons we are also in deed when present.

12 For we do not dare to classify or compare ourselves with some of those who commend themselves, but when they measure themselves by themselves and compare themselves with themselves, they are without understanding.

13 But we will not boast beyond *our* measure, but within the measure of the area of influence which God apportioned to us as a measure, to reach even as far as you.

14 For we are not overextending ourselves, as if we did not reach you, (for we were the first to come even as far as you in the gospel of Christ),

15 not boasting beyond *our* measure in other men's labors, but having the hope—that as your faith grows—to be enlarged even more by you within our area of influence,

16 so as to proclaim the gospel even to the regions beyond you, *and* not to boast in what has been accomplished in the area of influence of another.

17 But HE WHO BOASTS IS TO BOAST IN THE LORD.

18 For it is not the one who commends himself that is approved, but the one whom the Lord commends.

CHAPTER 11

Paul Defends His Apostleship

I wish that you would bear with me in a little foolishness, but indeed you are bearing with me.

2 For I am jealous for you with a godly jealousy, for I betrothed you to one husband, so that I might present you *as* a pure virgin to Christ.

3 But I fear that, as the serpent deceived Eve by his craftiness, your minds will be corrupted from the simplicity and purity *of devotion* to Christ.

4 For if one comes and preaches another Jesus whom we did not preach, or you receive a different spirit which you did not receive, or a different gospel which you did not accept, you bear *this* beautifully.

5 For I consider myself in no way inferior to the most-eminent apostles.

6 But even if I am unskilled in word, yet I am not *so* in knowledge; in fact, in every way we have made *this* evident to you in all things.

7 Or did I commit a sin in humbling myself so that you might be exalted, because I proclaimed the gospel of God to you without charge?

8 I robbed other churches by taking wages *from them* to minister to you.

9 And when I was present with you and was in need, I was not a burden to anyone; for when the brothers came from Macedonia they fully supplied my need, and in everything I kept and will keep myself from being a burden to you.

10 As the truth of Christ is in me, this boasting of mine will not be stopped in the regions of Achaia.

11 Why? Because I do not love you? God knows I *do*!

12 But what I am doing I will continue to do, so that I may cut off opportunity from those who desire an opportunity to be found just as we are in the matter about which they are boasting.

13 For such men are false apostles, deceitful workers, disguising themselves as apostles of Christ.

14 And no wonder, for even Satan disguises himself as an angel of light.

15 Therefore it is not surprising if his ministers also disguise themselves as ministers of righteousness, whose end will be according to their deeds.

16 Again I say, let no one think me foolish; but if *you do*, receive me even as foolish, so that I also may boast a little.

17 What I am saying, I am not saying according to the Lord, but as in foolishness, in this confidence of boasting.

18 Since many boast according to the flesh, I will boast also.

19 For you, being *so* wise, are bearing the foolish gladly.

20 For you bear it if anyone enslaves you, anyone devours you, anyone takes advantage of you, anyone exalts himself, anyone hits you in the face.

21 To *my* shame I *must* say that we have been weak *by comparison.*

But in whatever respect anyone *else* is daring—I speak in foolishness— I am just as daring myself.

22 Are they Hebrews? So am I. Are they Israelites? So am I. Are they Abraham's seed? So am I.

23 Are they ministers of Christ?—I speak as if insane—I more so; in far more labors, in far more imprisonments, in beatings without number, in frequent danger of death.

24 Five times I received from the Jews forty *lashes* less one.

25 Three times I was beaten with rods, once I was stoned, three times I was shipwrecked—a night and a day I have spent in the deep.

26 *I have been* on frequent journeys, in dangers from rivers, dangers from robbers, dangers from *my* countrymen, dangers from the Gentiles, dangers in the city, dangers in the desolate places, dangers on the sea, dangers among false brothers.

27 *I have been* in labor and hardship, in many sleepless nights, in starvation and thirst, often hungry, in cold and without enough clothing.

28 Apart from *such* external things, there is the daily pressure on me *of* concern for all the churches.

29 Who is weak without my being weak? Who is made to stumble without my burning concern?

30 If I have to boast, I will boast of what pertains to my weakness.

31 The God and Father of the Lord Jesus, He who is blessed forever, knows that I am not lying.

32 In Damascus the ethnarch under Aretas the king was guarding the city of the Damascenes in order to seize me,

33 and I was let down in a basket through a window in the wall, and *so* escaped his hands.

CHAPTER 12

A Vision of Paradise

IT is necessary to boast, though it is not profitable, but I will go on to visions and revelations of the Lord.

2 I know a man in Christ who fourteen years ago—whether in the body I do not know, or out of the body I do not know, God knows—such a man was caught up to the third heaven.

3 And I know how such a man—whether in the body or apart from the body I do not know, God knows—

4 was caught up into Paradise and heard inexpressible words, which a man is not permitted to speak.

5 On behalf of such a man I will boast, but on my own behalf I will not boast, except in weaknesses.

6 For if I do wish to boast I will not be foolish, for I will be speaking the truth; but I refrain *from this*, so that no one will consider me beyond what he sees *in* me or hears from me.

A Thorn in the Flesh

7 Because of the surpassing greatness of the revelations, for this reason, to keep me from exalting myself, there was given me a thorn in the flesh, a messenger of Satan to torment me—to keep me from exalting myself!

8 Concerning this I pleaded with the Lord three times that it might leave me.

9 And He has said to me, "My grace is sufficient for you, for power is perfected in weakness." Most gladly, therefore, I will rather boast in my weaknesses, so that the power of Christ may dwell in me.

10 Therefore I am well content with weaknesses, with insults, with distresses, with persecutions and hardships, for the sake of Christ, for when I am weak, then I am strong.

Concern for the Corinthian Church

11 I have become foolish; you yourselves compelled me. For I ought to have been commended by you, for in no respect was I inferior to the most-eminent apostles, even if I am nothing.

12 The signs of a true apostle were worked out among you with all perseverance, by signs and wonders and miracles.

13 For in what respect were you treated as less than the rest of the churches, except that I myself did not become a burden to you? Forgive me this wrong!

14 Here for this third time I am ready to come to you, and I will not be a burden to you; for I do not seek what is yours, but you. For children ought not to save up for *their* parents, but parents for *their* children.

15 So I will most gladly spend and be fully spent for your souls. If I love you more, am I to be loved less?

16 But be that as it may, I did not burden you myself. Nevertheless,

crafty fellow that I am, I took you in by deceit.

17 Have I taken advantage of you through any of those whom I have sent to you?

18 I encouraged Titus *to go*, and I sent the brother with him. Did Titus take any advantage of you? Did we not walk in the same spirit—in the very same steps?

19 All this time you think we are defending ourselves to you. We speak in Christ in the sight of God. And all *these* things, beloved, are for your building up.

20 For I am afraid that perhaps when I come I may find you to be not what I wish and may be found by you to be not what you wish; that perhaps *there will be* strife, jealousy, outbursts of anger, selfish ambition, slanders, gossip, arrogance, disturbances.

21 *I am afraid that* when I come again my God may humiliate me before you, and I may mourn over many of those who have sinned in the past and not repented of the impurity, sexual immorality, and sensuality which they have practiced.

CHAPTER 13

Examine Yourselves

THIS is the third time I am coming to you. By the mouth of two or three witnesses every matter shall be confirmed.

2 I have previously said when present the second time, and though now absent I say in advance to those who have sinned in the past and to all the rest *as well*, that if I come again I will not spare *anyone*,

3 since you are seeking proof that Christ speaks in me; He is not weak toward you, but mighty in you.

4 For indeed He was crucified because of weakness, yet He lives because of the power of God. For we also are weak in Him, yet we will live with Him because of the power of God toward you.

5 Test yourselves *to see* if you are in the faith; examine yourselves! Or do you not recognize about yourselves that Jesus Christ is in you— unless indeed you fail the test?

6 But I hope that you will realize that we ourselves do not fail the test.

7 Now we pray to God that you do no wrong, not that we ourselves may appear approved, but that you may do what is right, even though we may appear unapproved.

8 For we can do nothing against the truth, but *only* for the truth.

9 For we rejoice when we ourselves are weak but you are strong. This we also pray for, that you be restored.

10 For this reason I am writing these things while absent, so that when present I *need* not use severity, in accordance with the authority which the Lord gave me for building up and not for tearing down.

11 Finally, brothers, rejoice, be restored, be comforted, be like-minded,

live in peace, and the God of love and peace will be with you.

12 Greet one another with a holy kiss.

13 All the saints greet you.

14 The grace of the Lord Jesus Christ, and the love of God, and the fellowship of the Holy Spirit, be with you all.

THE LETTER OF PAUL TO THE

GALATIANS

CHAPTER 1

Greetings and Grace

PAUL, an apostle—not *sent* from men nor through man, but through Jesus Christ and God the Father, who raised Him from the dead—

2 and all the brothers who are with me,

To the churches of Galatia:

3 Grace to you and peace from God our Father and the Lord Jesus Christ,

4 who gave Himself for our sins so that He might rescue us from this present evil age, according to the will of our God and Father,

5 to whom *be* the glory forever and ever. Amen.

Distorting the Gospel

6 I marvel that you are so quickly deserting Him who called you by the grace of Christ for a different gospel,

7 which is *really* not another, only there are some who are disturbing you and want to distort the gospel of Christ.

8 But even if we, or an angel from heaven, should proclaim to you a gospel contrary to the gospel we have proclaimed to you, let him be accursed!

9 As we have said before, so I say again now, if any man is proclaiming to you a gospel contrary to what you received, let him be accursed!

10 For am I now seeking the favor of men, or of God? Or am I striving to please men? If I were still trying to please men, I would not be a slave of Christ.

Paul Called by God

11 For I make known to you, brothers, that the gospel which I am proclaiming as good news is not according to man.

12 For I neither received it from man, nor was I taught it, but *I received it* through a revelation of Jesus Christ.

13 For you have heard of my former conduct in Judaism, how I used to persecute the church of God beyond measure and tried to destroy it.

14 And I was advancing in Judaism beyond many of my contemporaries among my countrymen, being far more zealous for the traditions of my fathers.

15 But when God, who had set me apart from my mother's womb and called me through His grace, was pleased

16 to reveal His Son in me so that I might proclaim Him as good news among the Gentiles, I did not immediately consult with flesh and blood,

17 nor did I go up to Jerusalem to those who were apostles before me, but I went away to Arabia, and returned once more to Damascus.

18 Then three years later I went up to Jerusalem to become acquainted with Cephas, and stayed with him fifteen days.

19 But I did not see any other of the apostles except James, the Lord's brother

20 (now in what I am writing to you, I assure you before God that I am not lying!)

21 Then I went into the regions of Syria and Cilicia.

22 And I was *still* unknown by sight to the churches of Judea which are in Christ;

23 but only, they kept hearing, "He who once persecuted us is now proclaiming the good news of the faith which he once tried to destroy."

24 And they were glorifying God because of me.

CHAPTER 2

Paul Accepted by the Apostles

THEN after fourteen years I went up again to Jerusalem with Barnabas, taking Titus along also.

2 And I went up because of a revelation, and I laid out to them the gospel which I preach among the Gentiles, but I did so in private to those who were of reputation, lest somehow I might be running, or had run, in vain.

3 But not even Titus, who was with me, though he was a Greek, was compelled to be circumcised.

4 But *this was* because of the false brothers secretly brought in, who had sneaked in to spy out our freedom which we have in Christ Jesus, in order to enslave us.

5 But we did not yield in subjection to them for even a moment, so that the truth of the gospel would remain with you.

6 But from those who were of high reputation (what they were makes no difference to me; God shows no partiality)—well, those who were of reputation contributed nothing to me.

7 But on the contrary, seeing that I had been entrusted with the gospel to the uncircumcised, just as Peter *had been* to the circumcised

8 (for He who worked in Peter unto *his* apostleship to the circumcised worked in me also unto the Gentiles),

9 and recognizing the grace that had been given to me, James and

Cephas and John, who were reputed to be pillars, gave to me and Barnabas the right hand of fellowship, so that we *might go* to the Gentiles and they to the circumcised.

10 Only *they asked* us to remember the poor—the very thing I also was eager to do.

Paul Opposes Peter (Cephas)

11 But when Cephas came to Antioch, I opposed him to his face, because he stood condemned.

12 For prior to the coming of certain men from James, he used to eat with the Gentiles, but when they came, he *began to* shrink back and separate himself, fearing the party of the circumcision.

13 And the rest of the Jews joined him in hypocrisy, with the result that even Barnabas was carried away by their hypocrisy.

14 But when I saw that they were not straightforward about the truth of the gospel, I said to Cephas before everyone, "If you, being a Jew, live like the Gentiles and not like the Jews, how *is it that* you compel the Gentiles to live like Jews?

15 "We *are* Jews by nature and not sinners from among the Gentiles;

16 nevertheless knowing that a man is not justified by the works of the Law but through faith in Jesus Christ, even we have believed in Christ Jesus, so that we may be justified by faith in Christ and not by the works of the Law; since by the works of the Law no flesh will be justified.

17 "But if, while seeking to be justified in Christ, we ourselves have also been found sinners, is Christ then a minister of sin? May it never be!

18 "For if I rebuild what I have *once* destroyed, I prove myself to be a transgressor.

19 "For through the Law I died to the Law, so that I might live to God.

20 "I have been crucified with Christ, and it is no longer I who live, but Christ lives in me. And the *life* which I now live in the flesh I live by faith in the Son of God, who loved me and gave Himself up for me.

21 "I do not set aside the grace of God, for if righteousness *comes* through the Law, then Christ died needlessly."

CHAPTER 3

The Righteous Shall Live by Faith

O foolish Galatians, who bewitched you, before whose eyes Jesus Christ was publicly portrayed *as* crucified?

2 This is the only thing I want to learn from you: did you receive the Spirit by the works of the Law, or by hearing with faith?

3 Are you so foolish? Having begun by the Spirit, are you now being perfected by the flesh?

4 Did you suffer so many things for nothing—if indeed it was for nothing?

5 So then, does He who provides you with the Spirit and works miracles among you, do it by the works of the Law, or by hearing with faith?

6 Just as Abraham BELIEVED GOD AND IT WAS COUNTED TO HIM AS RIGHTEOUSNESS,

7 so know that those who are of faith, those are sons of Abraham.

8 And the Scripture, foreseeing that God would justify the Gentiles by faith, proclaimed the gospel beforehand to Abraham, *saying,* "ALL THE NATIONS WILL BE BLESSED IN YOU."

9 So then those who are of faith are blessed with Abraham, the believer.

10 For as many as are of the works of the Law are under a curse, for it is written, "CURSED IS EVERYONE WHO DOES NOT ABIDE BY ALL THINGS WRITTEN IN THE BOOK OF THE LAW, TO DO THEM."

11 Now that no one is justified by the Law before God is evident, for "THE RIGHTEOUS SHALL LIVE BY FAITH."

12 However, the Law is not of faith; rather, "HE WHO DOES THEM SHALL LIVE BY THEM."

13 Christ redeemed us from the curse of the Law, having become a curse for us—for it is written, "CURSED IS EVERYONE WHO HANGS ON A TREE"—

14 in order that in Christ Jesus the blessing of Abraham might come to the Gentiles, so that we would receive the promise of the Spirit through faith.

The Promise by Faith

15 Brothers, I speak in human terms: even though it is *only* a man's covenant, yet when it has been ratified, no one sets it aside or adds conditions to it.

16 Now the promises were spoken to Abraham and to his seed. He does not say, "And to seeds," as *referring* to many, but *rather* to one, "And TO YOUR SEED," that is, Christ.

17 And what I am saying is this: the Law, which came 430 years later, does not invalidate a covenant previously ratified by God, so as to abolish the promise.

18 For if the inheritance is by law, it is no longer by promise, but God has granted it to Abraham through promise.

19 Why the Law then? It was added because of trespasses, having been ordained through angels by the hand of a mediator, until the seed would come to whom the promise had been made.

20 Now a mediator is not for one *person only,* whereas God is one.

21 Is the Law then contrary to the promises of God? May it never be! For if a law had been given which was able to impart life, then righteousness would indeed be by law.

22 But the Scripture has shut up everyone under sin, so that the promise by faith in Jesus Christ might be given to those who believe.

23 But before faith came, we were held in custody under the Law, being shut up for the coming faith to be revealed.

24 Therefore the Law has become our tutor unto Christ, so that we may be justified by faith.

25 But now that faith has come, we are no longer under a tutor.

26 For you are all sons of God through faith in Christ Jesus.

27 For all of you who were baptized into Christ have clothed yourselves with Christ.

28 There is neither Jew nor Greek, there is neither slave nor free man, there is no male and female, for you are all one in Christ Jesus.

29 And if you belong to Christ, then you are Abraham's seed, heirs according to promise.

CHAPTER 4

Sonship in Christ

NOW I say, as long as the heir is a child, he does not differ at all from a slave although he is owner of everything,

2 but he is under guardians and stewards until the date set by the father.

3 So also we, while we were children, were enslaved under the elemental things of the world.

4 But when the fullness of the time came, God sent forth His Son, born of a woman, born under the Law,

5 so that He might redeem those who were under the Law, that we might receive the adoption as sons.

6 And because you are sons, God sent forth the Spirit of His Son into our hearts, crying, "Abba! Father!"

7 Therefore you are no longer a slave, but a son; and if a son, then an heir through God.

8 However at that time, when you did not know God, you were slaves to those which by nature are no gods.

9 But now, having known God, or rather having been known by God, how is it that you turn back again to the weak and worthless elemental things, to which you want to be enslaved all over again?

10 You observe days and months and seasons and years.

11 I fear for you, that perhaps I have labored over you for nothing.

12 I beg of you, brothers, become as I *am*, for I also *have become* as you *are*. You have done me no wrong.

13 But you know that it was because of a bodily illness that I proclaimed the gospel to you the first time;

14 and that which was a trial to you in my bodily condition you did not despise or loathe, but you received me as an angel of God, as Christ Jesus *Himself*.

15 Where then is that sense of blessing you had? For I testify to you that, if possible, you would have plucked out your eyes and given them to me.

16 So have I become your enemy by telling you the truth?

17 They zealously seek you, not commendably, but they wish to shut you out so that you will zealously seek them.

18 But it is good always to be zealously sought in a commendable manner, and not only when I am present with you.

19 My children, with whom I am again in labor until Christ is formed in you—

20 but I could wish to be present with you now and to change my tone, because I am perplexed about you.

An Allegory of Two Covenants

21 Tell me, you who want to be under law, do you not listen to the Law?

22 For it is written that Abraham had two sons, one by the servant-woman and one by the free woman.

23 But the son by the servant-woman had been born according to the flesh, while the son by the free woman through the promise.

24 This is spoken with allegory, for these women are two covenants: one from Mount Sinai bearing children into slavery; she is Hagar.

25 Now this Hagar is Mount Sinai in Arabia and corresponds to the present Jerusalem, for she is in slavery with her children.

26 But the Jerusalem above is free; she is our mother.

27 For it is written,

"REJOICE, BARREN WOMAN WHO
    DOES NOT GIVE BIRTH;
BREAK FORTH AND SHOUT, YOU
    WHO ARE NOT IN LABOR;
FOR MORE NUMEROUS ARE
    THE CHILDREN OF THE
    DESOLATE ONE
THAN OF THE ONE WHO HAS A
    HUSBAND."

28 And you brothers, in accordance with Isaac, are children of promise.

29 But as at that time he who was born according to the flesh was persecuting him *who was born* according to the Spirit, so it is now also.

30 But what does the Scripture say?

"CAST OUT THE SERVANT-WOMAN
    AND HER SON,
FOR THE SON OF THE SERVANT-
    WOMAN SHALL NOT BE AN
    HEIR WITH THE SON OF THE
    FREE WOMAN."

31 So then, brothers, we are not children of a servant-woman, but of the free woman.

CHAPTER 5

Christ Set Us Free

IT was for freedom that Christ set us free. Therefore, stand firm and do not be subject again to a yoke of slavery.

2 Behold I, Paul, say to you that if you receive circumcision, Christ will be of no benefit to you.

3 And I testify again to every man who receives circumcision, that he is under obligation to keep the whole Law.

4 You have been severed from Christ, you who are being justified by law; you have fallen from grace!

5 For we through the Spirit, by faith, are eagerly waiting for the hope of righteousness.

6 For in Christ Jesus neither circumcision nor uncircumcision means anything, but faith working through love.

7 You were running well; who hindered you from obeying the truth?

8 This persuasion *is* not from Him who calls you.

9 A little leaven leavens the whole lump.

10 I have confidence in you in the

Lord that you will adopt no other view. But the one who is disturbing you will bear his judgment, whoever he is.

11 But I, brothers, if I still preach circumcision, why am I still persecuted? Then the stumbling block of the cross would have been abolished.

12 I wish that those who are upsetting you would even mutilate themselves.

13 For you were called to freedom, brothers; only *do* not *turn* your freedom into an opportunity for the flesh, but through love serve one another.

14 For the whole Law is fulfilled in one word, in this: "YOU SHALL LOVE YOUR NEIGHBOR AS YOURSELF."

15 But if you bite and devour one another, beware that you are not consumed by one another.

Walk by the Spirit

16 But I say, walk by the Spirit and you will not carry out the desire of the flesh.

17 For the flesh sets its desire against the Spirit, and the Spirit against the flesh; for these are in opposition to one another, so that you do not do the things that you want.

18 But if you are led by the Spirit, you are not under the Law.

19 Now the deeds of the flesh are evident, which are: sexual immorality, impurity, sensuality,

20 idolatry, sorcery, enmities, strife, jealousy, outbursts of anger, selfish ambition, dissensions, factions,

21 envying, drunkenness, carousing, and things like these, of which I forewarn you, just as I have forewarned you, that those who practice such things will not inherit the kingdom of God.

22 But the fruit of the Spirit is love, joy, peace, patience, kindness, goodness, faithfulness,

23 gentleness, self-control. Against such things there is no law.

24 Now those who belong to Christ Jesus crucified the flesh with its passions and desires.

25 If we live by the Spirit, let us also walk in step with the Spirit.

26 Let us not become *those* with vain glory, challenging one another, envying one another.

CHAPTER 6

Bear One Another's Burdens

BROTHERS, even if anyone is caught in any transgression, you who are spiritual, restore such a one in a spirit of gentleness, *each of you* looking to yourself, so that you too will not be tempted.

2 Bear one another's burdens, and so fulfill the law of Christ.

3 For if anyone thinks he is something when he is nothing, he deceives himself.

4 But each one must examine his own work, and then he will have *reason for* boasting in regard to himself alone, and not in regard to another.

5 For each one will bear his own load.

6 And the one who is instructed in the word is to share in all good things with the one who instructs *him*.

7 Do not be deceived, God is not mocked, for whatever a man sows, this he will also reap.

8 For the one who sows to his own flesh will from the flesh reap corruption, but the one who sows to the Spirit will from the Spirit reap eternal life.

9 And let us not lose heart in doing good, for in due time we will reap if we do not grow weary.

10 So then, while we have opportunity, let us do good to all people, and especially to those who are of the household of the faith.

11 See with what large letters I am writing to you with my own hand!

12 As many as are wanting to make a good showing in the flesh, these are trying to compel you to be circumcised, simply so that they will not be persecuted for the cross of Christ.

13 For those who are circumcised do not even keep the Law themselves, but they want to have you circumcised so that they may boast in your flesh.

14 But may it never be that I would boast, except in the cross of our Lord Jesus Christ, through which the world has been crucified to me, and I to the world.

15 For neither is circumcision anything, nor uncircumcision, but a new creation.

16 And those who will walk in step with this rule, peace and mercy *be* upon them, and upon the Israel of God.

17 From now on let no one cause trouble for me, for I bear on my body the marks of Jesus.

18 The grace of our Lord Jesus Christ be with your spirit, brothers. Amen.

THE LETTER OF PAUL TO THE

EPHESIANS

CHAPTER 1

Spiritual Blessings in Christ

PAUL, an apostle of Christ Jesus by the will of God,

To the saints who are at Ephesus and *who are* faithful in Christ Jesus:

2 Grace to you and peace from God our Father and the Lord Jesus Christ.

3 Blessed *be* the God and Father of our Lord Jesus Christ, who has blessed us with every spiritual blessing in the heavenly *places* in Christ,

4 just as He chose us in Him before the foundation of the world, that we would be holy and blameless before Him in love,

5 by predestining us to adoption as sons through Jesus Christ to Himself,

according to the good pleasure of His will,

6 to the praise of the glory of His grace, which He graciously bestowed on us in the Beloved.

7 In Him we have redemption through His blood, the forgiveness of our transgressions, according to the riches of His grace

8 which He caused to abound to us in all wisdom and insight,

9 making known to us the mystery of His will, according to His good pleasure which He purposed in Him

10 for an administration of the fullness of the times, *that is*, the summing up of all things in Christ, things in the heavens and things on the earth in Him.

11 In Him, we also have been made an inheritance, having been predestined according to the purpose of Him who works all things according to the counsel of His will,

12 to the end that we who first have hoped in Christ would be to the praise of His glory.

13 In Him, you also, after listening to the word of truth, the gospel of your salvation—having also believed, you were sealed in Him with the Holy Spirit of promise,

14 who is given as a pledge of our inheritance, unto the redemption of *God's own* possession, to the praise of His glory.

15 For this reason I too, having heard of the faith in the Lord Jesus which *exists* among you and your love for all the saints,

16 do not cease giving thanks for you, while making mention *of you* in my prayers:

17 that the God of our Lord Jesus Christ, the Father of glory, may give to you *the* Spirit of wisdom and of revelation in the full knowledge of Him,

18 so that you—the eyes of your heart having been enlightened—will know what is the hope of His calling, what are the riches of the glory of His inheritance in the saints,

19 and what is the surpassing greatness of His power toward us who believe according to the working of the might of His strength,

20 which He worked in Christ, by raising Him from the dead and seating Him at His right hand in the heavenly *places*,

21 far above all rule and authority and power and dominion, and every name that is named, not only in this age but also in the one to come.

22 And HE PUT ALL THINGS IN SUBJECTION UNDER HIS FEET, and gave Him as head over all things to the church,

23 which is His body, the fullness of Him who fills all in all.

CHAPTER 2

By Grace Through Faith

AND you were dead in your transgressions and sins,

2 in which you formerly walked according to the course of this world, according to the ruler of the power of

the air, the spirit that is now working in the sons of disobedience,

3 among whom we all also formerly conducted ourselves in the lusts of our flesh, doing the desires of the flesh and of the mind, and were by nature children of wrath, even as the rest.

4 But God, being rich in mercy because of His great love with which He loved us,

5 even when we were dead in our transgressions, made us alive together with Christ—by grace you have been saved—

6 and raised us up with Him, and seated us with Him in the heavenly *places* in Christ Jesus,

7 so that in the ages to come He might show the surpassing riches of His grace in kindness toward us in Christ Jesus.

8 For by grace you have been saved through faith, and this not of yourselves, *it is* the gift of God;

9 not of works, so that no one may boast.

10 For we are His workmanship, created in Christ Jesus for good works, which God prepared beforehand so that we would walk in them.

11 Therefore, remember that formerly you—the Gentiles in the flesh, who are called "Uncircumcision" by the so-called "Circumcision," *which is* performed in the flesh by *human* hands—

12 *remember* that you were at that time without Christ, alienated from the citizenship of Israel, and strangers to the covenants of promise, having no hope and without God in the world.

13 But now in Christ Jesus you who formerly were far off have been brought near by the blood of Christ.

14 For He Himself is our peace, who made both *groups* one and broke down the dividing wall of the partition

15 by abolishing in His flesh the enmity, the Law of commandments *contained* in ordinances, so that in Himself He might create the two into one new man, making peace,

16 and might reconcile them both in one body to God through the cross, having in Himself put to death the enmity.

17 AND HE CAME AND PREACHED THE GOOD NEWS OF PEACE TO YOU WHO WERE FAR AWAY, AND PEACE TO THOSE WHO WERE NEAR;

18 for through Him we both have our access in one Spirit to the Father.

19 So then you are no longer strangers and sojourners, but you are fellow citizens with the saints, and are of God's household,

20 having been built on the foundation of the apostles and prophets, Christ Jesus Himself being the corner *stone*,

21 in whom the whole building, being joined together, is growing into a holy sanctuary in the Lord,

22 in whom you also are being built together into a dwelling of God in the Spirit.

CHAPTER 3

The Mystery of Christ Revealed

FOR this reason I, Paul, the prisoner of Christ Jesus on behalf of you Gentiles—

2 if indeed you heard of the stewardship of God's grace which was given to me for you;

3 that by revelation there was made known to me the mystery, as I wrote before in brief.

4 About which, when you read you can understand my insight into the mystery of Christ,

5 which in other generations was not made known to the sons of men, as it was now revealed to His holy apostles and prophets in the Spirit:

6 that the Gentiles are fellow heirs and fellow members of the body, and fellow partakers of the promise in Christ Jesus through the gospel,

7 of which I was made a minister, according to the gift of God's grace which was given to me according to the working of His power.

8 To me, the very least of all saints, this grace was given, to proclaim to the Gentiles the good news of the unfathomable riches of Christ,

9 and to bring to light for all what is the administration of the mystery which for ages has been hidden in God who created all things;

10 so that the manifold wisdom of God might now be made known through the church to the rulers and the authorities in the heavenly *places*.

11 *This was* in accordance with the eternal purpose which He carried out in Christ Jesus our Lord,

12 in whom we have boldness and confident access through faith in Him.

13 Therefore I ask you not to lose heart at my afflictions on your behalf, which are your glory.

Prayer for Spiritual Power

14 For this reason I bow my knees before the Father,

15 from whom every family in heaven and on earth is named,

16 that He would give you, according to the riches of His glory, to be strengthened with power through His Spirit in the inner man,

17 so that Christ may dwell in your hearts through faith; *and* that you, being firmly rooted and grounded in love,

18 may be able to comprehend with all the saints what is the breadth and length and height and depth,

19 and to know the love of Christ which surpasses knowledge, that you may be filled up to all the fullness of God.

20 Now to Him who is able to do far more abundantly beyond all that we ask or understand, according to the power that works within us,

21 to Him *be* the glory in the church and in Christ Jesus to all generations forever and ever. Amen.

CHAPTER 4

Unity of the Spirit

THEREFORE I, the prisoner in the Lord, exhort you to walk worthy of the calling with which you have been called,

2 with all humility and gentleness, with patience, bearing with one another in love,

3 being diligent to keep the unity of the Spirit in the bond of peace.

4 *There is* one body and one Spirit, just as also you were called in one hope of your calling;

5 one Lord, one faith, one baptism;

6 one God and Father of all who is over all and through all and in all.

7 But to each one of us grace was given according to the measure of Christ's gift.

8 Therefore it says,

"WHEN HE ASCENDED ON HIGH,
HE LED CAPTIVE A HOST OF
    CAPTIVES,
And HE GAVE GIFTS TO MEN."

9 (Now this *expression*, "He ascended," what does it mean except that He also descended into the lower parts of the earth?

10 He who descended is Himself also He who ascended far above all the heavens, so that He might fill all things.)

11 And He Himself gave some *as* apostles, and some *as* prophets, and some *as* evangelists, and some *as* pastors and teachers,

12 for the equipping of the saints for the work of service, to the building up of the body of Christ,

13 until we all attain to the unity of the faith, and of the full knowledge of the Son of God, to a mature man, to the measure of the stature which belongs to the fullness of Christ,

14 so that we are no longer to be children, tossed here and there by waves and carried about by every wind of doctrine, by the trickery of men, by craftiness in deceitful scheming,

15 but speaking the truth in love, we are to grow up in all *aspects* into Him who is the head, *that is* Christ,

16 from whom the whole body, being joined and held together by what every joint supplies, according to the properly measured working of each individual part, causes the growth of the body for the building up of itself in love.

Put On the New Man

17 Therefore this I say, and testify in the Lord, that you walk no longer just as the Gentiles also walk, in the futility of their mind,

18 being darkened in their mind, alienated from the life of God because of the ignorance that is in them, because of the hardness of their heart.

19 *And* they, having become callous, have given themselves over to sensuality for the practice of every kind of impurity with greediness.

20 But you did not learn Christ in this way—

21 if indeed you heard Him and were taught in Him, just as truth is in Jesus,

22 to lay aside, in reference to your former conduct, the old man, which is being corrupted in accordance with the lusts of deceit,

23 and to be renewed in the spirit of your mind,

24 and to put on the new man, which in *the likeness of* God has been created in righteousness and holiness of the truth.

25 Therefore, laying aside falsehood, SPEAK TRUTH EACH ONE *of you* WITH HIS NEIGHBOR, for we are members of one another.

26 BE ANGRY, AND *yet* DO NOT SIN; do not let the sun go down on your anger,

27 and do not give the devil an opportunity.

28 He who steals must steal no longer, but rather he must labor, performing with his own hands what is good, so that he will have *something* to share with one who has need.

29 Let no unwholesome word proceed from your mouth, but only such *a word* as is good for building up what is needed, so that it will give grace to those who hear.

30 And do not grieve the Holy Spirit of God, by whom you were sealed for the day of redemption.

31 Let all bitterness and anger and wrath and shouting and slander be put away from you, along with all malice.

32 Instead, be kind to one another, tender-hearted, graciously forgiving each other, just as God in Christ also has graciously forgiven you.

CHAPTER 5

Be Imitators of God

THEREFORE be imitators of God, as beloved children,

2 and walk in love, just as Christ also loved us and gave Himself up for us, an offering and a sacrifice to God as a fragrant aroma.

3 But sexual immorality or any impurity or greed must not even be named among you, as is proper among saints;

4 *nor* filthiness and foolish talk, or coarse jesting, which are not fitting, but rather giving of thanks.

5 For this you know with certainty, that no one sexually immoral or impure or greedy, who is an idolater, has an inheritance in the kingdom of Christ and God.

6 Let no one deceive you with empty words, for because of these things the wrath of God comes upon the sons of disobedience.

7 Therefore do not be partakers with them;

8 for you were formerly darkness, but now you are light in the Lord; walk as children of light

9 (for the fruit of that light *consists* in all goodness and righteousness and truth),

10 trying to learn what is pleasing to the Lord.

11 And do not participate in the unfruitful works of darkness, but instead even expose them.

12 For it is disgraceful even to speak of the things which are done by them in secret.

13 But all things become visible when they are exposed by the light, for everything that becomes visible is light.

14 For this reason it says,
"Awake, sleeper,
And arise from the dead,
And Christ will shine on you."

15 Therefore look carefully how you walk, not as unwise but as wise,

16 redeeming the time, because the days are evil.

17 On account of this, do not be foolish, but understand what the will of the Lord is.

18 And do not get drunk with wine, for that is dissipation, but be filled with the Spirit,

19 speaking to one another in psalms and hymns and spiritual songs, singing and making melody with your heart to the Lord;

20 always giving thanks for all things in the name of our Lord Jesus Christ to God, even the Father;

21 and being subject to one another in the fear of Christ.

Wives and Husbands

22 Wives, *be subject* to your own husbands, as to the Lord.

23 For the husband is the head of the wife, as Christ also is the head of the church, He Himself *being* the Savior of the body.

24 But as the church is subject to Christ, so also the wives *ought to be* to their husbands in everything.

25 Husbands, love your wives, just as Christ also loved the church and gave Himself up for her,

26 so that He might sanctify her, having cleansed her by the washing of water with the word,

27 that He might present to Himself the church in all her glory, having no spot or wrinkle or any such thing, but that she would be holy and blameless.

28 So husbands ought also to love their own wives as their own bodies. He who loves his own wife loves himself;

29 for no one ever hated his own flesh, but nourishes and cherishes it, just as Christ also *does* the church,

30 because we are members of His body.

31 FOR THIS REASON A MAN SHALL LEAVE HIS FATHER AND MOTHER AND BE JOINED TO HIS WIFE, AND THE TWO SHALL BECOME ONE FLESH.

32 This mystery is great, but I am speaking with reference to Christ and the church.

33 Nevertheless, each individual among you also is to love his own wife even as himself, and the wife must *see to it* that she respects her husband.

CHAPTER 6

Children and Parents

CHILDREN, obey your parents in the Lord, for this is right.

2 HONOR YOUR FATHER AND MOTHER (which is the first commandment with a promise),

3 SO THAT IT MAY BE WELL WITH YOU, AND THAT YOU MAY LIVE LONG IN THE LAND.

4 Fathers, do not provoke your children to anger, but bring them up in the discipline and instruction of the Lord.

5 Slaves, be obedient to those who are your masters according to the flesh, with fear and trembling, in the integrity of your heart, as to Christ;

6 not by way of eyeservice, as men-pleasers, but as slaves of Christ, doing the will of God from the heart,

7 serving with good will as to the Lord, and not to men,

8 knowing that whatever good thing each one does, this he will receive back from the Lord, whether slave or free.

9 And masters, do the same things to them, giving up threatening, knowing that both their Master and yours is in heaven, and there is no partiality with Him.

The Armor of God

10 Finally, be strong in the Lord and in the might of His strength.

11 Put on the full armor of God, so that you will be able to stand firm against the schemes of the devil.

12 For our struggle is not against flesh and blood, but against the rulers, against the authorities, against the *world forces of this* darkness, against the spiritual *forces* of wickedness in the heavenly *places*.

13 Therefore, take up the full armor of God, so that you will be able to resist in the evil day, and having done everything, to stand firm.

14 Stand firm therefore, HAVING GIRDED YOUR LOINS WITH TRUTH, and HAVING PUT ON THE BREASTPLATE OF RIGHTEOUSNESS,

15 and having shod YOUR FEET WITH THE PREPARATION OF THE GOSPEL OF PEACE.

16 In addition to all, having taken up the shield of faith with which you will be able to extinguish all the flaming arrows of the evil one,

17 also receive THE HELMET OF SALVATION, and the sword of the Spirit, which is the word of God,

18 praying at all times with all prayer and petition in the Spirit, and to this end, being on the alert with all perseverance and petition for all the saints,

19 as well as on my behalf, that words may be given to me in the opening of my mouth, to make known with boldness the mystery of the gospel—

20 for which I am an ambassador in chains—so that in *proclaiming* it I may speak boldly, as I ought to speak.

21 But that you also may know about all my affairs, how I am doing, Tychicus, the beloved brother and faithful servant in the Lord, will make everything known to you.

22 I have sent him to you for this very purpose, so that you may know our circumstances, and that he may encourage your hearts.

23 Peace be to the brothers, and love with faith, from God the Father and the Lord Jesus Christ.

24 Grace be with all those who love our Lord Jesus Christ with incorruptible *love*.

THE LETTER OF PAUL TO THE

PHILIPPIANS

CHAPTER 1

Thanksgiving

PAUL and Timothy, slaves of Christ Jesus,

To all the saints in Christ Jesus who are in Philippi, with the overseers and deacons:

2 Grace to you and peace from God our Father and the Lord Jesus Christ.

3 I thank my God in all my remembrance of you,

4 always offering prayer with joy in my every prayer for you all,

5 because of your fellowship in the gospel from the first day until now.

6 *For I am* confident of this very thing, that He who began a good work in you will perfect it until the day of Christ Jesus.

7 For it is only right for me to think this way about you all, because I have you in my heart, since both in my chains and in the defense and confirmation of the gospel, you all are fellow partakers with me in this grace.

8 For God is my witness, how I long for you all with the affection of *Christ Jesus.*

9 And this I pray, that your love may abound still more and more in full knowledge and all discernment,

10 so that you may approve the things that are excellent, in order to be sincere and without fault until the day of Christ,

11 having been filled with the fruit of righteousness which *comes* through Jesus Christ, to the glory and praise of God.

The Progress of the Gospel

12 Now I want you to know, brothers, that my circumstances have turned out for the greater progress of the gospel,

13 so that my chains in Christ have become well known throughout the whole praetorian guard and to everyone else,

14 and that most of the brothers, having become confident in the Lord because of my chains, have far more courage to speak the word of God without fear.

15 Some, to be sure, are preaching Christ even from envy and strife, but some also from good will;

16 the latter *do it* out of love, knowing that I am appointed for the defense of the gospel;

17 the former proclaim Christ out of selfish ambition rather than from pure motives, thinking to cause me affliction in my chains.

18 What then? Only that in every way, whether in pretense or in truth, Christ is proclaimed, and in this I rejoice.

Yes, and I will rejoice,

19 for I know that THIS WILL TURN OUT FOR MY SALVATION through your prayers and the provision of the Spirit of Jesus Christ,

20 according to my earnest expectation and hope, that I will not be put to shame in anything, but *that* with all boldness, Christ will even now, as always, be magnified in my body, whether by life or by death.

To Live Is Christ

21 For to me, to live is Christ and to die is gain.

22 But if *I am* to live *on* in the flesh, this *will mean* fruitful labor for me; and I do not know what I will choose.

23 But I am hard-pressed between the two, having the desire to depart and be with Christ, for *that* is very much better,

24 yet to remain on in the flesh is more necessary for your sake.

25 And convinced of this, I know that I will remain and continue with you all for your progress and joy in the faith,

26 so that your reason for boasting may abound in Christ Jesus in me, through my coming to you again.

27 Only live your lives in a manner worthy of the gospel of Christ, so that whether I come and see you or remain absent, I will hear about your circumstances, that you are standing firm in one spirit, with one mind contending together for the faith of the gospel,

28 in no way alarmed by *your* opponents—which is a sign of destruction for them, but of salvation for you, and that *too*, from God.

29 For to you it has been granted for Christ's sake, not only to believe in Him, but also to suffer for His sake,

30 having the same struggle which you saw in me, and now hear *to be* in me.

CHAPTER 2

Christ's Humility and Exaltation

THEREFORE if there is any encouragement in Christ, if there is any consolation of love, if there is any fellowship of the Spirit, if any affection and compassion,

2 fulfill my joy, that you think the same *way*, by maintaining the same love, *being* united in spirit, thinking on one purpose,

3 doing nothing from selfish ambition or vain glory, but with humility of mind regarding one another as more important than yourselves,

4 not *merely* looking out for your own personal interests, but also for the interests of others.

5 Have this *way of* thinking in yourselves which was also in Christ Jesus,

6 who, although existing in the form of God, did not regard equality with God a thing to be grasped,

7 but emptied Himself, by taking the form of a slave, by being made in the likeness of men.

8 Being found in appearance as a man, He humbled Himself by becoming obedient to the point of death, even death on a cross.

9 Therefore, God also highly exalted Him, and bestowed on Him the name which is above every name,

10 so that at the name of Jesus EVERY KNEE WILL BOW, of those who are in heaven and on earth and under the earth,

11 and that EVERY TONGUE WILL CONFESS that Jesus Christ is LORD, to the glory of God the Father.

12 So then, my beloved, just as you have always obeyed, not as in my presence only, but now much more in my absence, work out your salvation with fear and trembling;

13 for it is God who is at work in you, both to will and to work for *His* good pleasure.

14 Do all things without grumbling or disputing,

15 so that you will be blameless and innocent, children of God without blemish in the midst of a crooked and perverse generation, among whom you shine as lights in the world,

16 holding fast the word of life, so that in the day of Christ I will have reason to boast because I did not run in vain nor labor in vain.

17 But even if I am being poured out as a drink offering upon the sacrifice and service of your faith, I rejoice and share my joy with you all.

18 And you also, rejoice in the same way and share your joy with me.

Timothy and Epaphroditus Sent

19 But I hope in the Lord Jesus to send Timothy to you shortly, so that I also may be in good spirits when I learn of your circumstances.

20 For I have no one *else* of kindred spirit who will genuinely be concerned about your circumstances.

21 For they all seek after their own interests, not those of Christ Jesus.

22 But you know of his proven worth, that he served with me in the furtherance of the gospel like a child *serving* his father.

23 Therefore I hope to send him immediately, as soon as I evaluate my own circumstances,

24 and I am confident in the Lord that I myself also will be coming shortly.

25 But I regarded it necessary to send to you Epaphroditus, my brother and fellow worker and fellow soldier, who is also your messenger and minister to my need;

26 because he was longing for you all and was distressed because you had heard that he was sick.

27 For indeed he was sick to the point of death, but God had mercy on him, and not on him only but also on me, so that I would not have sorrow upon sorrow.

28 Therefore I have sent him all the more eagerly so that when you see him again you may rejoice and I may be less concerned.

29 Receive him then in the Lord with all joy, and hold men like him in high regard

30 because he came close to death for the work of Christ, risking his life to fulfill what was lacking in your service to me.

CHAPTER 3

Righteousness Through Faith in Christ

FINALLY, my brothers, rejoice in the Lord. To write the same things *again* is no trouble to me, and it is a safeguard for you.

2 Beware of the dogs! Beware of the evil workers! Beware of the mutilation!

3 For we are the circumcision, who worship in the Spirit of God and boast in Christ Jesus and put no confidence in the flesh,

4 although I myself might have confidence even in the flesh. If anyone else has a mind to put confidence in the flesh, I far more:

5 circumcised the eighth day, of the nation of Israel, of the tribe of Benjamin, a Hebrew of Hebrews; as to the Law, a Pharisee;

6 as to zeal, a persecutor of the church; as to the righteousness which is in the Law, found blameless.

7 But whatever things were gain to me, those things I have counted as loss for the sake of Christ.

8 More than that, I count all things to be *loss because of* the surpassing value of knowing Christ Jesus my Lord, for whom I have suffered the loss of all things, and count them but rubbish that I may gain Christ

9 and be found in Him, not having a righteousness of my own which is from *the* Law, but that which is through faith in Christ, the righteousness which *is* from God upon faith,

10 that I may know Him and the power of His resurrection and the fellowship of His sufferings, being conformed to His death,

11 in order that I may attain to the resurrection from the dead.

Pressing On Toward the Goal

12 Not that I have already obtained *it* or have already become perfect, but I press on so that I may lay hold of that for which also I was laid hold of by Christ Jesus.

13 Brothers, I do not consider myself as having laid hold of *it* yet, but one thing I *do:* forgetting what *lies* behind and reaching forward to what *lies* ahead,

14 I press on toward the goal for the prize of the upward call of God in Christ Jesus.

15 Let us therefore, as many as are perfect, think this way; and if in anything you think differently, God will reveal that also to you.

16 However, *let us* keep walking in step with the same *standard* to which we have attained.

17 Brothers, join in following my example, and look for those who walk according to the pattern you have in us.

18 For many walk—of whom I often told you, and now tell you even crying—as enemies of the cross of Christ,

19 whose end is destruction, whose god is *their* stomach and glory is in their shame, who set their thoughts on earthly things.

20 For our citizenship is in heaven, from which also we eagerly wait for a Savior, the Lord Jesus Christ,

21 who will transform the body of our humble state into conformity with the body of His glory, by His working through which He is able to even subject all things to Himself.

CHAPTER 4

Rejoice in the Lord Always

THEREFORE my brothers, loved and longed for, my joy and crown, in this way stand firm in the Lord, my beloved.

2 I urge Euodia and I urge Syntyche to think the same way in the Lord.

3 Indeed, I ask you also, genuine companion, help these women who have contended together alongside of me in the gospel, with also Clement and the rest of my fellow workers, whose names are in the book of life.

4 Rejoice in the Lord always; again I will say, rejoice!

5 Let your considerate *spirit* be known to all men. The Lord is near.

6 Be anxious for nothing, but in everything by prayer and petition with thanksgiving let your requests be made known to God.

7 And the peace of God, which surpasses all comprehension, will guard your hearts and your minds in Christ Jesus.

8 Finally, brothers, whatever is true, whatever is dignified, whatever is right, whatever is pure, whatever is lovely, whatever is commendable, if there is any excellence and if anything worthy of praise, consider these things.

9 The things you have learned and received and heard and seen in me, practice these things, and the God of peace will be with you.

God Will Fill Your Needs

10 But I rejoiced in the Lord greatly, that now at last you have revived thinking about me; indeed, you were thinking about me *before*, but you lacked opportunity.

11 Not that I speak from want, for I learned to be content in whatever circumstances I am.

12 I know how to get along with humble means, and I also know how to live in abundance; in any and all things I have learned the secret of being filled and going hungry, both of having abundance and suffering need.

13 I can do all things through Him who strengthens me.

14 Nevertheless, you have done well to fellowship *with me* in my affliction.

15 And you yourselves also know, Philippians, that at the first preaching of the gospel, after I left Macedonia, no church fellowshipped with me in the matter of giving and receiving but you alone.

16 For even in Thessalonica you sent *a gift* more than once for my needs.

17 Not that I seek the gift itself, but I seek the fruit which increases to your account.

18 But I have received everything in *full* and have an abundance; I have been filled, having received from Epaphroditus what you have sent, a fragrant aroma, an acceptable sacrifice, pleasing to God.

19 And my God will fulfill all your needs according to His riches in glory in Christ Jesus.

20 Now to our God and Father *be* the glory forever and ever. Amen.

21 Greet every saint in Christ Jesus. The brothers who are with me greet you.

22 All the saints greet you, especially those of Caesar's household.

23 The grace of the Lord Jesus Christ be with your spirit.

THE LETTER OF PAUL TO THE

COLOSSIANS

CHAPTER 1

Thanksgiving and Prayer

PAUL, an apostle of Christ Jesus by the will of God, and Timothy our brother,

2 To the saints and faithful brothers in Christ in Colossae: Grace to you and peace from God our Father.

3 We give thanks to God, the Father of our Lord Jesus Christ, praying always for you,

4 since we heard of *your faith* in Christ Jesus *and the* love which you *have for* all the saints,

5 because of the hope laid up for you in heaven, of which you previously heard in the word of truth, the gospel

6 which has come to you, just as in all the world also it is constantly bearing fruit and multiplying, just as *it has been doing* in you also since

the day you heard and understood the grace of God in truth;

7 just as you learned *it* from Epaphras, our beloved fellow slave, who is a faithful servant of Christ on our behalf,

8 who also informed us of your love in the Spirit.

9 For this reason also, since the day we heard, we have not ceased to pray for you and to ask that you may be filled *with* the full knowledge of *His* will in all spiritual wisdom and understanding,

10 so that you may walk in a manner worthy of the Lord, to please *Him* in all respects, bearing fruit in every good work and multiplying in the full knowledge of God;

11 being strengthened with all power, according to His glorious might, for the attaining of all steadfastness and patience; joyously

12 giving thanks to the Father, who has qualified us to share in the inheritance of the saints in light.

13 Who rescued us from the authority of darkness, and transferred us to the kingdom of the Son of His love,

14 in whom we have redemption, the forgiveness of sins.

The Firstborn of All Creation

15 Who is the image of the invisible God, the firstborn of all creation.

16 For in Him all things were created, *both* in the heavens and on earth, visible and invisible, whether thrones or dominions or rulers or authorities—all things have been created through Him and for Him.

17 And He is before all things,
And in Him all things hold together.

18 And He is the head of the body, the church;

Who is the beginning, the firstborn from the dead, so that He Himself will come to have first place in everything.

19 For in Him all the fullness *of God* was pleased to dwell,

20 And through Him to reconcile *all things* to Himself, having made peace *through* the blood of His cross—through Him—whether things on earth or things in heaven.

21 And although you were formerly alienated and enemies in mind *and* in evil deeds,

22 but now He reconciled you in the body of His flesh through death, in order to present you before Him holy and blameless and beyond reproach—

23 if indeed you continue in the faith firmly grounded and steadfast, and not moved away from the hope of the gospel, which you have heard, which was proclaimed in all creation under heaven, and of which I, Paul, was made a minister.

24 Now I rejoice in my sufferings for your sake, and I fill up what is lacking of Christ's afflictions in my flesh, on behalf of His body, which is the church,

25 of which I was made a minister according to the stewardship from God given to me for you, so that I might fully carry out *the preaching of* the word of God,

26 *that is*, the mystery which has been hidden from the *past* ages and generations, but has now been manifested to His saints,

27 to whom God willed to make known what is the riches of the glory of this mystery among the Gentiles, which is Christ in you, the hope of glory.

28 Him we proclaim, admonishing every man and teaching every man with all wisdom, so that we may present every man complete in Christ.

29 For this purpose I also labor, striving according to His working, which He works in me in power.

CHAPTER 2

Alive with Christ

FOR I want you to understand how great a struggle I have on your behalf and for those who are at Laodicea, and for all those who have not seen my face in the flesh,

2 so that their hearts may be encouraged, having been held together in love, even unto all the wealth of the full assurance of understanding, unto the full knowledge of God's mystery, *that is,* Christ *Himself,*

3 in whom are hidden all the treasures of wisdom and knowledge.

4 I say this so that no one will delude you with persuasive argument.

5 For even though I am absent in body, nevertheless I am with you in spirit, rejoicing to see your good order and the stability of your faith in Christ.

6 Therefore as you received Christ Jesus the Lord, *so* walk in Him,

7 having been firmly rooted and being built up in Him, and having been established in your faith—just as you were instructed—*and* abounding with thanksgiving.

8 *See to it that* no one takes you captive through philosophy and empty deception, according to the tradition of men, according to the elementary principles of the world, and not according to Christ.

9 For in Him all the fullness of Deity dwells bodily,

10 and in Him you have been filled, who is the head over all rule and authority;

11 in whom you were also circumcised with a circumcision made without hands, in the removal of the body of the flesh, in the circumcision of Christ,

12 having been buried with Him in baptism, in which you were also raised up with Him through faith in the working of God, who raised Him from the dead.

13 And you being dead in your transgressions and the uncircumcision of your flesh, He made you alive with Him, having graciously forgiven us all our transgressions.

14 Having canceled out the certificate of debt consisting of decrees against us which was hostile to us, He also has taken it out of the way, having nailed it to the cross.

15 Having disarmed the rulers and authorities, He made a public display of them, having triumphed over them in Him.

16 Therefore, no one is to judge you in food and drink, or in respect to a festival or a new moon or a Sabbath day—

17 *things* which are *only* a shadow of what is to come; but the substance belongs to Christ.

18 Let no one keep defrauding you of your prize by delighting in self-abasement and the worship of the angels, going into detail about *visions* he has seen, being puffed up for nothing by his fleshly mind,

19 and not holding fast to the head, from whom the entire body, being supplied and held together by the

joints and ligaments, grows with a growth that is from God.

20 If you have died with Christ to the elementary principles of the world, why, as if you were living in the world, do you submit yourself to decrees:

21 "Do not handle, nor taste, nor touch"?

22 Which deal with everything destined to perish with use, *which are* in accordance with the commands and teachings of men;

23 which are matters having, to be sure, a word of wisdom in self-made religion and self-abasement and severe treatment of the body, *but are* of no value against fleshly indulgence.

CHAPTER 3

Put On the New Man

THEREFORE, if you have been raised up with Christ, keep seeking the things above, where Christ is, seated at the right hand of God.

2 Set your mind on the things above, not on the things that are on earth.

3 For you died and your life has been hidden with Christ in God.

4 When Christ, who is our life, is manifested, then you also will be manifested with Him in glory.

5 Therefore, consider the members of *your earthly body* as dead to sexual immorality, impurity, passion, evil desire, and greed, which is idolatry.

6 On account of these things, the wrath of God is coming upon the sons of disobedience,

7 and in them you also once walked, when you were living in them.

8 But now you also, lay them all aside: wrath, anger, malice, slander, *and* abusive speech from your mouth.

9 Do not lie to one another, since you put off the old man with its *evil* practices,

10 and have put on the new man who is being renewed to a full knowledge according to the image of the One who created him—

11 *a renewal* in which there is no *distinction between* Greek and Jew, circumcised and uncircumcised, barbarian, Scythian, slave, *and* freeman, but Christ is all and in all.

12 So, as the elect of God, holy and beloved, put on a heart of compassion, kindness, humility, gentleness, *and* patience;

13 bearing with one another, and graciously forgiving each other, whoever has a complaint against anyone, just as the Lord graciously forgave you, so also should you.

14 Above all these things *put on* love, which is the perfect bond of unity.

15 And let the peace of Christ rule in your hearts, to which indeed you were called in one body, and be thankful.

16 Let the word of Christ dwell in you richly, with all wisdom teaching and admonishing one another with psalms *and* hymns *and* spiritual songs, singing with gratefulness in your hearts to God.

17 And whatever you do in word or

deed, *do* all in the name of the Lord Jesus, giving thanks to God the Father through Him.

Family and Work

18 Wives, be subject to your husbands, as is fitting in the Lord.

19 Husbands, love your wives and do not be embittered against them.

20 Children, obey your parents in all things, for this is pleasing to the Lord.

21 Fathers, do not exasperate your children, so that they will not lose heart.

22 Slaves, in all things obey those who are your masters according to the flesh, not with eyeservice, as men-pleasers, but with integrity of heart, fearing the Lord.

23 Whatever you do, do your work heartily, as for the Lord rather than for men,

24 knowing that from the Lord you will receive the reward of the inheritance. Serve the Lord Christ.

25 For he who does wrong will receive the consequences of the wrong which he has done, and that without partiality.

CHAPTER 4

Final Instructions and Greetings

MASTERS, show to your slaves what is right and fair, knowing that you too have a Master in heaven.

2 Devote yourselves to prayer, being watchful in it with thanksgiving;

3 praying at the same time for us as well, that God will open up to us a door for the word, so that we may speak the mystery of Christ, for which I have also been bound,

4 that I may make it manifest in the way I ought to speak.

5 Walk in wisdom toward outsiders, redeeming the time.

6 Let your words always be with grace, seasoned with salt, so that you will know how you should answer each person.

7 Tychicus, *our* beloved brother and faithful servant and fellow slave in the Lord, will make known to you all my affairs,

8 whom I have sent to you for this very purpose, that you may know about our circumstances and that he may encourage your hearts;

9 and with him Onesimus, *our* faithful and beloved brother, who is one of you. They will inform you about the whole situation here.

10 Aristarchus, my fellow prisoner, sends you his greetings; and *also* Mark, the cousin of Barnabas (about whom you received instructions; if he comes to you, welcome him);

11 and *also* Jesus who is called Justus. These are the only fellow workers for the kingdom of God who are from the circumcision, and they have proved to be a comfort to me.

12 Epaphras, who is one of your number, a slave of Christ Jesus, sends you his greetings, always striving for you in his prayers, that you may stand complete and fully assured in all the will of God.

13 For I testify for him that he has a deep concern for you and for those who are in Laodicea and Hierapolis.

14 Luke, the beloved physician, sends you his greetings, and *also* Demas.

15 Greet the brothers who are in Laodicea and also Nympha and the church that is in her house.

16 And when this letter is read among you, have it also read in the church of the Laodiceans; and you, for your part read my letter *that is coming* from Laodicea.

17 And say to Archippus, "Take heed to the ministry which you have received in the Lord, that you may fulfill it."

18 The greeting is in my own hand—Paul. Remember my chains. Grace be with you.

THE FIRST LETTER OF PAUL TO THE

THESSALONIANS

CHAPTER 1

Thanksgiving

PAUL and Silvanus and Timothy,

To the church of the Thessalonians in God the Father and the Lord Jesus Christ: Grace to you and peace.

2 We give thanks to God always for all of you, making mention *of you* in our prayers;

3 remembering without ceasing your work of faith and labor of love and steadfastness of hope in our Lord Jesus Christ before our God and Father,

4 knowing, brothers beloved by God, your election,

5 for our gospel did not come to you in word only, but also in power and in the Holy Spirit and with full assurance; just as you know what kind of men we proved to be among you for your sake.

6 You also became imitators of us and of the Lord, having received the word in much affliction with the joy of the Holy Spirit,

7 so that you became a model to all the believers in Macedonia and in Achaia.

8 For the word of the Lord has sounded forth from you, not only in Macedonia and Achaia, but also in every place your faith toward God has gone forth, so that we have no need to say anything.

9 For they themselves report about us what kind of an entrance we had with you, and how you turned to God from idols to serve a living and true God,

10 and to wait for His Son from heaven, whom He raised from the dead, Jesus, who rescues us from the wrath to come.

CHAPTER 2

Entrusted with the Gospel

FOR you yourselves know, brothers, that our entrance to you was not in vain,

2 but after we had already suffered and been mistreated in Philippi, as you know, we had the boldness in our God to speak to you the gospel of God amid much struggle.

3 For our exhortation does not *come* from error or impurity or by way of deceit;

4 but just as we have been approved by God to be entrusted with the gospel, so we speak, not as pleasing men, but God who examines our hearts.

5 For we never came with a flattering word, as you know, nor with a pretext for greed—God is witness—

6 nor seeking glory from men, either from you or from others, even though as apostles of Christ we could have been a burden to *you.*

7 But we proved to be gentle among you, as a nursing *mother* tenderly cares for her own children.

8 In this way, having fond affection for you, we were pleased to impart to you not only the gospel of God but also our own lives, because you had become beloved to us.

9 For you remember, brothers, our labor and hardship, *how* working night and day so as not to be a burden to any of you, we proclaimed to you the gospel of God.

10 You are witnesses, and *so is* God, of how devoutly and righteously and blamelessly we behaved toward you believers;

11 just as you know how we *were* exhorting and encouraging and bearing witness to each one of you as a father *would* his own children,

12 so that you would walk in a manner worthy of the God who calls you into His own kingdom and glory.

13 And for this reason we also thank God without ceasing that when you received the word of God which you heard from us, you accepted *it* not *as* the word of men, but *for* what it really is, the word of God, which also is at work in you who believe.

14 For you, brothers, became imitators of the churches of God in Christ Jesus that are in Judea, for you also suffered the same things at the hands of your own countrymen, even as they *did* from the Jews,

15 who both killed the Lord Jesus and the prophets, and drove us out, and do not please God, and *are* hostile to all men,

16 hindering us from speaking to the Gentiles so that they may be saved; with the result that they always fill up the measure of their sins. But wrath has come upon them to the utmost.

17 But we, brothers, having been taken away from you for a short while—in face but not in heart—were all the more eager with great desire to see your face.

18 For we wanted to come to you—I, Paul, more than once—and *yet* Satan hindered us.

19 For who is our hope or joy or

crown of boasting? Is it not even you, before our Lord Jesus at His coming?

20 For you are our glory and joy.

CHAPTER 3

Timothy's Good Report

THEREFORE when we could endure *it* no longer, we were pleased to be left behind at Athens alone,

2 and we sent Timothy, our brother and God's fellow worker in the gospel of Christ, to strengthen and encourage you as to your faith,

3 so that no one would be shaken by these afflictions, for you yourselves know that we have been destined for this.

4 For indeed when we were with you, we *kept* telling you in advance that we were going to suffer affliction, just as it happened and *as* you know.

5 For this reason, when I could endure *it* no longer, I also sent to know about your faith, lest somehow the tempter has tempted you, and our labor be in vain.

6 But now that Timothy has come to us from you, and has brought us good news of your faith and love, and that you always remember us kindly, longing to see us just as we also long to see you,

7 for this reason, brothers, in all our distress and affliction we were comforted about you through your faith;

8 for now we *really* live, if you stand firm in the Lord.

9 For what thanks can we render to God for you in return for all the joy with which we rejoice before our God because of you,

10 as we night and day keep praying most earnestly that we may see your face, and may complete what is lacking in your faith?

11 Now may our God and Father Himself and Jesus our Lord direct our way to you,

12 and may the Lord cause you to increase and abound in love for one another, and for all people, just as we also *do* for you,

13 so that He may strengthen your hearts blameless in holiness, before our God and Father, at the coming of our Lord Jesus with all His saints.

CHAPTER 4

Sanctification and Love

FINALLY then, brothers, we ask and exhort you in the Lord Jesus, that as you received from us as to how you ought to walk and please God (just as you actually do walk), that you excel still more.

2 For you know what commandments we gave you through the Lord Jesus.

3 For this is the will of God, your sanctification: that you abstain from sexual immorality;

4 that each of you know how to possess his own vessel in sanctification and honor,

5 not in lustful passion, like the Gentiles who do not know God;

6 *and* that no man transgress and defraud his brother in the matter because the Lord is *the* avenger in all

these things, just as we also told you before and solemnly warned *you*.

7 For God did not call us to impurity, but in sanctification.

8 Consequently, he who sets *this* aside is not setting aside man but the God who gives His Holy Spirit to you.

9 Now concerning love of the brothers, you have no need for *anyone* to write to you, for you yourselves are taught by God to love one another,

10 for indeed you do practice it toward all the brothers who are in all Macedonia. But we urge you, brothers, to excel still more,

11 and to make it your ambition to lead a quiet life and attend to your own business and work with your hands, just as we commanded you,

12 so that you will walk properly toward outsiders and not be in any need.

The Dead in Christ Will Rise

13 But we do not want you to be uninformed, brothers, about those who are asleep, so that you will not grieve as do the rest who have no hope.

14 For if we believe that Jesus died and rose again, even so God will bring with Him those who have fallen asleep in Jesus.

15 For this we say to you by the word of the Lord, that we who are alive and remain until the coming of the Lord, will not precede those who have fallen asleep.

16 For the Lord Himself will descend from heaven with a shout, with the voice of *the* archangel and with the trumpet of God, and the dead in Christ will rise first.

17 Then we who are alive and remain will be caught up together with them in the clouds to meet the Lord in the air, and so we shall always be with the Lord.

18 Therefore comfort one another with these words.

CHAPTER 5

The Day of the Lord

NOW concerning the times and the seasons, brothers, you have no need of anything to be written to you.

2 For you yourselves know full well that the day of the Lord will come just like a thief in the night.

3 While they are saying, "Peace and safety!" then destruction will come upon them suddenly like labor pains upon a woman who is pregnant, and they will never escape.

4 But you, brothers, are not in darkness, that the day would overtake you like a thief,

5 for you are all sons of light and sons of day. We are not of night nor of darkness;

6 so then let us not sleep as others do, but let us be awake and sober.

7 For those who sleep, sleep at night, and those who get drunk, get drunk at night.

8 But since we are of *the* day, let us be sober, having put on the breastplate of faith and love, and as a helmet, the hope of salvation.

9 For God has not appointed us for wrath, but for obtaining salvation through our Lord Jesus Christ,

10 who died for us, so that whether we are awake or asleep, we will live together with Him.

11 Therefore comfort one another and build up one another, just as you also are doing.

Admonishment and Instruction

12 But we ask of you, brothers, that you know those who labor among you, and lead you in the Lord and admonish you,

13 and that you regard them very highly in love because of their work. Live in peace with one another.

14 And we urge you, brothers, admonish the unruly, encourage the fainthearted, help the weak, be patient with everyone.

15 See that no one repays another with evil for evil, but always seek after that which is good for one another and for all people.

16 Rejoice always;

17 pray without ceasing;

18 in everything give thanks, for this is God's will for you in Christ Jesus.

19 Do not quench the Spirit;

20 do not despise prophecies;

21 but examine all things; hold fast to that which is good;

22 abstain from every form of evil.

23 Now may the God of peace Himself sanctify you entirely, and may your spirit and soul and body be preserved complete, without blame at the coming of our Lord Jesus Christ.

24 Faithful is He who calls you, who also will do it.

25 Brothers, pray for us.

26 Greet all the brothers with a holy kiss.

27 I implore you by the Lord to have this letter read to all the brothers.

28 The grace of our Lord Jesus Christ be with you.

THE SECOND LETTER OF PAUL TO THE
THESSALONIANS

CHAPTER 1

Greetings of Grace and Thanksgiving

PAUL and Silvanus and Timothy,

To the church of the Thessalonians in God our Father and the Lord Jesus Christ:

2 Grace to you and peace from God the Father and the Lord Jesus Christ.

3 We ought always to give thanks to God for you, brothers, as is *only* fitting, because your faith is growing abundantly, and the love of each one of you all toward one another increases *all the more,*

4 so that we ourselves boast about you among the churches of God for your perseverance and faith in the midst of all your persecutions and afflictions which you endure.

God's Righteous Judgment

5 *This is* a plain indication of God's righteous judgment so that you will be considered worthy of the kingdom of God, for which indeed you are suffering.

6 Since it is right for God to repay with affliction those who afflict you,

7 and *to give* rest to you who are afflicted and to us as well at the revelation of the Lord Jesus from heaven with His mighty angels in flaming fire,

8 executing vengeance on those who do not know God and to those who do not obey the gospel of our Lord Jesus.

9 These will pay the penalty of eternal destruction, AWAY FROM THE PRESENCE OF THE LORD AND FROM THE GLORY OF HIS MIGHT,

10 when He comes to be glorified in His saints on that day, and to be marveled at among all who have believed—for our witness to you was believed.

11 To this end also we pray for you always, that our God will count you worthy of your calling, and fulfill all *your* good pleasure for goodness and the work of faith with power,

12 so that the name of our Lord Jesus will be glorified in you, and you in Him, according to the grace of our God and *the* Lord Jesus Christ.

CHAPTER 2

The Man of Lawlessness

NOW we ask you, brothers, with regard to the coming of our Lord Jesus Christ and our gathering together to Him,

2 that you not be quickly shaken in your mind or be alarmed whether by a spirit or a word or a letter as if from us, to the effect that the day of the Lord has come.

3 Let no one in any way deceive you, for *it has not come* unless the apostasy comes first, and the man of lawlessness is revealed, the son of destruction,

4 who opposes and exalts himself above every so-called god or object of worship, so that he takes his seat in the sanctuary of God, exhibiting himself as being God.

5 Do you not remember that while I was still with you, I was telling you these things?

6 And you know what restrains him now, so that in his time he will be revealed.

7 For the mystery of lawlessness is already at work; only he who now restrains *will do so* until he is taken out of the way.

8 And then that lawless one will be revealed—whom the Lord Jesus WILL SLAY WITH THE BREATH OF HIS MOUTH and bring to an end by the appearance of His coming—

9 whose coming is in accord with the working of Satan, with all power and signs and false wonders,

10 and with all the deception of unrighteousness for those who perish, because they did not receive the love of the truth so as to be saved.

11 And for this reason God sends upon them a deluding influence so that they will believe what is false,

12 in order that they all may be judged who did not believe the truth, but took pleasure in unrighteousness.

13 But we should always give thanks to God for you, brothers beloved by the Lord, because God has chosen you as the first fruits for salvation through sanctification by the Spirit and faith in the truth.

14 It was for this He called you through our gospel, that you may obtain the glory of our Lord Jesus Christ.

15 So then, brothers, stand firm and hold to the traditions which you were taught, whether by word *of mouth* or by letter from us.

16 Now may our Lord Jesus Christ Himself and God our Father, who has loved us and given us eternal comfort and good hope by grace,

17 encourage your hearts and strengthen *them* in every good work and word.

CHAPTER 3

Disobedient Brothers

FINALLY, brothers, pray for us that the word of the Lord will spread rapidly and be glorified, just as *it did* also with you;

2 and that we will be rescued from perverse and evil men, for not all have faith.

3 But the Lord is faithful, who will strengthen and guard you from the evil one.

4 And we have confidence in the Lord about you, that you are doing and will *continue to* do what we command.

5 And may the Lord direct your hearts into the love of God and into the steadfastness of Christ.

6 Now we command you, brothers, in the name of our Lord Jesus Christ, that you keep away from every brother who walks in an unruly manner and not according to the tradition which they received from us.

7 For you yourselves know how you ought to imitate us, because we did not act in an unruly manner among you,

8 nor did we eat anyone's bread without paying for it, but with labor and hardship we *kept* working night and day so that we would not be a burden to any of you;

9 not because we do not have the authority, but in order to offer ourselves as a model for you, so that you would imitate us.

10 For even when we were with you, we used to command this to you: if anyone is not willing to work, neither let him eat.

11 For we hear that some among you are walking in an unruly manner, doing no work at all, but acting like busybodies.

12 Now such persons we command and exhort in the Lord Jesus Christ, that working with quietness, they eat their own bread.

13 But as for you, brothers, do not lose heart in doing good.

14 And if anyone does not obey our word in this letter, take special note of that person to not associate with him, so that he will be put to shame.

15 And *yet* do not regard him as an enemy, but admonish him as a brother.

16 Now may the Lord of peace Himself continually give you peace in every circumstance. The Lord be with you all!

17 The greeting is in my own hand—Paul, which is a distinguishing mark in every letter; this is the way I write.

18 The grace of our Lord Jesus Christ be with you all.

THE FIRST LETTER OF PAUL TO

TIMOTHY

CHAPTER 1

Instructions in Doctrine and Living

PAUL, an apostle of Christ Jesus according to the commandment of God our Savior, and of Christ Jesus, our hope,

2 To Timothy, *my* genuine child in *the* faith: Grace, mercy *and* peace from God the Father and Christ Jesus our Lord.

3 As I exhorted you when going to Macedonia, remain on at Ephesus so that you may command certain ones not to teach a different doctrine,

4 nor to pay attention to myths and endless genealogies, which give rise to mere speculation rather than *furthering* the stewardship from God which is by faith.

5 But the goal of our command is love from a pure heart and a good conscience and an unhypocritical faith.

6 For some, straying from these things, have turned aside to fruitless discussion,

7 wanting to be teachers of the Law, even though they do not understand either what they are saying or the matters about which they make confident assertions.

8 But we know that the Law is good, if one uses it lawfully,

9 knowing this, that law is not made for a righteous person, but for those who are lawless and rebellious, for the ungodly and sinners, for the unholy and godless, for those who kill their fathers or mothers, for murderers,

10 for sexually immoral persons, for homosexuals, for kidnappers, for liars, for perjurers, and whatever else is contrary to sound teaching,

11 according to the gospel of the glory of the blessed God, with which I have been entrusted.

12 I am grateful to Christ Jesus our Lord, who has strengthened me, because He regarded me faithful, putting me into service,

13 even though I was formerly a blasphemer and a persecutor and a violent aggressor. Yet I was shown mercy because I acted ignorantly in unbelief;

14 and the grace of our Lord was more than abundant, with the faith and love which *are* in Christ Jesus.

15 It is a trustworthy saying and deserving full acceptance: that Christ Jesus came into the world to save sinners, among whom I am foremost.

16 Yet for this reason I was shown mercy, so that in me as the foremost, Christ Jesus might demonstrate all His patience as an example for those who are going to believe upon Him for eternal life.

17 Now to the King of the ages, immortal, invisible, the only God, *be* honor and glory forever and ever. Amen.

18 This command I entrust to you, Timothy, *my* child, in accordance with the prophecies previously made concerning you, that by them you may fight the good fight,

19 keeping faith and a good conscience, which some, having rejected, suffered shipwreck in regard to their faith.

20 Among these are Hymenaeus and Alexander, whom I have handed over to Satan, so that they will be taught not to blaspheme.

CHAPTER 2

Exhortation to Prayer

FIRST of all, then, I exhort that petitions *and* prayers, requests *and* thanksgivings, be made for all men,

2 for kings and all who are in authority, so that we may lead a tranquil and quiet life in all godliness and dignity.

3 This is good and acceptable in the sight of God our Savior,

4 who desires all men to be saved and to come to the full knowledge of the truth.

5 For there is one God, *and* one mediator also between God and men, *the* man Christ Jesus,

6 who gave Himself as a ransom for all, the witness for this proper time.

7 For this I was appointed a preacher and an apostle (I am telling the truth, I am not lying) as a teacher of the Gentiles in faith and truth.

8 Therefore I want the men in every place to pray, lifting up holy hands, without wrath and dissension.

Instructions for Women

9 Likewise, I *want* women to adorn themselves with proper clothing, with modesty and self-restraint, not with braided hair and gold or pearls or costly clothing,

10 but rather by means of good

works, as is proper for women professing godliness.

11 A woman must learn in quietness, in all submission.

12 But I do not allow a woman to teach or exercise authority over a man, but to remain quiet.

13 For it was Adam who was first formed, *and* then Eve.

14 And *it was* not Adam *who* was deceived, but the woman being deceived, fell into trespass.

15 But she will be saved through the bearing of children, if they continue in faith and love and sanctification with self-restraint.

CHAPTER 3

Overseers and Deacons

IT is a trustworthy saying: if any man aspires to the office of overseer, he desires a good work.

2 An overseer, then, must be above reproach, the husband of one wife, temperate, sensible, respectable, hospitable, able to teach,

3 not addicted to wine or pugnacious, but considerate, peaceable, free from the love of money;

4 leading his own household well, having his children in submission with all dignity

5 (but if a man does not know how to lead his own household, how will he take care of the church of God?),

6 *and* not a new convert, so that he will not become conceited and fall into the condemnation of the devil.

7 And he must have a good reputation with those outside *the church*, so that he will not fall into reproach and the snare of the devil.

8 Deacons likewise *must be* dignified, not double-tongued, not indulging in much wine, not fond of dishonest gain,

9 *but* holding to the mystery of the faith with a clear conscience.

10 And these men must also first be tested; then let them serve as deacons if they are beyond reproach.

11 Women *must* likewise *be* dignified, not malicious gossips, but temperate, faithful in all things.

12 Deacons must be husbands of *only* one wife, leading *their* children and their own households well.

13 For those who have served well as deacons obtain for themselves a high standing and great boldness in the faith that is in Christ Jesus.

14 I am writing these things to you, hoping to come to you soon,

15 but in case I am delayed, *I write* so that you will know how one ought to conduct himself in the household of God, which is the church of the living God, the pillar and support of the truth.

16 And by common confession, great is the mystery of godliness:

He who was manifested in the flesh,
Was vindicated in the Spirit,
Seen by angels,
Proclaimed among the nations,
Believed on in the world,
Taken up in glory.

CHAPTER 4

Some Will Fall Away

BUT the Spirit explicitly says that in later times some will fall away from the faith, paying attention to deceitful spirits and doctrines of demons,

2 by the hypocrisy of liars, who have been seared in their own conscience,

3 who forbid marriage *and advocate* abstaining from foods which God created to be shared in with thanksgiving by those who believe and know the truth.

4 For everything created by God is good, and nothing is to be rejected if it is received with thanksgiving,

5 for it is sanctified by the word of God and prayer.

A Good Minister's Discipline

6 In pointing out these things to the brothers, you will be a good servant of Christ Jesus, being nourished on the words of the faith and of the sound doctrine which you have been following.

7 But refuse godless myths fit only for old women. On the other hand, train yourself for the purpose of godliness,

8 for bodily training is only of little profit, but godliness is profitable for all things, since it holds promise for *the present life* and *also* for the *life* to come.

9 It is a trustworthy saying and deserving full acceptance.

10 For it is for this we labor and strive, because we have fixed our hope on the living God, who is the Savior of all men, especially of believers.

11 Command and teach these things.

12 Let no one look down on your youthfulness, but show yourself as a model to those who believe in word, conduct, love, faith, *and* purity.

13 Until I come, give attention to the public reading *of Scripture*, to exhortation and teaching.

14 Do not neglect the gift within you, which was given to you through prophetic utterance with the laying on of hands by the council of elders.

15 Take pains with these things; be *absorbed* in them, so that your progress will be evident to all.

16 Pay close attention to yourself and to your teaching; persevere in these things, for as you do this you will save both yourself and those who hear you.

CHAPTER 5

Honor Widows

DO not sharply rebuke an older man, but *rather* plead with *him* as a father, *to* the younger men as brothers,

2 the older women as mothers, *and* the younger women as sisters, in all purity.

3 Honor widows who are widows indeed,

4 but if any widow has children or grandchildren, they must first learn to practice piety in regard to their own family and to make some return

to their parents; for this is acceptable in the sight of God.

5 Now she who is a widow indeed and who has been left alone, has fixed her hope on God and continues in petitions and prayers night and day.

6 But she who lives in self-indulgence is dead even while she lives.

7 And command these things as well, so that they may be above reproach.

8 But if anyone does not provide for his own, and especially for those of his household, he has denied the faith and is worse than an unbeliever.

9 A widow is to be put on the list only if she is not less than sixty years old, *having been* the wife of one man,

10 having a reputation for good works; if she has brought up children, if she has shown hospitality to strangers, if she has washed the saints' feet, if she has assisted those in affliction, if she has devoted herself to every good work.

11 But refuse *to put* younger widows *on the list*, for when they feel sensual desires in disregard of Christ, they want to get married,

12 *thus* incurring condemnation, because they have set aside their previous pledge.

13 And at the same time they also learn *to be* idle, as they go around from house to house. And not merely idle, but also gossips and busybodies, talking about things not proper *to mention.*

14 Therefore, I want younger *widows* to get married, bear children,

keep house, *and* give the enemy no opportunity for reviling,

15 for some have already turned aside after Satan.

16 If any believing woman has widows, she must assist them and the church must not be burdened, so that it may assist those who are widows indeed.

Honoring the Elders

17 The elders who lead well are to be considered worthy of double honor, especially those who labor at *preaching* the word and teaching.

18 For the Scripture says, "You SHALL NOT MUZZLE THE OX WHILE IT IS THRESHING," and "THE LABORER IS WORTHY OF HIS WAGES."

19 Do not receive an accusation against an elder except on the basis of two or three witnesses.

20 Those who continue in sin, reprove in the presence of all, so that the rest also will be fearful.

21 I solemnly charge you in the presence of God and of Christ Jesus and of *His* elect angels, to observe these *instructions* without bias, doing nothing in partiality.

22 Do not lay hands upon anyone hastily and thereby share *responsibility for* the sins of others; keep yourself pure.

23 No longer drink water *only*, but use a little wine for the sake of your stomach and your frequent ailments.

24 The sins of some men are quite evident, going before them to judgment; for others, their *sins* follow after.

25 So also good works are quite evident, and those which are otherwise cannot be concealed.

CHAPTER 6

Instructions to Those Who Serve

ALL who are under the yoke as slaves are to regard their own masters as worthy of all honor so that the name of God and *our* doctrine will not be slandered.

2 But those who have believers as their masters must not be disrespectful to them because they are brothers, but must serve them all the more, because those who partake of the benefit are believers and beloved. Teach and exhort these *things*.

3 If anyone teaches a different doctrine and does not agree with sound words—those of our Lord Jesus Christ—and with the doctrine conforming to godliness,

4 he is conceited, understanding nothing but having a morbid interest in controversial questions and disputes about words, out of which arise envy, strife, slander, evil suspicions,

5 and constant friction between men of depraved mind and deprived of the truth, who suppose that godliness is a means of gain.

6 But godliness *actually* is a means of great gain, when accompanied by contentment.

7 For we have brought nothing into the world, so we cannot take anything out of it either.

8 And if we have food and covering, with these we shall be content.

9 But those who want to get rich fall into temptation and a snare and many foolish and harmful desires which plunge men into ruin and destruction.

10 For the love of money is a root of all sorts of evils, and some by aspiring to it have wandered away from the faith and pierced themselves with many griefs.

11 But you, O man of God, flee from these things, and pursue righteousness, godliness, faith, love, perseverance, gentleness.

12 Fight the good fight of faith. Take hold of the eternal life to which you were called, and you made the good confession in the presence of many witnesses.

13 I charge you in the presence of God, who gives life to all things, and of Christ Jesus, who testified the good confession before Pontius Pilate,

14 that you keep the commandment without stain or reproach until the appearing of our Lord Jesus Christ,

15 which He will bring about at the proper time—He who is the blessed and only Sovereign, the King of kings and Lord of lords,

16 who alone has immortality and dwells in unapproachable light, whom no man has seen or can see. To Him *be* honor and eternal might! Amen.

17 Command those who are rich in this present age not to be haughty or to set their hope on the uncertainty of riches, but on God, who richly supplies us with all things to enjoy.

18 *Command them* to do good, to be

rich in good works, to be generous and ready to share,

19 storing up for themselves the treasure of a good foundation for the future, so that they may take hold of that which is life indeed.

20 O Timothy, guard what has been entrusted to you, turning aside from godless *and* empty chatter *and* the opposing arguments of what is falsely called knowledge—

21 which some, while professing, have gone astray from the faith.

Grace be with you.

THE SECOND LETTER OF PAUL TO
TIMOTHY

CHAPTER 1

Guard the Treasure Entrusted to You

PAUL, an apostle of Christ Jesus by the will of God, according to the promise of life in Christ Jesus,

2 To Timothy, my beloved child: Grace, mercy, *and* peace from God the Father and Christ Jesus our Lord.

3 I am grateful to God, whom I serve with a clear conscience the way my forefathers did, as I unceasingly remember you in my prayers night and day,

4 longing to see you, having remembered your tears, so that I may be filled with joy,

5 being reminded of the unhypocritical faith within you, which first dwelt in your grandmother Lois and your mother Eunice, and I am convinced that *it is* in you as well.

6 For this reason I remind you to kindle afresh the gift of God which is in you through the laying on of my hands.

7 For God has not given us a spirit of timidity, but of power and love and self-discipline.

8 Therefore do not be ashamed of either the witness about our Lord or me His prisoner, but join with *me* in suffering for the gospel according to the power of God,

9 who has saved us and called us with a holy calling, not according to our works, but according to His own purpose and grace which was given to us in Christ Jesus from all eternity,

10 but now has been manifested by the appearing of our Savior Christ Jesus, who abolished death and brought life and immortality to light through the gospel,

11 for which I was appointed a preacher and an apostle and a teacher.

12 For this reason I also suffer these things, but I am not ashamed; for I

know whom I have believed and I am convinced that He is able to guard what I have entrusted to Him until that day.

13 Hold to the standard of sound words which you have heard from me, in the faith and love which are in Christ Jesus.

14 Guard, through the Holy Spirit who dwells in us, the treasure which has been entrusted to *you*.

15 You are aware of this: that all who are in Asia turned away from me, among whom are Phygelus and Hermogenes.

16 The Lord give mercy to the house of Onesiphorus, for he often refreshed me and was not ashamed of my chains,

17 but when he was in Rome, he eagerly searched for me and found me—

18 the Lord grant to him to find mercy from the Lord on that day— and you know very well what services he rendered at Ephesus.

CHAPTER 2

Remember Jesus Christ

YOU therefore, my child, be strong in the grace that is in Christ Jesus.

2 And the things which you have heard from me in the presence of many witnesses, entrust these to faithful men who will be able to teach others also.

3 *Suffer hardship with me*, as a good soldier of Christ Jesus.

4 No soldier in active service entangles himself in the affairs of everyday life, so that he may please the one who enlisted him as a soldier.

5 And also if anyone competes as an athlete, he is not crowned unless he competes according to the rules.

6 The hard-working farmer ought to be the first to receive his share of the crops.

7 Understand what I say, for the Lord will give you insight in everything.

8 Remember Jesus Christ, risen from the dead, of the seed of David, according to my gospel,

9 for which I endure hardship even to chains as a criminal. But the word of God has not been chained.

10 For this reason I endure all things for the sake of the elect, so that they also may obtain the salvation, which is in Christ Jesus, with eternal glory.

11 It is a trustworthy saying:
For if we died with Him, we will
    also live with Him;

12 If we endure, we will also reign
    with Him;
If we will deny Him, He also will
    deny us;

13 If we are faithless, He remains
    faithful, for He cannot deny
    Himself.

Accurately Handle the Word of Truth

14 Remind *them* of these things, solemnly charging *them* in the presence of God not to dispute about words, which is useless *and leads* to the ruin of the hearers.

15 Be diligent to present yourself approved to God as a workman who does not need to be ashamed, accurately handling the word of truth.

16 But avoid godless *and*

empty chatter, for it will lead to further ungodliness,

17 and their word will spread like gangrene. Among them are Hymenaeus and Philetus,

18 who have gone astray from the truth saying that the resurrection has already taken place, and they upset the faith of some.

19 Nevertheless, the firm foundation of God stands, having this seal, "THE LORD KNOWS THOSE WHO ARE HIS," and, "EVERYONE WHO NAMES THE NAME OF THE LORD IS TO DEPART FROM WICKEDNESS."

20 Now in a large house there are not only gold and silver vessels, but also vessels of wood and of clay, and some to honor and some to dishonor.

21 Therefore, if anyone cleanses himself from these *things*, he will be a vessel for honor, sanctified, useful to the Master, having been prepared for every good work.

22 Now flee from youthful lusts and pursue righteousness, faith, love, *and* peace, with those who call on the Lord from a pure heart.

23 But refuse foolish and ignorant speculations, knowing that they produce quarrels.

24 And the Lord's slave must not be quarrelsome, but be kind to all, able to teach, patient when wronged,

25 with gentleness correcting those who are in opposition, if perhaps God may give them repentance leading to the full knowledge of the truth,

26 and they may come to their senses *and escape* from the snare of the devil, having been held captive by him to do his will.

CHAPTER 3

Difficult Times Will Come

BUT know this, that in the last days difficult times will come.

2 For men will be lovers of self, lovers of money, boastful, arrogant, blasphemers, disobedient to parents, ungrateful, unholy,

3 unloving, irreconcilable, malicious gossips, without self-control, without gentleness, without love for good,

4 treacherous, reckless, conceited, lovers of pleasure rather than lovers of God,

5 holding to a form of godliness, but having denied its power. Keep away from such men as these.

6 For among them are those who enter into households and take captive weak women weighed down with sins, being led on by various desires,

7 always learning and never able to come to the full knowledge of the truth.

8 Just as Jannes and Jambres opposed Moses, so these *men* also oppose the truth, men of depraved mind, disqualified in regard to the faith.

9 But they will not make further progress, for their folly will be obvious to all, just as theirs was also.

10 But you followed my teaching, conduct, purpose, faith, patience, love, perseverance,

11 persecutions, *and* sufferings, such as happened to me at Antioch, at

Iconium, *and* at Lystra. What persecutions I endured, and out of them all the Lord rescued me!

12 Indeed, all who desire to live godly in Christ Jesus will be persecuted.

13 But evil men and impostors will proceed *from bad* to worse, deceiving and being deceived.

14 But you, continue in the things you learned and became convinced of, knowing from whom you learned *them*,

15 and that from childhood you have known the sacred writings which are able to make you wise unto salvation through faith which is in Christ Jesus.

16 All Scripture is God-breathed and profitable for teaching, for reproof, for correction, for training in righteousness,

17 so that the man of God may be equipped, having been thoroughly equipped for every good work.

CHAPTER 4

Preach the Word

I solemnly charge *you* in the presence of God and of Christ Jesus, who is to judge the living and the dead, and by His appearing and His kingdom:

2 preach the word; be ready in season *and* out of season; reprove, rebuke, exhort, with great patience and teaching.

3 For the time will come when they will not endure sound doctrine, but *wanting* to have their ears tickled, they will accumulate for themselves teachers in accordance to their own desires,

4 and will turn away their ears from the truth and will turn aside to myths.

5 But you, be sober in all things, endure hardship, do the work of an evangelist, fulfill your ministry.

6 For I am already being poured out as a drink offering, and the time of my departure has come.

7 I have fought the good fight, I have finished the course, I have kept the faith.

8 In the future there is laid up for me the crown of righteousness, which the Lord, the righteous Judge, will award to me on that day, and not only to me, but also to all who have loved His appearing.

Personal Concerns

9 Be diligent to come to me soon,

10 for Demas, having loved this present age, has deserted me and gone to Thessalonica; Crescens *has gone* to Galatia, Titus to Dalmatia.

11 Only Luke is with me. Pick up Mark and bring him with you, for he is useful to me for service.

12 But Tychicus I sent to Ephesus.

13 When you come bring the cloak which I left at Troas with Carpus, and the scrolls, especially the parchments.

14 Alexander the coppersmith showed me much harm; the Lord will award him according to his deeds.

15 Be on guard against him yourself, for he vigorously opposed our words.

16 At my first defense no one supported me, but all deserted me. May it not be counted against them.

17 But the Lord stood with me and strengthened me, so that through me the preaching might be fulfilled, and

that all the Gentiles might hear. And I was rescued out of the lion's mouth.

18 The Lord will rescue me from every evil deed, and will save me unto His heavenly kingdom; to Him *be* the glory forever and ever. Amen.

19 Greet Prisca and Aquila, and the household of Onesiphorus.

20 Erastus remained at Corinth, but Trophimus I left sick at Miletus.

21 Be diligent to come before winter. Eubulus greets you, also Pudens and Linus and Claudia and all the brothers.

22 The Lord be with your spirit. Grace be with all of you.

THE LETTER OF PAUL TO
TITUS

CHAPTER 1

Greetings and Grace

PAUL, a slave of God and an apostle of Jesus Christ, for the faith of God's elect and the full knowledge of the truth which is according to godliness,

2 in the hope of eternal life, which the God who cannot lie promised from all eternity,

3 but at the proper time manifested His word in preaching, with which I was entrusted according to the commandment of God our Savior,

4 To Titus, my genuine child according to our common faith: Grace and peace from God the Father and Christ Jesus our Savior.

Qualifications of Elders

5 For this reason I left you in Crete, that you would set in order what

remains and appoint elders in every city as I directed you,

6 *namely*, if any man is beyond reproach, the husband of one wife, having faithful children, *who are* not accused of dissipation, or rebellious.

7 For the overseer must be beyond reproach as God's steward, not self-willed, not quick-tempered, not addicted to wine, not pugnacious, not fond of dishonest gain,

8 but hospitable, loving what is good, sensible, righteous, holy, self-controlled,

9 holding fast the faithful word which is in accordance with the teaching, so that he will be able both to exhort in sound doctrine and to reprove those who contradict.

10 For there are many rebellious men, empty talkers and deceivers, especially those of the circumcision,

11 who must be silenced because

they are upsetting whole families, teaching things they should not *teach* for the sake of dishonest gain.

12 One of themselves, a prophet of their own, said, "Cretans are always liars, evil beasts, lazy gluttons."

13 This testimony is true. For this reason reprove them severely so that they may be sound in the faith,

14 not paying attention to Jewish myths and commandments of men who turn away from the truth.

15 To the pure, all things are pure, but to those who are defiled and unbelieving, nothing is pure, but both their mind and their conscience are defiled.

16 They profess to know God, but by *their* works they deny *Him*, being detestable and disobedient and unfit for any good work.

CHAPTER 2

Instructions for the Older and Younger

BUT as for you, speak the things which are proper for sound doctrine.

2 Older men are to be temperate, dignified, sensible, sound in faith, in love, in perseverance.

3 Older women likewise are to be reverent in their behavior, not malicious gossips nor enslaved to much wine, *teaching what is good,*

4 so that they may instruct the young women in sensibility: to love their husbands, to love their children,

5 *to be* sensible, pure, workers at home, kind, being subject to their own husbands, so that the word of God will not be slandered.

6 Likewise urge the younger men to be sensible;

7 in all things show yourself to be a model of good works, *with* purity in doctrine, dignified,

8 sound *in* word which is irreproachable, so that the opponent will be put to shame, having nothing bad to say about us.

9 *Urge* slaves to be subject to their own masters in everything, to be pleasing, not contradicting,

10 not pilfering, but demonstrating all good faith so that they will adorn the doctrine of God our Savior in everything.

11 For the grace of God has appeared, bringing salvation to all men,

12 instructing us that, denying ungodliness and worldly desires, we should live sensibly, righteously, and godly in the present age,

13 looking for the blessed hope and the appearing of the glory of our great God and Savior, Jesus Christ,

14 who gave Himself for us that He might redeem us from all lawlessness, and purify for Himself a people for His own possession, zealous for good works.

15 These things speak and exhort and reprove with all authority. Let no one disregard you.

CHAPTER 3

Be Ready for Every Good Work

REMIND them to be subject to rulers,

to authorities, to be obedient, to be ready for every good work,

2 to slander no one, to be peaceable, considerate, demonstrating all gentleness to all men.

3 For we ourselves also once were foolish, disobedient, deceived, enslaved to various lusts and pleasures, spending our life in malice and envy, despicable, hating one another.

4 But when the kindness and affection of God our Savior appeared,

5 He saved us, not by works which we did in righteousness, but according to His mercy, through the washing of regeneration and renewing by the Holy Spirit,

6 whom He poured out upon us richly through Jesus Christ our Savior,

7 so that having been justified by His grace, we would become heirs according to *the* hope of eternal life.

8 This is a trustworthy saying. And concerning these things I want you to speak confidently, so that those who have believed God will be intent to lead in good works. These things are good and profitable for men.

9 But avoid foolish controversies and genealogies and strife and conflicts about the Law, for they are unprofitable and worthless.

10 Reject a factious man after a first and second warning,

11 knowing that such a man is perverted and is sinning, being self-condemned.

Personal Instructions and Greetings

12 When I send Artemas or Tychicus to you, be diligent to come to me at Nicopolis, for I have decided to spend the winter there.

13 Diligently help send Zenas the lawyer and Apollos on their way so that nothing is lacking for them.

14 And our people must also learn to lead in good works to meet pressing needs, so that they will not be unfruitful.

15 All who are with me greet you. Greet those who love us in *the* faith.

Grace be with you all.

THE LETTER OF PAUL TO

PHILEMON

Philemon's Love and Faith

PAUL, a prisoner of Christ Jesus, and Timothy our brother,

To Philemon our beloved *brother* and fellow worker,

2 and to Apphia our sister, and to Archippus our fellow soldier, and to the church in your house:

3 Grace to you and peace from God our Father and the Lord Jesus Christ.

4 I thank my God, always making mention of you in my prayers,

5 because I hear of your love and of the faith which you have toward the Lord Jesus and toward all the saints;

6 *and I pray* that the fellowship of your faith may become effective through the full knowledge of every good thing which is in you for the sake of Christ.

7 For I have come to have much joy and comfort in your love, because the hearts of the saints have been refreshed through you, brother.

8 Therefore, though I have much boldness in Christ to command you *to do* what is proper,

9 yet for love's sake I rather plead with *you*—since I am such a person as Paul, the aged, and now also a prisoner of Christ Jesus—

Plea for Onesimus

10 I plead with you for my child Onesimus, of whom I became a father in my chains,

11 who formerly was useless to you, but now is useful both to you and to me.

12 I have sent him back to you in person, that is, my very heart,

13 whom I intended to keep with me, so that on your behalf he might minister to me in my chains for the gospel,

14 but without your consent I did not want to do anything, so that your goodness would not be, in effect, by compulsion but voluntary.

15 For perhaps he was for this reason separated *from you* for a while, that you would have him back forever,

16 no longer as a slave, but more than a slave, a beloved brother, especially to me, but how much more to you, both in the flesh and in the Lord.

17 If then you regard me a partner, accept him as *you would accept* me.

18 But if he has wronged you in any way or owes you anything, charge that to my account.

19 I, Paul, am writing this with my own hand, I will repay it (not to mention to you that you owe to me even your own self as well).

20 Yes, brother, let me benefit from you in the Lord. Refresh my heart in Christ!

21 Having confidence in your obedience, I write to you, since I know that you will do even more than what I say.

22 And at the same time also prepare me a lodging, for I hope that through your prayers I will be graciously given to you.

23 Epaphras, my fellow prisoner in Christ Jesus, greets you,

24 *as do* Mark, Aristarchus, Demas, Luke, my fellow workers.

25 The grace of the Lord Jesus Christ be with your spirit.

THE LETTER TO THE
HEBREWS

CHAPTER 1

God's Final Word in His Son

GOD, having spoken long ago to the fathers in the prophets in many portions and in many ways,

2 in these last days spoke to us in *His* Son, whom He appointed heir of all things, through whom also He made the worlds,

3 who is the radiance of His glory and the exact representation of His nature, and upholds all things by the word of His power; who, having accomplished cleansing for sins, sat down at the right hand of the Majesty on high,

4 having become so much better than the angels, as He has inherited a more excellent name than they.

5 For to which of the angels did He ever say,

"YOU ARE MY SON,
TODAY I HAVE BEGOTTEN YOU"?
And again,
"I WILL BE A FATHER TO HIM
AND HE SHALL BE A SON
TO ME"?

6 And when He again brings the firstborn into the world, He says,

"AND LET ALL THE ANGELS OF GOD
WORSHIP HIM."

7 And of the angels He says,

"WHO MAKES HIS ANGELS WINDS,
AND HIS MINISTERS FLAMING
FIRE."

8 But of the Son He says,

"YOUR THRONE, O GOD, IS FOREV-
ER AND EVER,
AND THE SCEPTER OF
UPRIGHTNESS IS THE SCEPTER
OF YOUR KINGDOM.

9 "YOU HAVE LOVED RIGHTEOUSNESS
AND HATED LAWLESSNESS;
THEREFORE GOD, YOUR GOD, HAS
ANOINTED YOU
WITH THE OIL OF GLADNESS
ABOVE YOUR COMPANIONS."

10 And,

"YOU, LORD, IN THE BEGINNING
FOUNDED THE EARTH,
AND THE HEAVENS ARE THE
WORKS OF YOUR HANDS;

11 THEY WILL PERISH, BUT YOU REMAIN;
AND THEY ALL WILL WEAR OUT
LIKE A GARMENT,

12 AND LIKE A MANTLE YOU WILL
ROLL THEM UP;
LIKE A GARMENT THEY WILL ALSO
BE CHANGED.
BUT YOU ARE THE SAME,
AND YOUR YEARS WILL NOT COME
TO AN END."

13 But to which of the angels has He ever said,

"SIT AT MY RIGHT HAND,
UNTIL I PUT YOUR ENEMIES
AS A FOOTSTOOL FOR YOUR FEET"?

14 Are they not all ministering spirits, sent to render service for the sake of those who will inherit salvation?

CHAPTER 2

Warning Against Neglecting Salvation

FOR this reason we must pay much closer attention to what we have heard, lest we drift away.

2 For if the word spoken through angels proved unalterable, and every trespass and disobedience received a just penalty,

3 how will we escape if we neglect so great a salvation? That *salvation*, first spoken by the Lord, was confirmed to us by those who heard,

4 God also testifying with them, both by signs and wonders and by various miracles and by gifts of the Holy Spirit according to His own will.

Jesus, the Author of Salvation

5 For He did not subject to angels the world to come, concerning which we are speaking.

6 But one has testified somewhere, saying,

"WHAT IS MAN, THAT YOU REMEMBER HIM?
OR THE SON OF MAN, THAT YOU ARE CONCERNED ABOUT HIM?

7 "YOU HAVE MADE HIM FOR A LITTLE WHILE LOWER THAN THE ANGELS;
YOU HAVE CROWNED HIM WITH GLORY AND HONOR,
AND HAVE APPOINTED HIM OVER THE WORKS OF YOUR HANDS;

8 YOU HAVE PUT ALL THINGS IN SUBJECTION UNDER HIS FEET."

For in subjecting all things to him, He left nothing that is not subject to him. But now we do not yet see all things subjected to him.

9 But we do see Him who was made for a little while lower than the angels—Jesus, because of the suffering of death crowned with glory and honor, so that by the grace of God He might taste death for everyone.

10 For it was fitting for Him, for whom are all things, and through whom are all things, in bringing many sons to glory, to perfect the author of their salvation through sufferings.

11 For both He who sanctifies and those who are being sanctified are all of One; for which reason He is not ashamed to call them brothers,

12 saying,

"I WILL RECOUNT YOUR NAME TO MY BROTHERS,
IN THE MIDST OF THE ASSEMBLY I WILL SING YOUR PRAISE."

13 And again,

"I WILL PUT MY TRUST IN HIM."

And again,

"BEHOLD, I AND THE CHILDREN WHOM GOD HAS GIVEN ME."

14 Therefore, since the children share in flesh and blood, He Himself likewise also partook of the same, that through death He might render powerless him who had the power of death, that is, the devil,

15 and might free those who through fear of death were subject to slavery all their lives.

16 For assuredly He does not give help to angels, but He gives help to the seed of Abraham.

17 Therefore, He had to be made

like His brothers in all things, so that He might become a merciful and faithful high priest in things pertaining to God, to make propitiation for the sins of the people. 18 For since He Himself was tempted in that which He has suffered, He is able to come to help those who are tempted.

CHAPTER 3

Jesus Greater than Moses

THEREFORE, holy brothers, partakers of a heavenly calling, consider the Apostle and High Priest of our confession—Jesus; 2 who was faithful to Him who appointed Him, as Moses also was in all His house. 3 For He has been counted worthy of more glory than Moses, in so much as the builder of the house has more honor than the house. 4 For every house is built by someone, but the builder of all things is God. 5 Now Moses was FAITHFUL IN ALL HIS HOUSE AS A SERVANT, for a testimony of those things which were to be spoken later, 6 but Christ *was faithful* as a Son over His house—whose house we are, if we hold fast our confidence and the boast of our hope.

7 Therefore, just as the Holy Spirit says,

"TODAY IF YOU HEAR HIS VOICE,
8 DO NOT HARDEN YOUR HEARTS AS
WHEN THEY PROVOKED ME,

AS IN THE DAY OF TRIAL IN THE
WILDERNESS,
9 WHERE YOUR FATHERS TRIED *Me*
BY TESTING Me,
AND SAW My WORKS FOR FORTY
YEARS.
10 "THEREFORE I WAS ANGRY WITH
THIS GENERATION,
AND SAID, 'THEY ALWAYS GO
ASTRAY IN THEIR HEART,
AND THEY DID NOT KNOW My
WAYS';
11 AS I SWORE IN My WRATH,
'THEY SHALL NOT ENTER My
REST.'"

Warning Against Unbelief

12 See to it brothers, that there not be in any one of you an evil, unbelieving heart that falls away from the living God. 13 But encourage one another day after day, as long as it is *still* called "Today," so that none of you will be hardened by the deceitfulness of sin. 14 For we have become partakers of Christ, if we hold fast the beginning of our assurance firm until the end, 15 while it is said,

"TODAY IF YOU HEAR HIS VOICE,
DO NOT HARDEN YOUR HEARTS, AS
WHEN THEY PROVOKED ME."

16 For who provoked *Him* when they had heard? Indeed, did not all those who came out of Egypt led by Moses? 17 And with whom was He angry for forty years? Was it not with those who sinned, whose corpses fell in the wilderness?

18 And to whom did He swear that they would not enter His rest, but to those who were disobedient?

19 So we see that they were not able to enter because of unbelief.

CHAPTER 4

The Believer's Rest

THEREFORE, let us fear, lest, while a promise remains of entering His rest, any one of you may seem to have fallen short of it.

2 For indeed we have had good news proclaimed to us, just as they also; but the word that was heard did not profit those who were not united with faith among those who heard.

3 For we who have believed enter that rest, just as He has said,

"AS I SWORE IN MY WRATH,

THEY SHALL NOT ENTER MY REST,"

although His works were finished from the foundation of the world.

4 For He has spoken somewhere in this way concerning the seventh day: "AND GOD RESTED ON THE SEVENTH DAY FROM ALL HIS WORKS";

5 and again in this passage, "THEY SHALL NOT ENTER MY REST."

6 Therefore, since it remains for some to enter it, and those who formerly had good news proclaimed to them failed to enter because of disobedience,

7 He again determines a certain day, "Today," saying through David after so long a time just as has been said before,

"TODAY IF YOU HEAR HIS VOICE,

DO NOT HARDEN YOUR HEARTS."

8 For if Joshua had given them rest, He would not have spoken of another day after that.

9 So there remains a Sabbath rest for the people of God.

10 For the one who has entered His rest has himself also rested from his works, as God did from His.

11 Therefore let us be diligent to enter that rest, lest anyone fall into the same example of disobedience.

12 For the word of God is living and active and sharper than any two-edged sword, and piercing as far as the division of soul and spirit, of both joints and marrow, and able to judge the thoughts and intentions of the heart.

13 And there is no creature hidden from His sight, but all things are uncovered and laid bare to the eyes of Him to whom we have an account to give.

Jesus Our Great High Priest

14 Therefore, since we have a great high priest who has passed through the heavens, Jesus the Son of God, let us take hold of our confession.

15 For we do not have a high priest who cannot sympathize with our weaknesses, but One who has been tempted in all things like we are, yet without sin.

16 Therefore let us draw near with confidence to the throne of grace, so that we may receive mercy and find grace to help in time of need.

CHAPTER 5

FOR every high priest taken from among men is appointed on behalf of men in things pertaining to God, in order to offer both gifts and sacrifices for sins,

2 being able to deal gently with the ignorant and misguided, since he himself also is beset with weakness;

3 and because of it, he is obligated, just as for the people, to also offer *sacrifices* for sins in the same way for himself.

4 And no one takes this honor to himself, but *receives it* when he is called by God, even as Aaron was.

5 In this way also Christ did not glorify Himself to become a high priest, but He who said to Him,

"YOU ARE MY SON,

TODAY I HAVE BEGOTTEN YOU";

6 just as He says also in another *passage*,

"YOU ARE A PRIEST FOREVER

ACCORDING TO THE ORDER OF

MELCHIZEDEK."

7 He, in the days of His flesh, offered up both prayers and supplications with loud crying and tears to the One able to save Him from death, and He was heard because of His reverence.

8 Although He was a Son, He learned obedience from the things which He suffered.

9 And having been made perfect, He became to all those who obey Him the source of eternal salvation,

10 being designated by God as a high priest according to the order of Melchizedek.

11 Concerning him we have much to say, and *it is* hard to explain, since you have become dull of hearing.

12 For though by this time you ought to be teachers, you have need again for someone to teach you the elementary principles of the oracles of God, and you have come to need milk and not solid food.

13 For everyone who partakes *only* of milk is not accustomed to the word of righteousness, for he is an infant.

14 But solid food is for the mature, who because of practice have their senses trained to discern both good and evil.

CHAPTER 6

Warning Against Falling Away

THEREFORE leaving the elementary teaching about the Christ, let us press on to maturity, not laying again a foundation of repentance from dead works and of faith toward God,

2 of teaching about washings and laying on of hands, and the resurrection of the dead and eternal judgment.

3 And this we will do, if God permits.

4 For in the case of those once having been enlightened and having tasted of the heavenly gift and having become partakers of the Holy Spirit,

5 and having tasted the good word of God and the powers of the age to come,

6 and having fallen away, it is

impossible to renew them again to repentance, since they again crucify to themselves the Son of God and put Him to open shame.

7 For ground that drinks the rain which often falls on it and brings forth vegetation useful to those for whose sake it is also tilled, receives a blessing from God;

8 but if it yields thorns and thistles, it is unfit and close to being cursed, and its end is to be burned.

The Inheritance of the Promises

9 But we are convinced about you, beloved, of things that are better and that belong to salvation, though we are speaking in this way.

10 For God is not unrighteous so as to forget your work and the love which you have shown toward His name, in having ministered and continuing to minister to the saints.

11 And we desire that each one of you show the same diligence so as to realize the full assurance of hope until the end,

12 so that you may not become dull, but imitators of those who through faith and patience inherit the promises.

13 For when God made the promise to Abraham, since He could swear by no one greater, He swore by Himself,

14 saying, "I WILL GREATLY BLESS YOU AND I WILL GREATLY MULTIPLY YOU."

15 And so, having patiently waited, he obtained the promise.

16 For men swear by one greater *than themselves*, and with them an oath *given* as confirmation is an end of every dispute.

17 In the same way God, desiring even more to show to the heirs of the promise the unchangeableness of His purpose, guaranteed *it* with an oath,

18 so that by two unchangeable things in which it is impossible for God to lie, we who have taken refuge would have strong encouragement to take hold of the hope set before us.

19 This hope we have as an anchor of the soul, a *hope* both sure and confirmed and one which enters within the veil,

20 where a forerunner has entered as for us—Jesus, having become a high priest forever according to the order of Melchizedek.

CHAPTER 7

The Priesthoods of Melchizedek and Christ

FOR this MELCHIZEDEK, KING OF SALEM, PRIEST OF THE MOST HIGH GOD, who met ABRAHAM AS HE WAS RETURNING FROM THE SLAUGHTER OF THE KINGS and BLESSED HIM,

2 TO WHOM ALSO ABRAHAM APPORTIONED A TENTH PART OF ALL, was first of all, by the translation *of his name*, king of righteousness, and then also king of Salem, which is king of peace.

3 Without father, without mother, without genealogy, having neither beginning of days nor end of life, but made like the Son of God, he remains a priest continually.

4 Now observe how great this man was TO WHOM ABRAHAM, the patriarch, GAVE A TENTH of the spoils.

5 And those indeed of the sons of Levi, who receive the priest's office, have a commandment in the Law to collect a tenth from the people, that is, from their brothers, although these are descended from Abraham.

6 But the one whose genealogy is not traced from them had collected a tenth from Abraham and blessed the one who had the promises.

7 But without any dispute the lesser is blessed by the greater.

8 And in this case mortal men receive tithes, but in that case one *receives them,* of whom it is witnessed that he lives on.

9 And, so to speak, through Abraham even Levi, who received tithes, paid tithes,

10 for he was still in the loins of his father when Melchizedek met him.

11 Now if perfection was through the Levitical priesthood (for on the basis of it the people received the Law), what further need *was there* for another priest to arise according to the order of Melchizedek, and not be designated according to the order of Aaron?

12 For when the priesthood is changed, of necessity there takes place a change of law also.

13 For the one concerning whom these things are spoken belongs to another tribe, from which no one has officiated at the altar.

14 For it is evident that our Lord was descended from Judah, a tribe with reference to which Moses spoke nothing concerning priests.

15 And this is clearer still, if another priest arises according to the likeness of Melchizedek,

16 who has become *such* not according to a law of physical requirement, but according to the power of an indestructible life.

17 For it is witnessed *about Him,*

"YOU ARE A PRIEST FOREVER
ACCORDING TO THE ORDER OF
  MELCHIZEDEK."

18 For, on the one hand, there is a setting aside of a former commandment because of its weakness and uselessness

19 (for the Law made nothing perfect), and on the other hand there is a bringing in of a better hope, through which we draw near to God.

20 And inasmuch as *it was* not without an oath

21 (for they indeed became priests without an oath, but He with an oath through the One who said to Him,

"THE LORD HAS SWORN
AND WILL NOT CHANGE HIS MIND,
'YOU ARE A PRIEST FOREVER' ");

22 so much more Jesus also has become the guarantee of a better covenant.

23 And the *former* priests, on the one hand, existed in greater numbers because they were prevented by death from continuing,

24 but *Jesus,* on the other hand, because He continues forever, holds His priesthood permanently.

25 Therefore He is able also to save

forever those who draw near to God through Him, since He always lives to make intercession for them.

26 For it was fitting for us to have such a high priest, holy, innocent, undefiled, separated from sinners and exalted above the heavens;

27 who does not need daily, like those high priests, to offer up sacrifices, first for His own sins and then for the *sins* of the people, because this He did once for all when He offered up Himself.

28 For the Law appoints men as high priests who are weak, but the word of the oath, which came after the Law, *appoints* a Son, who has been made perfect forever.

CHAPTER 8

Jesus, High Priest of a New Covenant

NOW the main point in what is being said *is this*: we have such a high priest, who sat down at the right hand of the throne of the Majesty in the heavens,

2 a minister in the holy places and in the true tabernacle, which the Lord pitched, not man.

3 For every high priest is appointed to offer both gifts and sacrifices; so it is necessary that this *high priest* also have something to offer.

4 Now if He were on earth, He would not be a priest at all, since there are those who offer the gifts according to the Law;

5 who serve a copy and shadow of the heavenly things, just as Moses was warned *by God* when he was about to erect the tabernacle; for, "SEE," He says, "THAT YOU MAKE all things ACCORDING TO THE PATTERN WHICH WAS SHOWN YOU ON THE MOUNTAIN."

6 But now He has obtained a more excellent ministry, by as much as He is also the mediator of a better covenant, which has been enacted on better promises.

7 For if that first *covenant* had been faultless, there would have been no occasion sought for a second.

8 For finding fault with them, He says,
"BEHOLD, DAYS ARE COMING, SAYS THE LORD,
WHEN I WILL COMPLETE A NEW COVENANT
WITH THE HOUSE OF ISRAEL AND WITH THE HOUSE OF JUDAH;

9 NOT LIKE THE COVENANT WHICH I MADE WITH THEIR FATHERS
IN THE DAY WHEN I TOOK THEM BY THE HAND
TO LEAD THEM OUT OF THE LAND OF EGYPT;
FOR THEY DID NOT CONTINUE IN MY COVENANT,
AND I DID NOT CARE FOR THEM, SAYS THE LORD.

10 "FOR THIS IS THE COVENANT THAT I WILL MAKE WITH THE HOUSE OF ISRAEL
AFTER THOSE DAYS, SAYS THE LORD:
I WILL PUT MY LAWS INTO THEIR MINDS,
AND UPON THEIR HEARTS I WILL WRITE THEM.
AND I WILL BE THEIR GOD,
AND THEY SHALL BE MY PEOPLE.

11 "AND THEY SHALL NOT TEACH
    EVERYONE HIS FELLOW
    CITIZEN,
AND EVERYONE HIS BROTHER,
    SAYING, 'KNOW THE LORD,'
FOR ALL WILL KNOW ME,
FROM THE LEAST TO THE
    GREATEST OF THEM.
12 "FOR I WILL BE MERCIFUL TO THEIR
    INIQUITIES,
AND I WILL REMEMBER THEIR SINS
    NO MORE."

13 When He said, "A new *covenant*," He has made the first obsolete. But whatever is becoming obsolete and growing old is ready to disappear.

CHAPTER 9

The Old Covenant

NOW even the first *covenant* had requirements of divine worship and the earthly sanctuary.

2 For there was a tabernacle prepared: the first part, in which *were* the lampstand and the table and the sacred bread, which is called the holy place.

3 And behind the second veil there was a tabernacle which is called the Holy of Holies,

4 having a golden altar of incense and the ark of the covenant covered on all sides with gold, in which was a golden jar holding the manna, and Aaron's rod which budded, and the tablets of the covenant.

5 And above it *were* the cherubim of glory overshadowing the mercy seat. Of these things we cannot now speak in detail.

6 Now when these things have been so prepared, the priests are continually entering the first part *of the* tabernacle performing the divine worship,

7 but into the second, only the high priest *enters* once a year, not without *taking* blood, which he offers for himself and for the sins of the people committed in ignorance.

8 The Holy Spirit *is* indicating this, that the way into the holy places has not yet been manifested while that first part *of the* tabernacle is still standing,

9 which *is* a symbol for the present time. Accordingly both gifts and sacrifices are offered which cannot make the worshiper perfect in conscience,

10 since they *relate* only to food and drink and various washings, requirements for the body imposed until a time of reformation.

The New Covenant

11 But when Christ appeared *as* a high priest of the good things to come, *He entered* through the greater and more perfect tabernacle, not made with hands, that is to say, not of this creation,

12 and not through the blood of goats and calves, but through His own blood, He entered the holy places once for all, having obtained eternal redemption.

13 For if the blood of goats and bulls and the ashes of a heifer sprinkling those who have been defiled sanctify for the cleansing of the flesh,

14 how much more will the blood of Christ, who through the eternal Spirit offered Himself without blemish to God, cleanse your conscience from dead works to serve the living God?

15 And for this reason He is the mediator of a new covenant, so that, since a death has taken place for the redemption of the trespasses that were *committed* under the first covenant, those who have been called may receive the promise of the eternal inheritance.

16 For where a covenant is, there must of necessity be the death of the one who made it.

17 For a covenant is valid *only* when men are dead, for it is never in force while the one who made it lives.

18 Therefore not even the first *covenant* was inaugurated without blood.

19 For when every commandment had been spoken by Moses to all the people according to the Law, he took the blood of the calves and the goats, with water and scarlet wool and hyssop, and sprinkled both the book itself and all the people,

20 saying, "THIS IS THE BLOOD OF THE COVENANT WHICH GOD COMMANDED YOU."

21 And in the same way, both the tabernacle and all the vessels of the ministry he sprinkled with the blood.

22 And according to the Law, *one may* almost *say*, all things are cleansed with blood, and without shedding of blood there is no forgiveness.

23 Therefore it was necessary for the copies of the things in the heavens to be cleansed with these, but the heavenly things themselves with better sacrifices than these.

24 For Christ did not enter holy places made with hands, *mere* copies of the true ones, but into heaven itself, now to appear in the presence of God for us;

25 nor was it that He would offer Himself often, as the high priest enters the holy places year by year with blood that is not his own.

26 Otherwise, He would have needed to suffer often since the foundation of the world; but now once at the consummation of the ages He has been manifested to put away sin by the sacrifice of Himself.

27 And inasmuch as it is appointed for men to die once and after this *comes* judgment,

28 so Christ also, having been offered once to bear the sins of many, will appear a second time for salvation without *reference to* sin, to those who eagerly await Him.

CHAPTER 10

Christ's Sacrifice Once for All

FOR the Law, since it has *only* a shadow of the good things to come *and* not the very form of things, can never, by the same sacrifices which they offer continually year by year, make perfect those who draw near.

2 Otherwise, would they not have ceased to be offered, because the worshipers, having once been cleansed,

would no longer have consciousness of sins?

3 But in those *sacrifices* there is a reminder of sins year by year.

4 For it is impossible for the blood of bulls and goats to take away sins.

5 Therefore, when He comes into the world, He says,

"SACRIFICE AND OFFERING YOU
     HAVE NOT DESIRED,
BUT A BODY YOU HAVE PREPARED
     FOR ME;

6 IN BURNT OFFERINGS AND
     sacrifices FOR SIN YOU HAVE
     TAKEN NO PLEASURE.

7 "THEN I SAID, 'BEHOLD, I HAVE
     COME,
IN THE SCROLL OF THE BOOK IT IS
     WRITTEN OF ME,
TO DO YOUR WILL, O GOD.' "

8 After saying above, "SACRIFICES AND OFFERINGS AND BURNT OFFERINGS AND *sacrifices* FOR SIN YOU HAVE NOT DESIRED, NOR HAVE YOU TAKEN PLEASURE *in them*" (which are offered according to the Law),

9 then He said, "BEHOLD, I HAVE COME TO DO YOUR WILL." He takes away the first in order to establish the second.

10 By this will we have been sanctified through the offering of the body of Jesus Christ once for all.

11 And every priest stands daily ministering and offering time after time the same sacrifices, which can never take away sins;

12 but He, having offered one sacrifice for sins for all time, SAT DOWN AT THE RIGHT HAND OF GOD,

13 waiting from that time UNTIL HIS ENEMIES ARE PUT AS A FOOTSTOOL FOR HIS FEET.

14 For by one offering He has perfected for all time those who are being sanctified.

15 And the Holy Spirit also testifies to us, for after saying,

16 "THIS IS THE COVENANT THAT I
     WILL MAKE WITH THEM
AFTER THOSE DAYS, SAYS THE LORD:
I WILL PUT MY LAWS UPON THEIR
     HEART,
AND ON THEIR MIND I WILL WRITE
     THEM,"

He then says,

17 "AND THEIR SINS AND THEIR LAW-
     LESS DEEDS
I WILL REMEMBER NO MORE."

18 Now where there is forgiveness of these things, there is no longer *any* offering for sin.

A New and Living Way

19 Therefore, brothers, since we have confidence to enter the holy places by the blood of Jesus,

20 by a new and living way which He inaugurated for us through the veil, that is, His flesh,

21 and since *we have* a great priest over the house of God,

22 let us draw near with a sincere heart in full assurance of faith, having our hearts sprinkled from an evil conscience and our bodies washed with pure water.

23 Let us hold fast the confession of our hope without wavering, for He who promised is faithful.

24 And let us consider how to

stimulate one another to love and good deeds,

25 not forsaking our own assembling together, as is the habit of some, but encouraging *one another*, and all the more as you see the day drawing near.

Warning Against Willful Sin

26 For if we go on sinning willfully after receiving the knowledge of the truth, there no longer remains a sacrifice for sins,

27 but a terrifying expectation of judgment and THE FURY OF A FIRE WHICH WILL CONSUME THE ADVERSARIES.

28 Anyone who has set aside the Law of Moses dies without mercy by *the mouth of* two or three witnesses.

29 How much worse punishment do you think he will deserve who has trampled underfoot the Son of God, and has regarded as defiled the blood of the covenant by which he was sanctified, and has insulted the Spirit of grace?

30 For we know Him who said, "VENGEANCE IS MINE, I WILL REPAY." And again, "THE LORD WILL JUDGE HIS PEOPLE."

31 It is a terrifying thing to fall into the hands of the living God.

32 But remember the former days, when, after being enlightened, you endured a great conflict of sufferings,

33 partly by being made a public spectacle through reproaches and afflictions, and partly by becoming sharers with those who were so treated.

34 For you also showed sympathy to the prisoners and accepted with joy the seizure of your possessions, knowing that you have for yourselves a better and lasting possession.

35 Therefore, do not throw away that confidence of yours, which has a great reward.

36 For you have need of endurance, so that when you have done the will of God, you may receive the promise.

37 FOR YET IN A VERY LITTLE WHILE,
HE WHO IS COMING WILL COME,
   AND WILL NOT DELAY.

38 BUT MY RIGHTEOUS ONE SHALL
   LIVE BY FAITH,
AND IF HE SHRINKS BACK, MY SOUL
   HAS NO PLEASURE IN HIM.

39 But we are not of those who shrink back to destruction, but of those who have faith to the preserving of the soul.

CHAPTER 11

By Faith

NOW faith is the assurance of *things* hoped for, the conviction of things not seen.

2 For by it the men of old gained approval.

3 By faith we understand that the worlds were prepared by the word of God, so that what is seen was not made out of things which are visible.

4 By faith Abel offered to God a better sacrifice than Cain, through which he was approved as being righteous—God approving his gifts—and through faith, though he is dead, he still speaks.

5 By faith Enoch was taken up so

that he would not see death; AND HE WAS NOT FOUND BECAUSE GOD TOOK HIM UP; for prior to being taken up, he was approved as being pleasing to God.

6 And without faith it is impossible to please *Him*, for he who draws near to God must believe that He is and *that* He is a rewarder of those who seek Him.

7 By faith Noah, being warned about things not yet seen, in reverence prepared an ark for the salvation of his household, by which he condemned the world, and became an heir of the righteousness which is according to faith.

8 By faith Abraham, when he was called, obeyed by going out to a place which he was to receive for an inheritance; and he went out, not knowing where he was going.

9 By faith he sojourned in the land of promise, as in a foreign *land*, dwelling in tents with Isaac and Jacob, fellow heirs of the same promise,

10 for he was looking for the city which has foundations, whose architect and builder is God.

11 By faith even Sarah herself received ability to conceive, even beyond the proper time of life, since she regarded Him faithful who had promised.

12 Therefore there were born even of one man, and him as good as dead at that, *as many* AS THE STARS OF HEAVEN IN NUMBER, AND INNUMERABLE AS THE SAND WHICH IS BY THE SEASHORE.

13 All these died in faith, without receiving the promises, but having seen them and having welcomed them from a distance, and having confessed that they were strangers and exiles on the earth.

14 For those who say such things make it clear that they are seeking a country of their own.

15 And indeed if they had been remembering that *country* from which they went out, they would have had opportunity to return.

16 But now, they aspire to a better *country*, that is, a heavenly one. Therefore God is not ashamed to be called their God, for He prepared a city for them.

17 By faith Abraham, when he was tested, offered up Isaac, and he who had received the promises was offering up his only *son*,

18 to whom it was said, "IN ISAAC YOUR SEED SHALL BE CALLED."

19 He considered that God is able to raise *people* even from the dead, from which, figuratively speaking, he also received him back.

20 By faith Isaac blessed Jacob and Esau, even regarding things to come.

21 By faith Jacob, as he was dying, blessed each of the sons of Joseph, and WORSHIPED, *leaning* ON THE TOP OF HIS STAFF.

22 By faith Joseph, when he was dying, made mention of the exodus of the sons of Israel, and gave commands concerning his bones.

23 By faith Moses, when he was born, was hidden for three months by his parents, because they saw he was a beautiful child, and they were not afraid of the king's edict.

24 By faith Moses, when he had grown up, refused to be called the son of Pharaoh's daughter,

25 choosing rather to be mistreated with the people of God than to enjoy the passing pleasures of sin,

26 regarding the reproach of Christ greater riches than the treasures of Egypt; for he was looking to the reward.

27 By faith he left Egypt, not fearing the rage of the king; for he endured, as seeing Him who is unseen.

28 By faith he kept the Passover and the sprinkling of the blood, so that he who destroyed the firstborn would not touch them.

29 By faith they passed through the Red Sea as though *they were passing* through dry land, and the Egyptians, when they attempted it, were drowned.

30 By faith the walls of Jericho fell down after they had been encircled for seven days.

31 By faith Rahab the harlot did not perish along with those who were disobedient, after welcoming the spies in peace.

32 And what more shall I say? For time will fail me if I recount Gideon, Barak, Samson, Jephthah, as well as David and Samuel and the prophets,

33 who through faith conquered kingdoms, performed righteousness, obtained promises, shut the mouths of lions,

34 quenched the power of fire, escaped the edge of the sword, were made strong from weakness, became mighty in war, put foreign armies to flight.

35 Women received *back* their dead by resurrection; and others were tortured, not accepting their release, so that they might obtain a better resurrection;

36 and others experienced mockings and floggings, yes, also chains and imprisonment.

37 They were stoned, they were sawn in two, they were tempted, they were put to death with the sword. They went about in sheepskins, in goatskins, being destitute, afflicted, mistreated

38 (of whom the world was not worthy), wandering in desolate places and mountains and caves and holes in the ground.

39 And all these, having gained approval through their faith, did not receive what was promised,

40 because God had provided something better for us, so that apart from us they would not be made perfect.

CHAPTER 12

Jesus, the Author and Perfecter of Faith

THEREFORE, since we have so great a cloud of witnesses surrounding us, laying aside every weight and the sin which so easily entangles us, let us run with endurance the race that is set before us,

2 fixing our eyes on Jesus, the author and perfecter of faith, who for the joy set before Him endured the cross, despising the shame, and has sat down at the right hand of the throne of God.

3 For consider Him who has endured such hostility by sinners against

Himself, so that you will not grow weary, fainting in heart.

The Father's Discipline

4 You have not yet resisted to the point of shedding blood in your striving against sin.

5 And you have forgotten the exhortation which is addressed to you as sons,

"MY SON, DO NOT REGARD LIGHTLY
    THE DISCIPLINE OF THE LORD,
NOR FAINT WHEN YOU ARE
    REPROVED BY HIM;

6 FOR THOSE WHOM THE LORD
    LOVES HE DISCIPLINES,
AND HE FLOGS EVERY SON WHOM
    HE RECEIVES."

7 It is for discipline that you endure; God deals with you as with sons; for what son is there whom *his* father does not discipline?

8 But if you are without discipline, of which all have become partakers, then you are illegitimate children and not sons.

9 Furthermore, we had earthly fathers to discipline us, and we respected them. Shall we not much rather be subject to the Father of spirits, and live?

10 For they disciplined us for a short time as seemed best to them, but He *disciplines us* for our benefit, so that we may share His holiness.

11 And all discipline for the moment seems not to be joyful, but sorrowful, but to those who have been trained by it, afterwards it yields the peaceful fruit of righteousness.

12 Therefore, STRENGTHEN THE HANDS THAT ARE WEAK AND THE KNEES THAT ARE FEEBLE,

13 and make straight paths for your feet, so that what is lame may not be put out of joint, but rather be healed.

14 Pursue peace with all men, and the sanctification without which no one will see the Lord,

15 seeing to it that no one falls short of the grace of God; that no ROOT OF BITTERNESS SPRINGING UP CAUSES TROUBLE, and by it many be defiled;

16 that *also there be* no sexually immoral or godless person like Esau, who sold his own birthright for a *single* meal.

17 For you know that even afterwards, when he desired to inherit the blessing, he was rejected, for he found no place for repentance, though he sought for it with tears.

Contrast of Sinai and Zion

18 For you have not come to *a mountain* that can be touched and to a blazing fire, and to darkness and gloom and whirlwind,

19 and to the blast of a trumpet and the sound of words which *was such that* those who heard begged that no further word be spoken to them.

20 For they could not bear what was being commanded, "IF EVEN A BEAST TOUCHES THE MOUNTAIN, IT WILL BE STONED."

21 And so terrible was what appeared, *that* Moses said, "I AM FULL OF FEAR and trembling."

22 But you have come to Mount Zion and to the city of the living God,

the heavenly Jerusalem, and to myriads of angels,

23 to the festal gathering and assembly of the firstborn who are enrolled in heaven, and to God, the Judge of all, and to the spirits of *the* righteous made perfect,

24 and to Jesus, the mediator of a new covenant, and to the sprinkled blood, which speaks better than *the blood* of Abel.

An Unshakable Kingdom

25 See to it that you do not refuse Him who is speaking. For if those did not escape when they refused him who warned *them* on earth, much less *will* we *escape* who turn away from Him who *warns* from heaven.

26 And His voice shook the earth then, but now He has promised, saying, "YET ONCE MORE I WILL SHAKE NOT ONLY THE EARTH, BUT ALSO THE HEAVEN."

27 Now this *expression,* "Yet once more," indicates the removing of those things which can be shaken, as of created things, so that those things which cannot be shaken may remain.

28 Therefore, since we are receiving a kingdom which cannot be shaken, let us show gratitude, by which we may offer to God an acceptable service with reverence and awe;

29 for OUR GOD IS A CONSUMING FIRE.

CHAPTER 13

Sacrifices Pleasing to God

LET love of the brothers continue.

2 Do not neglect to show hospitality to strangers, for by this some have entertained angels without knowing it.

3 Remember the prisoners, as though in prison with them, *and* those who are mistreated, since you yourselves also are in the body.

4 Marriage *is to be held* in honor among all, and the *marriage* bed *is to be* undefiled, for the sexually immoral and adulterers God will judge.

5 *Make sure that* your way *of life* is free from the love of money, being content with what you have; for He Himself has said, "I WILL NEVER DESERT YOU, NOR WILL I EVER FORSAKE YOU,"

6 so that we confidently say,

"THE LORD IS MY HELPER, I WILL
    NOT BE AFRAID.
WHAT WILL MAN DO TO ME?"

7 Remember your leaders, who spoke the word of God to you; and considering the result of their conduct, imitate their faith.

8 Jesus Christ *is* the same yesterday and today and forever.

9 Do not be carried away by varied and strange teachings; for it is good for the heart to be strengthened by grace, not by foods, through which those who were so occupied were not benefited.

10 We have an altar from which those who serve the tabernacle have no authority to eat.

11 For the bodies of those animals whose blood is brought into the holy places by the high priest *as an offering* for sin, are burned outside the camp.

12 Therefore Jesus also, that He might sanctify the people through His own blood, suffered outside the gate.

13 So, let us go out to Him outside the camp, bearing His reproach.

14 For here we do not have a lasting city, but we are seeking *the one* to come.

15 Through Him then, let us continually offer up a sacrifice of praise to God, that is, the fruit of lips that confess His name.

16 And do not neglect doing good and sharing, for with such sacrifices God is pleased.

17 Obey your leaders and submit *to them*—for they keep watch over your souls as those who will give an account—so that they will do this with joy and not with groaning, for this would be unprofitable for you.

18 Pray for us, for we are convinced that we have a good conscience, desiring to conduct ourselves well in all things.

19 And I urge *you* all the more to do this, so that I may be restored to you the sooner.

Benediction

20 Now the God of peace, who brought up from the dead the great Shepherd of the sheep through the blood of the eternal covenant, our Lord Jesus,

21 equip you in every good thing to do His will, by doing in us what is pleasing in His sight, through Jesus Christ, to whom *be* the glory forever and ever. Amen.

22 But I urge you, brothers, bear with this word of exhortation, for I have written to you briefly.

23 Know that our brother Timothy has been released, with whom, if he comes soon, I will see you.

24 Greet all of your leaders and all the saints. Those from Italy greet you.

25 Grace be with you all.

THE LETTER OF
JAMES

CHAPTER 1

Testing Your Faith

JAMES, a slave of God and of the Lord Jesus Christ,

To the twelve tribes who are in the Dispersion: Greetings.

2 Consider it all joy, my brothers, when you encounter various trials,

3 knowing that the testing of your faith brings about perseverance.

4 And let perseverance have *its* perfect work, so that you may be perfect and complete, lacking in nothing.

5 But if any of you lacks wisdom, let him ask of God, who gives to all generously and without reproach, and it will be given to him.

6 But he must ask in faith, doubting nothing, for the one who doubts is like the surf of the sea, driven and tossed by the wind.

7 For that man ought not to expect that he will receive anything from the Lord,

8 *being* a double-minded man, unstable in all his ways.

9 But the brother of humble circumstances is to boast in his high position;

10 and the rich man *is to boast* in his humiliation, because like flowering grass he will pass away.

11 For the sun rises with a scorching heat and withers the grass; and its flower falls off and the beauty of its appearance is destroyed; so too the rich man in the midst of his pursuits will fade away.

12 Blessed is a man who perseveres under trial; for once he has been approved, he will receive the crown of life which *the Lord* has promised to those who love Him.

13 Let no one say when he is tempted, "I am being tempted by God"; for God cannot be tempted by evil, and He Himself does not tempt anyone.

14 But each one is tempted when he is carried away and enticed by his own lust.

15 Then when lust has conceived, it gives birth to sin, and when sin is fully matured, it brings forth death.

16 Do not be deceived, my beloved brothers.

17 Every good thing given and every perfect gift is from above, coming down from the Father of lights, with whom there is no variation or shifting shadow.

18 In the exercise of His will He brought us forth by the word of truth, so that we would be a kind of first fruits among His creatures.

Doers of the Word

19 Know *this*, my beloved brothers. But everyone must be quick to hear, slow to speak *and* slow to anger;

20 for the anger of man does not achieve the righteousness of God.

21 Therefore, laying aside all filthiness and *all* that remains of wickedness, in gentleness receive the implanted word, which is able to save your souls.

22 But become doers of the word, and not merely hearers who delude themselves.

23 For if anyone is a hearer of the word and not a doer, he is like a man who looks at his natural face in a mirror;

24 for *once* he looked at himself and has gone away, he immediately forgot what kind of person he was.

25 But one who looks intently at the perfect law, the *law* of freedom, and abides by it, not having become a forgetful hearer but a doer of the work, this man will be blessed in what he does.

26 If anyone thinks himself to be religious while not bridling his tongue but deceiving his *own* heart, this man's religion is worthless.

27 Pure and undefiled religion before

our God and Father is this: to visit orphans and widows in their affliction, *and* to keep oneself unstained by the world.

CHAPTER 2

The Sin of Favoritism

MY brothers, do not hold your faith in our glorious Lord Jesus Christ with *an attitude of* personal favoritism.

2 For if a man comes into your assembly with a gold ring and dressed in bright clothes, and there also comes in a poor man in dirty clothes,

3 and you pay special attention to the one who is wearing the bright clothes, and say, "You sit here in a good place," and you say to the poor man, "You stand over there, or sit down by my footstool,"

4 have you not made distinctions among yourselves, and become judges with evil thoughts?

5 Listen, my beloved brothers: did not God choose the poor of this world *to be* rich in faith and heirs of the kingdom which He promised to those who love Him?

6 But you have dishonored the poor man. Is it not the rich who oppress you and they themselves drag you into court?

7 Do they not blaspheme the good name by which you have been called?

8 If, however, you are fulfilling the royal law according to the Scripture, "YOU SHALL LOVE YOUR NEIGHBOR AS YOURSELF," you are doing well.

9 But if you show partiality, you are committing sin, being convicted by the law as transgressors.

10 For whoever keeps the whole law and yet stumbles in one *point*, he has become guilty of all.

11 For He who said, "DO NOT COMMIT ADULTERY," also said, "DO NOT MURDER." Now if you do not commit adultery, but murder, you have become a transgressor of the law.

12 So speak and so act as those who are to be judged by *the* law of freedom.

13 For judgment *will be* merciless to one who has shown no mercy. Mercy triumphs over judgment.

Faith and Works

14 What use is it, my brothers, if someone says he has faith but he has no works? Can that faith save him?

15 If a brother or sister is without clothing and in need of daily food,

16 and one of you says to them, "Go in peace, be warmed and be filled," and yet you do not give them what is necessary for *their* body, what use is that?

17 Even so faith, if it has no works, is dead by itself.

18 But someone will say, "You have faith; and I have works. Show me your faith without the works, and I will show you my faith by my works."

19 You believe that God is one. You do well; the demons also believe, and shudder.

20 But are you willing to recognize, you foolish fellow, that faith without works is useless?

21 Was not Abraham our father justified by works when he offered up Isaac his son on the altar?

22 You see that faith was working with his works, and as a result of the works, faith was perfected.

23 And the Scripture was fulfilled which says, "AND ABRAHAM BELIEVED GOD, AND IT WAS COUNTED TO HIM AS RIGHTEOUSNESS," and he was called the friend of God.

24 You see that a man is justified by works and not by faith alone.

25 And in the same way, was not Rahab the harlot also justified by works when she received the messengers and sent them out by another way?

26 For just as the body without the spirit is dead, so also faith without works is dead.

CHAPTER 3

The Tongue Is a Fire

DO not, many of you, become teachers, my brothers, knowing that we will receive a stricter judgment.

2 For we all stumble in many ways. If anyone does not stumble in what he says, he is a perfect man, able to bridle the entire body as well.

3 Now if we put the bits into the horses' mouths so that they will obey us, we direct their entire body as well.

4 Look at the ships also, though they are so great and are driven by strong winds, they are still directed by a very small rudder wherever the inclination of the pilot wills.

5 So also the tongue is a small part of the body, and yet it boasts of great things.

Behold how great a forest is set aflame by such a small fire!

6 And the tongue is a fire, the very world of unrighteousness; the tongue is set among our members as that which defiles the entire body, and sets on fire the course of our existence, and is set on fire by hell.

7 For every kind of beasts and birds, of reptiles and creatures of the sea, is tamed and has been tamed by mankind.

8 But no one can tame the tongue; it is a restless evil and full of deadly poison.

9 With it we bless our Lord and Father, and with it we curse men, who have been made in the likeness of God.

10 From the same mouth come blessing and cursing. My brothers, these things ought not to be so.

11 Does a fountain pour forth from the same opening fresh and bitter water?

12 Can a fig tree, my brothers, produce olives, or a vine produce figs? Nor can saltwater produce fresh.

Wisdom from Above

13 Who among you is wise and understanding? Let him show by his good conduct his works in the gentleness of wisdom.

14 But if you have bitter jealousy and selfish ambition in your heart, do not be arrogant and so lie against the truth.

15 This wisdom is not coming down from above, but is earthly, natural, demonic.

16 For where jealousy and selfish ambition exist, there is disorder and every evil practice.

17 But the wisdom from above is first pure, then peaceable, considerate, submissive, full of mercy and good fruits, without doubting, without hypocrisy.

18 And the fruit of righteousness is sown in peace by those who make peace.

CHAPTER 4

Draw Near to God

WHAT is the source of quarrels and conflicts among you? Is not the source your pleasures that wage war in your members?

2 You lust and do not have, *so you* murder. You are envious and cannot obtain, *so you* fight and quarrel. You do not have because you do not ask.

3 You ask and do not receive, because you ask with wrong motives, so that you may spend *it* on your pleasures.

4 You adulteresses, do you not know that friendship with the world is enmity *toward* God? Therefore, whoever wishes to be a friend of the world sets himself as an enemy of God.

5 Or do you think that the Scripture speaks to no purpose: "He jealously desires the Spirit which He has made to dwell in us"?

6 But He gives a greater grace. Therefore *it* says, "GOD IS OPPOSED TO THE PROUD, BUT GIVES GRACE TO THE HUMBLE."

7 Be subject therefore to God. Resist the devil and he will flee from you.

8 Draw near to God and He will draw near to you. Cleanse your hands, you sinners, and purify your hearts, you double-minded.

9 Be miserable and mourn and cry. Let your laughter be turned into mourning and your joy to gloom.

10 Humble yourselves in the presence of the Lord, and He will exalt you.

11 Do not slander one another, brothers. He who slanders a brother or judges his brother, slanders the law and judges the law; but if you judge the law, you are not a doer of the law but a judge *of it*.

12 There is *only* one Lawgiver and Judge, the One who is able to save and to destroy. But who are you who judge your neighbor?

Life Is a Vapor

13 Come now, you who say, "Today or tomorrow we will go to such and such a city, and spend a year there and engage in business and make a profit."

14 Yet you do not know what your life will be like tomorrow. You are a vapor that appears for a little while and then vanishes away.

15 Instead, you ought to say, "If the Lord wills, we will live and also do this or that."

16 But as it is, you boast in your arrogance. All such boasting is evil.

17 Therefore, to one who knows to do *the* right thing and does not do it, to him it is sin.

CHAPTER 5

Miseries of the Rich

COME now, you rich, cry, howling over your miseries which are coming upon you.

2 Your riches have rotted and your garments have become moth-eaten.

3 Your gold and your silver have rusted, and their corrosion will be a witness against you and will consume your flesh like fire. You have stored up *such* treasure in the last days!

4 Behold, the pay of the laborers who mowed your fields—that which has been withheld by you—cries out *against you*; and the outcries of those who did the harvesting have reached the ears of the Lord of Sabaoth.

5 You have lived luxuriously on the earth and lived in self-indulgence. You have fattened your hearts in a DAY OF SLAUGHTER.

6 You have condemned and murdered the righteous *man*; he does not resist you.

Patience and Perseverance

7 Therefore be patient, brothers, until the coming of the Lord. Behold, the farmer waits for the precious fruit of the soil, being patient about it, until it receives the early and late rains.

8 You too be patient; strengthen your hearts, for the coming of the Lord is at hand.

9 Do not groan, brothers, against one another, so that you yourselves may not be judged. Behold, the Judge is standing right at the door.

10 As an example, brothers, of suffering and patience, take the prophets who spoke in the name of the Lord.

11 Behold, we count those blessed who persevere. You have heard of the perseverance of Job and have seen the outcome of the Lord's dealings, that the Lord is full of compassion and *is* merciful.

12 But above all, my brothers, do not swear, either by heaven or by earth or with any other oath. But let your yes be yes, and your no, no, so that you may not fall under judgment.

13 Is anyone among you suffering? *Then* he must pray. Is anyone cheerful? He is to sing praises.

14 Is anyone among you sick? *Then* he must call for the elders of the church and they are to pray over him, anointing him with oil in the name of the Lord.

15 And the prayer offered in faith will save the one who is sick, and the Lord will raise him up, and if he has committed sins, they will be forgiven him.

16 Therefore, confess your sins to one another, and pray for one another so that you may be healed. The effective prayer of a righteous man can accomplish much.

17 Elijah was a man with a nature

like ours, and he prayed earnestly that it would not rain, and it did not rain on the earth for three years and six months.

18 Then he prayed again, and the sky gave rain and the earth produced its fruit.

19 My brothers, if any among you strays from the truth and one turns him back,

20 let him know that he who turns a sinner from the error of his way will save his soul from death and will COVER A MULTITUDE OF SINS.

THE FIRST LETTER OF

PETER

CHAPTER 1

A Living Hope

PETER, an apostle of Jesus Christ,

To those who reside as exiles, scattered throughout Pontus, Galatia, Cappadocia, Asia, and Bithynia, who are chosen

2 according to the foreknowledge of God the Father, by the sanctifying work of the Spirit, to the obedience of Jesus Christ and the sprinkling of His blood: May grace and peace be multiplied to you.

3 Blessed be the God and Father of our Lord Jesus Christ, who according to His great mercy has caused us to be born again to a living hope through the resurrection of Jesus Christ from the dead,

4 to *obtain* an inheritance incorruptible and undefiled and unfading, having been kept in heaven for you,

5 who are protected by the power of God through faith for a salvation ready to be revealed in the last time.

6 In this you greatly rejoice, even though now for a little while, if necessary, you have been grieved by various trials,

7 so that the proof of your faith, *being* more precious than gold which is perishable, even though tested by fire, may be found to result in praise and glory and honor at the revelation of Jesus Christ.

8 And though you have not seen Him, you love Him, and though you do not see Him now, but believe in Him, you rejoice with joy inexpressible and full of glory,

9 receiving as the outcome of your faith the salvation of your souls.

10 Concerning this salvation, the prophets, who prophesied of the grace that *would come* to you, made careful searches and inquiries,

11 inquiring to know what *time* or

what kind of time the Spirit of Christ within them was indicating as He was predicting the sufferings of Christ and the glories to follow.

12 It was revealed to them that they were not serving themselves, but you, in these things which now have been declared to you through those who proclaimed the gospel to you by the Holy Spirit sent from heaven— things into which angels long to look.

13 Therefore, having girded your minds for action, being sober *in spirit*, fix your hope completely on the grace to be brought to you at the revelation of Jesus Christ.

14 As obedient children, not being conformed to the former lusts *which were yours* in your ignorance,

15 but like the Holy One who called you, be holy yourselves also in all *your* conduct;

16 because it is written, "YOU SHALL BE HOLY, FOR I AM HOLY."

17 And if you address as Father the One who impartially judges according to each one's work, conduct yourselves in fear during the time of your sojourn,

18 knowing that you were not redeemed with corruptible things like silver or gold from your futile conduct inherited from your forefathers,

19 but with precious blood, as of a lamb unblemished and spotless, *the blood* of Christ.

20 He was foreknown before the foundation of the world, but appeared in these last times for the sake of you

21 who through Him are believers in God, who raised Him from the dead and gave Him glory, so that your faith and hope are in God.

22 Since you have in obedience to the truth purified your souls for a love of the brothers without hypocrisy, fervently love one another from the heart,

23 for you have been born again not of corruptible seed but incorruptible, *that is*, through the living and enduring word of God.

24 For,

"ALL FLESH IS LIKE GRASS,
AND ALL ITS GLORY LIKE THE
  FLOWER OF GRASS.
THE GRASS WITHERS,
AND THE FLOWER FALLS OFF,
25 BUT THE WORD OF THE LORD
  ENDURES FOREVER."

And this is the word which was proclaimed to you as good news.

CHAPTER 2

As Living Stones, God's Chosen Family

THEREFORE, laying aside all malice and all deceit and hypocrisy and envy and all slander,

2 like newborn babies, long for the pure milk of the word, so that by it you may grow in respect to salvation,

3 if you have TASTED THE KINDNESS OF THE LORD.

4 *And* coming to Him as to a living stone which has been rejected by men, but is choice and precious in the sight of God,

5 you also, as living stones, are being built up as a spiritual house for a holy priesthood, to offer up spiritual sacrifices acceptable to God through Jesus Christ.

6 For *this* is contained in Scripture:
"Behold, I lay in Zion a choice stone, a precious corner *stone*,
And he who believes upon Him will not be put to shame."

7 This precious value, then, is for you who believe; but for those who disbelieve,
"The stone which the builders rejected,
This has become the chief corner *stone*,"

8 and,
"A stone of stumbling and a rock of offense."
They stumble because they are disobedient to the word, and to this *stumbling* they were also appointed.

9 But you are a chosen family, a royal priesthood, a holy nation, a people for *God's* own possession, so that you may proclaim the excellencies of Him who has called you out of darkness into His marvelous light;

10 for you once were not a people, but now you are the people of God; you had not received mercy, but now you have received mercy.

11 Beloved, I urge you as sojourners and exiles to abstain from fleshly lusts which wage war against the soul,

12 by keeping your conduct excellent among the Gentiles, so that in the thing which they slander you as evildoers, they may because of your good works, as they observe *them*, glorify God in the day of visitation.

Be Subject to Authority

13 Be subject for the sake of the Lord to every human institution, whether to a king as the one in authority,

14 or to governors as sent by him for the punishment of evildoers and the praise of those who do good.

15 For such is the will of God that by doing good you may silence the ignorance of foolish men.

16 *Act* as free people, and do not use your freedom as a covering for evil, but *use it* as slaves of God.

17 Honor all people, love the brethren, fear God, honor the king.

18 Servants, be subject to your masters with all fear, not only to those who are good and considerate, but also to those who are crooked.

19 For this *finds* favor, if for the sake of conscience toward God a person bears up under sorrows when suffering unrighteously.

20 For what credit is there if, when you sin and are harshly treated, you endure? But if when you do good and suffer *for it*, you endure, this *finds* favor with God.

Christ, Our Example

21 For to this you have been called, since Christ also suffered for you, leaving you an example that you should follow in His steps,

22 who did no sin, nor was any deceit found in His mouth;

23 who being reviled, was not reviling in return; while suffering, He was uttering no threats, but kept entrusting *Himself* to Him who judges righteously.

24 Who Himself bore our sins in His body on the tree, so that having died to sin, we might live to righteousness; by His WOUNDS YOU WERE HEALED.

25 For you were continually straying like sheep, but now you have returned to the Shepherd and Overseer of your souls.

CHAPTER 3

Wives and Husbands

IN the same way, you wives, be subject to your own husbands so that even if any *of them* are disobedient to the word, they may be won without a word by the conduct of their wives,

2 as they observe your pure conduct with fear.

3 Your adornment must not be *merely* external—braiding the hair, and wearing gold jewelry, or putting on garments;

4 but *let it be* the hidden person of the heart, with the incorruptible quality of a lowly and quiet spirit, which *is* precious in the sight of God.

5 For in this way in former times the holy women also, who hoped in God, used to adorn themselves, being subject to their own husbands,

6 just as Sarah obeyed Abraham, calling him lord. You have become her children if you do good, NOT FEARING ANY INTIMIDATION.

7 You husbands in the same way, live with *your wives* in an understanding way, as with a weaker vessel, since she is a woman; and show her honor as a fellow heir of the grace of life, so that your prayers will not be hindered.

8 Now to sum up, all of you be likeminded, sympathetic, brotherly, tenderhearted, and humble in spirit;

9 not returning evil for evil or reviling for reviling, but giving a blessing instead, for you were called for the very purpose that you might inherit a blessing.

10 For,

"THE ONE WHO DESIRES LIFE, TO
    LOVE AND SEE GOOD DAYS,
MUST KEEP HIS TONGUE FROM
    EVIL AND HIS LIPS FROM
    SPEAKING DECEIT.

11 "HE MUST TURN AWAY FROM EVIL
    AND DO GOOD;
HE MUST SEEK PEACE AND
    PURSUE IT.

12 "FOR THE EYES OF THE LORD ARE
    TOWARD THE RIGHTEOUS,
AND HIS EARS ATTEND TO THEIR
    PRAYER,
BUT THE FACE OF THE LORD
    IS AGAINST THOSE WHO
    DO EVIL."

Suffering for Righteousness

13 And who is there to harm you if you prove zealous for what is good?

14 But even if you should suffer

for the sake of righteousness, you are blessed. AND DO NOT FEAR THEIR FEAR, AND DO NOT BE TROUBLED,

15 but sanctify Christ as Lord in your hearts, always *being* ready to make a defense to everyone who asks you to give an account for the hope that is in you, yet with gentleness and fear,

16 having a good conscience so that in the thing in which you are slandered, those who disparage your good conduct in Christ will be put to shame.

17 For it is better, if God should will it so, that you suffer for doing good rather than for doing wrong.

18 For Christ also suffered for sins once for all, *the* righteous for *the* unrighteous, so that He might bring you to God, having been put to death in the flesh, but made alive in the spirit;

19 in which also He went and made proclamation to the spirits *now* in prison,

20 who once were disobedient, when the patience of God kept waiting in the days of Noah, during the construction of the ark, in which a few, that is, eight persons, were brought safely through *the* water.

21 Corresponding to that, baptism now saves you—not the removal of dirt from the flesh, but an appeal of a good conscience to God—through the resurrection of Jesus Christ,

22 who is at the right hand of God, having gone into heaven, after angels and authorities and powers had been subjected to Him.

CHAPTER 4

Keep Fervent in Your Love

THEREFORE, since Christ has suffered in the flesh, arm yourselves also with the same purpose— because he who has suffered in the flesh has ceased from sin—

2 so as to no longer live the rest of the time in the flesh for the lusts of men, but for the will of God.

3 For the time already past is sufficient *for you* to have worked out the desire of the Gentiles, having pursued a course of sensuality, lusts, drunkenness, carousing, drinking parties, and abominable idolatries.

4 In *all* this, they are surprised that you do not run with *them* into the same excesses of dissipation, maligning *you*,

5 but they will give account to Him who is ready to judge the living and the dead.

6 For to this the gospel has been proclaimed even to those who are *now* dead, so that though they were judged in the flesh as men, they live in the spirit according to *the will of* God.

7 The end of all things is at hand; therefore, be of sound thinking and sober *spirit* for the purpose of prayer.

8 Above all, keep fervent in your love for one another, because LOVE COVERS A MULTITUDE OF SINS.

9 Be hospitable to one another without grumbling.

10 As each one has received a gift, employ it in serving one another as

good stewards of the manifold grace of God—

11 whoever speaks, as one *speaking* the oracles of God; whoever serves, as one *serving* by the strength which God supplies; so that in all things God may be glorified through Jesus Christ, to whom belongs the glory and might forever and ever. Amen.

Sharing the Suffering of Christ

12 Beloved, do not be surprised at the fiery trial among you, which comes upon you for your testing, as though some strange thing were happening to you.

13 But to the degree you are sharing the sufferings of Christ, keep on rejoicing, so that also at the revelation of His glory you may rejoice with exultation.

14 If you are insulted for the name of Christ, you are blessed, because the Spirit of glory and of God rests on you.

15 Make sure that none of you suffers as a murderer, or thief, or evildoer, or a troublesome meddler;

16 but if *anyone suffers* as a Christian, he is not to be put to shame, but is to glorify God in this name.

17 For *it is* time for judgment to begin with the house of God; and if *it begins* with us first, what *will be* the outcome for those who do not obey the gospel of God?

18 AND IF IT IS WITH DIFFICULTY THAT THE RIGHTEOUS IS SAVED, WHAT WILL BECOME OF THE GODLESS MAN AND THE SINNER?

19 Therefore, those also who suffer according to the will of God must entrust their souls to a faithful Creator in doing good.

CHAPTER 5

Shepherd the Flock of God

THEREFORE, I exhort the elders among you, as *your* fellow elder and witness of the sufferings of Christ, and a partaker also of the glory that is to be revealed,

2 shepherd the flock of God among you, overseeing not under compulsion, but willingly, according to God; and not for dishonest gain, but with eagerness;

3 nor yet as lording it over those allotted to you, but being examples to the flock.

4 And when the Chief Shepherd appears, you will receive the unfading crown of glory.

5 You younger men, likewise, be subject to *your* elders. And all of you, clothe yourselves with humility toward one another, for GOD IS OPPOSED TO THE PROUD, BUT GIVES GRACE TO THE HUMBLE.

6 Therefore humble yourselves under the mighty hand of God, that He may exalt you at the proper time,

7 CASTING ALL YOUR ANXIETY ON HIM, because He cares for you.

8 Be of sober *spirit*, be watchful. Your adversary, the devil, prowls around like a roaring lion, seeking someone to devour.

9 But resist him, firm in the faith, knowing that the same experiences of suffering are being accomplished among your brethren who are in the world.

10 And after you have suffered for a little while, the God of all grace, who called you to His eternal glory in Christ, will Himself restore, strengthen, confirm, *and* ground you.

11 To Him *be* might forever and ever. Amen.

12 Through Silvanus, our faithful brother as I regard *him*, I have written to you briefly, exhorting and bearing witness that this is the true grace of God. Stand firm in it!

13 She who is in Babylon, chosen together with you, sends you greetings, and *so does* my son, Mark.

14 Greet one another with a kiss of love.

Peace be to you all who are in Christ.

THE SECOND LETTER OF
PETER

CHAPTER 1

Precious and Magnificent Promises

SIMEON Peter, a slave and apostle of Jesus Christ,

To those who have received the same kind of faith as ours, by the righteousness of our God and Savior, Jesus Christ:

2 Grace and peace be multiplied to you in the full knowledge of God and of Jesus our Lord;

3 seeing that His divine power has granted to us everything pertaining to life and godliness, through the full knowledge of Him who called us by His own glory and excellence.

4 For by these He has granted to us His precious and magnificent promises, so that by them you may become partakers of *the* divine nature, having escaped the corruption that is in the world by lust.

5 Now for this very reason also, applying all diligence, in your faith supply moral excellence, and in *your* moral excellence, knowledge,

6 and in *your* knowledge, self-control, and in *your* self-control, perseverance, and in *your* perseverance, godliness,

7 and in *your* godliness, brotherly kindness, and in *your* brotherly kindness, love.

8 For if these things are yours and are increasing, they render you neither useless nor unfruitful in the full knowledge of our Lord Jesus Christ.

9 For in whom these things are not present, *that one* is blind, being near-sighted, having forgotten the purification from his former sins.

10 Therefore, brothers, be all the more diligent to make your calling and choosing sure; for in doing these things, you will never stumble;

11 for in this way the entrance into the eternal kingdom of our Lord and Savior Jesus Christ will be abundantly supplied to you.

12 Therefore, I will always be ready to remind you of these things, even though you *already* know *them*, and have been strengthened in the truth which is present with *you.*

13 I consider it right, as long as I am in this *earthly* dwelling, to stir you up by way of reminder,

14 knowing that the laying aside of my *earthly* dwelling is imminent, as also our Lord Jesus Christ has indicated to me.

15 And I will also be diligent that at any time after my departure you will be able to call these things to mind.

Eyewitnesses of Jesus

16 For we did not make known to you the power and coming of our Lord Jesus Christ, following cleverly devised myths, but being eyewitnesses of His majesty.

17 For when He received honor and glory from God the Father, such an utterance as this was made to Him by the Majestic Glory, "This is My beloved Son with whom I am well-pleased"—

18 and we ourselves heard this utterance made from heaven when we were with Him on the holy mountain.

19 And we have as more sure the prophetic word, to which you do well to pay attention as to a lamp shining in a dark place, until the day dawns and the morning star arises in your hearts.

20 Know this first of all, that no prophecy of Scripture comes by one's own interpretation.

21 For no prophecy was ever made by the will of man, but men being moved by the Holy Spirit spoke from God.

CHAPTER 2

The Rise of False Prophets

BUT false prophets also arose among the people, just as there will also be false teachers among you, who will secretly introduce destructive heresies, even denying the Master who bought them, bringing swift destruction upon themselves.

2 And many will follow their sensuality, and because of them the way of the truth will be maligned.

3 And in *their* greed they will exploit you with false words, their judgment from long ago is not idle, and their destruction is not asleep.

4 For if God did not spare angels who sinned, but cast them into the pit and delivered them to chains of darkness, being kept for judgment;

5 and did not spare the ancient world, but preserved Noah, a preacher of righteousness, with seven others,

when He brought a flood upon the world of the ungodly;

6 and *if* He condemned the cities of Sodom and Gomorrah to destruction by reducing *them* to ashes, having made them an example to those who would live ungodly *lives* thereafter;

7 and *if* He rescued righteous Lot, oppressed by the sensual conduct of unprincipled men

8 (for by what he saw and heard *that* righteous man, while living among them, felt *his* righteous soul tormented day after day by *their* lawless deeds),

9 *then* the Lord knows how to rescue the godly from trial, and to keep the unrighteous under punishment for the day of judgment,

10 and especially those who go after the flesh in *its* corrupt lust and despise authority.

Daring, self-willed, they do not tremble when they blaspheme glorious ones,

11 whereas angels who are greater in strength and power do not bring a reviling judgment against them before the Lord.

12 But these, like unreasoning animals, born as creatures of instinct to be captured and killed, blaspheming where they have no knowledge, will in the destruction of those creatures also be destroyed,

13 suffering unrighteousness as the wages of *their* unrighteousness, considering it a pleasure to revel in the daytime—*they are* stains and blemishes, reveling in their deceptions, as they feast with you,

14 having eyes full of adultery and unceasing sin, enticing unstable souls, having a heart trained in greed—*they are* accursed children.

15 Forsaking the right way, they have gone astray, having followed the way of Balaam, the *son* of Beor, who loved the wages of unrighteousness,

16 but he received a rebuke for his own lawlessness, *for* a mute donkey, speaking out with a voice of a man, restrained the madness of the prophet.

17 These are springs without water and mists driven by a storm, for whom the black darkness has been kept.

18 For speaking out arrogant *words* of vanity, they entice by sensual lusts of the flesh, those who barely escape from the ones who conducted themselves in error,

19 promising them freedom while they themselves are slaves of corruption; for by what a man is overcome, by this he is enslaved.

20 For if they are overcome, having *both* escaped the defilements of the world by the knowledge of the Lord and Savior Jesus Christ and having again been entangled in them, *then* the last state has become worse for them than the first.

21 For it would be better for them not to have known the way of righteousness, than having known it, to turn away from the holy commandment handed on to them.

22 The *message* of the true proverb has happened to them, "A DOG RETURNS TO ITS OWN VOMIT," and, "A

sow, after washing, *returns* to wallowing in the mire."

CHAPTER 3

The Day of the Lord Will Come

THIS is now, beloved, the second letter I am writing to you in which I am stirring up your sincere mind by way of reminder,

2 that you should remember the words spoken beforehand by the holy prophets and the commandment of the Lord and Savior *spoken* by your apostles,

3 knowing this first of all, that in the last days mockers will come with *their* mocking, following after their own lusts,

4 and saying, "Where is the promise of His coming? For since the fathers fell asleep, all continues just as it was from the beginning of creation."

5 For when they maintain this, it escapes their notice that by the word of God *the* heavens existed long ago and *the* earth was formed out of water and by water,

6 through which the world at that time was destroyed, being deluged with water.

7 But by His word the present heavens and earth are being reserved for fire, being kept for the day of judgment and destruction of ungodly men.

8 But do not let this one *fact* escape your notice, beloved, that with the Lord one day is like a thousand years, and a thousand years like one day.

9 The Lord is not slow about His promise, as some consider slowness, but is patient toward you, not willing for any to perish but for all to come to repentance.

10 But the day of the Lord will come like a thief, in which the heavens will pass away with a roar and the elements will be destroyed with intense heat, and the earth and its works will be found *out*.

11 Since all these things are to be destroyed in this way, what sort of people ought you to be in holy conduct and godliness,

12 looking for and hastening the coming of the day of God, because of which the heavens burning will be destroyed, and the elements will melt with intense heat!

13 But according to His promise we are looking for NEW HEAVENS AND A NEW EARTH, in which righteousness dwells.

Be on Your Guard

14 Therefore, beloved, since you are looking for these things, be diligent to be found by Him in peace, spotless and blameless,

15 and consider the patience of our Lord *as* salvation, just as also our beloved brother Paul, according to the wisdom given him, wrote to you,

16 as also in all *his* letters, speaking in them of these things, in which are some things hard to understand, which the untaught and unstable distort, as *they do* also the rest of the Scriptures, to their own destruction.

17 You therefore, beloved, knowing

this beforehand, be on your guard lest you, having been carried away by the error of unprincipled men, fall from your own steadfastness,

18 but grow in the grace and knowledge of our Lord and Savior Jesus Christ. To Him *be* the glory, both now and to the day of eternity. Amen.

THE FIRST LETTER OF

JOHN

CHAPTER 1

The Word of Life

WHAT was from the beginning, what we have heard, what we have seen with our eyes, what we beheld and touched with our hands, concerning the Word of Life—

2 and the life was manifested, and we have seen and bear witness and proclaim to you the eternal life, which was with the Father and was manifested to us—

3 what we have seen and heard we proclaim to you also, so that you may also have fellowship with us; and indeed our *fellowship* is with the Father, and with His Son Jesus Christ.

4 And these things we are writing, so that our joy may be made complete.

God Is Light

5 And this is the message we have heard from Him and declare to you, that God is Light, and in Him there is no darkness at all.

6 If we say that we have fellowship with Him and *yet* walk in the darkness, we lie and do not do the truth;

7 but if we walk in the Light as He Himself is in the Light, we have fellowship with one another, and the blood of Jesus His Son cleanses us from all sin.

8 If we say that we have no sin, we deceive ourselves and the truth is not in us.

9 If we confess our sins, He is faithful and righteous to forgive us our sins and to cleanse us from all unrighteousness.

10 If we say that we have not sinned, we make Him a liar and His word is not in us.

CHAPTER 2

Jesus Christ Our Advocate

MY little children, I am writing these things to you so that you may not sin. And if anyone sins, we have an Advocate with the Father, Jesus Christ the righteous;

2 and He Himself is the propitiation for our sins, and not for ours only, but also for *those of* the whole world.

3 And by this we know that we have come to know Him, if we keep His commandments.

4 The one who says, "I have come to know Him," and does not keep His commandments, is a liar, and the truth is not in him;

5 but whoever keeps His word, truly in him the love of God has been perfected. By this we know that we are in Him:

6 the one who says he abides in Him ought himself to walk in the same manner as He walked.

7 Beloved, I am not writing a new commandment to you, but an old commandment which you have had from the beginning; the old commandment is the word which you have heard.

8 On the other hand, I am writing a new commandment to you, which is true in Him and in you, because the darkness is passing away and the true Light is already shining.

9 The one who says he is in the Light and *yet* hates his brother is in the darkness until now.

10 The one who loves his brother abides in the Light and there is no cause for stumbling in him.

11 But *the one who hates his broth-*er is in the darkness and walks in the darkness, and does not know where he is going because the darkness blinded his eyes.

12 I am writing to you, little children,

because your sins have been forgiven you for His name's sake.

13 I am writing to you, fathers, because you have known Him who has been from the beginning. I am writing to you, young men, because you have overcome the evil one. I have written to you, children, because you have known the Father.

14 I have written to you, fathers, because you have known Him who has been from the beginning. I have written to you, young men, because you are strong, and the word of God abides in you, and you have overcome the evil one.

Do Not Love the World

15 Do not love the world nor the things in the world. If anyone loves the world, the love of the Father is not in him.

16 For all that is in the world, the lust of the flesh and the lust of the eyes and the boastful pride of life, is not from the Father, but is from the world.

17 And the world is passing away, and *also* its lusts, but the one who does the will of God abides forever.

18 Children, it is the last hour; and just as you heard that antichrist is coming, even now many antichrists have appeared. From this we know that it is the last hour.

19 They went out from us, but they were not *really* of us; for if they were of us, they would have remained with us; but *they went out*, so that it would be manifested that they all are not of us.

20 But you have an anointing from the Holy One, and you all know.

21 I have not written to you because you do not know the truth, but because you do know it, and because no lie is of the truth.

22 Who is the liar but the one who denies that Jesus is the Christ? This is the antichrist, the one who denies the Father and the Son.

23 Everyone who denies the Son does not have the Father; the one who confesses the Son has the Father also.

24 As for you, let that which you heard from the beginning abide in you. If what you heard from the beginning abides in you, you also will abide in the Son and in the Father.

25 And this is the promise which He Himself made to us: eternal life.

26 These things I have written to you about those who are trying to deceive you.

27 And as for you, the anointing whom you received from Him abides in you, and you have no need for anyone to teach you. But as His anointing teaches you about all things, and is true and is not a lie, and just as He has taught you, abide in Him.

28 And now, little children, abide in Him, so that when He is manifested, we may have confidence and not shrink away from Him in shame at His coming.

29 If you know that He is righteous, you know that everyone also who does righteousness has been born of Him.

CHAPTER 3

Children of God, Love One Another

SEE how great a love the Father has given to us, that we would be called children of God; and we are. For this reason the world does not know us, because it did not know Him.

2 Beloved, now we are children of God, and it has not been manifested as yet what we will be. We know that when He is manifested, we will be like Him, because we will see Him just as He is.

3 And everyone who has this hope *fixed* on Him purifies himself, just as He is pure.

4 Everyone who does sin also does lawlessness; and sin is lawlessness.

5 And you know that He was manifested in order to take away sins, and in Him there is no sin.

6 No one who abides in Him sins; no one who sins has seen Him or has come to know Him.

7 Little children, let no one deceive you. The one who does righteousness is righteous, just as He is righteous.

8 The one who does sin is of the devil, because the devil sins from the beginning. The Son of God was manifested for this purpose, to destroy the works of the devil.

9 Everyone who has been born of God does not sin, because His seed abides in him; and he cannot sin, because he has been born of God.

10 By this the children of God and the children of the devil are

manifested: everyone who does not do righteousness is not of God, as well as the one who does not love his brother.

11 For this is the message which you have heard from the beginning, that we should love one another;

12 not as Cain, *who* was of the evil one and slew his brother. And for what reason did he slay him? Because his deeds were evil, and his brother's *were* righteous.

13 Do not marvel, brothers, if the world hates you.

14 We know that we have passed out of death into life, because we love the brothers. The one who does not love abides in death.

15 Everyone who hates his brother is a murderer, and you know that no murderer has eternal life abiding in him.

16 By this we have known love, that He laid down His life for us; and we ought to lay down our lives for the brothers.

17 But whoever has the world's goods, and sees his brother in need and closes his heart against him, how does the love of God abide in him?

18 Little children, let us not love with word or with tongue, but in deed and truth.

19 And by this we will know that we are of the truth, and will assure our heart before Him

20 in whatever our heart condemns us; for God is greater than our heart and knows all things.

21 Beloved, if our heart does not condemn us, we have confidence before God;

22 and whatever we ask we receive from Him, because we keep His commandments and do the things that are pleasing in His sight.

23 And this is His commandment, that we believe in the name of His Son Jesus Christ, and love one another, just as He gave a commandment to us.

24 And the one who keeps His commandments abides in Him, and He in him. We know by this that He abides in us, by the Spirit whom He gave us.

CHAPTER 4

Test the Spirits

BELOVED, do not believe every spirit, but test the spirits to see whether they are from God, because many false prophets have gone out into the world.

2 By this you know the Spirit of God: every spirit that confesses that Jesus Christ has come in the flesh is from God,

3 and every spirit that does not confess Jesus is not from God. This is the *spirit* of the antichrist, of which you have heard that it is coming, and now it is already in the world.

4 You are from God, little children, and have overcome them; because greater is He who is in you than he who is in the world.

5 They are from the world; therefore

they speak *as* from the world, and the world hears them.

6 We are from God. The one who knows God hears us; the one who is not from God does not hear us. From this we know the spirit of truth and the spirit of error.

God Is Love

7 Beloved, let us love one another, for love is from God; and everyone who loves has been born of God and knows God.

8 The one who does not love does not know God, because God is love.

9 By this the love of God was manifested in us, that God has sent His only begotten Son into the world so that we might live through Him.

10 In this is love, not that we have loved God, but that He loved us and sent His Son *to be* the propitiation for our sins.

11 Beloved, if God so loved us, we also ought to love one another.

12 No one has beheld God at any time; if we love one another, God abides in us, and His love is perfected in us.

13 By this we know that we abide in Him and He in us, because He has given us of His Spirit.

14 We have beheld and bear witness that the Father has sent the Son *to be* the Savior of the world.

15 Whoever confesses that Jesus is the Son of God, God abides in him, and he in God.

16 And we have come to know and have believed the love which God has in us. God is love, and the one who abides in love abides in God, and God abides in him.

17 By this, love has been perfected with us, so that we may have confidence in the day of judgment, because as He is, so also are we in this world.

18 There is no fear in love; but perfect love casts out fear, because fear involves punishment, and the one who fears is not perfected in love.

19 We love, because He first loved us.

20 If someone says, "I love God," and hates his brother, he is a liar; for the one who does not love his brother whom he has seen, cannot love God whom he has not seen.

21 And this commandment we have from Him, that the one who loves God should love his brother also.

CHAPTER 5

Overcoming the World

EVERYONE who believes that Jesus is the Christ has been born of God, and everyone who loves the One who gives *new* birth loves also the one who has been born of Him.

2 By this we know that we love the children of God, when we love God and do His commandments.

3 For this is the love of God, that we keep His commandments; and His commandments are not burdensome.

4 For everything that has been born of God overcomes the world; and this is the overcoming that has overcome the world—our faith.

5 Who is the one who overcomes the world, but he who believes that Jesus is the Son of God?

6 This is the One who came by water and blood, Jesus Christ; not with the water only, but with the water and with the blood. It is the Spirit who bears witness, because the Spirit is the truth.

7 For there are three that bear witness:

8 the Spirit and the water and the blood; and the three are in agreement.

9 If we receive the witness of men, the witness of God is greater; for the witness of God is this, that He has borne witness about His Son.

10 The one who believes in the Son of God has this witness in himself. The one who does not believe God has made Him a liar, because he has not believed in the witness which God has borne witness about His Son.

11 And the witness is this, that God gave us eternal life, and this life is in His Son.

12 He who has the Son has the life; he who does not have the Son of God does not have that life.

That You May Know

13 These things I have written to you who believe in the name of the Son of God, so that you may know that you have eternal life.

14 And this is the confidence which we have before Him, that, if we ask anything according to His will, He hears us.

15 And if we know that He hears us *in* whatever we ask, we know that we have the requests which we have asked from Him.

16 If anyone sees his brother committing a sin not *leading* to death, he shall ask and *God* will for him give life to those who commit sin not *leading* to death. There is a sin *leading* to death; I do not say that he should make request for this.

17 All unrighteousness is sin, and there is a sin not *leading* to death.

18 We know that no one who has been born of God sins; but He who was begotten of God keeps him, and the evil one does not touch him.

19 We know that we are of God, and that the whole world lies in *the power of* the evil one.

20 And we know that the Son of God has come, and has given us understanding so that we may know Him who is true; and we are in Him who is true, in His Son Jesus Christ. This is the true God and eternal life.

21 Little children, guard yourselves from idols.

THE SECOND LETTER OF
JOHN

Walk in Truth and Love

THE elder to the elect lady and her children, whom I love in truth, and not only I, but also all who know the truth,

2 for the sake of the truth which abides in us and will be with us forever:

3 Grace, mercy *and* peace will be with us, from God the Father and from Jesus Christ, the Son of the Father, in truth and love.

4 I rejoiced greatly to find *some* of your children walking in truth, just as we received commandment from the Father.

5 Now I ask you, lady, not as though I *were* writing to you a new commandment, but the one which we have had from the beginning, that we love one another.

6 And this is love, that we walk according to His commandments. This is the commandment, just as you have heard from the beginning, that you should walk in it.

7 For many deceivers have gone out into the world, those who do not confess Jesus Christ *as* coming in the flesh. This is the deceiver and the antichrist.

8 See to yourselves, that you do not lose what we accomplished, but that you may receive a full reward.

9 Anyone who goes too far and does not abide in the teaching of Christ, does not have God. The one who abides in the teaching, he has both the Father and the Son.

10 If anyone comes to you and does not bring this teaching, do not receive him into *your* house, and do not give him a greeting,

11 for the one who gives him a greeting participates in his evil deeds.

12 Though I have many things to write to you, I do not want to *do so* with paper and ink; but I hope to come to you and speak face to face, so that your joy may be made complete.

13 The children of your elect sister greet you.

JOHN

Walking in the Truth

THE elder to the beloved Gaius, whom I love in truth.

2 Beloved, I pray that in all respects you may prosper and be in good health, just as your soul prospers.

3 For I rejoiced greatly when brothers came and bore witness to your truth, *that is*, how you are walking in truth.

4 I have no greater joy than this, to hear that my children are walking in the truth.

5 Beloved, you are acting faithfully in whatever work you do for the brothers, and *are doing* this *though they are* strangers;

6 and they bore witness to your love before the church. You will do well to send them on their way in a manner worthy of God.

7 For they went out for the sake of the Name, receiving nothing from the Gentiles.

8 Therefore we ought to support such men, so that we may be fellow workers with the truth.

9 I wrote something to the church, but Diotrephes, who loves to be first among them, does not welcome what we say.

10 For this reason, if I come, I will bring to remembrance his deeds which he does, unjustly disparaging us with wicked words. And not satisfied with this, he himself does not welcome the brothers either, and he forbids those who want *to do so* and puts *them* out of the church.

11 Beloved, do not imitate what is evil, but what is good. The one who does good is of God; the one who does evil has not seen God.

12 Demetrius has received a *good* witness from everyone, and from the truth itself; and we add our witness, and you know that our witness is true.

13 I had many things to write to you, but I am not willing to write *them* to you with pen and ink;

14 but I hope to see you shortly, and we will speak face to face.

15 Peace *be* to you. The friends greet you. Greet the friends by name.

THE LETTER OF

JUDE

Contend Earnestly for the Faith

JUDE, a slave of Jesus Christ, and brother of James,

To those who are the called, beloved in God the Father, and kept for Jesus Christ:

2 May mercy and peace and love be multiplied to you.

3 Beloved, while I was making every effort to write you about our common salvation, I felt the necessity to write to you exhorting that you contend earnestly for the faith which was once for all handed down to the saints.

4 For certain persons have crept in unnoticed, those who were long beforehand marked out for this condemnation, ungodly persons who turn the grace of our God into sensuality and deny our only Master and Lord, Jesus Christ.

5 Now I want to remind you, though you know all things, that Jesus, having once saved a people out of the land of Egypt, subsequently destroyed those who did not believe.

6 And angels who did not keep their own domain, but abandoned their proper abode, He has kept in eternal bonds under darkness for the judgment of the great day,

7 just as Sodom and Gomorrah and the cities around them, having indulged in the same way as these in gross sexual immorality and having gone after strange flesh, are exhibited as an example in undergoing the punishment of eternal fire.

8 Yet in the same way these men, also by dreaming, defile the flesh, and reject authority, and blaspheme glorious ones.

9 But Michael the archangel, when he, disputing with the devil, was arguing about the body of Moses, did not dare pronounce against him a blasphemous judgment, but said, "The Lord rebuke you!"

10 But these men blaspheme the things which they do not understand; and the things which they know by instinct, like unreasoning animals, by these things they are destroyed.

11 Woe to them! For they have gone the way of Cain, and for pay they have poured themselves into the error of Balaam, and perished in the rebellion of Korah.

12 These are the men who are hidden reefs in your love feasts when they feast with you without fear, caring for themselves; clouds without water, carried along by winds; autumn trees without fruit, doubly dead, uprooted;

13 wild waves of the sea, casting up their own shame like foam; wandering stars, for whom the black darkness has been reserved forever.

14 But Enoch, *in* the seventh *generation* from Adam, also prophesied about these men, saying, "Behold, the Lord came with many thousands of His holy ones,

15 to execute judgment upon all, and to convict all the ungodly of all their ungodly deeds which they have done in an ungodly way, and of all the harsh things which ungodly sinners have spoken against Him."

16 These are grumblers, finding fault, following after their *own* lusts; and their mouth speaks arrogantly, flattering people for the sake of *their own* benefit.

Keep Yourselves in the Love of God

17 But you, beloved, must remember the words that were spoken beforehand by the apostles of our Lord Jesus Christ,

18 that they were saying to you, "In the last time there will be mockers, following after their own ungodly lusts."

19 These are the ones who cause divisions, worldly-minded, not having the Spirit.

20 But you, beloved, building yourselves up on your most holy faith, praying in the Holy Spirit,

21 keep yourselves in the love of God, waiting for the mercy of our Lord Jesus Christ to eternal life.

22 And on some, who are doubting, have mercy;

23 and for others, save, snatching them out of the fire; and on others have mercy with fear, hating even the tunic polluted by the flesh.

24 Now to Him who is able to keep you from stumbling, and to make you stand in the presence of His glory blameless with great joy,

25 to the only God our Savior, through Jesus Christ our Lord, *be* glory, majesty, might, and authority, before all time and now and forever. Amen.

THE REVELATION
TO JOHN

CHAPTER 1

The Revelation of Jesus Christ

THE Revelation of Jesus Christ, which God gave Him to show to His slaves the things which must soon happen; and He indicated *this* by sending *it* through His angel to His slave John,

2 who bore witness to the word of God and to the witness of Jesus Christ, *even* to all that he saw.

3 Blessed is he who reads and those who hear the words of the

prophecy and keep the things which are written in it, for the time is near.

Message to the Seven Churches

4 John to the seven churches that are in Asia: Grace to you and peace, from the One who is and who was and who is to come, and from the seven Spirits who are before His throne,
5 and from Jesus Christ, the faithful witness, the firstborn of the dead, and the ruler of the kings of the earth. To Him who loves us and released us from our sins by His blood—
6 and He has made us *to be* a kingdom, priests to His God and Father—to Him *be* the glory and the might forever and ever. Amen.
7 BEHOLD, HE IS COMING WITH THE CLOUDS, and EVERY EYE WILL SEE HIM, EVEN THOSE WHO PIERCED HIM; and all the tribes of the earth will MOURN OVER HIM. Yes, amen.
8 "I am the Alpha and the Omega," says the Lord God, "who is and who was and who is to come, the Almighty."

The Vision of the Son of Man

9 I, John, your brother and fellow partaker in the tribulation and kingdom and perseverance *which are* in Jesus, was on the island called Patmos because of the word of God and the witness of Jesus.
10 I was in the Spirit on the Lord's day, and I heard behind me a loud voice like a trumpet,
11 saying, "Write in a scroll what you see, and send *it* to the seven churches: to Ephesus and to Smyrna and to Pergamum and to Thyatira and to Sardis and to Philadelphia and to Laodicea."
12 Then I turned to see the voice that was speaking with me. And having turned I saw seven golden lampstands;
13 and in the middle of the lampstands I saw one like a son of man, clothed in a robe reaching to the feet, and girded across His chest with a golden sash.
14 And His head and His hair were white like white wool, like snow; and His eyes were like a flame of fire.
15 His feet *were* like burnished bronze, when it has been made to glow in a furnace, and His voice *was* like the sound of many waters,
16 and having in His right hand seven stars, and a sharp two-edged sword which comes out of His mouth, and His face was like the sun shining in its power.
17 And when I saw Him, I fell at His feet like a dead man. And He placed His right hand on me, saying, "Do not fear; I am the first and the last,
18 and the living One; and I was dead, and behold, I am alive forever and ever, and I have the keys of death and of Hades.
19 Therefore write the things which you have seen, and the things which are, and the things which will take place after these things.
20 As for the mystery of the seven stars which you saw in My right

hand, and the seven golden lampstands: the seven stars are the angels of the seven churches, and the seven lampstands are the seven churches.

CHAPTER 2

To the Church in Ephesus

1 "TO the angel of the church in Ephesus write:

This is what the One who holds the seven stars in His right hand, the One who walks among the seven golden lampstands, says:

2 'I know your deeds and your toil and perseverance, and that you cannot bear with those who are evil, and you put to the test those who call themselves apostles, and they are not, and you found them *to be* false;

3 and you have perseverance and have endured for My name's sake, and you have not grown weary.

4 'But I have *this* against you, that you have left your first love.

5 'Therefore remember from where you have fallen, and repent and do the deeds you did at first; or else I am coming to you and will remove your lampstand out of its place, unless you repent.

6 'Yet this you do have, that you hate the deeds of the Nicolaitans, which I also hate.

7 'He who has an ear, let him hear what the Spirit says to the churches. To him who overcomes, I will grant to eat of the tree of life which is in the Paradise of God.'

To the Church in Smyrna

8 "And to the angel of the church in Smyrna write:

This is what the FIRST AND THE LAST, who was dead, and has come to life, says:

9 'I know your tribulation and your poverty (but you are rich), and the blasphemy by those who say they are Jews and are not, but are a synagogue of Satan.

10 'Do not fear what you are about to suffer. Behold, the devil is about to cast some of you into prison, so that you will be tested, and you will have tribulation for ten days. Be faithful until death, and I will give you the crown of life.

11 'He who has an ear, let him hear what the Spirit says to the churches. He who overcomes will never be hurt by the second death.'

To the Church in Pergamum

12 "And to the angel of the church in Pergamum write:

This is what the One who has the sharp two-edged sword says:

13 'I know where you dwell, where Satan's throne is; and you hold fast My name, and did not deny My faith even in the days of Antipas, My witness, My faithful one, who was killed among you, where Satan dwells.

14 'But I have a few things against you, that you have there some who hold the teaching of Balaam, who kept teaching Balak to put a stumbling block before the sons of Israel,

to eat things sacrificed to idols and to commit sexual immorality.

15 'So you also have some who in the same way hold the teaching of the Nicolaitans.

16 'Therefore repent. But if not, I am coming to you quickly, and I will make war against them with the sword of My mouth.

17 'He who has an ear, let him hear what the Spirit says to the churches. To him who overcomes, to him I will give *some* of the hidden manna, and I will give him a white stone, and a new name written on the stone which no one knows but he who receives it.'

To the Church in Thyatira

18 "And to the angel of the church in Thyatira write:

This is what the Son of God, the One who has eyes like a flame of fire and His feet are like burnished bronze, says:

19 'I know your deeds, and your love and faith and service and perseverance, and that your last deeds are greater than at first.

20 'But I have *this* against you, that you tolerate the woman Jezebel, who calls herself a prophetess, and she teaches and deceives My slaves so that they commit sexual immorality and eat things sacrificed to idols.

21 'And I gave her time to repent, and she does not wish to repent of her sexual immorality.

22 'Behold, I will throw her on a bed *of sickness*, and those who commit adultery with her into great tribulation, unless they repent of her deeds.

23 'And I will kill her children with pestilence, and all the churches will know that I am He who searches the minds and hearts; and I will give to each one of you according to your deeds.

24 'But I say to you, the rest who are in Thyatira, who do not have this teaching, who have not known the deep things of Satan, as they call them—I place no other burden on you.

25 'Nevertheless what you have, hold fast until I come.

26 'And he who overcomes, and he who keeps My deeds until the end, TO HIM I WILL GIVE AUTHORITY OVER THE NATIONS;

27 AND HE SHALL RULE THEM WITH A ROD OF IRON, AS THE VESSELS OF THE POTTER ARE BROKEN TO PIECES, as I also have received *authority* from My Father;

28 and I will give him the morning star.

29 'He who has an ear, let him hear what the Spirit says to the churches.'

CHAPTER 3

To the Church in Sardis

"AND to the angel of the church in Sardis write:

This is what He who has the seven Spirits of God and the seven stars, says: 'I know your deeds, that you have a name that you are alive, but you are dead.

2 'Wake up, and strengthen the things that remain, which were about to die, for I have not found your deeds complete in the sight of My God.

3 'So remember what you have received and heard; and keep *it*, and repent. Therefore if you do not wake up, I will come like a thief, and you will not know at what hour I will come to you.

4 'But you have a few names in Sardis who have not defiled their garments, and they will walk with Me in white, for they are worthy.

5 'He who overcomes will thus be clothed in white garments, and I will never erase his name from the book of life, and I will confess his name before My Father and before His angels.

6 'He who has an ear, let him hear what the Spirit says to the churches.'

To the Church in Philadelphia

7 "And to the angel of the church in Philadelphia write:

This is what He who is holy, who is true, who has the key of David, who opens and no one will shut, and who shuts and no one opens, says:

8 'I know your deeds. Behold, I have given before you an open door which no one can shut, because you have a little power, and have kept My word, and have not denied My name.

9 'Behold, I am giving *up those* of the synagogue of Satan, those who say that they are Jews and are not, but lie. Behold, I will make them come and bow down before your feet, and *make them* know that I have loved you.

10 'Because you have kept the word of My perseverance, I also will keep you from the hour of testing, which is about to come upon the whole world, to test those who dwell on the earth.

11 'I am coming quickly; hold fast what you have, so that no one will take your crown.

12 'He who overcomes, I will make him a pillar in the sanctuary of My God, and he will never go out from it anymore. And I will write on him the name of My God, and the name of the city of My God, the new Jerusalem, which comes down out of heaven from My God, and My new name.

13 'He who has an ear, let him hear what the Spirit says to the churches.'

To the Church in Laodicea

14 "And to the angel of the church in Laodicea write:

This is what the Amen, the faithful and true Witness, the Beginning of the creation of God, says:

15 'I know your deeds, that you are neither cold nor hot. I wish that you were cold or hot.

16 'So because you are lukewarm, and neither hot nor cold, I will spit you out of My mouth.

17 'Because you say, "I am rich, and have become wealthy, and have need of nothing," and you do not know that you are wretched and pitiable and poor and blind and naked.

18 I advise you to buy from Me gold refined by fire so that you may become rich, and white garments so that you may clothe yourself, and

that the shame of your nakedness will not be manifested; and eye salve to anoint your eyes so that you may see.

19 'Those whom I love, I reprove and discipline. Therefore be zealous and repent.

20 'Behold, I stand at the door and knock. If anyone hears My voice and opens the door, I will come in to him and will dine with him, and he with Me.

21 'He who overcomes, I will grant to him to sit down with Me on My throne, as I also overcame and sat down with My Father on His throne.

22 'He who has an ear, let him hear what the Spirit says to the churches.'"

CHAPTER 4

The Throne in Heaven

AFTER these things I looked, and behold, a door *standing* open in heaven, and the first voice which I had heard, like *the sound* of a trumpet speaking with me, said, "Come up here, and I will show you what must take place after these things."

2 Immediately I was in the Spirit, and behold, a throne was standing in heaven, and One sitting on the throne.

3 And He who was sitting *was* like a jasper stone and a sardius in appearance; and *there was* a rainbow around the throne, like an emerald in appearance.

4 Around the throne *were* twenty-four thrones, and upon those thrones *I saw* twenty-four elders sitting, clothed in white garments, and golden crowns on their heads.

5 And out from the throne come flashes of lightning and sounds and peals of thunder. And *there were* seven lamps of fire burning before the throne, which are the seven Spirits of God.

6 And before the throne *there was something* like a sea of glass, like crystal. And in the center and around the throne, four living creatures full of eyes in front and behind.

7 And the first creature *was* like a lion, and the second creature like a calf, and the third creature had a face like that of a man, and the fourth creature *was* like a flying eagle.

8 And the four living creatures, each one of them having six wings, are full of eyes around and within, and day and night they do not cease to say,

"HOLY, HOLY, HOLY *is* THE LORD GOD, THE ALMIGHTY, WHO WAS AND WHO IS AND WHO IS TO COME."

9 And when the living creatures give glory and honor and thanks to Him who sits on the throne, to Him who lives forever and ever,

10 the twenty-four elders will fall down before Him who sits on the throne, and will worship Him who lives forever and ever, and will cast their crowns before the throne, saying,

11 "Worthy are You, our Lord and our God, to receive glory and

honor and power, for You created all things, and because of Your will they existed, and were created."

CHAPTER 5

The Scroll and the Lamb

THEN I saw in the right hand of Him who sits on the throne a scroll written inside and on the back, sealed up with seven seals.

2 Then I saw a strong angel proclaiming with a loud voice, "Who is worthy to open the scroll and to break its seals?"

3 And no one in heaven or on the earth or under the earth was able to open the scroll or to look into it.

4 Then I was crying greatly because no one was found worthy to open the scroll or to look into it.

5 And one of the elders *said to me, "Stop crying! Behold, the Lion that is from the tribe of Judah, the Root of David, has overcome so as to open the scroll and its seven seals."

6 Then I saw in the midst of the throne and the four living creatures and in the midst of the elders a Lamb standing, as if slain, having seven horns and seven eyes, which are the seven Spirits of God, sent out into all the earth.

7 And He came and took *the scroll* out of the right hand of Him who sits on the throne.

8 And when He had taken the scroll, the four living creatures and the twenty-four elders fell down before the Lamb, each one having a harp and golden bowls full of incense, which are the prayers of the saints.

9 And they *sang a new song, saying, "Worthy are You to take the scroll and to open its seals, because You were slain and purchased for God with Your blood *people* from every tribe and tongue and people and nation.

10 "And You made them *to be* a kingdom and priests to our God, and they will reign upon the earth."

Angels Worship the Lamb

11 Then I looked, and I heard the voice of many angels around the throne and the living creatures and the elders; and the number of them was myriads of myriads, and thousands of thousands,

12 saying with a loud voice,
"Worthy is the Lamb that was slain to receive power and riches and wisdom and strength and honor and glory and blessing."

13 And every created thing which is in heaven and on the earth and under the earth and on the sea, and all things in them, I heard saying,
"To Him who sits on the throne, and to the Lamb, *be* the blessing and the honor and the glory and the might forever and ever."

14 And the four living creatures kept saying, "Amen." And the elders fell down and worshiped.

CHAPTER 6

The Seven Seals

THEN I looked when the Lamb opened one of the seven seals, and I heard one of the four living creatures saying as with a voice of thunder, "Come."

2 Then I looked, and behold, a white horse, and he who sits on it had a bow; and a crown was given to him, and he went out overcoming and to overcome.

3 And when He opened the second seal, I heard the second living creature saying, "Come."

4 And another, a red horse, went out; and to him who sits on it, it was given to him to take peace from the earth, and that *men* would slay one another; and a great sword was given to him.

5 And when He opened the third seal, I heard the third living creature saying, "Come." Then I looked, and behold, a black horse; and he who sits on it had a pair of scales in his hand.

6 And I heard *something* like a voice in the midst of the four living creatures saying, "One ¹choinix of wheat for one ²denarius, and three ¹choinix of barley for one ²denarius, and do not harm the oil and the wine."

7 And when He opened the fourth seal, I heard the voice of the fourth living creature saying, "Come."

8 Then I looked, and behold, a pale horse; and he who sits on it had the name Death, and Hades was following with him. Authority was given to them over a fourth of the earth, to kill with sword and with famine and with pestilence and by the wild beasts of the earth.

9 And when He opened the fifth seal, I saw underneath the altar the souls of those who had been slain because of the word of God, and because of the witness which they had maintained;

10 and they cried out with a loud voice, saying, "How long, O Master, holy and true? Will You not judge and avenge our blood on those who dwell on the earth?"

11 And a white robe was given to each of them; and it was told to them that they should rest for a little while longer, until *the number of* their fellow slaves and their brothers who were to be killed even as they had been, would be completed also.

12 Then I looked when He opened the sixth seal, and there was a great earthquake; and the sun became black as sackcloth *made* of hair, and the whole moon became like blood;

13 and the stars of the sky fell to the earth, as a fig tree casts its unripe figs when shaken by a great wind.

14 And the sky was split apart like a scroll when it is rolled up, and every mountain and island were moved out of their places.

15 Then the kings of the earth and

---

¹ A choinix was approx. 1 qt. or 1 l   ² A Roman silver coin, approx. a laborer's daily wage

the great men and the commanders and the rich and the strong and every slave and free man HID THEMSELVES IN THE CAVES and among the rocks of the mountains;

16 and they *SAID TO THE MOUNTAINS AND TO THE ROCKS, "FALL ON US AND HIDE US from the presence of Him who sits on the throne, and from the wrath of the Lamb,

17 for the great DAY OF their WRATH has come, and who is able to stand?"

CHAPTER 7

The 144,000

AFTER this I saw four angels standing at the four corners of the earth, holding back the four winds of the earth, so that no wind would blow on the earth or on the sea or on any tree.

2 Then I saw another angel ascending from the rising of the sun, having the seal of the living God; and he cried out with a loud voice to the four angels to whom it was granted to harm the earth and the sea,

3 saying, "Do not harm the earth or the sea or the trees until we have sealed the slaves of our God on their foreheads."

4 And I heard the number of those having been sealed, 144,000 sealed from every tribe of the sons of Israel:

5 from the tribe of Judah, 12,000 having been sealed, from the tribe of Reuben 12,000, from the tribe of Gad 12,000,

6 from the tribe of Asher 12,000,

from the tribe of Naphtali 12,000, from the tribe of Manasseh 12,000,

7 from the tribe of Simeon 12,000, from the tribe of Levi 12,000, from the tribe of Issachar 12,000,

8 from the tribe of Zebulun 12,000, from the tribe of Joseph 12,000, from the tribe of Benjamin, 12,000 having been sealed.

A Multitude from Every Nation

9 After these things I looked, and behold, a great multitude which no one could count, from every nation and *all* tribes and peoples and tongues, standing before the throne and before the Lamb, clothed in white robes, and palm branches *were* in their hands;

10 and they cry out with a loud voice, saying,

"Salvation *belongs* to our God who sits on the throne, and to the Lamb."

11 And all the angels were standing around the throne and the elders and the four living creatures, and they fell on their faces before the throne and worshiped God,

12 saying,

"Amen, the blessing and the glory and the wisdom and the thanksgiving and the honor and the power and the strength, *be* to our God forever and ever. Amen."

13 Then one of the elders answered, saying to me, "These, clothed in the white robes, who are they, and from where have they come?"

14 And I said to him, "My lord, you know." And he said to me, "These are the ones who come out of the great tribulation, and they washed their robes and made them white in the blood of the Lamb.

15 "For this reason, they are before the throne of God; and they serve Him day and night in His sanctuary; and He who sits on the throne will dwell over them.

16 "THEY WILL HUNGER NO LONGER, NOR THIRST ANYMORE; NOR WILL THE SUN BEAT DOWN ON THEM, NOR ANY HEAT;

17 for the Lamb at the center of the throne will shepherd them and will guide them to springs of the water of life. And God WILL WIPE EVERY TEAR FROM THEIR EYES."

CHAPTER 8

The Seventh Seal

WHEN He opened the seventh seal, there was silence in heaven for about half an hour.

2 Then I saw the seven angels who stand before God, and seven trumpets were given to them.

3 And another angel came and stood at the altar, having a golden censer; and much incense was given to him, so that he might add it to the prayers of all the saints on the golden altar which was before the throne.

4 And the smoke of the incense went up with the prayers of the saints, out of the angel's hand, before God.

5 Then the angel took the censer and filled it with the fire of the altar, and threw it to the earth; and there followed peals of thunder and sounds and flashes of lightning and an earthquake.

The Seven Trumpets

6 And the seven angels who had the seven trumpets prepared themselves to sound them.

7 And the first sounded, and there came hail and fire, mixed with blood, and they were thrown to the earth; and a third of the earth was burned up, and a third of the trees were burned up, and all the green grass was burned up.

8 And the second angel sounded, and *something* like a great mountain burning with fire was thrown into the sea; and a third of the sea became blood,

9 and a third of the creatures which were in the sea—those which had life—died; and a third of the ships were destroyed.

10 And the third angel sounded, and a great star fell from heaven, burning like a torch, and it fell on a third of the rivers and on the springs of waters.

11 And the name of the star is called Wormwood; and a third of the waters became wormwood, and many men died from the waters, because they were made bitter.

12 And the fourth angel sounded, and a third of the sun and a third of the moon and a third of the stars were

struck, so that a third of them would be darkened and the day would not shine for a third of it, and the night in the same way.

13 Then I looked, and I heard an eagle flying in midheaven, saying with a loud voice, "Woe, woe, woe to those who dwell on the earth, because of the remaining blasts of the trumpet of the three angels who are about to sound!"

CHAPTER 9

THEN the fifth angel sounded. Then I saw a star from heaven which had fallen to the earth, and the key of the pit of the abyss was given to him.

2 And he opened the pit of the abyss and smoke went up out of the pit, like the smoke of a great furnace, and the sun and the air were darkened by the smoke of the pit.

3 Then out of the smoke came locusts upon the earth, and power was given them, as the scorpions of the earth have power.

4 And they were told not to hurt the grass of the earth, nor any green thing, nor any tree, but only the men who do not have the seal of God on their foreheads.

5 And they were not permitted to kill anyone, but to torment for five months, and their torment was like the torment of a scorpion when it stings a man.

6 And in those days men will seek death and will never find it; they will long to die, and death flees from them.

7 And the appearance of the locusts was like horses prepared for battle. And on their heads appeared to be crowns like gold, and their faces were like the faces of men.

8 And they had hair like the hair of women, and their teeth were like *the teeth* of lions.

9 And they had breastplates like breastplates of iron, and the sound of their wings was like the sound of chariots, of many horses running to battle.

10 And they have tails like scorpions, and stings; and in their tails is their power to hurt men for five months.

11 They have as king over them, the angel of the abyss. His name in Hebrew is Abaddon, and in the Greek he has the name Apollyon.

12 One woe is past; behold, two woes are still coming after these things.

13 Then the sixth angel sounded, and I heard a voice from the four horns of the golden altar which is before God,

14 one saying to the sixth angel who had the trumpet, "Release the four angels who have been bound at the great river Euphrates."

15 And the four angels were released, who had been prepared for the hour and day and month and year, so that they would kill a third of mankind.

16 And the number of the armies of the horsemen was two hundred million; I heard the number of them.

17 And this is how I saw in the vision the horses and those who sit on them: *the riders* had breastplates *the color* of fire and of hyacinth and of brimstone; and the heads of the horses are like the heads of lions; and out of their mouths come fire and smoke and brimstone.

18 A third of mankind was killed by these three plagues, by the fire and the smoke and the brimstone which came out of their mouths.

19 For the power of the horses is in their mouths and in their tails; for their tails are like serpents, having heads, and with them they do harm.

20 And the rest of mankind, who were not killed by these plagues, did not repent of the works of their hands, so as not to worship demons, and the idols of gold and of silver and of brass and of stone and of wood, which can neither see nor hear nor walk.

21 And they did not repent of their murders nor of their sorceries nor of their sexual immorality nor of their thefts.

CHAPTER 10

The Angel and the Little Scroll

THEN I saw another strong angel coming down out of heaven, clothed with a cloud, and the rainbow was upon his head, and his face was like the sun, and his feet like pillars of fire;

2 and he had in his hand a little scroll which was open. He placed his right foot on the sea and his left on the earth,

3 and he cried out with a loud voice, as when a lion roars. And when he had cried out, the seven peals of thunder uttered their voices.

4 And when the seven peals of thunder had spoken, I was about to write; and I heard a voice from heaven saying, "Seal up the things which the seven peals of thunder have spoken and do not write them."

5 Then the angel, whom I saw standing on the sea and on the earth, lifted up his right hand to heaven,

6 and swore by Him who lives forever and ever, WHO CREATED HEAVEN AND THE THINGS IN IT, AND THE EARTH AND THE THINGS IN IT, AND THE SEA AND THE THINGS IN IT, that there will be delay no longer,

7 but in the days of the voice of the seventh angel, when he is about to sound, then the mystery of God is finished, as He proclaimed good news to His slaves, the prophets.

8 Then the voice which I heard from heaven, *I heard* again speaking with me, and saying, "Go, take the scroll which is open in the hand of the angel who stands on the sea and on the earth."

9 So I went to the angel, telling him to give me the little scroll. And he *said to me, "Take it and eat it; it will make your stomach bitter, but in your mouth it will be sweet as honey."

10 And I took the little scroll out of the angel's hand and ate it, and in my

mouth it was sweet as honey; and when I had eaten it, my stomach was made bitter.

11 And they *said to me, "You must prophesy again about many peoples and nations and tongues and kings."

CHAPTER 11

The Two Witnesses

THEN a measuring rod like a staff was given to me, saying, "Get up and measure the sanctuary of God and the altar, and those who worship in it.

2 "And leave out the court which is outside the sanctuary and do not measure it, for it has been given to the Gentiles, and they will trample the holy city under foot for forty-two months.

3 "And I will give *authority* to my two witnesses, and they will prophesy for 1,260 days, clothed in sackcloth."

4 These are the two olive trees and the two lampstands that stand before the Lord of the earth.

5 And if anyone wishes to harm them, fire comes out of their mouth and devours their enemies; so if anyone wishes to harm them, he must be killed in this way.

6 These have the authority to shut up the sky, so that rain will not fall during the days of their prophesying; they also have authority over the waters to turn them into blood, and to strike the earth with every plague, as often as they wish.

7 And when they have finished their witness, the beast that comes up out of the abyss will make war with them and overcome them and kill them.

8 And their dead bodies *will lie* in the street of the great city which spiritually is called Sodom and Egypt, where also their Lord was crucified.

9 And those from the peoples and tribes and tongues and nations *will* look at their dead bodies for three and a half days, and will not permit their dead bodies to be laid in a tomb.

10 And those who dwell on the earth *will* rejoice over them and celebrate and send gifts to one another, because these two prophets tormented those who dwell on the earth.

11 But after the three and a half days, the breath of life from God came into them, and they stood on their feet, and great fear fell upon those who were watching them.

12 And they heard a loud voice from heaven saying to them, "Come up here." Then they went up into heaven in the cloud, and their enemies watched them.

13 And in that hour there was a great earthquake, and a tenth of the city fell; seven thousand people were killed in the earthquake, and the rest were terrified and gave glory to the God of heaven.

14 The second woe is past; behold, the third woe is coming quickly.

The Seventh Trumpet

15 Then the seventh angel sounded, and there were loud voices in heaven, saying,

"The kingdom of the world has become *the kingdom* of our Lord and of His Christ, and He will reign forever and ever."

16 And the twenty-four elders, who sit on their thrones before God, fell on their faces and worshiped God,

17 saying,

"We give You thanks, O Lord God, the Almighty, who is and who was, because You have taken Your great power and have begun to reign.

18 "And the nations were enraged, and Your rage came, and the time *came* for the dead to be judged, and to give reward to Your slaves—the prophets and the saints and those who fear Your name, the small and the great—and to destroy those who destroy the earth."

19 And the sanctuary of God which is in heaven was opened, and the ark of His covenant appeared in His sanctuary, and there were flashes of lightning and sounds and peals of thunder and an earthquake and a great hailstorm.

CHAPTER 12

The Woman, the Child, and the Dragon

AND a great sign appeared in heaven: a woman clothed with the sun, and the moon under her feet, and on her head a crown of twelve stars.

2 And she was with child, and she *cried out, being in labor and in pain to give birth.

3 Then another sign appeared in heaven: and behold, a great red dragon having seven heads and ten horns, and on his heads *were* seven diadems.

4 And his tail *swept away a third of the stars of heaven and threw them to the earth. And the dragon stood before the woman who was about to give birth, so that when she gave birth he might devour her child.

5 And she gave birth to a son, a male *child*, who is to rule all the nations with a rod of iron; and her child was caught up to God and to His throne.

6 Then the woman fled into the wilderness where she *had a place prepared by God, so that there she would be nourished for 1,260 days.

War in Heaven

7 And there was war in heaven, Michael and his angels waging war with the dragon. The dragon and his angels waged war,

8 and they were not strong enough, and there was no longer a place found for them in heaven.

9 And the great dragon was thrown down, the serpent of old who is called the devil and Satan, who deceives the whole world. He was thrown down to the earth, and his angels were thrown down with him.

10 Then I heard a loud voice in heaven, saying,

"Now the salvation, and the power, and the kingdom of our God and the authority of His Christ have come, for the accuser of our brothers has been thrown down, he who accuses them before our God day and night.

11 "And they overcame him because of the blood of the Lamb and because of the word of their witness, and they did not love their life even to death.

12 "For this reason, rejoice, O heavens and you who dwell in them. Woe to the earth and the sea, because the devil has come down to you, having great wrath, knowing that he has *only* a short time."

13 And when the dragon saw that he was thrown down to the earth, he persecuted the woman who gave birth to the male *child*.

14 But the two wings of the great eagle were given to the woman, so that she could fly into the wilderness to her place, where she *was nourished for a time and times and half a time, from the presence of the serpent.

15 And the serpent poured water like a river out of his mouth after the woman, so that he might cause her to be swept away with the flood.

16 But the earth helped the woman, and the earth opened its mouth and drank up the river which the dragon poured out of his mouth.

17 So the dragon was enraged with the woman and went off to make war with the rest of her seed, who keep the commandments of God and have the witness of Jesus.

CHAPTER 13

The Beast from the Sea

AND the dragon stood on the sand of the seashore.

Then I saw a beast coming up out of the sea, having ten horns and seven heads, and on his horns *were* ten diadems, and on his heads *were* blasphemous names.

2 And the beast which I saw was like a leopard, and his feet were like *those* of a bear, and his mouth like the mouth of a lion. And the dragon gave him his power and his throne and great authority.

3 And *I saw* one of his heads as if it had been slain fatally, and his fatal wound was healed. And the whole earth marveled *and followed* after the beast.

4 And they worshiped the dragon because he gave his authority to the beast, and they worshiped the beast, saying, "Who is like the beast, and who is able to wage war with him?"

5 And there was given to him a mouth speaking great boasts and blasphemies, and authority to act for forty-two months was given to him.

6 And he opened his mouth in blasphemies against God, to blaspheme His name and His tabernacle, *that is,* those who dwell in heaven.

7 And it was also given to him to make war with the saints and to overcome them, and authority over every tribe and people and tongue and nation was given to him.

8 And all who dwell on the earth will worship him, *everyone* whose name has not been written from the foundation of the world in the book of life of the Lamb who has been slain.

9 If anyone has an ear, let him hear.

10 If anyone *is destined* for captivity, to captivity he goes; if anyone kills with the sword, with the sword he must be killed. Here is the perseverance and the faith of the saints.

The Beast from the Earth

11 Then I saw another beast coming up out of the earth, and he had two horns like a lamb and he was speaking as a dragon.

12 And he exercises all the authority of the first beast in his presence. And he makes the earth and those who dwell in it to worship the first beast, whose fatal wound was healed.

13 And he does great signs, so that he even makes fire come down out of heaven to the earth in the presence of men.

14 And he deceives those who dwell on the earth because of the signs which were given to him to do in the presence of the beast, telling those who dwell on the earth to make an image to the beast who *had the wound of the sword and has come to life.

15 And it was given to him to give breath to the image of the beast, so that the image of the beast would even speak and cause as many as do not worship the image of the beast to be killed.

16 And he causes all, the small and the great, and the rich and the poor, and the free men and the slaves, that they be given a mark on their right hand or on their forehead,

17 and that no one will be able to buy or to sell, except the one who has the mark, *either* the name of the beast or the number of his name.

18 Here is wisdom. Let him who has understanding calculate the number of the beast, for it is the number of man; and his number is 666.

CHAPTER 14

The Lamb and the 144,000

THEN I looked, and behold, the Lamb *was* standing on Mount Zion, and with Him 144,000, having His name and the name of His Father written on their foreheads.

2 And I heard a voice from heaven, like the sound of many waters and like the sound of loud thunder, and the voice which I heard *was* like *the sound* of harpists playing on their harps.

3 And they *sang a new song before the throne and before the four living creatures and the elders. And no one could learn that song except the 144,000 who had been purchased from the earth.

4 These are the ones who are not defiled with women, for they are virgins. These *are* the ones who follow the Lamb wherever He goes. These have been purchased from among men as first fruits to God and to the Lamb.

5 And NO LIE WAS FOUND IN THEIR MOUTH; they are blameless.

The Messages of the Three Angels

6 Then I saw another angel flying in midheaven, having an eternal

gospel to proclaim to those who inhabit the earth, and to every nation and tribe and tongue and people.

7 And he said with a loud voice, "Fear God, and give Him glory, because the hour of His judgment has come; worship Him who made the heaven and the earth and sea and springs of waters."

8 And another angel, a second one, followed, saying, "FALLEN, FALLEN IS BABYLON THE GREAT, she who has made all the nations drink of the wine of the wrath of her sexual immorality."

9 Then another angel, a third one, followed them, saying with a loud voice, "If anyone worships the beast and his image, and receives a mark on his forehead or on his hand,

10 and he also will drink of the wine of the wrath of God, which is mixed in full strength in the cup of His rage, and he will be tormented with fire and brimstone in the presence of the holy angels and in the presence of the Lamb.

11 "And the smoke of their torment goes up forever and ever; they have no rest day and night, those who worship the beast and his image, and whoever receives the mark of his name."

12 Here is the perseverance of the saints who keep the commandments of God and their faith in Jesus.

13 And I heard a voice from heaven, saying, "Write, 'Blessed are the dead who die in the Lord from now on!'" "Yes," says the Spirit, "so that they may rest from their labors, for their deeds follow with them."

Reaping the Earth's Harvest

14 Then I looked, and behold, a white cloud, and sitting on the cloud *was* one like a son of man, having a golden crown on His head and a sharp sickle in His hand.

15 And another angel came out of the sanctuary, crying out with a loud voice to Him who sits on the cloud, "Put in Your sickle and reap, for the hour to reap has come, because the harvest of the earth is ripe."

16 Then He who sits on the cloud swung His sickle over the earth, and the earth was reaped.

17 And another angel came out of the sanctuary which is in heaven, and he also had a sharp sickle.

18 Then another angel, the one who has authority over fire, came out from the altar; and he called with a loud voice to him who had the sharp sickle, saying, "Put in your sharp sickle and gather the clusters from the vine of the earth, because her grapes are ripe."

19 So the angel swung his sickle to the earth and gathered *the clusters from* the vine of the earth, and threw them into the great wine press of the wrath of God.

20 And the wine press was trodden outside the city, and blood came out from the wine press, up to the horses' bridles, for a distance of [1]1,600 stadia.

---

[1] Approx. 184 mi. or 296 km, a stadion was approx. 607 ft. or 185 m

CHAPTER 15

Seven Angels, Seven Plagues

THEN I saw another sign in heaven, great and marvelous, seven angels who have seven plagues, *which are* the last, because in them the wrath of God is finished.

2 Then I saw something like a sea of glass mixed with fire, and those who have overcome the beast and his image and the number of his name, standing on the sea of glass, having harps of God.

3 And they *sang the song of Moses, the slave of God, and the song of the Lamb, saying,

"GREAT AND MARVELOUS ARE
    YOUR WORKS,
O LORD GOD, THE ALMIGHTY;
RIGHTEOUS AND TRUE ARE YOUR
    WAYS,
KING OF THE NATIONS!
4 "WHO WILL NOT FEAR, O LORD,
    AND GLORIFY YOUR NAME?
For You alone are holy;
FOR ALL THE NATIONS WILL COME
    AND WORSHIP BEFORE YOU,
FOR YOUR RIGHTEOUS ACTS HAVE
    BEEN REVEALED."

5 And after these things I looked, and the sanctuary of the tabernacle of testimony in heaven was opened,

6 and the seven angels who have the seven plagues came out of the sanctuary, clothed in linen, clean *and* bright, and girded around their chests with golden sashes.

7 Then one of the four living creatures gave to the seven angels seven golden bowls full of the wrath of God, who lives forever and ever.

8 And the sanctuary was filled with smoke from the glory of God and from His power; and no one was able to enter the sanctuary until the seven plagues of the seven angels were finished.

CHAPTER 16

The Seven Bowls of God's Wrath

THEN I heard a loud voice from the sanctuary, saying to the seven angels, "Go and pour out on the earth the seven bowls of the wrath of God."

2 So the first *angel* went and poured out his bowl on the earth; and it became a loathsome and malignant sore on the people who have the mark of the beast and who worship his image.

3 And the second *angel* poured out his bowl into the sea, and it became blood like *that* of a dead man, and every living thing in the sea died.

4 Then the third *angel* poured out his bowl into the rivers and the springs of waters, and they became blood.

5 And I heard the angel of the waters saying, "Righteous are You, who is and who was, O Holy One, because You judged these things;

6 for they poured out the blood of saints and prophets, and You have given them blood to drink. They deserve it."

7 And I heard the altar saying, "Yes, O Lord God, the Almighty, true and righteous are Your judgments."

8 And the fourth *angel* poured out his bowl upon the sun, and it was given to it to scorch men with fire.

9 And men were scorched with fierce heat, and they blasphemed the name of God who has the authority over these plagues, and they did not repent so as to give Him glory.

10 Then the fifth *angel* poured out his bowl on the throne of the beast, and his kingdom became darkened; and they gnawed their tongues because of pain,

11 and they blasphemed the God of heaven because of their pains and their sores, and they did not repent of their deeds.

12 And the sixth *angel* poured out his bowl on the great river, the Euphrates, and its water was dried up, so that the way would be prepared for the kings from the east.

13 Then I saw *coming* out of the mouth of the dragon and out of the mouth of the beast and out of the mouth of the false prophet, three unclean spirits like frogs;

14 for they are spirits of demons, doing signs, which go out to the kings of the whole world, to gather them together for the war of the great day of God, the Almighty.

15 ("Behold, I am coming like a thief. Blessed is the one who stays awake and keeps his garments, so that he will not walk about naked and men will not see his shame.")

16 And they gathered them together to the place which in Hebrew is called Har-Magedon.

The Seventh Bowl

17 Then the seventh *angel* poured out his bowl upon the air, and a loud voice came out of the sanctuary from the throne, saying, "It is done."

18 And there were flashes of lightning and sounds and peals of thunder; and there was a great earthquake, such as there had not been since man came to be upon the earth, so great an earthquake *was it, and* so mighty.

19 And the great city was split into three parts, and the cities of the nations fell. Babylon the great was remembered before God, to give her the cup of the wine of the wrath of His rage.

20 And every island fled away, and the mountains were not found.

21 And huge hailstones, about one ¹talent each, *came down from heaven upon men; and men blasphemed God because of the plague of the hail, because its plague *was extremely severe.

CHAPTER 17

The Woman and the Beast

THEN one of the seven angels who have the seven bowls came and spoke with me, saying, "Come here, I will show you the judgment of the great harlot who sits on many waters,

---

¹ Approx. 100 lb. or 45 kg

2 with whom the kings of the earth committed sexual immorality, and those who dwell on the earth were made drunk with the wine of her sexual immorality."

3 And he carried me away in the Spirit into a wilderness; then I saw a woman sitting on a scarlet beast, full of blasphemous names, having seven heads and ten horns.

4 And the woman was clothed in purple and scarlet, and adorned with gold and precious stones and pearls, having in her hand a gold cup full of abominations and of the unclean things of her sexual immorality,

5 and on her forehead a name *was* written, a mystery, "BABYLON THE GREAT, THE MOTHER OF HARLOTS AND OF THE ABOMINATIONS OF THE EARTH."

6 Then I saw the woman drunk with the blood of the saints, and with the blood of the witnesses of Jesus. When I saw her, I wondered greatly.

7 And the angel said to me, "Why do you wonder? I will tell you the mystery of the woman and of the beast that carries her, which has the seven heads and the ten horns.

8 "The beast that you saw was, and is not, and is about to come up out of the abyss and go to destruction. And those who dwell on the earth, whose name has not been written in the book of life from the foundation of the world, will wonder when they see the beast, that he was and is not and will come.

9 "Here is the mind which has wisdom. The seven heads are seven mountains on which the woman sits,

10 and they are seven kings; five have fallen, one is, the other has not yet come; and when he comes, he must remain a little while.

11 "And the beast which was and is not, is himself also an eighth and is *one* of the seven, and he goes to destruction.

12 "And the ten horns which you saw are ten kings who have not yet received a kingdom, but they receive authority as kings with the beast for one hour.

13 "These have one purpose, and they give their power and authority to the beast.

14 "These will wage war against the Lamb, and the Lamb will overcome them, because He is Lord of lords and King of kings, and those who are with Him *are the* called and elect and faithful."

15 And he *said to me, "The waters which you saw where the harlot sits, are peoples and crowds and nations and tongues.

16 "And the ten horns which you saw, and the beast, these will hate the harlot and will lay waste to her and make *her* naked, and will eat her flesh and will burn her up with fire.

17 "For God gave *it* in their hearts to do His purpose both by doing *their own* common purpose and by giving their kingdom to the beast, until the words of God will be finished.

18 "And the woman whom you saw is the great city, which has a kingdom over the kings of the earth."

CHAPTER 18

Fallen Is Babylon

AFTER these things I saw another angel coming down from heaven, having great authority, and the earth was illumined with his glory.

2 And he cried out with a mighty voice, saying, "FALLEN, FALLEN IS BABYLON THE GREAT! And she has become a dwelling place of demons and a prison of every unclean spirit, and a prison of every unclean bird and a prison of every unclean and hateful beast.

3 "For all the nations have drunk of the wine of the wrath of her sexual immorality, and the kings of the earth have committed sexual immorality with her, and the merchants of the earth have become rich by the power of her sensuality."

4 And I heard another voice from heaven, saying, "Come out of her, my people, so that you will not participate in her sins and receive of her plagues;

5 for her sins have piled up as high as heaven, and God has remembered her iniquities.

6 "Pay her back even as she paid, and give *her* back double according to her deeds; in the cup which she has mixed, mix double for her.

7 "To the degree that she glorified herself and lived sensuously, to the same degree give her torment and mourning, for she says in her heart, 'I SIT *as* A QUEEN AND I AM NOT A WIDOW, and will never see mourning.'

8 "For this reason in one day her plagues will come, pestilence and mourning and famine, and she will be burned up with fire; for the Lord God who judges her is strong.

9 "And the kings of the earth, who committed sexual immorality and lived sensuously with her, will cry and lament over her when they see the smoke of her burning,

10 standing at a distance because of the fear of her torment, saying, 'Woe, woe, the great city, Babylon, the strong city! For in one hour your judgment has come.'

11 "And the merchants of the earth cry and mourn over her, because no one buys their cargo anymore—

12 cargo of gold and silver and precious stones and pearls and fine linen and purple and silk and scarlet, and every *kind of* citron wood and every article of ivory and every article *made* from precious wood and bronze and iron and marble,

13 and cinnamon and amomum and incense and perfume and frankincense and wine and olive oil and fine flour and wheat and cattle and sheep, and *cargo of* horses and carriages and human beings and human lives.

14 "And the fruit you long for has gone from you, and all things that were splendid and shining have passed away from you and *men* will no longer find them.

15 "The merchants of these things, who became rich from her, will stand at a distance because of the fear of her torment, crying and mourning,

16 saying, 'Woe, woe, the great city, she who was clothed in fine linen and purple and scarlet, and adorned with gold and precious stones and pearls;

17 for in one hour such great wealth has been laid waste!' And every ship-master and every passenger and sail-or, and as many as make their living by the sea, stood at a distance,

18 and were crying out as they saw the smoke of her burning, saying, 'What is like the great city?'

19 "And they threw dust on their heads and were crying out, crying and mourning, saying, 'Woe, woe, the great city, in which all who have ships at sea became rich by her wealth, for in one hour she has been laid waste!'

20 "Rejoice over her, O heaven, and you saints and apostles and proph-ets, because God has pronounced judgment for you against her."

21 Then a strong angel picked up a stone like a great millstone and threw it into the sea, saying, "So will Babylon, the great city, be thrown down with violence, and will not be found any longer.

22 "And the sound of harpists and musicians and flute-players and trumpeters will not be heard in you any longer; and no craftsman of any craft will be found in you any longer; and the sound of a mill will not be heard in you any longer;

23 and the light of a lamp will not shine in you any longer; and the voice of the bridegroom and bride will not be heard in you any longer; for your merchants were the great men of the earth, because all the na-tions were deceived by your sorcery.

24 "And in her was found the blood of prophets and of saints and of all who have been slain on the earth."

CHAPTER 19

Hallelujah!

AFTER these things I heard some-thing like a loud voice of a great crowd in heaven, saying,

"Hallelujah! Salvation and glory and power belong to our God;

2 BECAUSE HIS JUDGMENTS ARE TRUE AND RIGHTEOUS; for He has judged the great harlot who was corrupting the earth with her sexual immorality, and HE HAS AVENGED THE BLOOD OF HIS SLAVES *shed* BY HER HAND."

3 And a second time they said, "Hallelujah! HER SMOKE RISES UP FOR-EVER AND EVER."

4 And the twenty-four elders and the four living creatures fell down and worshiped God who sits on the throne saying, "Amen. Hallelujah!"

5 And a voice came from the throne, saying,

"Give praise to our God, all you His slaves, you who fear Him, the small and the great."

6 Then I heard *something* like the voice of a great crowd and like the sound of many waters and like the sound of mighty peals of thun-der, saying,

"Hallelujah! For the Lord our God, the Almighty, reigns.

The Marriage Supper of the Lamb

7 "Let us rejoice and be glad and give the glory to Him, for the marriage of the Lamb has come and His bride has made herself ready."

8 And it was given to her to clothe herself in fine linen, bright *and* clean; for the fine linen is the righteous acts of the saints.

9 Then he *said to me, "Write, 'Blessed are those who are invited to the marriage supper of the Lamb.'" And he *said to me, "These are true words of God."

10 Then I fell at his feet to worship him. But he *said to me, "Do not do that! I am a fellow slave with you and your brothers who have the witness of Jesus. Worship God! For the witness of Jesus is the spirit of prophecy."

The Rider on a White Horse

11 Then I saw heaven opened, and behold, a white horse, and He who sits on it *is* called Faithful and True, and in righteousness He judges and wages war.

12 His eyes *are* a flame of fire, and on His head *are* many diadems; having a name written *on Him* which no one knows except Himself,

13 and being clothed with a garment dipped in blood, His name is also called The Word of God.

14 And the armies which are in heaven, clothed in fine linen, white *and* clean, were following Him on white horses.

15 And from His mouth comes a sharp sword, so that with it He may STRIKE DOWN THE NATIONS, and He will RULE THEM WITH A ROD OF IRON; and HE TREADS THE WINE PRESS OF THE WRATH OF THE RAGE OF GOD, the Almighty.

16 And He has on His garment and on His thigh a name written, "KING OF KINGS, AND LORD OF LORDS."

17 Then I saw an angel standing in the sun, and he cried out with a loud voice, saying to all the birds which fly in midheaven, "Come, assemble for the great supper of God,

18 so that you may eat the flesh of kings and the flesh of commanders and the flesh of strong men and the flesh of horses and of those who sit on them and the flesh of all men, both free men and slaves, and small and great."

19 Then I saw the beast and the kings of the earth and their armies assembled to make war with Him who sits on the horse and with His army.

The Beast and False Prophet Are Seized

20 And the beast was seized, and with him the false prophet who did the signs in his presence, by which he deceived those who had received the mark of the beast and those who worshiped his image. These two were thrown alive into the lake of fire which burns with brimstone.

21 And the rest were killed with the

sword which came from the mouth of Him who sits on the horse, and all the birds were filled with their flesh.

CHAPTER 20

Christ's Thousand Year Reign

THEN I saw an angel coming down from heaven, having the key of the abyss and a great chain in his hand.

2 And he laid hold of the dragon, the serpent of old, who is the devil and Satan, and bound him for a thousand years;

3 and he threw him into the abyss, and shut *it* and sealed *it* over him, so that he would not deceive the nations any longer, until the thousand years were finished. After these things he must be released for a short time.

4 Then I saw thrones, and they sat on them, and judgment was given to them. And I *saw* the souls of those who had been beheaded because of their witness of Jesus and because of the word of God, and who also had not worshiped the beast or his image, and had not received the mark on their forehead and on their hand. And they came to life and reigned with Christ for a thousand years.

5 The rest of the dead did not come to life until the thousand years were finished. This is the first resurrection.

6 Blessed and holy is the one who has a part in the first resurrection. Over these the second death has no authority, but they will be priests of God and of Christ and will reign with Him for a thousand years.

The Defeat of Satan

7 And when the thousand years are finished, Satan will be released from his prison,

8 and will come out to deceive the nations which are in the four corners of the earth, Gog and Magog, to gather them together for the war; the number of them is like the sand of the seashore.

9 And they came up on the broad plain of the earth and surrounded the camp of the saints and the beloved city, and fire came down from heaven and devoured them.

10 And the devil who deceived them was thrown into the lake of fire and brimstone, where the beast and the false prophet are also, and they will be tormented day and night forever and ever.

The Great White Throne Judgment

11 Then I saw a great white throne and Him who sits upon it, from whose presence earth and heaven fled away, and no place was found for them.

12 Then I saw the dead, the great and the small, standing before the throne, and books were opened; and another book was opened, which is *the book* of life. And the dead were judged from the things which were written in the books, according to their deeds.

13 And the sea gave up the dead which were in it, and death and Hades

gave up the dead which were in them, and they were judged, every one *of them* according to their deeds.

14 Then death and Hades were thrown into the lake of fire. This is the second death, the lake of fire.

15 And if anyone's name was not found written in the book of life, he was thrown into the lake of fire.

CHAPTER 21

The New Heaven and Earth

THEN I saw a new heaven and a new earth; for the first heaven and the first earth passed away, and there is no longer *any* sea.

2 And I saw the holy city, new Jerusalem, coming down out of heaven from God, made ready as a bride adorned for her husband.

3 And I heard a loud voice from the throne, saying, "Behold, the tabernacle of God is among men, and He will dwell among them, and they shall be His people, and God Himself will be among them,

4 and He will WIPE AWAY EVERY TEAR FROM THEIR EYES; and there will no longer be *any* death; there will no longer be *any* mourning, or crying, or pain. The first things passed away."

5 And He who sits on the throne said, "Behold, I am making all things new." And He *said, "Write, for these words are faithful and true."

6 Then He said to me, "They are done. I am the Alpha and the Omega, the beginning and the end. I will give to the one who thirsts from the spring of the water of life without cost.

7 "He who overcomes will inherit these things, and I WILL BE HIS GOD AND HE WILL BE MY SON.

8 "But for the cowardly and unbelieving and abominable and murderers and sexually immoral persons and sorcerers and idolaters and all liars, their part *will be* in the lake that burns with fire and brimstone, which is the second death."

9 Then one of the seven angels who have the seven bowls full of the seven last plagues came and spoke with me, saying, "Come here, I will show you the bride, the wife of the Lamb."

New Jerusalem, the Holy City

10 And he carried me away in the Spirit to a great and high mountain, and showed me the holy city, Jerusalem, coming down out of heaven from God,

11 having the glory of God. Her brilliance was like precious stone, as a stone of crystal-clear jasper.

12 It had a great and high wall. It had twelve gates and at those gates, twelve angels; and names have been written on *those gates*, which are *the names* of the twelve tribes of the sons of Israel.

13 *There were* three gates on the east and three gates on the north and three gates on the south and three gates on the west.

14 And the wall of the city had twelve foundation stones, and on

them *were* the twelve names of the twelve apostles of the Lamb.

15 And the one who spoke with me had a gold measuring rod to measure the city and its gates and its wall.

16 And the city is laid out as a square, and its length is as great as the width; and he measured the city with the rod, [1]12,000 stadia; its length and width and height are equal.

17 And he measured its wall, [2]144 cubits, *according to* human measurements, which are *also* angelic *measurements*.

18 And the material of the wall was jasper, and the city was pure gold, like pure glass.

19 The foundation stones of the city wall were adorned with every kind of precious stone. The first foundation stone was jasper; the second, sapphire; the third, chalcedony; the fourth, emerald;

20 The fifth, sardonyx; the sixth, sardius; the seventh, chrysolite; the eighth, beryl; the ninth, topaz; the tenth, chrysoprase; the eleventh, jacinth; the twelfth, amethyst.

21 And the twelve gates were twelve pearls; each one of the gates was a single pearl. And the street of the city was pure gold, like transparent glass.

22 And I saw no sanctuary in it, for the Lord God the Almighty and the Lamb are its sanctuary.

23 And the city has no need of the sun or of the moon to shine on it, for the glory of God has illumined it, and its lamp *is* the Lamb.

24 And the nations will walk by its light, and the kings of the earth will bring their glory into it.

25 And its gates will never be closed by day, for there will be no night there;

26 and they will bring the glory and the honor of the nations into it.

27 And nothing defiled, and no one who practices abomination and lying, shall ever come into it, but only those whose names are written in the Lamb's book of life.

CHAPTER 22

The River and the Tree of Life

THEN he showed me a river of the water of life, bright as crystal, coming from the throne of God and of the Lamb,

2 in the middle of its street. On either side of the river was the tree of life, bearing twelve *kinds of* fruit, yielding its fruit every month; and the leaves of the tree were for the healing of the nations.

3 And there will no longer be any curse; and the throne of God and of the Lamb will be in it, and His slaves will serve Him;

4 and they will see His face, and His name *will be* on their foreheads.

5 And there will no longer be *any* night, and they will not have need of

---

[1] Approx. 1,380 mi. or 2,220 km, a stadion was approx. 607 ft. or 185 m   [2] Approx. 216 ft. or 66 m, a cubit was approx. 18 in. or 45 cm

the light of a lamp nor the light of the sun, because the Lord God will illumine them, and they will reign forever and ever.

6 And he said to me, "These words are faithful and true"; and the Lord, the God of the spirits of the prophets, sent His angel to show to His slaves the things which must soon take place.

7 "And behold, I am coming quickly. Blessed is he who keeps the words of the prophecy of this book."

8 I, John, am the one who was hearing and seeing these things. And when I heard and saw, I fell down to worship at the feet of the angel who showed me these things.

9 But he *said to me, "Do not do that! I am a fellow slave with you and your brothers the prophets and with those who keep the words of this book. Worship God!"

The Final Message: Come

10 And he *said to me, "Do not seal up the words of the prophecy of this book, for the time is near.

11 "Let the one who does unrighteousness, still do unrighteousness; and the one who is filthy, still be filthy; and let the one who is righteous, still do righteousness; and the one who is holy, still keep himself holy."

12 "Behold, I am coming quickly, and My reward *is* with Me, to render to every man according to his work.

13 "I am the Alpha and the Omega, THE FIRST AND THE LAST, the beginning and the end."

14 Blessed are those who wash their robes, so that they may have the authority to the tree of life and may enter by the gates into the city.

15 Outside are the dogs and the sorcerers and the sexually immoral persons and the murderers and the idolaters, and everyone who loves and practices lying.

16 "I, Jesus, sent My angel to bear witness to you of these things for the churches. I am the root and the descendant of David, the bright morning star."

17 And the Spirit and the bride say, "Come." And let the one who hears say, "Come." And let the one who is thirsty come. Let the one who wishes receive the water of life without cost.

18 I bear witness to everyone who hears the words of the prophecy of this book: if anyone adds to them, God will add to him the plagues which are written in this book.

19 And if anyone takes away from the words of the book of this prophecy, God will take away his part from the tree of life and from the holy city, which are written in this book.

20 He who bears witness to these things says, "Yes, I am coming quickly." Amen. Come, Lord Jesus.

21 The grace of the Lord Jesus be with all. Amen.

PSALMS AND PROVERBS

LEGACY STANDARD BIBLE

THE PSALMS

The following expressions occur often in the Psalms:

Selah   Possibly indicates *Pause*, *Crescendo*, or *Musical Interlude*
Maskil   Possibly *Contemplative*, *Didactic*, or *Skillful Psalm*
Mikhtam   Possibly *Epigrammatic Poem* or *Atonement Psalm*

BOOK 1

PSALM 1

The Way of the Righteous and Wicked

1 HOW blessed is the man who
does not walk in the counsel
of the wicked,
Nor stand in the way of sinners,
Nor sit in the seat of scoffers!
2 But his delight is in the law of
[1]Yahweh,
And in His law he meditates day
and night.
3 And he will be like a tree *firmly*
planted by streams of water,
Which yields its fruit in its season
And its leaf does not wither;
And in whatever he does, he
prospers.

4 The wicked are not so,
But they are like chaff which the
wind drives away.
5 Therefore the wicked will not
rise in the judgment,
Nor sinners in the congregation
of the righteous.

6 For Yahweh knows the way of
the righteous,
But the way of the wicked will
perish.

PSALM 2

The Reign of Yahweh's Anointed

1 WHY do the nations rage
And the peoples meditate on a
vain thing?
2 The kings of the earth take their
stand
And the rulers take counsel
together
Against Yahweh and against His
Anointed, *saying,*
3 "Let us tear their fetters apart
And cast away their cords from us!"

4 He who sits in the heavens
laughs,
The Lord mocks them.
5 Then He speaks to them in His
anger
And terrifies them in His fury,
saying,

[1] The personal covenant name of God, a form of I AM WHO I AM, cf. Exod 3:14–15

6 "But as for Me, I have installed
    My King
    Upon Zion, My holy mountain."

7 "I will surely tell of the decree of
    Yahweh:
    He said to Me, 'You are My Son,
    Today I have begotten You.
8 'Ask of Me, and I will surely give the
    nations as Your inheritance,
    And the ends of the earth as
    Your possession.
9 'You shall break them with a rod
    of iron,
    You shall shatter them like a
    potter's vessel.'"

10 So now, O kings, show
    insight;
    Take warning, O judges of the
    earth.
11 Serve Yahweh with fear
    And rejoice with trembling.
12 Kiss the Son, lest He become
    angry, and you perish *in*
    the way,
    For His wrath may soon be
    kindled.
    How blessed are all who take
    refuge in Him!

PSALM 3

Yahweh, Save Me

A Psalm of David. When he
fled from Absalom his son.

1 O Yahweh, how my adversaries
    have become many!
    Many are rising up against me.

2 Many are saying of my soul,
    "There is no salvation for
    him in God."   Selah.

3 But You, O Yahweh, are a shield
    about me,
    My glory, and the One who lifts
    my head.
4 I was calling to Yahweh with my
    voice,
    And He answered me from His
    holy mountain.   Selah.
5 I lay down and slept;
    I awoke, for Yahweh sustains me.
6 I will not be afraid of ten
    thousands of people
    Who *all* around have set
    themselves against me.

7 Arise, O Yahweh; save me,
    O my God!
    For You have struck all my
    enemies on the cheek;
    You have shattered the teeth of
    the wicked.
8 Salvation belongs to Yahweh;
    Your blessing *be* upon Your
    people!   Selah.

PSALM 4

Yahweh Makes Me Abide in Safety

For the choir director. With stringed
instruments. A Psalm of David.

1 ANSWER me when I call, O God
    of my righteousness!
    You have relieved me in *my* distress;
    Be gracious to me and hear my
    prayer.

2 O sons of men, how long will my
  glory become a reproach?
  How long will you love what
    is worthless and seek
    falsehood?   Selah.
3 But know that Yahweh has
    set apart the holy one for
    Himself;
  Yahweh hears when I call
    to Him.

4 Tremble, and do not sin;
  Ponder in your heart upon your
    bed, and be still.   Selah.
5 Offer the sacrifices of
    righteousness,
  And trust in Yahweh.

6 Many are saying, "Who will
    show us good?"
  Lift up the light of Your face
    upon us, O Yahweh!
7 You have put gladness in my
    heart,
  More than when their grain and
    new wine abound.
8 In peace I will both lie down and
    sleep,
  For You alone, O Yahweh, make
    me to abide in safety.

PSALM 5

Lead Me in Your Righteousness

For the choir director. For the
flutes. A Psalm of David.
1 GIVE ear to my words,
    O Yahweh,
  Consider my meditation.

2 Give heed to the sound of my
    cry for help, my King and
    my God,
  For to You I pray.
3 O Yahweh, in the morning,
    You will hear my voice;
  In the morning I will order *my
    prayer* to You and *eagerly*
    watch.

4 For You are not a God who
    delights in wickedness;
  Evil does not sojourn
    with You.
5 The boastful shall not stand
    before Your eyes;
  You hate all workers of
    iniquity.
6 You destroy those who speak
    falsehood;
  Yahweh abhors the man of
    bloodshed and deceit.
7 But as for me, in the
    abundance of Your
    lovingkindness I will enter
    Your house,
  At Your holy temple I will
    worship in fear of You.

8 O Yahweh, lead me in Your
    righteousness because of
    my foes;
  Make Your way straight
    before me.
9 There is nothing reliable in their
    mouth;
  Their inward part is destruction
    itself.
  Their throat is an open grave;
  They flatter with their tongue.

10 Hold them guilty, O God;
By their own devices let them fall!
In the abundance of their
transgressions thrust
them out,
For they are rebellious
against You.

11 But let all who take refuge in
You be glad,
Let them ever sing for joy;
And may You shelter them,
That those who love Your name
may exult in You.

12 For it is You who blesses the
righteous one, O Yahweh,
You surround him with favor as
with a large shield.

PSALM 6

Yahweh, Rescue My Soul

For the choir director. With stringed
instruments. According to the
Sheminith. A Psalm of David.

1 O Yahweh, do not reprove me in
Your anger,
Nor discipline me in Your wrath.

2 Be gracious to me, O Yahweh, for
I *am* pining away;
Heal me, O Yahweh, for my
bones are dismayed.

3 And my soul is greatly dismayed;
But You, O Yahweh—how long?

4 Return, O Yahweh, rescue
my soul;
Save me because of Your
lovingkindness.

5 For there is no remembrance of
You in death;
In Sheol who will give You
thanks?

6 I am weary with my sighing;
Every night I make my bed
swim,
I flood my couch with my tears.

7 My eye has wasted away
with grief;
It has become old because of all
my adversaries.

8 Depart from me, all you workers
of iniquity,
For Yahweh has heard the sound
of my weeping.

9 Yahweh has heard my
supplication,
Yahweh receives my prayer.

10 All my enemies will be ashamed
and greatly dismayed;
They shall turn back, they will
suddenly be ashamed.

PSALM 7

In You I Have Taken Refuge

A Shiggaion of David, which he
sang to Yahweh concerning the
words of Cush, a Benjamite.

1 O Yahweh my God, in You I have
taken refuge;
Save me from all those who
pursue me, and deliver me,

2 Lest he tear my soul like a lion,
Rending me in pieces, while
there is none to deliver.

3 O Yahweh my God, if I have
   done this,
If there is injustice in my hands,
4 If I have rewarded evil to him
   who is at peace with me,
Or have plundered my adversary
   without cause,
5 Let the enemy pursue my soul
   and overtake *it*;
And let him trample my life
   down to the ground
And cause my glory to dwell in
   the dust.   Selah.

6 Arise, O Yahweh, in Your anger;
Lift up Yourself against the fury
   of my adversaries,
And arouse Yourself for me; You
   have appointed judgment.
7 Let the congregation of the
   peoples encompass You,
And over them return on high.
8 Yahweh judges the peoples;
Give justice to me, O Yahweh,
   according to my
   righteousness and my
   integrity that is in me.
9 O let the evil of the wicked come
   to an end, but establish the
   righteous;
For the righteous God tests the
   hearts and minds.
10 My shield is with God,
Who saves the upright in heart.
11 God is a righteous judge,
And a God who has indignation
   every day.

12 If a man does not repent, He will
   sharpen His sword;

He has bent His bow and
   prepared it.
13 He has also prepared for
   Himself deadly weapons;
He makes His arrows fiery shafts.
14 Behold, he travails with
   wickedness,
And he conceives mischief and
   gives birth to falsehood.
15 He has dug a pit and hollowed
   it out,
And has fallen into the hole
   which he made.
16 His mischief will return upon
   his own head,
And his violence will descend
   upon his own skull.

17 I will give thanks to Yahweh
   according to His righteousness
And will sing praise to the name
   of Yahweh Most High.

PSALM 8

How Majestic Is Your Name

For the choir director. According
to the Gittith. A Psalm of David.
1 O Yahweh, our Lord,
How majestic is Your name in all
   the earth,
Who displays Your splendor
   above the heavens!
2 From the mouth of infants and
   nursing babies You have
   established strength
Because of Your adversaries,
To make the enemy and the
   revengeful cease.

3 When I see Your heavens, the
    work of Your fingers,
  The moon and the stars,
    which You have
    established;
4 What is man that You remember
    him,
  And the son of man that You
    care for him?
5 Yet You have made him a little
    lower than *the* angels,
  And You crown him with glory
    and majesty!
6 You make him to rule over the
    works of Your hands;
  You have put all things under
    his feet,
7 All sheep and oxen,
  And also the animals of the
    field,
8 The birds of the heavens and the
    fish of the sea,
  Whatever passes through the
    paths of the seas.

9 O Yahweh, our Lord,
  How majestic is Your name in all
    the earth!

PSALM 9

*Yahweh Will Judge the World
    in Righteousness*

For the choir director. Almuth-
labben. A Psalm of David.
1 I will give thanks to Yahweh
    with all my heart;
  I will recount all Your wondrous
    deeds.

2 I will be glad and exult in You;
  I will sing praise to Your name,
    O Most High.

3 When my enemies turn back,
  They stumble and perish
    before You.
4 For You have maintained my
    justice and my cause;
  You have sat on the throne
    judging righteously.
5 You have rebuked the nations,
  You have made the wicked
    perish;
  You have blotted out their name
    forever and ever.
6 The enemy has come to an end
    in perpetual ruins,
  And You have uprooted the
    cities;
  The very memory of them has
    perished.

7 But Yahweh abides forever;
  He has established His throne
    for judgment,
8 And He will judge the world in
    righteousness;
  He will render justice for the
    peoples with equity.
9 Yahweh also will be a stronghold
    for the oppressed,
  A stronghold in times of
    distress;
10 And those who know Your
    name will put their trust
    in You,
  For You, O Yahweh, have not
    forsaken those who
    seek You.

11 Sing praises to Yahweh, who
      abides in Zion;
  Declare among the peoples
      His acts.
12 For He who requires blood
      remembers them;
  He does not forget the cry of the
      afflicted.
13 Be gracious to me, O Yahweh;
  See my affliction from those
      who hate me,
  You who lift me up from the
      gates of death,
14 That I may recount all Your
      praises,
  That in the gates of the daughter
      of Zion
  I may rejoice in Your salvation.
15 The nations have sunk down
      in the pit which they
      have made;
  In the net which they hid, their
      own foot has been caught.
16 Yahweh has made Himself known;
  He has executed judgment.
  In the work of his own hands
      the wicked is snared.
              Higgaion Selah.

17 The wicked will return to Sheol,
  Even all the nations who
      forget God.
18 For the needy will not always be
      forgotten,
  Nor the hope of the afflicted
      perish forever.
19 Arise, O Yahweh, do not let man
      prevail;
  Let the nations be judged
      before You.

20 Put them in fear, O Yahweh;
  Let the nations know that they
      are but men.   Selah.

PSALM 10

Do Not Forget the Afflicted

1 WHY do You stand afar off,
      O Yahweh?
  Why do You hide *Yourself* in
      times of distress?
2 In *his* lofty pride the wicked
      hotly pursues the afflicted;
  Let them be caught in the thoughts
      which they have devised.

3 For the wicked boasts of his
      soul's desire,
  And the greedy man curses *and*
      spurns Yahweh.
4 The wicked, in the haughtiness
      of his countenance, does
      not seek *Him*.
  All his thoughts are, "There is
      no God."

5 His ways prosper at all times;
  Your judgments are on high, out
      of his sight;
  As for all his adversaries, he
      snorts at them.
6 He says in his heart, "I will not
      be shaken;
  From generation to generation
      I will not be in adversity."
7 His mouth is full of curses and
      deceit and oppression;
  Under his tongue is mischief
      and wickedness.

8 He sits in the places of the
villages *where one* lies in
wait;
In the hiding places he kills the
innocent;
His eyes stealthily watch for the
unfortunate.

9 He lies in wait in a hiding place
as a lion in his lair;
He lies in wait to catch the
afflicted;
He catches the afflicted when he
draws him into his net.

10 He crouches, he bows down,
And the unfortunate fall by his
mighty ones.

11 He says in his heart, "God has
forgotten;
He has hidden His face; He will
never see it."

12 Arise, O Yahweh; O God, lift up
Your hand.
Do not forget the afflicted.

13 Why has the wicked spurned
God?
He has said in his heart, "You
will not require *it.*"

14 You have seen *it,* for You have
beheld mischief and
vexation to take it into
Your hand.
The unfortunate commits
himself to You;
You have been the helper of the
orphan.

15 Break the arm of the wicked and
the evildoer,
Seek out his wickedness until
You find none.

16 Yahweh is King forever and ever;
Nations have perished from His
land.

17 O Yahweh, You have heard the
desire of the humble;
You will strengthen their heart,
You will cause Your ear to
give heed

18 To give justice to the orphan and
the oppressed,
So that man who is of the earth
will no longer cause terror.

PSALM 11

Yahweh Is in His Holy Temple

For the choir director. Of David.

1 IN Yahweh I take refuge;
How can you say to my soul,
"Flee *as* a bird to your
mountain;

2 For, behold, the wicked bend
the bow,
They make ready their arrow
upon the string
To shoot in darkness at the
upright in heart.

3 "If the foundations are
destroyed,
What can the righteous do?"

4 Yahweh is in His holy temple;
Yahweh's throne is in
heaven;
His eyes behold, His eyelids test
the sons of men.

5 Yahweh tests the righteous,
But the wicked and the one who
loves violence His soul hates.

6 May He rain snares upon the
    wicked;
  Fire and brimstone and burning
    wind will be the portion of
    their cup.
7 For Yahweh is righteous, He
    loves righteousness;
  The upright will behold
    His face.

PSALM 12

Yahweh Will Set the
Needy in Safety

For the choir director. According to
the Sheminith. A Psalm of David.
1 SAVE, O Yahweh, for the holy
    man ceases to be,
  For the faithful disappear from
    among the sons of men.
2 They speak worthlessness to
    one another;
  With a flattering lip and with
    a double heart they
    speak.
3 May Yahweh cut off all flattering
    lips,
  The tongue that speaks great
    things;
4 Who have said, "With our
    tongue we will prevail;
  Our lips are our own; who is lord
    over us?"
5 "Because of the devastation of
    the afflicted, because of the
    groaning of the needy,
  Now I will arise," says Yahweh;
    "I will set him in the safety
    for which he longs."

6 The words of Yahweh are pure
    words;
  As silver tried in a furnace on
    the ground, refined seven
    times.
7 You, O Yahweh, will keep
    them;
  You will guard him from this
    generation forever.
8 The wicked strut about on every
    side
  When vileness is exalted among
    the sons of men.

PSALM 13

How Long, O Yahweh?

For the choir director.
    A Psalm of David.
1 HOW long, O Yahweh? Will You
    forget me forever?
  How long will You hide Your
    face from me?
2 How long shall I take counsel in
    my soul,
  Having sorrow in my heart all
    the day?
  How long will my enemy be
    exalted over me?

3 Look *and* answer me, O Yahweh
    my God;
  Give light to my eyes, lest
    I sleep the *sleep of*
    death,
4 Lest my enemy says, "I have
    overcome him,"
  And my adversaries rejoice that I
    am shaken.

5 But I have trusted in Your
   lovingkindness;
   My heart shall rejoice in Your
      salvation.
6 I will sing to Yahweh,
   Because He has dealt
      bountifully with me.

PSALM 14

There Is No One Who Does Good

For the choir director. Of David.

1 THE wicked fool says in his
   heart, "There is no God."
   They act corruptly, they commit
      abominable deeds;
   There is no one who does good.
2 Yahweh looks down from heaven
      upon the sons of men
   To see if there is anyone who
      has insight,
   Anyone who seeks after God.
3 They have all turned aside,
      altogether they have
      become worthless;
   There is no one who does good,
      not even one.

4 Do all the workers of iniquity
      not know,
   Who eat up my people *as* they
      eat bread,
   And do not call upon Yahweh?
5 There they are in great dread,
   For God is with the righteous
      generation.
6 You would put to shame the
      counsel of the afflicted,
   But Yahweh is his refuge.

7 Oh, that the salvation of
   Israel would come out
   of Zion!
   When Yahweh restores His
      captive people,
   May Jacob rejoice, may Israel
      be glad.

PSALM 15

*Who May Dwell on Your Holy
Mountain?*

A Psalm of David.

1 O Yahweh, who may sojourn in
   Your tent?
   Who may dwell on Your holy
      mountain?
2 He who walks blamelessly, and
      works righteousness,
   And speaks truth in his
      heart.
3 He does not slander with his
      tongue,
   Nor does evil to his
      neighbor,
   Nor takes up a reproach against
      his friend;
4 In whose eyes a reprobate is
      despised,
   But who honors those who fear
      Yahweh;
   He swears to his own hurt and
      does not change;
5 He does not put out his money
      at interest,
   Nor does he take a bribe against
      the innocent.
   He who does these things will
      never be shaken.

PSALM 16

You Will Not Forsake My Soul

A Mikhtam of David.

1 KEEP me, O God, for I take
      refuge in You.
2 *O my soul*, you have said to
      Yahweh, "You are my Lord;
   I have no good without You."
3 As for the saints who are in the
      earth,
   They are the majestic ones in
      whom is all my delight.
4 The pains of those who have
      bartered for another *god*
      will be multiplied;
   I shall not pour out their drink
      offerings of blood,
   Nor will I take their names upon
      my lips.

5 Yahweh is the portion of my
      inheritance and my cup;
   You support my lot.
6 The lines have fallen to me in
      pleasant places;
   Indeed, my inheritance is
      beautiful to me.

7 I will bless Yahweh who has
      counseled me;
   Indeed, my mind instructs me in
      the night.
8 I have set Yahweh continually
      before me;
   Because He is at my right hand, I
      will not be shaken.
9 Therefore my heart is glad and
      my glory rejoices;
   My flesh also will dwell securely.

10 For You will not forsake my soul
      to Sheol;
   You will not give Your Holy One
      over to see corruption.
11 You will make known to me the
      path of life;
   In Your presence is fullness
      of joy;
   In Your right hand there are
      pleasures forever.

PSALM 17

In the Shadow of Your Wings

A Prayer of David.

1 HEAR a righteous cause,
      O Yahweh, give heed to my
      cry of lamentation;
   Give ear to my prayer, which
      is not from deceitful
      lips.
2 May my judgment come from
      Your presence;
   May Your eyes behold what is
      upright.
3 You have tested my heart;
   You have visited *me* by night;
   You have tried me and You find
      nothing;
   I have purposed that my mouth
      will not transgress.
4 As for the deeds of men, by the
      word of Your lips
   I have kept from the paths of the
      violent.
5 My steps have held fast to Your
      paths.
   My footsteps have not
      stumbled.

6 I have called upon You, for You
  will answer me, O God;
Incline Your ear to me, hear my
  speech.
7 Marvelously show Your
  lovingkindnesses,
O Savior of those who take
  refuge at Your right hand
From those who rise up *against
  them.*
8 Keep me as the apple of the eye;
Hide me in the shadow of Your
  wings
9 From the wicked who
  devastate me,
My deadly enemies who
  surround me.
10 They have closed their unfeeling
  heart,
With their mouth they speak
  proudly.
11 They have now surrounded us
  in our steps;
They set their eyes to cast *us*
  down to the ground.
12 He is like a lion that is eager to
  tear,
And as a young lion lurking in
  hiding places.

13 Arise, O Yahweh, confront him,
  bring him low;
Protect my soul from the wicked
  with Your sword,
14 From men *with* Your hand,
  O Yahweh,
From men of the world, whose
  portion is in *this* life,
And whose belly You fill with
  Your treasure;

They are satisfied with children,
And leave their excess to their
  infants.
15 As for me, I shall behold Your
  face in righteousness;
I will be satisfied with Your
  likeness when I awake.

PSALM 18

*Yahweh Is My Rock and
My Fortress*

For the choir director. Of the servant
  of Yahweh, of David, who spoke to
  Yahweh the words of this song in
  the day that Yahweh delivered him
  from the hand of all his enemies
  and from the hand of Saul.
1 HE said, "I love You, O Yahweh,
  my strength."
2 Yahweh is my rock and my
  fortress and my deliverer,
My God, my rock, in whom I
  take refuge;
My shield and the horn of my
  salvation, my stronghold.
3 I call upon Yahweh, who is
  worthy to be praised,
And I am saved from my
  enemies.

4 The cords of death
  encompassed me,
And the torrents of vileness
  terrified me.
5 The cords of Sheol
  surrounded me;
The snares of death
  confronted me.

6 In my distress I called upon
  Yahweh,
  And cried to my God for help;
  He heard my voice out of His
  temple,
  And my cry for help before Him
  came into His ears.

7 Then the earth shook and
  quaked;
  And the foundations of the
  mountains were trembling
  And were shaken, because He
  was angry.
8 Smoke went up out of His
  nostrils,
  And fire from His mouth
  devoured;
  Coals were kindled by it.
9 He bowed the heavens and
  came down
  With thick darkness under
  His feet.
10 He rode upon a cherub and flew;
  And He sped upon the wings of
  the wind.
11 He made darkness His hiding
  place, His canopy
  around Him,
  Darkness of waters, thick clouds
  of the skies.
12 From the brightness before
  Him passed His thick
  clouds,
  Hailstones and coals of fire.
13 Yahweh also thundered in the
  heavens,
  And the Most High gave forth
  His voice,
  Hailstones and coals of fire.

14 He sent out His arrows, and
  scattered them,
  And lightning flashes in
  abundance, and threw them
  into confusion.
15 Then the channels of water
  appeared,
  And the foundations of the
  world were laid bare
  At Your rebuke, O Yahweh,
  At the blast of the breath of Your
  nostrils.

16 He sent from on high, He
  took me;
  He drew me out of many
  waters.
17 He delivered me from my strong
  enemy,
  And from those who hated me,
  for they were too mighty
  for me.
18 They confronted me in the day
  of my disaster,
  But Yahweh was my support.
19 He brought me forth also into a
  broad place;
  He rescued me, because He
  delighted in me.

20 Yahweh has rewarded
  me according to my
  righteousness;
  According to the cleanness
  of my hands He has
  recompensed me.
21 For I have kept the ways of
  Yahweh,
  And have not wickedly departed
  from my God.

22 For all His judgments were
before me,
And I did not put away His
statutes from me.
23 I was also blameless with Him,
And I kept myself from my
iniquity.
24 Therefore Yahweh has
recompensed me according
to my righteousness,
According to the cleanness of
my hands before His eyes.

25 With the kind You show Yourself
kind;
With the blameless You show
Yourself blameless;
26 With the pure You show Yourself
pure,
And with the crooked You show
Yourself astute.
27 For You save an afflicted people,
But eyes *which are* lifted up, You
bring down.
28 For You light my lamp;
Yahweh my God illumines my
darkness.
29 For by You I can run upon a
troop;
And by my God I can leap over
a wall.

30 As for God, His way is
blameless;
The word of Yahweh is tried;
He is a shield to all who take
refuge in Him.
31 For who is God, but Yahweh?
And who is a rock, except
our God,

32 The God who girds me with
strength
And makes my way blameless?
33 He makes my feet like hinds'
feet,
And sets me upon my high
places.
34 He trains my hands for battle,
So that my arms can bend a bow
of bronze.
35 You have also given me the
shield of Your salvation,
And Your right hand
upholds me;
And Your gentleness makes me
great.
36 You enlarge my steps under me,
And my ankles have not
given way.

37 I pursued my enemies and
overtook them,
And I did not turn back until
they were consumed.
38 I crushed them, so that they
were not able to rise;
They fell under my feet.
39 For You have girded me with
strength for battle;
You have subdued under me
those who rose up
against me.
40 You have also made my enemies
turn their backs to me,
And I destroyed those who
hated me.
41 They cried for help, but there
was none to save,
Even to Yahweh, but He did not
answer them.

42 Then I beat them fine as the
     dust before the wind;
   I emptied them out as the mire
     of the streets.

43 You have delivered me from the
     contentions of the people;
   You have placed me as head of
     the nations;
   A people whom I have not
     known serve me.
44 As soon as they hear, they obey me;
   Foreigners cower before me.
45 Foreigners fade away,
   And come trembling out of their
     fortresses.

46 Yahweh lives, and blessed be my
     rock;
   And let the God of my salvation
     be lifted high,
47 The God who executes
     vengeance for me,
   And subdues peoples under me.
48 Who delivers me from my
     enemies;
   Surely You lift me above those
     who rise up against me;
   You rescue me from the
     violent man.
49 Therefore I will give thanks to
     You among the nations,
     O Yahweh,
   And I will sing praises to Your
     name.
50 He gives great salvation to His
     king,
   And shows lovingkindness to
     His anointed,
   To David and his seed forever.

PSALM 19

The Law of Yahweh Is Perfect

   For the choir director.
   A Psalm of David.
1 THE heavens are telling of the
     glory of God;
   And the expanse is declaring the
     work of His hands.
2 Day to day pours forth speech,
   And night to night reveals
     knowledge.
3 There is no speech, nor are there
     words;
   Their voice is not heard.
4 Their line has gone out through
     all the earth,
   And their utterances to the end
     of the world.
   In them He has placed a tent for
     the sun,
5 Which is as a bridegroom
     coming out of his
     chamber;
   It rejoices as a strong man to run
     his course.
6 Its rising is from one end of the
     heavens,
   And its circuit to the other end
     of them;
   And there is nothing hidden
     from its heat.

7 The law of Yahweh is perfect,
     restoring the soul;
   The testimony of Yahweh is
     sure, making wise the
     simple.
8 The precepts of Yahweh are
     right, rejoicing the heart;

The commandment of Yahweh
is pure, enlightening the
eyes.
9 The fear of Yahweh is clean,
enduring forever;
The judgments of Yahweh are
true; they are righteous
altogether.
10 *They are* more desirable than
gold, even more than much
fine gold;
Sweeter also than honey
and the drippings of the
honeycomb.
11 Moreover, by them Your slave is
warned;
In keeping them there is great
reward.
12 Who can discern *his* errors?
Acquit me of hidden *faults*.
13 Also keep back Your slave from
presumptuous *sins*;
Let them not rule over me;
Then I will be blameless,
And I shall be acquitted of great
transgression.
14 Let the words of my mouth and
the meditation of my heart
Be acceptable in Your sight,
O Yahweh, my rock and my
Redeemer.

PSALM 20

We Will Boast in the Name of Yahweh

For the choir director.
A Psalm of David.
1 MAY Yahweh answer you in the
day of distress!

May the name of the God of
Jacob set you *securely*
on high!
2 May He send you help from the
sanctuary
And uphold you from Zion!
3 May He remember all your meal
offerings
And find your burnt offering
acceptable!   Selah.

4 May He grant you your heart's
desire
And fulfill all your counsel!
5 We will sing for joy over your
salvation,
And in the name of our God
we will set up our
banners.
May Yahweh fulfill all your
petitions.

6 Now I know that Yahweh saves
His anointed;
He will answer him from His
holy heaven
With the saving might of His
right hand.
7 Some *boast* in chariots and
some in horses,
But we will boast in the
name of Yahweh,
our God.
8 They have bowed down and
fallen,
But we have risen and stood
upright.
9 Save, O Yahweh;
May the King answer us in the
day we call.

PSALM 21

The King Trusts in Yahweh

For the choir director.
A Psalm of David.

1 O Yahweh, in Your strength the
king will be glad,
And in Your salvation how
greatly he will rejoice!
2 You have given him his heart's
desire,
And You have not withheld the
request of his lips.   Selah.
3 For You meet him with the
blessings of good things;
You set a crown of fine gold on
his head.
4 He asked life of You,
You gave it to him,
Length of days forever and ever.
5 His glory is great through Your
salvation,
Splendor and majesty You
bestow upon him.
6 For You make him most blessed
forever;
You make him joyful with
gladness in Your presence.

7 For the king trusts in Yahweh,
And through the lovingkindness
of the Most High he will not
be shaken.
8 Your hand will find out all your
enemies;
Your right hand will find out
those who hate you.
9 You will make them as a fiery
oven in the time of your
anger;

Yahweh will swallow them up in
His wrath,
And fire will devour them.
10 Their offspring You will destroy
from the earth,
And their seed from among the
sons of men.
11 Though they intended evil
against You
And devised a scheme,
They will not succeed.
12 For You will make them turn
their back;
You will aim with Your
bowstrings at their faces.
13 Be exalted, O Yahweh, in Your
strength;
We will sing and praise Your
might.

PSALM 22

Why Have You Forsaken Me?

For the choir director.
According to Aijeleth Hashshahar.
A Psalm of David.

1 MY God, my God, why have You
forsaken me?
Far from my salvation are the
words of my groaning.
2 O my God, I call by day, but You
do not answer;
And by night, but I have no rest.
3 Yet You are holy,
Enthroned upon the praises of
Israel.
4 In You our fathers trusted;
They trusted and You rescued
them.

5 To You they cried out and were
   granted escape;
   In You they trusted and were not
   disappointed.

6 But I am a worm and not
   a man,
   A reproach of men and despised
   by the people.

7 All who see me mock me;
   They smack *their* lip, they wag
   their head, *saying,*

8 "Commit *yourself* to Yahweh; let
   Him rescue him;
   Let Him deliver him, because He
   delights in him."

9 Yet You are He who brought me
   out of the womb;
   You made me trust *when* upon
   my mother's breasts.

10 Upon You I was cast from
   birth;
   You have been my God from my
   mother's womb.

11 Be not far from me, for distress
   is near;
   For there is none to help.

12 Many bulls have surrounded me;
   Strong *bulls* of Bashan have
   encircled me.

13 They open wide their mouth
   at me,
   As a lion that tears and roars.

14 I am poured out like water,
   And all my bones are out of
   joint;
   My heart is like wax;
   It is melted within me.

15 My strength is dried up like a
   potsherd,
   And my tongue cleaves to my
   jaws;
   And You lay me in the dust of
   death.

16 For dogs have surrounded me;
   A band of evildoers has
   encompassed me;
   They pierced my hands and my
   feet.

17 I count all my bones.
   They look, they stare at me;

18 They divide my garments
   among them,
   And for my clothing they
   cast lots.

19 But You, O Yahweh, be not
   far off;
   O my Strength, hasten to
   my help.

20 Deliver my soul from the sword,
   My only *life* from the power of
   the dog.

21 Save me from the mouth of
   the lion;
   From the horns of the wild oxen
   You have answered me.

22 I will *surely* recount Your name
   to my brothers;
   In the midst of the assembly I
   will praise You.

23 You who fear Yahweh, praise
   Him;
   All you seed of Jacob, glorify
   Him,
   And stand in awe of Him, all you
   seed of Israel.

24 For He has not despised and
    He has not abhorred the
    affliction of the afflicted;
   And He has not hidden His face
    from him;
   But when he cried to Him for
    help, He heard.

25 Of You *is* my praise in the great
    assembly;
   I shall pay my vows before those
    who fear Him.
26 The afflicted will eat and be
    satisfied;
   Those who seek Him will praise
    Yahweh.
   May your heart live forever!
27 All the ends of the earth will
    remember and turn to
    Yahweh,
   And all the families of the
    nations will worship
    before You.
28 For the kingdom is Yahweh's
   And He rules over the
    nations.
29 All the prosperous of the earth
    will eat and worship,
   All those who go down to the
    dust *will* bow *before Him*,
   Even he who cannot keep his
    soul alive.
30 *Their* seed will serve Him;
   It will be recounted about
    the Lord to the *coming*
    generation.
31 They will come and will declare
    His righteousness
   To a people who will be born,
    that He has done *it*.

PSALM 23

Yahweh Is My Shepherd

A Psalm of David.

1 YAHWEH is my shepherd,
  I shall not want.
2 He makes me lie down in green
   pastures;
  He leads me beside quiet waters.
3 He restores my soul;
  He guides me in the paths of
   righteousness
  For His name's sake.

4 Even though I walk through
   the valley of the shadow of
   death,
  I fear no evil, for You are with me;
  Your rod and Your staff, they
   comfort me.
5 You prepare a table before me in
   the presence of my enemies;
  You have anointed my head
   with oil;
  My cup overflows.
6 Surely goodness and
   lovingkindness will pursue
   me all the days of my life,
  And I will dwell in the house of
   Yahweh forever.

PSALM 24

The King of Glory

Of David. A Psalm.

1 THE earth is Yahweh's, as well
   as its fullness,
  The world, and those who dwell
   in it.

2 For He has founded it upon
    the seas
  And established it upon the
    rivers.
3 Who may ascend into the
    mountain of Yahweh?
  And who may rise in His holy
    place?
4 He who has innocent hands and
    a pure heart,
  Who has not lifted up his soul
    to worthlessness
  And has not sworn
    deceitfully.
5 He shall lift up a blessing from
    Yahweh
  And righteousness from
    the God of his
    salvation.
6 This is the generation of those
    who seek Him,
  Who seek Your face—*pay heed*
    O Jacob.   Selah.

7 Lift up your heads, O gates,
  And be lifted up, O ancient
    doors,
  That the King of glory may
    come in!
8 Who is this King of glory?
  Yahweh strong and mighty,
  Yahweh mighty in battle.
9 Lift up your heads, O gates,
  And lift *yourselves* up, O ancient
    doors,
  That the King of glory may
    come in!
10 Who is He, this King of glory?
  Yahweh of hosts,
  He is the King of glory.   Selah.

PSALM 25

Lead Me in Your Truth
    Of David.
1 TO You, O Yahweh, I lift up
    my soul.
2 O my God, in You I trust,
  Do not let me be ashamed;
  Do not let my enemies exult
    over me.
3 Indeed, let none who hope in
    You be ashamed;
  Let those who deal
    treacherously without
    cause be ashamed.

4 Make me know Your ways,
    O Yahweh;
  Teach me Your paths.
5 Lead me in Your truth and
    teach me,
  For You are the God of my
    salvation;
  In You I hope all the day.
6 Remember, O Yahweh, Your
    compassion and Your
    lovingkindnesses,
  For they have been from
    of old.
7 Do not remember the sins
    of my youth or my
    transgressions;
  According to Your lovingkindness
    remember me,
  For the sake of Your goodness,
    O Yahweh.

8 Good and upright is Yahweh;
  Therefore He instructs sinners
    in the way.

9 May He lead the humble in
   justice,
   And may He teach the humble
   His way.
10 All the paths of Yahweh are
   lovingkindness and truth
   To those who guard His
   covenant and His
   testimonies.
11 For Your name's sake, O Yahweh,
   Pardon my iniquity, for it is
   great.

12 Who is the man who fears
   Yahweh?
   He will instruct him in the way
   he should choose.
13 His soul will abide in goodness,
   And his seed will inherit the land.
14 The secret of Yahweh is for
   those who fear Him,
   And He will make them know
   His covenant.
15 My eyes are continually toward
   Yahweh,
   For He will bring my feet out of
   the net.

16 Turn to me and be gracious to me,
   For I am alone and afflicted.
17 The troubles of my heart are
   enlarged;
   Bring me out of my distresses.
18 See my affliction and my
   trouble,
   And forgive all my sins.
19 See my enemies, for they are
   many,
   And they hate me with violent
   hatred.

20 Keep my soul and deliver me;
   Do not let me be ashamed, for
   I take refuge in You.
21 Let integrity and uprightness
   guard me,
   For I hope in You.
22 Redeem Israel, O God,
   Out of all his troubles.

PSALM 26

Give Justice to Me, O Yahweh

Of David.

1 GIVE justice to me, O Yahweh,
   for I have walked in my
   integrity,
   And I have trusted in Yahweh;
   I will not waver.
2 Test me, O Yahweh, and
   try me;
   Refine my mind and my heart.
3 For Your lovingkindness is
   before my eyes,
   And I have walked in Your
   truth.
4 I do not sit with worthless men,
   And I will not go with
   pretenders.
5 I hate the assembly of evildoers,
   And I will not sit with the
   wicked.
6 I shall wash my hands in
   innocence,
   So I will go around Your altar,
   O Yahweh,
7 In order to proclaim with the
   voice of thanksgiving
   And to recount all Your
   wondrous deeds.

8 O Yahweh, I love the habitation
    of Your house
  And the place where Your glory
    dwells.
9 Do not take my soul away *along*
    with sinners,
  Nor my life with men of
    bloodshed,
10 In whose hands is a *wicked*
    scheme,
  And whose right hand is full of
    bribes.
11 But as for me, I shall walk in my
    integrity;
  Redeem me, and be gracious
    to me.
12 My foot stands on level ground;
  In the congregations I shall bless
    Yahweh.

PSALM 27

Yahweh Is My Light and My Salvation
  Of David.
1 YAHWEH is my light and my
    salvation;
  Whom shall I fear?
  Yahweh is the strong defense of
    my life;
  Whom shall I dread?
2 When evildoers came upon me
    to devour my flesh,
  My adversaries and my enemies,
    they stumbled and fell.
3 Though a host encamp
    against me,
  My heart will not fear;
  Though war arise against me,
  In this I trust.

4 One thing I have asked from
    Yahweh, that I shall seek:
  That I may dwell in the house
    of Yahweh all the days of
    my life,
  To behold the beauty of Yahweh
  And to inquire in His temple.
5 For in the day of calamity He
    will conceal me in His
    shelter;
  In the secret place of His tent He
    will hide me;
  He will lift me up on a rock.
6 And now my head will be lifted
    up above my enemies
    around me,
  And I will offer in His tent
    sacrifices with loud shouts
    of joy;
  I will sing, and I will sing praises
    to Yahweh.

7 Hear, O Yahweh, when I call
    with my voice,
  And be gracious to me and
    answer me.
8 On Your *behalf* my heart says,
    "Seek My face,"
  "Your face, O Yahweh, I shall
    seek."
9 Do not hide Your face from me,
  Do not turn Your slave away in
    anger;
  You have been my help;
  Do not abandon me and do not
    forsake me,
  O God of my salvation!
10 For my father and my mother
    have forsaken me,
  But Yahweh will take me up.

11 Instruct me in Your way,
    O Yahweh,
And lead me in a level path
Because of my foes.
12 Do not give me over to the
    desire of my adversaries,
For false witnesses have risen
    against me,
And such as breathe out
    violence.
13 *I would have despaired* unless
    I had believed that I would
    see the goodness of Yahweh
In the land of the living.
14 Hope in Yahweh;
Be strong and let your heart take
    courage;
Hope in Yahweh.

PSALM 28

Yahweh Is My Strength and My Shield

Of David.
1 TO You, O Yahweh, I call;
My rock, do not be silent to me,
Lest if You are hesitant toward me,
I will become like those who go
    down to the pit.
2 Hear the voice of my
    supplications when I cry to
    You for help,
When I lift up my hands toward
    Your holy sanctuary.
3 Do not drag me away with the
    wicked
And with workers of iniquity,
Who speak peace with their
    neighbors,
While evil is in their hearts.

4 Give to them according to their
    work and according to the
    evil of their actions;
Give to them according to the
    deeds of their hands;
Return their dealings upon
    them.
5 Because they do not regard the
    works of Yahweh
Nor the deeds of His hands,
He will tear them down and not
    build them up.

6 Blessed be Yahweh,
Because He has heard the voice
    of my supplications.
7 Yahweh is my strength and my
    shield;
My heart trusts in Him, and I am
    helped;
Therefore my heart exults,
And with my song I shall thank
    Him.
8 Yahweh is their strength,
And He is a strong defense of
    salvation to His anointed.
9 Save Your people and bless Your
    inheritance;
Be their shepherd also, and
    carry them forever.

PSALM 29

The Voice of Yahweh

A Psalm of David.
1 ASCRIBE to Yahweh, O sons of
    the mighty,
Ascribe to Yahweh glory and
    strength.

2 Ascribe to Yahweh the glory of
His name;
Worship Yahweh in the splendor
of holiness.

3 The voice of Yahweh is upon the
waters;
The God of glory thunders,
Yahweh is over many waters.
4 The voice of Yahweh is
powerful,
The voice of Yahweh is *full of*
splendor.
5 The voice of Yahweh breaks the
cedars;
Indeed, Yahweh breaks in pieces
the cedars of Lebanon.
6 He makes Lebanon skip like
a calf,
And Sirion like a young wild ox.
7 The voice of Yahweh hews out
flames of fire.
8 The voice of Yahweh causes the
wilderness to tremble;
Yahweh causes the wilderness of
Kadesh to tremble.
9 The voice of Yahweh makes the
deer to calve
And strips the forests bare;
And in His temple everything
says, "Glory!"

10 Yahweh sat *enthroned over* the
flood;
Indeed, Yahweh sits as King
forever.
11 Yahweh will give strength to His
people;
Yahweh will bless His people
with peace.

PSALM 30

*You Have Turned My Mourning into
Dancing*

A Psalm. A Song at the Dedication
of the House. Of David.
1 I will exalt You, O Yahweh, for
You have lifted me up,
And have not let my enemies be
glad over me.
2 O Yahweh my God,
I cried to You for help, and You
healed me.
3 O Yahweh, You have brought up
my soul from Sheol;
You have kept me alive, that I
would not go down to the pit.
4 Sing praise to Yahweh, you His
holy ones,
And give thanks for the
remembrance of His
holy *name.*
5 For His anger is but for a
moment,
His favor is for a lifetime;
Weeping may last for the night,
But a shout of joy *comes* in the
morning.

6 Now as for me, I said in my
prosperity,
"I will never be shaken."
7 O Yahweh, by Your favor You
have made my mountain to
stand strong;
You hid Your face, I was
dismayed.
8 To You, O Yahweh, I called,
And to the Lord I made
supplication:

9 "What profit is there in my blood,
        if I go down to the pit?
   Will the dust praise You? Will it
        declare Your truth?

10 "Hear, O Yahweh, and be gra-
        cious to me;
   O Yahweh, be my helper."
11 You have turned for me my
        mourning into dancing;
   You have loosed my sackcloth
        and girded me with
        gladness,
12 That *my* glory may sing praise to
        You and not be silent.
   O Yahweh my God, I will give
        thanks to You forever.

PSALM 31

Into Your Hand I Commit My Spirit

        For the choir director.
            A Psalm of David.
1 IN You, O Yahweh, I have taken
        refuge;
   Let me never be ashamed;
   In Your righteousness protect me.
2 Incline Your ear to me, deliver
        me quickly;
   Be to me a rock of strength,
   A fortress to save me.
3 For You are my high rock and my
        fortress;
   For Your name's sake You will
        lead me and guide me.
4 You will bring me out of the net
        which they have secretly
        laid for me,
   For You are my strength.

5 Into Your hand I commit my
        spirit;
   You have ransomed me,
        O Yahweh, God of truth.

6 I hate those who regard
        worthless idols,
   But I trust in Yahweh.
7 I will rejoice and be glad in Your
        lovingkindness,
   Because You have seen my
        affliction;
   You have known the troubles of
        my soul,
8 And You have not given me over
        into the hand of the enemy;
   You have set my feet in a large
        place.

9 Be gracious to me, O Yahweh, for
        I am in distress;
   My eye is wasted away from
        grief, my soul and my
        body *also*.
10 For my life is worn down with
        sorrow
   And my years with sighing;
   My strength fails because of my
        iniquity,
   And my bones waste away.
11 Among all my adversaries, I
        have become a reproach,
   Especially to my neighbors,
   And an object of dread to my
        acquaintances;
   Those who see me in the street
        flee from me.
12 I am forgotten like a dead
        man—out of mind—
   I am like a broken vessel.

13 For I have heard the bad report
      of many,
   Terror is on every side;
   While they took counsel
      together against me,
   They schemed to take my life.

14 But as for me, I trust in You,
      O Yahweh,
   I say, "You are my God."
15 My times are in Your hand;
   Deliver me from the hand of
      my enemies and from those
      who pursue me.
16 Make Your face to shine upon
      Your slave;
   Save me in Your lovingkindness.
17 O Yahweh, let me not be put to
      shame, for I call upon You;
   Let the wicked be put to shame,
      let them be silent in Sheol.
18 Let the lying lips be mute,
   Which speak arrogantly against
      the righteous
   With lofty pride and contempt.

19 How great is Your goodness,
   Which You have stored up for
      those who fear You,
   Which You have worked for those
      who take refuge in You,
   Before the sons of men!
20 You hide them in the secret
      place of Your presence from
      the conspiracies of man;
   You keep them secretly in a
      shelter from the strife of
      tongues.
21 Blessed be Yahweh,
   For He has made marvelous His

      lovingkindness to me in a
      besieged city.
22 As for me, I said in my alarm,
   "I am cut off from before Your
      eyes";
   Nevertheless, You heard the
      voice of my supplications
   When I cried to You for help.

23 Oh, love Yahweh, all you His
      holy ones!
   Yahweh guards the faithful
   But repays fully the one who
      acts in lofty pride.
24 Be strong and let your heart take
      courage,
   All you who wait for Yahweh.

PSALM 32

You Forgave the Iniquity of My Sin

   Of David. A Maskil.
1 HOW blessed is he whose
      transgression is forgiven,
   Whose sin is covered!
2 How blessed is the man whose
      iniquity Yahweh will not
      take into account,
   And in whose spirit there is no
      deceit!

3 When I kept silent *about my sin*,
      my bones wasted away
   Through my groaning all day long.
4 For day and night Your hand was
      heavy upon me;
   My vitality was drained away *as*
      with the heat of summer.
                              Selah.

5 I acknowledged my sin to You,
     And my iniquity I did not
          cover up;
   I said, "I will confess my
          transgressions to
          Yahweh;"
   And You forgave the iniquity
          of my sin.   Selah.
6 Therefore, let every holy one
          pray to You at a time when
          You may be found;
   Surely in a flood of great
          waters they will not
          reach him.
7 You are my hiding place; You
          guard me from trouble;
   You surround me with songs
          of deliverance.   Selah.

8 I will give you insight and teach
          you in the way which you
          should go;
   I will counsel you with My eye
          upon you.
9 Do not be as the horse or as
          the mule which have no
          understanding,
   Whose harness are bit and
          bridle to control them,
   Otherwise they will not come
          near you.
10 Many are the sorrows of the
          wicked,
    But he who trusts in Yahweh,
          lovingkindness shall
          surround him.
11 Be glad in Yahweh and rejoice,
          you righteous ones;
    And shout for joy, all you who
          are upright in heart.

PSALM 33

Yahweh Is Our Help and Our Shield

1 SING for joy in Yahweh,
          O righteous ones;
   Praise is becoming to the
          upright.
2 Give thanks to Yahweh with
          the lyre;
   Sing praises to Him with a harp
          of ten strings.
3 Sing to Him a new song;
   Play skillfully with a loud
          shout.
4 For the word of Yahweh is
          upright,
   And all His work is *done* in
          faithfulness.
5 He loves righteousness and
          justice;
   The earth is full of the
          lovingkindness of Yahweh.

6 By the word of Yahweh the
          heavens were made,
   And by the breath of His mouth
          all their host.
7 He gathers the waters of the sea
          as a heap;
   He lays up the deeps in
          storehouses.
8 Let all the earth fear Yahweh;
   Let all the inhabitants of the
          world stand in awe of Him.
9 For He spoke, and it was;
   He commanded, and it stood.
10 Yahweh nullifies the counsel of
          the nations;
    He frustrates the thoughts of
          the peoples.

11 The counsel of Yahweh stands
forever,
The thoughts of His heart from
generation to generation.
12 Blessed is the nation whose God
is Yahweh,
The people whom He has
chosen for His own
inheritance.

13 Yahweh looks from heaven;
He sees all the sons of men;
14 From the place of His habitation
He gazes
On all the inhabitants of the
earth,
15 He who forms the hearts of
them all,
He who understands all their
works.
16 The king is not saved by a
mighty army;
A warrior is not delivered by
great strength.
17 A horse is a false hope for
salvation;
Nor does it provide escape to
anyone by its great
strength.

18 Behold, the eye of Yahweh is on
those who fear Him,
On those who wait for His
lovingkindness,
19 *To deliver their soul from
death*
And to keep them alive in
famine.
20 Our soul is patient for Yahweh;
He is our help and our shield.

21 For our heart is glad in Him,
Because we trust in His holy
name.
22 Let Your lovingkindness,
O Yahweh, be upon us,
As we wait for You.

PSALM 34

Taste and See That Yahweh Is Good

Of David. When he feigned madness
before Abimelech, so that he drove
him away and he departed.

1 I will bless Yahweh at all times;
His praise shall continually be in
my mouth.
2 My soul will make its boast in
Yahweh;
The humble will hear it and
rejoice.
3 O magnify Yahweh with me,
And let us exalt His name
together.

4 I inquired of Yahweh, and He
answered me,
And delivered me from all that
I dread.
5 They looked to Him and were
radiant,
And their faces will never be
humiliated.
6 This poor man called out, and
Yahweh heard him
And saved him out of all his
troubles.
7 The angel of Yahweh encamps
around those who fear Him,
And rescues them.

8 O taste and see that Yahweh is
    good;
  How blessed is the man who
    takes refuge in Him!
9 Oh, fear Yahweh, you His saints;
  For there is no want to those
    who fear Him.
10 The young lions do lack and
    suffer hunger;
  But they who inquire of Yahweh
    shall not be in want of any
    good thing.
11 Come, you children, listen to me;
  I will teach you the fear of Yahweh.
12 Who is the man who delights
    in life
  And loves *many* days that he
    may see good?
13 Guard your tongue from evil
  And your lips from speaking
    deceit.
14 Depart from evil and do good;
  Seek peace and pursue it.

15 The eyes of Yahweh are toward
    the righteous
  And His ears are *open* to their
    cry for help.
16 The face of Yahweh is against
    evildoers,
  To cut off the memory of them
    from the earth.
17 *The righteous* cry, and Yahweh
    hears
  And delivers them out of all
    their troubles.
18 Yahweh is near to the
    brokenhearted
  And saves those who are
    crushed in spirit.

19 Many are the evils *against* the
    righteous,
  But Yahweh delivers him out of
    them all.
20 He keeps all his bones,
  Not one of them is broken.
21 Evil shall slay the wicked,
  And those who hate the
    righteous will be
    condemned.
22 Yahweh redeems the soul of His
    slaves,
  And all those who take refuge
    in Him will not be
    condemned.

PSALM 35

Yahweh Be Magnified

Of David.

1 CONTEND, O Yahweh, with
    those who contend
    with me;
  Fight against those who fight
    against me.
2 Take hold of shield and large
    shield
  And rise up for my help.
3 Draw also the spear and the
    battle-axe to meet those
    who pursue me;
  Say to my soul, "I am your
    salvation."
4 Let those be ashamed and
    dishonored who seek
    my life;
  Let those who devise evil
    against me be turned back
    and humiliated.

5 Let them be like chaff before the
    wind,
  With the angel of Yahweh
    driving *them* on.

6 Let their way be dark and
    slippery,
  With the angel of Yahweh
    pursuing them.

7 For without cause they hid their
    net for me;
  Without cause they dug a pit for
    my soul.

8 Let destruction, which he does
    not know, come upon him,
  And let the net, which he hid,
    catch him;
  Let him fall into it in
    destruction.

9 And my soul shall rejoice in
    Yahweh;
  It shall be joyful in His salvation.

10 All my bones will say, "Yahweh,
    who is like You,
  Who delivers the afflicted from
    him who is too strong
    for him,
  And the afflicted and the needy
    from him who robs him?"

11 Malicious witnesses rise up,
  Who ask me of things that I do
    not know.

12 They repay me evil for good,
  It is bereavement to my soul.

13 *But as for me, when they were*
    sick, my clothing was
    sackcloth;
  I humbled my soul with fasting,
  And my prayer kept returning to
    my bosom.

14 I walked about as though it
    were my friend or
    brother;
  I bowed down mourning, as
    one who sorrows for a
    mother.

15 But at my stumbling they
    were glad and gathered
    themselves together;
  The smiters whom I did not
    know gathered together
    against me,
  They tore at me and never were
    silent.

16 Amongst the godless jesters at a
    feast,
  They gnashed at me with their
    teeth.

17 Lord, how long will You
    look on?
  Bring back my soul from their
    ravages,
  My only *life* from the lions.

18 I will give You thanks in the
    great assembly;
  I will praise You among a mighty
    people.

19 Let those who are wrongfully
    my enemies not be glad
    over me;
  Nor let those who hate me
    without cause wink
    maliciously.

20 For they do not speak
    peace,
  But they devise deceitful
    words against those
    who are quiet in
    the land.

21 They opened their mouth wide
        against me;
    They said, "Aha, aha, our eyes
        have seen it!"

22 You have seen it, O Yahweh, do
        not keep silent;
    O Lord, do not be far from me.
23 Stir up Yourself, and awake to
        my justice
    And to my cause, my God and
        my Lord.
24 Judge me, O Yahweh my
        God, according to Your
        righteousness,
    And do not let them be glad
        over me.
25 Do not let them say in their
        heart, "Aha, our desire!"
    Do not let them say, "We have
        swallowed him up!"
26 Let those be ashamed and
        humiliated altogether who
        are glad at the evil *done*
        to me;
    Let those be clothed with
        shame and dishonor who
        magnify themselves
        over me.

27 Let them shout for joy and be
        glad, who delight in my
        righteousness;
    And let them say continually,
        "Yahweh be magnified,
    Who delights in the peace of His
        slave."
28 And my tongue shall utter Your
        righteousness
    And Your praise all day long.

PSALM 36

In Your Light We See Light

For the choir director. Of the
servant of Yahweh, of David.
1 TRANSGRESSION declares to
        the ungodly within his heart;
    There is no dread of God before
        his eyes.
2 For it flatters him in his eyes
    For one to discover his iniquity
        and hate *it.*
3 The words of his mouth are
        wickedness and deceit;
    He has ceased to consider to
        do good.
4 He devises wickedness upon
        his bed;
    He sets himself on a path that is
        not good;
    He does not despise evil.

5 Your lovingkindness, O Yahweh,
        is in the heavens,
    Your faithfulness *reaches* to
        the skies.
6 Your righteousness is like the
        mountains of God;
    Your judgments are *like* a
        great deep.
    O Yahweh, You save man and
        beast.
7 How precious is Your
        lovingkindness, O God!
    And the sons of men take refuge
        in the shadow of Your wings.
8 They are satisfied from the
        richness of Your house;
    And You give them to drink of
        the river of Your delights.

9 For with You is the fountain
  of life;
  In Your light we see light.

10 Continue Your lovingkindness
   to those who know You,
   And Your righteousness to the
   upright in heart.
11 Let not the foot of pride come
   upon me,
   And let not the hand of the
   ungodly drive me away.
12 There the workers of
   wickedness have fallen;
   They have been thrust down
   and cannot rise.

PSALM 37

Delight Yourself in Yahweh

Of David.

1 DO not fret because of evildoers,
  Be not envious toward doers of
  unrighteousness.
2 For they will wither quickly like
  the grass
  And fade like the green herb.
3 Trust in Yahweh and do good;
  Dwell in the land and cultivate
  faithfulness.
4 Delight yourself in Yahweh;
  And He will give you the desires
  of your heart.
5 *Commit your* way to Yahweh,
  Trust in Him, and He will do it.
6 He will bring forth your
  righteousness as the light
  And your judgment as the
  noonday.

7 Be still in Yahweh and wait
  patiently for Him;
  Do not fret because of him who
  prospers in his way,
  Because of the man who carries
  out schemes of wickedness.
8 Cease from anger and forsake
  wrath;
  Do not fret; *it leads* only to
  evildoing.
9 For evildoers will be cut off,
  But those who hope for Yahweh,
  they will inherit the land.
10 Yet a little while and the wicked
   man will be no more;
   You will look carefully at his place,
   and he will not be *there*.
11 But the lowly will inherit the
   land
   And will delight themselves in
   abundant peace.

12 The wicked schemes against the
   righteous
   And gnashes at him with his teeth.
13 The Lord laughs at him,
   For He sees that his day is coming.
14 The wicked have drawn the
   sword and bent their bow
   To cast down the afflicted and
   the needy,
   To slay those who are upright in
   conduct.
15 Their sword will enter their own
   heart,
   And their bows will be broken.

16 Better is the little of the righteous
   Than the abundance of many
   wicked.

17 For the arms of the wicked will
    be broken,
  But Yahweh sustains the righteous.

18 Yahweh knows the days of the
    blameless,
  And their inheritance will be
    forever.

19 They will not be ashamed in the
    time of evil,
  And in the days of famine they
    will be satisfied.

20 But the wicked will perish;
  And the enemies of Yahweh
    will be like the glory of the
    pastures,
  They vanish—in smoke they
    vanish away.

21 The wicked borrows and does
    not pay back,
  But the righteous is gracious and
    gives.

22 For those blessed by Him will
    inherit the land,
  But those cursed by Him will be
    cut off.

23 The footsteps of a man are
    established by Yahweh,
  And He delights in his way.

24 When he falls, he will not be
    hurled headlong,
  Because Yahweh is the One who
    sustains his hand.

25 I was young and now I am old,
  Yet I have not seen the righteous
    forsaken
  Or his seed begging bread.

26 All day long he is gracious and
    lends,
  And his seed is a blessing.

27 Depart from evil and do good,
  So you will dwell forever.

28 For Yahweh loves justice
  And will not forsake His
    holy ones;
  They are kept forever,
  But the seed of the wicked will
    be cut off.

29 The righteous will inherit
    the land
  And dwell in it forever.

30 The mouth of the righteous
    utters wisdom,
  And his tongue speaks justice.

31 The law of his God is in his
    heart;
  His steps do not slip.

32 The wicked spies upon the
    righteous
  And seeks to put him to death.

33 Yahweh will not forsake him in
    his hand;
  He will not condemn him when
    he is judged.

34 Hope for Yahweh and keep
    His way,
  And He will exalt you to inherit
    the land;
  When the wicked are cut off,
    you will see it.

35 I have seen a wicked,
    ruthless man
  Spreading himself like a
    luxuriant tree in its
    native soil.

36 Then he passed away, and
    behold, he was no more;
  I sought for him, but he could
    not be found.

37 Observe the blameless man, and
behold the upright;
For the man of peace will have a
posterity.

38 But transgressors will be
altogether destroyed;
The posterity of the wicked will
be cut off.

39 But the salvation of the
righteous is from Yahweh;
He is their strength in time of
distress.

40 Yahweh helps them and protects
them;
He protects them from the
wicked and saves them,
Because they take refuge in Him.

PSALM 38

Do Not Forsake Me, O Yahweh

A Psalm of David. To bring
to remembrance.

1 O Yahweh, reprove me not in
Your wrath,
And discipline me not in Your
burning anger.

2 For Your arrows have pressed
deep into me,
And Your hand has pressed
down upon me.

3 There is no soundness in my
flesh because of Your
indignation;
There is no health in my bones
because of my sin.

4 For my iniquities go over my head;
As a heavy burden they weigh
too much for me.

5 My wounds stink *and* rot
Because of my folly.

6 I am bent over and greatly
bowed down;
I go mourning all day long.

7 For my loins are filled with
burning,
And there is no soundness in
my flesh.

8 I am faint and badly crushed;
I groan because of the agitation
of my heart.

9 Lord, all my desire is before You;
And my sighing is not hidden
from You.

10 My heart throbs, my strength
forsakes me;
And the light of my eyes, even
that has gone from me.

11 My loved ones and my friends
stand aloof from my plague;
And my kinsmen stand afar off.

12 Those who search for my life lay
snares *for me*;
And those who seek *to do* me
evil have threatened
destruction,
And they meditate on deception
all day long.

13 But I, like a deaf man, do not hear;
And *I am* like a mute man who
does not open his mouth.

14 And I am like a man who does
not hear,
And in whose mouth are no
reproofs.

15 For I wait on You, O Yahweh;
You will answer, O Lord my God.

16 For I said, "*Save*, lest they be
      glad over me,
   Who, when my foot stumbles,
      magnify themselves
      against me."
17 For I am ready to fall,
   And my sorrow is continually
      before me.
18 For I confess my iniquity;
   I am full of anxiety because of
      my sin.
19 But my enemies are vigorous
      and strong,
   And those who wrongfully hate
      me abound.
20 And those who repay evil for good,
   They accuse me, for I pursue
      what is good.
21 Do not forsake me, O Yahweh;
   O my God, do not be far from me!
22 Make haste to help me,
   O Lord, my salvation!

PSALM 39

Yahweh, Make Me Know My End

   For the choir director. For
   Jeduthun. A Psalm of David.
1 I said, "I will keep watch *over*
      my ways
   That I may not sin with my tongue;
   I will keep watch *over* my mouth
      as with a muzzle
   While the wicked are in my
      presence."
2 I was mute with silence,
   I *even* kept silent from *speaking*
      good,
   And my anguish grew worse.

3 My heart was hot within me,
   While I meditated the fire was
      burning;
   Then I spoke with my tongue:
4 "Yahweh, cause me to know
      my end
   And what is the extent of my
      days;
   Let me know how transient
      I am.
5 "Behold, You have made my days
      as handbreadths,
   And my lifetime as nothing
      before You;
   Surely every man, *even* standing
      firm, is altogether vanity.
                              Selah.
6 "Surely every man walks about
      as a shadow;
   Surely they make an uproar
      in vain;
   He piles up *riches* and does not
      know who will gather them.
7 "And now, Lord, what do I
      hope in?
   My expectation is in You.
8 "Deliver me from all my
      transgressions;
   Make me not the reproach of the
      wicked fool.
9 "I have become mute, I do not
      open my mouth,
   Because it is You who have
      done *it*.
10 "Remove Your plague from me;
   Because of the opposition of Your
      hand I am wasting away.
11 "With reproofs You chasten a
      man for iniquity;

You consume as a moth what is
    precious to him;
Surely every man is vanity.

                          Selah.

12 "Hear my prayer, O Yahweh, and
    give ear to my cry for help;
Do not be silent at my tears;
For I am a sojourner with You,
A foreign resident like all my
    fathers.
13 "Turn Your gaze away from me,
    that I may smile *again*
Before I go and am no more."

PSALM 40

The One Who Rescues Me

For the choir director.
    Of David. A Psalm.
1 I hoped earnestly for Yahweh;
And He inclined to me and
    heard my cry for help.
2 He brought me up out of the pit
    of destruction, out of the
    miry clay,
And He set my feet upon a
    high rock, He established
    my steps.
3 He put a new song in my mouth,
    a song of praise to our God;
Many will see and fear
And will trust in Yahweh.

4 How blessed is the man who has
    made Yahweh his trust,
And has not turned to the
    proud, nor to those who
    stray into falsehood.

5 Many, O Yahweh my God, are
    the wondrous deeds You
    have done,
And Your thoughts toward us;
There is none to compare
    with You.
I would declare and speak of them,
But they are too numerous to
    recount.

6 Sacrifice and meal offering You
    have not desired;
My ears You have opened;
Burnt offering and sin offering
    You have not required.
7 Then I said, "Behold, I come;
In the scroll of the book it is
    written of me.
8 "I desire to do Your will, O my God;
Your law is within my inner being."

9 I proclaim good news of
    righteousness in the great
    assembly;
Behold, I do not restrain my lips,
O Yahweh, You know.
10 I do not conceal Your
    righteousness within
    my heart;
I speak of Your faithfulness and
    Your salvation;
I do not hide Your lovingkindness
    and Your truth from the
    great assembly.

11 You, O Yahweh, will not withhold
    Your compassion from me;
Your lovingkindness and Your
    truth will continually
    guard me.

12 For evils beyond number have
　　surrounded me;
　My iniquities have overtaken me,
　　so that I am not able to see;
　They are more numerous than
　　the hairs of my head,
　And my heart has failed me.

13 Be pleased, O Yahweh, to
　　deliver me;
　Make haste, O Yahweh, to help me.
14 Let those be ashamed and
　　humiliated together
　Who seek my life to sweep it away;
　Let those be turned back and
　　dishonored
　Who delight in evil *against* me.
15 Let those be appalled because of
　　their shame
　Who say to me, "Aha, aha!"
16 Let all who seek You rejoice and
　　be glad in You;
　Let those who love Your
　　salvation say continually,
　　"Yahweh be magnified!"
17 As for me, I am afflicted and needy,
　May the Lord think of me.
　You are my help and the One
　　who rescues me;
　Do not delay, O my God.

PSALM 41

O Yahweh, Be Gracious to Me

For the choir director. A Psalm of David.
　1 HOW blessed is he who
　　considers the poor;
　Yahweh will provide him escape
　　in a day of calamity.

2 Yahweh will keep him and keep
　　him alive,
　And he shall be blessed upon
　　the earth;
　And do not give him over to the
　　desire of his enemies.
3 Yahweh will sustain him upon
　　his sickbed;
　In his illness, You restore him to
　　health.

4 As for me, I said, "O Yahweh, be
　　gracious to me;
　Heal my soul, for I have sinned
　　against You."
5 My enemies speak evil against me,
　　"When will he die, and his name
　　perish?"
6 And when he comes to see *me*,
　　he speaks worthlessness;
　His heart gathers wickedness
　　to itself;
　When he goes outside, he
　　speaks it.
7 All who hate me whisper
　　together against me;
　Against me, they devise for me
　　calamity, *saying*,
8 "A vile thing is poured out
　　upon him,
　That when he lies down, he will
　　not rise up again."
9 Even my close friend in whom I
　　trusted,
　Who ate my bread,
　Has lifted up his heel against me.

10 But You, O Yahweh, be gracious
　　to me and raise me up,
　That I may repay them.

11 By this I know that You delight
in me,
Because my enemy makes no
shout in triumph over me.
12 As for me, You uphold me in my
integrity,
And You make me stand firm in
Your presence forever.

13 Blessed be Yahweh, the God of
Israel,
From everlasting to everlasting.
Amen and Amen.

BOOK 2

PSALM 42

My Soul Thirsts for God

For the choir director. A Maskil
of the sons of Korah.

1 AS the deer pants for the water
brooks,
So my soul pants for You, O God.
2 My soul thirsts for God, for the
living God;
When shall I come and appear
before God?
3 My tears have been my food day
and night,
While *they* say to me all day
long, "Where is your God?"
4 These things I remember and I
pour out my soul within me.
For I used to go along with the
throng *and* lead them in
procession to the house
of God,
With the sound of a shout of

joy and thanksgiving, a
multitude keeping festival.

5 Why are you in despair, O my soul?
And *why* are you disturbed
within me?
Wait for God, for I shall still
praise Him,
For the salvation of His presence.
6 O my God, my soul is in despair
within me;
Therefore I remember You from
the land of the Jordan
And the peaks of Hermon, from
Mount Mizar.
7 Deep calls to deep at the sound
of Your waterfalls;
All Your breakers and Your
waves have rolled over me.
8 By day, Yahweh will command
His lovingkindness;
And by night, His song will be
with me,
A prayer to the God of my life.

9 I say to God my rock, "Why have
You forgotten me?
Why do I go mourning because of
the oppression of the enemy?"
10 As a shattering of my bones, my
adversaries reproach me,
While they say to me all day
long, "Where is your God?"
11 Why are you in despair, O my soul?
And why are you disturbed
within me?
Wait for God, for I shall still
praise Him,
The salvation of my presence
and my God.

PSALM 43

Send Out Your Light and Your Truth

1 GIVE justice to me, O God, and
plead my case against an
unholy nation;
Oh protect me from the deceitful
and unrighteous man!
2 For You are the God of my strength;
why have You rejected me?
Why do I go mourning because of
the oppression of the enemy?

3 Oh send out Your light and Your
truth, let them lead me;
Let them bring me to Your holy
mountain
And to Your dwelling places.
4 Then I will go to the altar of God,
To God my exceeding joy;
And upon the lyre I shall praise
You, O God, my God.

5 Why are you in despair, O my soul?
And why are you disturbed
within me?
Wait for God, for I shall still
praise Him,
The salvation of my presence
and my God.

PSALM 44

Rise Up, Be Our Help

For the choir director. Of the
sons of Korah. A Maskil.

1 O God, we have heard with
our ears,
Our fathers have recounted to us

The work that You did in
their days,
In the days of old.
2 You with Your own hand
dispossessed the
nations;
Then You planted them;
You afflicted the peoples,
Then You cast them out.
3 For by their own sword they did
not possess the land,
And their own arm did not
save them,
But Your right hand and Your
arm and the light of
Your presence,
For You favored them.

4 You are my King, O God;
Command salvation for Jacob.
5 Through You we will push back
our adversaries;
Through Your name we will
tread down those who rise
up against us.
6 For I will not trust in my bow,
And my sword will not save me.
7 But You have saved us from our
adversaries,
And You have put to shame
those who hate us.
8 In God we have boasted all
day long,
And we will give thanks to Your
name forever.   Selah.

9 Yet You have rejected *us* and
brought us to dishonor,
And do not go out with our
armies.

10 You cause us to turn back from
     the adversary;
   And those who hate us
     have plundered *us* for
     themselves.
11 You give us as sheep to be eaten
   And have scattered us among
     the nations.
12 You sell Your people for no
     amount,
   And You have not profited from
     their price.
13 You make us a reproach to our
     neighbors,
   A mockery and a derision to
     those around us.
14 You make us a byword among
     the nations,
   A laughingstock among the
     peoples.
15 All day long my dishonor is
     before me
   And the shame of my face has
     covered me,
16 Because of the voice of him who
     reproaches and reviles,
   Because of the presence of the
     enemy and the avenger.

17 All this has come upon us, but
     we have not forgotten You,
   And we have not dealt falsely
     with Your covenant.
18 Our heart has not turned back,
   Nor have our steps deviated
     from Your path,
19 Yet You have crushed us in a
     place of jackals
   And covered us with the shadow
     of death.

20 If we had forgotten the name of
     our God
   Or spread our hands to a
     strange god,
21 Would not God find this out?
   For He knows the secrets of the
     heart.
22 But for Your sake we are killed
     all day long;
   We are counted as sheep for the
     slaughter.
23 Arouse Yourself, why do You
     sleep, O Lord?
   Awake, do not reject us forever.
24 Why do You hide Your face
   And forget our affliction and our
     oppression?
25 For our soul has sunk down into
     the dust;
   Our body cleaves to the earth.
26 Rise up, be our help,
   And redeem us for the sake of
     Your lovingkindness.

PSALM 45

Your Throne, O God, Is Forever

For the choir director. According
to Shoshannim. Of the sons of
Korah. A Maskil. A Song of Love.
1 MY heart overflows with a good
     theme;
   I address my verses to the
     King;
   My tongue is the pen of a skillful
     scribe.
2 You are fairer than the sons
     of men;
   Grace is poured upon Your lips;

Therefore God has blessed You
forever.

3 Gird Your sword on *Your* thigh,
O Mighty One,
In Your splendor and Your
majesty!
4 And in Your majesty ride on
victoriously,
For the cause of truth
and meekness *and*
righteousness;
Let Your right hand teach You
awesome things.
5 Your arrows are sharp;
The peoples fall under You;
Your arrows are in the heart of
the King's enemies.

6 Your throne, O God, is forever
and ever;
A scepter of uprightness is the
scepter of Your kingdom.
7 You have loved righteousness
and hated wickedness;
Therefore God, Your God, has
anointed You
With the oil of joy above Your
companions.
8 All Your garments are *fragrant
with* myrrh and aloes *and*
cassia;
Out of ivory palaces stringed
instruments have made
You glad.
9 Kings' daughters are among
Your noble ladies;
At Your right hand stands
the queen in gold from
Ophir.

10 Listen, O daughter, give
attention and incline
your ear:
Forget your people and your
father's house;
11 Then the King will desire your
beauty.
Because He is your Lord, bow
down to Him.
12 The daughter of Tyre *will come*
with a present;
The rich among the people will
seek your favor.

13 The King's daughter is all
glorious within *her
chamber*;
Her clothing is interwoven
with gold.
14 She will be led to the King in
embroidered work;
The virgins, her companions
who follow her,
Will be brought to You.
15 They will be led forth with
gladness and rejoicing;
They will enter into the King's
palace.

16 In place of your fathers will be
your sons;
You shall set them up as princes
in all the earth.
17 I will cause Your name to
be remembered from
generation to every
generation;
Therefore the peoples will
give You thanks forever
and ever.

PSALM 46

God Is Our Refuge and Strength

For the choir director. Of the sons of
Korah. According to Alamoth. A Song.

1 GOD is our refuge and strength,
   A very present help in trouble.
2 Therefore we will not fear,
         though the earth should
         change
   And though the mountains shake
         into the heart of the sea;
3 Though its waters roar *and* foam,
   Though the mountains quake at
         its lofty pride.   Selah.

4 There is a river whose streams
         make glad the city of God,
   The holy dwelling places of the
         Most High.
5 God is in the midst of her, she
         will not be shaken;
   God will help her when morning
         dawns.
6 The nations roar, the kingdoms
         shake;
   He gives His voice, the earth melts.
7 Yahweh of hosts is with us;
   The God of Jacob is our
         stronghold.   Selah.

8 Come, behold the works of
         Yahweh,
   Who has appointed desolations
         in the earth.
9 He makes wars to cease to the
         end of the earth;
   He breaks the bow and cuts up
         the spear;
   He burns the chariots with fire.

10 "Cease *striving* and know that
         I am God;
   I will be exalted among the
         nations, I will be exalted in
         the earth."
11 Yahweh of hosts is with us;
   The God of Jacob is our
         stronghold.   Selah.

PSALM 47

God Is King of All the Earth

For the choir director. Of the
sons of Korah. A Psalm.

1 O clap your hands, all peoples;
   Make a loud shout to God with
         the sound of a shout of joy.
2 For Yahweh Most High is
         fearsome,
   A great King over all the earth.
3 He subdues peoples under us
   And nations under our feet.
4 He chooses our inheritance for us,
   The pride of Jacob whom He
         loves.   Selah.

5 God has ascended with a loud
         shout,
   Yahweh, with the sound of a
         trumpet.
6 Sing praises to God, sing praises;
   Sing praises to our King, sing
         praises.
7 For God is the King of all the
         earth;
   Sing praises with a skillful
         psalm.
8 God reigns over the nations,
   God sits on His holy throne.

9 The nobles of the peoples have
assembled themselves *with*
the people of the God of
Abraham,
For the shields of the earth
belong to God;
He is highly exalted.

PSALM 48

The City of Our God

A Song. A Psalm of the
sons of Korah.

1 GREAT is Yahweh, and greatly
to be praised,
In the city of our God, His holy
mountain.
2 Beautiful in elevation, the joy of
the whole earth,
Is Mount Zion *in* the far
north,
The city of the great King.
3 God, in her palaces,
Has made Himself known as a
stronghold.

4 For, behold, the kings assembled
themselves,
They passed by together.
5 They saw *it*, then they were
astonished;
They were dismayed, they fled
in alarm.
6 Panic seized them there,
Anguish, as of a woman in
childbirth.
7 With the east wind
You break the ships of
Tarshish.

8 As we have heard, so have we
seen
In the city of Yahweh of hosts, in
the city of our God;
God will establish her forever.
Selah.

9 We have thought on Your
lovingkindness, O God,
In the midst of Your temple.
10 As is Your name, O God,
So is Your praise to the ends of
the earth;
Your right hand is full of
righteousness.
11 Let Mount Zion be glad,
Let the daughters of Judah rejoice
Because of Your judgments.
12 Walk about Zion and go
around her;
Count her towers;
13 Consider her ramparts;
Go through her palaces,
That you may recount *it* to the
next generation.
14 For this is God,
Our God forever and ever;
He will guide us over death.

PSALM 49

Why Should I Fear in Days of Evil?

For the choir director. Of the
sons of Korah. A Psalm.

1 HEAR this, all peoples;
Give ear, all inhabitants of the
world,
2 Both low and high,
Rich and poor together.

3 My mouth will speak wisdom,
  And the meditation of my heart
    will be discernment.
4 I will incline my ear to a proverb;
  I will express my riddle on the
    harp.

5 Why should I fear in days of evil,
  When the iniquity of my
    supplanters surrounds me,
6 Even those who trust in their
    wealth
  And boast in the abundance of
    their riches?
7 Truly, no man can redeem *his*
    brother;
  He cannot give to God a ransom
    for him—
8 For the redemption price for
    their soul is costly,
  And *it* ceases forever—
9 That he should live on eternally,
  That he should not see
    corruption.

10 For he sees *that even* wise
    men die;
  The fool and the senseless alike
    perish
  And leave their wealth to others.
11 Their inner thought is *that* their
    houses are forever
  And their dwelling places from
    generation to generation;
  They have called their lands
    after their own names.
12 But man in *his* honor will not
    endure;
  He is like the animals that
    perish.

13 This is the way of those who are
    foolish,
  And of those after them who are
    pleased with their words.
                              Selah.
14 As sheep they are appointed
    for Sheol;
  Death will shepherd them;
  And the upright shall have
    dominion over them in
    the morning,
  And their form shall be for
    Sheol to consume,
  Far away from his habitation.
15 But God will redeem my soul
    from the power of Sheol,
  For He will receive me.   Selah.

16 Do not be afraid when a man
    becomes rich,
  When the glory of his house
    increases;
17 For when he dies he will not
    take any of it;
  His glory will not descend
    after him.
18 For while he lives he blesses
    his soul—
  And *men* will praise you
    when you do well for
    yourself—
19 *But his soul* shall go to the
    generation of his
    fathers;
  They will eternally not
    see light.
20 Man in *his* honor, but *who* does
    not understand,
  Is like the animals that
    perish.

PSALM 50

God Himself Is Judge

A Psalm of Asaph.

1 THE Mighty One, God, Yahweh,
   has spoken,
   And called the earth from the
   rising of the sun to its setting.

2 Out of Zion, the perfection of
   beauty,
   God has shone forth.

3 May our God come and not be
   silent;
   Fire devours before Him,
   And a *storm* whirls around Him.

4 He calls the heavens above,
   And the earth, to render justice
   to His people:

5 "Gather My holy ones to Me,
   Those who have cut a
   covenant with Me
   by sacrifice."

6 And the heavens declare His
   righteousness,
   For God Himself is judge.   Selah.

7 "Hear, O My people, and I will
   speak;
   O Israel, I will testify against you;
   I am God, your God.

8 "I do not reprove you for your
   sacrifices,
   And your burnt offerings are
   continually before Me.

9 "I shall take no young bull out of
   your house
   Nor male goats out of your folds.

10 "For every beast of the forest
   is Mine,
   The cattle on a thousand hills.

11 "I know every bird of the
   mountains,
   And everything that moves in
   the field is Mine.

12 "If I were hungry I would not
   tell you,
   For the world is Mine, as well as
   its fullness.

13 "Shall I eat the flesh of bulls
   Or drink the blood of male
   goats?

14 "Offer to God a sacrifice of
   thanksgiving
   And pay your vows to the
   Most High;

15 Call upon Me in the day of
   distress;
   I shall rescue you, and you will
   glorify Me."

16 But to the wicked God says,
   "What right have you to recount
   My statutes
   And to take My covenant in your
   mouth?

17 "For you hate discipline,
   And you cast My words
   behind you.

18 "When you see a thief, you are
   pleased with him,
   And you associate with
   adulterers.

19 "You let your mouth loose
   in evil
   And you harness your tongue
   for deceit.

20 "You sit and speak against your
   brother;
   You slander your own
   mother's son.

21 "These things you have done
        and I kept silent;
    You thought that I was just
        like you;
    I will reprove you and state
        the case in order before
        your eyes.

22 "Now consider this, you who
        forget God,
    Lest I tear *you* in pieces, and
        there will be none to deliver.
23 "He who offers a sacrifice of
        thanksgiving glorifies Me;
    And he who orders *his* way,
    I shall show the salvation of God."

PSALM 51

Create in Me a Clean Heart, O God

For the choir director. A Psalm
    of David. When Nathan the
    prophet came to him, after he
    had gone in to Bathsheba.

1 BE gracious to me, O God,
        according to Your
        lovingkindness;
    According to the abundance of
        Your compassion blot out
        my transgressions.

2 Wash me thoroughly from my
        iniquity
    And cleanse me from my sin.

3 For I know my transgressions,
    And my sin is ever before me.

4 Against You, You only, I have
        sinned
    And done what is evil in Your
        sight,

So that You are justified when
        You speak
    And pure when You judge.

5 Behold, I was brought forth in
        iniquity,
    And in sin my mother
        conceived me.

6 Behold, You delight in truth in
        the innermost being,
    And in the hidden part You
        will make me know
        wisdom.

7 Purify me with hyssop, and I
        shall be clean;
    Wash me, and I shall be whiter
        than snow.

8 Make me to hear joy and
        gladness,
    Let the bones which You have
        crushed rejoice.

9 Hide Your face from my sins
    And blot out all my iniquities.

10 Create in me a clean heart,
        O God,
    And renew a steadfast spirit
        within me.

11 Do not cast me away from Your
        presence
    And do not take Your Holy Spirit
        from me.

12 Restore to me the joy of Your
        salvation
    And sustain me with a willing
        spirit.

13 *Then* I will teach transgressors
        Your ways,
    And sinners will be converted
        to You.

14 Deliver me from bloodguiltiness,
    O God, the God of my salvation;
Then my tongue will joyfully
    sing of Your righteousness.
15 O Lord, open my lips,
    That my mouth may declare
    Your praise.
16 For You do not delight in sacrifice,
    otherwise I would give it;
You are not pleased with burnt
    offering.
17 The sacrifices of God are a
    broken spirit;
A broken and a contrite heart,
    O God, You will not despise.

18 By Your favor do good to Zion;
    Build the walls of Jerusalem.
19 Then You will delight in
    righteous sacrifices,
In burnt offering and whole
    burnt offering;
Then young bulls will be offered
    on Your altar.

PSALM 52

I Trust in the Lovingkindness of God

For the choir director. A Maskil of
David. When Doeg the Edomite came
and told Saul and said to him, "David
has come to the house of Ahimelech."
1 WHY do you boast in evil,
    O mighty man?
The lovingkindness of God
    endures all day long.
2 Your tongue devises destruction,
    Like a sharp razor, O worker of
    deceit.

3 You love evil more than good,
    Falsehood more than speaking
        what is right.   Selah.
4 You love all words that devour,
    O deceitful tongue.

5 But God will break you down
    forever;
He will snatch you up and tear
    you away from *your* tent,
And uproot you from the land of
    the living,   Selah.
6 So that the righteous will see
    and fear,
And will laugh at him, *saying*,
7 "Behold, the man who would
    not set God as his strength,
But trusted in the abundance of
    his riches
And was strong in his destruction."

8 But as for me, I am like a green
    olive tree in the house
    of God;
I trust in the lovingkindness of
    God forever and ever.
9 I will give You thanks forever,
    because You have done *it*,
And I will hope on Your
    name, for *it is* good, in the
    presence of Your holy ones.

PSALM 53

There Is No One Who Does Good

For the choir director. According
to Mahalath. A Maskil of David.
1 THE wicked fool says in his
    heart, "There is no God,"

They act corruptly, and
commit abominable
injustice;
There is no one who does
good.

2 God looks down from heaven
upon the sons of men
To see if there is anyone who
has insight,
Anyone who seeks after
God.

3 Every one of them has
turned back; together
they have become
worthless;
There is no one who does good,
not even one.

4 Do the workers of iniquity not
know,
Who eat up my people *as* they
eat bread
And do not call upon
God?

5 There they were in great
dread *where* no dread
had been;
For God scattered the bones
of him who encamped
against you;
You put *them* to shame,
because God had rejected
them.

6 Oh, that the salvation of
Israel would come out
of Zion!
When God restores His captive
people,
May Jacob rejoice, may Israel
be glad.

PSALM 54

God Is My Helper

For the choir director. With
stringed instruments. A Maskil of
David. When the Ziphites came
and said to Saul, "Is not David
hiding himself among us?"

1 O God, save me by Your
name,
And render justice to me by
Your might.

2 O God, hear my prayer;
Give ear to the words of my
mouth.

3 For strangers have risen
against me
And ruthless men have sought
my life;
They have not set God before
them.　　　　　Selah.

4 Behold, God is my helper;
The Lord is among those
who sustain my
soul.

5 He will return the evil to
my foes;
Destroy them in Your truth.

6 With a freewill offering I will
sacrifice to You;
I will give thanks to Your
name, O Yahweh, for
it is good.

7 For He has delivered me
from all distress,
And my eye has looked
in triumph upon my
enemies.

PSALM 55

*He Will Never Allow the Righteous to
Be Shaken*

For the choir director. With stringed
   instruments. A Maskil of David.

1 GIVE ear to my prayer,
        O God;
   And do not hide Yourself from
        my supplication.
2 Give heed to me and answer me;
   I am restless in my complaint
        and am surely distracted,
3 Because of the voice of the
        enemy,
   Because of the pressure of the
        wicked;
   For they shake wickedness
        down upon me
   And in anger they bear a grudge
        against me.

4 My heart is in anguish
        within me,
   And the terrors of death have
        fallen upon me.
5 Fear and trembling come
        upon me,
   And horror has covered me.
6 I said, "Oh, that I had wings like
        a dove!
   I would fly away and be at rest.
7 "Behold, I would wander far
        away,
   I would lodge in the wilderness.
                                    Selah.
8 "I would hasten to my place of
        refuge
   From the stormy wind *and*
        tempest."

9 Confuse, O Lord, divide their
        tongues,
   For I have seen violence and
        strife in the city.
10 Day and night they go around
        her upon her walls,
   And wickedness and mischief
        are in her midst.
11 Destruction is in her midst;
   Oppression and deceit do not
        depart from her streets.

12 For it is not an enemy who
        reproaches me,
   Then I could bear *it*;
   Nor is it one who hates me
        who has magnified himself
        against me,
   Then I could hide myself
        from him.
13 But it is you, a man my equal,
   My close companion and my
        familiar friend;
14 We who had sweet counsel
        together
   Walked in the house of God in
        the throng.
15 Let death come deceitfully
        upon them;
   Let them go down alive to
        Sheol,
   For evil is in their dwelling, in
        their midst.

16 As for me, I shall call upon God,
   And Yahweh will save me.
17 Evening and morning and
        at noon, I will bring my
        complaint and moan,
   And He will hear my voice.

18 He will redeem my soul in
    peace from the battle
    which is against me,
  For they are many *who strive*
    with me.
19 God will hear and answer
    them—
  Even the one who sits
    enthroned from of old—
                                    Selah.
  Because they do not
    change,
  And do not fear God.
20 *My companion* has put forth
    his hands against those
    who were at peace
    with him;
  He has violated his
    covenant.
21 His speech was smoother
    than butter,
  But his heart was war;
  His words were softer
    than oil,
  Yet they were drawn
    swords.

22 Cast your burden upon
    Yahweh and He will
    sustain you;
  He will never allow the
    righteous to be
    shaken.
23 But You, O God, will bring
    them down *to* the pit of
    corruption;
  Men of bloodshed and deceit
    will not live out half
    their days.
  But I will trust in You.

PSALM 56

In God I Trust, I Shall Not Be Afraid

For the choir director. According to
  Jonath Elem Rehokim. A Mikhtam
  of David. When the Philistines
  seized him in Gath.

1 BE gracious to me, O God, for
    man has trampled upon me;
  All day long, an attacker
    oppresses me.
2 My foes have trampled upon me
    all day long,
  For many attack me proudly.
3 When I am afraid,
  I will trust in You.
4 In God, whose word I praise,
  In God I trust;
  I shall not be afraid.
  What can *mere* man do to me?
5 All day long they distort my
    words;
  All their thoughts are against me
    for evil.
6 They attack, they lurk,
  They watch my heels,
  As they have hoped *to take* my
    life.
7 On account of *their* wickedness,
    will they have an escape?
  In anger, bring down the
    peoples, O God!

8 You have taken account of my
    wanderings;
  Put my tears in Your bottle.
  Are *they* not in Your book?
9 Then my enemies will turn back
    in the day when I call;
  This I know, that God is for me.

10 In God, *whose* word I praise,
In Yahweh, *whose* word I praise,
11 In God I trust, I shall not be
        afraid.
What can man do to me?
12 Your vows are *binding* upon me,
        O God;
I will fulfill thank offerings to You.
13 For You have delivered my soul
        from death,
Indeed my feet from stumbling,
So that I may walk before God
In the light of the living.

PSALM 57

Let Your Glory Be Above All the Earth

For the choir director. Al-tashheth.
    Of David. A Mikhtam. When he
    fled from Saul in the cave.
1 BE gracious to me, O God, be
        gracious to me,
For my soul takes refuge in You;
And in the shadow of Your
        wings I will take refuge
Until destruction passes by.
2 I will call to God Most High,
To God who accomplishes *all
        things* for me.
3 He will send from heaven and
        save me;
He reproaches him who
        tramples upon me.   Selah.
God will send His lovingkindness
        and His truth.

4 My soul is among lions;
I am lying down among those
        who breathe forth fire,

Sons of men whose teeth are
        spears and arrows
And their tongue a sharp sword.
5 Be exalted above the heavens,
        O God;
Let Your glory *be* above all the earth.
6 They have set a net for my steps;
My soul is bowed down;
They dug a pit before me;
They *themselves* have fallen into
        the midst of it.   Selah.

7 My heart is set, O God, my heart
        is set;
I will sing, yes, I will sing praises!
8 Awake, my glory!
Awake, harp and lyre!
I will awaken the dawn.
9 I will give thanks to You, O Lord,
        among the peoples;
I will sing praises to You among
        the nations.
10 For Your lovingkindness is great
        to the heavens
And Your truth to the skies.
11 Be exalted above the heavens,
        O God;
Let Your glory *be* above all the
        earth.

PSALM 58

There Is a God Who Judges on Earth

For the choir director. Al-tashheth.
    Of David. A Mikhtam.
1 DO you indeed speak
        righteousness, O gods?
Do you judge with equity, O sons
        of men?

2 No, in heart you work
    unrighteousness;
On earth you prepare a path
    for the violence of your
    hands.

3 The wicked are estranged from
    the womb;
These who speak falsehood
    wander in error from birth.

4 They have venom like the
    venom of a serpent;
Like a deaf cobra that stops up
    its ear,

5 So that it does not hear the voice
    of charmers,
Or a skillful caster of spells.

6 O God, shatter their teeth in
    their mouth;
Break out the fangs of the young
    lions, O Yahweh.

7 Let them flow away like water
    that runs off;
When he aims his arrows, let
    them be as headless shafts.

8 *Let them be* as a snail which
    melts away as it goes along,
Like the miscarriages of a
    woman which never behold
    the sun.

9 Before your pots can feel *the fire*
    of thorns
He will sweep them away with
    a whirlwind, the living and
    the burning alike.

10 The righteous will be glad when
    he beholds the vengeance;
He will wash his feet in the
    blood of the wicked.

11 And men will say, "Surely there
    is a reward for the righteous;
Surely there is a God who judges
    on earth!"

PSALM 59

Deliver Me from My Enemies

For the choir director. Al-tashheth.
Of David. A Mikhtam. When Saul
sent *men* and they watched the
house in order to put him to death.

1 DELIVER me from my enemies,
    O my God;
Set me *securely* on high away
    from those who rise up
    against me.

2 Deliver me from workers of
    iniquity
And save me from men of
    bloodshed.

3 For behold, they have lain in
    wait for my soul;
Fierce men launch an attack
    against me,
Not for my transgression nor for
    my sin, O Yahweh,

4 For no guilt of *mine*, they run
    and set themselves
    against me.
Arouse Yourself to meet me,
    and see!

5 You, O Yahweh God of hosts, the
    God of Israel,
Awake to punish all the
    nations;
Do not be gracious to any *who*
    are treacherous in iniquity.
                Selah.

6 They return at evening, they
    howl like a dog,
And go around the city.
7 Behold, they pour forth *speech*
    with their mouth;
Swords are in their lips,
For, *they say,* "Who hears?"
8 But You, O Yahweh, laugh at
    them;
You mock all the nations.

9 *Because of* his strength I will
    watch for You,
For God is my stronghold.
10 My God in His lovingkindness
    will approach me;
God will let me look
    triumphantly upon my foes.
11 Do not slay them, or my people
    will forget;
Make them wander about by
    Your power, and bring
    them down,
O Lord, our shield.
12 *On account of* the sin of their
    mouth *and* the word of
    their lips,
Let them even be caught in
    their pride,
And on account of curses and
    lies which they utter.
13 Destroy *them* in wrath, destroy
    them that they may be
    no more;
That *men* may know that God
    rules in Jacob
To the ends of the earth.   Selah.
14 They return at evening, they
    howl like a dog,
And go around the city.

15 They wander about for food
And growl if they are not
    satisfied.

16 But as for me, I shall sing of Your
    strength;
And I shall joyfully sing of
    Your lovingkindness in the
    morning,
For You have been my
    stronghold
And a refuge in the day of my
    distress.
17 O my strength, I will sing praises
    to You;
For God is my stronghold,
    the God who shows me
    lovingkindness.

PSALM 60

Through God We Shall Do Valiantly

For the choir director. According to
Shushan Eduth. A Mikhtam of David.
For teaching. When he struggled with
Aram-naharaim and with Aram-zobah,
and Joab returned, and smote twelve
thousand of Edom in the Valley of Salt.
1 O God, You have rejected us. You
    have broken us;
You have been angry; Oh,
    restore us.
2 You have made the land quake,
    You have split it open;
Heal its breaches, for it shakes.
3 You have caused Your people to
    see hardship;
You have given us wine to drink
    that causes reeling.

4 You have given a banner to
 those who fear You,
In order to flee *to it* from
 the bow.   Selah.
5 That Your beloved may be
 rescued,
Save with Your right hand, and
 answer us!

6 God has spoken in His
 holiness:
"I will exult, I will portion out
 Shechem and measure out
 the valley of Succoth.
7 "Gilead is Mine, and Manasseh
 is Mine;
Ephraim also is the helmet of
 My head;
Judah is My scepter.
8 "Moab is My washbowl;
Over Edom I shall throw My
 shoe;
Make a loud shout, O Philistia,
 because of Me!"

9 Who will bring me into the
 fortified city?
Who will lead me to Edom?
10 Have You Yourself, O God, not
 rejected us?
And will You, O God, not go
 forth with our armies?
11 Oh give us help against the
 adversary,
For *salvation* by man is
 worthless.
12 Through God we shall do
 valiantly,
And it is He who will tread down
 our adversaries.

PSALM 61

Lead Me to the Rock

For the choir director.
On a stringed instrument.
Of David.

1 HEAR my cry of lamentation,
 O God;
Give heed to my prayer.
2 From the end of the earth I call
 to You when my heart is
 faint;
Lead me to the rock that is
 higher than I.
3 For You have been a refuge
 for me,
A tower of strength before the
 enemy.
4 Let me sojourn in Your tent
 forever;
Let me take refuge in the shelter
 of Your wings.   Selah.

5 For You, O God, have heard my
 vows;
You have given *me* the
 inheritance of those who
 fear Your name.
6 You will add days to the king's
 life;
His years will be from
 generation to generation.
7 He will sit enthroned before
 God forever;
Appoint lovingkindness and
 truth that they may
 guard him.
8 So I will sing praise to Your
 name forever,
As I pay my vows day by day.

PSALM 62

God Is a Refuge for Us

For the choir director. According
to Jeduthun. A Psalm of David.

1 SURELY my soul *waits* in
    silence for God;
  From Him is my salvation.
2 Surely He is my rock and my
    salvation,
  My stronghold; I shall not be
    greatly shaken.

3 How long will you assail a man,
  That you may murder *him*, all
    of you,
  Like a leaning wall, like a fence
    thrust down?
4 Surely they have counseled to
    thrust him down from his
    high position;
  They find pleasure in falsehood;
  They bless with their mouth,
  But inwardly they curse.   Selah.

5 Surely wait in silence for God,
    O my soul,
  For my hope is from Him.
6 Surely He is my rock and my
    salvation,
  My stronghold; I shall not be
    shaken.
7 On God my salvation and my
    glory *rest*;
  The rock of my strength, my
    refuge is in God.
8 Trust in Him at all times,
    O people;
  Pour out your heart before Him;
  God is a refuge for us.   Selah.

9 Surely men of low degree are
    merely vanity and men of
    rank are a lie;
  In the balances they go up;
  They are together lighter than
    a breath of vanity.
10 Do not trust in oppression
   And do not put vain hope in
     robbery;
   If riches increase, do not set
     your heart *upon them.*

11 Once God has spoken;
   Twice I have heard this:
   That strength belongs
     to God;
12 And that to You, O Lord, belongs
     lovingkindness,
   For You repay a man according
     to his work.

PSALM 63

My Soul Thirsts for You

A Psalm of David. When he was
  in the wilderness of Judah.

1 O God, You are my God; I shall
    seek You earnestly;
  My soul thirsts for You, my flesh
    yearns for You,
  In a dry and weary land without
    water.
2 Thus I have beheld You in the
    sanctuary,
  To see Your power and Your
    glory.
3 Because Your lovingkindness is
    better than life,
  My lips will laud You.

4 Thus I will bless You as long as
  I live;
  I will lift up my hands in Your
    name.
5 My soul is satisfied as with
    fatness and richness,
  And my mouth offers praises
    with lips of joyful songs.

6 When I remember You on my bed,
  I meditate on You in the night
    watches,
7 For You have been my help,
  And in the shadow of Your
    wings I sing for joy.
8 My soul clings to You;
  Your right hand upholds me.

9 But those who seek my life to
    destroy it,
  Will go into the depths of the
    earth.
10 They will be delivered over to
    the power of the sword;
   They will be a portion for foxes.
11 But the king will be glad in God;
   Everyone who swears by Him
     will boast,
   For the mouths of those who
     speak lies will be closed.

PSALM 64

The Righteous Will Be Glad in Yahweh

For the choir director. A Psalm of David.
1 HEAR my voice, O God, in my
    complaint;
  Guard my life from dread of the
    enemy.

2 Hide me from the secret counsel
    of evildoers,
  From the tumult of the workers
    of iniquity,
3 Who have sharpened their
    tongue like a sword.
  They aimed bitter speech *as*
    their arrow,
4 To shoot from places of hiding
    at the blameless;
  Suddenly they shoot at him, and
    do not fear.
5 They hold fast to themselves an
    evil purpose;
  They talk of laying snares secretly;
  They say, "Who can see them?"
6 They searched out
    unrighteousness, *saying*,
  "We have completed a diligent
    search";
  For the inward thought of a man
    and *his* heart are deep.

7 But God will shoot them with an
    arrow;
  Suddenly they will be wounded.
8 So they will cause their own
    tongue to turn against them;
  All who see them will shake
    their head.
9 Then all men will fear,
  And they will declare the work
    of God,
  And will consider what He has
    done.
10 The righteous man will be glad
    in Yahweh and will take
    refuge in Him;
   And all the upright in heart will
    boast.

PSALM 65

Blessed Is the One Whom You Choose

For the choir director. A
Psalm of David. A Song.

1 TO You, there will be silence
and praise in Zion, O God,
And to You the vow will be paid.
2 O You who hear prayer,
To You all flesh comes.
3 Words of iniquity prevail
against me;
As for our transgressions, You
atone for them.
4 How blessed is the one whom You
choose and bring near *to You*
That he would dwell in Your
courts.
We will be satisfied with the
goodness of Your house,
Your holy temple.

5 By fearsome *deeds* You answer
us in righteousness, O God
of our salvation,
You who are the trust of all the
ends of the earth and of the
farthest sea;
6 Who establishes the mountains
by His strength,
Being girded with might;
7 Who stills the rumbling of the
seas,
The rumbling of their waves,
And the tumult of the peoples.
8 They who inhabit the ends
of the earth are in fear on
account of Your signs;
You make the dawn and the
sunset shout for joy.

9 You visit the earth and cause it
to overflow;
You greatly enrich it;
The stream of God is full of water;
You establish their grain, for
thus You establish the earth.
10 You water its furrows
abundantly,
You smooth its ridges,
You soften it with showers,
You bless its growth.
11 You crown the year with Your
goodness,
And Your paths drip *with* richness.
12 The pastures of the wilderness
drip,
And the hills gird themselves
with rejoicing.
13 The meadows are clothed with
flocks
And the valleys are covered with
grain;
They make a loud shout, indeed,
they sing.

PSALM 66

Come and See the Works of God

For the choir director. A Song. A Psalm.

1 MAKE a loud shout to God, all
the earth;
2 Sing praise for the glory of His
name;
Establish His praise as glorious.
3 Say to God, "How fearsome are
Your works!
Because of the abundance of
Your strength Your enemies
will cower before You.

4 "All the earth will worship You,
  And will sing praises to You;
  They will sing praises to Your
        name."   Selah.

5 Come and see the works of God,
  Who is fearsome in *His* deeds
        toward the sons of men.
6 He turned the sea into dry land;
  They passed through the river
        on foot;
  There let us be glad in Him!
7 He rules by His might forever;
  His eyes keep watch on the
        nations;
  Let not the rebellious exalt
        themselves.   Selah.

8 Bless our God, O peoples,
  And make the sound of His
        praise heard,
9 Who establishes us among the
        living
  And does not allow our feet to
        stumble.
10 For You have tested us, O God;
  You have refined us as silver is
        refined.
11 You brought us into the net;
  You established an oppressive
        burden upon our loins.
12 You made men ride over our
        heads;
  We went through fire and
        through water,
  Yet You brought us out into *a
        place of* abundance.
13 I shall come into Your house
        with burnt offerings;
  I shall pay You my vows,

14 Which my lips uttered
  And my mouth spoke when
        I was in distress.
15 I shall offer to You burnt
        offerings of fat beasts,
  With the smoke of rams;
  I shall make *an offering of* bulls
        with male goats.   Selah.

16 Come *and* hear, all who fear God,
  And I will recount what He has
        done for my soul.
17 I called out to Him with my
        mouth,
  And He was exalted with my
        tongue.
18 If I see wickedness in my heart,
  The Lord will not hear;
19 But certainly God has heard;
  He has given heed to the voice
        of my prayer.
20 Blessed be God,
  Who has not turned away my
        prayer
  Nor His lovingkindness from me.

PSALM 67

Cause Your Face to Shine upon Us

For the choir director. With stringed
  instruments. A Psalm. A Song.
1 GOD be gracious to us and
        bless us,
  And cause His face to shine
        upon us—   Selah.
2 That Your way may be known
        on the earth,
  Your salvation among all
        nations.

3 Let the peoples praise You,
     O God;
Let all the peoples praise You.
4 Let the nations be glad and sing
     for joy;
For You will judge the peoples
     with uprightness
And lead the nations on the
     earth.   Selah.
5 Let the peoples praise You,
     O God;
Let all the peoples praise You.
6 The earth has yielded its
     produce;
God, our God, blesses us.
7 God blesses us,
That all the ends of the earth
     may fear Him.

PSALM 68

Let God's Enemies Be Scattered

     For the choir director. A
     Psalm of David. A Song.
1 LET God arise, let His enemies
     be scattered,
And let those who hate Him flee
     before Him.
2 As smoke is driven away, *so*
     drive *them* away;
As wax melts before the fire,
So let the wicked perish
     before God.
3 But let the righteous be glad; let
     them exult before God;
And let them rejoice with
     gladness.

4 Sing to God, sing praises to His
     name;
Lift up *a song* for Him who rides
     through the deserts,
Whose name is [1]Yah, and exult
     before Him.

5 A father of the fatherless and a
     judge for the widows,
Is God in His holy habitation.
6 God causes the lonely to inhabit
     a home;
He leads out the prisoners into
     prosperity,
Only the rebellious dwell in a
     parched land.

7 O God, when You went forth
     before Your people,
When You marched through the
     wasteland,   Selah.
8 The earth quaked;
The heavens also dripped *rain* at
     the presence of God;
Sinai itself *quaked* at the presence
     of God, the God of Israel.
9 You caused abundant rain to
     sprinkle down, O God;
You established Your inheritance
     when it was parched.
10 Your creatures inhabited it;
You established it in Your
     goodness for the poor,
     O God.

11 The Lord gives the word;
The women who proclaim the
     good news are a great host:

---

[1] The shortened form of Yahweh, found in poetry and praise (e.g. Halleluj*ah*), and in names (e.g. Zechar*iah*)

12 "Kings of armies retreat, they
      retreat,
   And she who remains at home
      will divide the spoil!"
13 If you *men* lie down among the
      sheepfolds,
   You all would be like the wings
      of a dove covered with
      silver,
   And its pinions with glistening
      gold.
14 When the Almighty dispersed
      the kings there,
   It was snowing in Zalmon.

15 A mountain of God is the
      mountain of Bashan;
   A mountain *of many* peaks
      is the mountain of
      Bashan.
16 Why do you look with envy,
      O mountains with *many*
      peaks,
   At the mountain which God has
      prized for His habitation?
   Surely Yahweh will dwell *there*
      forever.
17 The chariots of God are
      myriads, thousands upon
      thousands;
   The Lord is among them *as at*
      Sinai, in holiness.
18 You have ascended on high,
      You have led captive *Your*
      captives;
   You have received gifts
      among men,
   Even *among* the rebellious also,
      that Yah—God—may
      dwell *there*.

19 Blessed be the Lord, who daily
      bears our burden,
   The God *who* is our salvation.
                              Selah.
20 God is to us a God of salvation;
   And to Yahweh the Lord
      belong escapes from
      death.
21 Surely God will crush the head
      of His enemies,
   The hairy skull of him who goes
      on in his guilty deeds.
22 The Lord said, "I will bring *them*
      back from Bashan.
   I will bring *them* back from the
      depths of the sea;
23 That your foot may crush *them*
      in blood,
   The tongue of your dogs *may
      have* its portion from *your*
      enemies."

24 They have seen Your procession,
      O God,
   The procession of my God, my
      King, into the sanctuary.
25 The singers went on, the
      musicians after *them*,
   In the midst of the maidens
      beating tambourines.
26 Bless God in the congregations,
   Yahweh, the fountain of
      Israel.
27 There is Benjamin, the
      youngest, having dominion
      over them,
   The princes of Judah *in* their
      throng,
   The princes of Zebulun, the
      princes of Naphtali.

28 Your God has commanded your
strength;
Show Yourself strong, O God,
who has worked on our
behalf.
29 Because of Your temple at
Jerusalem
Kings will bring gifts to You.
30 Rebuke the beast in the
reeds,
The herd of bulls with the calves
of the peoples,
Trampling under foot the pieces
of silver;
He has cast out the peoples who
delight in war.
31 Envoys will come out of
Egypt;
Ethiopia will quickly stretch
out her hands to God.

32 Sing to God, O kingdoms of the
earth,
Sing praises to the Lord,   Selah.
33 To Him who rides upon the
highest heavens, which are
from ancient times;
Behold, He gives forth His
voice, a voice *that is*
strong.
34 Ascribe strength to God;
His majesty is over Israel
And His strength is in the
skies.
35 O God, *You are* awesome from
Your sanctuary.
The God of Israel Himself gives
strength and might to the
people.
Blessed be God!

PSALM 69

Save Me, O God

For the choir director. According
to Shoshannim. Of David.
1 SAVE me, O God,
For the waters have threatened
my life.
2 I have sunk in deep clay, and
there is no foothold;
I have come into deep
waters, and a flood
overflows me.
3 I am weary with my calling out;
my throat is parched;
My eyes fail while I wait for
my God.
4 Those who hate me without
cause are more than the
hairs of my head;
Those who would destroy
me are powerful, being
wrongfully my enemies;
What I did not steal, I then have
to restore.

5 O God, it is You who knows
my folly,
And all my guilt is not hidden
from You.
6 May those who hope for You
not be ashamed through
me, O Lord Yahweh of
hosts;
May those who seek You not
be dishonored through me,
O God of Israel,
7 Because for Your sake I have
borne reproach;
Dishonor has covered my face.

8 I have become estranged from
my brothers
And a foreigner to my mother's
sons.

9 For zeal for Your house has
consumed me,
And the reproaches of those
who reproach You have
fallen on me.

10 When I wept in my soul with
fasting,
It became my reproach.

11 When I made sackcloth my
clothing,
I became a byword to them.

12 Those who dwell at the gate
moan about me,
And I *am* the drunkards' songs.

13 But as for me, my prayer is
to You, O Yahweh, at an
acceptable time;
O God, in the abundance of Your
lovingkindness,
Answer me with the truth of
Your salvation.

14 Deliver me from the mire and do
not let me sink;
May I be delivered from my foes
and from the deep waters.

15 May the flood of water not
overflow me
Nor the deep swallow me up,
Nor the pit shut its mouth on me.

16 Answer me, O Yahweh, for Your
lovingkindness is good;
According to the abundance
of Your compassion, turn
to me,

17 And do not hide Your face from
Your slave,
For I am in distress; answer me
quickly.

18 Oh draw near to my soul *and*
redeem it;
Ransom me because of my
enemies!

19 You know my reproach and my
shame and my dishonor;
All my adversaries are
before You.

20 Reproach has broken my heart
and I am so sick.
And I hoped for sympathy, but
there was none,
And for comforters, but I found
none.

21 They also gave *me* gall for my food
And for my thirst they gave me
vinegar to drink.

22 May their table before them
become a snare;
And when they are in peace,
may it become a trap.

23 May their eyes darken so that
they cannot see,
And make their loins quake
continually.

24 Pour out Your indignation on
them,
And may Your burning anger
overtake them.

25 May their camp be desolate;
May none dwell in their tents.

26 For they have persecuted him
whom You Yourself have
struck down,

And they recount the pain
　　of those whom You have
　　wounded.
27 Add iniquity to their iniquity,
And may they not come into
　　Your righteousness.
28 May they be blotted out of the
　　book of life
And may they not be recorded
　　with the righteous.

29 But I am afflicted and in pain;
May Your salvation, O God, set
　　me *securely* on high.
30 I will praise the name of God
　　with song
And magnify Him with
　　thanksgiving.
31 And this will please Yahweh
　　better than an ox
Or a young bull with horns and
　　hoofs.
32 The humble see *it and* are glad;
You who seek God, let your
　　heart revive.
33 For Yahweh hears the needy
And does not despise His *who
　are* prisoners.

34 Let heaven and earth praise Him,
The seas and everything that
　　moves in them.
35 For God will save Zion and build
　　the cities of Judah,
That they may dwell there and
　　possess it.
36 The seed of His slaves will
　　inherit it,
And those who love His name
　　will dwell in it.

PSALM 70

O Yahweh, Do Not Delay

For the choir director. Of David.
　　To bring to remembrance.
1 O God, *hasten* to deliver me;
O Yahweh, hasten to my help!
2 Let those be ashamed and
　　humiliated
Who seek my life;
Let those be turned back and
　　dishonored
Who delight in evil *against* me.
3 Let those turn back because of
　　their shame
Who say, "Aha, aha!"

4 Let those be joyful and glad
　　in You
All who seek You
And let them say continually,
"Let God be magnified,"
Those who love Your salvation.
5 But I am afflicted and needy;
Hasten to me, O God!
You are my help and my
　　protector;
O Yahweh, do not delay.

PSALM 71

O God, Do Not Forsake Me

1 IN You, O Yahweh, I have taken
　　refuge;
Let me never be ashamed.
2 In Your righteousness deliver
　　me and protect me;
Incline Your ear to me and
　　save me.

3 Be to me a rock of habitation to
   which I may continually come;
You have given the command to
   save me,
For You are my rock and my
   fortress.
4 Protect me, O my God, out of the
   hand of the wicked,
Out of the grasp of the
   unrighteous and
   ruthless man,
5 For You are my hope;
O Lord Yahweh, *You are* my trust
   from my youth.
6 By You I have been sustained
   from *my* birth;
You are He who took me from
   my mother's womb;
My praise is continually of You.

7 I have become a marvel to many,
For You are my strong refuge.
8 My mouth is filled with Your
   praise
And with Your beauty all day
   long.
9 Do not cast me off in the time of
   old age;
Do not forsake me when my
   strength fails.
10 For my enemies have spoken
   against me;
And those who watch my life
   have counseled together,
11 Saying, "God has forsaken him;
Pursue and seize him, for there
   is no one to deliver."

12 O God, do not be far from me;
O my God, hasten to my help!

13 Let those who accuse my soul be
   ashamed *and* consumed;
Let them be wrapped up with
   reproach and dishonor, who
   seek *to do* me evil.
14 But as for me, I will wait
   continually,
And will praise You yet more
   and more.
15 My mouth shall recount Your
   righteousness
And Your salvation all day long;
For I do not know the sum *of
   them.*
16 I will come with the mighty
   deeds of Lord Yahweh;
I will bring to remembrance
   Your righteousness, Yours
   alone.

17 O God, You have taught me from
   my youth,
And I still declare Your
   wondrous deeds.
18 And even when *I am* old and
   gray, O God, do not
   forsake me,
Until I declare Your strength to
   this generation,
Your might to all who are to
   come.
19 For Your righteousness, O God,
   reaches to the heavens,
You who have done great things;
O God, who is like You?
20 You, who have shown me many
   troubles and evils,
Will revive me again,
And will bring me up again from
   the depths of the earth.

21 May You increase my greatness
   And turn *to* comfort me.

22 I will also praise You with
   a harp,
   Even Your truth, O my God;
   To You I will sing praises with
   the lyre,
   O Holy One of Israel.

23 My lips will sing for joy when
   I sing praises to You;
   And my soul, which You have
   redeemed.

24 My tongue also will utter
   Your righteousness all
   day long;
   For they are ashamed, for they
   are humiliated who seek *to
   do* me evil.

PSALM 72

Give the King Your Judgments

   Of Solomon.

1 O God, give the king Your
   judgments,
   And Your righteousness to the
   king's son.

2 May he render judgment to
   Your people with
   righteousness
   And Your afflicted with justice.

3 Let the mountains lift up peace
   to the people,
   And the hills, in righteousness.

4 May he give justice to the
   afflicted of the people,
   Save the children of the needy,
   And crush the oppressor.

5 Let them fear You while the sun
   endures,
   And as long as the moon, *from*
   generation to *all* generations.

6 May he come down like rain
   upon the mown grass,
   Like showers that water the earth.

7 May the righteous flourish in
   his days,
   And abundance of peace until
   the moon is no more.

8 May he also have dominion
   from sea to sea
   And from the River to the ends
   of the earth.

9 Let the desert creatures kneel
   before him,
   And his enemies lick the dust.

10 Let the kings of Tarshish and of the
   coastlands bring a present;
   The kings of Sheba and Seba
   offer tribute.

11 And let all kings bow down to him,
   All nations serve him.

12 For he will deliver the needy
   when he cries for help,
   The afflicted also, and him who
   has no helper.

13 He will have compassion on the
   poor and needy,
   And the lives of the needy he
   will save.

14 He will redeem their life from
   oppression and violence,
   And their blood will be precious
   in his sight;

15 So may he live! And may they
   give to him the gold of Sheba;

And let each pray for him
    continually;
Let each bless him all day long.

16 May there be abundance of
    grain in the earth on top of
    the mountains;
May its fruit wave like *the cedars
    of* Lebanon;
And may those from the city
    blossom like vegetation of
    the earth.

17 May his name endure forever;
May his name increase as long
    as the sun *shines*;
Let *all nations* be blessed in
    him;
Let all nations call him blessed.

18 Blessed be Yahweh God, the God
    of Israel,
Who alone works wondrous deeds.

19 And blessed be His glorious
    name forever;
And may the whole earth be
    filled with His glory.
Amen, and Amen.

20 The prayers of David, the son of
    Jesse, are completed.

BOOK 3

PSALM 73

The Nearness of God Is My Good

A Psalm of Asaph.

1 SURELY God is good to Israel,
To those who are pure in heart!

2 But as for me, my feet had
    almost stumbled,
My steps had almost slipped.

3 For I was envious of the
    boastful,
I saw the peace of the wicked.

4 For there are no pains in their
    death,
And their body is fat.

5 They are not in trouble *as other*
    men,
And they are not stricken
    along with *the rest of*
    mankind.

6 Therefore lofty pride is their
    necklace;
The garment of violence covers
    them.

7 Their eye bulges from fatness;
The delusions of *their* heart
    overflow.

8 They scoff and wickedly speak
    of oppression;
They speak from on high.

9 They have set their mouth
    against the heavens,
And their tongue goes through
    the earth.

10 Therefore his people return
    here, *to his place*,
And waters of fullness are drunk
    by them.

11 They say, "How does God
    know?
And is there knowledge with the
    Most High?"

12 Behold, these are the wicked;
And always at ease, they have
    increased *in* wealth.

13 Surely in vain I have kept my
    heart pure
    And washed my hands in
    innocence;
14 For I have been stricken all day
    long
    And reproved every morning.

15 If I had said, "I will recount
    thus,"
    Behold, I would have betrayed
    the generation of Your
    children.
16 When I gave thought to know
    this,
    It was trouble in my sight
17 Until I came into the sanctuary
    of God;
    Then I understood their end.
18 Surely You set them in slippery
    places;
    You cause them to fall to
    destruction.
19 How they become desolate in a
    moment!
    They are completely swept away
    by terrors!
20 Like a dream when one awakes,
    O Lord, when aroused, You will
    despise their form.

21 When my heart was embittered
    And I was pierced within,
22 Then I was senseless and
    ignorant;
    I was *like* an animal before You.
23 Nevertheless I am continually
    with You;
    You have taken hold of my right
    hand.

24 With Your counsel You will
    lead me,
    And afterward take me in
    glory.

25 Whom have I in heaven *but You*?
    And besides You, I desire
    nothing on earth.
26 My flesh and my heart fail,
    But God is the rock of my heart
    and my portion forever.
27 For, behold, those who are far
    from You will perish;
    You have destroyed everyone
    who is unfaithful to You.
28 But as for me, the nearness of
    God is my good;
    I have set Lord Yahweh as my
    refuge,
    That I may recount all Your
    works.

PSALM 74

Yet God Is My King

A Maskil of Asaph.

1 WHY, O God? Have You rejected
    us forever?
    Why does Your anger smoke
    against the sheep of Your
    pasture?
2 Remember Your congregation,
    which You have purchased
    of old,
    Which You have redeemed
    to be the tribe of Your
    inheritance;
    And this Mount Zion, where You
    have dwelt.

3 Lift up Your steps toward the
   perpetual ruins;
   The enemy has damaged
   everything within the
   sanctuary.
4 Your adversaries have roared in
   the midst of Your meeting
   place;
   They have set up their own
   signs for signs.
5 Each seems like one who lifts up
   An axe against the undergrowth
   of trees.
6 And now its carved work
   altogether
   They smash with hatchet and
   hammers.
7 They have set Your sanctuary
   on fire;
   By bringing it to the ground,
   they have defiled the
   dwelling place of Your
   name.
8 They said in their heart, "Let us
   completely subdue them."
   They have burned all the
   meeting places of God in
   the land.
9 We do not see our signs;
   There is no longer any prophet,
   Nor is there any among us who
   knows how long.
10 How long, O God, will the
   adversary reproach?
   Will the enemy spurn Your
   name forever?
11 Why do You turn back Your
   hand, even Your right hand?
   From within Your bosom,
   destroy *them*!

12 Yet God is my King from of old,
   Who works deeds of salvation in
   the midst of the earth.
13 You divided the sea by Your
   strength;
   You broke the heads of the sea
   monsters in the waters.
14 You crushed the heads of
   Leviathan;
   You gave him as food for the
   creatures of the desert.
15 You split open spring and river;
   You dried up ever-flowing rivers.
16 Yours is the day, Yours also is the
   night;
   You have established the light
   and the sun.
17 You have caused all the
   boundaries of the earth to
   stand firm;
   You have formed summer and
   winter.

18 Remember this, O Yahweh,
   that the enemy has
   reproached,
   And a wickedly foolish people
   has spurned Your name.
19 Do not deliver the soul of Your
   turtledove to the wild beast;
   Do not forget the life of Your
   afflicted forever.
20 Look to the covenant;
   For the dark places of the land
   are full of the haunts of
   violence.
21 Let not the oppressed return
   dishonored;
   Let the afflicted and needy
   praise Your name.

22 Arise, O God, *and* plead Your
      own cause;
   Remember how the wicked fool
      reproaches You all day long.
23 Do not forget the voice of Your
      adversaries,
   The rumbling of those who rise
      against You which ascends
      continually.

PSALM 75

God Judges with Equity

For the choir director. Al-tashheth.
   A Psalm of Asaph. A Song.
1 WE give thanks to You, O God,
      we give thanks,
   For Your name is near;
   Men recount Your wondrous deeds.
2 "For I select an appointed time,
   It is I who judge with equity.
3 "The earth and all who dwell in
      it melt;
   It is I who have firmly set its
      pillars.   Selah.
4 "I said to the boastful, 'Do not
      boast,'
   And to the wicked, 'Do not raise
      up the horn;
5 Do not raise up your horn on high,
   Nor speak with insolent pride.'"

6 For *one's* rising up does not *come*
      from the east, nor from
      the west,
   And not from the desert;
7 But God is the Judge;
   He puts down one and raises up
      another.

8 For a cup is in the hand of
      Yahweh, and the wine foams;
   It is full of *His* mixture, and He
      pours from this;
   Surely all the wicked of the
      earth must drain *and* drink
      down its dregs.

9 But as for me, I will declare *it*
      forever;
   I will sing praises to the God of
      Jacob.
10 And all the horns of the wicked
      I will cut off,
   But the horns of the righteous
      will be raised up.

PSALM 76

God's Name Is Great in Israel

For the choir director.
   With stringed instruments.
   A Psalm of Asaph. A Song.
1 GOD is known in Judah;
   His name is great in Israel.
2 So His tabernacle is in Salem;
   His dwelling place is in Zion.
3 There He broke the flaming
      arrows,
   The shield and the sword and
      the battle.   Selah.

4 You are shining,
   Majestic from the mountains
      of prey.
5 The stouthearted were plundered,
   They sank into sleep;
   And none of the warriors could
      use his hands.

6 At Your rebuke, O God of Jacob,
  Both chariot rider and horse
      slumbered *into* a deep
      sleep.
7 But You, You are fearsome;
  And who can stand in Your
      presence when once You
      are angry?

8 You made *Your* cause to be
      heard from heaven;
  The earth feared and was quiet
9 When God arose to judgment,
  To save all the humble of the
      earth.   Selah.
10 For the wrath of man shall
      praise You;
   With a remnant of wrath You
      will gird Yourself.

11 Make vows to Yahweh your God
      and pay *them*;
   Let all who are around Him
      bring gifts to the
      Fearsome One.
12 He will cut off the spirit of
      princes;
   He is feared by the kings of the
      earth.

PSALM 77

In My Distress I Sought the Lord

For the choir director. According
to Jeduthun. Of Asaph. A Psalm.
1 MY voice *rises* to God, and I
      must cry aloud;
  My voice *rises* to God, and He
      will hear me.

2 In the day of my distress
      I sought the Lord;
  In the night my hand was stretched
      out without weariness;
  My soul refused to be comforted.
3 I remember God and I am
      disturbed;
  I muse and my spirit faints.
                            Selah.
4 You have held my eyelids *open*;
  I am so troubled that I cannot
      speak.
5 I give thought to the days of old,
  The years of long ago.
6 I remember my music in the
      night;
  I am musing with my heart,
  And my spirit is searching:

7 Will the Lord reject evermore?
  And will He not be favorable
      again?
8 Has His lovingkindness ceased
      forever?
  Has *His* word ended from
      generation to generation?
9 Has God forgotten to be
      gracious,
  Or has He in anger shut up His
      compassion?   Selah.
10 Then I said, "It is my grief,
   That the right hand of the Most
      High has changed."

11 I shall remember the deeds
      of Yah;
   Surely I will remember Your
      wonders of old.
12 I will meditate on all Your work
   And muse on Your deeds.

13 O God, Your way is holy;
What god is great like God?
14 You are the God who works
wonders;
You have made known Your
strength among the peoples.
15 You have by *Your* arm redeemed
Your people,
The sons of Jacob and Joseph.
Selah.

16 The waters saw You, O God;
The waters saw You, they were
in anguish;
The deeps also trembled.
17 The clouds poured out water;
The skies gave forth a sound;
Your arrows went here and there.
18 The sound of Your thunder was
in the whirlwind;
The lightnings lit up the world;
The earth trembled and shook.
19 Your way was in the sea
And Your paths in the mighty
waters,
But Your footprints were not
known.
20 You led Your people like a flock
By the hand of Moses and Aaron.

PSALM 78

*That the Generation to Come
Might Know*

A Maskil of Asaph.
1 GIVE ear, O my people, to my
instruction;
Incline your ears to the words of
my mouth.

2 I will open my mouth in a
parable;
I will pour forth dark sayings
of old,
3 Which we have heard and
known,
And our fathers have recounted
to us.
4 We will not conceal them from
their children,
But recount to the generation to
come the praises of Yahweh,
And His strength and His
wondrous deeds that He
has done.

5 For He established a testimony
in Jacob
And set a law in Israel,
Which He commanded our
fathers
That they should teach them to
their children,
6 That the generation to come
might know, *even* the
children *yet* to be born,
That they may arise and recount
them to their children,
7 That they should set their
confidence in God
And not forget the deeds of God,
But observe His
commandments,
8 And not be like their fathers,
A stubborn and rebellious
generation,
A generation that did not
prepare its heart
And whose spirit was not
faithful to God.

9 The sons of Ephraim were
archers equipped with
bows,
Yet they turned back in the day
of battle.

10 They did not keep the covenant
of God
And refused to walk in His law;

11 So they forgot His acts
And His wondrous deeds that
He had shown them.

12 He did wonders before their
fathers
In the land of Egypt, in the field
of Zoan.

13 He split the sea and caused
them to pass through,
And He made the waters stand
up like a heap.

14 Then He led them with the
cloud by day
And all the night with a light
of fire.

15 He was splitting the rocks in the
wilderness
And so gave *them* abundant
drink like the ocean depths.

16 He brought forth streams also
from the cliff face
And caused waters to run down
like rivers.

17 Yet they still continued to sin
against Him,
To rebel against the Most High
in the desert.

18 And in their heart they put God
to the test
By asking for food according to
their desire.

19 Then they spoke against God;
They said, "Can God prepare a
table in the wilderness?

20 "Behold, He struck the rock so
that waters gushed out,
And streams were overflowing;
Can He give bread also?
Will He prepare meat for His
people?"

21 Therefore Yahweh heard and
was full of wrath;
And a fire was kindled against
Jacob
And anger also mounted against
Israel,

22 Because they did not believe
in God
And did not trust in His
salvation.

23 Yet He commanded the skies
above
And opened the doors of heaven;

24 He rained down manna upon
them to eat
And gave them grain from
heaven.

25 Man ate the bread of angels;
He sent them provision to satisfy.

26 He led forth the east wind in the
heavens
And by His strength He guided
the south wind.

27 Then He rained meat upon them
like the dust,
Even winged fowl like the sand
of the seas,

28 He caused *them* to fall in the
midst of His camp,
All around His dwelling places.

29 So they ate and were very
   satisfied,
   And their desire He brought to
   them.
30 Before they had satisfied their
   desire,
   While their food was in their
   mouths,
31 The anger of God rose against
   them
   And killed some of their stoutest
   ones,
   And subdued the choice men of
   Israel.
32 In spite of all this they still sinned
   And did not believe in His
   wondrous deeds.
33 So He brought their days to an
   end in futility
   And their years in sudden terror.

34 When He killed them, then they
   sought Him,
   And returned and sought
   earnestly for God;
35 And they remembered that God
   was their rock,
   And the Most High God their
   Redeemer.
36 But they deceived Him with
   their mouth
   And lied to Him with their
   tongue.
37 For their heart was not prepared
   to remain with Him,
   Nor were they faithful in His
   covenant.
38 But He, being compassionate,
   atoned for *their* iniquity and
   did not destroy *them*;

And He abounded in turning
   back His anger
And did not arouse all His
   wrath.
39 Thus He remembered that they
   were but flesh,
   A wind that goes and does not
   return.

40 How often they rebelled against
   Him in the wilderness
   And grieved Him in the
   wasteland!
41 Again and again they tested
   God,
   And pained the Holy One of
   Israel.
42 They did not remember His
   power,
   The day when He redeemed
   them from the adversary,
43 When He performed His signs
   in Egypt
   And His miracles in the field of
   Zoan,
44 And turned their rivers to blood,
   And their streams, they could
   not drink.
45 He sent among them swarms of
   flies which devoured them,
   And frogs which destroyed
   them.
46 He gave also their crops to the
   grasshopper
   And the fruit of their labor to
   the locust.
47 He killed their vines with
   hailstones
   And their sycamore trees with
   frost.

48 He gave over their cattle also to
the hailstones
And their herds to bolts of
lightning.
49 He sent upon them His burning
anger,
Fury and indignation and distress,
A band of destroying angels.
50 He leveled a path for His anger;
He did not hold back their soul
from death,
But gave over their life to the
plague,
51 So He struck all the firstborn in
Egypt,
The first of their vigor in the
tents of Ham.
52 But He led forth His own people
like sheep
And guided them in the
wilderness like a flock;
53 He led them safely, so that they
did not fear;
But the sea covered their enemies.

54 So He brought them to His holy
land,
To this hill country which His
right hand had acquired.
55 He also drove out the nations
before them
And apportioned them
for an inheritance by
measurement,
And made the tribes of Israel
dwell in their tents.
56 Yet they tested and rebelled
against the Most High God
And did not keep His
testimonies,

57 But turned back and acted
treacherously like their
fathers;
They turned aside like a
treacherous bow.
58 For they provoked Him with
their high places
And aroused His jealousy with
their graven images.
59 God heard and was filled with
wrath
And greatly rejected Israel;
60 So that He abandoned the
dwelling place at Shiloh,
The tent which He caused to
dwell among men,
61 And gave up His strength to
captivity
And His beauty into the hand of
the adversary.
62 He also gave over His people to
the sword,
And was filled with wrath at His
inheritance.
63 Fire devoured His choice
men,
And His virgins had no wedding
songs.
64 His priests fell by the sword,
And His widows could not
weep.

65 Then the Lord awoke as *if from*
sleep,
As *if He were a* warrior
overcome by wine.
66 He struck His adversaries
backward;
He put on them an everlasting
reproach.

67 He also rejected the tent of
    Joseph,
    And did not choose the tribe of
    Ephraim,
68 But chose the tribe of Judah,
    Mount Zion which He loved.
69 And He built His sanctuary like
    the heights,
    Like the earth which He has
    founded forever.
70 He also chose David His
    servant
    And took him from the
    sheepfolds;
71 From following the nursing ewes
    He brought him
    To shepherd Jacob His people,
    And Israel His inheritance.
72 So he shepherded them
    according to the integrity of
    his heart,
    And led them with his skillful
    hands.

PSALM 79

How Long, O Yahweh?

    A Psalm of Asaph.
1 O God, the nations have come
    into Your inheritance;
    They have defiled Your holy
    temple;
    They have laid Jerusalem in
    ruins.
2 They have given the dead bodies
    of Your slaves for food to the
    birds of the heavens,
    The flesh of Your holy ones to
    the beasts of the earth.

3 They have poured out their
    blood like water round
    about Jerusalem;
    And there was no one to bury
    them.
4 We have become a reproach to
    our neighbors,
    A mockery and derision to those
    around us.
5 How long, O Yahweh? Will You
    be angry forever?
    Will Your jealousy burn like
    fire?
6 Pour out Your wrath upon the
    nations which do not
    know You,
    And upon the kingdoms
    which do not call upon
    Your name.
7 For they have devoured Jacob
    And laid waste his abode.

8 Do not remember *our* former
    iniquities against us;
    Let Your compassion quickly
    approach us,
    For we are brought very low.
9 Help us, O God of our salvation,
    for the glory of Your
    name;
    And deliver us and atone for
    our sins for Your name's
    sake.
10 Why should the nations say,
    "Where is their God?"
    Let it be known among the
    nations before our eyes:
    Vengeance for the blood of
    Your slaves which has been
    poured out.

11 Let the groaning of the prisoner
     come before You;
   According to the greatness of
     Your power preserve those
     who are doomed to die.
12 And return to our neighbors
     sevenfold into their bosom
   The reproach with which they
     have reproached You,
     O Lord.
13 But as for us, as Your people and
     the sheep of Your pasture,
   We will give thanks to You
     forever;
   From generation to generation
     we will recount Your praise.

PSALM 80

O God, Restore Us

For the choir director. El Shoshannim.
Eduth. Of Asaph. A Psalm.
 1 O Shepherd of Israel, give ear,
   You who guide Joseph like a
     flock;
   You who are enthroned *above*
     the cherubim, shine forth!
 2 Before Ephraim and Benjamin
     and Manasseh, stir up Your
     might
   And come to save us!
 3 O God, restore us
   And cause Your face to shine *upon
     us*, that we would be saved.

 4 O Yahweh God *of* hosts,
   How long will You smolder
     against the prayer of Your
     people?

 5 You have fed them with the
     bread of tears,
   And You have made them to
     drink tears in large measure.
 6 You set us as an object of strife
     to our neighbors,
   And our enemies mock *us*
     among themselves.
 7 O God *of* hosts, restore us
   And cause Your face to shine *upon
     us*, that we might be saved.

 8 You removed a vine from Egypt;
   You drove out the nations and
     then You planted it.
 9 You cleared *the ground* before it,
   And it took deep root and filled
     the land.
10 The mountains were covered
     with its shadow,
   And the cedars of God with its
     boughs.
11 It sent out its branches to the sea
   And its shoots to the River.
12 Why have You broken down its
     hedges,
   So that all who pass *that* way
     pick its *fruit*?
13 A boar from the forest devours it
   And whatever moves in the field
     feeds on it.

14 O God *of* hosts, return now, we
     beseech You;
   Look down from heaven and
     see, and visit this vine,
15 Even the sapling which Your
     right hand has planted,
   And on the son whom You have
     strengthened for Yourself.

16 It is burned with fire, it is cut
      down;
   They perish at the rebuke of
      Your face.
17 Let Your hand be upon the man
      of Your right hand,
   Upon the son of man whom
      You made strong for
      Yourself.
18 Then we shall not turn back
      from You;
   Revive us, and we will call upon
      Your name.
19 O Yahweh God of hosts,
      restore us;
   Cause Your face to shine *upon
      us*, that we might be saved.

PSALM 81

*Oh That My People Would
Listen to Me*

For the choir director. According
      to the Gittith. Of Asaph.
1 SING for joy to God our
      strength;
   Make a loud shout to the God
      of Jacob.
2 Lift up a song of praise, strike
      the tambourine,
   The sweet sounding lyre with
      the harp.
3 Blow the trumpet at the new
      moon,
   At the full moon, on our
      feast day.
4 For it is a statute for Israel,
   A judgment of the God of
      Jacob.

5 He established it for a testimony
      in Joseph
   When he went forth over the
      land of Egypt.
   I heard a language that I did not
      know:

6 "I relieved his shoulder of the
      burden,
   His hands were freed from the
      basket.
7 "You called in distress and
      I rescued you;
   I answered you in the hiding
      place of thunder;
   I tested you at the waters of
      Meribah.   Selah.
8 "Hear, O My people, and I will
      testify against you;
   O Israel, if you would listen
      to Me!
9 "Let there be no strange god
      among you;
   And you shall not worship a
      foreign god.
10 "I am Yahweh your God,
   Who brought you up from the
      land of Egypt;
   Open your mouth wide and
      I will fill it.

11 "But My people did not listen to
      My voice,
   And Israel was not willing *to
      obey* Me.
12 "So I released them over to the
      stubbornness of their
      heart,
   That they would walk in their
      own devices.

13 "Oh that My people would listen
to Me,
That Israel would walk in My ways!
14 "I would quickly subdue their
enemies
And I would turn My hand
against their adversaries.
15 "Those who hate Yahweh would
cower before Him,
And their time *of punishment*
would be forever.
16 "But I would feed you with the
finest of the wheat,
And with honey from the rock I
would satisfy you."

PSALM 82

God Stands in Judgment

A Psalm of Asaph.

1 GOD takes His stand in the
congregation of God;
He judges in the midst of gods.
2 How long will you judge
unrighteously
And show partiality to the
wicked?   Selah.
3 Give justice to the poor and the
orphan;
Justify the afflicted and destitute.
4 Protect the poor and needy;
Deliver *them* out of the hand of
the wicked.

5 They do not know and do not
understand;
They walk about in darkness;
All the foundations of the earth
are shaken.

6 I said, "You are gods,
And all of you are sons of the
Most High.
7 "Nevertheless you will die
like men
And you will fall like *any* one of
the princes."
8 Arise, O God, judge the earth!
For it is You who will inherit all
the nations.

PSALM 83

O God, Do Not Be Quiet

A Song. A Psalm of Asaph.

1 O God, do not remain at rest;
Do not be silent and, O God, do
not be quiet.
2 For behold, Your enemies roar,
And those who hate You have
lifted up their heads.
3 They make shrewd plans against
Your people,
And conspire together against
Your treasured ones.
4 They have said, "Come, and let
us wipe them out as a nation,
That the name of Israel be
remembered no more."
5 For they have conspired
together with one heart;
Against You they cut a
covenant:
6 The tents of Edom and the
Ishmaelites,
Moab and the Hagrites;
7 Gebal and Ammon and Amalek,
Philistia with the inhabitants
of Tyre;

8 Assyria also has joined with them;
They have become the power of
the children of Lot.   Selah.

9 Do to them as to Midian,
As to Sisera, *and* Jabin at the
river of Kishon,

10 Who were destroyed at En-dor,
Who were as dung for the
ground.

11 Make their nobles like Oreb and
Zeeb
And all their princes like Zebah
and Zalmunna,

12 Who said, "Let us possess for
ourselves
The pastures of God."

13 O my God, make them like the
whirling dust,
Like chaff before the wind.

14 Like fire that burns the forest
And like a flame that burns up
the mountains,

15 So pursue them with Your
tempest
And dismay them with Your
storm.

16 Fill their faces with disgrace,
That *they may seek* Your name,
O Yahweh.

17 Let them be ashamed and
dismayed forever,
And let them be humiliated and
perish,

18 That they may know that
You alone—Your name is
Yahweh—
Are the Most High over all the
earth.

PSALM 84

Blessed Is the Man Who Trusts in You

For the choir director. According to the
Gittith. Of the sons of Korah. A Psalm.

1 HOW lovely are Your dwelling
places,
O Yahweh of hosts!

2 My soul has longed and even
fainted for the courts of
Yahweh;
My heart and my flesh sing for
joy to the living God.

3 Even the bird has found a home,
And the swallow a nest for
herself, where she sets her
young,
At Your altars, O Yahweh of hosts,
My King and my God.

4 How blessed are those who
dwell in Your house!
They are ever praising You.
Selah.

5 How blessed is the man whose
strength is in You,
In whose heart are the highways
to Zion!

6 Passing through the valley of
Baca they make it a spring;
The early rain also wraps it up
with blessings.

7 They go from strength to
strength,
Each one of them appears before
God in Zion.

8 O Yahweh God of hosts, hear my
prayer;
Give ear, O God of Jacob!   Selah.

9 See our shield, O God,
  And look upon the face of Your
    anointed.
10 For better is a day in Your
    courts than a thousand
    elsewhere.
  I would choose to stand at the
    threshold of the house of
    my God
  Than dwell in the tents of
    wickedness.
11 For Yahweh God is a sun and
    shield;
  Yahweh gives grace and glory;
  No good thing does He withhold
    from those who walk
    blamelessly.
12 O Yahweh of hosts,
  How blessed is the man who
    trusts in You!

PSALM 85

Turn Us Back, O God

For the choir director. Of the
  sons of Korah. A Psalm.
1 O Yahweh, You showed favor to
    Your land;
  You returned the fortunes of
    Jacob.
2 You forgave the iniquity of Your
    people;
  You covered all their sin.   Selah.
3 *You withdrew all Your fury;*
  You turned back from Your
    burning anger.

4 Turn us back, O God of our
    salvation,

And cause Your vexation toward
    us to cease.
5 Will You be angry with us
    forever?
  Will You prolong Your anger
    from generation to
    generation?
6 Will You not Yourself return to
    revive us,
  That Your people may be glad
    in You?
7 Show us, O Yahweh, Your
    lovingkindness,
  And give us Your salvation.

8 Let me hear what the God,
    Yahweh, will speak;
  For He will speak peace to His
    people, to His holy ones;
  But let them not turn back
    to folly.
9 Surely His salvation is near to
    those who fear Him,
  That glory may dwell in our
    land.
10 Lovingkindness and truth have
    met together;
  Righteousness and peace have
    kissed each other.
11 Truth springs up from the earth,
  And righteousness looks down
    from heaven.
12 Indeed, Yahweh will give what
    is good,
  And our land will yield its
    produce.
13 Righteousness will go
    before Him
  And will establish the way of
    His steps.

PSALM 86

To You, O Lord, I Lift Up My Soul

A Prayer of David.

1 INCLINE Your ear, O Yahweh,
    and answer me;
  For I am afflicted and needy.
2 Keep my soul, for I am a holy one;
    O You my God, save Your slave
      who trusts in You.
3 Be gracious to me, O Lord,
    For to You I call all day long.
4 Make glad the soul of Your slave,
    For to You, O Lord, I lift up
      my soul.
5 For You, Lord, are good, and by
      nature forgiving,
    And abundant in lovingkindness
      to all who call upon You.
6 Give ear, O Yahweh, to my prayer;
    And give heed to the voice of my
      supplications!
7 In the day of my distress I shall
      call upon You,
    For You will answer me.
8 There is no one like You among
      the gods, O Lord,
    Nor are there any works like
      Yours.
9 All nations whom You have
      made shall come and
      worship before You, O Lord,
    And they shall glorify Your name.
10 For You are great and do
      wondrous deeds;
    You alone are God.

11 Teach me Your way, O Yahweh;
    I will walk in Your truth;
    Unite my heart to fear Your name.

12 I will give thanks to You, O Lord
      my God, with all my heart,
    And will glorify Your name
      forever.
13 For Your lovingkindness toward
      me is great,
    And You have delivered my soul
      from Sheol below.

14 O God, arrogant men have risen
      up against me,
    And a band of ruthless men
      have sought my life,
    And they have not set You
      before them.
15 But You, O Lord, are a God
      compassionate and gracious,
    Slow to anger and abundant in
      lovingkindness and truth.
16 Turn to me, and be gracious to me;
    Oh grant Your strength to Your
      slave,
    And save the son of Your
      maidservant.
17 Show me a sign for good,
    That those who hate me may see
      it and be ashamed,
    Because You, O Yahweh, have
      helped me and comforted me.

PSALM 87

Yahweh Loves the Gates of Zion

Of the sons of Korah. A Psalm. A Song.

1 HIS foundation is in the holy
      mountains.
2 Yahweh loves the gates of Zion
    More than all the dwelling
      places of Jacob.

3 Glorious things are spoken of you,
   O city of God.   Selah.
4 "I shall mention Rahab and
      Babylon among those who
      know Me;
   Behold, Philistia and Tyre with
      Ethiopia:
   'This one was born there.' "
5 But of Zion it shall be said, "This
      one and that one were born
      in her";
   And the Most High Himself will
      establish her.
6 Yahweh will count when He
      registers the peoples,
   "This one was born there."
                                Selah.
7 And singers, just like the
      dancers, *will all say,*
   "All my springs are in you."

PSALM 88

Incline Your Ear to My Cry

A Song. A Psalm of the sons of
Korah. For the choir director.
According to Mahalath Leannoth.
A Maskil of Heman the Ezrahite.

1 O Yahweh, the God of my
      salvation,
   I have cried out by day and
      throughout the night
      before You.
2 Let my prayer come before You;
   Incline Your ear to my cry of
      lamentation!
3 For my soul has been saturated
      with calamities,
   And my life has reached Sheol.

4 I am counted among those who
      go down to the pit;
   I am like a man without
      strength,
5 Released among the dead,
   Like the slain who lie in the
      grave,
   Whom You remember no more,
   And they are cut off from Your
      hand.
6 You have put me in the pit far
      below,
   In dark places, in the depths.
7 Your wrath lies upon me,
   And You afflict me with all
      Your breaking waves.   Selah.
8 You have removed my
      acquaintances far from me;
   You have set me as an
      abomination to them;
   I am shut up and cannot
      go out.
9 My eye has wasted away because
      of affliction;
   I have called upon You every
      day, O Yahweh;
   I have spread out my hands
      to You.

10 Will You do wonders for the
      dead?
   Will the departed spirits rise
      and praise You?   Selah.
11 Will Your lovingkindness be
      recounted in the grave,
   Your faithfulness in Abaddon?
12 Will Your wonders be known in
      the darkness?
   And Your righteousness in the
      land of forgetfulness?

13 But as for me, O Yahweh, I have
    cried out to You for help,
  And in the morning my prayer
    comes before You.
14 O Yahweh, why do You reject my
    soul?
  Why do You hide Your face
    from me?
15 I *have been* afflicted and about
    to breathe my last from *my*
    youth on;
  I bear Your terrors; I am
    overcome.
16 Your burning anger has passed
    over me;
  Your horrors have destroyed me.
17 They have surrounded me like
    water all day long;
  They have encompassed me
    altogether.
18 You have removed lover and
    friend far from me;
  My acquaintances are *in*
    darkness.

PSALM 89

*Sing of the Lovingkindness
of Yahweh Forever*

A Maskil of Ethan the Ezrahite.
1 I will sing of the lovingkindnesses
    of Yahweh forever;
  From generation to generation
    I will make known Your
    faithfulness with my mouth.
2 For I have said, "Lovingkindness
    will be built up forever;
  In the heavens You will establish
    Your faithfulness."

3 "I have cut a covenant with My
    chosen;
  I have sworn to David My servant,
4 I will establish your seed forever
  And build up your throne from
    generation to generation."
                  Selah.

5 The heavens will praise Your
    wonders, O Yahweh;
  Your faithfulness also in the
    assembly of the holy ones.
6 For who in the sky is
    comparable to Yahweh?
  Who among the sons of the
    mighty is like Yahweh,
7 A God greatly dreaded in the
    council of the holy ones,
  And fearsome above all those
    who are around Him?
8 O Yahweh God of hosts, who is
    like You, O mighty Yah?
  Your faithfulness also
    surrounds You.
9 You rule the swelling of the sea;
  When its waves rise, You still
    them.
10 You Yourself crushed Rahab like
    one who is slain;
  You scattered Your enemies with
    Your strong arm.
11 The heavens are Yours, the earth
    also is Yours;
  The world and its fullness, You
    have founded them.
12 The north and the south, You
    have created them;
  Tabor and Hermon sing with joy
    at Your name.

13 You have a mighty arm;
   Your hand is strong, Your right
     hand is exalted.
14 Righteousness and justice are
     the foundation of Your
     throne;
   Lovingkindness and truth go
     before You.
15 How blessed are the people who
     know the loud shout of joy!
   O Yahweh, they walk in the light
     of Your face.
16 In Your name they rejoice all
     the day,
   And by Your righteousness they
     are exalted.
17 For You are the beauty of their
     strength,
   And by Your favor our horn is
     exalted.
18 For our shield belongs to Yahweh,
   And our king to the Holy One
     of Israel.

19 Formerly You spoke in vision to
     Your holy ones,
   And said, "I have bestowed help
     to a mighty one;
   I have exalted one chosen from
     the people.
20 "I have found David My servant;
   With My holy oil I have
     anointed him,
21 With whom My hand will be
     established;
   My arm also will strengthen
     him.
22 "The enemy will not deceive him,
   Nor the son of unrighteousness
     afflict him.

23 "But I shall crush his adversaries
     before him,
   And strike those who hate him.
24 "My faithfulness and My
     lovingkindness will be
     with him,
   And in My name his horn will be
     exalted.
25 "I shall also set his hand on
     the sea
   And his right hand on the rivers.
26 "He will call to Me, 'You are my
     Father,
   My God, and the rock of my
     salvation.'
27 "I also shall make him *My*
     firstborn,
   The highest of the kings of the
     earth.
28 "My lovingkindness I will keep
     for him forever,
   And My covenant shall be
     confirmed to him.
29 "So I will set up his seed *to*
     endure forever
   And his throne as the days of
     heaven.

30 "If his sons forsake My law
   And do not walk in My
     judgments,
31 If they profane My statutes
   And do not keep My
     commandments,
32 Then I will punish their
     transgression with the rod
   And their iniquity with striking.
33 "But I will not break off My
     lovingkindness from him,
   Nor deal falsely in My faithfulness.

34 "My covenant I will not
    profane,
  Nor will I alter what comes forth
    from My lips.

35 "Once I have sworn by My
    holiness,
  I will not lie to David.

36 "His seed shall endure
    forever
  And his throne as the sun
    before Me.

37 "It shall be established forever
    like the moon,
  And the witness in the sky is
    faithful."   Selah.

38 But You have cast off and
    rejected,
  You have been full of wrath
    against Your anointed.

39 You have spurned the covenant
    of Your slave;
  You have profaned his crown to
    the ground.

40 You have broken down all his
    walls;
  You have beset his strongholds
    with ruin.

41 All who pass along the way
    plunder him;
  He has become a reproach to his
    neighbors.

42 You have exalted the right hand
    of his adversaries;
  You have made all his enemies
    be glad.

43 You also turn back the edge of
    his sword
  And have not made him arise in
    battle.

44 You have made his splendor
    to cease
  And cast his throne to the
    ground.

45 You have shortened the days of
    his youth;
  You have wrapped him up
    with shame.   Selah.

46 How long, O Yahweh?
  Will You hide Yourself forever?
  Will Your wrath burn like fire?

47 Remember what my span of
    life is;
  For what vanity You have
    created all the sons
    of men!

48 What man can live and not see
    death?
  Can he provide his soul escape
    from the power of Sheol?
        Selah.

49 Where are Your former
    lovingkindnesses, O Lord,
  Which You swore to David in
    Your faithfulness?

50 Remember, O Lord, the reproach
    of Your slaves;
  How I bear in my bosom *the
    reproach of* all the many
    peoples,

51 With which Your enemies have
    reproached, O Yahweh,
  With which they have
    reproached the footsteps of
    Your anointed.

52 Blessed be Yahweh forever!
  Amen and Amen.

BOOK 4

PSALM 90

*From Everlasting to Everlasting,
You Are God*

A Prayer of Moses, the man of God.

1 LORD, You have been our
dwelling place from
generation to generation.

2 Before the mountains were born
Or You brought forth the earth
and the world,
Even from everlasting to
everlasting, You are God.

3 You turn man back into dust
And say, "Return, O sons of men."

4 For a thousand years in Your
sight
Are like yesterday when it
passes by,
Or *as* a watch in the night.

5 You have swept them away like a
flood, they fall asleep;
In the morning they are like
grass which sprouts anew.

6 In the morning it blossoms and
sprouts anew;
Toward evening it withers away
and dries up.

7 For we have been consumed by
Your anger
And by Your wrath we have been
dismayed.

8 You have set our iniquities
before You,
Our secret *sins* in the light of
Your presence.

9 For all our days have declined in
Your fury;
We have finished our years like
a sigh.

10 As for the days of our life, they
contain seventy years,
Or if due to might, eighty
years,
Yet their pride is *but* labor and
wickedness;
For soon it is gone and we
fly away.

11 Who knows the power of Your
anger
And Your fury, according to the
fear that is due You?

12 So teach us to number our days,
That we may present *to You* a
heart of wisdom.

13 Return, O Yahweh; how long *will
it be*?
And be sorry for Your slaves.

14 O satisfy us in the morning with
Your lovingkindness,
That we may sing for joy and be
glad all our days.

15 Make us glad according to the
days You have afflicted us,
And the years we have seen
evil.

16 Let Your work appear to Your
slaves
And Your majesty to their sons.

17 Let the favor of the Lord our
God be upon us;
And establish for us the work of
our hands;
Establish the work of our
hands.

PSALM 91

In the Shadow of the Almighty

1 HE who abides in the shelter of
the Most High
Will abide in the shadow of the
Almighty.
2 I will say to Yahweh, "My refuge
and my fortress,
My God, in whom I trust!"
3 For it is He who delivers you
from the snare of the trapper
And from the destructive
pestilence.
4 He will cover you with His
pinions,
And under His wings you will
take refuge;
His truth is a large shield and
bulwark.

5 You will not be afraid of terror
by night,
Or arrow that flies by day;
6 Of pestilence that moves in
darkness,
Or of destruction that
devastates at noon.
7 A thousand may fall at your side
And ten thousand at your right
hand,
But it shall not approach you.
8 You will only look on with
your eyes
And see the recompense of the
wicked.
9 For you have made Yahweh—my
refuge,
The Most High—your dwelling
place.

10 No evil will befall you,
And no plague will come near
your tent.

11 For He will command His angels
concerning you,
To guard you in all your ways.
12 On their hands they will bear
you up,
Lest you strike your foot against
a stone.
13 You will tread upon the fierce
lion and cobra,
The young lion and the serpent
you will trample down.

14 "Because he has loved Me,
therefore I will protect him;
I will set him *securely* on high,
because he has known
My name.
15 "He will call upon Me, and I will
answer him;
I will be with him in *his*
distress;
I will rescue him and honor him.
16 "With a long life I will
satisfy him
And I will show him My
salvation."

PSALM 92

How Great Are Your Works, O Yahweh

A Psalm. A Song for the Sabbath day.
1 IT is good to give thanks to
Yahweh
And to sing praises to Your
name, O Most High;

2 To declare Your lovingkindness
in the morning
And Your faithfulness by night,
3 With the ten-stringed lute and
with the harp,
With resounding music upon
the lyre.
4 For You, O Yahweh, have made
me glad by what You have
done,
I will sing for joy at the works of
Your hands.

5 How great are Your works,
O Yahweh!
Your thoughts are very deep.
6 A senseless man does not know,
And a fool does not understand
this:
7 That when the wicked
flourished like grass
And all *the* workers of iniquity
blossomed,
It *was only* that they might be
destroyed forevermore.
8 But You are on high forever,
O Yahweh.
9 For, behold, Your enemies,
O Yahweh,
For, behold, Your enemies will
perish;
All *the* workers of iniquity will
be scattered.

10 But You have raised up my horn
like *that of* the wild ox;
I have been anointed with
fresh oil.
11 And my eye has looked
exultantly upon my foes,

My ears hear of the evildoers
who rise up against me.
12 The righteous man will flourish
like the palm tree,
He will grow like a cedar in
Lebanon.
13 Planted in the house of Yahweh,
They will flourish in the courts
of our God.
14 They will still yield fruit in old age;
They shall be rich and fresh,
15 To declare that Yahweh is upright;
He is my rock, and there is no
unrighteousness in Him.

PSALM 93

Yahweh Reigns Forevermore

1 YAHWEH reigns, He is clothed
with majesty;
Yahweh has clothed and girded
Himself with strength;
Indeed, the world is established,
it will not be shaken.
2 Your throne is established from
of old;
You are from everlasting.

3 The rivers have lifted up,
O Yahweh,
The rivers have lifted up their
voice,
The rivers lift up their pounding
waves.
4 More than the voices of many
waters,
Than the mighty breakers of
the sea,
Yahweh on high is mighty.

5 Your testimonies are very
    faithful;
Holiness befits Your house,
O Yahweh, forevermore.

PSALM 94

God of Vengeance, Shine Forth

1 O Yahweh, God of vengeance,
God of vengeance, shine forth!
2 Be lifted up, O Judge of the
    earth,
Render recompense to the
    proud.
3 How long shall the wicked,
    O Yahweh,
How long shall the wicked exult?
4 They pour forth *words*, they
    speak arrogantly;
All workers of iniquity vaunt
    themselves.
5 They crush Your people,
    O Yahweh,
And afflict Your inheritance.
6 They slay the widow and the
    sojourner
And murder the orphans.
7 They have said, "Yah does not see,
Nor does the God of Jacob
    discern."

8 Discern, you senseless among
    the people;
And when will you have insight,
    you fools?
9 He who planted the ear, does He
    not hear?
He who formed the eye, does He
    not see?

10 He who disciplines the nations,
    will He not rebuke,
Even He who teaches man
    knowledge?
11 Yahweh knows the thoughts
    of man,
That they are vanity.

12 Blessed is the man whom You
    discipline, O Yah,
And whom You teach out of
    Your law;
13 That You may grant him calm
    from the days of calamity,
Until a pit is dug for the
    wicked.
14 For Yahweh will not abandon
    His people,
Nor will He forsake His
    inheritance.
15 For judgment will again be
    righteous,
And all the upright in heart will
    follow it.
16 Who will arise for me against
    evildoers?
Who will take his stand for me
    against workers of iniquity?

17 If Yahweh had not been my help,
My soul would soon have dwelt
    in *the abode of* silence.
18 If I should say, "My foot has
    stumbled,"
Your lovingkindness, O Yahweh,
    will hold me up.
19 When my anxious thoughts
    multiply within me,
Your consolations delight
    my soul.

20 Can a throne of destruction be
allied with You,
One which forms trouble by
statute?
21 They band themselves together
against the life of the
righteous
And condemn the innocent to
death.
22 But Yahweh has been my
stronghold,
And my God the rock of my
refuge.
23 He has brought back their
iniquity upon them
And will destroy them in their evil;
Yahweh our God will destroy them.

PSALM 95

Let Us Kneel Before Yahweh Our Maker

1 OH come, let us sing for joy to
Yahweh,
Let us make a loud shout to the
rock of our salvation.
2 Let us come before His presence
with thanksgiving,
Let us make a loud shout to Him
with songs of praise.
3 For Yahweh is a great God
And a great King above all gods,
4 In whose hand are the depths of
the earth,
The peaks of the mountains are
His also.
5 The sea is His, for it was He who
made it,
And His hands formed the
dry land.

6 Come, let us worship and bow
down,
Let us kneel before Yahweh our
Maker.
7 For He is our God,
And we are the people of His
pasture and the sheep
of His hand.
Today, if you hear His voice,
8 Do not harden your hearts, as at
Meribah,
As in the day of Massah in the
wilderness,
9 "When your fathers tried Me,
They tested Me, though they
had seen My work.
10 "For forty years I loathed *that*
generation,
And said they are a people who
wander in their heart,
And they do not know My
ways.
11 "Therefore I swore in My
anger,
They shall never enter into
My rest."

PSALM 96

Ascribe to Yahweh Glory and Strength

1 SING to Yahweh a new song;
Sing to Yahweh, all the earth.
2 Sing to Yahweh, bless His name;
Proclaim good news of His
salvation from day to day.
3 Recount His glory among the
nations,
His wondrous deeds among all
the peoples.

4 For great is Yahweh and greatly
       to be praised;
   He is more fearsome than
       all gods.
5 For all the gods of the peoples
       are idols,
   But Yahweh made the
       heavens.
6 Splendor and majesty are
       before Him,
   Strength and beauty are in His
       sanctuary.

7 Ascribe to Yahweh, O families of
       the peoples,
   Ascribe to Yahweh glory and
       strength.
8 Ascribe to Yahweh the glory of
       His name;
   Lift up an offering and come
       into His courts.
9 Worship Yahweh in the splendor
       of holiness;
   Tremble before Him, all the
       earth.
10 Say among the nations, "Yahweh
       reigns;
   Indeed, the world is established,
       it will not be shaken;
   He will render justice to the
       peoples with equity."

11 Let the heavens be glad, and let
       the earth rejoice;
   Let the sea roar, as well as its
       fullness;
12 Let the field exult, and all that is
       in it.
   Then all the trees of the forest
       will sing for joy

13 Before Yahweh, for He is
       coming,
   For He is coming to judge the
       earth.
   He will judge the world in
       righteousness
   And the peoples in His
       faithfulness.

PSALM 97

Remember His Holy Name

1 YAHWEH reigns, let the earth
       rejoice;
   Let the many coastlands be glad.
2 Clouds and thick darkness are
       all around Him;
   Righteousness and justice
       are the foundation of His
       throne.
3 Fire goes before Him
   And burns up His adversaries all
       around.
4 His lightnings light up the
       world;
   The earth sees and trembles.
5 The mountains melt like wax at
       the presence of Yahweh,
   At the presence of the Lord of all
       the earth.
6 The heavens declare His
       righteousness,
   And all the peoples see His
       glory.

7 Let all those be ashamed who
       serve graven images,
   Who boast of idols;
   Worship Him, all you gods!

3 I will set no vile thing before
my eyes;
I hate the work of those who fall
away;
It shall not cling to me.
4 A crooked heart shall depart
from me;
I will know no evil.
5 Whoever secretly slanders his
neighbor, him I will destroy;
Whoever has a haughty look
and an arrogant heart, I will
not endure.

6 My eyes shall be upon the
faithful of the land, that
they may abide with me;
He who walks in the way of the
blameless is the one who
will minister to me.
7 He who practices deceit shall
not dwell within my house;
He who speaks lies shall not be
established before my eyes.
8 Every morning I will destroy all
the wicked of the land,
To cut off from the city of
Yahweh all the workers of
iniquity.

PSALM 102

Do Not Hide Your Face from Me

A Prayer of the afflicted when
he is faint and pours out his
complaint before Yahweh.
1 O Yahweh, hear my prayer!
And let my cry for help come
to You.

2 Do not hide Your face from me
in the day of my distress;
Incline Your ear to me;
In the day when I call answer me
quickly.
3 For my days have vanished in
smoke,
And my bones have been
scorched like a hearth.
4 My heart has been stricken like
grass and it has dried up,
Indeed, I forget to eat my
bread.
5 Because of the sound of my
groaning
My bones cling to my flesh.
6 I resemble a pelican of the
wilderness;
I have become like an owl of the
waste places.
7 I lie awake,
I have become like a lonely bird
on a roof.

8 My enemies have reproached me
all day long;
Those who ridicule me swear
against me.
9 For I have eaten ashes like
bread
And mixed my drinks with
weeping
10 Because of Your indignation and
Your wrath,
For You have lifted me up and
cast me away.
11 My days are like an outstretched
shadow,
And as for me, I dry up like
grass.

12 But You, O Yahweh, abide forever,
And the remembrance of Your
name from generation to
generation.

13 You will arise *and* have
compassion on Zion—
For it is time to be gracious to it,
For the appointed time has come.

14 For Your slaves find pleasure in
its stones
And show grace to its dust—

15 So the nations will fear the
name of Yahweh
And all the kings of the earth
Your glory.

16 For Yahweh has built up Zion;
He has appeared in His glory.

17 He has turned toward the prayer
of the destitute
And has not despised their prayer.

18 This will be written for the
generation to come,
And a people yet to be created
will praise Yah.

19 For He looked down from His
holy height;
From heaven Yahweh gazed
upon the earth,

20 To hear the groaning of the
prisoner,
To set free those who were
doomed to death,

21 To recount the name of Yahweh
in Zion
And His praise in Jerusalem,

22 When the peoples are gathered
together,
And the kingdoms, to serve
Yahweh.

23 He has afflicted my strength in
the way;
He has shortened my days.

24 I say, "O my God, do not take me
away in the midst of my days,
Your years are from generation
to *all* generations.

25 "Of old You founded the earth,
And the heavens are the work of
Your hands.

26 "Even they will perish, but You
will remain;
And all of them will wear out
like a garment;
Like clothing You will change them
and they will be changed.

27 "But You are the same,
And Your years will not come to
an end.

28 "The children of Your slaves will
dwell *securely*,
And their seed will be
established before You."

PSALM 103

Bless Yahweh, O My Soul

Of David.

1 BLESS Yahweh, O my soul,
And all that is within me, *bless*
His holy name.

2 Bless Yahweh, O my soul,
And forget none of His benefits;

3 Who pardons all your iniquities,
Who heals all your diseases;

4 Who redeems your life from
the pit,
Who crowns you with lovingkindness and compassion;

5 Who satisfies your years with
good things,
So that your youth is renewed
like the eagle.

6 Yahweh performs righteous
deeds
And judgments for all who are
oppressed.
7 He made known His ways to
Moses,
His acts to the sons of Israel.
8 Yahweh is compassionate and
gracious,
Slow to anger and abounding in
lovingkindness.
9 He will not always contend
with us,
And He will not keep *His anger*
forever.
10 He has not dealt with us
according to our sins,
And He has not rewarded us
according to our iniquities.
11 For as high as the heavens are
above the earth,
So great is His lovingkindness
toward those who
fear Him.
12 As far as the east is from
the west,
So far has He removed our
transgressions from us.
13 As a father has compassion on
his children,
So Yahweh has compassion on
those who fear Him.
14 For He Himself knows our form;
He remembers that we are
but dust.

15 As for man, his days are like grass;
As a flower of the field, so he
flowers.
16 When the wind has passed over
it, it is no more,
And its place acknowledges it no
longer.
17 But the lovingkindness of
Yahweh is from everlasting
to everlasting on those who
fear Him,
And His righteousness to
children's children,
18 To those who keep His covenant
And remember His precepts to
do them.

19 Yahweh has established His
throne in the heavens,
And His kingdom rules over all.
20 Bless Yahweh, you His angels,
Mighty in strength, who
perform His word,
Obeying the voice of His word!
21 Bless Yahweh, all *you* His hosts,
You who serve Him, doing His will.
22 Bless Yahweh, all you works
of His,
In all places of His rule;
Bless Yahweh, O my soul!

PSALM 104

The Glory of Yahweh Endures Forever

1 BLESS Yahweh, O my soul!
O Yahweh my God, You are
very great;
You are clothed with splendor
and majesty,

2 Wrapping Yourself with light as
    with a cloak,
  Stretching out the heavens like a
    tent curtain.
3 He lays the beams of His upper
    chambers in the waters;
  He sets up the clouds *to be* His
    chariot;
  He walks upon the wings of the
    wind;
4 He makes His angels the winds,
  His ministers flaming fire.

5 He founded the earth upon its
    place,
  So that it will not shake forever
    and ever.
6 You covered it with the deep as
    with a garment;
  The waters were standing above
    the mountains.
7 At Your rebuke they fled,
  At the sound of Your thunder
    they hurried away in alarm.
8 The mountains went up; the
    valleys went down
  To the place which You founded
    for them.
9 You set a boundary that they
    may not pass over,
  So that they will not return to
    cover the earth.

10 He sends forth springs in the
    valleys;
  They flow between the mountains;
11 They give water to every beast
    of the field;
  The wild donkeys quench their
    thirst.

12 Above them the birds of the
    heavens dwell;
  They give forth *their* voices
    among the branches.
13 He gives water to the mountains
    from His upper chambers;
  The earth is satisfied with the
    fruit of His works.

14 He causes the grass to grow for
    the cattle,
  And vegetation for man's
    cultivation,
  To bring forth food from the
    earth,
15 And wine which makes man's
    heart glad,
  To make *his* face glisten more
    than oil,
  And food which sustains man's
    heart.
16 The trees of Yahweh are satisfied,
  The cedars of Lebanon which
    He planted,
17 Where the birds build their nests,
  The stork's home is in the fir
    trees.

18 The high mountains are for the
    wild goats;
  The cliffs are a refuge for the
    shephanim.
19 He made the moon for the
    seasons;
  The sun knows the place of its
    setting.
20 You appoint darkness so that it
    becomes night,
  In which all the beasts of the
    forest creep about.

21 The young lions roar *to go*
    after their prey
  And to seek their food
    from God.
22 *When* the sun rises they gather
    together
  And lie down in their dens.
23 Man goes forth to his work
  And to his labor until evening.

24 How numerous are Your works,
    O Yahweh!
  In wisdom You have made
    them all;
  The earth is full of Your
    possessions.
25 This is the sea, great and broad,
  There *the* creeping things are
    without number,
  Creatures both small and great.
26 There the ships move along,
  And Leviathan, which You have
    formed to play in it.

27 They all wait for You
  To give them their food in due
    season.
28 You give to them, they gather
    it up;
  You open Your hand, they are
    satisfied with good.
29 You hide Your face, they are
    dismayed;
  You take away their spirit, they
    breathe *their* last
  And return to their dust.
30 You send forth Your Spirit, they
    are created;
  And You renew the face of the
    ground.

31 Let the glory of Yahweh endure
    forever;
  Let Yahweh be glad in His works;
32 He looks at the earth, and it
    trembles;
  He touches the mountains, and
    they smoke.
33 I will sing to Yahweh throughout
    my life;
  I will sing praise to my God
    while I have *my* being.
34 Let my musing be pleasing to Him;
  As for me, I shall be glad in Yahweh.
35 Let sinners be consumed from
    the earth
  And let the wicked be no more.
  Bless Yahweh, O my soul.
  Praise Yah!

PSALM 105

Remember His Wondrous Deeds

1 OH give thanks to Yahweh, call
    upon His name;
  Make known His acts among the
    peoples.
2 Sing to Him, sing praises to Him;
  Muse on all His wondrous
    deeds.
3 Boast in His holy name;
  Let the heart of those who seek
    Yahweh be glad.
4 Inquire of Yahweh and His
    strength;
  Seek His face continually.
5 Remember His wondrous deeds
    which He has done,
  His miracles and the judgments
    uttered by His mouth,

6 O seed of Abraham, His servant,
O sons of Jacob, His chosen
ones!
7 He is Yahweh our God;
His judgments are in all the earth.

8 He has remembered His
covenant forever,
The word which He commanded
for a thousand generations,
9 Which He cut with Abraham,
And His oath to Isaac.
10 Then He confirmed it to Jacob
for a statute,
To Israel as an everlasting
covenant,
11 Saying, "To you I will give the
land of Canaan
As the portion of your
inheritance,"
12 When they were only a few men
in number,
Of little account, and sojourners
in it.
13 And they wandered about from
nation to nation,
From *one* kingdom to another
people.
14 He permitted no man to oppress
them,
And He reproved kings for
their sakes:
15 "Do not touch My anointed
ones,
And to My prophets do no evil."

16 And He called for a famine upon
the land;
He broke the whole staff of
bread.

17 He sent a man before them,
Joseph, *who* was sold as a slave.
18 They afflicted his feet with
fetters,
He himself was laid in irons;
19 Until the time that his word
came to pass,
The word of Yahweh refined him.
20 The king sent and released him,
The ruler of peoples *sent* and set
him free.
21 He set him up as lord of his
house
And ruler over all his
possessions,
22 To imprison his princes at will,
And that he might teach his
elders wisdom.
23 Then Israel came to Egypt;
And Jacob sojourned in the land
of Ham.
24 And He caused His people to be
very fruitful,
And He caused them to
be stronger than their
adversaries.

25 He turned their heart to hate His
people,
To deal craftily with His slaves.
26 He sent Moses His servant,
And Aaron, whom He had
chosen.
27 They set forth the words of His
signs among them,
And miracles in the land of Ham.
28 He sent darkness and made
it dark;
And they did not rebel against
His words.

29 He turned their waters into
blood
And caused their fish to die.
30 Their land swarmed with frogs
Even in the chambers of their
kings.
31 He spoke, and there came a
swarm of flies
And gnats in all their territory.
32 He gave them hail for rain,
And flaming fire in their land.
33 He also struck down their vines
and their fig trees,
And He shattered the trees of
their territory.
34 He spoke, and locusts came,
And creeping locusts, without
number,
35 And they ate up all vegetation in
their land,
And they ate up the fruit of their
ground.
36 He also struck down all the
firstborn in their land,
The first of all their vigor.

37 Then He brought them out with
silver and gold,
And there was none among His
tribes who stumbled.
38 Egypt was glad when they
went out,
For the dread of them had fallen
upon them.
39 *He spread a cloud for* a covering,
And fire to give light by night.
40 They asked, and He brought
quail,
And He satisfied them with the
bread of heaven.

41 He opened the rock and water
flowed out;
It ran in the dry places *like* a river.
42 For He remembered His holy word
With Abraham His servant;
43 And He brought His people out
with joy,
His chosen ones with a shout
of joy.
44 He gave them also the lands of
the nations,
That they might take possession
of *the fruit of* the peoples'
labor,
45 So that they might keep His
statutes
And observe His laws,
Praise Yah!

PSALM 106

Remember Me, O Yahweh

1 PRAISE Yah!
Oh give thanks to Yahweh, for
He is good;
For His lovingkindness endures
forever.
2 Who can speak of the mighty
deeds of Yahweh,
Or can make all His praise to be
heard?
3 How blessed are those who keep
justice,
And he who does righteousness
at all times!

4 Remember me, O Yahweh, in *Your*
favor toward Your people;
Visit me with Your salvation,

5 That I may see the goodness of
Your chosen ones,
That I may rejoice in the
gladness of Your nation,
That I may boast with Your
inheritance.

6 We have sinned with our
fathers,
We have committed iniquity, we
have acted wickedly.

7 Our fathers in Egypt did not
consider Your wondrous
deeds;
They did not remember Your
abundant lovingkindnesses,
But they rebelled by the sea, at
the Red Sea.

8 Yet He saved them for the sake
of His name,
That He might make His might
known.

9 Thus He rebuked the Red Sea
and it dried up,
And He led them through
the deeps, as through the
wilderness.

10 So He saved them from the hand
of the one who hated them,
And redeemed them from the
hand of the enemy.

11 The waters covered their
adversaries;
Not one of them was left.

12 Then they believed His words;
They sang His praise.

13 They quickly forgot His works;
They did not wait for His
counsel,

14 But craved intensely in the
wilderness,
And put God to the test in the
wasteland.

15 So He gave them their request,
But sent a wasting disease
against their lives.

16 Then they became envious of
Moses in the camp,
And of Aaron, the holy one of
Yahweh.

17 The earth opened and
swallowed up Dathan,
And covered up the company of
Abiram.

18 And a fire burned up in their
company;
The flame consumed the
wicked.

19 They made a calf in Horeb
And worshiped a molten image.

20 Thus they exchanged their glory
For the image of an ox that eats
grass.

21 They forgot God their Savior,
Who had done great things in
Egypt,

22 Wondrous deeds in the land
of Ham
And awesome things by the
Red Sea.

23 Therefore He said that He would
destroy them,
Had not Moses His chosen one
stood in the breach
before Him,
To turn away His wrath from
eradicating them.

24 Then they despised the pleasant land;
They did not believe in His word,

25 But grumbled in their tents;
They did not listen to the voice of Yahweh.

26 So He swore to them
To make them fall in the wilderness,

27 And to make their seed fall among the nations
And to scatter them in the lands.

28 They then joined themselves to Baal-peor,
And ate sacrifices offered to the dead.

29 Thus they provoked *Him* to anger with their actions,
And the plague broke out among them.

30 Then Phinehas stood up and interceded,
And so the plague was checked.

31 And it was counted to him for righteousness,
From generation to generation forever.

32 They also provoked *Him* to wrath at the waters of Meribah,
So that it went badly with Moses on their account;

33 Because they were rebellious against His Spirit,
He spoke rashly with his lips.

34 They did not destroy the peoples,
As Yahweh commanded them,

35 But they mingled with the nations
And learned their works,

36 And served their idols,
Which became a snare to them.

37 They sacrificed their sons and their daughters to the demons,

38 And they shed innocent blood,
The blood of their sons and their daughters,
Whom they sacrificed to the idols of Canaan;
And the land was polluted with the blood.

39 Thus they became unclean in their works,
And played the harlot in their actions.

40 So the anger of Yahweh was kindled against His people
And He abhorred His inheritance.

41 Then He gave them into the hand of the nations,
And those who hated them ruled over them.

42 Their enemies oppressed them,
And they were subdued under their hand.

43 Many times He would deliver them;
But they were rebellious in their counsel,
And so they sank down in their iniquity.

44 Nevertheless He looked upon
their distress
When He heard their cry of
lamentation;
45 And He remembered for them
His covenant,
And relented according to
the abundance of His
lovingkindness.
46 He also made them *objects* of
compassion
In the presence of all their
captors.

47 Save us, O Yahweh our God,
And gather us from among the
nations,
To give thanks to Your holy name
And revel in Your praise.
48 Blessed be Yahweh, the God of
Israel,
From everlasting to everlasting.
And let all the people say,
"Amen."
Praise Yah!

BOOK 5

PSALM 107

Yahweh Saves in Times of Trouble

1 OH give thanks to Yahweh, for
He is good,
For His lovingkindness endures
forever.
2 Let the redeemed of Yahweh
say *so*,
Whom He has redeemed from
the hand of the adversary

3 And gathered from the lands,
From the east and from the
west,
From the north and from
the south.

4 They wandered in the
wilderness along the way of
the wasteland;
They did not find an inhabited
city.
5 Hungry and thirsty,
Their soul fainted within them.
6 Then they cried out to Yahweh
in their trouble;
He delivered them out of their
distresses.
7 He led them by a straight way,
To go to an inhabited city.
8 Let them give thanks to Yahweh
for His lovingkindness,
And for His wondrous deeds to
the sons of men!
9 For He has satisfied the thirsty
soul,
And the hungry soul He has
filled with what is good.

10 There were those who inhabited
darkness and the shadow of
death,
Prisoners in affliction and irons,
11 Because they had rebelled
against the words of God
And spurned the counsel of the
Most High.
12 So He subdued their heart with
labor;
They stumbled and there was
none to help.

13 Then they cried out to Yahweh
   in their trouble;
   He saved them out of their
   distresses.
14 He brought them out of
   darkness and the shadow
   of death
   And broke their bands apart.
15 Let them give thanks to Yahweh
   for His lovingkindness,
   And for His wondrous deeds to
   the sons of men!
16 For He has shattered the doors
   of bronze
   And cut through the bars of iron.

17 Ignorant fools, because of their
   way of transgression,
   And because of their iniquities,
   were afflicted.
18 Their soul abhorred all kinds
   of food,
   And they reached the gates of
   death.
19 Then they cried out to Yahweh
   in their trouble;
   He saved them out of their
   distresses.
20 He sent His word and healed
   them,
   And provided *them* escape from
   their destructions.
21 Let them give thanks to Yahweh
   for His lovingkindness,
   And for His wondrous deeds to
   the sons of men!
22 Let them also offer sacrifices of
   thanksgiving,
   And recount His works with
   joyful singing.

23 Those who go down to the sea
   in ships,
   Who do business on many
   waters;
24 They have seen the works of
   Yahweh,
   And His wondrous deeds in the
   deep.
25 He spoke and set up a stormy
   wind,
   Which raised up the waves of
   the sea.
26 They went up to the heavens,
   they went down to the
   depths;
   Their soul melted away in *the*
   calamity.
27 They staggered and swayed like
   a drunken man,
   And all their wisdom was
   swallowed up.
28 Then they cried to Yahweh in
   their trouble,
   And He brought them out of
   their distresses.
29 He caused the storm to
   stand still,
   So that its waves were hushed.
30 Then they were glad because
   they were quiet,
   So He led them to their desired
   haven.
31 Let them give thanks to Yahweh
   for His lovingkindness,
   And for His wondrous deeds to
   the sons of men!
32 Let them exalt Him also in the
   assembly of the people,
   And praise Him at the seat of
   the elders.

33 He makes rivers into a wilderness
And springs of water into a
thirsty ground;
34 A fruitful land into a salt waste,
Because of the evil of those who
inhabited it.
35 He makes a wilderness into a
pool of water
And a dry land into springs of
water;
36 And there He causes the hungry
to inhabit,
So that they may establish an
inhabited city,
37 And sow fields and plant
vineyards,
And produce a fruitful harvest.
38 Also He blesses them and they
multiply greatly,
And He does not let their cattle
decrease.

39 But when they decrease and are
bowed down
Through oppression, evil, and
sorrow,
40 He pours contempt upon nobles
And makes them wander in a
pathless void.
41 But He sets the needy securely
on high away from affliction,
And makes *his* families like a
flock.
42 The upright see it and are glad;
But all unrighteousness shuts its
mouth.
43 Who is wise? Let him keep these
things,
And carefully consider the
lovingkindnesses of Yahweh.

PSALM 108

He Will Tread Down Our Adversaries

A Song. A Psalm of David.

1 MY heart is set, O God;
I will sing, I will sing praises,
even with my glory.
2 Awake, harp and lyre;
I will awaken the dawn!
3 I will give thanks to You,
O Yahweh, among the peoples,
And I will sing praises to You
among the nations.
4 For Your lovingkindness is great
above the heavens,
And Your truth *reaches* to the
skies.
5 Be exalted above the heavens,
O God,
And Your glory above all the
earth.
6 That Your beloved may be
rescued,
Save with Your right hand, and
answer me!

7 God has spoken in His holiness:
"I will exult, I will portion out
Shechem
And measure out the valley of
Succoth.
8 "Gilead is Mine, Manasseh is
Mine;
Ephraim also is the helmet of
My head;
Judah is My scepter.
9 "Moab is My washbowl;
Over Edom I shall throw My shoe;
Over Philistia I will make a loud
shout."

10 Who will bring me into the
     well-defended city?
   Who will lead me to Edom?
11 Have You, O God, not rejected us?
   And will You, O God, not go
        forth with our armies?
12 Oh give us help against the
        adversary,
   For salvation by man is worthless.
13 Through God we shall do valiantly,
   And it is He who will tread down
        our adversaries.

PSALM 109

O God, Do Not Be Silent

For the choir director.
     Of David. A Psalm.
1 O God of my praise,
   Do not be silent!
2 For they have opened a wicked
        mouth and a deceitful
        mouth against me;
   They have spoken to me with a
        lying tongue.
3 They have also surrounded me
        with words of hatred,
   And fought against me without
        cause.
4 In return for my love they
        accuse me;
   But I am *in* prayer.
5 Thus they have set upon me evil
        for good
   And hatred for my love.

6 Appoint a wicked man over him,
   And let an accuser stand at his
        right hand.

7 When he is judged, let him
        come forth a wicked man,
   And let his prayer become sin.
8 Let his days be few;
   Let another take his office.
9 Let his sons be orphans
   And his wife a widow.
10 Let his sons wander aimlessly
        and beg;
   And let them search *for
        food* from their ruined
        homes.
11 Let the creditor seize all that
        he has,
   And let strangers plunder the
        fruit of his labor.
12 Let there be none to extend
        lovingkindness to him,
   And let there be none to be
        gracious to his orphans.
13 Let *those who* follow him be
        cut off;
   In a following generation let
        their name be blotted out.

14 Let the iniquity of his fathers
        be remembered before
        Yahweh,
   And let not the sin of his mother
        be blotted out.
15 Let them be before Yahweh
        continually,
   That He may cut off their
        memory from the earth;
16 Because he did not remember to
        show lovingkindness,
   But persecuted the afflicted, the
        needy man,
   And the disheartened to put
        them to death.

17 He also loved cursing, so it came
      to him;
   And he did not delight in blessing,
      so it was far from him.
18 But he clothed himself with
      cursing as his garment,
   And it came into his inward
      parts like water
   And like oil into his bones.
19 Let it be to him as a garment
      with which he wraps
      himself,
   And for a belt with which he
      constantly girds himself.
20 This is the reward of my
      accusers from Yahweh,
   And of those who speak evil
      against my soul.

21 But as for You, O Yahweh,
      O Lord, deal with me for
      Your name's sake;
   Because Your lovingkindness is
      good, deliver me;
22 For I am afflicted and needy,
   And my heart is pierced within me.
23 I am passing like a shadow when
      it is stretched out;
   I am shaken off like the locust.
24 My knees are feeble from fasting,
   And my flesh has grown lean,
      without fatness.
25 As for me, I have become a
      reproach to them;
   They see me, they wag their
      head.

26 Help me, O Yahweh my God;
   Save me according to Your
      lovingkindness.

27 And let them know that this is
      Your hand;
   You, O Yahweh, have done it.
28 Let them curse, but You
      bless;
   They arise and will be put to
      shame,
   But Your slave shall be
      glad.
29 Let my accusers be clothed
      with dishonor,
   And let them wrap themselves
      with their own shame as
      with a robe.

30 With my mouth I will give
      thanks abundantly to
      Yahweh;
   And in the midst of many I will
      praise Him.
31 For He stands at the right hand
      of the needy,
   To save him from those who
      judge his soul.

PSALM 110

You Are a Priest Forever

   Of David. A Psalm.
1 YAHWEH says to my Lord:
   "Sit at My right hand
   Until I put Your enemies
      as a footstool for
      Your feet."
2 Yahweh will stretch forth Your
      strong scepter from Zion,
      saying,
   "Have dominion in the midst
      of Your enemies."

3 Your people will offer themselves
  freely in the day of Your
  power;
  In the splendor of holiness,
  from the womb of the
  dawn,
  The dew of Your youthfulness
  will be Yours.

4 Yahweh has sworn and will not
  change His mind,
  "You are a priest forever
  According to the order of
  Melchizedek."
5 The Lord is at Your right hand;
  He will crush kings in the day of
  His anger.
6 He will render justice among the
  nations,
  He will fill *them* with corpses,
  He will crush the head *that is*
  over *the* wide earth.
7 He will drink from the brook by
  the wayside;
  Therefore He will lift up *His*
  head.

PSALM 111

*Yahweh Is Gracious and
Compassionate*

1 PRAISE Yah!
  I will give thanks to Yahweh
  with all *my* heart,
  In the council of the upright and
  in the congregation.
2 Great are the works of Yahweh;
  They are sought by all who
  delight in them.

3 Splendid and majestic is His
  work,
  And His righteousness stands
  forever.
4 He has made His wondrous
  deeds to be
  remembered;
  Yahweh is gracious and
  compassionate.
5 He has given food to those
  who fear Him;
  He will remember His
  covenant forever.
6 He has declared to His
  people the power of
  His works,
  In giving them an inheritance
  of the nations.

7 The works of His hands are
  truth and justice;
  All His precepts are
  faithful.
8 They are upheld forever
  and ever;
  They are done in truth and
  uprightness.
9 He has sent redemption to
  His people;
  He has commanded His
  covenant forever;
  Holy and fearsome is His
  name.
10 The fear of Yahweh is
   the beginning of
   wisdom;
   Good insight belongs to
   all those who do *His
   commandments*;
   His praise stands forever.

PSALM 112

*The Righteous Will Be
Remembered Forever*

1 PRAISE Yah!
How blessed is the man who
fears Yahweh,
Who greatly delights in His
commandments.

2 His seed will be mighty on earth;
The generation of the upright
will be blessed.

3 Wealth and riches are in his
house,
And his righteousness stands
forever.

4 Light arises in the darkness for
the upright;
He is gracious and
compassionate and
righteous.

5 It is well with the man who is
gracious and lends;
Who sustains his works with
justice.

6 For he will never be shaken;
The righteous will be
remembered forever.

7 He will not fear an evil report;
His heart is set, trusting in
Yahweh.

8 His heart is upheld, he will not
fear,
Until he looks *in triumph* on his
adversaries.

9 He has given freely to the needy,
His righteousness stands
forever;
His horn will be raised in glory.

10 The wicked will see it and be
vexed,
He will gnash his teeth and melt
away;
The desire of the wicked will
perish.

PSALM 113

Who Is like Yahweh Our God?

1 PRAISE Yah!
Praise, O slaves of Yahweh,
Praise the name of Yahweh.

2 May the name of Yahweh be
blessed
From now until forever.

3 From the rising of the sun to its
setting
The name of Yahweh is to be
praised.

4 Yahweh is high above all nations;
His glory is above the heavens.

5 Who is like Yahweh our God,
The One who sits on high,

6 The One who brings Himself
low to see
The things in heaven and on the
earth?

7 Who raises the poor from the
dust
And lifts high the needy from
the ash heap,

8 To make *them* sit with nobles,
With the nobles of His people.

9 He makes the barren woman of
the house sit
As a glad mother of children.
Praise Yah!

PSALM 114

When Israel Went Out from Egypt

1 WHEN Israel went out from
Egypt,
The house of Jacob from a
people of strange language,
2 Judah became His sanctuary,
Israel, His dominion.

3 The sea looked and fled;
The Jordan turned back.
4 The mountains skipped like rams,
The hills, like lambs.
5 What disturbs you, O sea, that
you flee?
O Jordan, that you turn back?
6 O mountains, that you skip like
rams?
O hills, like lambs?

7 Tremble, O earth, before the
Lord,
Before the God of Jacob,
8 Who turned the rock into a pool
of water,
The flint into a spring of water.

PSALM 115

To Yahweh's Name Give Glory

1 NOT to us, O Yahweh, not to us,
But to Your name give glory
Because of Your lovingkindness,
because of Your truth.
2 Why should the nations say,
"Where, now, is their God?"
3 But our God is in the heavens;
He does whatever He pleases.

4 Their idols are silver and gold,
The work of man's hands.
5 They have mouths, but they
do not speak;
They have eyes, but they do
not see;
6 They have ears, but they do not
hear;
They have noses, but they do
not smell;
7 As for their hands, they do not
feel;
As for their feet, they do not
walk;
They do not make a sound with
their throat.
8 Those who make them will
become like them,
Everyone who trusts in them.

9 O Israel, trust in Yahweh;
He is their help and their shield.
10 O house of Aaron, trust in
Yahweh;
He is their help and their shield.
11 You who fear Yahweh, trust in
Yahweh;
He is their help and their shield.
12 Yahweh remembered us; He will
bless!
He will bless the house of Israel.
He will bless the house of Aaron.
13 He will bless those who fear
Yahweh,
The small together with the
great.
14 May Yahweh give you increase,
You and your children.
15 May you be blessed of Yahweh,
Who made heaven and earth.

16 The heavens are the heavens of
   Yahweh,
   But the earth He has given to the
       sons of men.
17 It is not the dead that praise Yah,
   And it is none of those who go
       down to silence;
18 But as for us, we will bless Yah
   From now until forever.
   Praise Yah!

PSALM 116

I Love Yahweh

1 I love Yahweh, because He hears
   My voice *and* my supplications.
2 Because He has inclined His ear
       to me,
   So I shall call *upon Him* in all
       my days.
3 The cords of death
       encompassed me
   And the distresses of Sheol
       found me;
   I found distress and sorrow.
4 Then I called upon the name of
       Yahweh:
   "O Yahweh, I beseech You,
       provide my soul escape!"

5 Gracious is Yahweh, and
       righteous;
   And our God is compassionate.
6 Yahweh keeps the simple;
   I was brought low, and He
       saved me.
7 Return to your rest, O my soul,
   For Yahweh has dealt
       bountifully with you.

8 For You have rescued my soul
       from death,
   My eyes from tears,
   My feet from stumbling.
9 I shall walk before Yahweh
   In the land of the living.
10 I believed when I said,
   "I am greatly afflicted."
11 I said in my alarm,
   "All men are liars."

12 What shall I give to Yahweh in
       return
   For all His bountiful dealings
       with me?
13 I shall lift up the cup of
       salvation
   And call upon the name of
       Yahweh.
14 I shall pay my vows to Yahweh,
   Oh *may it be* in the presence of
       all His people.
15 Precious in the sight of Yahweh
   Is the death of His holy ones.
16 O Yahweh, surely I am Your
       slave,
   I am Your slave, the son of Your
       maidservant,
   You have loosed my bonds.
17 To You I shall offer a sacrifice of
       thanksgiving,
   And call upon the name of
       Yahweh.
18 I shall pay my vows to Yahweh,
   Oh *may it be* in the presence of
       all His people,
19 In the courts of the house of
       Yahweh,
   In the midst of you, O Jerusalem.
   Praise Yah!

PSALM 117

Yahweh's Lovingkindness Prevails

1 PRAISE Yahweh, all nations;
Laud Him, all peoples!
2 For His lovingkindness prevails
over us,
And the truth of Yahweh is
everlasting.
Praise Yah!

PSALM 118

*Yahweh's Lovingkindness
Endures Forever*

1 GIVE thanks to Yahweh, for He
is good;
For His lovingkindness endures
forever.
2 Oh let Israel say,
"His lovingkindness endures
forever."
3 Oh let the house of Aaron say,
"His lovingkindness endures
forever."
4 Oh let those who fear Yahweh say,
"His lovingkindness endures
forever."

5 From *my* distress I called
upon Yah;
Yah answered me *and set me* in a
large place.
6 Yahweh is for me; I will not fear;
What can man do to me?
7 Yahweh is for me among those
who help me;
Therefore I will look *in triumph*
on those who hate me.

8 It is better to take refuge in
Yahweh
Than to trust in man.
9 It is better to take refuge
in Yahweh
Than to trust in nobles.

10 All nations surrounded me;
In the name of Yahweh I will
surely cut them off.
11 They surrounded me, indeed,
they surrounded me;
In the name of Yahweh I will
surely cut them off.
12 They surrounded me like bees;
They were extinguished as a fire
of thorns;
In the name of Yahweh I will
surely cut them off.
13 You pushed me down violently
to *make* me fall,
But Yahweh helped me.
14 Yah is my strength and song,
And He has become my
salvation.

15 The sound of joyful shouting
and salvation is in the tents
of the righteous;
The right hand of Yahweh does
valiantly.
16 The right hand of Yahweh is
exalted;
The right hand of Yahweh does
valiantly.
17 I will not die; indeed I will live,
And recount the works of Yah.
18 Yah has disciplined me severely,
But He has not given me over to
death.

19 Open to me the gates of
     righteousness;
     I shall enter through them, I
         shall give thanks to Yah.
20 This is the gate of Yahweh;
     The righteous will enter
         through it.
21 I shall give thanks to You, for
         You have answered me,
     And You have become my
         salvation.

22 The stone which the builders
         rejected
     Has become the chief corner
         stone.
23 This is from Yahweh;
     It is marvelous in our eyes.
24 This is the day which Yahweh
         has made;
     Let us rejoice and be glad
         in it.
25 O Yahweh, save!
     O Yahweh, succeed!
26 Blessed is the one who comes in
         the name of Yahweh;
     We have blessed you from the
         house of Yahweh.
27 Yahweh is God, and He has
         given us light;
     Bind the festival sacrifice with
         cords to the horns of the
         altar.
28 You are my God, and I give
         thanks to You;
     You are my God, I exalt You.
29 Give thanks to Yahweh, for
         He is good;
     For His lovingkindness endures
         forever.

PSALM 119

I Love Your Law, O Yahweh

א
Aleph

1 HOW blessed are those whose
         way is blameless,
     Who walk in the law of Yahweh.
2 How blessed are those who
         observe His testimonies,
     They seek Him with all *their*
         heart.
3 They also do not work
         unrighteousness;
     They walk in His ways.
4 You have commanded *us,*
     To keep Your precepts
         diligently.
5 Oh may my ways be established
     To keep Your statutes!
6 Then I shall not be ashamed
     When I look upon all Your
         commandments.
7 I shall give thanks to You with
         uprightness of heart,
     When I learn Your righteous
         judgments.
8 I shall keep Your statutes;
     Do not forsake me utterly!

ב
Beth

9 How can a young man keep his
         way pure?
     By keeping *it* according to Your
         word.
10 With all my heart I have
         sought You;
     Do not let me stray from Your
         commandments.

11 Your word I have treasured in
   my heart,
   That I may not sin against You.
12 Blessed are You, O Yahweh;
   Teach me Your statutes.
13 With my lips I have recounted
   All the judgments of Your
   mouth.
14 I have rejoiced in the way of
   Your testimonies,
   As much as in all riches.
15 I will muse upon Your precepts
   And look upon Your ways.
16 I shall delight in Your statutes;
   I shall not forget Your word.

ב
Gimel

17 Deal bountifully with Your slave,
   That I may live and keep Your
   word.
18 Open my eyes, that I may
   behold
   Wonderful things from Your law.
19 I am a sojourner in the earth;
   Do not hide Your
   commandments from me.
20 My soul is crushed with longing
   For Your judgments at all times.
21 You rebuke the arrogant, the
   cursed,
   Who stray from Your
   commandments.
22 Take away reproach and
   contempt from me,
   For I observe Your testimonies.
23 Even though princes sit *and* talk
   against me,
   Your slave muses on Your
   statutes.

24 Your testimonies also are my
   delight;
   They are my counselors.

ד
Daleth

25 My soul clings to the dust;
   Revive me according to Your
   word.
26 I have recounted my ways, and
   You have answered me;
   Teach me Your statutes.
27 Make me understand the way of
   Your precepts,
   So I will muse on Your wondrous
   deeds.
28 My soul weeps because of grief;
   Raise me up according to Your
   word.
29 Remove the false way from me,
   And graciously grant me
   Your law.
30 I have chosen the faithful way;
   I have placed Your judgments
   before me.
31 I cling to Your testimonies;
   O Yahweh, do not put me to
   shame!
32 I shall run the way of Your
   commandments,
   For You will enlarge my heart.

ה
He

33 Instruct me, O Yahweh, in the
   way of Your statutes,
   That I may observe it to the end.
34 Cause me to understand, that
   I may observe Your law
   And keep it with all *my* heart.

35 Cause me to walk in the path of
       Your commandments,
    For I delight in it.
36 Cause my heart to incline to
       Your testimonies
    And not to *dishonest* gain.
37 Cause my eyes to turn
       away from looking at
       worthlessness,
    And revive me in Your ways.
38 Cause Your word to be
       established for Your slave,
    As that which produces fear
       for You.
39 Cause my reproach which I
       dread to pass away,
    For Your judgments are good.
40 Behold, I long for Your
       precepts;
    Revive me in Your
       righteousness.

ו
Vav

41 May Your lovingkindnesses also
       come to me, O Yahweh,
    Your salvation according to Your
       word;
42 So I will have an answer for him
       who reproaches me,
    For I trust in Your word.
43 And do not take away the word
       of truth utterly from my
       mouth,
    For I wait for Your judgments.
44 So I will keep Your law
       continually,
    Forever and ever.
45 And I will walk in a wide place,
    For I seek Your precepts.

46 I will also speak of Your
       testimonies before kings
    And I shall not be ashamed.
47 I shall delight in Your
       commandments,
    Which I love.
48 And I shall lift up my hands to
       Your commandments,
    Which I love;
    And I will muse on Your
       statutes.

ז
Zayin

49 Remember the word to Your
       slave,
    In which You have made me
       wait.
50 This is my comfort in my
       affliction,
    That Your word has revived me.
51 The arrogant utterly scoff
       at me,
    Yet I do not turn aside from
       Your law.
52 I have remembered Your
       judgments from of old,
       O Yahweh,
    And comfort myself.
53 Burning indignation has seized
       me because of the wicked,
    Who forsake Your law.
54 Your statutes have become my
       songs
    In the house of my sojourning.
55 I remember in the night Your
       name, O Yahweh,
    So I keep Your law.
56 This has become mine,
    That I observe Your precepts.

ח
Heth

57 Yahweh is my portion;
   I have promised to keep Your
      words.
58 I have sought to please Your face
      with all *my* heart;
   Be gracious to me according to
      Your word.
59 I thought upon my ways
   And I turned my feet to Your
      testimonies.
60 I hastened and did not delay
   To keep Your commandments.
61 The cords of the wicked have
      encircled me,
   But I have not forgotten
      Your law.
62 At midnight I shall rise to give
      thanks to You
   Because of Your righteous
      judgments.
63 I am a companion of all those
      who fear You,
   And of those who keep Your
      precepts.
64 The earth, O Yahweh, is full of
      Your lovingkindness;
   Teach me Your statutes.

ט
Teth

65 You have dealt well with Your
      slave,
   O Yahweh, according to Your
      word.
66 Teach me good discernment and
      knowledge,
   For I believe in Your
      commandments.

67 Before I was afflicted I went
      astray,
   But now I keep Your word.
68 You are good and do good;
   Teach me Your statutes.
69 The arrogant have smeared me
      with lying;
   With all *my* heart I will observe
      Your precepts.
70 Their heart is covered with fat,
   But I delight in Your law.
71 It is good for me that I was
      afflicted,
   That I may learn Your statutes.
72 The law of Your mouth is better
      to me
   Than thousands of gold and
      silver *pieces.*

י
Yodh

73 Your hands made me and
      established me;
   Give me understanding,
      that I may learn Your
      commandments.
74 May those who fear You see me
      and be glad,
   Because I wait for Your word.
75 I know, O Yahweh, that Your
      judgments are righteous,
   And that in faithfulness You
      have afflicted me.
76 Oh may Your lovingkindness
      comfort me,
   According to Your word to Your
      slave.
77 May Your compassion come to
      me that I may live,
   For Your law is my delight.

78 May the arrogant be ashamed,
      for they wrong me with
      lying;
   But I shall muse on Your precepts.
79 May those who fear You turn
      to me,
   And those who know Your
      testimonies.
80 May my heart be blameless in
      Your statutes,
   So that I will not be ashamed.

כ
Kaph

81 My soul fails *with longing* for
      Your salvation;
   I wait for Your word.
82 My eyes fail *with longing* for
      Your word,
   Saying, "When will You
      comfort me?"
83 For I am like a wineskin in the
      smoke,
   But I do not forget Your statutes.
84 How many are the days of Your
      slave?
   When will You execute
      judgment on those who
      persecute me?
85 The arrogant have dug pits for me,
   Men who are not in accord with
      Your law.
86 All Your commandments are
      faithful;
   They have persecuted me with
      lying; help me!
87 They almost made an end of me
      on the earth,
   But as for me, I did not forsake
      Your precepts.

88 Revive me according to Your
      lovingkindness,
   So that I may keep the testimony
      of Your mouth.

ל
Lamedh

89 Forever, O Yahweh,
   Your word stands firm in
      heaven.
90 Your faithfulness *endures* from
      generation to generation;
   You established the earth, and
      it stands.
91 They stand this day according to
      Your judgments,
   For all things are Your slaves.
92 If Your law had not been my
      delight,
   Then I would have perished in
      my affliction.
93 I will never forget Your precepts,
   For by them You have revived me.
94 I am Yours, save me;
   For I have sought Your precepts.
95 The wicked hope for me—to
      destroy me;
   I shall perceive Your testimonies.
96 I have seen a limit to all
      perfection;
   Your commandment is
      exceedingly broad.

מ
Mem

97 Oh how I love Your law!
   It is my meditation all the day.
98 Your commandments make me
      wiser than my enemies,
   For they are mine forever.

99 I have more insight than all my
    teachers,
  For Your testimonies are my
    meditation.
100 I perceive more than the aged,
  Because I have observed Your
    precepts.
101 I have restrained my feet from
    every evil way,
  That I may keep Your word.
102 I have not turned aside from
    Your judgments,
  For You Yourself have taught me.
103 How sweet is Your word to my
    taste!
  Sweeter than honey to my
    mouth!
104 From Your precepts I get
    perception;
  Therefore I hate every
    false way.

נ
Nun

105 Your word is a lamp to my feet
  And a light to my path.
106 I have sworn and I have
    confirmed,
  To keep Your righteous
    judgments.
107 I am exceedingly afflicted;
  O Yahweh, revive me according
    to Your word.
108 Oh be pleased with the freewill
    offerings of my mouth,
    O Yahweh,
  And teach me Your judgments.
109 My soul is continually in my
    hand,
  Yet I do not forget Your law.

110 The wicked have laid a snare
    for me,
  Yet I have not wandered from
    Your precepts.
111 I have inherited Your
    testimonies forever,
  For they are the joy of my heart.
112 I have inclined my heart to do
    Your statutes
  Forever, to the end.

ס
Samekh

113 I hate those who are
    double-minded,
  But I love Your law.
114 You are my hiding place and my
    shield;
  I wait for Your word.
115 Depart from me, evildoers,
  That I may observe the
    commandments of my God.
116 Sustain me according to Your
    word, that I may live;
  And do not put me to shame
    because of my hope.
117 Uphold me that I may be saved,
  That I may have regard for Your
    statutes continually.
118 You have rejected all those who
    stray from Your statutes,
  For their deceitfulness is a lie.
119 You remove all the wicked of the
    earth *like* dross;
  Therefore I love Your
    testimonies.
120 My flesh quakes for dread
    of You,
  And I am afraid of Your
    judgments.

ע
Ayin

121 I have done justice and
righteousness;
Do not leave me to my
oppressors.

122 Be for Your slave a guarantee
for good;
Do not let the arrogant
oppress me.

123 My eyes fail *with longing* for
Your salvation
And for Your righteous word.

124 Deal with Your slave according
to Your lovingkindness
And teach me Your statutes.

125 I am Your slave; give me
understanding,
That I may know Your
testimonies.

126 It is time for Yahweh to act,
For they have broken Your law.

127 Therefore I love Your
commandments
Above gold, even above
fine gold.

128 Therefore I deem all *Your*
precepts concerning
everything to be right,
I hate every false way.

פ
Pe

129 Your testimonies are wonderful;
Therefore my soul observes
them.

130 The unfolding of Your words
gives light;
It gives understanding to the
simple.

131 I opened my mouth wide and
panted,
For I longed for Your
commandments.

132 Turn to me and be gracious to me,
According to *Your* judgment for
those who love Your name.

133 Establish my steps in Your word,
And do not let any wickedness
overpower me.

134 Redeem me from the oppression
of man,
That I may keep Your precepts.

135 Make Your face shine upon Your
slave,
And teach me Your statutes.

136 My eyes shed streams of water,
Because they do not keep
Your law.

צ
Tsadhe

137 Righteous are You, O Yahweh,
And upright are Your judgments.

138 In righteousness, You have
commanded Your
testimonies
And in exceeding faithfulness.

139 My zeal has consumed me,
Because my adversaries have
forgotten Your words.

140 Your word is exceedingly refined,
Therefore Your slave loves it.

141 I am small and despised,
Yet I do not forget Your precepts.

142 Your righteousness is an
everlasting righteousness,
And Your law is truth.

143 Trouble and anguish have
found me,

Yet Your commandments are my
delight.
144 Righteous are Your testimonies
forever;
Give me understanding that
I may live.

ק
Qoph

145 I called with all my heart;
answer me, O Yahweh!
I will observe Your statutes.
146 I called to You; save me
And I shall keep Your
testimonies.
147 I eagerly greet the dawn and cry
for help;
I wait for Your words.
148 My eyes eagerly greet the night
watches,
That I may muse on Your word.
149 Hear my voice according to Your
lovingkindness;
O Yahweh, revive me, according
to Your judgments.
150 Near are those who pursue
wickedness;
They are far from Your law.
151 Near are You, O Yahweh,
And all Your commandments
are truth.
152 Of old I have known from Your
testimonies
That You have founded them
forever.

ר
Resh

153 See my affliction and rescue me,
For I do not forget Your law.

154 Plead my cause and redeem me;
Revive me according to Your word.
155 Salvation is far from the wicked,
For they do not seek Your
statutes.
156 Many are Your compassions,
O Yahweh;
Revive me according to Your
judgments.
157 Many are my persecutors and
my adversaries,
Yet I do not turn aside from Your
testimonies.
158 I see the treacherous and loathe
them,
Those who do not keep Your word.
159 See how I love Your precepts;
O Yahweh, revive me according
to Your lovingkindness.
160 The sum of Your word is truth,
And every one of Your righteous
judgments is everlasting.

ש
Sin / Shin

161 Princes persecute me without
cause,
But my heart is in dread of Your
words.
162 I rejoice at Your word,
As one who finds much spoil.
163 I hate and abhor lying,
But I love Your law.
164 Seven times a day I praise You,
Because of Your righteous
judgments.
165 Those who love Your law have
much peace,
And nothing causes them to
stumble.

166 I hope for Your salvation,
 O Yahweh,
And I do Your commandments.
167 My soul keeps Your testimonies,
And I love them exceedingly.
168 I keep Your precepts and Your
 testimonies,
For all my ways are before You.

ת
Tav

169 Let my cry of lamentation come
 near before You, O Yahweh;
Give me understanding
 according to Your word.
170 Let my supplication come
 before You;
Deliver me according to Your
 word.
171 Let my lips pour forth praise,
For You teach me Your statutes.
172 Let my tongue answer with Your
 word,
For all Your commandments are
 righteous.
173 Let Your hand be ready to
 help me,
For I have chosen Your
 precepts.
174 I long for Your salvation,
 O Yahweh,
And Your law is my delight.
175 Let my soul live that it may
 praise You,
And let Your judgments
 help me.
176 I have wandered off like a lost
 sheep; search for Your slave,
For I have not forgotten Your
 commandments.

PSALM 120

O Yahweh, Deliver My Soul

A Song of Ascents.

1 IN my distress I called to Yahweh,
And He answered me.
2 O Yahweh, deliver my soul from
 a lying lip,
From a deceitful tongue.
3 What shall He give to you, and
 what shall He add to you,
O deceitful tongue?
4 Sharp arrows of the warrior,
With the *burning* coals of the
 broom tree.

5 Woe is me, for I sojourn in
 Meshech,
 For I dwell among the tents of
 Kedar!
6 Too long has my soul had its
 dwelling
With those who hate peace.
7 I am *for* peace, but when I speak,
They are for war.

PSALM 121

My Help Comes from Yahweh

A Song of Ascents.

1 I will lift up my eyes to the
 mountains;
From where shall my help come?
2 My help *comes* from Yahweh,
Who made heaven and earth.
3 He will not allow your foot to
 stumble;
He who keeps you will not
 slumber.

4 Behold, He who keeps Israel
   Will not slumber and will not
      sleep.

5 Yahweh is your keeper;
   Yahweh is your shade on your
      right hand.
6 The sun will not strike you by day,
   Nor the moon by night.
7 Yahweh will keep you from
      all evil;
   He will keep your soul.
8 Yahweh will keep your going out
      and your coming in
   From now until forever.

PSALM 122

Go to the House of Yahweh

A Song of Ascents. Of David.
1 I was glad when they said to me,
   "Let us go to the house of
      Yahweh."
2 Our feet are standing
   Within your gates, O Jerusalem,
3 Jerusalem, which is built
   As a city joined altogether;
4 To which the tribes, the tribes of
      Yah, go up—
   A testimony for Israel—
   To give thanks to the name of
      Yahweh.
5 For there, thrones sit for
      judgment,
   The thrones of the house of
      David.

6 Pray for the peace of Jerusalem:
   "May they prosper who love you.

7 "May peace be within your
      walls,
   And tranquility within your
      palaces."
8 For the sake of my brothers and
      my friends,
   I will now say, "May peace be
      within you."
9 For the sake of the house of
      Yahweh our God,
   I will seek your good.

PSALM 123

To You I Lift Up My Eyes

A Song of Ascents.
1 TO You I lift up my eyes,
   The One enthroned in the
      heavens!
2 Behold, as the eyes of slaves
   look to the hand of their
      master,
   As the eyes of a servant-girl
      to the hand of her
      mistress,
   So our eyes *look* to Yahweh
      our God,
   Until He is gracious to us.

3 Be gracious to us, O Yahweh,
      be gracious to us,
   For we are greatly saturated
      with contempt.
4 Our soul is greatly
      saturated
   With the mockery of those
      who are at ease,
   And with the contempt of the
      proud.

PSALM 124

Yahweh Was on Our Side

A Song of Ascents. Of David.

1 "HAD it not been Yahweh who
  was on our side,"
Let Israel now say,
2 "Had it not been Yahweh who
  was on our side
When men rose up against us,
3 Then they would have
  swallowed us alive,
When their anger was kindled
  against us;
4 Then the waters would have
  flowed over us,
The stream would have swept
  over our soul;
5 Then the raging waters would
  have swept over our soul."

6 Blessed be Yahweh,
Who has not given us to be prey
  for their teeth.
7 Our soul has escaped as a bird out
  of the snare of the trapper;
The snare is broken and we have
  escaped.
8 Our help is in the name of Yahweh,
Who made heaven and earth.

PSALM 125

Yahweh Surrounds His People

A Song of Ascents.

1 THOSE who trust in Yahweh
Are as Mount Zion, which will
  not be shaken but will abide
  forever.

2 As the mountains surround
  Jerusalem,
So Yahweh surrounds His people
From now until forever.
3 For the scepter of wickedness
  shall not rest upon the land
  of the righteous,
So that the righteous would not
  send forth their hands in
  unrighteousness.

4 Do good, O Yahweh, to those
  who are good
And to those who are upright in
  their hearts.
5 But as for those who turn aside
  to their crooked ways,
Yahweh will lead them away
  with the workers of iniquity.
Peace be upon Israel.

PSALM 126

*Those Who Sow in Tears Shall Reap
with Joy*

A Song of Ascents.

1 WHEN Yahweh returned the
  captive ones of Zion,
We were like those who dream.
2 Then our mouth was filled with
  laughter
And our tongue with shouts
  of joy;
Then they said among the nations,
"Yahweh has done great things
  for them."
3 Yahweh has done great things
  for us;
We are glad.

4 Restore our captivity, O Yahweh,
As the streams in the Negev.
5 Those who sow in tears shall
reap with shouts of joy.
6 He who goes to and fro weeping,
carrying *his* bag of seed,
Shall indeed come again with
a shout of joy, carrying his
sheaves *with him.*

PSALM 127

Unless Yahweh Builds the House

A Song of Ascents. Of Solomon.
1 UNLESS Yahweh builds the
house,
They labor in vain who build it;
Unless Yahweh watches the city,
The watchman keeps awake
in vain.
2 It is in vain that you rise up early,
That you sit out late,
O you who eat the bread of
painful labors;
For in this manner, He gives
sleep to His beloved.

3 Behold, children are an
inheritance of Yahweh,
The fruit of the womb is a reward.
4 Like arrows in the hand of a
warrior,
So are the children of one's
youth.
5 How blessed is the man who fills
his quiver with them;
They will not be ashamed
When they speak with enemies
in the gate.

PSALM 128

Blessed Is Everyone Who Fears Yahweh

A Song of Ascents.
1 HOW blessed is everyone who
fears Yahweh,
Who walks in His ways.
2 When you shall eat of the fruit
of the labor of your hands,
How blessed will you be and
how well will it be for you.
3 Your wife shall be like a fruitful
vine
In the innermost parts of your
house,
Your children like olive plants
All around your table.
4 Behold, for thus shall the man
be blessed
Who fears Yahweh.

5 May Yahweh bless you from Zion,
That you may see the prosperity
of Jerusalem all the days of
your life.
6 Indeed, may you see your
children's children.
Peace be upon Israel!

PSALM 129

*Yahweh Has Cut the Cords
of the Wicked*

A Song of Ascents.
1 "MANY times they have assailed
me from my youth up,"
Let Israel now say,
2 "Many times they have assailed
me from my youth up;

Yet they have not prevailed
    against me.
3 "The plowers plowed upon my
    back;
They lengthened their furrows."
4 Yahweh is righteous;
He has cut up the cords of the
    wicked.

5 Let all who hate Zion
Be put to shame and turned
    backward;
6 Let them be like grass upon the
    rooftops,
Which dries up before it
    grows up;
7 With which the reaper does not
    fill his hand,
Nor the binder of sheaves the
    fold of his garment;
8 And those who pass by will
    not say,
"The blessing of Yahweh be
    upon you;
We bless you in the name of
    Yahweh."

PSALM 130

Yahweh Will Redeem Israel

A Song of Ascents.
1 OUT of the depths I called to
    You, O Yahweh.
2 O Lord, hear my voice!
Let Your ears be attentive
To the voice of my supplications.
3 If You should keep iniquities,
    O Yah,
O Lord, who could stand?

4 But with You there is
    forgiveness,
That You may be feared.

5 I hope for Yahweh, my soul
    does hope,
And for His word do I wait.
6 My soul *waits* for the Lord
More than the watchmen for the
    morning,
The watchmen for the morning.
7 O Israel, wait for Yahweh;
For with Yahweh there is
    lovingkindness,
And with Him is abundant
    redemption.
8 And it is He who will redeem
    Israel
From all his iniquities.

PSALM 131

I Have Quieted My Soul

A Song of Ascents. Of David.
1 O Yahweh, my heart is not
    exalted, and my eyes are not
    raised high;
And I do not involve myself in
    great matters,
Or in matters too marvelous
    for me.
2 Surely I have soothed and
    quieted my soul,
Like a weaned child with his
    mother,
Like a weaned child is my soul
    within me.
3 O Israel, wait for Yahweh
From now until forever.

PSALM 132

Yahweh Has Chosen Zion

A Song of Ascents.

1 REMEMBER, O Yahweh, on
    David's behalf,
  All his affliction;
2 How he swore to Yahweh
  And vowed to the Mighty One
    of Jacob,
3 "Surely I will not come into my
    house,
  Nor lie in the comfort of my bed;
4 I will not give sleep to my eyes
  Or slumber to my eyelids,
5 Until I find a place for Yahweh,
  A dwelling place for the Mighty
    One of Jacob."

6 Behold, we heard of it in
    Ephrathah,
  We found it in the fields of Jaar.
7 Let us come into His dwelling
    place;
  Let us worship at the footstool
    of His feet.
8 Arise, O Yahweh, to Your resting
    place,
  You and the ark of Your strength.
9 Let Your priests be clothed with
    righteousness,
  And let Your holy ones sing for joy.

10 For the sake of David Your
    servant,
  Do not turn away the face of
    Your anointed.
11 Yahweh has sworn to David
  A truth from which He will not
    turn back:

"Of the fruit of your body I will
    set upon your throne.
12 "If your sons keep My covenant
  And My testimony which I will
    teach them,
  Their sons also shall sit upon
    your throne forever."

13 For Yahweh has chosen Zion;
  He has desired it for His
    habitation.
14 "This is My resting place forever;
  Here I will inhabit, for I have
    desired it.
15 "I will abundantly bless her
    provision;
  I will satisfy her needy with
    bread.
16 "Her priests also I will clothe
    with salvation,
  And her holy ones will sing
    loudly for joy.
17 "There I will cause the horn of
    David to spring up;
  I have prepared a lamp for Mine
    anointed.
18 "His enemies I will clothe with
    shame,
  But upon him, his crown shall
    blossom."

PSALM 133

How Good and Pleasant Is Unity

A Song of Ascents. Of David.

1 BEHOLD, how good and how
    pleasant it is
  For brothers to dwell together
    in unity!

2 It is like the good oil upon the
    head,
  Coming down upon the beard,
    Aaron's beard,
  Coming down upon the edge of
    his robes.
3 It is like the dew of Hermon
  Coming down upon the
    mountains of Zion;
  For there, Yahweh commanded
    the blessing—life forever.

PSALM 134

Behold, Bless Yahweh

    A Song of Ascents.
1 BEHOLD, bless Yahweh, all *you*
    slaves of Yahweh,
  Who stand in the house of
    Yahweh by night!
2 Lift up your hands to the
    sanctuary
  And bless Yahweh.
3 May Yahweh bless you from
    Zion,
  Who made heaven and earth.

PSALM 135

O Yahweh, Your Name Is Everlasting

1 PRAISE Yah!
  Praise the name of Yahweh;
  Praise *Him*, O slaves of
    Yahweh,
2 You who stand in the house of
    Yahweh,
  In the courts of the house of
    our God!

3 Praise Yah, for Yahweh is good;
  Sing praises to His name, for it
    is lovely.
4 For Yah has chosen Jacob for
    Himself,
  Israel for His treasured
    possession.

5 For I know that Yahweh is great
  And that our Lord *is greater*
    than all gods.
6 Whatever Yahweh pleases,
    He does,
  In heaven and on earth, in the
    seas and in all deeps.
7 The One who causes the clouds
    to ascend from the end of
    the earth;
  Who makes lightnings for
    the rain,
  Who brings forth the wind from
    His storehouses.

8 He struck the firstborn of
    Egypt,
  From man to beast.
9 He sent signs and wonders into
    your midst, O Egypt,
  Amongst Pharaoh and all
    his slaves.
10 He struck many nations
  And slew mighty kings,
11 Sihon, king of the Amorites,
  And Og, king of Bashan,
  And all the kingdoms of
    Canaan,
12 And He gave their land as an
    inheritance,
  An inheritance to Israel His
    people.

13 O Yahweh, Your name is
      everlasting,
   O Yahweh, Your remembrance is
      from generation to generation.
14 For Yahweh will render justice
      for His people
   And will give comfort to His
      slaves.
15 The idols of the nations are
      silver and gold,
   The work of man's hands.
16 They have mouths, but they
      do not speak;
   They have eyes, but they do
      not see;
17 They have ears, but they do not
      hear,
   Surely, there is not any breath in
      their mouths.
18 Those who make them will be
      like them,
   All who trust in them.

19 O house of Israel, bless Yahweh;
   O house of Aaron, bless Yahweh;
20 O house of Levi, bless Yahweh;
   You who fear Yahweh, bless
      Yahweh.
21 Blessed be Yahweh from Zion,
   Who dwells in Jerusalem.
   Praise Yah!

PSALM 136

His Lovingkindness Endures Forever

1 GIVE thanks to Yahweh, for He
   is good,
   For His lovingkindness endures
      forever.

2 Give thanks to the God of gods,
   For His lovingkindness endures
      forever.
3 Give thanks to the Lord of lords,
   For His lovingkindness endures
      forever.

4 To Him who alone does great
      wonders,
   For His lovingkindness endures
      forever;
5 To Him who made the heavens
      with skill,
   For His lovingkindness endures
      forever;
6 To Him who spread out the
      earth above the waters,
   For His lovingkindness endures
      forever;
7 To Him who made *the* great
      lights,
   For His lovingkindness endures
      forever:
8 The sun to rule by day,
   For His lovingkindness endures
      forever,
9 The moon and stars to rule by
      night,
   For His lovingkindness endures
      forever.

10 To Him who struck the
      Egyptians through their
      firstborn,
   For His lovingkindness endures
      forever;
11 Then brought Israel out from
      their midst,
   For His lovingkindness endures
      forever,

12 With a strong hand and an
    outstretched arm,
   For His lovingkindness endures
    forever.

13 To Him who divided the Red Sea
    in two,
   For His lovingkindness endures
    forever,
14 And made Israel pass through
    the midst of it,
   For His lovingkindness endures
    forever,
15 But He overthrew Pharaoh and
    his army in the Red Sea,
   For His lovingkindness endures
    forever.

16 To Him who led His people
    through the wilderness,
   For His lovingkindness endures
    forever;

17 To Him who struck great
    kings,
   For His lovingkindness endures
    forever,
18 And killed mighty kings,
   For His lovingkindness endures
    forever:
19 Sihon, king of the Amorites,
   For His lovingkindness endures
    forever,
20 And Og, king of Bashan,
   For His lovingkindness endures
    forever,
21 And gave their land as an
    inheritance,
   For His lovingkindness endures
    forever,

22 Even an inheritance to Israel His
    servant,
   For His lovingkindness endures
    forever.

23 Who remembered us in our low
    estate,
   For His lovingkindness endures
    forever,
24 And has snatched us from our
    adversaries,
   For His lovingkindness endures
    forever;
25 Who gives food to all flesh,
   For His lovingkindness endures
    forever.
26 Give thanks to the God of
    heaven,
   For His lovingkindness endures
    forever.

PSALM 137

We Wept When We Remembered Zion

1 BY the rivers of Babylon,
   There we sat and also wept,
   When we remembered Zion.
2 Upon the willows in the midst of it
   We hung our lyres.
3 For there our captors asked us
    about the words of a song,
   And our tormentors *asked*
    joyfully, *saying,*
   "Sing for us one of the songs
    of Zion."

4 How can we sing a song of
    Yahweh
   In a foreign land?

5 If I forget you, O Jerusalem,
  May my right hand forget *her skill*.
6 May my tongue cling to the roof
  of my mouth
  If I do not remember you,
  If I do not exalt Jerusalem
  Above my chief joy.

7 Remember, O Yahweh, against
  the sons of Edom
  The day of Jerusalem,
  Who said, "Tear it down! Tear
  it down
  To its very foundation."
8 O daughter of Babylon, you
  devastated one,
  How blessed will be the one
  who repays you
  With the recompense with which
  you have recompensed us.
9 How blessed will be the one who
  seizes and dashes your infants
  Against the cliff.

PSALM 138

I Will Give Thanks to Your Name

Of David.

1 I will give You thanks with all
  my heart;
  I will sing praises to You before
  the gods.
2 I will worship toward Your holy
  temple
  And give thanks to Your name
  for Your lovingkindness and
  Your truth;
  For You have magnified Your word
  according to all Your name.

3 On the day I called, You
  answered me;
  You made me bold with strength
  in my soul.

4 All the kings of the earth,
  O Yahweh, will give You
  thanks,
  When they hear the words of
  Your mouth.
5 And they will sing of the ways of
  Yahweh,
  For great is the glory of Yahweh.
6 For Yahweh is high,
  Yet He sees the lowly,
  But the one who exalts *himself*
  He knows from afar.

7 Though I walk in the midst of
  distress, You will revive me;
  You will stretch forth Your hand
  against the wrath of my
  enemies,
  And Your right hand will
  save me.
8 Yahweh will accomplish what
  concerns me;
  O Yahweh, Your lovingkindness
  endures forever;
  Do not fail the works of Your
  hands.

PSALM 139

Where Can I Go from Your Spirit?

For the choir director.
Of David. A Psalm.

1 O Yahweh, You have searched
  me and known *me*.

2 You know when I sit down and
    when I rise up;
You understand my thought
    from afar.

3 You scrutinize my path and my
    lying down,
And are intimately acquainted
    with all my ways.

4 Even before there is a word on
    my tongue,
Behold, O Yahweh, You know
    it all.

5 You have enclosed me behind
    and before,
And You have put Your hand
    upon me.

6 *Such* knowledge is too
    wonderful for me;
It is *too* high, I cannot attain
    to it.

7 Where can I go from Your Spirit?
Or where can I flee from Your
    presence?

8 If I ascend to heaven, You are
    there;
If I make my bed in Sheol,
    behold, You are there.

9 If I lift up the wings of the
    dawn,
If I dwell in the remotest part
    of the sea,

10 Even there Your hand will
    lead me,
And Your right hand will lay
    hold of me.

11 If I say, "Surely the darkness will
    bruise me,
And the light around me will
    be night,"

12 Even the darkness is not too
    dark for You,
And the night is as bright as
    the day.
Darkness and light are alike
    to You.

13 For You formed my inward parts;
You wove me in my mother's
    womb.

14 I will give thanks to You, for I am
    fearfully and wonderfully
    made;
Wonderful are Your works,
And my soul knows it very well.

15 My frame was not hidden
    from You,
When I was made in secret,
And intricately woven in the
    depths of the earth;

16 Your eyes have seen my
    unshaped substance;
And in Your book all of them
    were written
The days that were formed *for me*,
When as yet there was not one
    of them.

17 How precious are Your thoughts
    to me, O God!
How vast is the sum of them!

18 If I should count them, they
    would outnumber the sand.
When I awake, I am still
    with You.

19 Oh that You would slay the
    wicked, O God!
O men of bloodshed, depart
    from me.

20 For they speak against You
    wickedly,
    And Your enemies take *Your*
      name in vain.
21 Do I not hate those who hate
    You, O Yahweh?
    And do I not revile those who
      rise up against You?
22 I hate them with the utmost
    hatred;
    They have become my
      enemies.

23 Search me, O God, and know my
    heart;
    Try me and know my anxious
      thoughts;
24 And see if there be any hurtful
    way in me,
    And lead me in the everlasting
      way.

PSALM 140

Rescue Me, O Yahweh,
from Evil Men

For the choir director.
A Psalm of David.
1 RESCUE me, O Yahweh, from
    evil men;
    Guard me from violent men
2 Who think up evil things in
    their hearts;
    They continually stir up
      wars.
3 They sharpen their tongues
    as a serpent;
    Poison of an asp is under
      their lips.   Selah.

4 Keep me, O Yahweh, from the
    hands of the wicked;
    Guard me from violent men
    Who give thought to trip up
      my steps.
5 The proud have hidden a trap
    for me, and cords;
    They have spread a net by the
      wayside;
    They have set snares for me.
                    Selah.

6 I said to Yahweh, "You are
    my God;
    Give ear, O Yahweh, to the voice
      of my supplications.
7 "O Yahweh, O Lord, the strength
    of my salvation,
    You have covered my head in the
      day of battle.
8 "Do not grant, O Yahweh, the
    desires of the wicked;
    Do not promote his *evil* scheme,
      that they *not* be exalted.
                    Selah.

9 "As for the head of those who
    surround me,
    May the trouble *from* their lips
      cover them.
10 "May burning coals be shaken
    out upon them;
    May He cause them to fall into
      the fire,
    Into bottomless pits from which
      they can never rise.
11 "May a slanderer not be
    established in the earth;
    May evil hunt the violent man
      speedily."

12 I know that Yahweh will maintain
    the cause for the afflicted
And judgment for the needy.
13 Surely the righteous will give
    thanks to Your name;
The upright will abide in Your
    presence.

PSALM 141

My Prayer as Incense Before You

A Psalm of David.

1 O Yahweh, I call upon You;
    hasten to me!
Give ear to my voice when I call
    to You!
2 May my prayer be established as
    incense before You;
The lifting up of my hands as
    the evening offering.
3 Set a guard, O Yahweh, over my
    mouth;
Keep watch over the door of
    my lips.
4 Do not incline my heart to any
    evil thing,
To practice deeds in wickedness
With men who are workers of
    iniquity;
And do not let me eat of their
    delicacies.

5 Let the righteous smite me in
    lovingkindness and
    reprove me;
It is oil upon the head;
Let not my head refuse it,
For still my prayer is against
    their evil deeds.

6 Their judges are thrown down
    by the sides of the cliff,
And they hear my words, for
    they are pleasant.
7 As when one plows and splits
    open the earth,
Our bones have been scattered
    at the mouth of Sheol.

8 For my eyes are toward You,
    O Yahweh, O Lord;
In You I take refuge; do not pour
    out my soul *to death*.
9 Keep me from the jaws of the trap
    which they have set for me,
And from the snares of workers
    of iniquity.
10 Let the wicked fall into their
    own nets,
As for myself—meanwhile, I am
    passing by.

PSALM 142

Give Heed to My Cry

A Maskil of David. When he
was in the cave. A Prayer.

1 WITH my voice to Yahweh,
    I cry aloud;
With my voice to Yahweh, I
    make supplication.
2 I pour out my complaint
    before Him;
I declare my distress before Him.
3 When my spirit was faint
    within me,
You knew my path.
In the way where I walk
They have hidden a trap for me.

4 Look to the right and see;
  That there is no one who
      regards me;
  A *way of* escape has been
      destroyed from me;
  No one cares for my soul.

5 I cried out to You, O Yahweh;
  I said, "You are my refuge,
  My portion in the land of the
      living.
6 "Give heed to my cry of
      lamentation,
  For I am brought very low;
  Deliver me from my
      persecutors,
  For they are too strong for me.
7 "Bring my soul out of prison,
  To give thanks to Your name;
  The righteous will encircle me,
  For You will deal bountifully
      with me."

PSALM 143

My Soul Reaches for You

A Psalm of David.

1 O Yahweh, hear my prayer,
  Give ear to my supplications!
  Answer me in Your faithfulness,
      in Your righteousness!
2 And do not enter into judgment
      with Your slave,
  For no one living is righteous in
      Your sight.
3 For the enemy has pursued
      my soul;
  He has crushed my life to the
      ground;

He has made me inhabit dark
    places, like those who have
    long been dead.
4 Therefore my spirit was faint
    within me;
  My heart was appalled
      within me.

5 I remember the days of old;
  I meditate on all You have done;
  I muse on the work of Your
      hands.
6 I stretch out my hands to You;
  My soul *reaches* for You like a
      weary land.   Selah.

7 Answer me quickly, O Yahweh,
      my spirit wastes away;
  Do not hide Your face from me,
  Or I will become like those who
      go down to the pit.
8 Cause me to hear Your
      lovingkindness in the
      morning;
  For I trust in You;
  Cause me to know the way in
      which I should walk;
  For to You I lift up my soul.
9 Deliver me from my enemies,
      O Yahweh,
  I have concealed *myself* in You.

10 Teach me to do Your will,
   For You are my God;
   Let Your good Spirit lead me on
       level ground.
11 For the sake of Your name,
       O Yahweh, revive me.
   In Your righteousness bring my
       soul out of distress.

12 And in Your lovingkindness, cut
off my enemies
And cause all those who assail
my soul to perish,
For I am Your slave.

PSALM 144

Blessed Be Yahweh, My Rock

Of David.

1 BLESSED be Yahweh, my rock,
Who trains my hands for war,
My fingers for battle;
2 My lovingkindness and my
fortress,
My stronghold and my
deliverer,
My shield and He in whom I
take refuge,
Who subdues my people
under me.
3 O Yahweh, what is man, that You
know him?
Or the son of man, that You
think of him?
4 Man is like a breath;
His days are like a passing
shadow.

5 O Yahweh, bow Your heavens,
and come down;
Touch the mountains, that they
may smoke.
6 Flash forth lightning and scatter
them;
Send out Your arrows and
confuse them.
7 Send forth Your hand from
on high;

Set me free and deliver me out
of many waters,
Out of the hand of foreigners
8 Whose mouth speaks
worthlessness,
And whose right hand is a right
hand of lying.

9 O God, I will sing a new song
to You;
Upon a harp of ten strings I will
sing praises to You,
10 Who gives salvation to kings,
Who sets David His servant free
from the evil sword.
11 Set me free and deliver me out
of the hand of the sons of a
foreigner,
Whose mouth speaks
worthlessness
And whose right hand is a right
hand of lying.

12 That our sons would be as grown-
up plants in their youth,
And our daughters as corner
pillars fashioned as for
a palace;
13 *That* our granaries would be
full, furnishing every kind
of produce,
And our flocks would bring
forth thousands and ten
thousands in our *fields*
outside;
14 That our cattle would bear
Without mishap and without
loss,
And without outcry in our
streets!

15 How blessed are the people for
     whom this is so;
   How blessed are the people for
     whom God is Yahweh!

PSALM 145

Yahweh's Greatness Is Unsearchable

A Praise of David.

1 I will exalt You, my God,
     O King,
   And I will bless Your name
     forever and ever.
2 Every day I will bless You,
   And I will praise Your name
     forever and ever.
3 Great is Yahweh, and highly to
     be praised,
   And His greatness is
     unsearchable.
4 One generation shall laud Your
     works to another,
   And shall declare Your mighty
     deeds.
5 On the glorious splendor of
     Your majesty
   And on the words of Your
     wondrous deeds, I will
     muse.
6 Men shall speak of the
     strength of Your
     fearsome acts,
   And I will recount Your
     greatness.
7 They shall pour forth the
     memory of Your abundant
     goodness
   And will shout joyfully of Your
     righteousness.

8 Yahweh is gracious and
     compassionate;
   Slow to anger and great in
     lovingkindness.
9 Yahweh is good to all,
   And His compassions are over
     all His works.
10 All Your works, O Yahweh, shall
     give thanks to You,
   And Your holy ones shall
     bless You.
11 They shall speak of the glory
     of Your kingdom
   And talk of Your might;
12 To make known to the sons of
     men His mighty deeds
   And the glory of the majesty
     of His kingdom.
13 Your kingdom is an everlasting
     kingdom,
   And Your dominion *endures*
     from generation to every
     generation.

14 Yahweh sustains all who fall
   And raises up all who are bowed
     down.
15 The eyes of all wait on You,
   And You give them their food in
     due time.
16 You open Your hand
   And satisfy the desire of every
     living thing.

17 Yahweh is righteous in all His ways
   And holy in all His works.
18 Yahweh is near to all who call
     upon Him,
   To all who call upon Him in
     truth.

19 He will work out the desire of
   those who fear Him;
   He will hear their cry for help
   and He will save them.
20 Yahweh keeps all who
   love Him,
   But all the wicked He will
   destroy.
21 My mouth will speak the praise
   of Yahweh,
   And all flesh will bless His holy
   name forever and ever.

PSALM 146

I Will Praise Yahweh Throughout
My Life

1 PRAISE Yah!
  Praise Yahweh, O my soul!
2 I will praise Yahweh throughout
  my life;
  I will sing praises to my God
  while I have my being.
3 Do not trust in nobles,
  In *merely* a son of man, in whom
  there is no salvation.
4 His spirit departs, he returns to
  the earth;
  In that very day his plans
  perish.
5 How blessed is he whose help is
  the God of Jacob,
  Whose hope is in Yahweh
  his God,
6 Who made heaven and earth,
  The sea and all that is in them;
  Who keeps truth forever;
7 Who does justice for the
  oppressed;

Who gives food to the hungry.
Yahweh sets the prisoners free.

8 Yahweh opens *the eyes of* the
  blind;
  Yahweh raises up those who are
  bowed down;
  Yahweh loves the righteous;
9 Yahweh keeps the
  sojourners;
  He helps up the orphan and the
  widow,
  But He bends the way of the
  wicked.
10 Yahweh will reign forever,
   Your God, O Zion, from
   generation to generation.
   Praise Yah!

PSALM 147

He Heals the Brokenhearted

1 PRAISE Yah!
  For it is good to sing praises to
  our God;
  For it is pleasant *and* praise is
  becoming.
2 Yahweh builds up
  Jerusalem;
  He gathers the outcasts of
  Israel.
3 *He is* the One who heals the
  brokenhearted
  And who binds up their
  wounds;
4 Who counts the number of the
  stars;
  He gives names to all of
  them.

5 Great is our Lord and abundant
 in power;
 His discernment is infinite.
6 Yahweh helps up the
 afflicted;
 He brings down the wicked to
 the ground.

7 Sing to Yahweh with
 thanksgiving;
 Sing praises to our God on
 the lyre.
8 *He is* the One who covers the
 heavens with clouds,
 The One who provides rain
 for the earth,
 The One who makes grass
 to sprout on the
 mountains,
9 Who gives to the animal its
 food,
 And to the young ravens which
 call out.
10 He does not delight in the
 might of the horse;
 He does not take pleasure
 in the legs of a man.
11 Yahweh is pleased with
 those who fear Him,
 Those who wait for His
 lovingkindness.

12 Laud Yahweh, O Jerusalem!
 Praise your God, O Zion!
13 For He strengthened the
 bars of your gates;
 He blessed your sons
 within you.
14 *He is* the One who sets peace
 in your borders,

He satisfies you with the finest
 of the wheat,
15 The One who sends forth His
 command to the earth;
 His word runs very swiftly,
16 The One who gives snow like
 wool;
 He scatters the frost like ashes,
17 Who casts forth His ice as
 fragments;
 Who can stand before His cold?
18 He sends forth His word and
 melts them;
 He causes His wind to blow and
 so the waters flow,
19 Who declares His words to
 Jacob,
 His statutes and His judgments
 to Israel.
20 He has not done so with any
 nation;
 So as for His judgments, they
 have not known them.
 Praise Yah!

PSALM 148

Praise Yahweh!

1 PRAISE Yah!
 Praise Yahweh from the
 heavens;
 Praise Him in the heights!
2 Praise Him, all His angels;
 Praise Him, all His hosts!
3 Praise Him, sun and moon;
 Praise Him, all stars of light!
4 Praise Him, heavens of heavens,
 And the waters that are above
 the heavens!

5 Let them praise the name of
     Yahweh,
   For He commanded and they
     were created.
6 He caused them to stand forever
     and ever;
   He gave a statute and it will
     never pass away.

7 Praise Yahweh from the
     earth,
   Sea monsters and all deeps;
8 Fire and hail, snow and
     clouds;
   Stormy wind, doing His word;
9 Mountains and all hills;
   Fruit trees and all cedars;
10 Beasts and all cattle;
   Creeping things and winged
     bird;
11 Kings of the earth and all
     peoples;
   Princes and all judges of the
     earth;
12 Both choice men as well as
     virgins;
   The old with the young.

13 Let them praise the name of
     Yahweh,
   For His name alone is set on
     high;
   His splendor is above earth and
     heaven.
14 And He has raised up a horn for
     His people,
   Praise for all His holy ones;
   For the sons of Israel, a people
     near to Him.
   Praise Yah!

PSALM 149

Yahweh Takes Pleasure in His People

1 PRAISE Yah!
   Sing to Yahweh a new song,
   His praise in the assembly of the
     holy ones.
2 Let Israel be glad in his Maker;
   Let the sons of Zion rejoice in
     their King.
3 Let them praise His name with
     dancing;
   With tambourine and lyre let
     them sing praises to Him.
4 For Yahweh takes pleasure in
     His people;
   He will beautify the afflicted
     ones with salvation.

5 Let the holy ones exult in
     glory;
   Let them sing for joy on
     their beds.
6 *Let* the exaltations of God *be* in
     their throats,
   And a two-edged sword in
     their hand,
7 To execute vengeance on the
     nations
   And punishments on the
     peoples,
8 To bind their kings with
     chains
   And their honored men with
     fetters of iron,
9 To execute on them the
     judgment written;
   This is the majesty of all His
     holy ones.
   Praise Yah!

PSALM 150

Praise Him, Praise Yah!

1 PRAISE Yah!
  Praise God in His sanctuary;
  Praise Him in His mighty
    expanse.
2 Praise Him for His mighty
    deeds;
  Praise Him according to the
    abundance of His
    greatness.

3 Praise Him with trumpet blast;
  Praise Him with harp and lyre.
4 Praise Him with tambourine
    and dancing;
  Praise Him with stringed
    instruments and pipe.
5 Praise Him with resounding
    cymbals;
  Praise Him with clashing cymbals.
6 Let everything that has breath
    praise Yah.
  Praise Yah!

THE PROVERBS

CHAPTER 1

To Know Wisdom

THE proverbs of Solomon the son of David, king of Israel:

2 To know wisdom and discipline,
To understand the sayings of understanding,

3 To receive discipline *that leads to* insight,
Righteousness, justice, and equity,

4 To give prudence to the simple,
To the youth knowledge and discretion;

5 Let the wise man hear and increase in learning,
And a man of understanding will acquire guidance,

6 To understand a proverb and an enigma,
The words of the wise and their riddles.

7 The fear of Yahweh is the beginning of knowledge;
Ignorant fools despise wisdom and discipline.

The Enticement of Sinners

8 Hear, my son, your father's discipline
And do not abandon your mother's instruction;

9 For they are a garland of grace for your head
And ornaments about your neck.

10 My son, if sinners entice you,
Do not be willing.

11 If they say, "Come with us,
Let us lie in wait for blood,
Let us ambush the innocent without cause;

12 Let us swallow them alive like Sheol,
And whole, as those who go down to the pit;

13 We will find all *kinds* of precious wealth,
We will fill our houses with spoil;

14 Cast in your lot with us,
We shall all have one purse,"

15 My son, do not walk in the way with them.
Withhold your feet from their pathway,

16 For their feet run to evil
And they hasten to shed blood.

17 For it is no use that a net is spread
In the sight of any bird;

18 But they lie in wait for their own blood;
They ambush their own lives.

19 So are the paths of everyone who is greedy for gain;
It takes away the life of its possessors.

The Call of Wisdom

20 Wisdom shouts in the street,
She gives forth her voice in the
square;

21 At the head of the noisy *streets*
she calls out;
At the entrance of the gates
in the city she utters her
sayings:

22 "How long, O simple ones, will
you love simplicity?
And scoffers delight in scoffing
And fools hate knowledge?

23 "Turn to my reproof,
Behold, I will pour out my spirit
on you;
I will make my words known
to you.

24 "Because I called and you
refused,
I stretched out my hand and no
one paid attention;

25 And you neglected all my
counsel
And were not willing to accept
my reproof;

26 I will also laugh at your
disaster;
I will mock when your dread
comes,

27 When your dread comes like a
storm
And your disaster comes like a
whirlwind,
When distress and anguish
come upon you.

28 "Then they will call on me, but I
will not answer;
They will seek me earnestly but
they will not find me,

29 Because they hated knowledge
And did not choose the fear of
Yahweh.

30 "They were not willing to accept
my counsel,
They spurned all my reproof.

31 "So they shall eat of the fruit of
their way
And be satisfied with their own
devices.

32 "For the turning away of the
simple will kill them,
And the complacency of fools
will destroy them.

33 "But he who listens to me shall
dwell securely
And will be at ease from the
dread of evil."

CHAPTER 2

Yahweh Gives Wisdom

1 MY son, if you will receive my
words
And treasure my
commandments within you,

2 To make your ear pay attention
to wisdom,
Incline your heart to
discernment;

3 For if you call out for
understanding,
Give your voice for discernment;

4 If you seek her as silver
And search for her as for hidden
treasures;

5 Then you will understand the
fear of Yahweh
And find the knowledge of God.

6 For Yahweh gives wisdom;
From His mouth *come* knowledge
and discernment.
7 He stores up sound wisdom for
the upright,
A shield to those who walk in
integrity,
8 To guard the paths of justice,
And He keeps the way of His
holy ones.
9 Then you will understand
righteousness and justice
And equity—every good track.
10 For wisdom will enter your
heart
And knowledge will be pleasant
to your soul;
11 Discretion will keep you,
Discernment will guard you,
12 To deliver you from the way
of evil,
From the man who speaks
perverse things;
13 From those who forsake the
paths of uprightness
To walk in the ways of darkness;
14 Who are glad to do evil
And they rejoice in the
perversity of evil;
15 Whose paths are crooked,
And who are devious in their
tracks;
16 To deliver you from the strange
woman,
From the foreign woman who
flatters with her words;
17 Who forsakes the close
companion of her youth
And forgets the covenant of
her God;

18 For her house sinks down to
death
And her tracks *descend* to the
dead;
19 All who go to her will not
return,
And they will not reach the
paths of life.
20 So that you will walk in the way
of good men
And keep to the paths of the
righteous.
21 For the upright will dwell in
the land
And the blameless will remain
in it;
22 But the wicked will be cut off
from the land
And the treacherous will be torn
away from it.

CHAPTER 3

Trust, Fear, and Honor Yahweh

1 MY son, do not forget my law,
But let your heart guard my
commandments;
2 For length of days and years
of life
And peace they will add
to you.
3 Do not let lovingkindness and
truth forsake you;
Bind them around your neck,
Write them on the tablet of your
heart.
4 So you will find favor and good
insight
In the eyes of God and man.

5 Trust in Yahweh with all your
    heart
  And do not lean on your own
    understanding.
6 In all your ways acknowledge
    Him,
  And He will make your paths
    straight.
7 Do not be wise in your own eyes;
  Fear Yahweh and turn away
    from evil.
8 It will be healing to your body
  And refreshment to your bones.
9 Honor Yahweh from your wealth
  And from the first of all your
    produce;
10 So your barns will be filled with
    plenty
  And your vats will burst with
    new wine.
11 My son, do not reject the
    discipline of Yahweh
  Or loathe His reproof,
12 For whom Yahweh loves He
    reproves,
  Even as a father *reproves* the son
    in whom he delights.

13 How blessed is the man who
    finds wisdom
  And the man who obtains
    discernment.
14 For her profit is better than the
    profit of silver
  And her produce better than
    fine gold.
15 She is more precious than
    pearls;
  And nothing you desire
    compares with her.

16 Length of days is in her right
    hand;
  In her left hand are riches and
    glory.
17 Her ways are pleasant ways
  And all her pathways are
    peace.
18 She is a tree of life to those who
    seize her,
  And all those who hold her fast
    are blessed.
19 Yahweh by wisdom founded the
    earth,
  By discernment He established
    the heavens.
20 By His knowledge the deeps
    were split up
  And the skies drip with dew.
21 My son, let them not deviate
    from your eyes;
  Guard sound wisdom and
    discretion,
22 So they will be life for your
    soul
  And grace for your neck.
23 Then you will walk in your way
    securely
  And your foot will not stumble.
24 When you lie down, you will not
    be in dread;
  You will lie down, and your
    sleep will be pleasant.
25 Do not be afraid of sudden
    dread
  Nor of the storm of the wicked
    when it comes;
26 For Yahweh will be your
    confidence
  And will keep your foot from
    being caught.

27 Do not withhold good from
those to whom it is due,
When it is in your hand to do *it*.

28 Do not say to your neighbor,
"Go, and come back,
And tomorrow I will give *it*,"
When it is there with you.

29 Do not devise harm against
your neighbor,
While he lives securely
beside you.

30 Do not contend with a man
without cause,
If he has dealt you no harm.

31 Do not envy a man of violence
And do not choose any of
his ways.

32 For the devious one is an
abomination to Yahweh;
But His secret council is with
the upright.

33 The curse of Yahweh is on the
house of the wicked one,
But He blesses the abode of the
righteous.

34 Though He scoffs at the
scoffers,
Yet He gives grace to the
humble.

35 The wise will inherit glory,
But fools raise up disgrace.

CHAPTER 4

A Father's Wise Instruction

1 HEAR, *O* sons, the discipline of
a father,
And pay attention that you may
know understanding,

2 For I give you sound learning;
Do not forsake my instruction.

3 When I was a son to my father,
Tender and the only son before
my mother,

4 Then he instructed me and said
to me,
"Let your heart hold fast my
words;
Keep my commandments
and live;

5 Acquire wisdom! Acquire
understanding!
Do not forget and do not turn
away from the sayings of
my mouth.

6 "Do not forsake her, and she
will keep you;
Love her, and she will guard
you.

7 "The beginning of wisdom *is*:
Acquire wisdom;
And with all your acquiring,
acquire understanding.

8 "Prize her, and she will
exalt you;
She will honor you if you
embrace her.

9 "She will give for your head a
garland of grace;
She will present you with a
crown of beauty."

10 Hear, my son, and receive my
sayings
And the years of your life will
be many.

11 I have instructed you in the way
of wisdom;
I have led you in upright tracks.

12 When you walk, your steps will
   not be impeded;
   And if you run, you will not
   stumble.
13 Seize discipline; do not let go.
   Guard her, for she is your life.
14 Do not enter the path of
   wicked men
   And do not step into the way of
   evil men.
15 Avoid it, do not pass by it;
   Stray from it and pass on.
16 For they do not sleep unless
   they do evil;
   And they are robbed of sleep
   unless they make *someone*
   stumble.
17 For they eat the bread of
   wickedness
   And drink the wine of violence.
18 But the path of the righteous is
   like the light of dawn,
   That shines brighter and
   brighter until the fullness
   of day.
19 The way of the wicked is like
   thick darkness;
   They do not know over what
   they stumble.

20 My son, pay attention to my
   words;
   Incline your ear to my sayings.
21 Do not let them deviate from
   your eyes;
   Keep them in the midst of your
   heart.
22 For they are life to those who
   find them
   And healing to all his flesh.

23 Guard your heart with all
   diligence,
   For from it *flow* the springs
   of life.
24 Put away from you a perverse
   mouth
   And put devious lips far
   from you.
25 Let your eyes look directly
   ahead
   And *even* let your eyelids be
   fixed straight in front
   of you.
26 Watch the track of your feet
   And all your ways will be
   established.
27 Do not turn to the right nor to
   the left;
   Turn your foot from evil.

CHAPTER 5

Warning Against Adultery

1 MY son, pay attention to my
   wisdom,
   Incline your ear to my
   discernment;
2 That you may keep discretion
   And that your lips may guard
   knowledge.
3 For the lips of a strange woman
   drip honey
   And smoother than oil is her
   speech;
4 But her end is bitter as
   wormwood,
   Sharp as a two-edged sword.
5 Her feet go down to death,
   Her steps take hold of Sheol,

6 Lest she watch the path of life;
   Her tracks are unstable, she
      does not know *it*.

7 So now, *my* sons, listen to me
   And do not turn away from the
      words of my mouth.

8 Keep your way far from her
   And do not go near the door of
      her house,

9 Lest you give your splendor to
      others
   And your years to the cruel one;

10 Lest strangers be satisfied by
      your strength
   And by your painful labor, *those*
      in the house of a foreigner;

11 And you groan at your end,
   When your flesh and your body
      are consumed;

12 And you say, "How I have hated
      discipline!
   And my heart spurned reproof!

13 "I have not listened to the voice
      of my instructors,
   And I have not inclined my ear
      to my teachers!

14 "I was almost in utter ruin
   In the midst of the assembly and
      congregation."

15 Drink water from your own
      cistern
   And fresh water from your
      own well.

16 Should your springs be
      dispersed abroad,
   Streams of water in the streets?

17 Let them be for you alone,
   And not for strangers with you.

18 Let your fountain be blessed,
   And be glad in the wife of your
      youth.

19 *As* a loving hind and a
      graceful doe,
   Let her breasts satisfy you at
      all times;
   Be intoxicated always with
      her love.

20 So why should you, my son, be
      intoxicated with a strange
      woman
   And embrace the bosom of a
      foreign woman?

21 For the ways of a man are before
      the eyes of Yahweh,
   And He watches all his tracks.

22 His own iniquities will capture
      him *who is* the wicked one,
   And with the cords of his sin he
      will be held fast.

23 He will die for lack of
      discipline,
   And in the abundance of his
      folly he will stumble in
      intoxication.

CHAPTER 6

Practical Warnings

1 MY son, if you have become a
      guarantor for your
      neighbor,
   Have struck your hands *in
      pledge* for a stranger,

2 *If* you have been snared with the
      words of your mouth,
   Have been caught with the
      words of your mouth,

3 Do this then, my son, and
   deliver yourself;
   Since you have come into the
   hand of your neighbor,
   Go, humble yourself, and badger
   your neighbor.
4 Give no sleep to your eyes,
   Nor slumber to your eyelids;
5 Deliver yourself like a gazelle
   from *the hunter's* hand
   And like a bird from the hand of
   the fowler.

6 Go to the ant, O sluggard,
   Observe her ways and be wise,
7 Which, having no chief,
   Officer or ruler,
8 Prepares her food in the summer
   And gathers her provision in the
   harvest.
9 How long will you lie down,
   O sluggard?
   When will you arise from your
   sleep?
10 "A little sleep, a little slumber,
   A little folding of the hands to
   rest"—
11 Your poverty will come in like a
   vagabond
   And your want like an armed man.

12 A vile person, a wicked man,
   Is the one who walks with a
   perverse mouth,
13 Who winks with *his* eyes, who
   signals with his feet,
   Who points with his fingers;
14 Who *with* perversity in his heart
   continually devises evil,
   Who spreads contentions.

15 Therefore his disaster will come
   suddenly;
   Instantly he will be broken
   and there will be no
   healing.

16 There are six things which
   Yahweh hates,
   Even seven which are an
   abomination to Him:
17 Haughty eyes, a lying tongue,
   And hands that shed innocent
   blood,
18 A heart that devises wicked
   thoughts,
   Feet that hasten to run to evil,
19 A false witness *who* breathes
   out lies,
   And one who spreads strife
   among brothers.

Warning Against Adultery

20 My son, observe the
   commandment of your
   father
   And do not abandon the law of
   your mother;
21 Bind them continually on your
   heart;
   Tie them around your neck.
22 When you walk about, they will
   lead you;
   When you sleep, they will keep
   watch over you;
   And when you awake, they will
   speak to you.
23 For the commandment is a lamp
   and the law is light;
   And reproofs for discipline are
   the way of life

24 To keep you from the evil
woman,
From the smooth tongue of the
foreign woman.

25 Do not desire her beauty in your
heart,
Nor let her capture you with her
eyelids.

26 For on account of a harlot *one is
reduced* to a loaf of bread,
And an adulteress hunts for the
precious life.

27 Can a man take fire in his bosom
And his clothes not be burned?

28 Or can a man walk on hot coals
And his feet not be scorched?

29 So is the one who goes in to his
neighbor's wife;
Whoever touches her will not go
unpunished.

30 *Men* do not despise a thief if he
steals
To fill himself when he is
hungry;

31 But when he is found, he must
repay sevenfold;
He must give all the substance
of his house.

32 The one who commits adultery
with a woman is lacking a
heart *of wisdom*;
He who would destroy his soul
does it.

33 Wounds and disgrace he will
find,
And his reproach will not be
blotted out.

34 For jealousy enrages a man,
And he will not spare in the day
of vengeance.

35 He will not accept any
ransom,
He will not be willing though
you give many bribes.

CHAPTER 7

The Adulteress' Trap

1 MY son, keep my words
And treasure my commandments
within you.

2 Keep my commandments
and live,
And my law as the apple of
your eye.

3 Bind them on your fingers;
Write them on the tablet of your
heart.

4 Say to wisdom, "You are my
sister,"
And call understanding *your*
intimate friend;

5 In order to keep you from the
strange woman,
From the foreign woman who
flatters with her words.

6 For at the window of my
house
I looked out through my
lattice,

7 And I saw among the simple,
And discerned among the sons
A young man lacking a heart *of
wisdom*,

8 Passing through the street near
her corner;
And he strides along the way to
her house,

9 In the twilight, in the evening of
    that day,
  In the middle of the night, and
    in the thick darkness.
10 And behold, a woman *comes* to
    meet him,
  Dressed as a harlot and cunning
    of heart.
11 She is boisterous and rebellious,
  Her feet do not dwell at home;
12 Stepping in the streets, stepping
    in the squares,
  And near every corner she lies
    in wait.
13 So she seizes him and kisses him
  And with a brazen face she says
    to him:
14 "The sacrifices of peace
    offerings are with me;
  Today I paid my vows.
15 "Therefore I have come out to
    meet you,
  To seek your face earnestly, and
    I have found you.
16 "I have spread my couch with
    coverings,
  With colored linens of Egypt.
17 "I have sprinkled my bed
  With myrrh, aloes, and cinnamon.
18 "Come, then, let us drink our fill
    as lovers until morning;
  Let us delight ourselves with the
    pleasures of love.
19 "For my husband is not at home,
  He has gone on a journey *far
    away*;
20 He took a bag of silver in his
    hand,
  On the day of the full moon he
    will come home."

21 With her abundant persuasions
    she entices him;
  With her flattering lips she
    drives him *to herself*.
22 He suddenly follows her
  As an ox goes to the slaughter,
  Or as *one in* fetters to the
    discipline of an ignorant fool,
23 Until an arrow pierces through
    his liver;
  As a bird hastens to the snare,
  And he does not know that it
    will cost him his soul.

24 So now, *my* sons, listen to me,
  And pay attention to the words
    of my mouth.
25 Do not let your heart go astray
    into her ways,
  Do not wander into her pathways.
26 For many are the slain *whom*
    she has cast down,
  And numerous are all those
    killed by her.
27 The ways to Sheol *are in* her
    house,
  Descending to the chambers of
    death.

CHAPTER 8

The Blessing of Wisdom

1 DOES not wisdom call,
  And discernment give forth her
    voice?
2 At the top of the heights upon
    the way,
  Where the pathways meet, she
    takes her stand;

3 Beside the gates, at the opening
     to the city,
  At the entrance of the doors, she
     makes a shout:
4 "To you, O men, I call,
  And my voice is to the sons
     of men.
5 "O simple ones, understand
     prudence;
  And, O fools, understand a heart
     of wisdom.
6 "Listen, for I will speak noble
     things;
  And the opening of my lips *will
     reveal* upright things.
7 "For my mouth will utter
     truth;
  And wickedness is an
     abomination to my lips.
8 "All the words of my mouth are
     in righteousness;
  There is nothing twisted or
     crooked in them.
9 "They are all straightforward to
     him who understands,
  And right to those who find
     knowledge.
10 "Take my discipline and not
     silver,
  And knowledge rather than
     choicest fine gold.
11 "For wisdom is better than
     pearls;
  And all desirable things cannot
     compare with her.

12 "I, wisdom, dwell with
     prudence,
  And I find knowledge *and*
     discretion.

13 "The fear of Yahweh is to
     hate evil;
  Pride and arrogance and the
     evil way
  And the mouth of perverted
     words, I hate.
14 "Counsel is mine and sound
     wisdom;
  I am understanding, might is
     mine.
15 "By me kings reign,
  And rulers mark out
     righteousness.
16 "By me princes rule, and nobles,
  All who judge rightly.
17 "I love those who love me;
  And those who earnestly seek
     me will find me.
18 "Riches and glory are with me,
  Enduring wealth and
     righteousness.
19 "My fruit is better than fine gold,
     even pure gold,
  And my produce *better* than
     choice silver.
20 "I walk in the path of
     righteousness,
  In the midst of the pathways of
     justice,
21 To give those who love me an
     inheritance of wealth,
  That I may fill their treasuries.

22 "Yahweh possessed me at the
     beginning of His way,
  Before His deeds of old.
23 "From everlasting I was
     installed,
  From the beginning, from the
     earliest times of the earth.

24 "When there were no depths
    I was brought forth,
    When there were no springs
    heavy with water.
25 "Before the mountains were
    settled,
    Before the hills I was brought
    forth;
26 While He had not yet made
    the earth and the *fields*
    outside,
    Nor the first dust of the world.
27 "When He established the
    heavens, I was there,
    When He marked out a circle on
    the face of the deep,
28 When He made firm the skies
    above,
    When the springs of the deep
    became strong,
29 When He set for the sea its
    boundary
    So that the water would not
    pass over His command,
    When He marked out the
    foundations of the earth;
30 Then I was beside Him, *as* a
    master workman;
    And I was a daily delight,
    Rejoicing always before Him,
31 Rejoicing in the world, His
    earth,
    My delight *is* in the sons
    of men.

32 "So now, O sons, listen to me,
    For blessed are they who keep
    my ways.
33 "Hear discipline and be wise,
    And do not neglect *it*.

34 "How blessed is the man who
    hears me,
    To watch daily at my doors,
    To keep watch at my doorposts.
35 "For he who finds me finds life
    And obtains favor from Yahweh.
36 "But he who sins against me does
    violence to his own soul;
    All those who hate me love death."

CHAPTER 9

Wisdom and Foolishness Call Out

1 WISDOM has built her house,
    She has hewn out her seven
    pillars;
2 She has slaughtered her cattle,
    she has mixed her wine;
    She has also prepared her table;
3 She has sent out her maidens,
    she calls
    From the tops of the heights of
    the city:
4 "Whoever is simple, let him turn
    in here!"
    To him who lacks a heart *of
    wisdom* she says,
5 "Come, eat of my bread
    And drink of the wine I have
    mixed.
6 "Forsake *your* simplicity and live,
    And step into the way of
    understanding."

7 He who disciplines a scoffer
    receives disgrace for himself,
    And he who reproves a wicked
    man *receives* injury for
    himself.

8 Do not reprove a scoffer, lest he
  hate you,
  Reprove a wise man and he will
  love you.
9 Give *knowledge* to a wise
  man and he will be
  still wiser,
  Make a righteous man know
  it and he will increase *his*
  learning.
10 The fear of Yahweh is the
  beginning of wisdom,
  And the knowledge of the Holy
  One is understanding.
11 For by me your days will
  become many,
  And years of life will be added
  to you.
12 If you are wise, you are wise for
  yourself,
  And if you scoff, you alone will
  bear it.

13 The woman of foolishness is
  boisterous,
  A woman of simplicity, and
  does not know
  anything.
14 She sits at the doorway of her
  house,
  On a seat by the high places of
  the city,
15 To call to those who pass by
  that way,
  Who are making their paths
  straight:
16 "Whoever is simple, let him turn
  in here,"
  And to him who lacks a heart *of*
  wisdom she says,

17 "Stolen water is sweet;
  And bread *eaten* in secret is
  pleasant."
18 But he does not know that the
  dead are there,
  That those she called are in the
  depths of Sheol.

CHAPTER 10

*Contrast of the Righteous
and the Wicked*

THE proverbs of Solomon.
  A wise son makes a father glad,
  But a foolish son is a grief to his
  mother.
2 Treasures *gained* by wickedness
  do not profit,
  But righteousness delivers from
  death.
3 Yahweh will not allow the
  soul of the righteous to
  hunger,
  But He will push away the
  craving of the wicked.
4 Poor is he who works with a
  slack hand,
  But the hand of the diligent
  makes rich.
5 He who gathers in summer
  is a son who acts
  insightfully,
  But he who sleeps in harvest
  is a son who acts
  shamefully.
6 Blessings are on the head of the
  righteous,
  But the mouth of the wicked
  covers up violence.

7 The remembrance of the
   righteous is blessed,
But the name of the wicked
   will rot.

8 The wise of heart will receive
   commandments,
But an ignorant fool of *loose* lips
   will be ruined.

9 He who walks in integrity walks
   securely,
But he who makes his ways
   crooked will be found out.

10 He who winks the eye causes
   pain,
And an ignorant fool of *loose*
   lips will be ruined.

11 The mouth of the righteous is a
   fountain of life,
But the mouth of the wicked
   covers up violence.

12 Hatred stirs up strife,
But love covers all
   transgressions.

13 On the lips of the one who has
   understanding, wisdom is
   found,
But a rod is for the back of
   him who lacks a heart *of*
   wisdom.

14 Wise men store up knowledge,
But the mouth of the ignorant
   fool draws ruin near.

15 The rich man's wealth is his
   strong city,
The ruin of the poor is their
   poverty.

16 The wages of the righteous
   is life,
The income of the wicked,
   punishment.

17 He is *on* the path of life who
   keeps discipline,
But he who forsakes reproof
   makes himself wander about.

18 He who covers up hatred *has*
   lying lips,
And he who spreads a bad
   report is a fool.

19 When there are many
   words, transgression is
   unavoidable,
But he who holds back his lips
   has insight.

20 The tongue of the righteous is
   as choice silver,
The heart of the wicked is *worth*
   little.

21 The lips of the righteous feed
   many,
But ignorant fools die for lack of
   a heart *of wisdom.*

22 It is the blessing of Yahweh that
   makes rich,
And He adds no pain with it.

23 Doing wickedness is like
   laughing to a fool,
And *so is* wisdom to a man of
   discernment.

24 What the wicked dreads will
   come upon him,
But the desire of the righteous
   will be granted.

25 When the whirlwind passes, the
   wicked is no more,
But the righteous *has* an
   everlasting foundation.

26 Like vinegar to the teeth and like
   smoke to the eyes,
So is the sluggard to those who
   send him.

27 The fear of Yahweh prolongs
life,
But the years of the wicked will
be shortened.

28 The expectation of the righteous
is gladness,
But the hope of the wicked will
perish.

29 The way of Yahweh is a
stronghold to the one with
integrity,
But ruin to the workers of
iniquity.

30 The righteous will never be
shaken,
But the wicked will not dwell in
the land.

31 The mouth of the righteous
bears wisdom,
But the tongue of perversions
will be cut out.

32 The lips of the righteous know
what is acceptable,
But the mouth of the wicked
what is perverse.

CHAPTER 11

1 A deceptive balance is an
abomination to Yahweh,
But a just weight is His delight.

2 When arrogance comes, then
comes disgrace,
But with the meek is wisdom.

3 The integrity of the upright will
lead them,
But the crookedness of the
treacherous will destroy
them.

4 Wealth will not profit in the day
of wrath,
But righteousness will deliver
from death.

5 The righteousness of the
blameless will make his way
straight,
But the wicked will fall by his
own wickedness.

6 The righteousness of the
upright will deliver
them,
But the treacherous will be
captured by *their own*
desire.

7 When a wicked man dies, *his*
hope will perish,
And the expectation of vigorous
men perishes.

8 The righteous is rescued from
distress,
But the wicked takes his
place.

9 With *his* mouth the godless man
corrupts his neighbor,
But through knowledge the
righteous will be
rescued.

10 When it goes well with the
righteous, the city exults,
And when the wicked perish,
there is joyful shouting.

11 By the blessing of the upright a
city is raised up,
But by the mouth of the wicked
it is torn down.

12 He who despises his neighbor
lacks a heart *of wisdom*,
But a man of discernment keeps
silent.

13 He who goes about as a
slanderer reveals secrets,
But he who is faithful in spirit
conceals a matter.

14 Where there is no guidance the
people fall,
But in abundance of counselors
there is salvation.

15 If one becomes a guarantor for
a stranger, he will surely
suffer,
But he who hates striking hands
in pledge is secure.

16 A gracious woman holds fast to
glory,
But ruthless men hold fast to
riches.

17 The man of lovingkindness
deals bountifully with his
soul,
But the cruel man brings trouble
on his flesh.

18 The wicked earns deceptive
wages,
But he who sows righteousness
gets a true reward.

19 He who is steadfast in
righteousness *will attain*
to life,
And he who pursues evil *will
bring about* his own death.

20 Those with a crooked heart
are an abomination to
Yahweh,
But those of a blameless way are
His delight.

21 Assuredly, the evil man will not
go unpunished,
But the seed of the righteous
will escape.

22 *As* a ring of gold in a swine's
snout
So is a beautiful woman who
turns away from discretion.

23 The desire of the righteous is
only good,
But the hope of the wicked is
wrath.

24 There is one who scatters, and
yet increases all the more,
And there is one who holds back
what is rightly due, *and yet
results* only in want.

25 The soul that blesses will be
enriched,
And he who waters will himself
be watered.

26 He who withholds grain, the
people will curse him,
But blessing will be on the head
of him who sells *it.*

27 He who earnestly seeks good
seeks favor,
But he who searches for evil, *evil*
will come to him.

28 He who trusts in his riches
will fall,
But the righteous will flourish
like the *green* leaf.

29 He who troubles his own house
will inherit wind,
And the ignorant fool will be a
slave to the wise of heart.

30 The fruit of the righteous is a
tree of life,
And he who is wise wins souls.

31 If the righteous will be repaid in
the earth,
How much more the wicked and
the sinner!

CHAPTER 12

1 WHOEVER loves discipline
    loves knowledge,
But he who hates reproof is
    senseless.

2 A good man will obtain favor
    from Yahweh,
But a man of evil schemes He
    will condemn.

3 A man will not be established by
    wickedness,
But the root of the righteous will
    not be shaken.

4 An excellent wife is the crown of
    her husband,
But she who causes shame is
    like rottenness in his
    bones.

5 The thoughts of the righteous
    are just,
But the guidance of the wicked
    is deceitful.

6 The words of the wicked lie in
    wait for blood,
But the mouth of the upright
    will deliver them.

7 The wicked are overthrown and
    are no more,
But the house of the righteous
    will stand.

8 A man will be praised according
    to his insight,
But one of perverse heart will be
    despised.

9 Better is he who is lightly
    esteemed and has a
    servant
Than he who honors himself
    and lacks bread.

10 A righteous man knows *the
    value of* the life of his
    animal,
But *even* the compassion of the
    wicked is cruel.

11 He who cultivates his land will
    be satisfied with bread,
But he who pursues empty
    things lacks a heart *of
    wisdom.*

12 The wicked man desires a
    stronghold of evil men,
But the root of the righteous
    gives *fruit.*

13 The snare of an evil man is
    in the transgression of
    his lips,
But the righteous *man* will come
    out from distress.

14 A man will be satisfied with
    good by the fruit of his
    mouth,
And the good deed of a man's
    hands will return to him.

15 The way of an ignorant fool is
    right in his own eyes,
But a wise man is he who listens
    to counsel.

16 An ignorant fool's anger is
    known at once,
But a prudent man conceals
    disgrace.

17 He who breathes out truth
    declares what is right,
But a false witness, deceit.

18 There is one who speaks
    rashly like the thrusts
    of a sword,
But the tongue of the wise
    brings healing.

19 Truthful lips will be established
forever,
But a lying tongue is only for a
moment.
20 Deceit is in the heart of those
who devise evil,
But counselors of peace have
gladness.
21 No misfortune befalls the
righteous,
But the wicked are filled with
calamity.
22 Lying lips are an abomination to
Yahweh,
But doers of faithfulness are His
delight.
23 A prudent man conceals
knowledge,
But the heart of fools proclaims
folly.
24 The hand of the diligent will
rule,
But the slack *hand* will be put to
forced labor.
25 Anxiety in a man's heart weighs
it down,
But a good word makes it
glad.
26 The righteous is a guide to his
neighbor,
But the way of the wicked makes
them wander about.
27 A slack *handed* man does not
roast his prey,
But the wealth of a man is
precious for the diligent.
28 In the path of righteousness is
life,
And in *its* pathway there is no
death.

CHAPTER 13

1 A wise son *accepts his* father's
discipline,
But a scoffer does not listen to
rebuke.
2 From the fruit of a man's mouth
he eats what is good,
But the soul of the treacherous
desires violence.
3 The one who guards his mouth
keeps his soul;
The one who opens wide his lips
comes to ruin.
4 The soul of the sluggard craves
and *gets* nothing,
But the soul of the diligent is
enriched.
5 A righteous man hates a lying
word,
But a wicked man acts odiously
and is humiliated.
6 Righteousness guards the one
whose way is blameless,
But wickedness subverts the
sinner.
7 There is one who pretends to be
rich, but has nothing;
Another pretends to be poor, but
has great wealth.
8 The ransom of a man's life is his
wealth,
But the poor hears no rebuke.
9 The light of the righteous is glad,
But the lamp of the wicked
goes out.
10 With arrogance comes only
quarreling,
But with those who receive
counsel is wisdom.

11 Wealth *obtained* from empty
   effort dwindles,
   But the one who gathers with *his*
   hand abounds.
12 Hope deferred makes the heart
   sick,
   But desire fulfilled is a tree
   of life.
13 The one who despises the word
   will be in debt to it,
   But the one who fears the
   commandment will be
   rewarded.
14 The instruction of the wise is a
   fountain of life,
   To turn aside from the snares of
   death.
15 Good insight gives grace,
   But the way of the treacherous is
   unrelenting.
16 Every prudent man acts with
   knowledge,
   But a fool spreads out folly.
17 A wicked messenger falls into
   evil,
   But a faithful envoy *brings*
   healing.
18 Poverty and disgrace *come*
   to him who neglects
   discipline,
   But he who keeps reproof will be
   honored.
19 Desire realized is pleasant to the
   soul,
   But it is an abomination to fools
   to turn away from evil.
20 He who walks with the wise will
   be wise,
   But the friend of fools will suffer
   harm.

21 Evil pursues sinners,
   But the righteous are repaid
   with good.
22 A good man leaves an
   inheritance to his children's
   children,
   And the wealth of the sinner is
   stored up for the righteous.
23 Abundant food *is in* the fallow
   ground of the poor,
   But it is swept away by
   injustice.
24 He who holds back his rod hates
   his son,
   But he who loves him disciplines
   him diligently.
25 The righteous eats to the
   satisfaction of his soul,
   But the stomach of the wicked
   lacks.

CHAPTER 14

1 THE wise woman builds her
   house,
   But the woman of folly tears it
   down with her own hands.
2 He who walks in his uprightness
   fears Yahweh,
   But he who is devious in his
   ways despises Him.
3 In the mouth of the ignorant
   fool is a rod of lofty pride,
   But the lips of the wise will keep
   them.
4 Where no oxen are, the manger
   is clean,
   But much revenue *comes* by the
   strength of the ox.

5 A faithful witness will not lie,
But a false witness breathes
out lies.

6 A scoffer seeks wisdom and
finds none,
But knowledge is easy to one
who has understanding.

7 Leave the presence of a fool,
As you have not known lips of
knowledge *there.*

8 The wisdom of the prudent is to
understand his way,
But the folly of fools is deceit.

9 Ignorant fools scoff at guilt,
But among the upright there is
favor.

10 The heart knows its own
bitterness,
And a stranger does not share
its gladness.

11 The house of the wicked will be
destroyed,
But the tent of the upright will
flourish.

12 There is a way *which seems* right
to a man,
But its end is the way of death.

13 Even in laughter the heart may
be in pain,
And the end of joy may be
grief.

14 The one who turns back in *his*
heart will be satisfied with
his ways,
But a good man will *be satisfied*
with his.

15 The simple believes
everything,
But the prudent one discerns
his steps.

16 A wise man fears and turns away
from evil,
But a fool gets angry and *feels*
secure.

17 A quick-tempered man acts in
folly,
And a man of evil schemes is
hated.

18 The simple inherit folly,
But the prudent are crowned
with knowledge.

19 The evil will bow down before
the good,
And the wicked at the gates of
the righteous.

20 The poor is hated even by his
neighbor,
But those who love the rich are
many.

21 He who despises his neighbor
sins,
But how blessed is he who is
gracious to the poor.

22 Will they not wander in error
who devise evil?
But lovingkindness and truth *will
be to* those who devise good.

23 In all painful labor there is profit,
But *mere* words from the lips
lead only to want.

24 The crown of the wise is their
riches,
But the folly of fools is folly.

25 A truthful witness delivers souls,
But he who breathes out lies is
deceitful.

26 In the fear of Yahweh there is
strong security,
And his children will have
refuge.

27 The fear of Yahweh is a fountain
   of life,
   To turn aside from the snares of
   death.
28 In a multitude of people is a
   king's splendor,
   But in the dearth of people is a
   prince's ruin.
29 He who is slow to anger has
   great discernment,
   But he who is quick-tempered
   raises up folly.
30 A tranquil heart is life to the
   body,
   But jealousy is rottenness to
   the bones.
31 He who oppresses the
   poor reproaches
   his Maker,
   But he who is gracious to the
   needy honors Him.
32 The wicked is thrust down by
   his own evil,
   But the righteous takes refuge
   even in his death.
33 Wisdom rests in the heart
   of one who has
   understanding,
   But in the midst of fools
   it is *merely* made
   known.
34 Righteousness exalts a
   nation,
   But sin is a disgrace to *any*
   people.
35 The king's favor is toward
   a servant who acts
   insightfully,
   But his fury is toward him who
   acts shamefully.

CHAPTER 15

1 A gentle answer turns away
  wrath,
  But a harsh word stirs up
  anger.
2 The tongue of the wise makes
  knowledge *look* good,
  But the mouth of fools pours
  forth folly.
3 The eyes of Yahweh are in every
  place,
  Watching the evil and the good.
4 A tongue that brings healing is a
  tree of life,
  But perversion in it breaks the
  spirit.
5 An ignorant fool spurns his
  father's discipline,
  But he who keeps reproof is
  prudent.
6 The house of the righteous has
  much treasure,
  But in the income of the wicked
  there is trouble.
7 The lips of the wise disperse
  knowledge,
  But the hearts of fools are
  not so.
8 The sacrifice of the wicked is an
  abomination to Yahweh,
  But the prayer of the upright is
  His delight.
9 The way of the wicked is an
  abomination to Yahweh,
  But He loves one who pursues
  righteousness.
10 Grievous discipline is for him
   who forsakes the way;
   He who hates reproof will die.

11 Sheol and Abaddon *lie open*
before Yahweh,
How much more the hearts of
the sons of men!

12 A scoffer does not love one who
reproves him,
He will not go to the wise.

13 A glad heart makes a face *look*
good,
But when the heart is pained,
the spirit is broken.

14 The heart of the one who
has understanding seeks
knowledge,
But the mouth of fools feeds on
folly.

15 All the days of the afflicted are
evil,
But a good heart *has* a continual
feast.

16 Better is a little with the fear of
Yahweh
Than great treasure and turmoil
with it.

17 Better is a dish of vegetables
where there is love
Than a fattened ox and hatred
in it.

18 A hot-tempered man stirs up
strife,
But the slow to anger quiets a
dispute.

19 The way of the sluggard is as a
hedge of thorns,
But the path of the upright is a
highway.

20 A wise son makes a father
glad,
But a foolish man despises his
mother.

21 Folly is gladness to him who
lacks a heart *of wisdom*,
But a man of discernment walks
straight.

22 Without consultation, plans are
frustrated,
But with many counselors they
succeed.

23 A man has gladness in an apt
answer,
And how good is a timely
word!

24 The path of life *leads* upward for
the one who has insight
That he may turn away from
Sheol below.

25 Yahweh will tear down the
house of the proud,
But He will cause the boundary
of the widow to stand.

26 Evil thoughts are an
abomination to Yahweh,
But pleasant words are pure.

27 He who is greedy for gain
troubles his own house,
But he who hates gifts *of bribery*
will live.

28 The heart of the righteous
ponders how to answer,
But the mouth of the wicked
pours forth evil things.

29 Yahweh is far from the wicked,
But He hears the prayer of the
righteous.

30 Bright eyes gladden the heart;
A good report puts fat on the
bones.

31 He whose ear listens to the life-
giving reproof
Will lodge among the wise.

32 He who neglects discipline
   despises his soul,
   But he who listens to reproof
   acquires a heart *of wisdom*.

33 The fear of Yahweh is the
   discipline leading to
   wisdom,
   And before glory *comes*
   humility.

CHAPTER 16

1 THE plans of the heart belong
   to man,
   But the answer of the tongue is
   from Yahweh.

2 All the ways of a man are pure in
   his own sight,
   But Yahweh weighs the motives.

3 Commit your works to Yahweh
   And your plans will be
   established.

4 Yahweh has made everything for
   its own purpose,
   Even the wicked for the day
   of evil.

5 Everyone who is proud in
   heart is an abomination to
   Yahweh;
   Assuredly, he will not be
   unpunished.

6 By lovingkindness and truth
   iniquity is atoned for,
   And by the fear of Yahweh one
   turns away from evil.

7 When a man's ways are pleasing
   to Yahweh,
   He makes even his enemies to
   be at peace with him.

8 Better is a little with
   righteousness
   Than great produce with
   injustice.

9 The heart of man plans his way,
   But Yahweh directs his steps.

10 A divine decision is in the lips of
   the king;
   His mouth should not err in
   judgment.

11 A just balance and scales belong
   to Yahweh;
   All the weights of the bag are
   His work.

12 It is an abomination for kings to
   commit wickedness,
   For in righteousness a throne is
   established.

13 Righteous lips are the delight of
   kings,
   And he who speaks uprightly is
   loved.

14 The wrath of a king is *like*
   messengers of death,
   But a wise man will atone for it.

15 In the light of a king's face
   is life,
   And his favor is like a cloud with
   the late rain.

16 How much better it is to acquire
   wisdom than fine gold!
   And to acquire understanding is
   to be chosen above silver.

17 The highway of the upright is to
   turn away from evil;
   He who guards his way keeps
   his soul.

18 Pride *goes* before destruction,
   And a haughty spirit before
   stumbling.

19 It is better to be humble in spirit
with the lowly
Than to divide the spoil with the
proud.

20 He who considers the word will
find good,
And how blessed is he who
trusts in Yahweh.

21 The wise in heart will be called
understanding,
And sweetness of lips increases
learning.

22 Insight is a fountain of life to
one who has it,
But the discipline of ignorant
fools is folly.

23 The heart of the wise gives
insight to his mouth
And increases learning to
his lips.

24 Pleasant words are a
honeycomb,
Sweet to the soul and healing to
the bones.

25 There is a way *which seems* right
to a man,
But its end is the way of death.

26 A worker's appetite works
for him,
For his mouth urges him *on.*

27 A vile man digs up evil,
And *the words* on his lips are
like scorching fire.

28 A perverse man spreads strife,
And a whisperer separates close
companions.

29 A man of violence entices his
neighbor
And leads him in a way that is
not good.

30 He who winks his eyes *does so* to
devise perverse things;
He who compresses his lips
brings evil to pass.

31 Gray hair is a crown of
beauty;
It is found in the way of
righteousness.

32 He who is slow to anger is better
than the mighty,
And he who rules his own spirit,
than he who captures a city.

33 The lot is cast into the lap,
But its every judgment is from
Yahweh.

CHAPTER 17

1 BETTER is a dry morsel and
tranquility with it
Than a house full of feasting
with strife.

2 A slave who acts insightfully
will rule over a son who acts
shamefully,
And will share in the
inheritance among
brothers.

3 The refining pot is for silver and
the furnace for gold,
But Yahweh tests hearts.

4 An evildoer gives heed to lips of
wickedness;
A liar gives ear to a destructive
tongue.

5 He who mocks the poor
reproaches his Maker;
He who is glad at disaster will
not go unpunished.

6 Grandchildren are the crown of
old men,
And the beauty of sons is their
fathers.

7 Excellent lips are not fitting for a
wicked fool,
Even less are lying lips for a
noble man.

8 A bribe is a charm in the eyes of
its owner;
Wherever he turns, he prospers.

9 He who covers a transgression
seeks love,
But he who repeats a matter
separates close companions.

10 A rebuke goes deeper into one
who understands
Than a hundred blows into a fool.

11 A rebellious man seeks only evil,
So a cruel messenger will be
sent against him.

12 Let a man meet a bear robbed of
her cubs,
Rather than a fool in his folly.

13 He who returns evil for good,
Evil will not depart from his
house.

14 The beginning of strife is *like*
letting out water,
So abandon the dispute before it
breaks out.

15 He who justifies the wicked
and he who condemns the
righteous,
Both of them alike are an
abomination to Yahweh.

16 Why is there a price in the hand
of a fool to acquire wisdom,
When he has no heart *of
wisdom*?

17 A friend loves at all times,
And a brother is born for
adversity.

18 A man lacking a heart *of
wisdom* strikes his hands
in pledge
And becomes guarantor in the
presence of his neighbor.

19 He who loves transgression
loves quarreling;
He who makes his doorway
high seeks destruction.

20 He who has a crooked heart
finds no good,
And he who is perverted in his
tongue falls into evil.

21 He who begets a fool *does so* to
his grief,
And the father of a wicked fool
is not glad.

22 A glad heart is good medicine,
But a broken spirit dries up the
bones.

23 A wicked man receives a bribe
from the bosom
To thrust aside the paths of
justice.

24 Wisdom is in the presence
of the one who
understands,
But the eyes of a fool are on the
ends of the earth.

25 A foolish son is a vexation to his
father
And bitterness to her who gave
birth to him.

26 It is also not good to punish the
righteous,
Nor to strike the noble for *their*
uprightness.

27 He who holds back his words
   has knowledge,
   And he who has a cool spirit is a
   man of discernment.
28 Even an ignorant fool, when he
   keeps silent, is considered
   wise;
   When he closes his lips, he is
   considered understanding.

CHAPTER 18

1 HE who separates himself seeks
   his own desire,
   He breaks out *in dispute* against
   all sound wisdom.
2 A fool does not delight in
   discernment,
   But only in revealing his own
   heart.
3 When a wicked man comes,
   despising also comes,
   And with disgrace *comes*
   reproach.
4 The words of a man's mouth are
   deep waters;
   The fountain of wisdom is a
   flowing brook.
5 To show partiality to the wicked
   is not good,
   Nor to thrust aside the righteous
   in judgment.
6 A fool's lips come with strife,
   And his mouth calls for beatings.
7 A fool's mouth is his ruin,
   And his lips are the snare of his
   soul.
8 The words of a whisperer are
   like dainty morsels,

And they go down into the
   innermost parts of the
   stomach.
9 He also who is slack in his
   work
   Is brother to him who
   destroys.
10 The name of Yahweh is a strong
   tower;
   The righteous runs into it and is
   set securely on high.
11 A rich man's wealth is his
   strong city,
   And like a high wall in his own
   delusion.
12 Before destruction the heart of
   man is haughty,
   But humility *goes* before glory.
13 He who responds with a word
   before he hears,
   It is folly and shame to him.
14 The spirit of a man can endure
   his sickness,
   But *as for* a broken spirit, who
   can bear it?
15 The heart of the understanding
   acquires knowledge,
   And the ear of the wise seeks
   knowledge.
16 A man's gift makes room for him
   And leads him into the presence
   of great men.
17 The first to plead his case *seems*
   right,
   Until another comes and
   examines him.
18 The *cast* lot puts an end to
   contentions
   And decides between the
   mighty ones.

19 A brother offended *is harder to win over* than a strong city,
And contentions are like the bars of a citadel.

20 From the fruit of a man's mouth his stomach will be satisfied;
With the produce of his lips he will be satisfied.

21 Death and life are in the power of the tongue,
And those who love it will eat its fruit.

22 He who finds a wife finds a good thing
And obtains favor from Yahweh.

23 The poor man speaks supplications,
But the rich man answers with strong *words*.

24 A man of *too many* friends *comes* to ruin,
But there is a friend who sticks closer than a brother.

CHAPTER 19

The Counsel of Yahweh Will Stand

1 BETTER is a poor man who walks in his integrity
Than he who is crooked in lips and is a fool.

2 Also it is not good for a person to be without knowledge,
And he who hurries his footsteps sins.

3 The folly of man subverts his way,
But his heart rages against Yahweh.

4 Wealth adds many friends,
But a poor man is separated from his friend.

5 A false witness will not go unpunished,
And he who breathes out lies will not escape.

6 Many will seek the favor of a noble man,
And everyone is a friend to a man who gives gifts.

7 All the brothers of a poor man hate him;
How much more do his friends distance *themselves* from him!
He pursues *them with* words, *but* they are no more.

8 He who acquires a heart *of wisdom* loves his own soul;
He who keeps discernment will find good.

9 A false witness will not go unpunished,
And he who breathes out lies will perish.

10 Luxury is not fitting for a fool;
Much less for a slave to rule over princes.

11 A man's insight makes him slow to anger,
And it is his honor to overlook a transgression.

12 The king's wrath is like the roaring of a lion,
But his favor is like dew on the grass.

13 A foolish son is destruction to his father,

And the contentions of a wife
are a constant dripping.

14 House and wealth are an
inheritance from fathers,
But a wife who has insight is
from Yahweh.

15 Laziness casts into a deep
sleep,
And a slack-handed soul will
suffer hunger.

16 He who keeps the
commandment keeps
his soul,
But he who despises his way
will die.

17 He who is gracious to a poor
man lends to Yahweh,
And He will repay him for his
bountiful deed.

18 Discipline your son while there
is hope,
And do not direct your soul to
put him to death.

19 *A man of* great wrath will bear
the penalty,
For if you deliver *him*, you
will only have to do it
again.

20 Listen to counsel and receive
discipline,
That you may be wise in the end
of your *days*.

21 Many thoughts are in a man's
heart,
But it is the counsel of Yahweh
that will stand.

22 What is desirable in a man is his
lovingkindness,
And better is a poor man than a
man of falsehood.

23 The fear of Yahweh *leads* to life,
So that one may sleep satisfied,
not visited by evil.

24 The sluggard buries his hand in
the dish,
But will not even bring it back to
his mouth.

25 Strike a scoffer and the simple
may become prudent,
But reprove one who has
understanding and he will
understand knowledge.

26 He who assaults *his* father *and*
causes *his* mother to flee
Is a son who brings shame and
humiliation.

27 Cease listening, my son, to
discipline,
And you will stray from the
words of knowledge.

28 A vile witness scoffs at justice,
And the mouth of the wicked
swallows up iniquity.

29 Judgments are established for
scoffers,
And beatings for the back of
fools.

CHAPTER 20

Hope in Yahweh and He Will Save You

1 WINE is a mocker, strong drink
a brawler,
And whoever is led astray by it
is not wise.

2 The terror of a king is like the
roar of a lion;
He who provokes him to anger
sins against his own soul.

3 It is a glory for a man to cease
   quarreling,
   But any ignorant fool will break
   out *in dispute.*

4 The sluggard does not plow
   from winter *on,*
   So he begs during the harvest
   and has nothing.

5 Counsel in the heart of a man is
   like deep water,
   But a man of discernment draws
   it out.

6 Many a man will call out his
   own lovingkindness,
   But a faithful man, who can
   find?

7 A righteous man who walks in
   his integrity—
   How blessed are his sons
   after him.

8 A king who sits on the throne of
   justice
   Disperses all evil with his eyes.

9 Who can say, "I have kept my
   heart pure,
   I am clean from my sin"?

10 Differing weights and differing
   measures,
   Both of them are an
   abomination to Yahweh.

11 It is by his deeds that a young
   man makes himself
   known
   If his conduct is pure and right.

12 The hearing ear and the
   seeing eye,
   Yahweh has made both of
   them.

13 Do not love sleep, lest you
   become poor;
   Open your eyes, *and* you will be
   satisfied with food.

14 "Bad, bad," says the buyer,
   But when he goes his way, then
   he boasts.

15 There is gold, and an abundance
   of pearls;
   But the lips of knowledge are a
   more precious vessel.

16 Take his garment when he
   becomes a guarantor for a
   stranger;
   And for foreigners, hold him in
   pledge.

17 Bread obtained by lying is sweet
   to a man,
   But afterward his mouth will be
   filled with gravel.

18 Thoughts are established by
   counsel,
   So make war by guidance.

19 He who goes about as a
   slanderer reveals secrets,
   Therefore do not associate with
   one of loose lips.

20 He who curses his father or his
   mother,
   His lamp will go out in the midst
   of darkness.

21 An inheritance gained hurriedly
   at the beginning
   In the end will not be
   blessed.

22 Do not say, "I will repay evil";
   Hope in Yahweh, and He will
   save you.

23 Differing weights are an
   abomination to Yahweh,
   And a deceitful balance is
   not good.

24 The steps of a man are from
   Yahweh,
   How then can man understand
   his way?

25 It is a trap for a man to say
   rashly, "It is holy!"
   And after the vows to make
   inquiry.

26 A wise king winnows the
   wicked,
   And turns the *threshing* wheel
   over them.

27 The breath of man is the lamp of
   Yahweh,
   Searching all the innermost
   parts of his body.

28 Lovingkindness and truth will
   guard the king,
   And he upholds his throne by
   lovingkindness.

29 The honor of young men is their
   strength,
   And the majesty of old men is
   their gray hair.

30 Stripes that wound scour away
   evil,
   And strokes *reach* the innermost
   parts of the body.

CHAPTER 21

Salvation Belongs to Yahweh

1 THE king's heart is *like* channels
   of water in the hand of
   Yahweh;
   He turns it wherever He pleases.

2 Every man's way is right in his
   own eyes,
   But Yahweh weighs the hearts.

3 To do righteousness and
   justice
   Is chosen by Yahweh over
   sacrifice.

4 Haughty eyes and a proud
   heart—
   The fallow ground of the
   wicked—are sin.

5 The thoughts of the diligent
   lead surely to profit,
   But everyone who is hasty
   comes surely to poverty.

6 Working for treasures by a lying
   tongue
   Is a fleeting breath, by those
   who pursue death.

7 The destruction of the wicked
   will drag them away,
   Because they refuse to do
   justice.

8 The way of a guilty man is
   perverse,
   But as for the pure, his work is
   upright.

9 It is better to live in a corner
   of a roof
   Than in a house shared with a
   contentious woman.

10 The soul of the wicked craves
   evil;
   His neighbor finds no favor in
   his eyes.

11 When the scoffer is punished,
   the simple becomes wise;
   And when one considers
   wisdom, he receives
   knowledge.

12 The righteous one considers the
   house of the wicked,
   Turning the wicked to ruin.

13 He who shuts his ear to the
outcry of the poor
Will himself also call and not be
answered.

14 A gift in secret subdues anger,
And a bribe in the bosom,
strong wrath.

15 To do justice is pleasure for the
righteous,
But is ruin to the workers of
iniquity.

16 A man who wanders from the
way of insight
Will rest in the assembly of
the dead.

17 He who loves pleasure *will
become* a poor man;
He who loves wine and oil will
not become rich.

18 The wicked is a ransom for the
righteous,
And the treacherous is in the
place of the upright.

19 It is better to live in a desert land
Than with a contentious and
vexing woman.

20 There is desirable treasure and
oil in the abode of the wise,
But a foolish man swallows it up.

21 He who pursues righteousness
and lovingkindness
Finds life, righteousness, and
glory.

22 A wise man goes up to the city
of the mighty
And brings down the stronghold
in which they trust.

23 He who keeps his mouth and his
tongue,
Keeps his soul from troubles.

24 "Arrogant," "Haughty," "Scoffer,"
are his names,
Who acts with arrogant fury.

25 The desire of the sluggard puts
him to death,
For his hands refuse to work;

26 All day long he is insatiably
craving,
While the righteous gives and
does not hold back.

27 The sacrifice of the wicked is an
abomination,
How much more when he brings
it with a wicked scheme!

28 A false witness will perish,
But the man who listens will
speak forever.

29 A wicked man displays a
brazen face,
But as for the upright, he
establishes his way.

30 There is no wisdom, there is no
discernment
And there is no counsel against
Yahweh.

31 The horse is set for the day of
battle,
But salvation belongs to Yahweh.

CHAPTER 22

Yahweh Is the Maker of All

1 A *good* name is to be chosen
over great wealth,
Favor is better than silver and
gold.

2 The rich and the poor meet
together *in this*—
Yahweh is the Maker of them all.

3 A prudent man sees evil and
    hides,
  But the simple pass on, and are
    punished.
4 The reward of humility—the
    fear of Yahweh—
  Is riches, glory, and life.
5 Thorns *and* snares are in the
    way of the crooked;
  He who keeps his soul will be far
    from them.
6 Train up a child according to
    his way,
  Even when he is old he will not
    depart from it.
7 The rich rules over the poor,
  And the borrower is the slave of
    the lender.
8 He who sows unrighteousness
    will reap iniquity,
  And the rod of his fury
    will end.
9 He who is generous will be
    blessed,
  For he gives from his food to the
    poor.
10 Drive out the scoffer, and strife
    will go out,
  Even contention and disgrace
    will cease.
11 He who loves purity of heart
  And grace on his lips, the king is
    his friend.
12 The eyes of Yahweh guard
    knowledge,
  But He subverts the words of the
    treacherous one.
13 The sluggard says, "There is a
    lion outside;
  I will be killed in the streets!"

14 The mouth of strange women is
    a deep pit;
  He who is cursed of Yahweh will
    fall into it.
15 Folly is bound up in the heart of
    a child;
  The rod of discipline will
    remove it far from him.
16 He who oppresses the poor
    to make more for
    himself
  Or who gives to the rich *will*
    only *come to* lack.

17 Incline your ear and hear the
    words of the wise,
  And set your heart on my
    knowledge;
18 For it will be pleasant if you
    keep them within you,
  That they may be established on
    your lips.
19 So that your trust may be in
    Yahweh,
  I have made you know today,
    even you.
20 Have I not written to you
    excellent things
  Of counsels and knowledge,
21 To make you know the
    veracity of the words
    of truth
  That you may respond with the
    words of truth to him who
    sent you?

22 Do not rob the poor because he
    is poor,
  And do not crush the afflicted at
    the gate;

23 For Yahweh will plead their
case
And rob the soul of those
who rob them.

24 Do not befriend a man of
anger;
And do not come along with a
man of great wrath,
25 Lest you learn his ways
And take *on* a snare against
your soul.

26 Do not be among those who
strike hands *in pledge*,
Among those who become
guarantors for debts.
27 If you have nothing with which
to pay,
Why should he take your bed
from under you?

28 Do not move the ancient
boundary
Which your fathers made.

29 Do you see a man skilled in his
work?
He will stand before kings;
He will not stand before
obscure men.

CHAPTER 23

Be Zealous in the Fear of Yahweh

1 WHEN you sit down to dine
with a ruler,
Understand well what is
before you,

2 So you should put a knife to
your throat
If you are a man of appetite.
3 Do not desire his delicacies,
For it is bread of falsehood.

4 Do not weary yourself to gain
wealth,
Because of your understanding,
cease!
5 Do you make your eyes fly
up to see it? But it is not
there!
Because it certainly makes itself
wings
Like an eagle that flies *toward*
the heavens.

6 Do not eat the bread of a
selfish man,
And do not desire his
delicacies;
7 For as he calculates in his soul,
so he is.
"Eat and drink!" he says to you,
But his heart is not with you.
8 You will vomit up the morsel
you have eaten,
And you will corrupt your
pleasant words.

9 Do not speak in the hearing of a
fool,
For he will despise the insight of
your speech.

10 Do not move the ancient
boundary
And do not come into the fields
of the orphans,

11 For their Redeemer is strong;
   He will plead their case
      against you.
12 Bring your heart to discipline
   And your ears to words of
      knowledge.

13 Do not withhold discipline from
      the child,
   Although you strike him with
      the rod, he will not die.
14 You shall strike him with the rod
   And deliver his soul from Sheol.

15 My son, if your heart is wise,
   My own heart also will be glad;
16 And my inmost being will exult
   When your lips speak upright
      things.

17 Do not let your heart be jealous
      of sinners,
   But *be zealous* in the fear of
      Yahweh always.
18 Surely there is a future,
   And your hope will not be cut off.
19 You, my son, listen and be wise,
   And direct your heart in the way.
20 Do not be with heavy drinkers of
      wine,
   Or with gluttonous eaters of meat;
21 For the heavy drinker and the
      glutton will come to poverty,
   And drowsiness will clothe *them*
      with rags.

22 Listen to your father who
      begot you,
   And do not despise your mother
      when she is old.

23 Buy truth, and do not sell *it*,
   Get wisdom and discipline and
      understanding.

24 The father of the righteous will
      greatly rejoice,
   And he who begets a wise son
      will be glad in him.
25 Let your father and your mother
      be glad,
   And let her rejoice who gave
      birth to you.

26 Give your heart to me,
      my son,
   And let your eyes delight in my
      ways.
27 For a harlot is a deep pit
   And a foreign woman is a
      narrow well.
28 Surely she lies in wait as a
      robber,
   And adds to the treacherous
      among men.

29 Who has woe? Who has
      sorrow?
   Who has contentions? Who has
      complaining?
   Who has wounds without
      cause?
   Who has redness of eyes?
30 Those who linger long over
      wine,
   Those who go to search out
      mixed wine.
31 Do not look on the wine when it
      glistens red,
   When it sparkles in the cup,
   When it goes down smoothly;

32 At the end—like a serpent it
        bites,
   And like a viper it stings.
33 Your eyes will see strange things
   And your heart will speak
        perverse things.
34 And you will be like one who
        lies down in the heart of
        the sea,
   Or like one who lies down on
        the top of a mast.
35 "They struck me, *but* I did not
        become ill;
   They beat me, *but* I did not
        know *it*.
   When shall I awake?
   I will seek yet another."

CHAPTER 24

My Son, Fear Yahweh

1 DO not be jealous of evil men,
   And do not desire to be with
        them;
2 For their heart meditates on
        destruction,
   And their lips talk of mischief.

3 By wisdom a house is built,
   And by discernment it is firmly
        established;
4 And by knowledge the rooms
        are filled
   With all precious and pleasant
        riches.

5 A wise man is strong,
   And a man of knowledge
        strengthens his power.

6 For by guidance you will
        make war,
   And in abundance of counselors
        there is salvation.

7 Wisdom is *too* exalted for an
        ignorant fool,
   He does not open his mouth in
        the gate.

8 One who deliberately thinks to
        do evil,
   Men will call a schemer.
9 The scheming of folly is sin,
   And the scoffer is an
        abomination to men.

10 If you are slack in the day of
        trouble,
   Your strength is in trouble.

11 Deliver those who are being
        taken away to death,
   And those who are stumbling to
        the slaughter, Oh hold *them*
        back.
12 If you say, "Behold, we did not
        know this,"
   Does not He who weighs the
        hearts understand?
   And *does not* He who guards
        your soul know?
   And will not He render to man
        according to his work?

13 Eat honey, my son, for it
        is good,
   Indeed, the honey from the
        comb is sweet to your
        taste;

14 Know *that* wisdom is thus for
your soul;
If you find *it*, then there will be
a future,
And your hope will not be cut off.

15 Do not lie in wait, O wicked
man, against the abode of
the righteous;
Do not destroy his resting place;

16 For a righteous man falls seven
times, and rises again,
But the wicked will stumble in
calamity.

17 When your enemy falls, do not
be glad,
And when he stumbles, do not
let your heart rejoice;

18 Lest Yahweh see *it* and it be evil
in His eyes,
And turn His anger away
from him.

19 Do not fret because of evildoers
Do not be jealous of the wicked;

20 For there will be no future for
the evil one;
The lamp of the wicked will
go out.

21 My son, fear Yahweh and the
king;
Do not associate with those
who change,

22 For suddenly their disaster
will rise,
And who knows the upheaval
that comes from both
of them?

23 These also are *sayings* of the
wise.
To show partiality in judgment
is not good.

24 He who says to the wicked, "You
are righteous,"
Peoples will curse him, nations
will be indignant with him;

25 But to those who reprove the
wicked, it will be pleasant,
And a good blessing will come
upon them.

26 He kisses the lips
Who responds with right
words.

27 Establish your work outside
And make it ready for yourself
in the field;
And afterwards, you shall build
your house.

28 Do not be a witness against your
neighbor without cause,
Nor deceive with your lips.

29 Do not say, "As he did to me so I
shall do to him;
I will render to the man
according to his work."

30 I passed by the field of the
sluggard
And by the vineyard of the man
lacking a heart *of wisdom*,

31 And behold, it was completely
overgrown with thistles;
Nettles have covered its
surface,
And its stone wall has been
torn down.

32 And I beheld, I set my heart
      upon it;
   I saw, I received discipline.
33 "A little sleep, a little slumber,
   A little folding of the hands
      to rest,"
34 Then your poverty will come
      as a robber
   And your want like an
      armed man.

CHAPTER 25

Analogies of Wisdom

THESE also are proverbs of Solomon
which the men of Hezekiah, king of
Judah, transcribed.
   2 It is the glory of God to conceal
      a matter,
      But the glory of kings is to
         search out a matter.
   3 *As* the heavens for height and
         the earth for depth,
      So the heart of kings is
         unsearchable.
   4 Take away the dross from the
         silver,
      And there comes out a vessel for
         the smith;
   5 Take away the wicked before
         the king,
      And his throne will
         be established in
         righteousness.
   6 Do not promote your majesty
         in the presence of the
         king,
      And in the place of great men do
         not stand;

7 For it is better that it be said to
      you, "Come up here,"
   Than for you to be placed
      lower in the presence
      of a noble,
   Whom your eyes have seen.

8 Do not go out hastily to plead
      your case;
   Lest, what will you do in
      the end,
   When your neighbor humiliates
      you?
9 Plead your case with your
      neighbor,
   And do not reveal the secret of
      another,
10 Lest he who hears *it* bring
      disgrace upon you,
   And the bad report about you
      will not turn away.

11 *Like* apples of gold in settings of
      silver
   Is a word spoken in right
      circumstances.
12 *Like* an earring of gold and an
      ornament of fine gold
   Is a wise reprover to a
      listening ear.
13 Like the cold of snow in the time
      of harvest
   Is a faithful envoy to those who
      send him,
   For he refreshes the soul of his
      masters.
14 *Like* clouds and wind without
      rain
   Is a man who boasts of his gifts
      falsely.

15 When one is slow to anger, a
ruler may be persuaded,
And a soft tongue breaks the
bone.

16 Have you found honey? Eat *only*
enough for you,
Lest you have more than your
fill and vomit it.

17 Let your foot rarely be in your
neighbor's house,
Lest he have more than his fill of
you and hate you.

18 *Like* a club and a sword and a
sharp arrow
Is a man who bears false witness
against his neighbor.

19 *Like* an aching tooth and a
slipping foot
Is trust in a treacherous man in
a day of distress.

20 *Like* one who takes off a
garment on a cold day, *or
like* vinegar on soda,
Is he who sings songs to an
aching heart.

21 If your enemy is hungry, give
him food to eat;
And if he is thirsty, give him
water to drink;

22 For you will heap burning coals
on his head,
And Yahweh will repay you.

23 The north wind brings forth
rain,
And a tongue of secrets, an
indignant face.

24 It is better to live in a corner of
the roof
Than in a house shared with a
contentious woman.

25 *Like* cold water to a weary soul,
So is a good report from a
distant land.

26 *Like* a muddied spring and a
corrupted well
Is a righteous man shaking
before the wicked.

27 To eat too much honey is not
good,
Nor is it glory to search out
one's own glory.

28 *Like* a city that is broken into
and without a wall
Is a man without restraint over
his spirit.

CHAPTER 26

1 LIKE snow in summer and like
rain in harvest,
So glory is not fitting for a fool.

2 Like a sparrow in *its* flitting, like
a swallow in flying,
So a curse without cause does
not come *to pass*.

3 A whip is for the horse, a bridle
for the donkey,
And a rod for the back of fools.

4 Do not answer a fool according
to his folly,
Lest you yourself also be
like him.

5 Answer a fool according to
his folly,
Lest he be wise in his own eyes.

6 He cuts off *his own* feet *and*
drinks violence
Who sends words by the hand
of a fool.

7 *Like* the legs *which* hang limp on the lame,
  So is a proverb in the mouth of fools.

8 Like one who binds a stone in a sling,
  So is he who gives glory to a fool.

9 *Like* a thorn *which* goes up into the hand of a drunkard,
  So is a proverb in the mouth of fools.

10 *Like* an archer who wounds everyone,
   So is he who hires a fool or who hires those who pass by.

11 Like a dog that returns to its vomit
   Is a fool who repeats his folly.

12 Do you see a man wise in his own eyes?
   There is more hope for a fool than for him.

13 The sluggard says, "There is a fierce lion in the road!
   A lion is among the streets!"

14 *As* the door turns on its hinges,
   So *does* the sluggard on his bed.

15 The sluggard buries his hand in the dish;
   He is *too* weary to return it to his mouth.

16 The sluggard is wiser in his own eyes
   Than seven men who can respond with a discreet answer.

17 *Like* one who seizes a dog by the ears
   Is he who passes by *and* becomes passionate about strife not belonging to him.

18 Like a madman who shoots
   Firebrands, arrows, and death,

19 So is the man who deceives his neighbor,
   And says, "Am I not joking?"

20 With no wood the fire goes out,
   And where there is no whisperer, strife quiets down.

21 *Like* charcoal to hot embers and wood to fire,
   So is a contentious man to kindle strife.

22 The words of a whisperer are like dainty morsels,
   And they go down into the innermost parts of the stomach.

23 *Like* an earthen vessel overlaid with silver dross
   Are fiery lips and an evil heart.

24 He who hates disguises *it* with his lips,
   But he sets up deceit within himself.

25 When he makes his voice gracious, do not believe him,
   For there are seven abominations in his heart.

26 *Though his* hatred covers itself with guile,
   His evil will be revealed in the assembly.

27 He who digs a pit will fall into it,
   And he who rolls a stone, it will turn back on him.

28 A lying tongue hates those it crushes,
   And a flattering mouth works ruin.

CHAPTER 27

Instructions and Warnings

1 DO not boast about tomorrow,
For you do not know what a day
may bring forth.

2 Let a stranger praise you, and
not your own mouth;
A foreigner, and not your
own lips.

3 A stone is heavy and the sand
weighty,
But the provocation of an
ignorant fool is heavier than
both of them.

4 Wrath is cruelty and anger is a
flood,
But who can stand before
jealousy?

5 Better is reproof that is revealed
Than love that is hidden.

6 Faithful are the wounds of a
friend,
But deceitful are the kisses
of an enemy.

7 A satisfied soul tramples the
honeycomb,
But to a hungry soul any bitter
thing is sweet.

8 Like a bird that wanders from
her nest,
So is a man who wanders from
his place.

9 Oil and incense make the
heart glad,
So counsel from the soul is
sweet to his friend.

10 Do not forsake your friend or
your father's friend,
And do not come to your
brother's house in the day of
your disaster;
Better is one who dwells near
than a brother far away.

11 Be wise, my son, and make my
heart glad,
That I may respond with a
word to him who
reproaches me.

12 A prudent man sees evil *and*
hides,
The simple pass on *and* are
punished.

13 Take his garment when he
becomes a guarantor for a
stranger;
And for a foreign woman seize it
as a pledge.

14 He who blesses his friend with
a loud voice early in the
morning,
It will be counted as a curse to
him.

15 A constant dripping on a day of
steady rain
And a contentious woman are
alike;

16 He who would restrain her
restrains the wind,
And grasps oil with his right
hand.

17 Iron sharpens iron,
So one man sharpens another.

18 He who guards the fig tree will
eat its fruit,
And he who keeps *watch for* his
master will be honored.

19 As in water face *reflects* face,
So the heart of man
reflects man.

20 Sheol and Abaddon are never
     satisfied,
   So the eyes of man are never
     satisfied.
21 The refining pot is for silver and
     the furnace for gold,
   And each *is tested* by the mouth
     that praises him.
22 Though you pound an ignorant
     fool in a mortar with a pestle
     in the midst of crushed grain,
   His folly will not turn aside
     from him.

23 Know well the condition of your
     flocks,
   And pay attention to your herds;
24 For wealth is not forever,
   Neither is a crown from
     generation to generation.
25 *When* the grass disappears and
     the vegetation appears,
   And the herbs of the mountains
     are gathered in,
26 The lambs *will be* for your
     clothing,
   And the goats *will bring* the
     price of a field,
27 And *there will be enough* goats'
     milk for your food,
   For the food of your household,
   And sustenance for your maidens.

CHAPTER 28

1 THE wicked flee when there is
     no one pursuing,
   But the righteous are secure as
     a lion.

2 By the transgression of a land
     many are its princes,
   But by a man who understands,
     who knows, so it endures.
3 A poor man who oppresses the
     lowly
   Is a driving rain which leaves
     no food.
4 Those who forsake the law
     praise the wicked,
   But those who keep the law
     strive with them.
5 Evil men do not understand
     justice,
   But those who seek Yahweh
     understand all things.
6 Better is the poor who walks in
     his integrity
   Than he who is crooked—double
     dealing—though he be rich.
7 He who observes the law is a
     son who understands,
   But he who befriends gluttons
     humiliates his father.
8 He who increases his wealth by
     interest and usury
   Gathers it for him who is
     gracious to the lowly.
9 He who turns away his ear from
     listening to the law,
   Even his prayer is an abomination.
10 He who leads the upright astray
     in an evil way
   Will himself fall into his own pit,
   But the blameless will inherit
     good.
11 The rich man is wise in his
     own eyes,
   But the lowly who understands
     searches him.

12 When the righteous exult, there
        is great honor,
    But when the wicked rise, man
        has to be sought out.

13 He who conceals his
        transgressions will not
        prosper,
    But he who confesses and
        forsakes *them* will receive
        compassion.

14 How blessed is the man who is
        always in dread,
    But he who hardens his heart
        will fall into calamity.

15 *Like* a roaring lion and a rushing
        bear
    Is a wicked ruler over a poor
        people.

16 A leader who lacks discernment
        abounds in oppressions,
    But he who hates greedy gain
        will prolong *his* days.

17 A man oppressed with the
        bloodguilt of life
    Will flee until death; let no one
        uphold him.

18 He who walks blamelessly will
        be saved,
    But he who is crooked—double
        dealing—will fall all
        at once.

19 He who cultivates his ground
        will be satisfied with food,
    But he who pursues empty
        things will be satisfied with
        poverty.

20 A faithful man will abound with
        blessings,
    But he who makes haste to be
        rich will not go unpunished.

21 To show partiality is not good,
    Even for a piece of bread a man
        will transgress.

22 A man with an evil eye hurries
        after wealth
    And does not know that want
        will come upon him.

23 He who reproves a man will
        afterward find *more* favor
    Than he who flatters with the
        tongue.

24 He who robs his father or his
        mother
    And says, "It is not a
        transgression,"
    Is the companion of a man who
        destroys.

25 An arrogant man stirs up strife,
    But he who trusts in Yahweh will
        be enriched.

26 He who trusts in his own heart
        is a fool,
    But he who walks wisely will
        escape.

27 He who gives to the poor will
        never want,
    But he who shuts his eyes will
        have many curses.

28 When the wicked rise, men hide
        themselves;
    But when they perish, the
        righteous increase.

CHAPTER 29

1 A man who hardens *his* neck
        after much reproof
    Will suddenly be broken beyond
        healing.

2 When the righteous increase,
　　the people are glad,
　But when a wicked man rules,
　　people groan.

3 A man who loves wisdom makes
　　his father glad,
　But he who befriends harlots
　　destroys *his* wealth.

4 By justice the king causes the
　　land to stand,
　But a man of bribes tears it
　　down.

5 A man who flatters his
　　neighbor
　Is spreading a net for his steps.

6 By transgression an evil man is
　　ensnared,
　But the righteous sings with joy
　　and is glad.

7 The righteous knows the cause
　　of the poor,
　The wicked does not understand
　　that knowledge.

8 Scoffers set a city aflame,
　But wise men turn away anger.

9 When a wise man is brought
　　into judgment with a man
　　who is an ignorant fool,
　The *ignorant fool* both rages
　　and laughs, and there is
　　no rest.

10 Men of bloodshed hate the
　　blameless,
　But the upright seek *the well-
　　being of* his soul.

11 A fool lets out all of his spirit,
　But a wise man holds it back.

12 *If* a ruler pays attention to a
　　lying word,
　All his ministers *become* wicked.

13 The poor man and the oppressor
　　meet together *in this*—
　Yahweh gives light to the eyes
　　of both.

14 If a king judges the poor with
　　truth,
　His throne will be established
　　forever.

15 The rod and reproof give
　　wisdom,
　But a child left *to himself* brings
　　shame to his mother.

16 When the wicked increase,
　　transgression increases;
　But the righteous will see
　　their fall.

17 Discipline your son, and he
　　will give you rest;
　And he will give delight to
　　your soul.

18 Where there is no vision,
　　the people are out of
　　control,
　But how blessed is he who keeps
　　the law.

19 A slave will not be corrected by
　　words *alone*;
　For though he understands,
　　there will be no answer.

20 Do you behold a man who is
　　hasty in his words?
　There is more hope for a fool
　　than for him.

21 He who pampers his slave from
　　childhood
　Will in the end find him to be
　　arrogant.

22 An angry man stirs up strife,
　And a hot-tempered man
　　abounds in transgression.

23 A man's lofty pride will bring
     him low,
   But a lowly spirit will take hold
     of glory.
24 He who divides *the spoil* with a
     thief hates his own soul;
   He hears the oath but declares
     nothing.
25 Trembling before man brings a
     snare,
   But he who trusts in Yahweh will
     be set securely on high.
26 Many seek the face of a ruler,
   But justice for man *comes* from
     Yahweh.
27 An unjust man is an abomination
     to the righteous,
   And he who is upright in the
     way is an abomination to
     the wicked.

CHAPTER 30

Every Word of God Is Tested

THE words of Agur the son of Jakeh,
the oracle.
   The man declares to Ithiel, to
Ithiel and Ucal:
2 Surely I am more senseless than
     any man,
   And I do not have the
     understanding of mankind.
3 Neither have I learned wisdom,
   Nor do I know the knowledge of
     the Holy One.
4 Who has ascended into heaven
     and descended?
   Who has gathered the wind in
     His fists?

Who has wrapped the waters in
     His garment?
Who has established all the
     ends of the earth?
What is His name? And what is
     His Son's name?
Surely you know!

5 Every word of God is tested;
   He is a shield to those who take
     refuge in Him.
6 Do not add to His words
   Lest He reprove you, and you be
     proved a liar.

7 Two things I asked of You,
   Do not withhold from me before
     I die:
8 Keep worthlessness and *every*
     false word far from me,
   Give me neither poverty nor
     riches;
   Feed me with the food that is my
     portion,
9 Lest I be full and deny *You* and
     say, "Who is Yahweh?"
   Or lest I be impoverished and
     steal,
   And profane the name of my God.

10 Do not slander a slave to his
     master,
   Lest he curse you and you be
     found guilty.

11 There is a generation that curses
     its father
   And does not bless its mother.
12 There is a generation that is
     clean in its own eyes,

Yet is not washed from its
filthiness.

13 There is a generation—oh how
haughty are its eyes!
And its eyelids are lifted up.

14 There is a generation whose
teeth are *like* swords
And its fangs *like* knives,
To devour the afflicted from
the earth
And the needy from among
men.

15 The leech has two daughters,
"Give," "Give."
There are three things that will
not be satisfied,
Four that will not say,
"Enough":

16 Sheol, and the barren womb,
Earth that is never satisfied with
water,
And fire that never says,
"Enough."

17 The eye that mocks a father
And despises obedience to a
mother,
The ravens of the valley will
pick it out,
And the young eagles will eat it.

18 There are three things which are
too wonderful for me,
Four which I do not understand:

19 The way of an eagle in the sky,
The way of a serpent on a rock,
The way of a ship in the heart of
the sea,
And the way of a man with a
virgin.

20 This is the way of an adulterous
woman:
She eats and wipes her mouth,
And says, "I have done no
wrong."

21 Under three things the earth
quakes,
And under four, it cannot
bear up:

22 Under a slave when he becomes
king,
And a wicked fool when he is
satisfied with food,

23 Under an unloved woman when
she gets a husband,
And a servant-girl when she
supplants her mistress.

24 Four things are small on the
earth,
But they are exceedingly wise:

25 The ants are not a strong
people,
But they prepare their food in
the summer;

26 The shephanim are not a mighty
people,
Yet they make their houses in
the cliff;

27 The locusts have no king,
Yet all of them go out in rank;

28 The lizard you may grasp with
the hands,
Yet it is in kings' palaces.

29 There are three things which are
stately in *their* march,
Even four which are stately
when they walk:

30 The lion *which* is mighty among
    the animals
    And does not turn back
    before any,
31 The strutting rooster, the male
    goat also,
    And a king *when his* army is
    with him.

32 If you have been wickedly foolish
    in lifting yourself up,
    Or if you have schemed *evil*,
    put your hand on your
    mouth.
33 For pressing milk brings forth
    butter,
    And pressing the nose brings
    forth blood;
    And pressing anger brings
    forth strife.

CHAPTER 31

A Mother's Oracle

THE words of King Lemuel, the oracle *unto* which his mother disciplined him:
  2 What, O my son?
    And what, O son of my womb?
    And what, O son of my vows?
  3 Do not give your excellence to
    women,
    Or your ways to that which blots
    out kings.
  4 It is not for kings, O Lemuel,
    It is not for kings to drink
    wine,
    Or for rulers to desire strong
    drink,

5 Lest he drink and forget what is
    decreed,
    And pervert the justice of all the
    afflicted.
6 Give strong drink to him who is
    perishing,
    And wine to those whose soul
    is bitter.
7 Let him drink and forget his
    poverty
    And he will not remember his
    trouble any longer.
8 Open your mouth for the mute,
    For the justice of all those
    passing away.
9 Open your mouth, judge
    righteously,
    And render justice to the
    afflicted and needy.

A Woman Who Fears Yahweh

10 An excellent wife, who can find?
    For her worth is far above
    pearls.
11 The heart of her husband trusts
    in her,
    And he will have no lack of gain.
12 She deals bountifully with him
    for good and not evil
    All the days of her life.
13 She searches for wool and flax
    And works with her hands in
    delight.
14 She is like merchant ships;
    She brings her food from afar.
15 And she rises while it is still
    night,
    And gives food to her household
    And a portion to her young
    women.

16 She makes plans for a field and
     buys it;
   From the fruit of her hands she
     plants a vineyard.
17 She girds herself with strength
   And makes her arms strong.
18 She senses that her gain is good;
   Her lamp does not go out at
     night.
19 She stretches out her hands to
     the distaff,
   And her hands hold fast the
     spindle.
20 She extends her hand to the
     poor,
   And she stretches out her hands
     to the needy.
21 She is not afraid of the snow for
     her household,
   For all her household are
     clothed with scarlet.
22 She makes coverings for
     herself;
   Her clothing is fine linen and
     purple.
23 Her husband is known in the
     gates,
   When he sits with the elders of
     the land.

24 She makes linen garments and
     sells *them*,
   And gives belts to the tradesmen.
25 Strength and majesty are her
     clothing,
   And she smiles at the future.
26 She opens her mouth in wisdom,
   And the instruction of
     lovingkindness is on her
     tongue.
27 She watches over the ways of
     her household,
   And does not eat the bread of
     idleness.
28 Her children rise up and bless her;
   As for her husband, he also
     praises her, *saying*:
29 "Many daughters have done
     excellently,
   But you have gone above
     them all."
30 Charm is deceitful and beauty
     is vain,
   But a woman who fears Yahweh,
     she shall be praised.
31 Give to her from the fruit of her
     hands,
   And let her works praise her in
     the gates.

TABLE OF
MONETARY UNITS

Assarion *(plural assaria)* .... A Roman copper coin, approximately
1/16 of a laborer's daily wage

Denarius *(plural denarii)* .... A Roman silver coin, approximately a
laborer's daily wage

Drachma *(plural drachmas)* ...... A Greek silver coin, approximately a laborer's
daily wage

Lepton *(plural lepta)*............ Smallest Greek copper coin, approximately
1/128 of a laborer's daily wage

Mina *(plural minas)* .... Greek monetary unit worth approximately
100 days of a laborer's wages

Quadrans...................... A Roman copper coin, approximately
1/64 of a laborer's daily wage

Shekel .... A coin weighing approximately
0.4 ounces or 11 grams

Stater .... Literally *standard coin*, approximately
4 days of a laborer's wages

Talent .... A talent was approximately worth more
than 15 years of a laborer's wages

This table contains values regarding monetary units, gathered from widely
accepted historical and archeological research. These values are based on the
most accurate information available.

TABLE OF
WEIGHTS AND MEASUREMENTS

Bath . . . . Hebrew measurement, a bath was approximately 8 gallons or 30 liters

Choinix . . . . A dry measure, approximately 1 quart or 1 liter

Cubit . . . . A cubit was approximately 18 inches or 45 centimeters

Fathom . . . . An ancient fathom was approximately 6 feet or 1.8 meters

Handbreadth . . . . Approximately 3 inches or 7.5 centimeters

Kor . . . . Hebrew measurement, a kor was approximately 11 bushels or 400 liters

Litra . . . . A Roman pound, a litra was approximately 12 ounces or 340 grams

Measure . . . . A measure was approximately 10 gallons or 38 liters

Sabbath day's journey . . . . Approximately 0.6 miles or 1 kilometer

Saton *(plural sata)* . . . . A Hebrew dry measure, a saton was approximately 16 pounds or 13 liters

Seah . . . . A dry measure, approximately 7 quarts or 7.7 liters

Stadion *(plural stadia)* . . . . A stadion was approximately 607 feet or 185 meters

Talent . . . . Approximately 100 pounds or 45 kilograms

This table contains data gathered from widely accepted historical and archeological research. The amounts listed as weights and measurements are not intended to be precise. Further discoveries may allow for more consistent and accurate data. Until then, these units remain approximations.

1:1
Answers
IN GENESIS®

Connect with Ken Ham

blogs.answersingenesis.org
facebook.com/aigkenham
x.com/aigkenham
instagram.com/aigkenham

Connect with Answers in Genesis

answersingenesis.org
facebook.com/answersingenesis
x.com/aig
instagram.com/answersingenesis

Answers in Genesis (AiG) exists to proclaim the authority of the Bible—from the very first verse—without compromise by using apologetics in its world-class attractions, dynamic resources, and creative media to communicate the message of God's Word and the gospel so that believers are equipped to defend the Christian faith and nonbelievers are challenged with the truth of the Bible and its message of salvation.

Connect with the Creation Museum

creationmuseum.org
facebook.com/creationmuseum
x.com/creationmuseum
instagram.com/creationmuseum

Connect with the Ark Encounter

arkencounter.com
facebook.com/arkencounter
x.com/arkencounter
instagram.com/arkencounter

The Ark Encounter and Creation Museum exist to be world-class, Christ-centered, family attractions impacting guests with life-changing experiences by providing immersive and captivating exhibits—tailored for all ages—that feature countless learning opportunities, entertainment, and adventure so guests can understand that the history and the saving gospel message of the Bible are true.

See the Glory of Christ through The Window of God's Word

A translation is like a window — it allows you to see through to the other side. While many Bible renderings focus on the reader's point of view, the Legacy Standard Bible began by asking a decidedly different question — what did the Author intend?

Explore insights from the scholars that did the translation work, comparison verses to other English translations, and a list of digital editions available.

 LSBible.org

3 Commitments of the LEGACY STANDARD BIBLE

The LSB aspires to be a legacy preserved:
to uphold the work and tradition that is found in translations from the KJV, ASV, to NASB.

The LSB aspires to be a legacy performed:
to advance the commitments of past translations by bringing forth features of the original text relative to accuracy and consistency.

The LSB aspires to be a legacy passed on:
to equip generations to study Scripture and continue the philosophy of being a window into the original text for the glory of God.

"It is the best English translation I have ever read!"
- JOHN MACARTHUR